STATE GUN LAWS
South Edition

As published by the ATF in 2017

The FFL Lawyer
www.FFLlawyer.com
info@FFLlawyer.com

Ordering Information:
Discounts are available on quantity purchases by government agencies, associations, and other. For details contact "Bulk Sales" at the email address above.

State Gun Laws, South Edition, Volume 3

ISBN: 978-1981557752

TABLE OF CONTENTS

Alabama Code

Titles 1-44 current through August 16, 2016 and through Acts 2016, No. 16-421 (end) of the 2016 Regular Session

Office of the Attorney General
State House
11 South Union Street
Montgomery, AL 36130
(334) 242-7300
http://www.ago.alabama.gov/

Nashville Field Division
5300 Maryland Way, Suite 200
Brentwood, Tennessee 37027
Voice: (615) 565-1400
https://www.atf.gov/nashville-field-division

PROTECTING THE PUBLIC
SERVING OUR NATION

Table of Contents

§ 11-80-11. Firearms. The authority to bring or settle any lawsuit in which the state has an exclusive interest or right to recover against any firearm or ammunition manufacturer, trade association, or dealer, and the authority to bring or settle any lawsuit on behalf of any governmental unit created by or pursuant to an act of the Legislature or the Constitution of Alabama of 1901, or any department, agency, or authority thereof, for damages, abatement, injunctive relief, or other equitable relief resulting from or relating to the design, manufacture, marketing, or lawful sale of firearms or ammunition, or both, shall be reserved exclusively to the Attorney General, by and with the consent of the Governor. This section shall not prohibit a county or municipal corporation from bringing an action against a firearms or ammunition manufacturer or dealer for breach of contract or warranty as to firearms or ammunition purchased by the political subdivision or local governmental authority.

TITLE 13A Criminal Code
Chapter 11 Offenses against Order and Safety
Article 3 Offenses Relating to Firearms and Weapons
Division 1 General Provisions

§ 13A-11-50. Carrying concealed weapon; generally. Except as otherwise provided in this Code, a person who carries concealed about his person a bowie knife or knife or instrument of like kind or description or a pistol or firearm of any other kind or an air gun shall, on conviction, be fined not less than $50 nor more than $500, and may also be imprisoned in the county jail or sentenced to hard labor for the county for not more than six months.

§ 13A-11-51. Carrying concealed weapon; apprehension of an attack. The defendant being tried under the provisions of § 13A-11-50 may give evidence that at the time of carrying the weapon concealed, he had good reason to apprehend an attack, which the jury may consider in mitigation of the punishment or in justification of the offense.

§ 13A-11-52. Carrying pistol. Except as otherwise provided in this article, no person shall carry a pistol about his person on private property not his own or under his control unless the person possesses a valid concealed weapon permit or the person has the consent of the owner or legal possessor of the premises; but this section shall not apply to any law enforcement officer in the lawful discharge of the duties of his office, or to United States marshal or his deputies, rural free delivery mail carriers in the discharge of their duties as such, bonded constables in the discharge of their duties as such, conductors, railway mail clerks and express messengers in the discharge of their duties.

§ 13A-11-54. Carrying rifle or shotgun walking cane. Any person who carries a rifle or shotgun walking cane shall, on conviction, be fined not less than $500 nor more than $1,000, and be imprisoned in the penitentiary not less than 2 years.

§ 13A-11-56. Use of firearm while fighting. Any person who, while fighting in the streets of any city or town, or at a militia muster, or at any public place, whether public in itself, or made public at the time by an assemblage of persons, uses or attempts to use, except in self-defense, any kind of firearms shall, on conviction, be fined not less than $200 nor more than $500, and may also be imprisoned in the county jail or sentenced to hard labor for the county for not less than 6 months.

§ 13A-11-57. Selling, giving or lending pistol or knife to minor.
(a) Any person who sells, gives or lends to any minor any pistol , except under the circumstances provided in § 13A-11-72, bowie knife, or other knife of like kind or description, shall, on conviction, be fined not less than $50 nor more than $ 500.
(b) This section does not apply to a transfer by inheritance of title to, but not possession of, a pistol, bowie knife, or other knife of like kind or description to a minor.

§ 13A-11-58. Sale or purchase of rifles, shotguns and ammunition in adjoining state.
(a) Any resident of Alabama authorized to sell and deliver rifles, shotguns, and ammunition may sell and deliver them to a resident of any state where the sale of the firearms and ammunition is legal. Any purchaser of the firearm or ammunition may take or send it out of the state or have it delivered to his or her place of residence.
(b) Any resident of Alabama who legally purchases rifles, shotguns, and ammunition in any state where the purchase is legal may take delivery of the weapons either in the state where they were purchased or in Alabama.

§ 13A-11-58.1. Soliciting, persuading, encouraging, or enticing an illegal firearms sale – Providing false information to dealer or seller.
(a) For the purposes of this section, the following words have the following meanings:
  (1) Ammunition. – Any cartridge, shell, or projectile designed for use in a firearm.
  (2) Licensed dealer. – A person who is licensed pursuant to 18 U.S.C.S. § 923 or § 13A-11-79, Code of Alabama 1975, to engage in the business of dealing in firearms.

(3) Materially false information. – Information that portrays an illegal transaction as legal or a legal transaction as illegal.

(4) Private seller. – A person who sells or offers for sale any firearm, as defined in § 13A-8-1(4), Code of Alabama 1975, or ammunition.

(b) A person who knowingly solicits, persuades, encourages, or entices a licensed dealer or private seller of a firearm or ammunition to transfer a firearm or ammunition under circumstances which the person knows would violate the laws of this state or the United States is guilty of a Class C felony.

(c) A person who provides to a licensed dealer or private seller of firearms or ammunition what the person knows to be materially false information with intent to deceive the dealer or seller about the legality of the transfer of a firearm or ammunition is guilty of a Class C felony.

(d) This section does not apply to a peace officer acting in his or her official capacity or to a person acting at the direction of a peace officer.

§ 13A-11-58.1. Soliciting, persuading, encouraging, or enticing an illegal firearms sale – Providing false information to dealer or seller.

(a) For the purposes of this section, the following words have the following meanings:

(1) Ammunition. – Any cartridge, shell, or projectile designed for use in a firearm.

(2) Licensed dealer. – A person who is licensed pursuant to 18 U.S.C.S. § 923 or § 13A-11-79, Code of Alabama 1975, to engage in the business of dealing in firearms.

(3) Materially false information. – Information that portrays an illegal transaction as legal or a legal transaction as illegal.

(4) Private seller. – A person who sells or offers for sale any firearm, as defined in § 13A-8-1(4), Code of Alabama 1975, or ammunition.

(b) A person who knowingly solicits, persuades, encourages, or entices a licensed dealer or private seller of a firearm or ammunition to transfer a firearm or ammunition under circumstances which the person knows would violate the laws of this state or the United States is guilty of a Class C felony.

(c) A person who provides to a licensed dealer or private seller of firearms or ammunition what the person knows to be materially false information with intent to deceive the dealer or seller about the legality of the transfer of a firearm or ammunition is guilty of a Class C felony.

(d) This section does not apply to a peace officer acting in his or her official capacity or to a person acting at the direction of a peace officer.

§ 13A-11-59. Possession of firearm at or near demonstration.

(a) For the purposes of this section, the following words and phrases shall have the meanings respectively ascribed to them in this subsection, except in those instances where the context clearly indicates a different meaning:

(1) Demonstration. – Demonstrating, picketing, speechmaking or marching, holding of vigils and all other like forms of conduct which involve the communication or expression of views or grievances engaged in by one or more persons, the conduct of which has the effect, intent or propensity to draw a crowd or onlookers. Such term shall not include casual use of property by visitors or tourists which does not have an intent or propensity to attract a crowd or onlookers.

(2) Firearm. – Any pistol, rifle, shotgun or firearm of any kind, whether loaded or not.

(3) Law enforcement officer. – Any duly appointed and acting federal, state, county or municipal law enforcement officer, peace officer or investigating officer, or any military or militia personnel called out or directed by constituted authority to keep the law and order, and any park ranger while acting as such on the grounds of a public park and who is on regular duty and present to actively police and control the demonstration, and who is assigned this duty by his department or agency. Such term does not include a peace officer on strike or a peace officer not on duty.

(4) Public place. – Any place to which the general public has access and a right to resort for business, entertainment or other lawful purpose, but does not necessarily mean a place devoted solely to the uses of the public. Such term shall include the front or immediate area or parking lot of any store, shop, restaurant, tavern, shopping center or other place of business. Such term shall also include any public building, the grounds of any public building, or within the curtilage of any public building, or in any public parking lot, public street, right-of-way, sidewalk right-of-way, or within any public park or other public grounds.

(b) It shall be unlawful for any person, other than a law enforcement officer, to have in his or her possession or on his or her person or in any vehicle any firearm while participating in or attending any demonstration being held at a public place.

(c) It shall be unlawful for any person, other than a law enforcement officer as defined in subsection (a) of this section, to have in his or her possession or about his or her person or in any vehicle at a point within 1,000 feet of a demonstration at a public place, any firearm after having first been advised by a law enforcement officer that a demonstration was taking place at a public place and after having been ordered by such officer to remove himself or herself from the prescribed area until such time as he or she no longer was in possession of any firearm. This subsection shall not apply to any person in possession of or having on his or her person any firearm within a private dwelling or other private building or structure.

(d) Any person violating any of the provisions of this section shall be guilty of a misdemeanor and shall be punished as provided by law.

§ 13A-11-60. Possession or sale of brass or steel teflon-coated handgun ammunition.
(a) Except as provided in subsection (b) of this section, the possession or sale of brass or steel teflon-coated handgun ammunition is illegal anywhere within the State of Alabama. The possession or sale of said ammunition or any ammunition of like kind designed to penetrate bullet-proof vests, shall be unlawful and punishable as provided in subsection (c) of this section.
(b) The provisions of this section shall not apply to state or local law enforcement officers; nor shall it apply to the possession or sale of teflon-coated lead or brass ammunition designed to expand upon contact.
(c) Any person who while armed with a firearm in the commission or attempted commission of any felony, has in his or her immediate possession, teflon-coated ammunition for such firearm, upon conviction of such felony or attempted felony, in addition and consecutive to the punishment prescribed for said felony or attempted felony, shall be punished by the imposition of an additional term of 3 years in the penitentiary.
(d) Any person violating the provisions of this section shall be guilty of a Class C felony as defined by § 13A-5-3.

§ 13A-11-61. Discharging firearm into building, train, etc.
(a) No person shall shoot or discharge a firearm, explosive or other weapon which discharges a dangerous projectile into any occupied or unoccupied dwelling or building or railroad locomotive or railroad car, aircraft, automobile, truck or watercraft in this state.
(b) Any person who commits an act prohibited by subsection (a) with respect to an occupied dwelling or building or railroad locomotive or railroad car, aircraft, automobile, truck or watercraft shall be deemed guilty of a Class B felony as defined by the state criminal code, and upon conviction, shall be punished as prescribed by law.
(c) Any person who commits any act prohibited by subsection (a) hereof with respect to an unoccupied dwelling or building or railroad locomotive or railroad car, aircraft, automobile, truck or watercraft shall be deemed guilty of a Class C felony as defined by the state criminal code, and upon conviction, shall be punished as prescribed by law.

§ 13A-11-61.1. Discharging a firearm into a unoccupied school bus or school building.
(a) No person shall shoot or discharge a firearm into an occupied or unoccupied school bus or school building.
(b) A person who shoots or discharges a firearm into an occupied school bus or school building shall be guilty of a Class B felony.
(c) A person who shoots or discharges a firearm into an unoccupied school bus or school building shall be guilty of a Class C felony.
(d) This section shall not be construed to repeal other criminal laws. Whenever conduct prescribed by any provision of this section is also prescribed by any other provision of law, the provision which carries the more serious penalty shall be applied.

§ 13A-11-61.2. Limitations on where firearms may be carried; notifications at premises.
(a) In addition to any other place limited or prohibited by state or federal law, a person, including a person with a permit issued under § 13A-11-75(a)(1) or recognized under § 13A-11-85, may not knowingly possess or carry a firearm in any of the following places without the express permission of a person or entity with authority over the premises:
    (1) Inside the building of a police, sheriff, or highway patrol station.
    (2) Inside or on the premises of a prison, jail, halfway house, community corrections facility, or other detention facility for those who have been charged with or convicted of a criminal or juvenile offense.
    (3) Inside a facility which provides inpatient or custodial care of those with psychiatric, mental, or emotional disorders.
    (4) Inside a courthouse, courthouse annex, a building in which a District Attorney's office is located, or a building in which a county commission or city council is currently having a regularly scheduled or specially called meeting.
    (5) Inside any facility hosting an athletic event not related to or involving firearms which is sponsored by a private or public elementary or secondary school or any private or public institution of postsecondary education, unless the person has a permit issued under § 13A-11-75(a)(1) or recognized under § 13A-11-85.
    (6) Inside any facility hosting a professional athletic event not related to or involving firearms, unless the person has a permit issued under § 13A-11-75(a)(1) or recognized under § 13A-11-85.
(b) Notwithstanding the provisions of subsection (a), a person, including a person with a permit issued under § 13A-11-75(a)(1) or recognized under § 13A-11-85, may not, without the express permission of a person or entity with authority over the premises, knowingly possess or carry a firearm inside any building or facility to which access of unauthorized persons and prohibited articles is limited during normal hours of operation by the continuous posting of guards and the use of other security features, including, but not limited to, magnetometers, key cards, biometric screening devices, or turnstiles or other physical barriers. Nothing in this subsection otherwise restricts the possession, transportation, or storage of a lawfully possessed firearm or ammunition in an employee's privately-owned motor vehicle while parked or operated in a public or private parking area provided the employee complies with the requirements of § 13A-11-90.
(c) The person or entity with authority over the premises set forth in subsections (a)(1)-(6) and subsection (b) shall place a notice at the public entrances of such premises or buildings alerting those entering that firearms are prohibited.
(d) Except as provided in subsections (a)(5) and (a)(6), any firearm on the premises of any facility set forth in subsection (a)(1), or subsections (a)(4)-(6), or subsection (b) must be kept from ordinary observation and locked within a compartment or in the interior of the person's motor vehicle or in a compartment or container securely affixed to the motor vehicle.
(e) A violation of subsections (a), (b), or (d) is a Class C misdemeanor.

(f) This section shall not prohibit any person from possessing a firearm within the person's residence or during ingress or egress thereto.

(g) Prohibitions regarding the carrying of a firearm under this section shall not apply to law enforcement officers engaged in the lawful execution of their official duties.

(h) Nothing in this section shall be construed to authorize the carrying or possession of a firearm where prohibited by federal law.

§ 13A-11-61.3. Legislative purpose of uniformity on firearm issues.

(b) For the purposes of this section, the following words shall have the following meanings:

(1) Ammunition. – Fixed cartridge ammunition, shotgun shells, the individual components of fixed cartridge ammunition and shotgun shells, projectiles for muzzle-loading firearms, and any propellant used in firearms or ammunition.

(2) Expressly authorized by a statute of this state. – The authority of a political subdivision to regulate firearms, ammunition, or firearm accessories that is granted by a duly enacted state law that specifically mentions firearms, a particular type of firearm, ammunition, or a particular type of ammunition.

(3) Firearm accessory. – A device specifically designed or adapted to enable the wearing or carrying about one's person, or the storage or mounting in or on a conveyance, of a firearm, or an attachment or device specifically designed or adapted to be inserted into or affixed onto a firearm to enable, alter, or improve the functioning or capabilities of the firearm.

(4) Firearm. – This term has the same meaning as in § 13A-8-1(4), Code of Alabama 1975.

(5) Person adversely affected. – Any of the following:

    a. A resident of this state who may legally possess a firearm under the laws of this state and the United States and who is either of the following:

        1. Subject to any manner of regulation alleged to be promulgated or enforced in violation of this section, whether or not specific enforcement action has been initiated or threatened against that person or another person.

        2. If the person were present in the political subdivision in question, subject to any manner of regulation alleged to be promulgated or enforced in violation of this section, whether or not specific enforcement action has been initiated or threatened against that person or another person.

    b. A person who otherwise has standing under the laws of this state to bring an action under subsection (f).

    c. A membership organization if its members would otherwise have standing to sue in their own right, if the interests it seeks to protect are germane to the organization's purpose, and neither the claim asserted nor the relief requested requires the participation of individual members in the lawsuit.

(6) Political subdivision. – A county, incorporated city, unincorporated city, public local entity, public-private partnership, and any other public entity of a county or city commonly considered to be a political subdivision of the state.

(7) Public official. – Any person elected to public office, whether or not that person has taken office, by the vote of the people of a political subdivision or its instrumentalities, including governmental corporations, and any person appointed to a position at the municipal level of government or its instrumentalities, including governmental corporations.

(8) Reasonable expenses. – The expenses involved in litigation, including, but not limited to, expert witness fees, court costs, and compensation for loss of income.

(c) Except as otherwise provided in Acts 2013, No. 13-283 or as expressly authorized by a statute of this state, the Legislature hereby occupies and preempts the entire field of regulation in this state touching in any way upon firearms, ammunition, and firearm accessories to the complete exclusion of any order, ordinance, or rule promulgated or enforced by any political subdivision of this state.

(d) The authority of a political subdivision to regulate firearms, ammunition, or firearm accessories shall not be inferred from its proprietary authority, home rule status, or any other inherent or general power.

(e) Any existing orders, ordinances, or rules promulgated or enforced contrary to the terms of this section are null and void and any future order, ordinance, or rules shall comply with this section.

(f) (1) A person adversely affected by any order, ordinance, or rule promulgated in violation of this section may file a petition with the Attorney General requesting that he or she bring an action in circuit court for declarative and injunctive relief. The petition must be signed under oath and under penalty of perjury and must include specific details regarding the alleged violations.

(2) If, after investigation of the enactment or adoption of the order, ordinance, or rule, the Attorney General determines that there is reasonable cause to proceed with an action, he or she shall provide the political subdivision or public official enacting or adopting the order, ordinance, or rule 60 days' notice of his or her intent to file an action. Upon the expiration of the 60 days' notice, the Attorney General may file the suit.

(3) If, after investigation of the enactment or adoption of the order, ordinance, or rule, the Attorney General determines that there is no reasonable cause to proceed with an action, he or she shall publicly state in writing the justification for the determination not to file suit.

(4) The Attorney General shall either bring an action or publicly state, within 90 days of receipt of the petition, in the written justification why a violation of the spirit of this section, specifically subsections (a) and (c), has not occurred.

(5) The court may award reimbursement for actual and reasonable expenses to a person adversely affected if an action under this subsection results in a final determination in favor of the person adversely affected.

(g) This section shall not be construed to prevent any of the following:

(1) A duly organized law enforcement agency of a political subdivision from promulgating and enforcing rules pertaining to firearms, ammunition, or firearm accessories that it issues to or that are used by the political subdivision's peace officers in the course of their official duties.

(2) An employer from regulating or prohibiting an employee's carrying or possession of firearms, firearm accessories, or ammunition during and in the course of the employee's official duties.

(3) A prosecutor, court or administrative law judge from hearing and resolving a case or controversy or issuing an opinion or order on a matter within its jurisdiction.

(4) The enactment or enforcement of a generally applicable zoning or business ordinance that includes firearms businesses along with other businesses, provided that an ordinance designed or enforced effectively to restrict or prohibit the sale, purchase, transfer, manufacture, or display of firearms, ammunition, or firearm accessories that is otherwise lawful under the laws of this state is in conflict with this section and is void.

(5) A political subdivision from enacting and enforcing rules of operation and use for any firearm range owned or operated by the political subdivision.

(6) A political subdivision from sponsoring or conducting any firearm-related competition or educational or cultural program and from enacting and enforcing rules for participation in or attendance at such program, provided that nothing in this section authorizes or permits a political subdivision to offer remuneration for the surrender or transfer of a privately owned firearm to the political subdivision or another party as a method of reducing the number of privately owned firearms within the political subdivision.

(7) Any official of a political subdivision, a sheriff, or other law enforcement officer with appropriate authority and jurisdiction from enforcing any law enacted by the Legislature.

(8) A sheriff of a county from acting on an application for a permit under § 13A-11-75, Code of Alabama 1975.

(9) A political subdivision from leasing public property to another person or entity for a gun show or other firearm-related event on terms agreeable to both parties.

(10) The adoption or enforcement by a county or municipality of ordinances which make the violation of a state firearm law a violation of an ordinance, provided that the elements of the local ordinance may not differ from the state firearm law, nor may the local ordinance impose a higher penalty than what is imposed under the state firearm law.

(11) A municipality from regulating the discharge of firearms within the limits of the municipality or a county from exercising any authority it has under law, to regulate the discharge of firearms within the jurisdiction of the county. The discharge of a firearm in defense of one's self or family or in defense of one's property may not be construed to be a violation of state law or any ordinance or rule of a political subdivision of this state.

(12) A county or a municipality from exercising any authority it has to assess, enforce, and collect generally applicable sales taxes, use taxes, and gross receipts taxes in the nature of sales taxes as defined by § 40-2A-3(8), Code of Alabama 1975, on the retail sale of firearms, ammunition, and firearm accessories along with other goods, provided that no such tax imposed by a county or municipality may apply at a higher rate to firearms, ammunition, or firearm accessories than the general sales tax rate of the jurisdiction.

Division 1A Rifles and Shotguns

§ 13A-11-62. Definitions. For purposes of this division, the following terms shall have the following meanings, unless the context clearly indicates otherwise:

(1) Firearm. – Definition is same as provided in § 13A-8-1(4).

(2) Rifle. – Any weapon designed or redesigned, made or remade, and intended to be fired from the shoulder and designed or redesigned and made or remade to use the energy of the explosive in a fixed metallic cartridge to fire only a single projectile through a rifled bore for each pull of the trigger.

(3) Shotgun. – A weapon designed or redesigned, made or remade, and intended to be fired from the shoulder and designed or redesigned and made or remade to use the energy of the explosive in a fixed shotgun shell to fire through a smooth bore either a number of ball shot or a single projectile for each single pull of the trigger.

(4) Short-barreled rifle. – A rifle having one or more barrels less than 16 inches in length and any weapon made from a rifle (whether by alteration, modification, or otherwise) if such weapon, as modified, has an overall length of less than 26 inches.

(5) Short-barreled shotgun. – A shotgun having one or more barrels less than 18 inches in length and any weapon made from a shotgun (whether by alteration, modification, or otherwise) if such weapon as modified has an overall length of less than 26 inches.

§ 13A-11-63. Short-barreled rifle or shotgun; possession, sale, etc.
(a) A person who possesses, obtains, receives, sells, or uses a short-barreled rifle or a short-barreled shotgun in violation of federal law is guilty of a Class C felony.
(b) This section does not apply to a peace officer who possesses, obtains, receives, sells, or uses a short-barreled rifle or a short-barreled shotgun in the course of or in connection with his or her official duties.

§ 13A-11-64. Identification number, mark or name; altering; possession after alteration. A person who either:
(1) Changes, alters, removes, or obliterates the name of the maker, model, manufacturer's number or other mark or identification of any firearm, or

(2) Possesses, obtains, receives, sells, or uses a firearm after the maker, model, manufacturer's number or other mark or identification has been changed, altered, removed, or obliterated, is guilty of a Class C felony.

§ 13A-11-65. Violation in connection with commission of other felony. Violation of § 13A-11-63(a) or § 13A-11-64 in the course of, or in connection with the commission of any other felony shall be a Class B felony, and the punishment imposed therefor shall be in addition to the punishment imposed for the other felony.

§ 13A-11-66. Supplement to other laws – Penalties provided by other laws. This division is supplemental to any other law and the penalties provided herein are in addition to any other penalties provided by law. This division shall not be construed to limit or in any way reduce the minimum and maximum penalties provided in any other law.

Division 2 Pistols

§ 13A-11-70. Definitions. For the purposes of this division, the following terms shall have the respective meanings ascribed by this section:

(1) Pistol. – Any firearm with a barrel less than 12 inches in length.

(2) Crime of violence. – Any of the following crimes or an attempt to commit any of them, namely, murder, manslaughter, (except manslaughter arising out of the operation of a vehicle), rape, mayhem, assault with intent to rob, assault with intent to ravish, assault with intent to murder, robbery, burglary, and kidnapping. "Crime of violence" shall also mean any Class A felony or any Class B felony that has as an element serious physical injury, the distribution or manufacture of a controlled substance, or is of a sexual nature involving a child under the age of 12.

(3) Person. – Such term includes any firm, partnership, association or corporation.

§ 13A-11-71. Committing crime of violence when armed with pistol. If any person shall commit or attempt to commit a crime of violence when armed with a pistol, he may, in addition to the punishment provided for the crime, be punished also as provided by this division. In the trial of a person for committing or attempting to commit a crime of violence, the fact that he was armed with a pistol and had no license to carry the same shall be prima facie evidence of his intention to commit said crime of violence.

§ 13A-11-72. Violent felons, drug addicts or drunkards; possession and ownership restrictions – School grounds; possession or carrying on prohibited.
(a) No person who has been convicted in this state or elsewhere of committing or attempting to commit a crime of violence, misdemeanor offense of domestic violence, violent offense as listed in § 12-25-32(15), anyone who is subject to a valid protection order for domestic abuse, or anyone of unsound mind shall own a firearm or have one in his or her possession or under his or her control.
(b) No person who is a minor, except under the circumstances provided in this section, a drug addict, or an habitual drunkard shall own a pistol or have one in his or her possession or under his or her control.
(c) Subject to the exceptions provided by § 13A-11-74, no person shall knowingly with intent to do bodily harm carry or possess a deadly weapon on the premises of a public school.
(d) Possession of a deadly weapon with the intent to do bodily harm on the premises of a public school in violation of subsection (c) of this section is a Class C felony.
(e) School security personnel and school resource officers qualified under subsection (a) of § 16-1-44.1, employed by a local board of education, and authorized by the employing local board of education to carry a deadly weapon while on duty are exempt from subsection (c) of this section. Law enforcement officers are exempt from this section, and persons with pistol permits issued pursuant to § 13A-11-75, are exempt from subsection (c) of this section.
(f) A person shall not be in violation of § 13A-11-57 or 13A-11-76 and a minor shall not be in violation of this section if the minor has permission to possess a pistol from a parent or legal guardian who is not prohibited from possessing a firearm under state or federal law, and any of the following are satisfied:
(1) The minor is attending a hunter education course or a firearms safety course under the supervision of an adult who is not prohibited from possessing a firearm under state or federal law.
(2) The minor is engaging in practice in the use of a firearm or target shooting at an established range under the supervision of an adult who is not prohibited from possessing a firearm under state or federal law.
(3) The minor is engaging in an organized competition involving the use of a firearm or participating in or practicing for a performance by an organized group under 26 U.S.C. § 501(c)(3) which uses firearms as part of the performance.
(4) The minor is hunting or fishing pursuant to a valid license, if required, and the person has the license in his or her possession; has written permission of the owner or legal possessor of the land on which the activities are being conducted; and the pistol, when loaded, is carried only in a manner discernible by ordinary observation.
(5) The minor is on real property under the control of the minor's parent, legal guardian, or grandparent.
(6) The minor is a member of the armed services or National Guard and the minor is acting in the line of duty.
(7) The minor is traveling by motor vehicle to any of the locations or activities listed in subdivisions (1) through (6), has written permission to possess the pistol by his or her parent or legal guardian, and the pistol is unloaded, locked in a compartment or container that is in or affixed securely to the motor vehicle and is out of reach of the driver and any passenger in the motor vehicle.
(g) This section does not apply to a minor who uses a pistol while acting in self-defense of himself or herself or other

persons against an intruder into the residence of the minor or a residence in which the minor is an invited guest.

(h) The term "school resource officer" as used in this section means an Alabama Peace Officers' Standards and Training Commissioner-certified law enforcement officer employed by a law enforcement agency who is specifically selected and specially trained for the school setting.

(i) The term "public school" as used in this section applies only to a school composed of grades K-12 and shall include a school bus used for grades K-12.

(j) The term "deadly weapon" as used in this section means a firearm or anything manifestly designed, made, or adapted for the purposes of inflicting death or serious physical injury, and such term includes, but is not limited to, a bazooka, hand grenade, missile, or explosive or incendiary device; a pistol, rifle, or shotgun;....

(k) (1) The term "convicted" as used in this section requires that the person was represented by counsel in the case, or knowingly and intelligently waived the right to counsel in the case if required by law, and either the case was tried before a judge, tried by a jury, or the person knowingly and intelligently waived the right to have the case tried, by guilty plea or otherwise.

(2) A person may not be considered to have been convicted for the purposes of this section if the person is not considered to have been convicted in the jurisdiction in which the proceedings were held or the conviction has been expunged, set aside, or is of an offense for which the person has been pardoned or has had civil rights restored, unless the pardon, expungement, or restoration of civil rights expressly provides that the person may not ship, transport, possess, or receive firearms.

(l) The term "misdemeanor offense of domestic violence" as used in this section means a misdemeanor offense that has, as its elements, the use or attempted use of physical force or the threatened use of a dangerous instrument or deadly weapon, and the victim is a current or former spouse, parent, child, person with whom the defendant has a child in common, or a present or former household member.

(m) The term "valid protection order" as used in this section means an order issued after a hearing of which the person received actual notice, and at which the person had an opportunity to participate, that does any of the following:

(1) Restrains the person from harassing, stalking, or threatening a qualified individual or child of the qualified individual or person or engaging in other conduct that would place a qualified individual in reasonable fear of bodily injury to the individual or child and that includes a finding that the person represents a credible threat to the physical safety of the qualified individual or child.

(2) By its terms, explicitly prohibits the use, attempted use, or threatened use of physical force against the qualified individual or child that would reasonably be expected to cause bodily injury.

(n) The term "qualified individual" as used in subsection (m), means a spouse or former spouse of the person, an individual who is a parent of a child of the person, or an individual who cohabitates or has cohabited with the person.

(o) The term "unsound mind" as used in this section includes any person who is subject to any of the findings listed below, and who has not had his or her rights to possess a firearm reinstated by operation of law or legal process:

(1) Found by a court, board, commission, or other lawful authority that, as a result of marked subnormal intelligence, mental illness, incompetency, condition, or disease, is a danger to himself or herself or others or lacks the mental capacity to contract or manage his or her own affairs.

(2) Found to be insane, not guilty by reason of mental disease or defect, found mentally incompetent to stand trial, or found not guilty by a reason of lack of mental responsibility by a court in a criminal case, to include state, federal and military courts.

(3) Involuntarily committed for a final commitment for inpatient treatment to the Department of Mental Health or a Veterans' Administration hospital by a court after a hearing.

§ 13A-11-73. License to carry pistol; generally.

(a) Except on land under his or her control or in his or her own abode or his or her own fixed place of business, no person shall carry a pistol in any vehicle or concealed on or about his or her person without a permit issued under § 13A-11-75(a)(1) or recognized under § 13A-11-85.

(b) Except as otherwise prohibited by law, a person legally permitted to possess a pistol, but who does not possess a valid concealed weapon permit, may possess an unloaded pistol in his or her motor vehicle if the pistol is locked in a compartment or container that is in or affixed securely to the vehicle and out of reach of the driver and any passenger in the vehicle.

§ 13A-11-74. License to carry pistol; exceptions. The provisions of § 13A-11-73 shall not apply to marshals, sheriffs, prison and jail wardens and their regularly employed deputies, policemen and other law enforcement officers of any state or political subdivision thereof, or to the members of the army, navy or marine corps of the United States or of the national guard, or to the members of the national guard organized reserves or state guard organizations when on duty or going to or from duty, or to the regularly enrolled members of any organization duly authorized to purchase or receive such weapons from the United States or from this state; provided, that such members are at or are going to or from their places of assembly or target practices, or to officers or employees of the United States duly authorized to carry a pistol, or to any person engaged in manufacturing, repairing or dealing in pistols, or the agent or representative of such person possessing, using, or carrying a pistol in the usual or ordinary course of such business, or to any common carrier, except taxicabs, licensed as a common carrier, or to any person permitted by law to possess a pistol while carrying it unloaded in

a secure wrapper, from the place of purchase to his home or place of business, or to or from a place of repair or in moving from one place of abode or business to another.

§ 13A-11-75. License to carry pistol; issuance; form and content; copies; fee; revocation.

(a) (1) a. The sheriff of a county, upon the application of any person residing in that county, within 30 days from receipt of a complete application and accompanying fee, shall issue or renew a permit for such person to carry a pistol in a vehicle or concealed on or about his or her person within this state for 1 to 5 year increments, as requested by the person seeking the permit, from date of issue, unless the sheriff determines that the person is prohibited from the possession of a pistol or firearm pursuant to state or federal law, or has a reasonable suspicion that the person may use a weapon unlawfully or in such other manner that would endanger the person's self or others. In making such determination, the sheriff may consider whether the applicant:

    1. Was found guilty but mentally ill in a criminal case.

    2. Was found not guilty in a criminal case by reason of insanity or mental disease or defect.

    3. Was declared incompetent to stand trial in a criminal case.

    4. Asserted a defense in a criminal case of not guilty by reason of insanity or mental disease or defect.

    5. Was found not guilty only by reason of lack of mental responsibility under the Uniform Code of Military Justice.

    6. Required involuntary inpatient treatment in a psychiatric hospital or similar treatment facility.

    7. Required involuntary outpatient treatment in a psychiatric hospital or similar treatment facility based on a finding that the person is an imminent danger to himself or herself or to others.

    8. Required involuntary commitment to a psychiatric hospital or similar treatment facility for any reason, including drug use.

    9. Is or was the subject of a prosecution or of a commitment or incompetency proceeding that could lead to a prohibition on the receipt or possession of a firearm under the laws of Alabama or the United States.

    10. Falsified any portion of the permit application.

    11. Caused justifiable concern for public safety.

    b. The sheriff shall take into account how recent any consideration under paragraph a. is in relation to the date of the application. The sheriff shall provide a written statement of the reasons for a denial of a permit and the evidence upon which it is based must be disclosed to the applicant, unless disclosure would interfere with a criminal investigation.

    c. Except as otherwise provided by the laws of this state, a permit issued under this subdivision is valid throughout the state, and a sheriff may not place conditions or requirements on the issuance of the permit or limit its scope or applicability.

    (2) a. The sheriff may revoke a permit issued under subdivision (1) for any reason that could lead to a denial of a permit under that subdivision.

    b. The sheriff shall provide a written statement of the reasons for the revocation and the evidence upon which it is based must be disclosed to the applicant, unless disclosure would interfere with a criminal investigation.

    (3) A person who is denied a permit under subdivision (1), or a person whose permit is revoked under subdivision (2), within 30 days of notification of the denial or revocation, may appeal the denial or revocation to the district court of the county where the denial or revocation was issued. Upon a review of a denial under this subdivision, the sheriff shall have the burden of proving by clear and convincing evidence that the person is prohibited from possession of a pistol or other firearm pursuant to state or federal law or, based on any of the considerations enumerated in the subsection (a)(1) that the person may use a weapon unlawfully or in such other manner as would endanger the person's self or others if granted a permit to carry a concealed weapon under this section.

    (4) Within 30 days of receipt of the appeal, the district court shall review the appeal and issue a determination providing the reasons for the determination.

    (5) If the district court issues a determination in favor of a person whose permit was denied or revoked, the person shall be issued a permit or the permit must be reinstated.

    (6) Nothing in this section shall be construed to permit a sheriff to disregard any federal law or regulation pertaining to the purchase or possession of a firearm.

(b) Each permit shall be written or in an electronic or digital form to be prescribed by the Secretary of State in consultation with the Alabama Sheriff's Association, and shall bear the name, address, description, and signature of the permittee. The original hardcopy of the permit shall be delivered to the permittee, and a duplicate shall, within 7 days, be sent by registered or certified mail to the Director of Public Safety. The application and a copy shall be preserved for 6 years by the authority issuing the same. The sheriff may charge a fee as provided by local law for the issuance of the permit under subdivision (1) of subsection (a). The amount of the fee for a period of 1 year up to 5 years shall be the amount of the fee as prescribed by local law multiplied by the number of years of the permit requested by the applicant. The fee shall be paid into the county treasury unless otherwise provided by local law. Prior to issuance or renewal of a permit, the sheriff shall contact available local, state, and federal criminal history data banks, including the National Instant Criminal Background Check System, to determine whether possession of a firearm by an applicant would be a violation of state or federal law.

(c) For the convenience of the applicant, the sheriff may provide for application or renewal of a permit under subdivision (1) of subsection (a) through electronic means. The sheriff may also accept payment for a permit by debit or credit card or other consumer electronic payment method. Any transaction or banking fee charged for the electronic payment method shall be paid by the applicant.

(d) If a person who is not a United States citizen applies for a permit under this section, the sheriff shall conduct an Immigration Alien Query through U.S. Immigration and Customs Enforcement, or any successor agency, and the application form shall require information relating to the applicant's country of citizenship, place of birth, and any alien or admission number issued by U.S. Immigration and Customs Enforcement, or any successor agency. The sheriff shall review the results of these inquiries before making a determination of whether to issue a permit or renewal permit. A person who is unlawfully present in this state may not be issued a permit under this section.

(e) The name, address, signature, photograph, and any other personally identifying information collected from an applicant or permittee under this section shall be kept confidential, shall be exempt from disclosure under § 36-12-40, and may only be used for law enforcement purposes except when a current permittee is charged in any state with a felony involving the use of a pistol. All other information on permits under this section, including information concerning the annual number of applicants, number of permits issued, number of permits denied or revoked, revenue from issuance of permits, and any other fiscal or statistical data otherwise, shall remain public writings subject to public disclosure. Except as provided above, the sheriff of a county shall redact the name, address, signature, photograph, and any other personally identifying information of an permit holder before releasing a copy of a permit for a non-law enforcement purpose. The sheriff may charge $1 per copy of any redacted permit record requested other than when requested for law enforcement purposes. To knowingly publish or release to the public in any form any information or records related to the licensing process, or the current validity of any permit, except as authorized in this subsection or in response to a court order or subpoena, is a Class A misdemeanor.

(f) A concealed pistol permit issued under this section shall be valid for the carrying of a pistol in a motor vehicle or concealed on the permittees person throughout the state, unless prohibited

(g) This section shall not be construed to limit or place any conditions upon a person's right to carry a pistol that is not in a motor vehicle or not concealed.

(h) If a person issued a pistol permit in this state establishes residence in another state, the pistol permit shall expire upon the establishment of residence in the other state.

§ 13A-11-75.1. Certain retired military personnel permitted to obtain free pistol permit.

(a) The words "retired military veteran" as used in this section, unless the context clearly requires a different meaning, means only those persons who are nondisability retirees from active duty in the Army, or the Navy, or the Marine Corps, or the Air Force, or the Coast Guard of the United States or any reserve or National Guard component thereof.

(b) Any retired military veteran who meets the conditions for issuance of a pistol permit pursuant to § 13A-11-75, Code of Alabama 1975, shall be eligible to obtain the pistol permit without paying a fee for the permit. Upon approval of the pistol permit application, the pistol permit shall be issued by the sheriff of the county in which the veteran resides upon presentation by the retired military veteran of the United States government issued Veteran Identification Card or a DD-214 Proof of Military Service form and sufficient proof that the person is a military retiree. The retired military veteran shall apply for renewal as required by law, but shall be eligible to obtain renewed pistol permits without paying a fee as long as he or she meets the conditions for renewal of the permit.

(c) In the event a retired veteran, to whom a pistol permit has been issued pursuant to subsection (b), is suspected of or is charged with any crime, then the sheriff of the county in which the retired veteran resides may revoke the pistol permit. The sheriff shall notify the retired veteran in writing and by registered mail that his or her pistol permit is revoked. The sheriff shall state the reasons for the revocation and order the retiree to return his or her pistol permit to that sheriff within 30 days. Should the retired veteran refuse to return the pistol permit within the 30-day limit and continue to carry the handgun, he or she shall be guilty of carrying a weapon without a license or carrying a concealed weapon, whichever might be the case.

§ 13A-11-76. Delivery to minors, violent felons, etc.

(a) Except as provided in subsection (b), no person shall deliver a pistol to any person who he or she has reasonable cause to believe is a minor, except under the circumstances provided in § 13A-11-72, a drug addict, or an habitual drunkard, has been convicted in this state or elsewhere of committing or attempting to commit a crime of violence, misdemeanor offense of domestic violence, a violent offense as listed in § 12-25-32(15), or anyone who is subject to a valid protection order for domestic abuse, or anyone of unsound mind.

(b) A person may deliver a pistol to a person otherwise prohibited from receiving a pistol under subsection (a), if the person has had his or her firearm rights restored by operation of law or legal process.

(c) For the purposes of this subsection, the terms "convicted," "misdemeanor offense of domestic violence," "valid protection order," and "unsound mind" shall have the same meanings as provided in § 13A-11-72.

§ 13A-11-78. License to sell pistol; generally.
No retail dealer shall sell or otherwise transfer, or expose for sale or transfer, or have in his possession with intent to sell, or otherwise transfer, any pistol without being licensed as hereinafter provided.

§ 13A-11-79. License to sell pistol; granting; term; conditions; fee.

(a) The duly constituted licensing authorities of any city, town or political subdivision of this state may grant licenses in forms prescribed by the secretary of state, effective for not more than one year from date of issue, permitting the licensee to sell pistols at retail within this state subject to the following conditions, for breach of any of which the license shall be forfeited and the licensee subject to punishment as provided in this division. The business shall be carried on only in the building designated in the license. The license or a copy thereof, certified by the issuing authority, shall be displayed on the premises where it can easily be read. The fee for issuing the license shall be $50, which fee shall be paid into the State Treasury.

(b) All records of pistol, revolver, or maxim silencer sales that are maintained or in the custody of dealers, the chief of police, the sheriff, or the Secretary of State pursuant to this section or § 40-12-143, including any records or databases compiled as a result of or based on the records or information so maintained or received, shall be permanently removed and destroyed without reproduction of the removed documents no later than February 28, 2016. This section does not apply to any record necessary for an active investigation or ongoing prosecution.

§ 13A-11-80. Loaning pistols. No person shall make any loan secured by a mortgage, deposit or pledge of a pistol contrary to this division, nor shall any person lend or give a pistol to another or otherwise deliver a pistol contrary to the provisions of this division.

§ 13A-11-81. False information or identification; purchase of pistol; application for license. No person shall, in purchasing or otherwise securing delivery of a pistol or in applying for a license to carry the same, give false information or offer false evidence of his identity.

§ 13A-11-83. Applicability; pistols as curiosities or ornaments. This division shall not apply to the purchase, possession or sale of pistols as curiosities or ornaments or to the transportation of such pistols unloaded and in a bag, box or securely wrapped package, but not concealed on the person.

§ 13A-11-84. Penalty – Seizure of pistol – Destruction or use by law enforcement officer.
(a) Every violation of subsection (a) of § 13A-11-72 or § 13A-11-81 shall be a Class C felony. Every violation of subsection (b) of § 13A-11-72 or §§ 13A-11-73, 13A-11-74, 13A-11-76, and 13A-11-77 through 13A-11-80 shall be a Class A misdemeanor. The punishment for violating § 13A-11-78 or 13A-11-79 may include revocation of license.
(b) It shall be the duty of any sheriff, policeman, or other peace officer of the State of Alabama, arresting any person charged with violating §§ 13A-11-71 through 13A-11-73, or any one or more of those sections, to seize the pistol or pistols in the possession or under the control of the person or persons charged with violating the section or sections, and to deliver the pistol or pistols to one of the following named persons: if a municipal officer makes the arrest, to the city clerk or custodian of stolen property of the municipality employing the arresting officer; if a county, state, or other peace officer makes the arrest, to the sheriff of the county in which the arrest is made. The person receiving the pistol or pistols from the arresting officer shall keep it in a safe place in as good condition as received until disposed of as hereinafter provided. Within five days after the final conviction of any person arrested for violating any of the above-numbered sections, the person receiving possession of the pistol or pistols, seized as provided in this section, shall report the seizure and detention of the pistol or pistols to the district attorney within the county where the pistol or pistols are seized, giving a full description thereof, the number, make and model thereof, the name of the person in whose possession it was found when seized, the person making claim to same or any interest therein, if the name can be ascertained or is known, and the date of the seizure. Upon receipt of the report from the person receiving possession of the pistol or pistols, it shall be the duty of the district attorney within the county wherein the pistol or pistols were seized to forthwith file a complaint in the circuit court of the proper county, praying that the seized pistol or pistols be declared contraband, be forfeited to the state and be destroyed. Any person, firm or corporation or association of persons in whose possession said pistol or pistols may be seized or who claim to own the same or any interest therein shall be made a party defendant to the complaint, and thereupon the matter shall proceed and be determined in the circuit court of the proper county in the same form and manner, as near as may be, as in the forfeiture and destruction of gaming devices, except as otherwise provided. When any judgment of condemnation and forfeiture is made in any case filed under this section, the judge making the judgment shall direct the destruction of the pistol or pistols by the person receiving possession of the pistol or pistols from the arresting officer in the presence of the clerk or register of the court, unless the judge is of the opinion that the non-destruction thereof is necessary or proper in the ends of justice, in which event and upon recommendation of the district attorney, the judge shall award the pistol or pistols to the sheriff of the county or to the chief of police of the municipality to be used exclusively by the sheriff or the chief of police in the enforcement of law, and the sheriff of the county and the chiefs of police of the municipalities shall keep a permanent record of all pistols awarded to them as provided for in this section, to be accounted for as other public property, and the order, in the event that no appeal is taken within 15 days from the rendition thereof, shall be carried out and executed before the expiration of 20 days from the date of the judgment. The court may direct in the judgment that the costs of the proceedings be paid by the person in whose possession the pistol or pistols were found when seized, or by any party or parties who claim to own the pistol or pistols, or any interest therein, and who contested the condemnation and forfeiture thereof.

§ 13A-11-85. Out-of-state license; reciprocity.
(a) A person licensed to carry a handgun in any state shall be authorized to carry a handgun in this state. This section shall apply to a license holder from another state only while the license holder is not a resident of this state. A license holder from another state shall carry the handgun in compliance with the laws of this state.
(b) The Attorney General is authorized to enter into reciprocal agreements with other states for the mutual recognition of licenses to carry handguns and shall periodically publish a list of states which recognize licenses issued pursuant to § 13A-11-75.

Division 3 Firearms in Place of Employment

§ 13A-11-90. Possession of firearm on employer's property.

(a) Except as provided in subdivision (b), a public or private employer may restrict or prohibit its employees, including those with a permit issued or recognized under § 13A-11-75, Code of Alabama 1975, from carrying firearms while on the employer's property or while engaged in the duties of the person's employment.

(b) A public or private employer may not restrict or prohibit the transportation or storage of a lawfully possessed firearm or ammunition in an employee's privately owned motor vehicle while parked or operated in a public or private parking area if the employee satisfies all of the following:

  (1) The employee either:

    a. Has a valid concealed weapon permit; or

    b. If the weapon is any firearm legal for use for hunting in Alabama other than a pistol:

      i. The employee possesses a valid Alabama hunting license;

      ii. The weapon is unloaded at all times on the property;

      iii. It is during a season in which hunting is permitted by Alabama law or regulation;

      iv. The employee has never been convicted of any crime of violence as that term is defined in § 13A-11-70, Code of Alabama 1975, nor of any crime set forth in Chapter 6 of Title 13A, Code of Alabama 1975, nor is subject to a Domestic Violence Order, as that term is defined in § 13A-6-141, Code of Alabama 1975;

      v. The employee does not meet any of the factors set forth in § 13A-11-75(a)(1)a.1-8; and

      vi. The employee has no documented prior workplace incidents involving the threat of physical injury or which resulted in physical injury.

  (2) The motor vehicle is operated or parked in a location where it is otherwise permitted to be.

  (3) The firearm is either of the following:

    a. In a motor vehicle attended by the employee, kept from ordinary observation within the person's motor vehicle.

    b. In a motor vehicle unattended by the employee, kept from ordinary observation and locked within a compartment, container, or in the interior of the person's privately owned motor vehicle or in a compartment or container securely affixed to the motor vehicle.

(c) If an employer believes that an employee presents a risk of harm to himself/herself or to others, the employer may inquire as to whether the employee possesses a firearm in his or her private motor vehicle. If the employee does possess a firearm in his or her private motor vehicle on the property of the employer, the employer may make any inquiry necessary to establish that the employee is in compliance with subsection (b).

  (1) If the employee is not in compliance with subsection (b), the employer may take adverse employment action against the employee, in the discretion of the employer.

  (2) If the employee has been in compliance with subsection (b) at all times, the employer may not take adverse employment action against the employee based solely on the presence of the firearm.

(d) If an employer discovers by other means that an employee is transporting or storing a firearm in his or her private motor vehicle, the employer may not take any adverse employment action against the employee based solely on the possession of that firearm if the employee has complied with the requirements in subsection (b).

(e) Nothing in this section shall prohibit an employer from reporting to law enforcement a complaint based upon information and belief that there is credible evidence of any of the following:

  (1) That the employee's motor vehicle contains:

    a. A firearm prohibited by state or federal law.

    b. Stolen property or a prohibited or illegal item other than a firearm.

  (2) A threat made by an employee to cause bodily harm to themselves or others.

(f) If law enforcement officers, pursuant to a valid search warrant or valid warrantless search based upon probable cause, exigent circumstances, or other lawful exception to the search warrant requirement, discover a firearm prohibited by state or federal law, stolen property, or a prohibited or illegal item other than a firearm, the employer may take adverse employment action against the employee.

(g) However, if the employee has fully complied with the requirements of subsection (b) and does not possess a firearm prohibited by state or federal law, that employee is entitled to recovery as specified in this subsection for any adverse employment action against the employee. If demand for the recovery has not been satisfied within 45 calendar days, the employee may file a civil action in the appropriate court of this state against the public or private employer. A plaintiff is entitled to seek an award of all of the following:

  (1) Compensation, if applicable, for lost wages or benefits.

  (2) Compensation, if applicable, for other lost remuneration caused by the termination, demotion, or other adverse action.

(h) The license requirements set forth in sections (b)(1)a. and (b)(1)b.i. are for the purposes of this section only in order to determine whether an employee may transport or store a lawfully possessed firearm or ammunition in an employee's privately owned motor vehicle while parked or operated in a public or private parking area owned by the employer and shall not be construed to otherwise expand the requirements for the lawful possession of a firearm. These requirements shall not be interpreted to mean that the laws of the State of Alabama create any new connection between the possession of a hunting license and the right of a citizen to keep and bear arms.

(i) Prohibitions regarding the carrying of a firearm under this section shall not apply to law enforcement officers engaged in the lawful execution of their official duties.

(j) Nothing in this section shall be construed to authorize the transportation, carrying, storing, or possession of a firearm or ammunition where prohibited by federal law.

§ 13A-11-91. Employer's or property owner's immunity from liability for firearm possession.

(a) Except as provided in subsection (g) of § 13A-11-90, an employer and the owner and/or lawful possessor of the property on which the employer is situated shall be absolutely immune from any claim, cause of action or lawsuit that may be brought by any person seeking any form of damages that are alleged to arise, directly or indirectly, as a result of any firearm brought onto the property of the employer, owner or lawful possessor by an employee, including a firearm that is transported in an employee's privately owned motor vehicle.

(b) The presence of a firearm or ammunition on an employer's property under the authority of Acts 2013, No. 13-283 does not, by itself, constitute the failure by the employer to provide a safe workplace.

(c) For the purposes of Acts 2013, No. 13-283, a public or private employer, or the employer's principal, officer, director, employee, or agent, does not have a duty:

(1) To patrol, inspect, or secure:

a. Any parking lot, parking garage, or other parking area the employer provides for employees; or

b. Any privately owned motor vehicle located in a parking lot, parking garage, or other parking area the employer provides for employees; or

(2) To investigate, confirm, or determine an employees compliance with laws related to the ownership or possession of a firearm or ammunition or the transportation and storage of a firearm or ammunition.

(d) Nothing in this section shall be construed to provide immunity from liability to an employer, business entity or property owner for his or her own affirmative wrongful acts that cause harm, damage or injury to another.

(e) The denial by a Court of a Motion to Dismiss based on immunity grounds shall be appealable in the same manner as a final order to the appellate court which would otherwise have jurisdiction over the appeal from a final order of the action. Such appeal may only be filed within 42 days of the order denying the Motion to Dismiss. The filing of such appeal, the failure to file an appeal, or the affirmance of the denial of the Motion to Dismiss shall in no way affect the right of the Defendant, after entry of judgment, to appeal the denial of immunity. During the pendency of such appeal, the action in the trial court shall be stayed in all respects.

(f) Nothing in Acts 2013, No. 13-283 is intended to expand or limit the rights an employer or employee currently has under § 25-5-1 et seq., Code of Alabama 1975.

TITLE 40 Revenue and Taxation
Chapter 12 Licenses
Article 2 Business, Vocation or Occupation

§ 40-12-143. Weapons dealers. Persons dealing in pistols, revolvers, maxim silencers, bowie knives, dirk knives, brass knucks or knucks of like kind, whether principal stock in trade or not shall pay the following license tax: In cities and towns of 35,000 inhabitants and over, $150; and in all other places, $100. The required license amounts shall be paid for each place of business from which sales of such items are made. In addition to any other required licenses, a person may organize and conduct a gun and knife show of no more than 7 days, by paying the maximum license tax prescribed in this section, as well as the maximum license taxes provided in §§ 40-12-158 and 40-12-174(d), for each such show. Participants shall not be required to pay the license taxes provided in this section, nor in § 40-12-158 or 40-12-174 for participating in such shows, provided the organizer has paid the license taxes prescribed in this section prior to the commencement of the event. It shall be the duty of the organizer of such show to determine if each participant is licensed under the sales tax laws of this state as well as the particular county and municipality in which the show is conducted. The organizer shall be responsible for providing a list of participants to the county and municipality in which the gun show is held and for collecting and remitting all state and local sales taxes for any participant not licensed under state or local sales tax laws. In the event the organizer does not provide the information required herein or pay the license taxes prescribed in this section, prior to the commencement of the event, each participant shall be responsible for his or her applicable licenses. The organizer and all participants shall abide by applicable federal, state, and local laws and regulations.

§ 40-12-158. Shotgun sales.

(a) Each person dealing in shotguns, rifles of .22 caliber or over, metallic ammunition or shotgun shells shall pay a license tax of $25 in cities of 100,000 inhabitants or over; $10 in cities or towns of 7,000 and less than 100,000 inhabitants; and $3 in all other places, whether incorporated or not.

(b) Regularly licensed rolling stores selling any or all of the articles enumerated in this section shall, in addition to the license provided in § 40-12-174, pay a license tax of $5 to the state and $5 to the county in each county in which they sell or offer such articles for sale.

§ 41-9-649. Firearm purchase background check – Mims-Russell Law Enforcement Protection Act. All transfers or purchases of firearms conducted by a licensed importer, licensed manufacturer, or licensed dealer shall be subject to the national instant criminal background check system (NICS) created by the federal "Brady Handgun Violence Prevention Act" (P.L. No. 103-159), the relevant portion of which is codified at 18 U.S.C.S. § 922(t). To the extent possible, all information from any state or local government agency that is necessary to complete a NICS check shall be provided to the Criminal Justice Information Center. The Criminal Justice Information Center Commission shall promulgate rules and regulations necessary to implement a complete NICS Check. The commission shall also ensure that all information received shall be used solely for the purposes of compliance with NICS and every effort is made to protect the privacy of this information. All proposed rules shall go through the privacy and security committee of the commission which shall seek consultation from the President of the Probate Judges' Association and the Commissioner of the Department of Mental Health and consumer advocates as recommended by the commissioner.

Arkansas Code

Current through the 2016 Second Extraordinary Session, 2016 Fiscal Session, and 2016 Third Extraordinary Session of the 90th General Assembly.

Office of the Attorney General
323 Center Street, Suite 200
Little Rock, Arkansas 72201
Voice: (501) 682-2007
http://www.ag.arkansas.gov/

New Orleans Field Division
One Galleria Boulevard, Suite 1700
Metairie, Louisiana 70001
Voice: (504) 841-7000
https://www.atf.gov/new-orleans-field-division

PROTECTING THE PUBLIC
SERVING OUR NATION

Table of Contents

TITLE 14, Subtitle 2, Chapter 16, Subchapter 5 — Regulation of Use of Firearms and Archery Equipment

TITLE 5: Criminal Offenses
Chapter 1: General Provisions

§ 5-1-102. Definitions. As used in the Arkansas Criminal Code:

(4) "**Deadly weapon**" means:

  (A) A firearm or anything manifestly designed, made, or adapted for the purpose of inflicting death or serious physical injury; or

  (B) Anything that in the manner of its use or intended use is capable of causing death or serious physical injury;

(6) (A) "**Firearm**" means any device designed, made, or adapted to expel a projectile by the action of an explosive or any device readily convertible to that use.

  (B) "Firearm" includes:

    (i) A device described in subdivision (6)(A) of this section that is not loaded or lacks a clip or another component to render it immediately operable; and

    (ii) Components that can readily be assembled into a device described in subdivision (6)(A) of this section;

(19) "**Sawed-off or short-barreled rifle**" means:

  (A) A rifle having 1 or more barrels less than 16 inches in length; or

  (B) Any weapon made from a rifle, whether by alteration, modification, or otherwise, if the weapon, as modified, has an overall length of less than 26 inches;

(20) "**Sawed-off or short-barreled shotgun**" means:

  (A) A shotgun having 1 or more barrels less than 18 inches in length; or

  (B) Any weapon made from a shotgun, whether by alteration, modification, or otherwise, if the weapon, as modified, has an overall length of less than 26 inches;

Chapter 73: Weapons
Subchapter 1: Possession and Use Generally

§ 5-73-102. Possessing instrument of crime.

(a) A person commits the offense of possessing an instrument of crime if he or she possesses any instrument of crime with a purpose to employ it criminally.

(b) Possessing an instrument of crime is a Class A misdemeanor.

5-73-103. Possession of firearms by certain persons.

(a) Except as provided in subsection (d) of this section or unless authorized by and subject to such conditions as prescribed by the Governor, or his or her designee, or the United States Bureau of Alcohol, Tobacco, Firearms, and Explosives, or other bureau or office designated by the United States Department of Justice, no person shall possess or own any firearm who has been:

  (1) Convicted of a felony;

  (2) Adjudicated mentally ill; or

  (3) Committed involuntarily to any mental institution.

(b) (1) Except as provided in subdivisions (b)(2) and (3) of this section, a determination by a jury or a court that a person committed a felony constitutes a conviction for purposes of subsection (a) of this section even though the court suspended imposition of sentence or placed the defendant on probation.

  (2) Subdivision (b)(1) of this section does not apply to a person whose case was dismissed and expunged under § 16-93-301 et seq. or § 16-98-303(g).

  (3) The determination by the jury or court that the person committed a felony does not constitute a conviction for purposes of subsection (a) of this section if the person is subsequently granted a pardon explicitly restoring the ability to possess a firearm.

(c) (1) A person who violates this section commits a Class B felony if:

  (A) The person has a prior violent felony conviction;

  (B) The person's current possession of a firearm involves the commission of another crime; or

  (C) The person has been previously convicted under this section or a similar provision from another jurisdiction.

  (2) A person who violates this section commits a Class D felony if he or she has been previously convicted of a felony and his or her present conduct or the prior felony conviction does not fall within subdivision (c)(1) of this section.

(3) Otherwise, the person commits a Class A misdemeanor.

(d) The Governor may restore without granting a pardon the right of a convicted felon or an adjudicated delinquent to own and possess a firearm upon the recommendation of the chief law enforcement officer in the jurisdiction in which the person resides, so long as the underlying felony or delinquency adjudication:

(1) Did not involve the use of a weapon; and

(2) Occurred more than 8 years ago.

5-73-104. Criminal use of prohibited weapons.

(a) A person commits the offense of criminal use of prohibited weapons if, except as authorized by law, he or she uses, possesses, makes, repairs, sells, or otherwise deals in any:

(1) Bomb;

(2) Machine gun;

(3) Sawed-off shotgun or rifle;

(4) Firearm specially made or specially adapted for silent discharge;

(6) Other implement for the infliction of serious physical injury or death.

(b) It is a defense to prosecution under this section that:

(1) The defendant was a law enforcement officer, prosecuting attorney, deputy prosecuting attorney, prison guard, or member of the armed forces acting in the course and scope of his or her duty at the time he or she used or possessed the prohibited weapon; or

(2) The defendant used, possessed, made, repaired, sold, or otherwise dealt in any article enumerated in subsection (a) of this section under circumstances negating any likelihood that the weapon could be used as a weapon.

(c) (1) Criminal use of prohibited weapons is a Class B felony if the weapon is a bomb, machine gun, or firearm specially made or specially adapted for silent discharge.

(3) Otherwise, criminal use of prohibited weapons is a Class D felony.

§ 5-73-105. Legitimate manufacture, repair, and transportation of prohibited weapons.
Section 5-73-104 shall not be construed to prohibit the manufacture, repair, transportation, or sale of the weapons enumerated in § 5-73-104 to or for an authorized representative of:

(1) The armed forces; or

(2) Any law enforcement agency.

§ 5-73-106. Defacing a firearm.

(a) A person commits the offense of defacing a firearm if he or she knowingly removes, defaces, mars, covers, alters, or destroys the manufacturer's serial number or identification mark of a firearm.

(b) Defacing a firearm is a Class D felony.

§ 5-73-107. Possession of a defaced firearm.

(a) A person commits the offense of possession of a defaced firearm if he or she knowingly possesses a firearm with a manufacturer's serial number or other identification mark required by law that has been removed, defaced, marred, altered, or destroyed.

(b) It is a defense to a prosecution under this section that the person reported the possession to the police or other governmental agency prior to arrest or the issuance of an arrest warrant or summons.

(c) (1) Possession of a defaced firearm is a Class D felony.

(2) However, possession of a defaced firearm is a Class A misdemeanor if the manufacturer's serial number or other identification mark required by law is merely covered or obstructed, but still retrievable.

§ 5-73-109. Furnishing a deadly weapon to a minor.

(a) A person commits the offense of furnishing a deadly weapon to a minor if he or she sells, barters, leases, gives, rents, or otherwise furnishes a firearm or other deadly weapon to a minor without the consent of a parent, guardian, or other person responsible for general supervision of the minor's welfare.

(b)(1) Furnishing a deadly weapon to a minor is a Class A misdemeanor.

(2) However, furnishing a deadly weapon to a minor is a Class B felony if the deadly weapon is:

(A) A handgun;

(B) A sawed-off or short-barreled shotgun, as defined in § 5-1-102;

(C) A sawed-off or short-barreled rifle, as defined in § 5-1-102;

(D) A firearm that has been specially made or specially adapted for silent discharge;

(E) A machine gun;

(H) A defaced firearm, as defined in § 5-73-107; or

(I) Another implement for the infliction of serious physical injury or death that serves no common lawful purpose

§ 5-73-110. Disarming minors and mentally defective or mentally irresponsible persons – Disposition of property seized.

(a) Subject to constitutional limitation, nothing in this section and §§ 5-73-101 – 5-73-109 shall be construed to prohibit a law enforcement officer from disarming, without arresting, a minor or person who reasonably appears to be mentally defective or otherwise mentally irresponsible when that person is in possession of a deadly weapon.

(b) Property seized under subsection (a) of this section shall be:

(1) Held for 72 hours by the law enforcement agency employing the law enforcement officer who seized the property; and

(2) After the 72-hour hold and upon request and presentation of valid proof of ownership, returned to the:

(A) Owner, if he or she is 18 years of age or older and may lawfully possess the property; or

(B) Parent or legal guardian of the owner, if the owner is a minor and the parent or legal guardian may lawfully possess the property.

§ 5-73-111. Unlawful procurement of a firearm.

(a) As used in this section:

(1) "Ammunition" means any cartridge, shell, or projectile designed for use in a firearm;

(2) "False information" means information that portrays an unlawful transaction as lawful or a lawful transaction as unlawful;

(3) "Licensed dealer" means a person who is licensed under 18 U.S.C. § 923, as it existed on January 1, 2013, to engage in the business of dealing in firearms; and

(4) "Private seller" means a person other than a licensed dealer who sells or offers for sale a firearm or ammunition.

(b) A person commits the offense of unlawful procurement of a firearm or ammunition if he or she knowingly:

(1) Solicits, persuades, encourages, or entices a licensed dealer or private seller to transfer a firearm or ammunition under unlawful circumstances; or

(2) Provides false information to a licensed dealer or private seller with a purpose to deceive the licensed dealer or private seller concerning the lawfulness of a transfer of a firearm or ammunition.

(c) It is a defense to prosecution under this section if the person is:

(1) A law enforcement officer acting in his or her official capacity; or

(2) Acting at the direction of a law enforcement officer.

(d) Unlawful procurement of a firearm or ammunition is a Class D felony.

§ 5-73-112. Certification by a chief law enforcement officer regarding receipt or manufacture of a firearm.

(a) As used in this section:

(1) "Certification" means the participation and assent of the chief law enforcement officer or his or her designee necessary under federal law for the approval of an application to transfer or manufacture a firearm; and

(2) "Firearm" means the same as defined in § 5845(a) of the National Firearms Act, 26 U.S.C. § 5801 et seq. as it existed on January 1, 2015.

(b) (1) When certification by the chief law enforcement officer of a jurisdiction is required by federal law or regulation for the transfer or manufacture of a firearm within 15 days of receipt of a request for certification, the chief law enforcement officer or his or her designee shall provide the certification if the applicant is not prohibited by law from receiving or manufacturing the firearm or is not the subject of a proceeding that could result in the applicant's being prohibited by law from receiving or manufacturing the firearm.

(2) If the applicant is prohibited by law from receiving or manufacturing the firearm or is the subject of a proceeding that could result in a prohibition against his or her receiving or manufacturing the firearm, the chief law enforcement officer or his or her designee shall provide written notification to the applicant that states the reasons for his or her findings and that the certification is denied.

(c) (1) An applicant whose request for certification is denied may appeal the denial to the circuit court where the applicant resides.

(2) The circuit court shall review the denial de novo.

(3) If the circuit court finds that the applicant is not prohibited by law from receiving or manufacturing the firearm or is not the subject of a proceeding that could result in a prohibition against his or her receiving or manufacturing the firearm, the circuit court shall order the chief law enforcement officer to issue the certification to the applicant.

§ 5-73-119. Handguns – Possession by minor or possession on school property.

(a)(1) No person in this state under 18 years of age shall possess a handgun.

(2)(A) A violation of subdivision (a)(1) of this section is a Class A misdemeanor.

(B) A violation of subdivision (a)(1) of this section is a Class D felony if the person has previously:

(i) Been adjudicated delinquent for a violation of subdivision (a)(1) of this section;

(ii) Been adjudicated delinquent for any offense that would be a felony if committed by an adult; or

(iii) Pleaded guilty or nolo contendere to or been found guilty of a felony in circuit court while under 18 years of age.

(b)(1) No person in this state shall possess a firearm:

(A) Upon the developed property of a public or private school, kindergarten through grade 12 (K-12);

(B) In or upon any school bus; or

(C) At a designated bus stop as identified on the route list published by a school district each year.

(2)(A) A violation of subdivision (b)(1) of this section is a Class D felony.

(B) No sentence imposed for a violation of subdivision (b)(1) of this section shall be suspended or probated or treated as a first offense under § 16-93-301 et seq.

(c)(1) Except as provided in § 5-73-322, a person in this state shall not possess a handgun upon the property of any private institution of higher education or a publicly supported institution of higher education in this state on or about his or her person, in a vehicle occupied by him or her, or otherwise readily available for use with a purpose to employ the handgun as a weapon against a person.

(2) A violation of subdivision (c)(1) of this section is a Class D felony.

(d) "Handgun" means a firearm capable of firing rimfire ammunition or centerfire ammunition and designed or constructed to be fired with one (1) hand.

(e) It is permissible to carry a handgun under this section if at the time of the act of possessing a handgun or firearm:

(1) The person is in his or her own dwelling or place of business or on property in which he or she has a possessory or proprietary interest, except upon the property of a public or private institution of higher learning;

(2) The person is a law enforcement officer, correctional officer, or member of the armed forces acting in the course and scope of his or her official duties;

(3) The person is assisting a law enforcement officer, correctional officer, or member of the armed forces acting in the course and scope of his or her official duties pursuant to the direction or request of the law enforcement officer, correctional officer, or member of the armed forces;

(4) The person is a registered commissioned security guard acting in the course and scope of his or her duties;

(5) The person is hunting game with a handgun or firearm that may be hunted with a handgun or firearm under the rules and regulations of the Arkansas State Game and Fish Commission or is en route to or from a hunting area for the purpose of hunting game with a handgun or firearm;

(6) The person is a certified law enforcement officer;

(7) The person is on a journey beyond the county in which the person lives, unless the person is 18 years of age or less;

(8) The person is participating in a certified hunting safety course sponsored by the commission or a firearm safety course recognized and approved by the commission or by a state or national nonprofit organization qualified and experienced in firearm safety;

(9) The person is participating in a school-approved educational course or sporting activity involving the use of firearms;

(10) The person is a minor engaged in lawful marksmanship competition or practice or other lawful recreational shooting under the supervision of his or her parent, legal guardian, or other person 21 years of age or older standing in loco parentis or is traveling to or from a lawful marksmanship competition or practice or other lawful recreational shooting with an unloaded handgun or firearm accompanied by his or her parent, legal guardian, or other person 21 years of age or older standing in loco parentis;

(11) The person has a license to carry a concealed handgun under § 5-73-301 et seq. and is carrying a concealed handgun on the developed property of:

(A) A kindergarten through grade 12 (K-12) private school operated by a church or other place of worship that:

(i) Is located on the developed property of the kindergarten through grade 12 (K-12) private school;

(ii) Allows the person to carry a concealed handgun into the church or other place of worship under § 5-73-306; and

(iii) Allows the person to possess a concealed handgun on the developed property of the kindergarten through grade 12 (K-12) private school; or

(B) A kindergarten through grade 12 (K-12) private school or a prekindergarten private school that through its governing board or director has set forth the rules and circumstances under which the licensee may carry a concealed handgun into a building or event of the kindergarten through grade 12 (K-12) private school or the prekindergarten private school; or

(12) (A) The person has a license to carry a concealed handgun under § 5-73-301 et seq. and is carrying a concealed handgun in his or her motor vehicle or has left the concealed handgun in his or her locked and unattended motor vehicle in a publicly owned and maintained parking lot.

(B) (i) As used in this subdivision (e)(12), "parking lot" means a designated area or structure or part of a structure intended for the parking of motor vehicles or a designated drop-off zone for children at a school.

(ii) "Parking lot" does not include a parking lot owned, maintained, or otherwise controlled by the Department of Correction or Department of Community Correction.

§ 5-73-120. Carrying a weapon.

(a) A person commits the offense of carrying a weapon if he or she possesses a handgun, knife, or club on or about his or her person, in a vehicle occupied by him or her, or otherwise readily available for use with a purpose to attempt to unlawfully employ the handgun, knife, or club as a weapon against a person.

(b) As used in this section:

(2) "Handgun" means any firearm with a barrel length of less than 12 inches that is designed, made, or adapted to be fired with 1 hand;

(3) "Journey" means travel beyond the county in which a person lives; and

(c) It is permissible to carry a weapon under this section if at the time of the act of carrying the weapon:

(1) The person is in his or her own dwelling or place of business or on property in which he or she has a possessory or proprietary interest;

(2) The person is a law enforcement officer, correctional officer, or member of the armed forces acting in the course and scope of his or her official duties;

(3) The person is assisting a law enforcement officer, correctional officer, or member of the armed forces acting in the course and scope of his or her official duties pursuant to the direction or request of the law enforcement officer, correctional officer, or member of the armed forces;

(4) The person is carrying a weapon when upon a journey, unless the journey is through a commercial airport when presenting at the security checkpoint in the airport or is in the person's checked baggage and is not a lawfully declared weapon;

(5) The person is a registered commissioned security guard acting in the course and scope of his or her duties;

(6) The person is hunting game with a handgun that may be hunted with a handgun under rules and regulations of the Arkansas State Game and Fish Commission or is en route to or from a hunting area for the purpose of hunting game with a handgun;

(7) The person is a certified law enforcement officer;

(8) The person is in possession of a concealed handgun and has a valid license to carry a concealed handgun under § 5-73-301 et seq., or recognized under § 5-73-321 and is not in a prohibited place as defined by § 5-73-306;

(9) The person is a prosecuting attorney or deputy prosecuting attorney carrying a firearm under § 16-21-147; or

(10) The person is in possession of a handgun and is a retired law enforcement officer with a valid concealed carry authorization issued under federal or state law.

(d) Carrying a weapon is a Class A misdemeanor.

§ 5-73-122. Carrying a firearm in publicly owned buildings or facilities.

(a) (1) Except as provided in § 5-73-322 and § 5-73-306(5), it is unlawful for any person other than a law enforcement officer or a security guard in the employ of the state or an agency of the state, or any city or county, or any state or federal military personnel, to knowingly carry or possess a loaded firearm or other deadly weapon in any publicly owned building or facility or on the State Capitol grounds.

(2) It is unlawful for any person other than a law enforcement officer or a security guard in the employ of the state or an agency of the state, or any city or county, or any state or federal military personnel, to knowingly carry or possess a firearm, whether loaded or unloaded, in the State Capitol Building or the Justice Building in Little Rock.

(3) However, this subsection does not apply to a person carrying or possessing a firearm or other deadly weapon in a publicly owned building or facility or on the State Capitol grounds:

(A) For the purpose of participating in a shooting match or target practice under the auspices of the agency responsible for the publicly owned building or facility or State Capitol grounds;

(B) If necessary to participate in a trade show, exhibit, or educational course conducted in the publicly owned building or facility or on the State Capitol grounds; or

(C) (i) If the person has a license to carry a concealed handgun under § 5-73-301 et seq. and is carrying a concealed handgun in his or her motor vehicle or has left the concealed handgun in his or her locked and unattended motor vehicle in a publicly owned and maintained parking lot.

(ii) *(a)* As used in this subdivision (a)(3)(C), "parking lot" means a designated area or structure or part of a structure intended for the parking of motor vehicles or a designated drop-off zone for children at school.

(b) "Parking lot" does not include a parking lot owned, maintained, or otherwise controlled by the Department of Correction or Department of Community Correction.

(4) As used in this section, "facility" means a municipally owned or maintained park, football field, baseball field, soccer field, or another similar municipally owned or maintained recreational structure or property.

(b) (1) Any person other than a law enforcement officer, officer of the court, or bailiff, acting in the line of duty, or any other person authorized by the court, who possesses a handgun in the courtroom of any court of this state is guilty of a Class D felony.

(2) Otherwise, any person violating a provision of this section is guilty of a Class A misdemeanor.

§ 5-73-125. Interstate sale and purchase of shotguns, rifles, and ammunition.

(a) The sale of shotguns and rifles and ammunition in this state to residents of other states is authorized under regulations issued by the United States Attorney General under the Gun Control Act of 1968, 18 U.S.C. § 921 et seq., as in effect on January 1, 2009.

(b) A resident of this state may purchase a rifle, shotgun, or ammunition in another state as expressly authorized under the regulations issued under the Gun Control Act of 1968, 18 U.S.C. § 921 et seq., as in effect on January 1, 2009.

§ 5-73-127. Possession of loaded center-fire weapons in certain areas.

(a) It is unlawful to possess a loaded center-fire weapon, other than a shotgun and other than in a residence or business of the owner, in the following areas:

(1) Baxter County:

(A) That part bounded on the south by Highway 178, on the west and north by Bull Shoals Lake, and on the east by the Central Electric Power Corporation transmission line from Howard Creek to Highway 178;

(B) That part of Bidwell Point lying south of the east-west road which crosses Highway 101 at the Pre

(C) That part of Bidwell Point lying west of Bennett's Bayou and north of the east-west road which crosses Highway 101 at the Presbyterian Church;

(D) That part of Baxter County between:

(i) County Road 139 and Lake Norfork to the north and west;

(ii) County Road 151 and Lake Norfork to the north, west, and south in the Diamond Bay area;

(iii) The Bluff Road and Lake Norfork to the west;

(iv) John Lewis Road (Timber Lake Manor) and Lake Norfork to the west and south;

(v) The south end of County Road 91 south of its intersection with John Lewis Road and Lake Norfork to the south and east; and

(vi) County Road 150 from its intersection with County Road 93 south and Lake Norfork to the south and east but not east of County Road 93;

(2) Benton County:

(A) That part of the Hobbs Estate north of State Highway 12, west of Rambo Road, and south and east of Van Hollow Creek and the Van Hollow Creek arm of Beaver Lake;

(B) All of Bella Vista Village; and

(C) That part bounded on the north by Beaver Lake, on the east by Beaver Lake, on the south by the Hobbs State Management Area boundary from the intersection of State Highway 12 eastward along the boundary to its intersection with the Van Hollow Creek arm of Beaver Lake;

(3) Benton and Carroll Counties: That part bounded on the north by Highway 62, on the east by Highway 187 and Henry Hollow Creek, and the south and west by Beaver Lake and the road from Beaver Dam north to Highway 62;

(4) Conway County: That part lying above the rimrock of Petit Jean Mountain;

(5) Garland County: All of Hot Springs Village and Diamondhead;

(6) Marion County:

(A) That part known as Bull Shoals Peninsula, bounded on the east and north by White River and Lake Bull Shoals, on the west by the Jimmie Creek arm of Lake Bull Shoals, and on the south by the municipal boundaries of the City of Bull Shoals;

(B) That part of Marion County bounded on the north, west, and south by Bull Shoals Lake and on the east by County Roads 355 and 322 from their intersections with State Highway 202 to the points where they respectively dead-end at arms of Bull Shoals Lake;

(C) The Yocum Bend Peninsula of Bull Shoals Lake bounded on the north and east by Bull Shoals Lake, on the west by Pine Mountain and Bull Shoals Lake, and on the south by County Road 30; and

(D) Those lands situated in Marion County known as the Frost Point Peninsula, not inundated by the waters of Bull Shoals Lake, being more particularly described as follows:

(i) Section Six, Township Twenty North, Range Fifteen West, (Sec. 6 – T.20 N. – R.15 W.), lying south of the White River channel;

(ii) Section One, Township Twenty North, Range Sixteen West, (Sec. 1 – T.20 N. – R.16 W.); and

(iii) East Half of Section Two, Township Twenty North, Range Sixteen West, (E 1/2 Sec. 2 – T.20 N. – R.16 W.); North Half of the Northeast Quarter of Section Eleven, Township Twenty North, Range Sixteen West (N 1/2 – NE 1/4 Sec. 11 – T.20 N. – R.16 W.); and

(7) A platted subdivision located in an unincorporated area.

(b) Nothing contained in this section shall be construed to limit or restrict or to make unlawful the discharge of a firearm in defense of a person or property within the areas described in this section.

(c) A person who is found guilty or who pleads guilty or nolo contendere to violating this section is guilty of a violation and shall be fined no less than $25 nor more than $500.

(d) This section does not apply to a:

(1) Law enforcement officer in the performance of his or her duties;

(2) Discharge of a center-fire weapon at a firing range maintained for the discharging of a center-fire weapon; or

(3) Person possessing a valid concealed handgun license under § 5-73-301 et seq.

§ 5-73-128. Offenses upon property of public schools.

(a) (1) The court shall prepare and transmit to the Department of Finance and Administration an order of denial of driving privileges for a person within 24 hours after the plea or finding, if a person who is less than 19 years of age at the time of the commission of the offense:

(A) Pleads guilty or nolo contendere to any criminal offense under § 5-73-101 et seq. or the Uniform Machine Gun Act, § 5-73-201 et seq., and the plea is accepted by the court, or is found guilty of any criminal offense under § 5-73-101 et seq. or the Uniform Machine Gun Act, § 5-73-201 et seq., if the state proves that the offense was committed upon the property of a public school or in or upon any school bus; or

(B) Is found by a juvenile division of circuit court to have committed an offense described in subdivision (a)(1)(A) of this section.

(2) In a case of extreme and unusual hardship, the order may provide for the issuance of a restricted driving permit to allow driving to and from a place of employment or driving to and from school.

(b) Upon receipt of an order of denial of driving privileges under this section, the department shall suspend the motor vehicle operator's license of the person for not less than 12 months nor more than 36 months.

(c) A penalty prescribed in this section is in addition to any other penalty prescribed by law for an offense covered by this section.

§ 5-73-129. Furnishing a handgun or a prohibited weapon to a felon.

(a) A person commits the offense of furnishing a handgun to a felon if he or she sells, barters, leases, gives, rents, or otherwise furnishes a handgun to a person who he or she knows has been found guilty of or pleaded guilty or nolo contendere to a felony.

(b) A person commits the offense of furnishing a prohibited weapon to a felon if he or she sells, barters, leases, gives, rents, or otherwise furnishes:

    (1) A sawed-off shotgun or rifle;

    (2) A firearm that has been specially made or specially adapted for silent discharge;

    (3) A machine gun;

    (6) A defaced firearm, as defined in § 5-73-107; or

    (7) Other implement for the infliction of serious physical injury or death that serves no common lawful purpose, to a person who has been found guilty of or who has pleaded guilty or nolo contendere to a felony.

(c) Furnishing a handgun or a prohibited weapon to a felon is a Class B felony.

§ 5-73-130. Seizure and forfeiture of firearm – Seizure and forfeiture of motor vehicle – Disposition of property seized.

(a) If a person under 18 years of age is unlawfully in possession of a firearm, the firearm shall be seized and, after an adjudication of delinquency or a conviction, is subject to forfeiture.

(b) If a felon or a person under 18 years of age is unlawfully in possession of a firearm in a motor vehicle, the motor vehicle is subject to seizure and, after an adjudication of delinquency or a conviction, subject to forfeiture.

(c) As used in this section, "unlawfully in possession of a firearm" does not include any act of possession of a firearm that is prohibited only by:

    (1) Section 5-73-127, unlawful to possess loaded center-fire weapons in certain areas; or

    (2) A regulation of the Arkansas State Game and Fish Commission.

(d) The procedures for forfeiture and disposition of the seized property are as follows:

    (1) The prosecuting attorney of the judicial district within whose jurisdiction the property is seized that is sought to be forfeited shall promptly proceed against the property by filing in the circuit court a petition for an order to show cause why the circuit court should not order forfeiture of the property; and

    (2) The petition shall be verified and shall set forth:

        (A) A statement that the action is brought pursuant to this section;

        (B) The law enforcement agency bringing the action;

        (C) A description of the property sought to be forfeited;

        (D) A statement that on or about a date certain there was an adjudication of delinquency or a conviction and a finding that the property seized is subject to forfeiture;

        (E) A statement detailing the facts in support of subdivision (d)(1) of this section; and

        (F) A list of all persons known to the law enforcement agency, after diligent search and inquiry, who may claim an ownership interest in the property by title or registration or by virtue of a lien allegedly perfected in the manner prescribed by law.

(e) (1) Upon receipt of a petition complying with the requirements of subdivision (d)(1) of this section, the circuit court judge having jurisdiction shall issue an order to show cause setting forth a statement that this subchapter is the controlling law.

    (2) In addition, the order shall set a date at least 41 days from the date of first publication of the order pursuant to subsection (f) of this section for all persons claiming an interest in the property to file such pleadings as they desire as to why the circuit court should not order the forfeiture of the property for use, sale, or other disposition by the law enforcement agency seeking forfeiture of the property.

    (3) The circuit court shall further order that any person who does not appear on that date is deemed to have defaulted and waived any claim to the subject property.

(f) (1) The prosecuting attorney shall give notice of the forfeiture proceedings by:

    (A) Causing a copy of the order to show cause to be published two (2) times each week for two (2) consecutive weeks in a newspaper having general circulation in the county where the property is located with the last publication being not less than 5 days before the show cause hearing; and

    (B) Sending a copy of the petition and order to show cause by certified mail, return receipt requested, to each person having ownership of or a security interest in the property or in the manner provided in Rule 4 of the Arkansas Rules of Civil Procedure if:

        (i) The property is of a type for which title or registration is required by law;

        (ii) The owner of the property is known in fact to the law enforcement agency at the time of seizure; or

        (iii) The property is subject to a security interest perfected in accordance with the Uniform Commercial Code, § 4-1-101 et seq.

    (2) The law enforcement agency is only obligated to make diligent search and inquiry as to the owner of the property, and if, after diligent search and inquiry, the law enforcement agency is unable to ascertain the owner, the requirement of actual notice by mail with respect to a person having a perfected security interest in the property is not applicable.

(g) At the hearing on the matter, the petitioner has the burden to establish that the property is subject to forfeiture by a preponderance of the evidence.

(i) The final order of forfeiture by the circuit court shall perfect in the law enforcement agency right, title, and interest in and to the property and shall relate back to the date of the seizure.

(j) Physical seizure of property is not necessary in order to allege in a petition under this section that the property is forfeitable.

(k) Upon filing the petition, the prosecuting attorney for the judicial district may also seek such protective orders as are necessary to prevent the transfer, encumbrance, or other disposal of any property named in the petition.
(l) The law enforcement agency to which the property is forfeited shall:
  (1) Destroy any forfeited firearm; and

§ 5-73-131. Possession or use of weapons by incarcerated persons.
(a) A person commits the offense of possession or use of weapons by incarcerated persons if, without approval of custodial authority he or she uses, possesses, makes, repairs, sells, or otherwise deals in any weapon, including, but not limited to, any bomb, firearm, knife, or other implement for the infliction of serious physical injury or death and that serves no common lawful purpose, while incarcerated in the Department of Correction, the Department of Community Correction, or a county or municipal jail or detention facility.
(b) Possession or use of weapons by incarcerated persons is a Class D felony.
(c) This section is not applicable to possession of a weapon by an incarcerated person before he or she completes the standard booking and search procedures in a jail facility after arrest.

§ 5-73-132. Sale, rental, or transfer of firearm to person prohibited from possessing firearms.
(a) A person shall not sell, rent, or transfer a firearm to any person who he or she knows is prohibited by state or federal law from possessing the firearm.
(b) (1) Violation of this section is a Class A misdemeanor, unless the firearm is:
  (A) A handgun;
  (B) A sawed-off or short-barrelled shotgun, as defined in § 5-1-102;
  (C) A sawed-off or short-barrelled rifle, as defined in § 5-1-102;
  (D) A firearm that has been specially made or specially adapted for silent discharge;
  (E) A machine gun;
  (F) An explosive or incendiary device, as defined in § 5-71-301;
  (G) A defaced firearm, as defined in § 5-73-107; or
  (H) Other implement for the infliction of serious physical injury or death that serves no common lawful purpose.
  (2) If the firearm is listed in subdivision (b)(1) of this section, a violation of this section is a Class B felony.

Subchapter 2: Uniform Machine Gun Act

§ 5-73-202. Definitions. As used in this subchapter:
(1) "Crime of violence" means any of the following crimes or an attempt to commit any of them:
  (A) Murder;
  (B) Manslaughter;
  (C) Kidnapping;
  (D) Rape;
  (E) Mayhem;
  (F) Assault to do great bodily harm;
  (G) Robbery;
  (H) Burglary;
  (I) Housebreaking;
  (J) Breaking and entering; and
  (K) Larceny;
(2) "Machine gun" means a weapon of any description by whatever name known, loaded or unloaded, from which more than five (5) shots or bullets may be rapidly, or automatically, or semi-automatically, discharged from a magazine, by a single function of the firing device; and
(3) "Person" includes a firm, partnership, association, or corporation.

§ 5-73-204. Possession or use for offensive or aggressive purposes unlawful. Possession or use of a machine gun for offensive or aggressive purpose is declared to be a crime punishable by imprisonment in the state penitentiary for a term of not less than 10 years.

§ 5-73-205. Presumption of offensive or aggressive purpose.
(a) Possession or use of a machine gun is presumed to be for an offensive or aggressive purpose:
  (1) When the machine gun is on premises not owned or rented for bona fide permanent residence or business occupancy by the person in whose possession the machine gun may be found;
  (2) When in the possession of or used by an unnaturalized foreign-born person or a person who has been convicted of a crime of violence in any court of record, state or federal, of the United States of America, its territories or insular possessions;
  (4) When empty or loaded pistol shells of 30 (.30 in. or 7.63 mm.) or larger caliber which have been or are susceptible of use in the machine gun are found in the immediate vicinity of the machine gun.
(b) A machine gun is exempt from the presumption of offensive or aggressive purpose if:

(1) The machine gun has been registered to a corporation in the business of manufacturing ammunition or a representative of the corporation under the National Firearms Act, 26 U.S.C. § 5801 et seq., or the Gun Control Act of 1968, 18 U.S.C. § 921 et seq.;

(2) The machine gun is being used primarily to test ammunition in a nonoffensive and nonaggressive manner by the corporation or the corporation's representative that the machine gun is registered to; and

(3) The corporation or the corporation's representative is not prohibited from the possession of a firearm by any state or federal law.

§ 5-73-206. Evidence of possession or use. The presence of a machine gun in any room, boat, or vehicle is evidence of the possession or use of the machine gun by each person occupying the room, boat, or vehicle where the machine gun is found.

§ 5-73-207. Manufacture for military, nonaggressive, or nonoffensive use. Nothing contained in this subchapter prohibits or interferes with:

(1) The manufacture for and sale of machine guns to the military forces or the peace officers of the United States or of any political subdivision of the United States, or the transportation required for that purpose;

(2) The possession of a machine gun for scientific purpose, or the possession of a machine gun not usable as a weapon and possessed as a curiosity, ornament, or keepsake; or

(3) The possession of a machine gun other than one adapted to use pistol cartridges of 30 (.30 in. or 7.63 mm.) or larger caliber, for a purpose manifestly not aggressive or offensive.

5-73-208. Registration by manufacturers.

(a) Every manufacturer shall keep a register of all machine guns manufactured or handled by the manufacturer.

(b) This register shall show:

(1) The model and serial number, date of manufacture, sale, loan, gift, delivery, or receipt, of every machine gun, the name, address, and occupation of the person to whom the machine gun was sold, loaned, given, or delivered, or from whom it was received; and

(2) The purpose for which it was acquired by the person to whom the machine gun was sold, loaned, given, or delivered, or from whom received.

(c) Upon demand every manufacturer shall permit any marshal, sheriff, or police officer to inspect the manufacturer's entire stock of machine guns, parts, and supplies therefor, and shall produce the register, required by this section, for inspection.

(d) A violation of this section is a violation punishable by a fine of not less than $100.

§ 5-73-211. Perpetrating or attempting crime. Possession or use of a machine gun in the course of a criminal offense is a Class A felony.

Subchapter 3: Concealed Handguns

§ 5-73-301. Definitions. As used in this subchapter:

(1) "Acceptable electronic format" means an electronic image produced on the person's own cellular phone or other type of portable electronic device that displays all of the information on a concealed handgun license as clearly as an original concealed handgun license;

(2) "Concealed" means to cover from observation so as to prevent public view;

(3) "Convicted" means that a person pleaded guilty or nolo contendere to or was found guilty of a criminal offense;

(4) "Handgun" means any firearm, other than a fully automatic firearm, with a barrel length of less than 12 inches that is designed, made, or adapted to be fired with 1 hand;

(5) "Licensee" means a person granted a valid license to carry a concealed handgun pursuant to this subchapter; and

(6) "Parking lot" means an area, structure, or part of a structure designated for the parking of motor vehicles or a designated drop-off zone for children at a school.

§ 5-73-302. Authority to issue license.

(a) The Director of the Department of Arkansas State Police may issue a license to carry a concealed handgun to a person qualified as provided in this subchapter.

(b) (1) For new licenses issued after July 31, 2007, the license to carry a concealed handgun is valid throughout the state for a period of 5 years from the date of issuance.

  (2) After July 31, 2007, upon renewal, an existing valid license to carry a concealed handgun shall be issued for a period of 5 years.

(c) (1) (A) After July 31, 2007, a license or renewal of a license issued to a former elected or appointed sheriff of any county of this state shall be issued for a period of 5 years.

  (B) The license issued to a former elected or appointed sheriff is revocable on the same grounds as other licenses.

  (2) (A) The former elected or appointed sheriff shall meet the same qualifications as all other applicants.

  (B) However, the former elected or appointed sheriff is exempt from the fee prescribed by § 5-73-311(a)(2) and from the training requirements of § 5-73-309(13) for issuance.

§ 5-73-304. Exemptions.

(a) (1) (A) A current or former certified law enforcement officer, chief of police, court bailiff, or county sheriff is exempt from the licensing requirements of this subchapter if otherwise authorized to carry a concealed handgun.

(B) A former certified law enforcement officer whose employment was terminated by a law enforcement agency due to disciplinary reasons or because he or she committed a disqualifying criminal offense is not exempt from the licensing requirements of this subchapter.

(2) Solely for purposes of this subchapter, an auxiliary law enforcement officer certified by the Arkansas Commission on Law Enforcement Standards and Training and approved by the county sheriff of the county where he or she is acting as an auxiliary law enforcement officer is deemed to be a certified law enforcement officer.

(b) An auxiliary law enforcement officer or employee of a local detention facility is exempt from the licensing requirements of this subchapter if the auxiliary law enforcement officer or employee of a local detention facility:

(1) If an auxiliary law enforcement officer, has completed the minimum training requirements and is certified as an auxiliary law enforcement officer in accordance with the commission; and

(2) Is authorized in writing as exempt from the licensing requirements of this subchapter by the chief of police or county sheriff that has appointed the auxiliary law enforcement officer or employs the employee of a local detention facility.

(c) The authorization prescribed in subdivision (b)(2) of this section shall be carried on the person of the auxiliary law enforcement officer or employee of a local detention facility and be produced upon demand at the request of any law enforcement officer or owner or operator of any of the prohibited places as set out in § 5-73-306.

(d) As used in this section, "employee of a local detention facility" means a person who:

(1) Is employed by a county sheriff or municipality that operates a local detention facility and whose job duties include:

(A) Securing a local detention facility;

(B) Monitoring inmates in a local detention facility; and

(C) Administering the daily operation of the local detention facility; and

(2) Has completed the minimum training requirements for his or her position

§ 5-73-305. Criminal penalty.

Any person who knowingly submits a false answer to any question on an application for a license issued pursuant to this subchapter, or who knowingly submits a false document when applying for a license issued pursuant to this subchapter upon conviction is guilty of a Class B misdemeanor.

§ 5-73-306. Prohibited places.

No license to carry a concealed handgun issued pursuant to this subchapter authorizes any person to carry a concealed handgun into:

(1) Any police station, sheriff's station, or Department of Arkansas State Police station;

(2) Any Arkansas Highway Police Division of the Arkansas State Highway and Transportation Department facility;

(3) (A) Any building of the Arkansas State Highway and Transportation Department or onto grounds adjacent to any building of the Arkansas State Highway and Transportation Department.

(B) However, subdivision (3)(A) of this section does not apply to:

(i) A rest area or weigh station of the Arkansas State Highway and Transportation Department; or

(ii) A publicly owned and maintained parking lot that is a publicly accessible parking lot if the licensee is carrying a concealed handgun in his or her motor vehicle or has left the concealed handgun in his or her locked and unattended motor vehicle in the publicly owned and maintained parking lot;

(4) Any part of a detention facility, prison, or jail, including without limitation a parking lot owned, maintained, or otherwise controlled by the Department of Correction or Department of Community Correction;

(5) Any courthouse, courthouse annex, or other building owned, leased, or regularly used by a county for conducting court proceedings or housing a county office unless:

(A) The licensee is either:

(i) Employed by the county; or

(ii) A countywide elected official;

(B) The licensee's principal place of employment is within the courthouse, the courthouse annex, or other building owned, leased, or regularly used by the county for conducting court proceedings or housing a county office; and

(C) The quorum court by ordinance approves a plan that allows licensees permitted under this subdivision (5) to carry a concealed handgun into the courthouse as set out by the local security and emergency preparedness plan;

(6) (A) Any courtroom.

(B) However, nothing in this subchapter precludes a judge from carrying a concealed weapon or determining who will carry a concealed weapon into his or her courtroom;

(7) Any meeting place of the governing body of any governmental entity;

(8) Any meeting of the General Assembly or a committee of the General Assembly;

(9) Any state office;

(10) Any athletic event not related to firearms;

(11) Any portion of an establishment, except a restaurant as defined in § 3-5-1202, licensed to dispense alcoholic beverages for consumption on the premises;

(12) Any portion of an establishment, except a restaurant as defined in § 3-5-1202, where beer or light wine is consumed on the premises;

(13) (A) A school, college, community college, or university campus building or event.

(B) However, subdivision (13)(A) of this section does not apply to:

(i) A kindergarten through grade 12 (K-12) private school operated by a church or other place of worship that:

(a) Is located on the developed property of the kindergarten through grade 12 (K-12) private school;

(b) Allows the licensee to carry a concealed handgun into the church or other place of worship under this section; and

(c) Allows the licensee to possess a concealed handgun on the developed property of the kindergarten through grade 12 (K-12) private school under § 5-73-119(e);

(ii) A kindergarten through grade 12 (K-12) private school or a prekindergarten private school that through its governing board or director has set forth the rules and circumstances under which the licensee may carry a concealed handgun into a building or event of the kindergarten through grade 12 (K-12) private school or the prekindergarten private school;

(iii) Participation in an authorized firearms-related activity;

(iv) Carrying a concealed handgun as authorized under § 5-73-322; or

(v) A publicly owned and maintained parking lot of a college, community college, or university if the licensee is carrying a concealed handgun in his or her motor vehicle or has left the concealed handgun in his or her locked and unattended motor vehicle;

(14) Inside the passenger terminal of any airport, except that no person is prohibited from carrying any legal firearm into the passenger terminal if the firearm is encased for shipment for purposes of checking the firearm as baggage to be lawfully transported on any aircraft;

(15) (A) Any church or other place of worship.

(B) However, this subchapter does not preclude a church or other place of worship from determining who may carry a concealed handgun into the church or other place of worship;

(16) Any place where the carrying of a firearm is prohibited by federal law;

(17) Any place where a parade or demonstration requiring a permit is being held, and the licensee is a participant in the parade or demonstration; or

(18) (A) (i) Any place at the discretion of the person or entity exercising control over the physical location of the place by placing at each entrance to the place a written notice clearly readable at a distance of not less than 10 feet that "carrying a handgun is prohibited".

(ii) *(a)* If the place does not have a roadway entrance, there shall be a written notice placed anywhere upon the premises of the place.

(b) In addition to the requirement of subdivision (18)(A)(ii)*(a)* of this section, there shall be at least one (1) written notice posted within every 3 acres of a place with no roadway entrance.

(iii) A written notice as described in subdivision (18)(A)(i) of this section is not required for a private home.

(iv) Any licensee entering a private home shall notify the occupant that the licensee is carrying a concealed handgun.

(B) Subdivision (18)(A) of this section does not apply if the physical location is:

(i) A public university, public college, or community college, as defined in § 5-73-322, and the licensee is carrying a concealed handgun as provided under § 5-73-322; or

(ii) A publicly owned and maintained parking lot if the licensee is carrying a concealed handgun in his or her motor vehicle or has left the concealed handgun in his or her locked and unattended motor vehicle.

§ 5-73-307. List of license holders.

(a) The Department of Arkansas State Police shall maintain an automated listing of license holders, and this information shall be available online, upon request, at any time, to any law enforcement agency through the Arkansas Crime Information Center.

(b) Nothing in this subchapter shall be construed to require or allow the registration, documentation, or providing of a serial number with regard to any firearm.

§ 5-73-308. License – Issuance or denial.

(a) (1) (A) The Director of the Department of Arkansas State Police may deny a license if within the preceding 5 years the applicant has been found guilty of 1 or more crimes of violence constituting a misdemeanor or for the offense of carrying a weapon.

(B) The director may revoke a license if the licensee has been found guilty of 1 or more crimes of violence within the preceding 3 years.

(2) Subdivision (a)(1) of this section does not apply to a misdemeanor that has been expunged or for which the imposition of sentence was suspended.

(3) Upon notification by any law enforcement agency or a court and subsequent written verification, the director shall suspend a license or the processing of an application for a license if the licensee or applicant is arrested or formally charged with a crime that would disqualify the licensee or applicant from having a license under this subchapter until final disposition of the case.

(b) (1) The director may deny a license to carry a concealed handgun if the county sheriff or chief of police, if applicable, of the applicant's place of residence or the director or the director's designee submits an affidavit that the applicant has been or is reasonably likely to be a danger to himself or herself or others or to the community at large, as demonstrated by past patterns of behavior or participation in an incident involving unlawful violence or threats of unlawful violence, or if the applicant is under a criminal investigation at the time of applying for a license to carry a concealed handgun.

(2) Within 120 days after the date of receipt of the items listed in § 5-73-311(a), the director shall:

(A) Issue the license; or

(B) Deny the application based solely on the ground that the applicant fails to qualify under the criteria listed in this subchapter.

(3) (A) If the director denies the application, the director shall notify the applicant in writing, stating the grounds for denial.

(B) The decision of the director is subject to appeal under the Arkansas Administrative Procedure Act, § 25-15-201 et seq.

§ 5-73-309. License – Requirements.
The Director of the Department of Arkansas State Police shall issue a license to carry a concealed handgun if the applicant:

(1) Is a citizen of the United States or a permanent legal resident;

(2) (A) Is a resident of the state and has been a resident continuously for 90 days or longer immediately preceding the filing of the application.

(B) However, subdivision (2)(A) of this section does not apply to any:

(i) Active duty member of the United States Armed Forces who submits documentation of his or her active duty status; or

(ii) Spouse of an active duty member of the United States Armed Forces who submits documentation of his or her spouse's active duty status;

(3) Is at least:

(A) Twenty-one (21) years of age; or

(B) Eighteen (18) years of age and is:

(i) Currently a federally recognized commissioned or noncommissioned officer or an enlisted member on active duty in the United States Armed Forces;

(ii) In the National Guard or a reserve component of the United States Armed Forces; or

(iii) A former member of the United States Armed Forces who has been honorably discharged;

(4) Does not suffer from a mental or physical infirmity that prevents the safe handling of a handgun and has not threatened or attempted suicide;

(5) (A) Has not been convicted of a felony in a court of this state, of any other state, or of the United States without having been pardoned for conviction and had firearms possession rights restored.

(B) A record of a conviction that has been sealed or expunged under Arkansas law does not render an applicant ineligible to receive a concealed handgun license if:

(i) The applicant was sentenced prior to March 13, 1995; or

(ii) The order sealing or expunging the applicant's record of conviction complies with § 16-90-605 [repealed];

(6) Is not subject to any federal, state, or local law that makes it unlawful to receive, possess, or transport any firearm, and has had his or her background check successfully completed through the Department of Arkansas State Police and the Federal Bureau of Investigation's National Instant Criminal Background Check System;

(7) (A) Does not chronically or habitually abuse a controlled substance to the extent that his or her normal faculties are impaired.

(B) It is presumed that an applicant chronically and habitually uses a controlled substance to the extent that his or her faculties are impaired if the applicant has been voluntarily or involuntarily committed to a treatment facility for the abuse of a controlled substance or has been found guilty of a crime under the provisions of the Uniform Controlled Substances Act, § 5-64-101 et seq., or a similar law of any other state or the United States relating to a controlled substance within the 3-year period immediately preceding the date on which the application is submitted;

(8) (A) Does not chronically or habitually use an alcoholic beverage to the extent that his or her normal faculties are impaired.

(B) It is presumed that an applicant chronically and habitually uses an alcoholic beverage to the extent that his or her normal faculties are impaired if the applicant has been voluntarily or involuntarily committed as an alcoholic to a treatment facility or has been convicted of 2 or more offenses related to the use of alcohol under a law of this state or similar law of any other state or the United States within the 3-year period immediately preceding the date on which the application is submitted;

(9) Desires a legal means to carry a concealed handgun to defend himself or herself;

(10) Has not been adjudicated mentally incompetent;

(11) Has not been voluntarily or involuntarily committed to a mental institution or mental health treatment facility;

(12) Is not a fugitive from justice or does not have an active warrant for his or her arrest;

(13) Has satisfactorily completed a training course as prescribed and approved by the director; and

(14) Signs a statement of allegiance to the United States Constitution and the Arkansas Constitution.

§ 5-73-310. Application form.
The application for a license to carry a concealed handgun shall be completed, under oath, on a form promulgated by the Director of the Department of Arkansas State Police and shall include only:

(1) The name, address, place and date of birth, race, and sex of the applicant;

(2) The driver's license number or Social Security number of the applicant;

(3) Any previous address of the applicant for the 2 years preceding the date of the application;

(4) A statement that the applicant is in compliance with criteria contained within §§ 5-73-308(a) and 5-73-309;

(5) A statement that the applicant has been furnished a copy of this subchapter and is acquainted with the truth and understanding of this subchapter;

(6) A conspicuous warning that the application is executed under oath, and that a knowingly false answer to any question or the knowing submission of any false document by the applicant subjects the applicant to:

  (A) Criminal prosecution and precludes any future license's being issued to the applicant; and

  (B) Immediate revocation if the license has already been issued;

(7) A statement that the applicant desires a legal means to carry a concealed handgun to defend himself or herself;

(8) (A) A statement of whether the applicant is applying for:

  (i) An unrestricted license, that allows the person to carry any handgun; or

  (ii) A restricted license, that allows the person to carry any handgun other than a semiautomatic handgun.

  (B) (i) An applicant requesting an unrestricted license shall establish proficiency in the use of a semiautomatic handgun.

  (ii) An applicant requesting a restricted license shall establish proficiency in the use of a handgun and may use any kind of handgun when establishing proficiency; and

(9) A statement of whether or not the applicant has been found guilty of a crime of violence or domestic abuse.

§ 5-73-311. Application procedure.

(a) The applicant for a license to carry a concealed handgun shall submit the following to the Department of Arkansas State Police:

(1) A completed application, as described in § 5-73-310;

(2) A nonrefundable license fee of $100, except that the nonrefundable license fee is $50 if the applicant is 65 years of age or older;

(3) (A) A full set of fingerprints of the applicant.

  (B) In the event a legible set of fingerprints, as determined by the department and the Federal Bureau of Investigation, cannot be obtained after a minimum of 2 attempts, the Director of the Department of Arkansas State Police shall determine eligibility in accordance with criteria that the department shall establish by promulgating rules.

  (C) Costs for processing the set of fingerprints as required in subdivision (a)(3)(A) of this section shall be borne by the applicant;

(4) (A) A waiver authorizing the department access to any medical, criminal, or other records concerning the applicant and permitting access to all of the applicant's criminal records.

  (B) If a check of the applicant's criminal records uncovers any unresolved felony arrests over 10 years old, then the applicant shall obtain a letter of reference from the county sheriff, prosecuting attorney, or circuit judge of the county where the applicant resides that states that to the best of the county sheriff's, prosecuting attorney's, or circuit judge's knowledge that the applicant is of good character and free of any felony convictions.

  (C) The department shall maintain the confidentiality of the medical, criminal, or other records; and

(5) A digital photograph of the applicant or a release authorization to obtain a digital photograph of the applicant from another source.

(b) (1) Upon receipt of the items listed in subsection (a) of this section, the department shall forward the full set of fingerprints of the applicant to the appropriate agencies for state and federal processing.

(2) (A) The department shall forward a notice of the applicant's application to the sheriff of the applicant's county of residence and, if applicable, the police chief of the applicant's municipality of residence.

  (B) (i) The sheriff of the applicant's county of residence and, if applicable, the police chief of the applicant's municipality of residence may participate, at his or her discretion, in the process by submitting a voluntary report to the department containing any readily discoverable information that he or she feels may be pertinent to the licensing of any applicant.

    (ii) The reporting under subdivision (b)(2)(B)(i) of this section shall be made within 30 days after the date the notice of the application was sent by the department.

(c) A concealed handgun license issued, renewed, or obtained under § 5-73-314 or § 5-73-319 after December 31, 2007, shall bear a digital photograph of the licensee.

§ 5-73-312. Revocation.

(a) (1) A license to carry a concealed handgun issued under this subchapter shall be revoked if the licensee becomes ineligible under the criteria set forth in § 5-73-308(a) or § 5-73-309.

(2) (A) Any law enforcement officer making an arrest of a licensee for a violation of this subchapter or any other statutory violation that requires revocation of a license to carry a concealed handgun shall confiscate the license and forward it to the Director of the Department of Arkansas State Police.

  (B) The license shall be held until a determination of the charge is finalized, with the appropriate disposition of the license after the determination.

(b) When the Department of Arkansas State Police receives notification from any law enforcement agency or court that a licensee has been found guilty or has pleaded guilty or nolo contendere to any crime involving the use of a weapon, the license issued under this subchapter is immediately revoked.

(c) The director shall revoke the license of any licensee who has pleaded guilty or nolo contendere to or been found guilty of an alcohol-related offense committed while carrying a handgun.

§ 5-73-313. Expiration and renewal.

(a) Except as provided in subdivision (f)(1) of this section, the licensee may renew his or her license no more than 90 days prior to the expiration date by submitting to the Department of Arkansas State Police:

    (1) A renewal form prescribed by the department;

    (2) A verified statement that the licensee remains qualified pursuant to the criteria specified in §§ 5-73-308(a) and 5-73-309;

    (3) A renewal fee of $35;

    (4) A certification or training form properly completed by the licensee's training instructor reflecting that the licensee's training was conducted; and

    (5) A digital photograph of the licensee or a release authorization to obtain a digital photograph of the licensee from another source.

(b) The license shall be renewed upon receipt of the completed renewal application, a digital photograph of the licensee, and appropriate payment of fees subject to a background investigation conducted pursuant to this subchapter that did not reveal any disqualifying offense or unresolved arrest that would disqualify a licensee under this subchapter.

(c) Additionally, a licensee who fails to file a renewal application on or before the expiration date shall renew his or her license by paying a late fee of $15.

(d) (1) No license shall be renewed 6 months or more after its expiration date, and the license is deemed to be permanently expired.

    (2) (A) A person whose license has been permanently expired may reapply for licensure.

      (B) An application for licensure and fees pursuant to §§ 5-73-308(a), 5-73-309, and 5-73-311(a) shall be submitted, and a new background investigation shall be conducted.

(e) A new criminal background investigation shall be conducted when an applicant applies for renewal of a license. Costs for processing a new background check shall be paid by the applicant.

(f) (1) An active duty member of the United States Armed Forces, a member of the National Guard, or a member of a reserve component of the United States Armed Forces, who is on active duty outside this state may renew his or her license within 30 days after the person returns to this state by submitting to the department:

    (A) Proof of assignment outside of this state on the expiration date of the license; and

    (B) The items listed in subdivisions (a)(1)-(5) of this section.

    (2) Subsections (c) and (d) of this section shall not apply to a person who renews his or her license under subdivision (f)(1) of this section.

5-73-314. Lost, destroyed, or duplicate license – Change of address.

(a) Within thirty (30) days after the changing of a permanent address, or within 30 days after having a license to carry a concealed handgun lost, the licensee shall notify the Director of the Department of Arkansas State Police in writing of the change or loss.

(b) If a license to carry a concealed handgun is lost or destroyed, or a duplicate is requested, the person to whom the license to carry a concealed handgun was issued shall comply with the provisions of subsection (a) of this section and may obtain a duplicate license or replacement license upon:

    (1) Paying the Department of Arkansas State Police a fee established by the director under the Arkansas Administrative Procedure Act, § 25-15-201 et seq.; and

    (2) Furnishing a notarized statement to the department that the license to carry a concealed handgun has been lost or destroyed or that a duplicate is requested.

(c) The fee described in subdivision (b)(1) of this section shall be reduced by 50% if a person 65 years of age or older is requesting a replacement or duplicate license under this section.

§ 5-73-315. Authority to carry concealed handgun – Identification of licensee.

(a) Any licensee possessing a valid license issued pursuant to this subchapter may carry a concealed handgun.

(b) The licensee shall:

    (1) Carry the license, or an electronic copy of the license in an acceptable electronic format, together with valid identification, at any time when the licensee is carrying a concealed handgun; and

    (2) Display both the license, or an electronic copy of the license in an acceptable electronic format, and proper identification upon demand by a law enforcement officer.

(c) The presentment of proof of a license to carry a concealed handgun in electronic form does not:

    (1) Authorize a search of any other content of an electronic device without a search warrant or probable cause; or

    (2) Expand or restrict the authority of a law enforcement officer to conduct a search or investigation.

§ 5-73-317. Rules and regulations.
The Director of the Department of Arkansas State Police may promulgate rules and regulations to permit the efficient administration of this subchapter.

§ 5-73-319. Transfer of a license to Arkansas.

(a) Any person who becomes a resident of Arkansas who has a valid license to carry a concealed handgun issued by a reciprocal state may apply to transfer his or her license to Arkansas by submitting the following to the Department of Arkansas State Police:

(1) The person's current reciprocal state license;

(2) Two (2) properly completed fingerprint cards;

(3) A nonrefundable license fee of $35;

(4) Any fee charged by a state or federal agency for a criminal history check; and

(5) A digital photograph of the person or a release authorization to obtain a digital photograph of the person from another source.

(b) After July 31, 2007, the newly transferred license is valid for a period of 5 years from the date of issuance and binds the holder to all Arkansas laws and regulations regarding the carrying of the concealed handgun.

§ 5-73-321. Recognition of other states' licenses. A person in possession of a valid license to carry a concealed handgun issued to the person by another state is entitled to the privileges and subject to the restrictions prescribed by this subchapter.

§ 5-73-322. Concealed handguns in a university, college, or community college building.

(a) As used in this section:

(1) (A) "Public university, public college, or community college" means an institution that:

(i) Regularly receives budgetary support from the state government;

(ii) Is part of the University of Arkansas or Arkansas State University systems; or

(iii) Is required to report to the Arkansas Higher Education Coordinating Board.

(B) "Public university, public college, or community college" does not include a private university or private college solely because:

(i) Students attending the private university or private college receive state-supported scholarships; or

(ii) The private university or private college voluntarily reports to the Arkansas Higher Education Coordinating Board; and

(2) "Staff member" means a person who is not enrolled as a full-time student at the university, college, or community college and is either employed by the university, college, or community college full time or is on a 9-month or 12-month appointment at the university, college, or community college as a faculty member.

(b) A licensee may possess a concealed handgun in the buildings and on the grounds, whether owned or leased by the public university, public college, or community college, of the public university, public college, or community college where he or she is employed unless otherwise prohibited by § 5-73-306 if:

(1) He or she is a staff member; and

(2) (A) The governing board of the public university, public college, or community college does not adopt a policy expressly disallowing the carrying of a concealed handgun by staff members in the buildings or on the grounds of the public university, public college, or community college and posts notices as described in § 5-73-306(18).

(B) A governing board of the public university, public college, or community college may adopt differing policies for the carrying of a concealed handgun by staff members for different campuses, areas of a campus, or individual buildings of the public university, public college, or community college for which the governing board is responsible.

(C) A policy disallowing the carrying of a concealed handgun by staff members into the public university, public college, or community college expires 1 year after the date of adoption and must be readopted each year by the governing board of the public university, public college, or community college to remain in effect.

(c) A licensee may possess a concealed handgun in the buildings and on the grounds of the private university or private college where he or she is employed unless otherwise prohibited by § 5-73-306 if:

(1) He or she is a staff member; and

(2) The private university or private college does not adopt a policy expressly disallowing the carrying of a concealed handgun in the buildings and on the grounds of the private university or private college and posts notices as described in § 5-73-306(18).

(d) The storage of a handgun in a university or college-operated student dormitory or residence hall is prohibited under § 5-73-119(c).

§ 5-73-323. Parole board exemptions. A member of the Parole Board, a board investigator, or a parole revocation judge who has been issued a license to carry a concealed handgun by the Department of Arkansas State Police under this subchapter may carry his or her concealed handgun into a building in which or a location on which a law enforcement officer may carry a handgun if the board member, board investigator, or parole revocation judge is on official business of the board.

TITLE 14. Local Government
Subtitle 2. County Government
Chapter 16 Powers Of Counties Generally
Subchapter 5 – Regulation of Use of Firearms and Archery Equipment

§ 14-16-501. Regulation upon request of suburban improvement district.

(a) Upon the written request of the governing body of a suburban improvement district, a county may by ordinance regulate the discharge of firearms and the shooting of archery equipment within all or any part of the suburban improvement district.

(b) As used in this section, "suburban improvement district" means a suburban improvement district which includes as one of its purposes for organization the construction or maintenance of roads or streets and which is governed by § 14-92-201 et seq. or its predecessor acts.

§ 14-16-502. Regulation upon request of property owners' association. Upon the written request of a property owners' association which has a population at least equal to that prescribed for cities of the first class and which is located outside the boundaries of a municipality, a county may by ordinance regulate the discharge of firearms and the shooting of archery equipment within all or any part of the area included in the property owners' association.

§ 14-16-503. Exemptions. Nothing in this subchapter shall be construed to prohibit:

(1) The discharge of a firearm or archery equipment in the defense of life or property;

(2) The discharge of a firearm or archery equipment at a public or private shooting range or gallery; or

(3) The discharge of a firearm by a law enforcement officer in the performance of his or her duty.

§ 14-16-504. Regulation by local unit of government.

(a) As used in this section, "local unit of government" means a city, town, or county.

(b)(1)(A) A local unit of government shall not enact any ordinance or regulation pertaining to, or regulate in any other manner, the ownership, transfer, transportation, carrying, or possession of firearms, ammunition for firearms, or components of firearms, except as otherwise provided in state or federal law.

(B) The provision in subdivision (b)(1)(A) of this section does not prevent the enactment of an ordinance regulating or forbidding the unsafe discharge of a firearm.

(2)(A) A local unit of government shall not have the authority to bring suit and shall not have the right to recover against any firearm or ammunition manufacturer, trade association, or dealer for damages, abatement, or injunctive relief resulting from or relating to the lawful design, manufacture, marketing, or sale of firearms or ammunition to the public.

(B) The authority to bring any suit and the right to recover against any firearm or ammunition manufacturer, trade association, or dealer for damages, abatement, or injunctive relief shall be reserved exclusively to the State of Arkansas.

(C) However, subdivisions (b)(1)(A) and (B) of this section do not prevent a local unit of government from bringing suit against a firearm or ammunition manufacturer or dealer for breach of contract or warranty as to firearms or ammunition purchased by the local unit of government.

(c)(1) The governing body of a local unit of government, following the proclamation by the Governor of a state of emergency, is prohibited from enacting an emergency ordinance regulating the transfer, transportation, or carrying of firearms or components of firearms.

(2) A person who has his or her firearm seized in violation of subdivision (c)(1) of this section may bring an action in the circuit court having jurisdiction for the return of the seized firearm.

Florida Statutes

The Florida Code and Constitution are updated through the 2016 regular session.

Office of the Attorney General
The Capitol PL-01
Tallahassee, FL 32399-1050
Phone Switchboard: (850) 414-3300
Citizens Services: (850) 414-3990
http://myfloridalegal.com/

Miami Field Division
11410 NW 20 Street, Suite 201
Miami, Florida 33172
Voice: (305) 597-4800
https://www.atf.gov/miami-field-division

Tampa Field Division
400 North Tampa Street, Suite 2100
Tampa, Florida 33602
Voice: (813) 202-7300
https://www.atf.gov/tampa-field-division

Table of Contents

Broward County Code of Ordinances

Martin County Municipal Code

Miami Dade County Municipal Code

Palm Beach County Municipal Code

TITLE XLVI
Chapter 790: Weapons and Firearms

790.001   Definitions. As used in this chapter, except where the context otherwise requires:

(1)   "Antique firearm" means any firearm manufactured in or before 1918 (including any matchlock, flintlock, percussion cap, or similar early type of ignition system) or replica thereof, whether actually manufactured before or after the year 1918, and also any firearm using fixed ammunition manufactured in or before 1918, for which ammunition is no longer manufactured in the United States and is not readily available in the ordinary channels of commercial trade.

(2)   "Concealed firearm" means any firearm, as defined in subsection (6), which is carried on or about a person in such a manner as to conceal the firearm from the ordinary sight of another person.

(3)(a)   "Concealed weapon" means any … tear gas gun, chemical weapon or device, or other deadly weapon carried on or about a person in such a manner as to conceal the weapon from the ordinary sight of another person.

(4)   "Destructive device" means any bomb, grenade, mine, rocket, missile, pipebomb, or similar device containing an explosive, incendiary, or poison gas and includes any frangible container filled with an explosive, incendiary, explosive gas, or expanding gas, which is designed or so constructed as to explode by such filler and is capable of causing bodily harm or property damage; any combination of parts either designed or intended for use in converting any device into a destructive device and from which a destructive device may be readily assembled; any device declared a destructive device by the Bureau of Alcohol, Tobacco, and Firearms; any type of weapon which will, is designed to, or may readily be converted to expel a projectile by the action of any explosive and which has a barrel with a bore of one-half inch or more in diameter; and ammunition for such destructive devices, but not including shotgun shells or any other ammunition designed for use in a firearm other than a destructive device. "Destructive device" does not include:

   (a)   A device which is not designed, redesigned, used, or intended for use as a weapon;

   (b)   Any device, although originally designed as a weapon, which is redesigned so that it may be used solely as a signaling, line-throwing, safety, or similar device;

   (c)   Any shotgun other than a short-barreled shotgun; or

   (d)   Any nonautomatic rifle (other than a short-barreled rifle) generally recognized or particularly suitable for use for the hunting of big game.

(5)   "Explosive" means any chemical compound or mixture that has the property of yielding readily to combustion or oxidation upon application of heat, flame, or shock, including but not limited to dynamite, nitroglycerin, trinitrotoluene, or ammonium nitrate when combined with other ingredients to form an explosive mixture, blasting caps, and detonators; but not including:

(a) Shotgun shells, cartridges, or ammunition for firearms;

(b) Fireworks as defined in § 791.01;

(c) Smokeless propellant powder or small arms ammunition primers, if possessed, purchased, sold, transported, or used in compliance with § 552.241;

(d) Black powder in quantities not to exceed that authorized by chapter 552, or by any rules adopted thereunder by the Department of Financial Services, when used for, or intended to be used for, the manufacture of target and sporting ammunition or for use in muzzle-loading flint or percussion weapons.

The exclusions contained in paragraphs (a)-(d) do not apply to the term "explosive" as used in the definition of "firearm" in subsection (6).

(6) **"Firearm"** means any weapon (including a starter gun) which will, is designed to, or may readily be converted to expel a projectile by the action of an explosive; the frame or receiver of any such weapon; any firearm muffler or firearm silencer; any destructive device; or any machine gun. The term "firearm" does not include an antique firearm unless the antique firearm is used in the commission of a crime.

(7) **"Indictment"** means an indictment or an information in any court under which a crime punishable by imprisonment for a term exceeding 1 year may be prosecuted.

(8) **"Law enforcement officer"** means:

(a) All officers or employees of the United States or the State of Florida, or any agency, commission, department, board, division, municipality, or subdivision thereof, who have authority to make arrests;

(b) Officers or employees of the United States or the State of Florida, or any agency, commission, department, board, division, municipality, or subdivision thereof, duly authorized to carry a concealed weapon;

(c) Members of the Armed Forces of the United States, the organized reserves, state militia, or Florida National Guard, when on duty, when preparing themselves for, or going to or from, military duty, or under orders;

(d) An employee of the state prisons or correctional systems who has been so designated by the Department of Corrections or by a warden of an institution;

(e) All peace officers;

(f) All state attorneys and United States attorneys and their respective assistants and investigators.

(9) **"Machine gun"** means any firearm, as defined herein, which shoots, or is designed to shoot, automatically more than one shot, without manually reloading, by a single function of the trigger.

(10) **"Short-barreled shotgun"** means a shotgun having one or more barrels less than 18 inches in length and any weapon made from a shotgun (whether by alteration, modification, or otherwise) if such weapon as modified has an overall length of less than 26 inches.

(11) **"Short-barreled rifle"** means a rifle having one or more barrels less than 16 inches in length and any weapon made from a rifle (whether by alteration, modification, or otherwise) if such weapon as modified has an overall length of less than 26 inches.

(12) **"Slungshot"** means a small mass of metal, stone, sand, or similar material fixed on a flexible handle, strap, or the like, used as a weapon.

(13) **"Weapon"** means any … tear gas gun, chemical weapon or device, or other deadly weapon except a firearm….

(16) **"Readily accessible for immediate use"** means that a firearm or other weapon is carried on the person or within such close proximity and in such a manner that it can be retrieved and used as easily and quickly as if carried on the person.

(17) **"Securely encased"** means in a glove compartment, whether or not locked; snapped in a holster; in a gun case, whether or not locked; in a zippered gun case; or in a closed box or container which requires a lid or cover to be opened for access.

(18) **"Sterile area"** means the area of an airport to which access is controlled by the inspection of persons and property in accordance with federally approved airport security programs.

(19) **"Ammunition"** means an object consisting of all of the following:

(a) A fixed metallic or nonmetallic hull or casing containing a primer.

(b) One or more projectiles, 1 or more bullets, or shot.

(c) Gunpowder.

All of the specified components must be present for an object to be ammunition.

790.01 Unlicensed carrying of concealed weapons or concealed firearms.—

(1) Except as provided in subsection (3), a person who is not licensed under § 790.06 and who carries a concealed weapon or electric weapon or device on or about his or her person commits a misdemeanor of the first degree, punishable as provided in § 775.082 or § 775.083.

(2) Except as provided in subsection (3), a person who is not licensed under § 790.06 and who carries a concealed firearm on or about his or her person commits a felony of the third degree, punishable as provided in § 775.082, § 775.083, or § 775.084.

(3) This section does not apply to:

(a) A person who carries a concealed weapon, or a person who may lawfully possess a firearm and who carries a concealed firearm, on or about his or her person while in the act of evacuating during a mandatory evacuation order issued during a state of emergency declared by the Governor pursuant to chapter 252 or declared by a local authority pursuant to chapter 870. As used in this subsection, the term "in the act of evacuating" means the immediate and urgent movement of a person away from the evacuation zone within 48 hours after a mandatory evacuation is ordered. The 48 hours may be extended by an order issued by the Governor.

790.015   Nonresidents who are United States citizens and hold a concealed weapons license in another state; reciprocity.—
(1)   Notwithstanding § 790.01, a nonresident of Florida may carry a concealed weapon or concealed firearm while in this state if the nonresident:
    (a)   Is 21 years of age or older.
    (b)   Has in his or her immediate possession a valid license to carry a concealed weapon or concealed firearm issued to the nonresident in his or her state of residence.
    (c)   Is a resident of the United States.
(2)   A nonresident is subject to the same laws and restrictions with respect to carrying a concealed weapon or concealed firearm as a resident of Florida who is so licensed.
(3)   If the resident of another state who is the holder of a valid license to carry a concealed weapon or concealed firearm issued in another state establishes legal residence in this state by:
    (a)   Registering to vote;
    (b)   Making a statement of domicile pursuant to § 222.17; or
    (c)   Filing for homestead tax exemption on property in this state, the license shall remain in effect for 90 days following the date on which the holder of the license establishes legal state residence.
(4)   This section applies only to nonresident concealed weapon or concealed firearm license holders from states that honor Florida concealed weapon or concealed firearm licenses.
(5)   The requirement of paragraph (1)(a) does not apply to a person who:
    (a)   Is a service member, as defined in § 250.01; or
    (b)   Is a veteran of the United States Armed Forces who was discharged under honorable conditions.

790.02   Officer to arrest without warrant and upon probable cause.—The carrying of a concealed weapon is declared a breach of peace, and any officer authorized to make arrests under the laws of this state may make arrests without warrant of persons violating the provisions of § 790.01 when said officer has reasonable grounds or probable cause to believe that the offense of carrying a concealed weapon is being committed.

790.051   Exemption from licensing requirements; law enforcement officers.—Law enforcement officers are exempt from the licensing and penal provisions of this chapter when acting at any time within the scope or course of their official duties or when acting at any time in the line of or performance of duty.

790.052   Carrying concealed firearms; off-duty law enforcement officers.—
(1)   All persons holding active certifications from the Criminal Justice Standards and Training Commission as law enforcement officers or correctional officers as defined in § 943.10(1), (2), (6), (7), (8), or (9) shall have the right to carry, on or about their persons, concealed firearms, during off-duty hours, at the discretion of their superior officers, and may perform those law enforcement functions that they normally perform during duty hours, utilizing their weapons in a manner which is reasonably expected of on-duty officers in similar situations. However, nothing in this subsection shall be construed to limit the right of a law enforcement officer, correctional officer, or correctional probation officer to carry a concealed firearm off duty as a private citizen under the exemption provided in § 790.06 that allows a law enforcement officer, correctional officer, or correctional probation officer as defined in § 943.10(1), (2), (3), (6), (7), (8), or (9) to carry a concealed firearm without a concealed weapon or firearm license. The appointing or employing agency or department of an officer carrying a concealed firearm as a private citizen under § 790.06 shall not be liable for the use of the firearm in such capacity. Nothing herein limits the authority of the appointing or employing agency or department from establishing policies limiting law enforcement officers or correctional officers from carrying concealed firearms during off-duty hours in their capacity as appointees or employees of the agency or department.
(2)   The superior officer of any police department or sheriff's office or the Florida Highway Patrol, if he or she elects to direct the officers under his or her supervision to carry concealed firearms while off duty, shall file a statement with the governing body of such department of his or her instructions and requirements relating to the carrying of said firearms.

790.053   Open carrying of weapons.—
(1)   Except as otherwise provided by law and in subsection (2), it is unlawful for any person to openly carry on or about his or her person any firearm or electric weapon or device. It is not a violation of this section for a person licensed to carry a concealed firearm as provided in § 790.06(1), and who is lawfully carrying a firearm in a concealed manner, to briefly and openly display the firearm to the ordinary sight of another person, unless the firearm is intentionally displayed in an angry or threatening manner, not in necessary self-defense.
(3)   Any person violating this section commits a misdemeanor of the second degree, punishable as provided in § 775.082 or § 775.083.

790.06   License to carry concealed weapon or firearm.—

(1) The Department of Agriculture and Consumer Services is authorized to issue licenses to carry concealed weapons or concealed firearms to persons qualified as provided in this section. Each such license must bear a color photograph of the licensee. For the purposes of this section, concealed weapons or concealed firearms are defined as a handgun, electronic weapon or device, tear gas gun, knife, or billie, but the term does not include a machine gun as defined in § 790.001(9). Such licenses shall be valid throughout the state for a period of 7 years from the date of issuance. Any person in compliance with the terms of such license may carry a concealed weapon or concealed firearm notwithstanding the provisions of § 790.01. The licensee must carry the license, together with valid identification, at all times in which the licensee is in actual possession of a concealed weapon or firearm and must display both the license and proper identification upon demand by a law enforcement officer. Violations of the provisions of this subsection shall constitute a noncriminal violation with a penalty of $25, payable to the clerk of the court.

(2) The Department of Agriculture and Consumer Services shall issue a license if the applicant:

(a) Is a resident of the United States and a citizen of the United States or a permanent resident alien of the United States, as determined by the United States Bureau of Citizenship and Immigration Services, or is a consular security official of a foreign government that maintains diplomatic relations and treaties of commerce, friendship, and navigation with the United States and is certified as such by the foreign government and by the appropriate embassy in this country;

(b) Is 21 years of age or older;

(c) Does not suffer from a physical infirmity which prevents the safe handling of a weapon or firearm;

(d) Is not ineligible to possess a firearm pursuant to § 790.23 by virtue of having been convicted of a felony;

(e) Has not been committed for the abuse of a controlled substance or been found guilty of a crime under the provisions of chapter 893 or similar laws of any other state relating to controlled substances within a 3-year period immediately preceding the date on which the application is submitted;

(f) Does not chronically and habitually use alcoholic beverages or other substances to the extent that his or her normal faculties are impaired. It shall be presumed that an applicant chronically and habitually uses alcoholic beverages or other substances to the extent that his or her normal faculties are impaired if the applicant has been committed under chapter 397 or under the provisions of former chapter 396 or has been convicted under § 790.151 or has been deemed a habitual offender under § 856.011(3), or has had two or more convictions under § 316.193 or similar laws of any other state, within the 3-year period immediately preceding the date on which the application is submitted;

(g) Desires a legal means to carry a concealed weapon or firearm for lawful self-defense;

(h) Demonstrates competence with a firearm by any one of the following:

1. Completion of any hunter education or hunter safety course approved by the Fish and Wildlife Conservation Commission or a similar agency of another state;

2. Completion of any National Rifle Association firearms safety or training course;

3. Completion of any firearms safety or training course or class available to the general public offered by a law enforcement agency, junior college, college, or private or public institution or organization or firearms training school, using instructors certified by the National Rifle Association, Criminal Justice Standards and Training Commission, or the Department of Agriculture and Consumer Services;

4. Completion of any law enforcement firearms safety or training course or class offered for security guards, investigators, special deputies, or any division or subdivision of a law enforcement agency or security enforcement;

5. Presents evidence of equivalent experience with a firearm through participation in organized shooting competition or military service;

6. Is licensed or has been licensed to carry a firearm in this state or a county or municipality of this state, unless such license has been revoked for cause; or

7. Completion of any firearms training or safety course or class conducted by a state-certified or National Rifle Association certified firearms instructor;

A photocopy of a certificate of completion of any of the courses or classes; an affidavit from the instructor, school, club, organization, or group that conducted or taught such course or class attesting to the completion of the course or class by the applicant; or a copy of any document that shows completion of the course or class or evidences participation in firearms competition shall constitute evidence of qualification under this paragraph. A person who conducts a course pursuant to subparagraph 2., subparagraph 3., or subparagraph 7., or who, as an instructor, attests to the completion of such courses, must maintain records certifying that he or she observed the student safely handle and discharge the firearm in his or her physical presence and that the discharge of the firearm included live fire using a firearm and ammunition as defined in § 790.001;

(i) Has not been adjudicated an incapacitated person under § 744.331, or similar laws of any other state, unless 5 years have elapsed since the applicant's restoration to capacity by court order;

(j) Has not been committed to a mental institution under chapter 394, or similar laws of any other state, unless the applicant produces a certificate from a licensed psychiatrist that he or she has not suffered from disability for at least 5 years before the date of submission of the application;

(k) Has not had adjudication of guilt withheld or imposition of sentence suspended on any felony unless 3 years have elapsed since probation or any other conditions set by the court have been fulfilled, or expunction has occurred;

(l) Has not had adjudication of guilt withheld or imposition of sentence suspended on any misdemeanor crime of domestic violence unless 3 years have elapsed since probation or any other conditions set by the court have been fulfilled, or the record has been expunged;

(m) Has not been issued an injunction that is currently in force and effect and that restrains the applicant from committing acts of domestic violence or acts of repeat violence; and

(n) Is not prohibited from purchasing or possessing a firearm by any other provision of Florida or federal law.

(3) The Department of Agriculture and Consumer Services shall deny a license if the applicant has been found guilty of, had adjudication of guilt withheld for, or had imposition of sentence suspended for one or more crimes of violence constituting a misdemeanor, unless 3 years have elapsed since probation or any other conditions set by the court have been fulfilled or the record has been sealed or expunged. The Department of Agriculture and Consumer Services shall revoke a license if the licensee has been found guilty of, had adjudication of guilt withheld for, or had imposition of sentence suspended for one or more crimes of violence within the preceding 3 years. The department shall, upon notification by a law enforcement agency, a court, or the Florida Department of Law Enforcement and subsequent written verification, suspend a license or the processing of an application for a license if the licensee or applicant is arrested or formally charged with a crime that would disqualify such person from having a license under this section, until final disposition of the case. The department shall suspend a license or the processing of an application for a license if the licensee or applicant is issued an injunction that restrains the licensee or applicant from committing acts of domestic violence or acts of repeat violence.

(4) The application shall be completed, under oath, on a form adopted by the Department of Agriculture and Consumer Services and shall include:

(a) The name, address, place of birth, date of birth, and race of the applicant;

(b) A statement that the applicant is in compliance with criteria contained within subsections (2) and (3);

(c) A statement that the applicant has been furnished a copy of this chapter and is knowledgeable of its provisions;

(d) A conspicuous warning that the application is executed under oath and that a false answer to any question, or the submission of any false document by the applicant, subjects the applicant to criminal prosecution under § 837.06;

(e) A statement that the applicant desires a concealed weapon or firearms license as a means of lawful self-defense; and

(f) Directions for an applicant who is a service member, as defined in § 250.01, or a veteran, as defined in § 1.01, to request expedited processing of his or her application.

(5) The applicant shall submit to the Department of Agriculture and Consumer Services or an approved tax collector pursuant to § 790.0625:

(a) A completed application as described in subsection (4).

(b) A nonrefundable license fee of up to $60 if he or she has not previously been issued a statewide license or of up to $50 for renewal of a statewide license. The cost of processing fingerprints as required in paragraph (c) shall be borne by the applicant. However, an individual holding an active certification from the Criminal Justice Standards and Training Commission as a law enforcement officer, correctional officer, or correctional probation officer as defined in § 943.10(1), (2), (3), (6), (7), (8), or (9) is exempt from the licensing requirements of this section. If such individual wishes to receive a concealed weapon or firearm license, he or she is exempt from the background investigation and all background investigation fees but must pay the current license fees regularly required to be paid by nonexempt applicants. Further, a law enforcement officer, a correctional officer, or a correctional probation officer as defined in § 943.10(1), (2), or (3) is exempt from the required fees and background investigation for 1 year after his or her retirement.

(c) A full set of fingerprints of the applicant administered by a law enforcement agency or the Division of Licensing of the Department of Agriculture and Consumer Services or an approved tax collector pursuant to § 790.0625 together with any personal identifying information required by federal law to process fingerprints.

(d) A photocopy of a certificate, affidavit, or document as described in paragraph (2)(h).

(e) A full frontal view color photograph of the applicant taken within the preceding 30 days, in which the head, including hair, measures 7/8 of an inch wide and 1-1/8 inches high.

(f) For expedited processing of an application:

1. A service member shall submit a copy of the Common Access Card, United States Uniformed Services Identification Card, or current deployment orders.

2. A veteran shall submit a copy of the DD Form 214, issued by the United States Department of Defense, or another acceptable form of identification as specified by the Department of Veterans' Affairs.

(6)(a) The Department of Agriculture and Consumer Services, upon receipt of the items listed in subsection (5), shall forward the full set of fingerprints of the applicant to the Department of Law Enforcement for state and federal processing, provided the federal service is available, to be processed for any criminal justice information as defined in § 943.045. The cost of processing such fingerprints shall be payable to the Department of Law Enforcement by the Department of Agriculture and Consumer Services.

(b) The sheriff's office shall provide fingerprinting service if requested by the applicant and may charge a fee not to exceed $5 for this service.

(c) The Department of Agriculture and Consumer Services shall, within 90 days after the date of receipt of the items listed in subsection (5):

1. Issue the license; or

2. Deny the application based solely on the ground that the applicant fails to qualify under the criteria listed in subsection (2) or subsection (3). If the Department of Agriculture and Consumer Services denies the application, it shall notify the applicant in writing, stating the ground for denial and informing the applicant of any right to a hearing pursuant to chapter 120.

3. In the event the department receives criminal history information with no final disposition on a crime which may disqualify the applicant, the time limitation prescribed by this paragraph may be suspended until receipt of the final disposition or proof of restoration of civil and firearm rights.

(d) In the event a legible set of fingerprints, as determined by the Department of Agriculture and Consumer Services or the Federal Bureau of Investigation, cannot be obtained after two attempts, the Department of Agriculture and Consumer Services shall determine eligibility based upon the name checks conducted by the Florida Department of Law Enforcement.

(e) A consular security official of a foreign government that maintains diplomatic relations and treaties of commerce, friendship, and navigation with the United States and is certified as such by the foreign government and by the appropriate embassy in this country must be issued a license within 20 days after the date of the receipt of a completed application, certification document, color photograph as specified in paragraph (5)(e), and a nonrefundable license fee of $300. Consular security official licenses shall be valid for 1 year and may be renewed upon completion of the application process as provided in this section.

(f) The Department of Agriculture and Consumer Services shall, upon receipt of a completed application and the identifying information required under paragraph (5)(f), expedite the processing of a service member's or a veteran's concealed weapon or firearm license application.

(7) The Department of Agriculture and Consumer Services shall maintain an automated listing of license holders and pertinent information, and such information shall be available online, upon request, at all times to all law enforcement agencies through the Florida Crime Information Center.

(8) Within 30 days after the changing of a permanent address, or within 30 days after having a license lost or destroyed, the licensee shall notify the Department of Agriculture and Consumer Services of such change. Failure to notify the Department of Agriculture and Consumer Services pursuant to the provisions of this subsection shall constitute a noncriminal violation with a penalty of $25.

(9) In the event that a concealed weapon or firearm license is lost or destroyed, the license shall be automatically invalid, and the person to whom the same was issued may, upon payment of $15 to the Department of Agriculture and Consumer Services, obtain a duplicate, or substitute thereof, upon furnishing a notarized statement to the Department of Agriculture and Consumer Services that such license has been lost or destroyed.

(10) A license issued under this section shall be suspended or revoked pursuant to chapter 120 if the licensee:

(a) Is found to be ineligible under the criteria set forth in subsection (2);

(b) Develops or sustains a physical infirmity which prevents the safe handling of a weapon or firearm;

(c) Is convicted of a felony which would make the licensee ineligible to possess a firearm pursuant to § 790.23;

(d) Is found guilty of a crime under the provisions of chapter 893, or similar laws of any other state, relating to controlled substances;

(e) Is committed as a substance abuser under chapter 397, or is deemed a habitual offender under § 856.011(3), or similar laws of any other state;

(f) Is convicted of a second violation of § 316.193, or a similar law of another state, within 3 years after a first conviction of such section or similar law of another state, even though the first violation may have occurred before the date on which the application was submitted;

(g) Is adjudicated an incapacitated person under § 744.331, or similar laws of any other state; or

(h) Is committed to a mental institution under chapter 394, or similar laws of any other state.

Notwithstanding § 120.60(5), service of a notice of the suspension or revocation of a concealed weapon or firearm license must be given by either certified mail, return receipt requested, to the licensee at his or her last known mailing address furnished to the Department of Agriculture and Consumer Services, or by personal service. If a notice given by certified mail is returned as undeliverable, a second attempt must be made to provide notice to the licensee at that address, by either first-class mail in an envelope, postage prepaid, addressed to the licensee at his or her last known mailing address furnished to the department, or, if the licensee has provided an e-mail address to the department, by e-mail. Such mailing by the department constitutes notice, and any failure by the licensee to receive such notice does not stay the effective date or term of the suspension or revocation. A request for hearing must be filed with the department within 21 days after notice is received by personal delivery, or within 26 days after the date the department deposits the notice in the United States mail (21 days plus 5 days for mailing). The department shall document its attempts to provide notice, and such documentation is admissible in the courts of this state and constitutes sufficient proof that notice was given.

(11)(a) At least 90 days before the expiration date of the license, the Department of Agriculture and Consumer Services shall mail to each licensee a written notice of the expiration and a renewal form prescribed by the Department of Agriculture and Consumer Services. The licensee must renew his or her license on or before the expiration date by filing with the Department of Agriculture and Consumer Services the renewal form containing an affidavit submitted under oath and under penalty of perjury stating that the licensee remains qualified pursuant to the criteria specified in subsections (2) and (3), a color photograph as specified in paragraph (5)(e), and the required renewal fee. Out-of-state residents must also submit a complete set of fingerprints and fingerprint processing fee. The license shall be renewed upon receipt of the completed renewal form, color photograph, appropriate payment of fees, and, if applicable, fingerprints. Additionally, a licensee who fails to file a renewal application on or before its expiration date must renew his or her license by paying a late fee of $15. A license may not be renewed 180 days or more after its expiration date, and such a license is deemed to be permanently expired. A person whose license has been permanently expired may reapply for licensure; however, an application for licensure and fees under subsection (5) must be submitted, and a background investigation shall be conducted pursuant to this section. A person who knowingly files false information under this subsection is subject to criminal prosecution under § 837.06.

(b) A license issued to a service member, as defined in § 250.01, is subject to paragraph (a); however, such a license does not expire while the service member is serving on military orders that have taken him or her over 35 miles from his or her residence and shall be extended, as provided in this paragraph, for up to 180 days after his or her return to such residence. If the license renewal requirements in paragraph (a) are met within the 180-day extension period, the service member may not be charged any additional costs, such as, but not limited to, late fees or delinquency fees, above the normal license fees. The service member must present to the Department of Agriculture and Consumer Services a copy of his or her official military orders or a written verification from the member's commanding officer before the end of the 180-day period in order to qualify for the extension.

(12)(a) A license issued under this section does not authorize any person to openly carry a handgun or carry a concealed weapon or firearm into:

  1. Any place of nuisance as defined in § 823.05;
  2. Any police, sheriff, or highway patrol station;
  3. Any detention facility, prison, or jail;
  4. Any courthouse;
  5. Any courtroom, except that nothing in this section would preclude a judge from carrying a concealed weapon or determining who will carry a concealed weapon in his or her courtroom;
  6. Any polling place;
  7. Any meeting of the governing body of a county, public school district, municipality, or special district;
  8. Any meeting of the Legislature or a committee thereof;
  9. Any school, college, or professional athletic event not related to firearms;
  10. Any elementary or secondary school facility or administration building;
  11. Any career center;
  12. Any portion of an establishment licensed to dispense alcoholic beverages for consumption on the premises, which portion of the establishment is primarily devoted to such purpose;
  13. Any college or university facility unless the licensee is a registered student, employee, or faculty member of such college or university and the weapon is a stun gun or nonlethal electric weapon or device designed solely for defensive purposes and the weapon does not fire a dart or projectile;
  14. The inside of the passenger terminal and sterile area of any airport, provided that no person shall be prohibited from carrying any legal firearm into the terminal, which firearm is encased for shipment for purposes of checking such firearm as baggage to be lawfully transported on any aircraft; or
  15. Any place where the carrying of firearms is prohibited by federal law.

(b) A person licensed under this section shall not be prohibited from carrying or storing a firearm in a vehicle for lawful purposes.

(c) This section does not modify the terms or conditions of § 790.251(7).

(d) Any person who knowingly and willfully violates any provision of this subsection commits a misdemeanor of the second degree, punishable as provided in § 775.082 or § 775.083.

(15) …The Department of Agriculture and Consumer Services shall implement and administer the provisions of this section. The Legislature does not delegate to the Department of Agriculture and Consumer Services the authority to regulate or restrict the issuing of licenses provided for in this section, beyond those provisions contained in this section. Subjective or arbitrary actions or rules which encumber the issuing process by placing burdens on the applicant beyond those sworn statements and specified documents detailed in this section or which create restrictions beyond those specified in this section are in conflict with the intent of this section and are prohibited. This section shall be liberally construed to carry out the constitutional right to bear arms for self-defense. This section is supplemental and additional to existing rights to bear arms, and nothing in this section shall impair or diminish such rights.

(16) The Department of Agriculture and Consumer Services shall maintain statistical information on the number of licenses issued, revoked, suspended, and denied.

(17) As amended by chapter 87-24, Laws of Florida, this section shall be known and may be cited as the "Jack Hagler Self Defense Act."

790.0601 Public records exemption for concealed weapons.—

(1) Personal identifying information of an individual who has applied for or received a license to carry a concealed weapon or firearm pursuant to § 790.06 held by the Division of Licensing of the Department of Agriculture and Consumer Services is confidential and exempt from § 119.07(1) and § 24(a), Art. I of the State Constitution. This exemption applies to such information held by the division before, on, or after the effective date of this section.

(2) Personal identifying information of an individual who has applied for a license to carry a concealed weapon or firearm pursuant to § 790.0625 which is held by a tax collector appointed by the Department of Agriculture and Consumer Services to receive applications and fees is confidential and exempt from § 119.07(1) and § 24(a), Art. I of the State

Constitution. This exemption applies to such information held by the tax collector before, on, or after the effective date of this subsection.

(3) Information made confidential and exempt by this section shall be disclosed:

  (a) With the express written consent of the applicant or licensee or his or her legally authorized representative.

  (b) By court order upon a showing of good cause.

  (c) Upon request by a law enforcement agency in connection with the performance of lawful duties, which shall include access to any automated database containing such information maintained by the Department of Agriculture and Consumer Services.

(4) Subsection (2) is subject to the Open Government Sunset Review Act in accordance with § 119.15 and shall stand repealed on October 2, 2019, unless reviewed and saved from repeal through reenactment by the Legislature.

790.061   Judges and justices; exceptions from licensure provisions. A county court judge, circuit court judge, district court of appeal judge, justice of the supreme court, federal district court judge, or federal court of appeals judge serving in this state is not required to comply with the provisions of § 790.06 in order to receive a license to carry a concealed weapon or firearm, except that any such justice or judge must comply with the provisions of § 790.06(2)(h). The Department of Agriculture and Consumer Services shall issue a license to carry a concealed weapon or firearm to any such justice or judge upon demonstration of competence of the justice or judge pursuant to § 790.06(2)(h).

790.062   Members and veterans of United States Armed Forces; exceptions from licensure provisions.—

(1) Notwithstanding § 790.06(2)(b), the Department of Agriculture and Consumer Services shall issue a license to carry a concealed weapon or firearm under § 790.06 if the applicant is otherwise qualified and:

  (a) Is a service member, as defined in § 250.01; or

  (b) Is a veteran of the United States Armed Forces who was discharged under honorable conditions.

(2) The Department of Agriculture and Consumer Services shall accept fingerprints of an applicant under this section administered by any law enforcement agency, military provost, or other military unit charged with law enforcement duties or as otherwise provided for in § 790.06(5)(c).

790.0625   Appointment of tax collectors to accept applications for a concealed weapon or firearm license; fees; penalties.—

(1) As used in this section, the term:

  (a) "Department" means the Department of Agriculture and Consumer Services.

  (b) "Division" means the Division of Licensing of the Department of Agriculture and Consumer Services.

(2) The department, at its discretion, may appoint tax collectors, as defined in § 1(d) of Art. VIII of the State Constitution, to accept applications on behalf of the division for concealed weapon or firearm licenses. Such appointment shall be for specified locations that will best serve the public interest and convenience in applying for these licenses.

(3) A tax collector seeking to be appointed to accept applications for new or renewal concealed weapon or firearm licenses must submit a written request to the division stating his or her name, address, telephone number, each location within the county at which the tax collector wishes to accept applications, and other information as required by the division.

  (a) Upon receipt of a written request, the division shall review it and at its discretion may decline to enter into a memorandum of understanding or, if approved, enter into a memorandum of understanding with the tax collector to accept applications for new or renewal concealed weapon or firearm licenses on behalf of the department.

  (b) The department or the division may rescind a memorandum of understanding for any reason at any time.

(4) All personal identifying information that is provided pursuant to § 790.06 and contained in the records of a tax collector appointed under this section is confidential and exempt as provided in § 790.0601.

(5) A tax collector appointed under this section may collect and retain a convenience fee of $22 for each new application and $12 for each renewal application and shall remit weekly to the department the license fees pursuant to § 790.06 for deposit in the Division of Licensing Trust Fund.

(6)(a) A tax collector appointed under this section may not maintain a list or record of persons who apply for or are granted a new or renewal license to carry a concealed weapon or firearm. A violation of this paragraph is subject to § 790.335.

  (b) A person may not handle an application for a concealed weapon or firearm for a fee or compensation of any kind unless he or she has been appointed by the department to do so.

(7) A person who willfully violates this section commits a misdemeanor of the second degree, punishable as provided in § 775.082 or § 775.083.

(8) Upon receipt of a completed renewal application, a new color photograph, and appropriate payment of fees, a tax collector authorized to accept renewal applications for concealed weapon or firearm licenses under this section may, upon approval and confirmation of license issuance by the department, print and deliver a concealed weapon or firearm license to a licensee renewing his or her license at the tax collector's office.

790.065   Sale and delivery of firearms.—

(1)(a) A licensed importer, licensed manufacturer, or licensed dealer may not sell or deliver from her or his inventory at her or his licensed premises any firearm to another person, other than a licensed importer, licensed manufacturer, licensed dealer, or licensed collector, until she or he has:

1. Obtained a completed form from the potential buyer or transferee, which form shall have been promulgated by the Department of Law Enforcement and provided by the licensed importer, licensed manufacturer, or licensed dealer, which shall include the name, date of birth, gender, race, and social security number or other identification number of such potential buyer or transferee and has inspected proper identification including an identification containing a photograph of the potential buyer or transferee.

2. Collected a fee from the potential buyer for processing the criminal history check of the potential buyer. The fee shall be established by the Department of Law Enforcement and may not exceed $8 per transaction. The Department of Law Enforcement may reduce, or suspend collection of, the fee to reflect payment received from the Federal Government applied to the cost of maintaining the criminal history check system established by this section as a means of facilitating or supplementing the National Instant Criminal Background Check System. The Department of Law Enforcement shall, by rule, establish procedures for the fees to be transmitted by the licensee to the Department of Law Enforcement. All such fees shall be deposited into the Department of Law Enforcement Operating Trust Fund, but shall be segregated from all other funds deposited into such trust fund and must be accounted for separately. Such segregated funds must not be used for any purpose other than the operation of the criminal history checks required by this section. The Department of Law Enforcement, each year prior to February 1, shall make a full accounting of all receipts and expenditures of such funds to the President of the Senate, the Speaker of the House of Representatives, the majority and minority leaders of each house of the Legislature, and the chairs of the appropriations committees of each house of the Legislature. In the event that the cumulative amount of funds collected exceeds the cumulative amount of expenditures by more than $2.5 million, excess funds may be used for the purpose of purchasing soft body armor for law enforcement officers.

3. Requested, by means of a toll-free telephone call, the Department of Law Enforcement to conduct a check of the information as reported and reflected in the Florida Crime Information Center and National Crime Information Center systems as of the date of the request.

4. Received a unique approval number for that inquiry from the Department of Law Enforcement, and recorded the date and such number on the consent form.

(b) However, if the person purchasing, or receiving delivery of, the firearm is a holder of a valid concealed weapons or firearms license pursuant to the provisions of § 790.06 or holds an active certification from the Criminal Justice Standards and Training Commission as a "law enforcement officer," a "correctional officer," or a "correctional probation officer" as defined in § 943.10(1), (2), (3), (6), (7), (8), or (9), this subsection does not apply.

(c) This subsection does not apply to the purchase, trade, or transfer of a rifle or shotgun by a resident of this state when the resident makes such purchase, trade, or transfer from a licensed importer, licensed manufacturer, or licensed dealer in another state.

(2) Upon receipt of a request for a criminal history record check, the Department of Law Enforcement shall, during the licensee's call or by return call, forthwith:

(a) Review any records available to determine if the potential buyer or transferee:

1. Has been convicted of a felony and is prohibited from receipt or possession of a firearm pursuant to § 790.23;

2. Has been convicted of a misdemeanor crime of domestic violence, and therefore is prohibited from purchasing a firearm;

3. Has had adjudication of guilt withheld or imposition of sentence suspended on any felony or misdemeanor crime of domestic violence unless 3 years have elapsed since probation or any other conditions set by the court have been fulfilled or expunction has occurred; or

4. Has been adjudicated mentally defective or has been committed to a mental institution by a court or as provided in sub-sub-subparagraph b.(II), and as a result is prohibited by state or federal law from purchasing a firearm.

a. As used in this subparagraph, "adjudicated mentally defective" means a determination by a court that a person, as a result of marked subnormal intelligence, or mental illness, incompetency, condition, or disease, is a danger to himself or herself or to others or lacks the mental capacity to contract or manage his or her own affairs. The phrase includes a judicial finding of incapacity under § 744.331(6)(a), an acquittal by reason of insanity of a person charged with a criminal offense, and a judicial finding that a criminal defendant is not competent to stand trial.

b. As used in this subparagraph, "committed to a mental institution" means:

(I) Involuntary commitment, commitment for mental defectiveness or mental illness, and commitment for substance abuse. The phrase includes involuntary inpatient placement as defined in § 394.467, involuntary outpatient placement as defined in § 394.4655, involuntary assessment and stabilization under § 397.6818, and involuntary substance abuse treatment under § 397.6957, but does not include a person in a mental institution for observation or discharged from a mental institution based upon the initial review by the physician or a voluntary admission to a mental institution; or

(II) Notwithstanding sub-sub-subparagraph (I), voluntary admission to a mental institution for outpatient or inpatient treatment of a person who had an involuntary examination under § 394.463, where each of the following conditions have been met:

(A) An examining physician found that the person is an imminent danger to himself or herself or others.

(B) The examining physician certified that if the person did not agree to voluntary treatment, a petition for involuntary outpatient or inpatient treatment would have been filed under § 394.463(2)(i)4., or the examining physician certified that a petition was filed and the person subsequently agreed to voluntary treatment prior to a court hearing on the petition.

(C) Before agreeing to voluntary treatment, the person received written notice of that finding and certification, and written notice that as a result of such finding, he or she may be prohibited from purchasing a firearm, and may not be eligible to apply for or retain a concealed weapon or firearms license under § 790.06 and the person acknowledged such notice in writing, in substantially the following form:

"I understand that the doctor who examined me believes I am a danger to myself or to others. I understand that if I do not agree to voluntary treatment, a petition will be filed in court to require me to receive involuntary treatment. I understand that if that petition is filed, I have the right to contest it. In the event a petition has been filed, I understand that I can subsequently agree to voluntary treatment prior to a court hearing. I understand that by agreeing to voluntary treatment in either of these situations, I may be prohibited from buying firearms and from applying for or retaining a concealed weapons or firearms license until I apply for and receive relief from that restriction under Florida law."

(D) A judge or a magistrate has, pursuant to sub-sub-subparagraph c.(II), reviewed the record of the finding, certification, notice, and written acknowledgment classifying the person as an imminent danger to himself or herself or others, and ordered that such record be submitted to the department.

c. In order to check for these conditions, the department shall compile and maintain an automated database of persons who are prohibited from purchasing a firearm based on court records of adjudications of mental defectiveness or commitments to mental institutions.

(I) Except as provided in sub-sub-subparagraph (II), clerks of court shall submit these records to the department within 1 month after the rendition of the adjudication or commitment. Reports shall be submitted in an automated format. The reports must, at a minimum, include the name, along with any known alias or former name, the sex, and the date of birth of the subject.

(II) For persons committed to a mental institution pursuant to sub-sub-subparagraph b.(II), within 24 hours after the person's agreement to voluntary admission, a record of the finding, certification, notice, and written acknowledgment must be filed by the administrator of the receiving or treatment facility, as defined in § 394.455, with the clerk of the court for the county in which the involuntary examination under § 394.463 occurred. No fee shall be charged for the filing under this sub-sub-subparagraph. The clerk must present the records to a judge or magistrate within 24 hours after receipt of the records. A judge or magistrate is required and has the lawful authority to review the records ex parte and, if the judge or magistrate determines that the record supports the classifying of the person as an imminent danger to himself or herself or others, to order that the record be submitted to the department. If a judge or magistrate orders the submittal of the record to the department, the record must be submitted to the department within 24 hours.

d. A person who has been adjudicated mentally defective or committed to a mental institution, as those terms are defined in this paragraph, may petition the court that made the adjudication or commitment, or the court that ordered that the record be submitted to the department pursuant to sub-sub-subparagraph c.(II), for relief from the firearm disabilities imposed by such adjudication or commitment. A copy of the petition shall be served on the state attorney for the county in which the person was adjudicated or committed. The state attorney may object to and present evidence relevant to the relief sought by the petition. The hearing on the petition may be open or closed as the petitioner may choose. The petitioner may present evidence and subpoena witnesses to appear at the hearing on the petition. The petitioner may confront and cross-examine witnesses called by the state attorney. A record of the hearing shall be made by a certified court reporter or by court-approved electronic means. The court shall make written findings of fact and conclusions of law on the issues before it and issue a final order. The court shall grant the relief requested in the petition if the court finds, based on the evidence presented with respect to the petitioner's reputation, the petitioner's mental health record and, if applicable, criminal history record, the circumstances surrounding the firearm disability, and any other evidence in the record, that the petitioner will not be likely to act in a manner that is dangerous to public safety and that granting the relief would not be contrary to the public interest. If the final order denies relief, the petitioner may not petition again for relief from firearm disabilities until 1 year after the date of the final order. The petitioner may seek judicial review of a final order denying relief in the district court of appeal having jurisdiction over the court that issued the order. The review shall be conducted de novo. Relief from a firearm disability granted under this sub-subparagraph has no effect on the loss of civil rights, including firearm rights, for any reason other than the particular adjudication of mental defectiveness or commitment to a mental institution from which relief is granted.

e. Upon receipt of proper notice of relief from firearm disabilities granted under sub-subparagraph d., the department shall delete any mental health record of the person granted relief from the automated database of persons who are prohibited from purchasing a firearm based on court records of adjudications of mental defectiveness or commitments to mental institutions.

f. The department is authorized to disclose data collected pursuant to this subparagraph to agencies of the Federal Government and other states for use exclusively in determining the lawfulness of a firearm sale or transfer. The department is also authorized to disclose this data to the Department of Agriculture and Consumer Services for purposes of determining eligibility for issuance of a concealed weapons or concealed firearms license and for determining whether a basis exists for revoking or suspending a previously issued license pursuant to § 790.06(10). When a potential buyer or transferee appeals a nonapproval based on these records, the clerks of court and mental institutions shall, upon request by the department, provide information to help determine whether the potential buyer or transferee is the same person as the subject of the record. Photographs and any other data that could confirm or negate identity must be made available to the department for such purposes, notwithstanding any other provision of state law to the contrary. Any such information that is made confidential or exempt from disclosure by law shall retain such confidential or exempt status when transferred to the department.

(b) Inform the licensee making the inquiry either that records demonstrate that the buyer or transferee is so prohibited and provide the licensee a nonapproval number, or provide the licensee with a unique approval number.

(c)1. Review any records available to it to determine whether the potential buyer or transferee has been indicted or has had an information filed against her or him for an offense that is a felony under either state or federal law, or, as mandated by federal law, has had an injunction for protection against domestic violence entered against the potential buyer or transferee under § 741.30, has had an injunction for protection against repeat violence entered against the potential buyer or transferee under § 784.046, or has been arrested for a dangerous crime as specified in § 907.041(4)(a) or for any of the following enumerated offenses:

    a. Criminal anarchy under §§. 876.01 and 876.02.
    b. Extortion under § 836.05.
    c. Explosives violations under § 552.22(1) and (2).
    d. Controlled substances violations under chapter 893.
    e. Resisting an officer with violence under § 843.01.
    f. Weapons and firearms violations under this chapter.
    g. Treason under § 876.32.
    h. Assisting self-murder under § 782.08.
    i. Sabotage under § 876.38.
    j. Stalking or aggravated stalking under § 784.048.

If the review indicates any such indictment, information, or arrest, the department shall provide to the licensee a conditional non-approval number.

    2. Within 24 working hours, the department shall determine the disposition of the indictment, information, or arrest and inform the licensee as to whether the potential buyer is prohibited from receiving or possessing a firearm. For purposes of this paragraph, "working hours" means the hours from 8 a.m. to 5 p.m. Monday through Friday, excluding legal holidays.

    3. The office of the clerk of court, at no charge to the department, shall respond to any department request for data on the disposition of the indictment, information, or arrest as soon as possible, but in no event later than 8 working hours.

    4. The department shall determine as quickly as possible within the allotted time period whether the potential buyer is prohibited from receiving or possessing a firearm.

    5. If the potential buyer is not so prohibited, or if the department cannot determine the disposition information within the allotted time period, the department shall provide the licensee with a conditional approval number.

    6. If the buyer is so prohibited, the conditional nonapproval number shall become a nonapproval number.

    7. The department shall continue its attempts to obtain the disposition information and may retain a record of all approval numbers granted without sufficient disposition information. If the department later obtains disposition information which indicates:

        a. That the potential buyer is not prohibited from owning a firearm, it shall treat the record of the transaction in accordance with this section; or

        b. That the potential buyer is prohibited from owning a firearm, it shall immediately revoke the conditional approval number and notify local law enforcement.

    8. During the time that disposition of the indictment, information, or arrest is pending and until the department is notified by the potential buyer that there has been a final disposition of the indictment, information, or arrest, the conditional nonapproval number shall remain in effect.

(3) In the event of scheduled computer downtime, electronic failure, or similar emergency beyond the control of the Department of Law Enforcement, the department shall immediately notify the licensee of the reason for, and estimated length of, such delay. After such notification, the department shall forthwith, and in no event later than the end of the next business day of the licensee, either inform the requesting licensee if its records demonstrate that the buyer or transferee is prohibited from receipt or possession of a firearm pursuant to Florida and Federal law or provide the licensee with a unique approval number. Unless notified by the end of said next business day that the buyer or transferee is so prohibited, and without regard to whether she or he has received a unique approval number, the licensee may complete the sale or transfer and shall not be deemed in violation of this section with respect to such sale or transfer.

(4)(a) Any records containing any of the information set forth in subsection (1) pertaining to a buyer or transferee who is not found to be prohibited from receipt or transfer of a firearm by reason of Florida and federal law which records are created by the Department of Law Enforcement to conduct the criminal history record check shall be confidential and exempt from the provisions of § 119.07(1) and may not be disclosed by the Department of Law Enforcement or any officer or employee thereof to any person or to another agency. The Department of Law Enforcement shall destroy any such records forthwith after it communicates the approval and nonapproval numbers to the licensee and, in any event, such records shall be destroyed within 48 hours after the day of the response to the licensee's request.

(b) Notwithstanding the provisions of this subsection, the Department of Law Enforcement may maintain records of NCIC transactions to the extent required by the Federal Government, and may maintain a log of dates of requests for criminal history records checks, unique approval and nonapproval numbers, license identification numbers, and transaction numbers corresponding to such dates for a period of not longer than 2 years or as otherwise required by law.

(c) Nothing in this chapter shall be construed to allow the State of Florida to maintain records containing the names of purchasers or transferees who receive unique approval numbers or to maintain records of firearm transactions.

(d) Any officer or employee, or former officer or employee of the Department of Law Enforcement or law enforcement agency who intentionally and maliciously violates the provisions of this subsection commits a felony of the third degree punishable as provided in § 775.082 or § 775.083.

(5) The Department of Law Enforcement shall establish a toll-free telephone number which shall be operational 7 days a week with the exception of Christmas Day and New Year's Day, for a period of 12 hours a day beginning at 9 a.m. and ending at 9 p.m., for purposes of responding to inquiries as described in this section from licensed manufacturers, licensed importers, and licensed dealers. The Department of Law Enforcement shall employ and train such personnel as are necessary expeditiously to administer the provisions of this section.

(6) Any person who is denied the right to receive or purchase a firearm as a result of the procedures established by this section may request a criminal history records review and correction in accordance with the rules promulgated by the Department of Law Enforcement.

(7) It shall be unlawful for any licensed dealer, licensed manufacturer, or licensed importer willfully and intentionally to request criminal history record information under false pretenses, or willfully and intentionally to disseminate criminal history record information to any person other than the subject of such information. Any person convicted of a violation of this subsection commits a felony of the third degree punishable as provided in § 775.082 or § 775.083.

(8) The Department of Law Enforcement shall promulgate regulations to ensure the identity, confidentiality, and security of all records and data provided pursuant to this section.

(9) This section shall become effective at such time as the Department of Law Enforcement has notified all licensed importers, licensed manufacturers, and licensed dealers in writing that the procedures and toll-free number described in this section are operational. This section shall remain in effect only during such times as the procedures described in subsection (2) remain operational.

(10) A licensed importer, licensed manufacturer, or licensed dealer is not required to comply with the requirements of this section in the event of:

(a) Unavailability of telephone service at the licensed premises due to the failure of the entity which provides telephone service in the state, region, or other geographical area in which the licensee is located to provide telephone service to the premises of the licensee due to the location of said premises; or the interruption of telephone service by reason of hurricane, tornado, flood, natural disaster, or other act of God, war, invasion, insurrection, riot, or other bona fide emergency, or other reason beyond the control of the licensee; or

(b) Failure of the Department of Law Enforcement to comply with the requirements of subsections (2) and (3).

(11) Compliance with the provisions of this chapter shall be a complete defense to any claim or cause of action under the laws of any state for liability for damages arising from the importation or manufacture, or the subsequent sale or transfer to any person who has been convicted in any court of a crime punishable by imprisonment for a term exceeding 1 year, of any firearm which has been shipped or transported in interstate or foreign commerce. The Department of Law Enforcement, its agents and employees shall not be liable for any claim or cause of action under the laws of any state for liability for damages arising from its actions in lawful compliance with this section.

(12)(a) Any potential buyer or transferee who willfully and knowingly provides false information or false or fraudulent identification commits a felony of the third degree punishable as provided in § 775.082 or § 775.083.

(b) Any licensed importer, licensed manufacturer, or licensed dealer who violates the provisions of subsection (1) commits a felony of the third degree punishable as provided in § 775.082 or § 775.083.

(c) Any employee or agency of a licensed importer, licensed manufacturer, or licensed dealer who violates the provisions of subsection (1) commits a felony of the third degree punishable as provided in § 775.082 or § 775.083.

(d) Any person who knowingly acquires a firearm through purchase or transfer intended for the use of a person who is prohibited by state or federal law from possessing or receiving a firearm commits a felony of the third degree, punishable as provided in § 775.082 or § 775.083.

(13) This section does not apply to employees of sheriff's offices, municipal police departments, correctional facilities or agencies, or other criminal justice or governmental agencies when the purchases or transfers are made on behalf of an employing agency for official law enforcement purposes.

790.0655 Purchase and delivery of handguns; mandatory waiting period; exceptions; penalties.—

(1)(a) There shall be a mandatory 3-day waiting period, which shall be 3 days, excluding weekends and legal holidays, between the purchase and the delivery at retail of any handgun. "Purchase" means the transfer of money or other valuable consideration to the retailer. "Handgun" means a firearm capable of being carried and used by one hand, such as a pistol or revolver. "Retailer" means and includes every person engaged in the business of making sales at retail or for distribution, or use, or consumption, or storage to be used or consumed in this state, as defined in § 212.02(13).

(b) Records of handgun sales must be available for inspection by any law enforcement agency, as defined in § 934.02, during normal business hours.

(2) The 3-day waiting period shall not apply in the following circumstances:

(a) When a handgun is being purchased by a holder of a concealed weapons permit as defined in § 790.06.

(b) To a trade-in of another handgun.

(3) It is a felony of the third degree, punishable as provided in § 775.082, § 775.083, or § 775.084:

(a) For any retailer, or any employee or agent of a retailer, to deliver a handgun before the expiration of the 3-day waiting period, subject to the exceptions provided in subsection (2).

(b) For a purchaser to obtain delivery of a handgun by fraud, false pretense, or false representation.

790.07   Persons engaged in criminal offense, having weapons.—

(1)   Whoever, while committing or attempting to commit any felony or while under indictment, displays, uses, threatens, or attempts to use any weapon or electric weapon or device or carries a concealed weapon is guilty of a felony of the third degree, punishable as provided in § 775.082, § 775.083, or § 775.084.

(2)   Whoever, while committing or attempting to commit any felony, displays, uses, threatens, or attempts to use any firearm or carries a concealed firearm is guilty of a felony of the second degree, punishable as provided in § 775.082, § 775.083, and § 775.084.

(3)   The following crimes are excluded from application of this section: Antitrust violations, unfair trade practices, restraints of trade, nonsupport of dependents, bigamy, or other similar offenses.

(4)   Whoever, having previously been convicted of a violation of subsection (1) or subsection (2) and, subsequent to such conviction, displays, uses, threatens, or attempts to use any weapon, firearm, or electric weapon or device, carries a concealed weapon, or carries a concealed firearm while committing or attempting to commit any felony or while under indictment is guilty of a felony of the first degree, punishable as provided in § 775.082, § 775.083, or § 775.084. Sentence shall not be suspended or deferred under the provisions of this subsection.

790.08   Taking possession of weapons and arms; reports; disposition; custody.—

(1)   Every officer making an arrest under § 790.07, or under any other law or municipal ordinance within the state, shall take possession of any weapons, electric weapons or devices, or arms mentioned in § 790.07 found upon the person arrested and deliver them to the sheriff of the county, or the chief of police of the municipality wherein the arrest is made, who shall retain the same until after the trial of the person arrested.

(2)   If the person arrested as aforesaid is convicted of violating § 790.07, or of a similar offense under any municipal ordinance, or any other offense involving the use or attempted use of such weapons, electric weapons or devices, or arms, such weapons, electric weapons or devices, or arms shall become forfeited to the state, without any order of forfeiture being necessary, although the making of such an order shall be deemed proper, and such weapons, electric weapons or devices, or arms shall be forthwith delivered to the sheriff by the chief of police or other person having custody thereof, and the sheriff is hereby made the custodian of such weapons, electric weapons or devices, and arms for the state.

(3)   If the person arrested as aforesaid is acquitted of the offenses mentioned in subsection (2), the said weapons, electric weapons or devices, or arms taken from the person as aforesaid shall be returned to him or her; however, if he or she fails to call for or receive the same within 60 days from and after his or her acquittal or the dismissal of the charges against him or her, the same shall be delivered to the sheriff as aforesaid to be held by the sheriff as hereinafter provided. This subsection shall likewise apply to persons and their weapons, electric weapons or devices, or arms who have heretofore been acquitted or the charges against them dismissed.

(4)   All such weapons, electric weapons or devices, and arms now in, or hereafter coming into, the hands of any of the peace officers of this state or any of its political subdivisions, which have been found abandoned or otherwise discarded, or left in their hands and not reclaimed by the owners shall, within 60 days, be delivered by such peace officers to the sheriff of the county aforesaid.

(5)   Weapons, electric weapons or devices, and arms coming into the hands of the sheriff pursuant to subsections (3) and (4) aforesaid shall, unless reclaimed by the owner thereof within 6 months from the date the same come into the hands of the said sheriff, become forfeited to the state, and no action or proceeding for their recovery shall thereafter be maintained in this state.

(6)   Weapons, electric weapons or devices, and arms coming into the hands of the sheriff as aforesaid shall be listed, kept, and held by him or her as custodian for the state. Any or all such weapons, electric weapons or devices, and arms suitable for use by the sheriff may be so used. All such weapons, electric weapons or devices, and arms not needed by the said sheriff may be loaned to any other department of the state or to any county or municipality having use for such weapons, electric weapons or devices, and arms. The sheriff shall take the receipt of such other department, county, or municipality for such weapons, electric weapons or devices, and arms loaned to them. All weapons, electric weapons or devices, and arms which are not needed or which are useless or unfit for use shall be destroyed or otherwise disposed of by the sheriff as provided in chapter 705 or as provided in the Florida Contraband Forfeiture Act. All sums received from the sale or other disposition of the said weapons, electric weapons or devices, or arms disposed of by the sheriff under chapter 705 as aforesaid shall be paid into the State Treasury for the benefit of the State School Fund and shall become a part thereof. All sums received from the sale or other disposition of any such weapons, electric weapons or devices, or arms disposed of by the sheriff under the Florida Contraband Forfeiture Act shall be disbursed as provided therein.

(7)   This section does not apply to any municipality in any county having home rule under the State Constitution.

790.10   Improper exhibition of dangerous weapons or firearms. If any person having or carrying any dirk, sword, sword cane, firearm, electric weapon or device, or other weapon shall, in the presence of one or more persons, exhibit the same in a rude, careless, angry, or threatening manner, not in necessary self-defense, the person so offending shall be guilty of a misdemeanor of the first degree, punishable as provided in § 775.082 or § 775.083.

790.115 Possessing or discharging weapons or firearms at a school-sponsored event or on school property prohibited; penalties; exceptions.—

(1) A person who exhibits any sword, sword cane, firearm, electric weapon or device, destructive device, or other weapon as defined in § 790.001(13), including a razor blade, box cutter, or common pocketknife, except as authorized in support of school-sanctioned activities, in the presence of one or more persons in a rude, careless, angry, or threatening manner and not in lawful self-defense, at a school-sponsored event or on the grounds or facilities of any school, school bus, or school bus stop, or within 1,000 feet of the real property that comprises a public or private elementary school, middle school, or secondary school, during school hours or during the time of a sanctioned school activity, commits a felony of the third degree, punishable as provided in § 775.082, § 775.083, or § 775.084. This subsection does not apply to the exhibition of a firearm or weapon on private real property within 1,000 feet of a school by the owner of such property or by a person whose presence on such property has been authorized, licensed, or invited by the owner.

(2)(a) A person shall not possess any firearm, electric weapon or device, destructive device, or other weapon as defined in § 790.001(13), including a razor blade or box cutter, except as authorized in support of school-sanctioned activities, at a school-sponsored event or on the property of any school, school bus, or school bus stop; however, a person may carry a firearm:

1. In a case to a firearms program, class or function which has been approved in advance by the principal or chief administrative officer of the school as a program or class to which firearms could be carried;

2. In a case to a career center having a firearms training range; or

3. In a vehicle pursuant to § 790.25(5); except that school districts may adopt written and published policies that waive the exception in this subparagraph for purposes of student and campus parking privileges.

For the purposes of this section, "school" means any preschool, elementary school, middle school, junior high school, secondary school, career center, or postsecondary school, whether public or nonpublic.

(b) A person who willfully and knowingly possesses any electric weapon or device, destructive device, or other weapon as defined in § 790.001(13), including a razor blade or box cutter, except as authorized in support of school-sanctioned activities, in violation of this subsection commits a felony of the third degree, punishable as provided in § 775.082, § 775.083, or § 775.084.

(c)1. A person who willfully and knowingly possesses any firearm in violation of this subsection commits a felony of the third degree, punishable as provided in § 775.082, § 775.083, or § 775.084.

2. A person who stores or leaves a loaded firearm within the reach or easy access of a minor who obtains the firearm and commits a violation of subparagraph 1. commits a misdemeanor of the second degree, punishable as provided in § 775.082 or § 775.083; except that this does not apply if the firearm was stored or left in a securely locked box or container or in a location which a reasonable person would have believed to be secure, or was securely locked with a firearm-mounted push-button combination lock or a trigger lock; if the minor obtains the firearm as a result of an unlawful entry by any person; or to members of the Armed Forces, National Guard, or State Militia, or to police or other law enforcement officers, with respect to firearm possession by a minor which occurs during or incidental to the performance of their official duties.

(d) A person who discharges any weapon or firearm while in violation of paragraph (a), unless discharged for lawful defense of himself or herself or another or for a lawful purpose, commits a felony of the second degree, punishable as provided in § 775.082, § 775.083, or § 775.084.

(e) The penalties of this subsection shall not apply to persons licensed under § 790.06. Persons licensed under § 790.06 shall be punished as provided in § 790.06(12), except that a license holder who unlawfully discharges a weapon or firearm on school property as prohibited by this subsection commits a felony of the second degree, punishable as provided in § 775.082, § 775.083, or § 775.084.

(3) This section does not apply to any law enforcement officer as defined in § 943.10(1), (2), (3), (4), (6), (7), (8), (9), or (14).

(4) Notwithstanding § 985.24, § 985.245, or § 985.25(1), any minor under 18 years of age who is charged under this section with possessing or discharging a firearm on school property shall be detained in secure detention, unless the state attorney authorizes the release of the minor, and shall be given a probable cause hearing within 24 hours after being taken into custody. At the hearing, the court may order that the minor continue to be held in secure detention for a period of 21 days, during which time the minor shall receive medical, psychiatric, psychological, or substance abuse examinations pursuant to § 985.18, and a written report shall be completed.

790.145 Crimes in pharmacies; possession of weapons; penalties.—

(1) Unless otherwise provided by law, any person who is in possession of a concealed "firearm," as defined in § 790.001(6), or a "destructive device," as defined in § 790.001(4), within the premises of a "pharmacy," as defined in chapter 465, is guilty of a felony of the third degree, punishable as provided in § 775.082, § 775.083, or § 775.084.

(2) The provisions of this section do not apply:

(a) To any law enforcement officer;

(b) To any person employed and authorized by the owner, operator, or manager of a pharmacy to carry a firearm or destructive device on such premises; or

(c) To any person licensed to carry a concealed weapon.

790.15 Discharging firearm in public or on residential property.—

(1) Except as provided in subsection (2) or subsection (3), any person who knowingly discharges a firearm in any public place or on the right-of-way of any paved public road, highway, or street, who knowingly discharges any firearm over the right-of-way of any paved public road, highway, or street or over any occupied premises, or who recklessly or negligently discharges a firearm outdoors on any property used primarily as the site of a dwelling as defined in § 776.013 or zoned exclusively for residential use commits a misdemeanor of the first degree, punishable as provided in § 775.082 or § 775.083. This section does not apply to a person lawfully defending life or property or performing official duties requiring the discharge of a firearm or to a person discharging a firearm on public roads or properties expressly approved for hunting by the Fish and Wildlife Conservation Commission or Florida Forest Service.

(2) Any occupant of any vehicle who knowingly and willfully discharges any firearm from the vehicle within 1,000 feet of any person commits a felony of the second degree, punishable as provided in § 775.082, § 775.083, or § 775.084.

(3) Any driver or owner of any vehicle, whether or not the owner of the vehicle is occupying the vehicle, who knowingly directs any other person to discharge any firearm from the vehicle commits a felony of the third degree, punishable as provided in § 775.082, § 775.083, or § 775.084.

(4) Any person who recreationally discharges a firearm outdoors, including target shooting, in an area that the person knows or reasonably should know is primarily residential in nature and that has a residential density of one or more dwelling units per acre, commits a misdemeanor of the first degree, punishable as provided in § 775.082 or § 775.083. This subsection does not apply:

  (a) To a person lawfully defending life or property or performing official duties requiring the discharge of a firearm;

  (b) If, under the circumstances, the discharge does not pose a reasonably foreseeable risk to life, safety, or property; or

  (c) To a person who accidentally discharges a firearm.

790.151 Using firearm while under the influence of alcoholic beverages, chemical substances, or controlled substances; penalties.—

(1) As used in §§ 790.151-790.157, to "use a firearm" means to discharge a firearm or to have a firearm readily accessible for immediate discharge.

(2) For the purposes of this section, "readily accessible for immediate discharge" means loaded and in a person's hand.

(3) It is unlawful and punishable as provided in subsection (4) for any person who is under the influence of alcoholic beverages, any chemical substance set forth in § 877.111, or any substance controlled under chapter 893, when affected to the extent that his or her normal faculties are impaired, to use a firearm in this state.

(4) Any person who violates subsection (3) commits a misdemeanor of the second degree, punishable as provided in § 775.082 or § 775.083.

(5) This section does not apply to persons exercising lawful self-defense or defense of one's property.

790.157 Presumption of impairment; testing methods.—

(1) It is unlawful and punishable as provided in § 790.151 for any person who is under the influence of alcoholic beverages or controlled substances, when affected to the extent that his or her normal faculties are impaired, to use a firearm in this state.

(2) Upon the trial of any civil or criminal action or proceeding arising out of acts alleged to have been committed by any person while using a firearm while under the influence of alcoholic beverages or controlled substances, when affected to the extent that his or her normal faculties were impaired or to the extent that the person was deprived of full possession of his or her normal faculties, the results of any test administered in accordance with § 790.153 or § 790.155 and this section shall be admissible into evidence when otherwise admissible, and the amount of alcohol in the person's blood at the time alleged, as shown by chemical analysis of the person's blood or chemical or physical analysis of the person's breath, shall give rise to the following presumptions:

  (a) If there was at that time 0.05 percent or less by weight of alcohol in the person's blood, it shall be presumed that the person was not under the influence of alcoholic beverages to the extent that his or her normal faculties were impaired.

  (b) If there was at that time in excess of 0.05 percent but less than 0.10 percent by weight of alcohol in the person's blood, such fact shall not give rise to any presumption that the person was or was not under the influence of alcoholic beverages to the extent that his or her normal faculties were impaired, but such fact may be considered with other competent evidence in determining whether the person was under the influence of alcoholic beverages to the extent that his or her normal faculties were impaired.

  (c) If there was at that time 0.10 percent or more by weight of alcohol in the person's blood, that fact shall be prima facie evidence that the person was under the influence of alcoholic beverages to the extent that his or her normal faculties were impaired.

  The percent by weight of alcohol in the blood shall be based upon grams of alcohol per 100 milliliters of blood. The foregoing provisions of this subsection shall not be construed as limiting the introduction of any other competent evidence bearing upon the question of whether the person was under the influence of alcoholic beverages to the extent that his or her normal faculties were impaired.

(3) A chemical analysis of a person's blood to determine its alcoholic content or a chemical or physical analysis of a person's breath, in order to be considered valid under the provisions of this section, must have been performed substantially in accordance with methods approved by the Florida Department of Law Enforcement and by an individual possessing a valid permit issued by the department for this purpose. Any insubstantial differences between approved techniques and actual testing procedures in an individual case shall not render the test or test results invalid. The Florida Department of Law Enforcement may approve satisfactory techniques or methods, ascertain the qualification and competence of individuals to conduct such analyses, and issue permits which shall be subject to termination or revocation in accordance with rules adopted by the department.

(4) Any person charged with using a firearm while under the influence of alcoholic beverages or controlled substances to the extent that his or her normal faculties were impaired, whether in a municipality or not, shall be entitled to trial by jury according to the Florida Rules of Criminal Procedure.

790.16 Discharging machine guns; penalty.—

(1) It is unlawful for any person to shoot or discharge any machine gun upon, across, or along any road, street, or highway in the state; upon or across any public park in the state; or in, upon, or across any public place where people are accustomed to assemble in the state. The discharge of such machine gun in, upon, or across such public street; in, upon, or across such public park; or in, upon, or across such public place, whether indoors or outdoors, including all theaters and athletic stadiums, with intent to do bodily harm to any person or with intent to do damage to property not resulting in the death of another person shall be a felony of the first degree, punishable as provided in § 775.082. A sentence not exceeding life imprisonment is specifically authorized when great bodily harm to another or serious disruption of governmental operations results.

(2) This section shall not apply to the use of such machine guns by any United States or state militia or by any law enforcement officer while in the discharge of his or her lawful duty in suppressing riots and disorderly conduct and in preserving and protecting the public peace or in the preservation of public property, or when said use is authorized by law.

790.161 Making, possessing, throwing, projecting, placing, or discharging any destructive device or attempt so to do, felony; penalties. A person who willfully and unlawfully makes, possesses, throws, projects, places, discharges, or attempts to make, possess, throw, project, place, or discharge any destructive device:

(1) Commits a felony of the third degree, punishable as provided in § 775.082 or § 775.084.

(2) If the act is perpetrated with the intent to do bodily harm to any person, or with the intent to do property damage, or if the act results in a disruption of governmental operations, commerce, or the private affairs of another person, commits a felony of the second degree, punishable as provided in § 775.082 or § 775.084.

(3) If the act results in bodily harm to another person or in property damage, commits a felony of the first degree, punishable as provided in § 775.082 or § 775.084.

(4) If the act results in the death of another person, commits a capital felony, punishable as provided in § 775.082. In the event the death penalty in a capital felony is held to be unconstitutional by the Florida Supreme Court or the United States Supreme Court, the court having jurisdiction over a person previously sentenced to death for a capital felony shall cause such person to be brought before the court, and the court shall sentence such person to life imprisonment if convicted of murder in the first degree or of a capital felony under this subsection, and such person shall be ineligible for parole. No sentence of death shall be reduced as a result of a determination that a method of execution is held to be unconstitutional under the State Constitution or the Constitution of the United States.

790.1612 Authorization for governmental manufacture, possession, and use of destructive devices. The governing body of any municipality or county and the Division of State Fire Marshal of the Department of Financial Services have the power to authorize the manufacture, possession, and use of destructive devices as defined in § 790.001(4).

790.1615 Unlawful throwing, projecting, placing, or discharging of destructive device or bomb that results in injury to another; penalty.—

(1) A person who perpetrates any unlawful throwing, projecting, placing, or discharging of a destructive device or bomb that results in any bodily harm to a firefighter or any other person, regardless of intent or lack of intent to cause such harm, commits a misdemeanor of the first degree, punishable as provided in § 775.082 or § 775.083.

(2) A person who perpetrates any unlawful throwing, projecting, placing, or discharging of a destructive device or bomb that results in great bodily harm, permanent disability, or permanent disfigurement to a firefighter or any other person, regardless of intent or lack of intent to cause such harm, commits a felony of the second degree, punishable as provided in § 775.082, § 775.083, or § 775.084.

(3) Upon conviction and adjudication of guilt, a person may be sentenced separately, pursuant to § 775.021(4), for any violation of this section and for any unlawful throwing, projecting, placing, or discharging of a destructive device or bomb committed during the same criminal episode. A conviction for any unlawful throwing, projecting, placing, or discharging of a destructive device or bomb, however, is not necessary for a conviction under this section.

790.162 Threat to throw, project, place, or discharge any destructive device, felony; penalty. It is unlawful for any person to threaten to throw, project, place, or discharge any destructive device with intent to do bodily harm to any person or with intent to do damage to any property of any person, and any person convicted thereof commits a felony of the second degree, punishable as provided in § 775.082, § 775.083, or § 775.084.

§ 790.163. False report concerning planting a bomb, an explosive, or a weapon of mass destruction, or concerning the use of firearms in a violent manner; penalty.

(1) It is unlawful for any person to make a false report, with intent to deceive, mislead, or otherwise misinform any person, concerning the placing or planting of any bomb, dynamite, other deadly explosive, or weapon of mass destruction as defined in § 790.166, or concerning the use of firearms in a violent manner against a person or persons. A person who violates this subsection commits a felony of the second degree, punishable as provided in § 775.082, § 775.083, or § 775.084.

(2) Notwithstanding any other law, adjudication of guilt or imposition of sentence for a violation of this section may not be suspended, deferred, or withheld. However, the state attorney may move the sentencing court to reduce or suspend the sentence of any person who is convicted of a violation of this section and who provides substantial assistance in the identification, arrest, or conviction of any of his or her accomplices, accessories, coconspirators, or principals.

(3) Proof that a person accused of violating this section knowingly made a false report is prima facie evidence of the accused person's intent to deceive, mislead, or otherwise misinform any person.

(4) In addition to any other penalty provided by law with respect to any person who is convicted of a violation of this section that resulted in the mobilization or action of any law enforcement officer or any state or local agency, a person convicted of a violation of this section may be required by the court to pay restitution for all of the costs and damages arising from the criminal conduct.

§ 790.164. False reports concerning planting a bomb, explosive, or weapon of mass destruction in, or committing arson against, state-owned property, or concerning the use of firearms in a violent manner; penalty; reward.

(1) It is unlawful for any person to make a false report, with intent to deceive, mislead, or otherwise misinform any person, concerning the placing or planting of any bomb, dynamite, other deadly explosive, or weapon of mass destruction as defined in § 790.166, concerning any act of arson or other violence to property owned by the state or any political subdivision, or concerning the use of firearms in a violent manner against a person or persons. A person who violates this subsection commits a felony of the second degree, punishable as provided in § 775.082, § 775.083, or § 775.084.

(2) Notwithstanding any other law, adjudication of guilt or imposition of sentence for a violation of this section may not be suspended, deferred, or withheld. However, the state attorney may move the sentencing court to reduce or suspend the sentence of any person who is convicted of a violation of this section and who provides substantial assistance in the identification, arrest, or conviction of any of his or her accomplices, accessories, coconspirators, or principals.

(3) Proof that a person accused of violating this section knowingly made a false report is prima facie evidence of the accused person's intent to deceive, mislead, or otherwise misinform any person.

(4) **(d)** In addition to any other penalty provided by law with respect to any person who is convicted of a violation of this section that resulted in the mobilization or action of any law enforcement officer or any state or local agency, a person convicted of a violation of this section may be required by the court to pay restitution for all of the costs and damages arising from the criminal conduct.

790.169 Juvenile offenders; release of names and addresses.
A law enforcement agency may release for publication the name and address of a child who has been convicted of any offense involving possession or use of a firearm.

790.17 Furnishing weapons to minors under 18 years of age or persons of unsound mind and furnishing firearms to minors under 18 years of age prohibited.—

(1) A person who sells, hires, barters, lends, transfers, or gives any minor under 18 years of age any dirk, electric weapon or device, or other weapon, other than an ordinary pocketknife, without permission of the minor's parent or guardian, or sells, hires, barters, lends, transfers, or gives to any person of unsound mind an electric weapon or device or any dangerous weapon, other than an ordinary pocketknife, commits a misdemeanor of the first degree, punishable as provided in § 775.082 or § 775.083.

(2)(a) A person may not knowingly or willfully sell or transfer a firearm to a minor under 18 years of age, except that a person may transfer ownership of a firearm to a minor with permission of the parent or guardian. A person who violates this paragraph commits a felony of the third degree, punishable as provided in § 775.082, § 775.083, or § 775.084.

(b) The parent or guardian must maintain possession of the firearm except pursuant to § 790.22.

790.174 Safe storage of firearms required.—

(1) A person who stores or leaves, on a premise under his or her control, a loaded firearm, as defined in § 790.001, and who knows or reasonably should know that a minor is likely to gain access to the firearm without the lawful permission of the minor's parent or the person having charge of the minor, or without the supervision required by law, shall keep the firearm in a securely locked box or container or in a location which a reasonable person would believe to be secure or shall secure it with a trigger lock, except when the person is carrying the firearm on his or her body or within such close proximity thereto that he or she can retrieve and use it as easily and quickly as if he or she carried it on his or her body.

(2) It is a misdemeanor of the second degree, punishable as provided in § 775.082 or § 775.083, if a person violates subsection (1) by failing to store or leave a firearm in the required manner and as a result thereof a minor gains access to the firearm, without the lawful permission of the minor's parent or the person having charge of the minor, and possesses or exhibits it, without the supervision required by law:

(a) In a public place; or

(b) In a rude, careless, angry, or threatening manner in violation of § 790.10.

This subsection does not apply if the minor obtains the firearm as a result of an unlawful entry by any person.

(3) As used in this act, the term "minor" means any person under the age of 16.

790.175 Transfer or sale of firearms; required warnings; penalties.—
(1) Upon the retail commercial sale or retail transfer of any firearm, the seller or transferor shall deliver a written warning to the purchaser or transferee, which warning states, in block letters not less than 1/4 inch in height:
"IT IS UNLAWFUL, AND PUNISHABLE BY IMPRISONMENT AND FINE, FOR ANY ADULT TO STORE OR LEAVE A FIREARM IN ANY PLACE WITHIN THE REACH OR EASY ACCESS OF A MINOR UNDER 18 YEARS OF AGE OR TO KNOWINGLY SELL OR OTHERWISE TRANSFER OWNERSHIP OR POSSESSION OF A FIREARM TO A MINOR OR A PERSON OF UNSOUND MIND."
(2) Any retail or wholesale store, shop, or sales outlet which sells firearms must conspicuously post at each purchase counter the following warning in block letters not less than 1 inch in height:
"IT IS UNLAWFUL TO STORE OR LEAVE A FIREARM IN ANY PLACE WITHIN THE REACH OR EASY ACCESS OF A MINOR UNDER 18 YEARS OF AGE OR TO KNOWINGLY SELL OR OTHERWISE TRANSFER OWNERSHIP OR POSSESSION OF A FIREARM TO A MINOR OR A PERSON OF UNSOUND MIND."
(3) Any person or business knowingly violating a requirement to provide warning under this section commits a misdemeanor of the second degree, punishable as provided in § 775.082 or § 775.083.

790.18 Sale or transfer of arms to minors by dealers. It is unlawful for any dealer in arms to sell or transfer to a minor any firearm, pistol, Springfield rifle or other repeating rifle.... A person who violates this section commits a felony of the second degree, punishable as provided in § 775.082, § 775.083, or § 775.084.

790.19 Shooting into or throwing deadly missiles into dwellings, public or private buildings, occupied or not occupied; vessels, aircraft, buses, railroad cars, streetcars, or other vehicles. Whoever, wantonly or maliciously, shoots at, within, or into, or throws any missile or hurls or projects a stone or other hard substance which would produce death or great bodily harm, at, within, or in any public or private building, occupied or unoccupied, or public or private bus or any train, locomotive, railway car, caboose, cable railway car, street railway car, monorail car, or vehicle of any kind which is being used or occupied by any person, or any boat, vessel, ship, or barge lying in or plying the waters of this state, or aircraft flying through the airspace of this state shall be guilty of a felony of the second degree, punishable as provided in § 775.082, § 775.083, or § 775.084.

790.22 Use of BB guns, air or gas-operated guns, or electric weapons or devices by minor under 16; limitation; possession of firearms by minor under 18 prohibited; penalties.—
(1) The use for any purpose whatsoever of BB guns, air or gas-operated guns, or electric weapons or devices, by any minor under the age of 16 years is prohibited unless such use is under the supervision and in the presence of an adult who is acting with the consent of the minor's parent.
(2) Any adult responsible for the welfare of any child under the age of 16 years who knowingly permits such child to use or have in his or her possession any BB gun, air or gas-operated gun, electric weapon or device, or firearm in violation of the provisions of subsection (1) of this section commits a misdemeanor of the second degree, punishable as provided in § 775.082 or § 775.083.
(3) A minor under 18 years of age may not possess a firearm, other than an unloaded firearm at his or her home, unless:
  (a) The minor is engaged in a lawful hunting activity and is:
    1. At least 16 years of age; or
    2. Under 16 years of age and supervised by an adult.
  (b) The minor is engaged in a lawful marksmanship competition or practice or other lawful recreational shooting activity and is:
    1. At least 16 years of age; or
    2. Under 16 years of age and supervised by an adult who is acting with the consent of the minor's parent or guardian.
  (c) The firearm is unloaded and is being transported by the minor directly to or from an event authorized in paragraph (a) or paragraph (b).
(4)(a) Any parent or guardian of a minor, or other adult responsible for the welfare of a minor, who knowingly and willfully permits the minor to possess a firearm in violation of subsection (3) commits a felony of the third degree, punishable as provided in § 775.082, § 775.083, or § 775.084.
  (b) Any natural parent or adoptive parent, whether custodial or noncustodial, or any legal guardian or legal custodian of a minor, if that minor possesses a firearm in violation of subsection (3) may, if the court finds it appropriate, be required to participate in classes on parenting education which are approved by the Department of Juvenile Justice, upon the first conviction of the minor. Upon any subsequent conviction of the minor, the court may, if the court finds it appropriate, require the parent to attend further parent education classes or render community service hours together with the child.
  (c) The juvenile justice circuit advisory boards or the Department of Juvenile Justice shall establish appropriate community service programs to be available to the alternative sanctions coordinators of the circuit courts in implementing this subsection. The boards or department shall propose the implementation of a community service program in each circuit, and may submit a circuit plan, to be implemented upon approval of the circuit alternative sanctions coordinator.

(5)(a) A minor who violates subsection (3) commits a misdemeanor of the first degree; for a first offense, may serve a period of detention of up to 3 days in a secure detention facility; and, in addition to any other penalty provided by law, shall be required to perform 100 hours of community service; and:

    1. If the minor is eligible by reason of age for a driver license or driving privilege, the court shall direct the Department of Highway Safety and Motor Vehicles to revoke or to withhold issuance of the minor's driver license or driving privilege for up to 1 year.

    2. If the minor's driver license or driving privilege is under suspension or revocation for any reason, the court shall direct the Department of Highway Safety and Motor Vehicles to extend the period of suspension or revocation by an additional period of up to 1 year.

    3. If the minor is ineligible by reason of age for a driver license or driving privilege, the court shall direct the Department of Highway Safety and Motor Vehicles to withhold issuance of the minor's driver license or driving privilege for up to 1 year after the date on which the minor would otherwise have become eligible.

  (b) For a second or subsequent offense, a minor who violates subsection (3) commits a felony of the third degree and shall serve a period of detention of up to 15 days in a secure detention facility and shall be required to perform not less than 100 nor more than 250 hours of community service, and:

    1. If the minor is eligible by reason of age for a driver license or driving privilege, the court shall direct the Department of Highway Safety and Motor Vehicles to revoke or to withhold issuance of the minor's driver license or driving privilege for up to 2 years.

    2. If the minor's driver license or driving privilege is under suspension or revocation for any reason, the court shall direct the Department of Highway Safety and Motor Vehicles to extend the period of suspension or revocation by an additional period of up to 2 years.

    3. If the minor is ineligible by reason of age for a driver license or driving privilege, the court shall direct the Department of Highway Safety and Motor Vehicles to withhold issuance of the minor's driver license or driving privilege for up to 2 years after the date on which the minor would otherwise have become eligible.

For the purposes of this subsection, community service shall be performed, if possible, in a manner involving a hospital emergency room or other medical environment that deals on a regular basis with trauma patients and gunshot wounds.

(6) Any firearm that is possessed or used by a minor in violation of this section shall be promptly seized by a law enforcement officer and disposed of in accordance with § 790.08(1)-(6).

(7) The provisions of this section are supplemental to all other provisions of law relating to the possession, use, or exhibition of a firearm.

(8) Notwithstanding § 985.24 or § 985.25(1), if a minor is charged with an offense that involves the use or possession of a firearm, including a violation of subsection (3), or is charged for any offense during the commission of which the minor possessed a firearm, the minor shall be detained in secure detention, unless the state attorney authorizes the release of the minor, and shall be given a hearing within 24 hours after being taken into custody. At the hearing, the court may order that the minor continue to be held in secure detention in accordance with the applicable time periods specified in § 985.26(1)-(5), if the court finds that the minor meets the criteria specified in § 985.255, or if the court finds by clear and convincing evidence that the minor is a clear and present danger to himself or herself or the community. The Department of Juvenile Justice shall prepare a form for all minors charged under this subsection which states the period of detention and the relevant demographic information, including, but not limited to, the gender, age, and race of the minor; whether or not the minor was represented by private counsel or a public defender; the current offense; and the minor's complete prior record, including any pending cases. The form shall be provided to the judge for determining whether the minor should be continued in secure detention under this subsection. An order placing a minor in secure detention because the minor is a clear and present danger to himself or herself or the community must be in writing, must specify the need for detention and the benefits derived by the minor or the community by placing the minor in secure detention, and must include a copy of the form provided by the department.

(9) Notwithstanding § 985.245, if the minor is found to have committed an offense that involves the use or possession of a firearm, as defined in § 790.001, other than a violation of subsection (3), or an offense during the commission of which the minor possessed a firearm, and the minor is not committed to a residential commitment program of the Department of Juvenile Justice, in addition to any other punishment provided by law, the court shall order:

  (a) For a first offense, that the minor shall serve a minimum period of detention of 15 days in a secure detention facility; and

    1. Perform 100 hours of community service; and may

    2. Be placed on community control or in a nonresidential commitment program.

  (b) For a second or subsequent offense, that the minor shall serve a mandatory period of detention of at least 21 days in a secure detention facility; and

    1. Perform not less than 100 nor more than 250 hours of community service; and may

    2. Be placed on community control or in a nonresidential commitment program.

The minor shall not receive credit for time served before adjudication.

(10) If a minor is found to have committed an offense under subsection (9), the court shall impose the following penalties in addition to any penalty imposed under paragraph (9)(a) or paragraph (9)(b):

  (a) For a first offense:

1. If the minor is eligible by reason of age for a driver license or driving privilege, the court shall direct the Department of Highway Safety and Motor Vehicles to revoke or to withhold issuance of the minor's driver license or driving privilege for up to 1 year.

2. If the minor's driver license or driving privilege is under suspension or revocation for any reason, the court shall direct the Department of Highway Safety and Motor Vehicles to extend the period of suspension or revocation by an additional period for up to 1 year.

3. If the minor is ineligible by reason of age for a driver license or driving privilege, the court shall direct the Department of Highway Safety and Motor Vehicles to withhold issuance of the minor's driver license or driving privilege for up to 1 year after the date on which the minor would otherwise have become eligible.

(b) For a second or subsequent offense:

1. If the minor is eligible by reason of age for a driver license or driving privilege, the court shall direct the Department of Highway Safety and Motor Vehicles to revoke or to withhold issuance of the minor's driver license or driving privilege for up to 2 years.

2. If the minor's driver license or driving privilege is under suspension or revocation for any reason, the court shall direct the Department of Highway Safety and Motor Vehicles to extend the period of suspension or revocation by an additional period for up to 2 years.

3. If the minor is ineligible by reason of age for a driver license or driving privilege, the court shall direct the Department of Highway Safety and Motor Vehicles to withhold issuance of the minor's driver license or driving privilege for up to 2 years after the date on which the minor would otherwise have become eligible.

790.221 Possession of short-barreled rifle, short-barreled shotgun, or machine gun; penalty.—
(1) It is unlawful for any person to own or to have in his or her care, custody, possession, or control any short-barreled rifle, short-barreled shotgun, or machine gun which is, or may readily be made, operable; but this section shall not apply to antique firearms.
(2) A person who violates this section commits a felony of the second degree, punishable as provided in § 775.082, § 775.083, or § 775.084.
(3) Firearms in violation hereof which are lawfully owned and possessed under provisions of federal law are excepted.

790.23 Felons and delinquents; possession of firearms, ammunition, or electric weapons or devices unlawful.—
(1) It is unlawful for any person to own or to have in his or her care, custody, possession, or control any firearm, ammunition, or electric weapon or device, or to carry a concealed weapon, including a tear gas gun or chemical weapon or device, if that person has been:
  (a) Convicted of a felony in the courts of this state;
  (b) Found, in the courts of this state, to have committed a delinquent act that would be a felony if committed by an adult and such person is under 24 years of age;
  (c) Convicted of or found to have committed a crime against the United States which is designated as a felony;
  (d) Found to have committed a delinquent act in another state, territory, or country that would be a felony if committed by an adult and which was punishable by imprisonment for a term exceeding 1 year and such person is under 24 years of age; or
  (e) Found guilty of an offense that is a felony in another state, territory, or country and which was punishable by imprisonment for a term exceeding 1 year.
(2) This section shall not apply to a person:
  (a) Convicted of a felony whose civil rights and firearm authority have been restored.
  (b) Whose criminal history record has been expunged pursuant to § 943.0515(1)(b).
(3) Except as otherwise provided in subsection (4), any person who violates this section commits a felony of the second degree, punishable as provided in § 775.082, § 775.083, or § 775.084.
(4) Notwithstanding the provisions of § 874.04, if the offense described in subsection (1) has been committed by a person who has previously qualified or currently qualifies for the penalty enhancements provided for in § 874.04, the offense is a felony of the first degree, punishable by a term of years not exceeding life or as provided in § 775.082, § 775.083, or § 775.084.

790.233 Possession of firearm or ammunition prohibited when person is subject to an injunction against committing acts of domestic violence, stalking, or cyberstalking; penalties.—
(1) A person may not have in his or her care, custody, possession, or control any firearm or ammunition if the person has been issued a final injunction that is currently in force and effect, restraining that person from committing acts of domestic violence, as issued under § 741.30 or from committing acts of stalking or cyberstalking, as issued under § 784.0485.
(2) A person who violates subsection (1) commits a misdemeanor of the first degree, punishable as provided in § 775.082 or § 775.083.
(3) It is the intent of the Legislature that the disabilities regarding possession of firearms and ammunition are consistent with federal law. Accordingly, this section does not apply to a state or local officer as defined in § 943.10(14), holding an active certification, who receives or possesses a firearm or ammunition for use in performing official duties on behalf of the officer's employing agency, unless otherwise prohibited by the employing agency.

790.235   Possession of firearm or ammunition by violent career criminal unlawful; penalty.—

(1)   Any person who meets the violent career criminal criteria under § 775.084(1)(d), regardless of whether such person is or has previously been sentenced as a violent career criminal, who owns or has in his or her care, custody, possession, or control any firearm, ammunition, or electric weapon or device, or carries a concealed weapon, including a tear gas gun or chemical weapon or device, commits a felony of the first degree, punishable as provided in § 775.082, § 775.083, or § 775.084. A person convicted of a violation of this section shall be sentenced to a mandatory minimum of 15 years' imprisonment; however, if the person would be sentenced to a longer term of imprisonment under § 775.084(4)(d), the person must be sentenced under that provision. A person convicted of a violation of this section is not eligible for any form of discretionary early release, other than pardon, executive clemency, or conditional medical release under § 947.149.

(2)   For purposes of this section, the previous felony convictions necessary to meet the violent career criminal criteria under § 775.084(1)(d) may be convictions for felonies committed as an adult or adjudications of delinquency for felonies committed as a juvenile. In order to be counted as a prior felony for purposes of this section, the felony must have resulted in a conviction sentenced separately, or an adjudication of delinquency entered separately, prior to the current offense, and sentenced or adjudicated separately from any other felony that is to be counted as a prior felony.

(3)   This section shall not apply to a person whose civil rights and firearm authority have been restored.

§ 790.25. Lawful ownership, possession, and use of firearms and other weapons.
(2) Uses not authorized.

(a) This section does not authorize carrying a concealed weapon without a permit, as prohibited by §§ 790.01 and 790.02.

(b) The protections of this section do not apply to the following:

1. A person who has been adjudged mentally incompetent, who is addicted to the use of narcotics or any similar drug, or who is a habitual or chronic alcoholic, or a person using weapons or firearms in violation of §§ 790.07-790.115, 790.145-790.19, 790.22-790.24;

2. Vagrants and other undesirable persons as defined in § 856.02;

3. A person in or about a place of nuisance as defined in § 823.05, unless such person is there for law enforcement or some other lawful purpose.

(3) Lawful uses. – The provisions of §§ 790.053 and 790.06 do not apply in the following instances, and, despite such sections, it is lawful for the following persons to own, possess, and lawfully use firearms and other weapons, ammunition, and supplies for lawful purposes:

(a) Members of the Militia, National Guard, Florida State Defense Force, Army, Navy, Air Force, Marine Corps, Coast Guard, organized reserves, and other armed forces of the state and of the United States, when on duty, when training or preparing themselves for military duty, or while subject to recall or mobilization;

(b) Citizens of this state subject to duty in the Armed Forces under § 2, Art. X of the State Constitution, under chapters 250 and 251, and under federal laws, when on duty or when training or preparing themselves for military duty;

(c) Persons carrying out or training for emergency management duties under chapter 252;

(d) Sheriffs, marshals, prison or jail wardens, police officers, Florida highway patrol officers, game wardens, revenue officers, forest officials, special officers appointed under the provisions of chapter 354, and other peace and law enforcement officers and their deputies and assistants and full-time paid peace officers of other states and of the Federal Government who are carrying out official duties while in this state;

(e) Officers or employees of the state or United States duly authorized to carry a concealed weapon;

(f) Guards or messengers of common carriers, express companies, armored car carriers, mail carriers, banks, and other financial institutions, while actually employed in and about the shipment, transportation, or delivery of any money, treasure, bullion, bonds, or other thing of value within this state;

(g) Regularly enrolled members of any organization duly authorized to purchase or receive weapons from the United States or from this state, or regularly enrolled members of clubs organized for target, skeet, or trap shooting, while at or going to or from shooting practice; or regularly enrolled members of clubs organized for modern or antique firearms collecting, while such members are at or going to or from their collectors' gun shows, conventions, or exhibits;

(h) A person engaged in fishing, camping, or lawful hunting or going to or returning from a fishing, camping, or lawful hunting expedition;

(i) A person engaged in the business of manufacturing, repairing, or dealing in firearms, or the agent or representative of any such person while engaged in the lawful course of such business;

(j) A person firing weapons for testing or target practice under safe conditions and in a safe place not prohibited by law or going to or from such place;

(k) A person firing weapons in a safe and secure indoor range for testing and target practice;

(l) A person traveling by private conveyance when the weapon is securely encased or in a public conveyance when the weapon is securely encased and not in the person's manual possession;

(m) A person while carrying a pistol unloaded and in a secure wrapper, concealed or otherwise, from the place of purchase to his or her home or place of business or to a place of repair or back to his or her home or place of business;

(n) A person possessing arms at his or her home or place of business;

(o) Investigators employed by the several public defenders of the state, while actually carrying out official duties, provided such investigators:

1. Are employed full time;

2. Meet the official training standards for firearms established by the Criminal Justice Standards and Training Commission as provided in § 943.12(5) and the requirements of §§ 493.6108(1)(a) and 943.13(1)-(4); and

3. Are individually designated by an affidavit of consent signed by the employing public defender and filed with the clerk of the circuit court in the county in which the employing public defender resides.

(p) Investigators employed by the capital collateral regional counsel, while actually carrying out official duties, provided such investigators:

1. Are employed full time;

2. Meet the official training standards for firearms as established by the Criminal Justice Standards and Training Commission as provided in § 943.12(1) and the requirements of §§ 493.6108(1)(a) and 943.13(1)-(4); and

3. Are individually designated by an affidavit of consent signed by the capital collateral regional counsel and filed with the clerk of the circuit court in the county in which the investigator is headquartered.

(4) Construction. – This act shall be liberally construed to carry out the declaration of policy herein and in favor of the constitutional right to keep and bear arms for lawful purposes. This act is supplemental and additional to existing rights to bear arms now guaranteed by law and decisions of the courts of Florida, and nothing herein shall impair or diminish any of such rights. This act shall supersede any law, ordinance, or regulation in conflict herewith.

(5) Possession in private conveyance. – Notwithstanding subsection (2), it is lawful and is not a violation of § 790.01 for a person 18 years of age or older to possess a concealed firearm or other weapon for self-defense or other lawful purpose within the interior of a private conveyance, without a license, if the firearm or other weapon is securely encased or is otherwise not readily accessible for immediate use. Nothing herein contained prohibits the carrying of a legal firearm other than a handgun anywhere in a private conveyance when such firearm is being carried for a lawful use. Nothing herein contained shall be construed to authorize the carrying of a concealed firearm or other weapon on the person. This subsection shall be liberally construed in favor of the lawful use, ownership, and possession of firearms and other weapons, including lawful self-defense as provided in § 776.012.

790.251   Protection of the right to keep and bear arms in motor vehicles for self-defense and other lawful purposes; prohibited acts; duty of public and private employers; immunity from liability; enforcement.—

(1)   SHORT TITLE.—This section may be cited as the "Preservation and Protection of the Right to Keep and Bear Arms in Motor Vehicles Act of 2008."

(2)   DEFINITIONS.—As used in this section, the term:

(a)   "Parking lot" means any property that is used for parking motor vehicles and is available to customers, employees, or invitees for temporary or long-term parking or storage of motor vehicles.

(b)   "Motor vehicle" means any automobile, truck, minivan, sports utility vehicle, motor home, recreational vehicle, motorcycle, motor scooter, or any other vehicle operated on the roads of this state and required to be registered under state law.

(c)   "Employee" means any person who possesses a valid license issued pursuant to § 790.06 and:

1.   Works for salary, wages, or other remuneration;

2.   Is an independent contractor; or

3.   Is a volunteer, intern, or other similar individual for an employer.

(d)   "Employer" means any business that is a sole proprietorship, partnership, corporation, limited liability company, professional association, cooperative, joint venture, trust, firm, institution, or association, or public sector entity, that has employees.

(e)   "Invitee" means any business invitee, including a customer or visitor, who is lawfully on the premises of a public or private employer.

As used in this section, the term "firearm" includes ammunition and accoutrements attendant to the lawful possession and use of a firearm.

(4)   PROHIBITED ACTS.—No public or private employer may violate the constitutional rights of any customer, employee, or invitee as provided in paragraphs (a)-(e):

(a)   No public or private employer may prohibit any customer, employee, or invitee from possessing any legally owned firearm when such firearm is lawfully possessed and locked inside or locked to a private motor vehicle in a parking lot and when the customer, employee, or invitee is lawfully in such area.

(b)   No public or private employer may violate the privacy rights of a customer, employee, or invitee by verbal or written inquiry regarding the presence of a firearm inside or locked to a private motor vehicle in a parking lot or by an actual search of a private motor vehicle in a parking lot to ascertain the presence of a firearm within the vehicle. Further, no public or private employer may take any action against a customer, employee, or invitee based upon verbal or written statements of any party concerning possession of a firearm stored inside a private motor vehicle in a parking lot for lawful purposes. A search of a private motor vehicle in the parking lot of a public or private employer to ascertain the presence of a firearm within the vehicle may only be conducted by on-duty law enforcement personnel, based upon due process and must comply with constitutional protections.

(c)   No public or private employer shall condition employment upon either:

1. The fact that an employee or prospective employee holds or does not hold a license issued pursuant to § 790.06; or

2. Any agreement by an employee or a prospective employee that prohibits an employee from keeping a legal firearm locked inside or locked to a private motor vehicle in a parking lot when such firearm is kept for lawful purposes.

(d) No public or private employer shall prohibit or attempt to prevent any customer, employee, or invitee from entering the parking lot of the employer's place of business because the customer's, employee's, or invitee's private motor vehicle contains a legal firearm being carried for lawful purposes, that is out of sight within the customer's, employee's, or invitee's private motor vehicle.

(e) No public or private employer may terminate the employment of or otherwise discriminate against an employee, or expel a customer or invitee for exercising his or her constitutional right to keep and bear arms or for exercising the right of self-defense as long as a firearm is never exhibited on company property for any reason other than lawful defensive purposes.

This subsection applies to all public sector employers, including those already prohibited from regulating firearms under the provisions of § 790.33.

(5) DUTY OF CARE OF PUBLIC AND PRIVATE EMPLOYERS; IMMUNITY FROM LIABILITY.—

(a) When subject to the provisions of subsection (4), a public or private employer has no duty of care related to the actions prohibited under such subsection.

(b) A public or private employer is not liable in a civil action based on actions or inactions taken in compliance with this section. The immunity provided in this subsection does not apply to civil actions based on actions or inactions of public or private employers that are unrelated to compliance with this section.

(c) Nothing contained in this section shall be interpreted to expand any existing duty, or create any additional duty, on the part of a public or private employer, property owner, or property owner's agent.

(6) ENFORCEMENT.—The Attorney General shall enforce the protections of this act on behalf of any customer, employee, or invitee aggrieved under this act. If there is reasonable cause to believe that the aggrieved person's rights under this act have been violated by a public or private employer, the Attorney General shall commence a civil or administrative action for damages, injunctive relief and civil penalties, and such other relief as may be appropriate under the provisions of § 760.51, or may negotiate a settlement with any employer on behalf of any person aggrieved under the act. However, nothing in this act shall prohibit the right of a person aggrieved under this act to bring a civil action for violation of rights protected under the act. In any successful action brought by a customer, employee, or invitee aggrieved under this act, the court shall award all reasonable personal costs and losses suffered by the aggrieved person as a result of the violation of rights under this act. In any action brought pursuant to this act, the court shall award all court costs and attorney's fees to the prevailing party.

(7) EXCEPTIONS.—The prohibitions in subsection (4) do not apply to:

(a) Any school property as defined and regulated under § 790.115.

(b) Any correctional institution regulated under § 944.47 or chapter 957.

(c) Any property where a nuclear-powered electricity generation facility is located.

(d) Property owned or leased by a public or private employer or the landlord of a public or private employer upon which are conducted substantial activities involving national defense, aerospace, or homeland security.

(e) Property owned or leased by a public or private employer or the landlord of a public or private employer upon which the primary business conducted is the manufacture, use, storage, or transportation of combustible or explosive materials regulated under state or federal law, or property owned or leased by an employer who has obtained a permit required under 18 U.S.C. § 842 to engage in the business of importing, manufacturing, or dealing in explosive materials on such property.

(f) A motor vehicle owned, leased, or rented by a public or private employer or the landlord of a public or private employer.

(g) Any other property owned or leased by a public or private employer or the landlord of a public or private employer upon which possession of a firearm or other legal product by a customer, employee, or invitee is prohibited pursuant to any federal law, contract with a federal government entity, or general law of this state.

790.27 Alteration or removal of firearm serial number or possession, sale, or delivery of firearm with serial number altered or removed prohibited; penalties.—

(1)(a) It is unlawful for any person to knowingly alter or remove the manufacturer's or importer's serial number from a firearm with intent to disguise the true identity thereof.

(b) Any person violating paragraph (a) is guilty of a felony of the third degree, punishable as provided in § 775.082, § 775.083, or § 775.084.

(2)(a) It is unlawful for any person to knowingly sell, deliver, or possess any firearm on which the manufacturer's or importer's serial number has been unlawfully altered or removed.

(b) Any person violating paragraph (a) is guilty of a misdemeanor of the first degree, punishable as provided in § 775.082 or § 775.083.

(3) This section shall not apply to antique firearms.

790.29 Paramilitary training; teaching or participation prohibited.—

(1) This act shall be known and may be cited as the "State Anti-paramilitary Training Act."

(2) As used in this section, the term "civil disorder" means a public disturbance involving acts of violence by an assemblage of three or more persons, which disturbance causes an immediate danger of, or results in, damage or injury to the property or person of any other individual within the United States.

(3)(a) Whoever teaches or demonstrates to any other person the use, application, or making of any firearm, destructive device, or technique capable of causing injury or death to persons, knowing or having reason to know or intending that the same will be unlawfully employed for use in, or in furtherance of, a civil disorder within the United States, is guilty of a felony of the third degree, punishable as provided in § 775.082, § 775.083, or § 775.084.

(b) Whoever assembles with one or more persons for the purpose of training with, practicing with, or being instructed in the use of any firearm, destructive device, or technique capable of causing injury or death to persons, intending to unlawfully employ the same for use in, or in furtherance of, a civil disorder within the United States, is guilty of a felony of the third degree, punishable as provided in § 775.082, § 775.083, or § 775.084.

(4) Nothing contained in this section shall be construed to prohibit any act of a law enforcement officer which is performed in connection with the lawful performance of his or her official duties or to prohibit the training or teaching of the use of weapons to be used for hunting, recreation, competition, self-defense or the protection of one's person or property, or other lawful use.

790.31 Armor-piercing or exploding ammunition or dragon's breath shotgun shells, bolo shells, or flechette shells prohibited.—
(1) As used in this section, the term:
(a) "Armor-piercing bullet" means any bullet which has a steel inner core or core of equivalent hardness and a truncated cone and which is designed for use in a handgun as an armor-piercing or metal-piercing bullet.
(b) "Exploding bullet" means any bullet that can be fired from any firearm, if such bullet is designed or altered so as to detonate or forcibly break up through the use of an explosive or deflagrant contained wholly or partially within or attached to such bullet. The term does not include any bullet designed to expand or break up through the mechanical forces of impact alone or any signaling device or pest control device not designed to impact on any target.
(c) "Handgun" means a firearm capable of being carried and used by one hand, such as a pistol or revolver.
(d) "Dragon's breath shotgun shell" means any shotgun shell that contains exothermic pyrophoric misch metal as the projectile and that is designed for the sole purpose of throwing or spewing a flame or fireball to simulate a flamethrower.
(e) "Bolo shell" means any shell that can be fired in a firearm and that expels as projectiles two or more metal balls connected by solid metal wire.
(f) "Flechette shell" means any shell that can be fired in a firearm and that expels two or more pieces of fin-stabilized solid metal wire or two or more solid dart-type projectiles.
(2)(a) Any person who manufactures, sells, offers for sale, or delivers any armor-piercing bullet or exploding bullet, or dragon's breath shotgun shell, bolo shell, or flechette shell is guilty of a felony of the third degree, punishable as provided in § 775.082, § 775.083, or § 775.084.
(b) Any person who possesses an armor-piercing bullet or exploding bullet with knowledge of its armor-piercing or exploding capabilities loaded in a handgun, or who possesses a dragon's breath shotgun shell, bolo shell, or flechette shell with knowledge of its capabilities loaded in a firearm, is guilty of a felony of the third degree, punishable as provided in § 775.082, § 775.083, or § 775.084.
(c) Any person who possesses with intent to use an armor-piercing bullet or exploding bullet or dragon's breath shotgun shell, bolo shell, or flechette shell to assist in the commission of a criminal act is guilty of a felony of the second degree, punishable as provided in § 775.082, § 775.083, or § 775.084.
(3) This section does not apply to:
(a) The possession of any item described in subsection (1) by any law enforcement officer, when possessed in connection with the performance of his or her duty as a law enforcement officer, or law enforcement agency.
(b) The manufacture of items described in subsection (1) exclusively for sale or delivery to law enforcement agencies.
(c) The sale or delivery of items described in subsection (1) to law enforcement agencies.

790.33 Field of regulation of firearms and ammunition preempted.—
(1) PREEMPTION.—Except as expressly provided by the State Constitution or general law, the Legislature hereby declares that it is occupying the whole field of regulation of firearms and ammunition, including the purchase, sale, transfer, taxation, manufacture, ownership, possession, storage, and transportation thereof, to the exclusion of all existing and future county, city, town, or municipal ordinances or any administrative regulations or rules adopted by local or state government relating thereto. Any such existing ordinances, rules, or regulations are hereby declared null and void.
(2) POLICY AND INTENT.—
(a) It is the intent of this section to provide uniform firearms laws in the state; to declare all ordinances and regulations null and void which have been enacted by any jurisdictions other than state and federal, which regulate firearms, ammunition, or components thereof; to prohibit the enactment of any future ordinances or regulations relating to firearms, ammunition, or components thereof unless specifically authorized by this section or general law; and to require local jurisdictions to enforce state firearms laws.
(b) It is further the intent of this section to deter and prevent the violation of this section and the violation of rights protected under the constitution and laws of this state related to firearms, ammunition, or components thereof, by the abuse of official authority that occurs when enactments are passed in violation of state law or under color of local or state authority.
(3) PROHIBITIONS; PENALTIES.—

(a) Any person, county, agency, municipality, district, or other entity that violates the Legislature's occupation of the whole field of regulation of firearms and ammunition, as declared in subsection (1), by enacting or causing to be enforced any local ordinance or administrative rule or regulation impinging upon such exclusive occupation of the field shall be liable as set forth herein.

(b) If any county, city, town, or other local government violates this section, the court shall declare the improper ordinance, regulation, or rule invalid and issue a permanent injunction against the local government prohibiting it from enforcing such ordinance, regulation, or rule. It is no defense that in enacting the ordinance, regulation, or rule the local government was acting in good faith or upon advice of counsel.

(c) If the court determines that a violation was knowing and willful, the court shall assess a civil fine of up to $5,000 against the elected or appointed local government official or officials or administrative agency head under whose jurisdiction the violation occurred.

(d) Except as required by applicable law, public funds may not be used to defend or reimburse the unlawful conduct of any person found to have knowingly and willfully violated this section.

(e) A knowing and willful violation of any provision of this section by a person acting in an official capacity for any entity enacting or causing to be enforced a local ordinance or administrative rule or regulation prohibited under paragraph (a) or otherwise under color of law shall be cause for termination of employment or contract or removal from office by the Governor.

(f) A person or an organization whose membership is adversely affected by any ordinance, regulation, measure, directive, rule, enactment, order, or policy promulgated or caused to be enforced in violation of this section may file suit against any county, agency, municipality, district, or other entity in any court of this state having jurisdiction over any defendant to the suit for declaratory and injunctive relief and for actual damages, as limited herein, caused by the violation. A court shall award the prevailing plaintiff in any such suit:

1. Reasonable attorney's fees and costs in accordance with the laws of this state, including a contingency fee multiplier, as authorized by law; and

2. The actual damages incurred, but not more than $100,000.

Interest on the sums awarded pursuant to this subsection shall accrue at the legal rate from the date on which suit was filed.

(4) EXCEPTIONS.—This section does not prohibit:

(a) Zoning ordinances that encompass firearms businesses along with other businesses, except that zoning ordinances that are designed for the purpose of restricting or prohibiting the sale, purchase, transfer, or manufacture of firearms or ammunition as a method of regulating firearms or ammunition are in conflict with this subsection and are prohibited;

(b) A duly organized law enforcement agency from enacting and enforcing regulations pertaining to firearms, ammunition, or firearm accessories issued to or used by peace officers in the course of their official duties;

(c) Except as provided in § 790.251, any entity subject to the prohibitions of this section from regulating or prohibiting the carrying of firearms and ammunition by an employee of the entity during and in the course of the employee's official duties;

(d) A court or administrative law judge from hearing and resolving any case or controversy or issuing any opinion or order on a matter within the jurisdiction of that court or judge; or

(e) The Florida Fish and Wildlife Conservation Commission from regulating the use of firearms or ammunition as a method of taking wildlife and regulating the shooting ranges managed by the commission.

(5) SHORT TITLE.—As created by chapter 87-23, Laws of Florida, this section may be cited as the "Joe Carlucci Uniform Firearms Act."

790.331 Prohibition of civil actions against firearms or ammunition manufacturers, firearms trade associations, firearms or ammunition distributors, or firearms or ammunition dealers.—

(1) The Legislature finds and declares that the manufacture, distribution, or sale of firearms and ammunition by manufacturers, distributors, or dealers duly licensed by the appropriate federal and state authorities is a lawful activity and is not unreasonably dangerous, and further finds that the unlawful use of firearms and ammunition, rather than their lawful manufacture, distribution, or sale, is the proximate cause of injuries arising from their unlawful use.

(2) Except as permitted by this section, a legal action against a firearms or ammunition manufacturer, firearms trade association, firearms or ammunition distributor, or firearms or ammunition dealer on behalf of the state or its agencies and instrumentalities, or on behalf of a county, municipality, special district, or any other political subdivision or agency of the state, for damages, abatement, or injunctive relief resulting from or arising out of the lawful design, marketing, distribution, or sale of firearms or ammunition to the public is prohibited. However, this subsection does not preclude a natural person from bringing an action against a firearms or ammunition manufacturer, firearms trade association, firearms or ammunition distributor, or firearms or ammunition dealer for breach of a written contract, breach of an express warranty, or injuries resulting from a defect in the materials or workmanship in the manufacture of a firearm or ammunition.

(3) A county, municipality, special district, or other political subdivision or agency of the state may not sue for or recover from a firearms or ammunition manufacturer, firearms trade association, firearms or ammunition distributor, or firearms or ammunition dealer damages, abatement, or injunctive relief in any case that arises out of or results from the lawful design, marketing, distribution, or sale of firearms or ammunition to the public.

(4) This section does not prohibit an action against a firearms or ammunition manufacturer, distributor, or dealer for:

(a) Breach of contract or warranty in connection with a firearm or ammunition purchased by a county, municipality, special district, or other political subdivision or agency of the state.

(b) Injuries resulting from the malfunction of a firearm or ammunition due to a defect in design or manufacture.

(5)(a) For the purposes of this section, the potential of a firearm or ammunition to cause serious injury, damage, or death as a result of normal function does not constitute a defective condition of the product.

(b) A firearm or ammunition may not be deemed defective on the basis of its potential to cause serious injury, damage, or death when discharged legally or illegally.

(6)(a) If a civil action is brought in violation of this section, the defendant may recover all expenses resulting from such action from the governmental entity bringing such action.

(b) In any civil action where the court finds that the defendant is immune as provided in this section, the court shall award the defendant all attorney's fees, costs and compensation for loss of income, and expenses incurred as a result of such action.

(7) This section applies to any action brought on or after the effective date of this section.

790.333 Sport shooting and training range protection; liability; claims, expenses, and fees; penalties; preemption; construction.—

(3) DEFINITIONS. As used in this act:

(a) "Department" means the Department of Environmental Protection.

(b) "Operator" means any person who operates or has operated a sport shooting or training range.

(c) "Owner" means any person who owns or has owned a sport shooting or training range or any interest therein.

(d) "Projectile" means any object expelled, propelled, discharged, shot, or otherwise released from a firearm, BB gun, airgun, or similar device, including, but not limited to, gunpowder, ammunition, lead, shot, skeet, and trap targets and associated chemicals, derivatives, and constituents thereof.

(e) "Environmental management practices" includes but is not limited to Best Management Practices for Environmental Stewardship of Florida Shooting Ranges as developed by the Department of Environmental Protection. Such practices include, but are not limited to, control and containment of projectiles, prevention of the migration of projectiles and their constituents to ground and surface water, periodic removal and recycling of projectiles, and documentation of actions taken.

(f) "Environment" means the air, water, surface water, sediment, soil, and groundwater and other natural and manmade resources of this state.

(g) "User" means any person, partner, joint venture, business or social entity, or corporation, or any group of the foregoing, organized or united for a business, sport, or social purpose.

(h) "Sport shooting and training range" or "range" means any area that has been designed, or operated for the use of, firearms, rifles, shotguns, pistols, silhouettes, skeet, trap, black powder, BB guns, airguns, or similar devices, or any other type of sport or training shooting.

(4) DUTIES.—

(a) No later than January 1, 2005, the department shall make a good faith effort to provide copies of the Best Management Practices for Environmental Stewardship of Florida Shooting Ranges to all owners or operators of sport shooting or training ranges. The department shall also provide technical assistance with implementing environmental management practices, which may include workshops, demonstrations, or other guidance, if any owner or operator of sport shooting or training ranges requests such assistance.

(b) No later than January 1, 2006, sport shooting or training range owners, operators, tenants, or occupants shall implement situation appropriate environmental management practices.

(c) If contamination is suspected or identified by any owner, operator, tenant, or occupant of sport shooting or training ranges, any owner, operator, tenant, or occupant of sport shooting or training ranges may request that the department assist with or perform contamination assessment, including, but not limited to, assistance preparing and presenting a plan to confirm the presence and extent of contamination.

(d) If contamination is suspected or identified by a third-party complaint or adjacent property sampling events, the department shall give 60 days' notice to the sport shooting or training range owner, operator, tenant, or occupant of the department's intent to enter the site for the purpose of investigating potential sources of contamination. The department may assist with or perform contamination assessment, including, but not limited to, assistance preparing and presenting a plan to confirm the presence and extent of contamination.

(e) If the department confirms contamination under paragraph (c) or paragraph (d), principles of risk-based corrective action pursuant to § 376.30701 shall be applied to sport shooting or training ranges. Application of the minimum risk-based corrective action principles shall be the primary responsibility of the sport shooting range or training range owner or operator for implementation, however, the department may assist in these efforts. Risk-based corrective action plans used for these cleanups shall be based upon the presumption that the sport shooting or training range is an industrial use and not a residential use and will continue to be operated as a sport shooting or training range.

(5) SPORT SHOOTING AND TRAINING RANGE PROTECTION.—

(a) Notwithstanding any other provision of law, any public or private owner, operator, employee, agent, contractor, customer, lender, insurer, or user of any sport shooting or training range located in this state shall have immunity from lawsuits and other legal actions from the state and any of its agencies, special purpose districts, or political subdivisions for any claims of any kind associated with the use, release, placement, deposition, or accumulation of any projectile in the environment, on or under that sport shooting or training range, or any other property over which the range has an easement, leasehold, or other legal right of use, if the sport shooting or training range owner or operator has made a good faith effort to comply with subsection (4).

(b) Nothing in this act is intended to impair or diminish the private property rights of owners of property adjoining a sport shooting or training range.

(c) The sport shooting and training range protections provided by this act are supplemental to any other protections provided by general law.

(6) WITHDRAWALS OF CLAIMS AND RECOVERY OF EXPENSES AND ATTORNEY'S FEES.—

(a) Within 90 days after the effective date of this act becoming law, all claims by the state and any of its agencies, special purpose districts, or political subdivisions against sport shooting or training ranges pending in any court of this state or before any administrative agency on January 1, 2004, shall be withdrawn. The termination of such cases shall have no effect on the defendant's cause of action for damages, reasonable attorney's fees, and costs.

(b) In any action filed in violation of this act after the effective date of this act, the defendant shall recover all expenses resulting from such action from the governmental body, person, or entity bringing such unlawful action.

(7) PENALTIES.—Any official, agent, or employee of a county, municipality, town, special purpose district, or other political subdivision or agent of the state, while he or she was acting in his or her official capacity and within the scope of his or her employment or office, who intentionally and maliciously violates the provisions of this section or is party to bringing an action in violation of this section commits a misdemeanor of the first degree, punishable as provided in §§ 775.082 and 775.083.

(8) PREEMPTION.—Except as expressly provided by general law, the Legislature hereby declares that it is occupying the whole field of regulation of firearms and ammunition use at sport shooting and training ranges, including the environmental effects of projectile deposition at sport shooting and training ranges.

(9) The provisions of this act shall supersede any conflicting provisions of chapter 376 or chapter 403.

(10) CONSTRUCTION.—This act shall be liberally construed to effectuate its remedial and deterrent purposes.

790.335 Prohibition of registration of firearms; electronic records.—

(2) PROHIBITIONS.—No state governmental agency or local government, special district, or other political subdivision or official, agent, or employee of such state or other governmental entity or any other person, public or private, shall knowingly and willfully keep or cause to be kept any list, record, or registry of privately owned firearms or any list, record, or registry of the owners of those firearms.

(3) EXCEPTIONS.—The provisions of this section shall not apply to:

(a) Records of firearms that have been used in committing any crime.

(b) Records relating to any person who has been convicted of a crime.

(c) Records of firearms that have been reported stolen that are retained for a period not in excess of 10 days after such firearms are recovered. Official documentation recording the theft of a recovered weapon may be maintained no longer than the balance of the year entered, plus 2 years.

(d) Firearm records that must be retained by firearm dealers under federal law, including copies of such records transmitted to law enforcement agencies. However, no state governmental agency or local government, special district, or other political subdivision or official, agent, or employee of such state or other governmental entity or any other person, private or public, shall accumulate, compile, computerize, or otherwise collect or convert such written records into any form of list, registry, or database for any purpose.

(e)1. Records kept pursuant to the recordkeeping provisions of § 790.065; however, nothing in this section shall be construed to authorize the public release or inspection of records that are made confidential and exempt from the provisions of § 119.07(1) by § 790.065(4)(a).

2. Nothing in this paragraph shall be construed to allow the maintaining of records containing the names of purchasers or transferees who receive unique approval numbers or the maintaining of records of firearm transactions.

(f) Firearm records, including paper pawn transaction forms and contracts on firearm transactions, required by chapters 538 and 539.

1. Electronic firearm records held pursuant to chapter 538 may only be kept by a secondhand dealer for 30 days after the date of the purchase of the firearm by the secondhand dealer.

2. Electronic firearm records held pursuant to chapter 539 may only be kept by a pawnbroker for 30 days after the expiration of the loan that is secured by a firearm or 30 days after the date of purchase of a firearm, whichever is applicable.

3. Except as required by federal law, any firearm records kept pursuant to chapter 538 or chapter 539 shall not, at any time, be electronically transferred to any public or private entity, agency, business, or enterprise, nor shall any such records be copied or transferred for purposes of accumulation of such records into lists, registries, or databases.

4. Notwithstanding subparagraph 3., secondhand dealers and pawnbrokers may electronically submit firearm transaction records to the appropriate law enforcement agencies as required by chapters 538 and 539; however, the law enforcement agencies may not electronically submit such records to any other person or entity and must destroy such records within 60 days after receipt of such records.

5. Notwithstanding subparagraph 3., secondhand dealers and pawnbrokers may electronically submit limited firearms records consisting solely of the manufacturer, model, serial number, and caliber of pawned or purchased firearms to a third-party private provider that is exclusively incorporated, exclusively owned, and exclusively operated in the United

States and that restricts access to such information to only appropriate law enforcement agencies for legitimate law enforcement purposes. Such records must be destroyed within 30 days by the third-party provider. As a condition of receipt of such records, the third-party provider must agree in writing to comply with the requirements of this section. Any pawnbroker or secondhand dealer who contracts with a third-party provider other than as provided in this act or electronically transmits any records of firearms transactions to any third-party provider other than the records specifically allowed by this paragraph commits a felony of the second degree, punishable as provided in § 775.082 or § 775.083.

(g)   Records kept by the Department of Law Enforcement of NCIC transactions to the extent required by federal law and a log of dates of requests for criminal history record checks, unique approval and nonapproval numbers, license identification numbers, and transaction numbers corresponding to such dates.

(h)   Records of an insurer that, as a condition to providing insurance against theft or loss of a firearm, identify such firearm. Such records may not be sold, commingled with records relating to other firearms, or transferred to any other person or entity. The insurer may not keep a record of such firearm more than 60 days after the policy of insurance expires or after notification by the insured that the insured is no longer the owner of such firearm.

(i)   Lists of customers of a firearm dealer retained by such dealer, provided that such lists do not disclose the particular firearms purchased. Such lists, or any parts thereof, may not be sold, commingled with records relating to other firearms, or transferred to any other person or entity.

(j)   Sales receipts retained by the seller of firearms or by a person providing credit for such purchase, provided that such receipts shall not serve as or be used for the creation of a database for registration of firearms.

(k)   Personal records of firearms maintained by the owner of such firearms.

(l)   Records maintained by a business that stores or acts as the selling agent of firearms on behalf of the lawful owner of the firearms.

(m)   Membership lists of organizations comprised of firearm owners.

(n)   Records maintained by an employer or contracting entity of the firearms owned by its officers, employees, or agents, if such firearms are used in the course of business performed on behalf of the employer.

(o)   Records maintained pursuant to § 790.06 by the Department of Agriculture and Consumer Services of a person who was a licensee within the prior 2 years.

(p)   Records of firearms involved in criminal investigations, criminal prosecutions, criminal appeals, and post-conviction motions, civil proceedings relating to the surrender or seizure of firearms including protective injunctions, Baker Act commitments, and sheriff's levies pursuant to court judgments, and voluntary surrender by the owner or custodian of the firearm.

(q)   Paper documents relating to firearms involved in criminal cases, criminal investigations, and criminal prosecutions, civil proceedings relating to the surrender or seizure of firearms including protective injunctions, Baker Act commitments, and sheriff's levies pursuant to court judgments, and voluntary surrender by the owner or custodian of the firearm.

(r)   Noncriminal records relating to the receipt, storage or return of firearms, including, but not limited to, records relating to firearms impounded for storage or safekeeping, receipts proving that a firearm was returned to the rightful owner and supporting records of identification and proof of ownership, or records relating to firearms impounded pursuant to levies or court orders, provided, however, that such records shall not be compiled, sorted, or otherwise arranged into any lists, indexes, or registries of firearms or firearms owners.

(4)   PENALTIES.—

(a)   Any person who, or entity that, violates a provision of this section commits a felony of the third degree, punishable as provided in § 775.082 or § 775.083.

(b)   Except as required by the provisions of § 16, Art. I of the State Constitution or the Sixth Amendment to the United States Constitution, no public funds shall be used to defend the unlawful conduct of any person charged with a violation of this section, unless the charges against such person are dismissed or such person is determined to be not guilty at trial. Notwithstanding this paragraph, public funds may be expended to provide the services of the office of public defender or court-appointed conflict counsel as provided by law.

(c)   The governmental entity, or the designee of such governmental entity, in whose service or employ a list, record, or registry was compiled in violation of this section may be assessed a fine of not more than $5 million, if the court determines that the evidence shows that the list, record, or registry was compiled or maintained with the knowledge or complicity of the management of the governmental entity. The Attorney General may bring a civil cause of action to enforce the fines assessed under this paragraph.

(d)   The state attorney in the appropriate jurisdiction shall investigate complaints of criminal violations of this section and, where evidence indicates a violation may have occurred, shall prosecute violators.

(5)   ELECTRONIC RECORDS.—Secondhand dealers and pawnbrokers who electronically submit firearms transaction records to the appropriate law enforcement agencies as required by chapters 538 and 539 shall submit the name of the manufacturer and caliber information of each firearm in Florida Crime Information Center coding, and shall include the model and serial number of each firearm.

(6)   CONSTRUCTION.—This section shall be construed to effectuate its remedial and deterrent purposes. This section may not be construed to grant any substantive, procedural privacy right or civil claim to any criminal defendant, and a violation of this section may not be grounds for the suppression of evidence in any criminal case.

790.336   Lists, records, or registries to be destroyed. Any list, record, or registry maintained or under construction on the effective date of this act shall be destroyed, unless prohibited by law, within 60 calendar days after this act becomes law. Thereafter, failure to destroy any such list, record, or registry may result in prosecution under this act.

790.338   Medical privacy concerning firearms; prohibitions; penalties; exceptions.—

(1)   A health care practitioner licensed under chapter 456 or a health care facility licensed under chapter 395 may not intentionally enter any disclosed information concerning firearm ownership into the patient's medical record if the practitioner knows that such information is not relevant to the patient's medical care or safety, or the safety of others.

(2)   A health care practitioner licensed under chapter 456 or a health care facility licensed under chapter 395 shall respect a patient's right to privacy and should refrain from making a written inquiry or asking questions concerning the ownership of a firearm or ammunition by the patient or by a family member of the patient, or the presence of a firearm in a private home or other domicile of the patient or a family member of the patient. Notwithstanding this provision, a health care practitioner or health care facility that in good faith believes that this information is relevant to the patient's medical care or safety, or the safety of others, may make such a verbal or written inquiry.

(3)   Any emergency medical technician or paramedic acting under the supervision of an emergency medical services medical director under chapter 401 may make an inquiry concerning the possession or presence of a firearm if he or she, in good faith, believes that information regarding the possession of a firearm by the patient or the presence of a firearm in the home or domicile of a patient or a patient's family member is necessary to treat a patient during the course and scope of a medical emergency or that the presence or possession of a firearm would pose an imminent danger or threat to the patient or others.

(4)   A patient may decline to answer or provide any information regarding ownership of a firearm by the patient or a family member of the patient, or the presence of a firearm in the domicile of the patient or a family member of the patient. A patient's decision not to answer a question relating to the presence or ownership of a firearm does not alter existing law regarding a physician's authorization to choose his or her patients.

(5)   A health care practitioner licensed under chapter 456 or a health care facility licensed under chapter 395 may not discriminate against a patient based solely upon the patient's exercise of the constitutional right to own and possess firearms or ammunition.

(6)   A health care practitioner licensed under chapter 456 or a health care facility licensed under chapter 395 shall respect a patient's legal right to own or possess a firearm and should refrain from unnecessarily harassing a patient about firearm ownership during an examination.

(7)   An insurer issuing any type of insurance policy pursuant to chapter 627 may not deny coverage, increase any premium, or otherwise discriminate against any insured or applicant for insurance on the basis of or upon reliance upon the lawful ownership or possession of a firearm or ammunition or the lawful use or storage of a firearm or ammunition. Nothing herein shall prevent an insurer from considering the fair market value of firearms or ammunition in the setting of premiums for scheduled personal property coverage.

(8)   Violations of the provisions of subsections (1)-(4) constitute grounds for disciplinary action under §§ 456.072(2) and 395.1055.

Broward County Code of Ordinances
Chapter 18: Law Enforcement
Article VI: Firearms Five-Day Waiting Period
Current through August 29, 2016

Sec. 18-96. - Waiting period; prohibition. There shall be a mandatory 5-day waiting period, which shall be 5 days, excluding weekends and legal holidays, in connection with the sale of firearms occurring within Broward County when the sale is a transfer of money or other valuable consideration, and any part of the sale transaction is conducted on property to which the public has the right of access. Some examples of properties to which the public has a right of access are: gun shows, firearm exhibits, wholesale and retail stores, and flea markets. No person shall transfer or receive a firearm to or from another person for five days from the hour of such sale, excluding weekends and legal holidays, when the sale is a transfer of money or other valuable consideration, and any part of the sale transaction is conducted on property to which the public has the right of access. An uninterrupted, continuous, and cumulative aggregate of 120 hours must elapse between such sale and receipt of the firearm, excluding the hours of weekends and legal holidays. A person who violates the prohibition of this Section is guilty of a violation of a county ordinance, punishable as provided in § 125.69, F.S. and the violation shall be prosecuted in the same manner as misdemeanors are prosecuted.

Sec. 18-97. - Criminal history records check; requirement; prohibition.

(a) *Legislative intent.* It is the intent of the Board of County Commissioners, in the exercise of its constitutionally-granted authority, to ensure that no firearm is sold, offered for sale, or transferred where any part of the transaction is conducted on property to which the public has a right of access unless a national criminal history background check is conducted. As of the dates of the enactment and effectiveness of this Ordinance, Florida statutory law only allows such checks to be performed for and by licensed dealers, licensed importers, and licensed manufacturers. Therefore, a buyer or seller who is not otherwise a licensed dealer, licensed importer, or licensed manufacturer must use a licensed dealer, licensed importer, or licensed manufacturer as an intermediary to ensure such checks are conducted.

(b) *Requirement; prohibition.* There shall be a mandatory national criminal history records check done in connection with the sale of firearms occurring within Broward County. No person shall transfer or receive a firearm when any part of the sale transaction is conducted on property to which the public has the right of access until all procedures and requirements of § 790.065, F.S. have been complied with by a person statutorily authorized to conduct background information checks, and an approval number has been obtained and documented, as provided by § 790.065, F.S. In case of repeal or amendment of § 790.065, F.S., no person shall transfer or receive a firearm by sale when any part of the sale transaction is conducted on property to which the public has the right of access until all procedures, requirements, and prohibitions set forth in other federal or state laws relating to background checks have been complied with by persons selling or buying firearms. A person who violates the prohibition of this Section is guilty of a violation of a county ordinance, punishable as provided in § 125.69, F.S. and the violation shall be prosecuted in the same manner as misdemeanors are prosecuted.

Sec. 18-98. - Non-applicability to holders of Florida concealed weapon permits. Pursuant to the Florida Constitution, when purchasing a firearm, holders of a Florida concealed weapon permit or license, as prescribed by general law, shall not be subject to the prohibitions and penalties of this article.

Sec. 18-99. - Penalty. Violation of a prohibition of this article shall be punishable by a fine not to exceed $500 or by imprisonment in the county jail not to exceed 60 days or by both such fine and imprisonment. Each violation of a prohibition of this article relating to a specific firearm shall constitute a separate and individual violation. Nothing contained herein shall be construed to preempt the imposition of higher penalties imposed by state or federal law.

Martin County Municipal Code
Chapter 75: Firearms
Current through May 24, 2016

Sec. 75.1. - Repeal of county firearm ordinances. Pursuant to F.S. § 790.33, any and all county ordinances regarding firearms, guns, shooting, or ammunition, not set forth as repealed by this ordinance, are hereby repealed. Pursuant to F.S. § 790.33(4), the sections of the Martin County Land Development Code regarding firing ranges and shooting ranges are excepted from this repeal.

Sec. 75.2 - Local option. In accordance with the authority granted by the Article VIII, Section 5.(b) of the Constitution of the State of Florida, Martin County hereby requires a three-day waiting period, excluding weekends and legal holidays, in connection with the sale of any firearm occurring within Martin County. For purposes of this section, the term "sale" means the transfer of money or other valuable consideration for any firearm when any part of the transaction is conducted on property to which the public has the right of access. Holders of a concealed weapons permit as prescribed by general law shall not be subject to the provisions of this section when purchasing a firearm.

Miami Dade County Municipal Code
Article III: Weapons
Current through August 31, 2016

Sec. 21-14. - Dangerous weapons; penalty; trial court.
(a) *Concealed dangerous weapons.* It shall be unlawful for any person to wear under his clothes, or concealed about his person, or to display in a threatening manner any dangerous or deadly weapon including, but not by way of limitation, any pistol, revolver, … or any other dangerous or deadly weapon, except as hereinafter provided.
Note— Florida Statutes § 790.33, as amended, preempts and declares null and void all local ordinances, administrative regulations and rules in the field of firearms and ammunition, with limited exceptions set forth in § 790.33, as amended.
(c) *Forfeiture in addition to other penalties.* Every person convicted of any violation of this section shall forfeit to the County such dangerous or deadly weapon so concealed or displayed.
(d) *Exception.* Nothing in this section shall be construed to forbid any regular, special or ex officio police officer from carrying or wearing, while on duty, such weapons as shall be necessary in the proper discharging of his duty.
(e) *Penalty.* Every person who is convicted for a violation of subsection (a) shall for first conviction thereof be punished by imprisonment for not less than 6 months and by a fine of not less than $1,000; for a second or subsequent conviction of a violation of subsection (a) such person shall be punished by imprisonment for not less than 1 year and by a fine of not less than $1,000.
(f) *Court of appropriate jurisdiction vested with trial jurisdiction.* All violations of Section 21-14(a) shall be prosecuted only in the court of appropriate jurisdiction which shall have original, exclusive jurisdiction to try all cases arising hereunder. Provided, however, that where an act is recognized by State law as a misdemeanor and by this section as an offense, complaints against persons charged with such unlawful acts may be filed and prosecuted in either the court of appropriate jurisdiction or the Criminal Court of Record of Miami-Dade County, Florida, as the prosecuting attorney shall direct.
(g) *Certain municipal ordinances superseded.* The provisions of Section 21-14, Miami-Dade Code, as amended by Ordinance 68-72, shall pertain to all violations thereof within the County and supersede and nullify those provisions of

any and all municipal ordinances, codes and laws which define or penalize any act prohibited by Section 21-14(a) except those municipal ordinances, codes and laws not in conflict therewith and which contain an identical penalty provision. (Ord. No. 58-5, § 22.01, 2-18-58; Ord. No. 68-72, §§ 1, 2, 11-19-68; Ord. No. 68-84, § 1, 12-17-68)

Editor's note— Ord. No. 68-72, amended § 21-14 by adding subsection (c). Subsection (f) of § 21-14, derived from § 2 of said Ord. No. 68-72, was codified as said subsection pursuant to the authority set out in § 3 of said Ord. No. 68-72. Ord. No. 68-84, § 1, amended Ord. No. 68-72 by adding thereto another section which the editors, in their discretion, have codified as subsection (g) of § 21-14.

Sec. 21-15. - Reserved. Editor's note— At the direction of the County Attorney as authorized by Ord. No. 11-80, § 21-15, concealed weapons permit, has been preempted and declared null and void by F.S. § 790.33, which is titled "Field of Regulation of Firearms and Ammunition Preempted." Former § 21-15 derived from Ord. No. 58-5, adopted Feb. 18, 1958; Ord. No. 75-101, adopted Nov. 4, 1975; Ord. No. 79-31, adopted April 17, 1979; and Ord. No. 79-55, adopted July 3, 1979.

Sec. 21-16. - Reserved. Editor's note— At the direction of the County Attorney as authorized by Ord. No. 11-80, § 21-16, sale, loan, etc., weapons to intoxicated persons, etc., has been preempted and declared null and void by F.S. § 790.33, which is titled "Field of Regulation of Firearms and Ammunition Preempted." Former § 21-16 derived from Ord. No. 58-5, adopted Feb. 18, 1958; and Ord. No. 73-95, adopted Nov. 12, 1973.

Sec. 21-17. - Possession of weapons by felons, intoxicated persons, etc. It shall be unlawful for any person who has been convicted of a felony, or who is under the influence of alcohol or a narcotic or drug to wear or have about his person or in any vehicle in which he is an occupant any firearm or other dangerous or deadly weapon.

Note— Florida Statutes § 790.33, as amended, preempts and declares null and void all local ordinances, administrative regulations and rules in the field of firearms and ammunition, with limited exceptions set forth in § 790.33, as amended.

Sec. 21-18. - Handling weapon in dangerous manner. It shall be unlawful for any person to display, flourish, or handle in a threatening manner, any dangerous or deadly weapons in the presence of one (1) or more persons, except in self-defense or in the defense of person or property.

Note— Florida Statutes § 790.33, as amended, preempts and declares null and void all local ordinances, administrative regulations and rules in the field of firearms and ammunition, with limited exceptions set forth in § 790.33, as amended.

Sec. 21-18.1. - Reserved. Editor's note— At the direction of the County Attorney as authorized by Ord. No. 11-80, § 21-18.1, discharge of firearms over private property, has been preempted and declared null and void by F.S. § 790.33, which is titled "Field of Regulation of Firearms and Ammunition Preempted." Former § 21-18.1 derived from Ord. No. 70-14, adopted Feb. 18, 1970; and Ord. No. 94-147, adopted July 14, 1994.

Sec. 21-19. - Disposition of weapons seized on arrest. It shall be the duty of every police officer, upon making any arrest and taking a weapon under any provision of this article, to deliver such weapon to the clerk of the court of appropriate jurisdiction, to be held by the clerk until the final determination of the prosecution. Upon a finding of guilt, it shall be the duty of the clerk to deliver the weapon or weapons forthwith to the Miami-Dade Police Department which shall dispose of the weapon. If the person charged be acquitted of the offense, the weapon taken from him shall be returned to him upon request; provided, however, that if it is not called for within 60 days from and after the date of his acquittal or the dismissal of the charges against him, the weapon shall be disposed of as in the case of conviction.

Note— Florida Statutes § 790.33, as amended, preempts and declares null and void all local ordinances, administrative regulations and rules in the field of firearms and ammunition, with limited exceptions set forth in § 790.33, as amended.

Sec. 21-19.1. - Reserved. Editor's note— At the direction of the County Attorney as authorized by Ord. No. 11-80, § 21-19.1, sale of Saturday night specials in Miami-Dade County prohibited, has been preempted and declared null and void by F.S. § 790.33, which is titled "Field of Regulation of Firearms and Ammunition Preempted." Former § 21-19.1 derived from Ord. No. 73-93, adopted Nov. 12, 1973.

Sec. 21-19.2. - Reserved. Editor's note— Section 21-19.2, pertaining to the sale, possession, etc., of armor-piercing, KTW, etc., bullets, has been deleted as preempted by F.S. §§ 125.0107, 166.044. The section was derived from Ord. No. 82-34, §§ 1—4, adopted May 4, 1982.

Sec. 21-20. - Reserved. Editor's note— At the direction of the County Attorney as authorized by Ord. No. 11-80, § 21-20, registration of sales and transfers required; penalty, has been preempted and declared null and void by F.S. § 790.33, which is titled "Field of Regulation of Firearms and Ammunition Preempted." Former § 21-20 derived from Ord. No. 58-5, adopted Feb. 18, 1958; Ord. No. 67-72, adopted Oct. 3, 1967; Ord. No. 68-71, adopted Nov. 19, 1968; and Ord. No. 73-95, adopted Nov. 12, 1973.

Division 2. – License to Sell Firearms

Secs. 21-20.1—21-20.14.1. - Reserved. Editor's note— At the direction of the County Attorney as authorized by Ord. No. 11-80, §§ 21-20.1—21-20.14.1, regarding license to sell firearms, has been preempted and declared null and void by F.S. § 790.33, which is titled "Field of Regulation of Firearms and Ammunition Preempted." Former §§ 21-20.1—21-14.1 derived from Ord. No. 66-17, adopted April 26, 1966; Ord. No. 66-53, adopted Oct. 18, 1966; Ord. No. 68-66, adopted Nov. 5, 1968; Ord. No. 73-93, adopted Nov. 12, 1973; Ord. No. 73-94, adopted Nov. 12, 1973; Ord. No. 73-95, adopted Nov. 12, 1973; Ord. No. 75-98, adopted Nov. 4, 1975; Ord. No. 79-31, adopted April 17, 1979; Ord. No. 81-79, adopted July 7, 1981; Ord. No. 87-31, adopted May 19, 1987; and Ord. No. 88-57, adopted June 21, 1988.

Sec. 21-20.15. - Penalty. Every person who is convicted of a violation of this division shall be punished by a fine not to exceed $500 or imprisonment in the County Jail for not more than 30 days, or by both such fine and imprisonment; for a second conviction of a violation of this division such person shall be punished by a fine not to exceed $1,000 or imprisonment in the County Jail not more than 12 months, or by both such fine and imprisonment.

Sec. 21-20.16. - Reserved. Editor's note— At the direction of the County Attorney as authorized by Ord. No. 11-80, § 21-20.16, handgun purchaser's instruction and qualification procedure, has been preempted and declared null and void by F.S. § 790.33, which is titled "Field of Regulation of Firearms and Ammunition Preempted." Former § 21-20.16 derived from Ord. No. 73-95, adopted Nov. 12, 1973.

Sec. 21-20.17. - Reserved. Editor's note— At the direction of the County Attorney as authorized by Ord. No. 11-80, § 21-20.17, unlawful to sell handguns to persons who have not qualified, has been preempted and declared null and void by F.S. § 790.33, which is titled "Field of Regulation of Firearms and Ammunition Preempted." Former § 21-20.17 derived from Ord. No. 73-95, adopted Nov. 12, 1973.

Sec. 21-20.18. - Five-day waiting period and criminal history records check on firearms sales.
(a) *Definitions.* For purposes of this section, the following terms shall be defined as follows:
(1) *Any part of the transaction* means any part of the sales transaction, including but not limited to, the offer of sale, negotiations, the agreement to sell, the transfer of consideration, or the transfer of the firearm.
(2) *Antique firearms* means any firearm (including any firearm with a matchlock, flintlock, percussion cap, or similar type of ignition system) manufactured in or before 1898; and any replica of any such firearm if such replica **(i)** is not designed or redesigned for using rimfire or conventional centerfire fixed ammunition, or **(ii)** uses rimfire or conventional centerfire fixed ammunition which is no longer manufactured in the United States and which is not readily available in the ordinary channels of commercial trade.
(3) *Firearm* means any weapon which will, is designed to, or may readily be converted to expel a projectile by the action of an explosive; the frame or receiver of any such weapon; and firearm muffler or firearm silencer; any destructive device; or any machine gun. Such term does not include an antique firearm.
(4) *Property to which the public has the right of access* means any real or personal property to which the public has a right of access, including property owned by either public or private individuals, firms and entities and expressly includes, but is not limited to, flea markets, gun shows and firearms exhibitions.
(5) *Sale* means the transfer of money or other valuable consideration.
(b) *Application and enforcement of section.* Law enforcement officers shall have the right to enforce the provisions of this section against any person found violating these provisions within their jurisdiction.
(c) *Sale and delivery of firearms; mandatory five-day waiting period.* There shall be a mandatory 5-day waiting period, which shall be 5 full days, excluding weekends and legal holidays, between the hour of the sale and the hour of the delivery of any firearm when any part of the transaction is conducted within Miami-Dade County on property to which the public has the right of access.
(d) *Sale and delivery of firearms; mandatory criminal records check.* No person, whether licensed or unlicensed, shall sell, offer for sale, transfer or deliver any firearm to another person when any part of the transaction is conducted on property to which the public has the right of access within Miami-Dade County until all procedures specified under section 790.065, Florida Statutes, have been complied with by a person authorized by that section to conduct a criminal history check of background information as specified in that section, and the approval number set forth by that section has been obtained and documented. Upon the repeal of section 790.065, Florida Statutes, no person, whether licensed or unlicensed, shall sell, offer for sale, transfer or deliver any firearm to another person when any part of the transaction is conducted on property to which the public has the right of access until all procedures specified under any other state or federal law which requires a national criminal history information or national criminal history check on potential buyer or transferee of firearms have been complied with by any person authorized by law to conduct the required national criminal history or background records check and any required approval under such state or federal law or rule has been obtained. "Person" for purposes of this subsection shall include any person, including, but not limited to a licensed importer, licensed manufacturer or licensed dealer and any unlicensed person.
In the case of a seller who is not a licensed importer, licensed manufacturer or licensed dealer, compliance with section 790.065 or its state or federal successor shall be achieved by the seller requesting that a licensed importer, licensed manufacturer or licensed dealer complete all the requirements of section 790.065 or its state or federal successor. Licensed importers, manufacturers and dealers may charge a reasonable fee of an unlicensed seller to cover costs associated with completing the requirements of section 790.065.

(e) *Exemptions.* Holders of a concealed weapons permit as prescribed by state law and holders of an active certification from the Criminal Justice Standards and Training Commission as a law enforcement officer, a correctional officer, or a correctional probation officer as set forth in state law shall not be subject to the provisions of this section. Sales to a licensed importer, licensed manufacturer or licensed dealer shall not be subject to the provisions of this section.

(f) *Penalties.* Any person violating any provision of this section shall be punished by a fine not to exceed $500 or by imprisonment not to exceed 60 days in the County Jail, or by both such fine and imprisonment. Nothing contained herein shall be construed to preempt the imposition of any higher penalties imposed by state or federal law.

(g) *Reporting of information.* To the fullest extent permissible by law, all information acquired in relation to a violation of this section shall be reported to appropriate federal and state officials.

Palm Beach County Municipal Code
Current through September 16, 2016
Chapter 28: Weapons

Sec. 28-21. - Definitions. As used in this article:

Business day means a 24-hour day (beginning at 12:01 a.m.), excluding weekends and legal holidays.

FDLE means the Florida Department of Law Enforcement.

Firearm means any weapon, including a starter gun or handgun, which will or is designed to or may readily be converted to expel a projectile by the action of an explosive; the frame or receiver of any such weapon; any firearm muffler or firearm silencer; and destructive device; or any machine gun.

Handgun means a firearm capable of being carried and used by 1 hand, such as a pistol or revolver.

Licensed dealer means a dealer licensed under the provisions of Title 27, Code of Federal Regulations, Part 478, or any successor federal regulations requiring licenses for firearm dealers.

Licensed importer means an importer licensed under the provisions of Title 27, Code of Federal Regulations, Part 478, or any successor federal regulations requiring licenses for firearm importers.

Licensed manufacturer means a manufacturer licensed under the provisions of Title 27, Code of Federal Regulations, Part 478, or any successor federal regulations requiring licenses for firearm manufacturers.

NICS means the National Instant Criminal Background Check System established pursuant to Title 18, United States Code, Section 922.

Person includes, but is not limited to, any individual, corporation, company, association, firm partnership, society, or joint stock company.

Sale means the transfer of money or other valuable consideration for any firearm when any part of the transaction is conducted on property to which the public has the right of access, which includes, but is not limited to, flea markets, gun shows and gun exhibitions.

Shotgun means a shoulder-held firearm with a smooth bore designed primarily to fire shells containing multiple projectiles (shotshells).

Shotshell means a metal, plastic or cardboard case containing a primer, propellant and multiple projectiles intended to be fired from a shotgun.

Structure means that which is 3 feet or more in height which is built or constructed or erected or tied down having a fixed location on the ground such as buildings, homes and mobile homes.

Sec. 28-22. - Reserved.

Editor's note— Ord. No. 2011-019, § 1, adopted Sept. 13, 2011, repealed § 28-22 which pertained to discharge of firearms and derived from Ord. No. 99-5, § 2, adopted Feb. 23, 1999.

Sec. 28-23. - Mandatory waiting period; criminal history records check requirement.

(a) No person shall deliver a firearm to another person, other than a licensed dealer, licensed manufacturer or licensed importer, in connection with the sale of such firearm for a period of 5 business days from the date of the sale.

(b) No person shall deliver a firearm to another person, other than a licensed dealer, licensed manufacturer or licensed importer, in connection with the sale of such firearm until the seller, either directly or through a licensed dealer, licensed manufacturer or licensed importer, has:

　(1) Requested a national criminal history records check of the potential purchaser or transferee of the firearm from FDLE or NICS, and

　(2) Received an approval/identification number from FDLE or NICS signifying the potential purchaser or transferee of the firearm would not be prohibited by state or federal law from receiving or possessing a firearm.

(c) The provisions of this section shall not apply to holders of a concealed weapons permit issued pursuant to general law of the State of Florida when purchasing a firearm.

Georgia Code

Current through the 2016 Regular Session

Office of the Attorney General
40 Capitol Square, SW
Atlanta, Ga 30334
Voice: (404) 656-3300
https://law.georgia.gov/

Atlanta Field Division
2600 Century Parkway, Suite 300
Atlanta, Georgia 30345
Voice: (404) 417-2600
https://www.atf.gov/atlanta-field-division

PROTECTING THE PUBLIC
SERVING OUR NATION

Table of Contents

TITLE 10. Commerce and Trade
Chapter 1. Selling and Other Trade Practices
Article 6. Interstate Purchase of Rifles and Shotguns

§ 10-1-100. Out of state purchase of rifles and shotguns by residents. Residents of the State of Georgia may purchase rifles and shotguns in any state of the United States, provided such residents conform to applicable provisions of statutes and regulations of the United States, of the State of Georgia, and of the state in which the purchase is made.

§ 10-1-101. Nonresidents may purchase rifles and shotguns in Georgia. Residents of any state of the United States may purchase rifles and shotguns in the State of Georgia, provided such residents conform to applicable provisions of statutes and regulations of the United States, of the State of Georgia, and of the state in which such persons reside.

TITLE 16. Crimes and Offenses
Chapter 11. Offenses Against Public Order and Safety
Article 4. Dangerous Instrumentalities and Practices
Part 1. General Provision

§ 16-11-101.1. Furnishing pistol or revolver to person under the age of 18 years
(a) For the purposes of this Code section, the term:
  (1) "Minor" means any person under the age of 18 years.
  (2) "Pistol or revolver" means a handgun as defined in subsection (a) of Code § 16-11-125.1.
(b) It shall be unlawful for a person intentionally, knowingly, or recklessly to sell or furnish a pistol or revolver to a minor, except that it shall be lawful for a parent or legal guardian to permit possession of a pistol or revolver by a minor for the purposes specified in subsection (c) of Code § 16-11-132 unless otherwise expressly limited by subsection (c) of this Code section.
(c)(1) It shall be unlawful for a parent or legal guardian to permit possession of a pistol or revolver by a minor if the parent or legal guardian knows of a minor's conduct which violates the provisions of Code § 16-11-132 and fails to make reasonable efforts to prevent any such violation of Code § 16-11-132.
  (2) Notwithstanding any provisions of subsection (c) of Code § 16-11-132 or any other law to the contrary, it shall be unlawful for any parent or legal guardian intentionally, knowingly, or recklessly to furnish to or permit a minor to possess a pistol or revolver if such parent or legal guardian is aware of a substantial risk that such minor will use a pistol or revolver to commit a felony offense or if such parent or legal guardian who is aware of such substantial risk fails to make reasonable efforts to prevent commission of the offense by the minor.
  (3) In addition to any other act which violates this subsection, a parent or legal guardian shall be deemed to have violated this subsection if such parent or legal guardian furnishes to or permits possession of a pistol or revolver by any minor who has been convicted of a forcible felony or forcible misdemeanor, as defined in Code § 16-1-3, or who has been adjudicated for committing a delinquent act under the provisions of Article 6 of Chapter 11 of Title 15 for an offense which would constitute a forcible felony or forcible misdemeanor, as defined in Code § 16-1-3, if such minor were an adult.
(d) Upon conviction of a violation of subsection (b) or (c) of this Code section, a person shall be guilty of a felony and punished by a fine not to exceed $5,000 or by imprisonment for not less than 3 nor more than 5 years, or both.

§ 16-11-102. Pointing or aiming gun or pistol at another. A person is guilty of a misdemeanor when he intentionally and without legal justification points or aims a gun or pistol at another, whether the gun or pistol is loaded or unloaded.

§ 16-11-103. Discharge of gun or pistol near public highway; penalty
(a) As used in this Code section, the term:
  (1) "Firearm" means any handgun, rifle, or shotgun.
  (2) "Public highway" means every public street, road, and highway in this state.
  (3) "Sport shooting range" means an area designated and operated by a person or entity for the sport shooting of firearms, target practice, trapshooting, skeet shooting, or shooting sporting clays and not available for such use by the general public without payment of a fee, membership contribution, or dues or without the invitation of an authorized person, or any area so designated and operated by a unit of government, regardless of the terms of admission thereto.
  (4) "Unit of government" means any of the departments, agencies, authorities, or political subdivisions of the state, cities, municipal corporations, townships, or villages and any of their respective departments, agencies, or authorities.
(b) Except as provided in subsection (c) of this Code section, it shall be unlawful for any person, without legal justification, to discharge a firearm on or within 50 yards of a public highway.
(c) This Code section shall not apply to a discharge of a firearm which occurs within 50 yards of a public highway if such discharge is shielded from the view of a traveler on the public highway and occurs at:
  (1) An indoor or outdoor sport shooting range;
  (2) Facilities used for firearm or hunting safety courses sponsored by a unit of government, nonprofit corporation, or commercial enterprise; or
  (3) The business location of any person, firm, retail dealer, wholesale dealer, pawnbroker, or corporation licensed as a firearm dealer pursuant to Chapter 16 of Title 43.
(d) Any person who violates subsection (b) of the Code section shall be guilty of a misdemeanor.

§ 16-11-104. Discharge of firearms on property of another
(a) It shall be unlawful for any person to fire or discharge a firearm on the property of another person, firm, or corporation without having first obtained permission from the owner or lessee of the property. This Code section shall not apply to:
    (1) Persons who fire or discharge a firearm in defense of person or property; and
    (2) Law enforcement officers.
(b) Any person who violates subsection (a) of this Code section is guilty of a misdemeanor.

§ 16-11-106. Possession of firearm or knife during commission of or attempt to commit certain crimes
(a) For the purposes of this Code section, the term "firearm" shall include stun guns and tasers. A stun gun or taser is any device that is powered by electrical charging units such as batteries and emits an electrical charge in excess of 20,000 volts or is otherwise capable of incapacitating a person by an electrical charge.
(b) Any person who shall have on or within arm's reach of his or her person a firearm or a knife having a blade of 3 or more inches in length during the commission of, or the attempt to commit:
    (1) Any crime against or involving the person of another;
    (2) The unlawful entry into a building or vehicle;
    (3) A theft from a building or theft of a vehicle;
    (4) Any crime involving the possession, manufacture, delivery, distribution, dispensing, administering, selling, or possession with intent to distribute any controlled substance or marijuana as provided in Code § 16-13-30, any counterfeit substance as defined in Code § 16-13-21, or any noncontrolled substance as provided in Code § 16-13-30.1; or
    (5) Any crime involving the trafficking of cocaine, marijuana, or illegal drugs as provided in Code § 16-13-31,
and which crime is a felony, commits a felony and, upon conviction thereof, shall be punished by confinement for a period of 5 years, such sentence to run consecutively to any other sentence which the person has received.
(c) Upon the second or subsequent conviction of a person under this Code section, the person shall be punished by confinement for a period of 10 years. Notwithstanding any other law to the contrary, the sentence of any person which is imposed for violating this Code section a second or subsequent time shall not be suspended by the court and probationary sentence imposed in lieu thereof.
(d) The punishment prescribed for the violation of subsections (b) and (c) of this Code section shall not be reducible to misdemeanor punishment as is provided by Code § 17-10-5.
(e) Any crime committed in violation of subsections (b) and (c) of this Code section shall be considered a separate offense.

§ 16-11-108. Misuse of firearm or archery tackle while hunting
(a) Any person who while hunting wildlife uses a firearm or archery tackle in a manner to endanger the bodily safety of another person by consciously disregarding a substantial and unjustifiable risk that his act or omission will cause harm to or endanger the safety of another person and the disregard constitutes a gross deviation from the standard of care which a reasonable person would exercise in the situation is guilty of a misdemeanor; provided, however, if such conduct results in serious bodily harm to another person, the person engaging in such conduct shall be guilty of a felony and, upon conviction thereof, shall be punished by a fine of not more than $5,000 or by imprisonment for not less than one nor more than 10 years, or both.
(b) Whenever a person is charged with violating subsection (a) of this Code section, the arresting law enforcement officer shall take the hunting license of the person so charged. The hunting license shall be attached to the court's copy of the citation, warrant, accusation, or indictment and shall be forwarded to the court having jurisdiction of the offense. A copy of the citation, warrant, accusation, or indictment shall be forwarded, within 15 days of its issuance, to the Game and Fish Division of the Department of Natural Resources.
(c) In order to obtain a temporary hunting license, a person charged with violating subsection (a) of this Code section must present to the director of the Game and Fish Division of the Department of Natural Resources a certificate of satisfactory completion, after the date of the incident for which the person was charged and regardless of the person's age or date of birth, of a hunter education course prescribed by the Board of Natural Resources. A temporary hunting license issued under such circumstances shall be valid until the next March 31 or until suspended or revoked under any provision of this title or of Title 27. The director of the Game and Fish Division of the Department of Natural Resources may renew the temporary hunting license during the pendency of charges.
(d)(1) If the person is convicted of violating subsection (a) of this Code section, the court shall, within 15 days of such conviction, forward the person's hunting license and a copy of the record of the disposition of the case to the Game and Fish Division of the Department of Natural Resources. At this time, the court shall also require the person to surrender any temporary hunting licenses issued pursuant to the provisions of subsection (c) of this Code section.
    (2) If the person is not convicted of violating subsection (a) of this Code section, the court shall return the hunting license to the person.

§ 16-11-113. Offense of transferring firearm to individual other than actual buyer
Any person who attempts to solicit, persuade, encourage, or entice any dealer to transfer or otherwise convey a firearm other than to the actual buyer, as well as any other person who willfully and intentionally aids or abets such person, shall be guilty of a felony. This Code section shall not apply to a federal law enforcement officer or a peace officer, as defined in Code § 16-1-3, in the performance of his or her official duties or other person under such officer's direct supervision.

Part 2. Possession of Dangerous Weapons

§ 16-11-120. Short title. This part shall be known and may be cited as the "Georgia Firearms and Weapons Act."

§ 16-11-121. Definitions. As used in this part, the term:

(1) "Dangerous weapon" means any weapon commonly known as a "rocket launcher," "bazooka," or "recoilless rifle" which fires explosive or nonexplosive rockets designed to injure or kill personnel or destroy heavy armor, or similar weapon used for such purpose. The term shall also mean a weapon commonly known as a "mortar" which fires high explosive from a metallic cylinder and which is commonly used by the armed forces as an antipersonnel weapon or similar weapon used for such purpose. The term shall also mean a weapon commonly known as a "hand grenade" or other similar weapon which is designed to explode and injure personnel or similar weapon used for such purpose.

(2) "Machine gun" means any weapon which shoots or is designed to shoot, automatically, more than 6 shots, without manual reloading, by a single function of the trigger.

(3) "Person" means any individual, partnership, company, association, or corporation.

(4) "Sawed-off rifle" means a weapon designed or redesigned, made or remade, and intended to be fired from the shoulder; and designed or redesigned, made or remade, to use the energy of the explosive in a fixed metallic cartridge to fire only a single projectile through a rifle bore for each single pull of the trigger; and which has a barrel or barrels of less than 16 inches in length or has an overall length of less than 26 inches.

(5) "Sawed-off shotgun" means a shotgun or any weapon made from a shotgun whether by alteration, modification, or otherwise having one or more barrels less than 18 inches in length or if such weapon as modified has an overall length of less than 26 inches.

(6) "Shotgun" means a weapon designed or redesigned, made or remade, and intended to be fired from the shoulder; and designed or redesigned, and made or remade, to use the energy of the explosive in a fixed shotgun shell to fire through a smooth bore either a number of ball shot or a single projectile for each single pull of the trigger.

(7) "Silencer" means any device for silencing or diminishing the report of any portable weapon such as a rifle, carbine, pistol, revolver, machine gun, shotgun, fowling piece, or other device from which a shot, bullet, or projectile may be discharged by an explosive.

§ 16-11-122. Possession of sawed-off shotgun or rifle, machine gun, silencer, or dangerous weapon prohibited
No person shall have in his possession any sawed-off shotgun, sawed-off rifle, machine gun, dangerous weapon, or silencer except as provided in Code § 16-11-124.

§ 16-11-123. Unlawful possession of firearms or weapons. A person commits the offense of unlawful possession of firearms or weapons when he or she knowingly has in his or her possession any sawed-off shotgun, sawed-off rifle, machine gun, dangerous weapon, or silencer, and, upon conviction thereof, he or she shall be punished by imprisonment for a period of 5 years.

§ 16-11-124. Exemptions from application of part. This part shall not apply to:

(1) A peace officer of any duly authorized police agency of this state or of any political subdivision thereof, or a law enforcement officer of any department or agency of the United States who is regularly employed and paid by the United States, this state, or any such political subdivision, or an employee of the Department of Corrections of this state who is authorized in writing by the commissioner of corrections to transfer or possess such firearms while in the official performance of his duties;

(2) A member of the National Guard or of the armed forces of the United States to wit: the army, navy, marine corps, air force, or coast guard who, while serving therein, possesses such firearm in the line of duty;

(3) Any sawed-off shotgun, sawed-off rifle, machine gun, dangerous weapon, or silencer which has been modified or changed to the extent that it is inoperative. Examples of the requisite modification include weapons with their barrel or barrels filled with lead, hand grenades filled with sand, or other nonexplosive materials;

(4) Possession of a sawed-off shotgun, sawed-off rifle, machine gun, dangerous weapon, or silencer by a person who is authorized to possess the same because he has registered the sawed-off shotgun, sawed-off rifle, machine gun, dangerous weapon, or silencer in accordance with the dictates of the National Firearms Act, 68A Stat. 725 (26 U.S.C. §§ 5841-5862); and

(5) A security officer employed by a federally licensed nuclear power facility or a licensee of such facility, including a contract security officer, who is trained and qualified under a security plan approved by the United States Nuclear Regulatory Commission or other federal agency authorized to regulate nuclear facility security; provided, however, that this exemption shall apply only while such security officer is acting in connection with his or her official duties on the premises of such nuclear power facility or on properties outside the facility property pursuant to a written agreement entered into with the local law enforcement agency having jurisdiction over the facility. The exemption under this paragraph does not include the possession of silencers.

§ 16-11-125. Burden of proof as to exemptions. In any complaint, accusation, or indictment and in any action or proceeding brought for the enforcement of this part it shall not be necessary to negative any exception, excuse, proviso, or exemption contained in this part, and the burden of proof of any such exception, excuse, proviso, or exemption shall be upon the defendant.

Part 3. Carrying and Possession of Firearms

§ 16-11-125.1. Definitions. As used in this part, the term:

(1) "Handgun" means a firearm of any description, loaded or unloaded, from which any shot, bullet, or other missile can be discharged by an action of an explosive where the length of the barrel, not including any revolving, detachable, or magazine breech, does not exceed 12 inches; provided, however, that the term "handgun" shall not include a gun which discharges a single shot of .46 centimeters or less in diameter.

(3) "License holder" means a person who holds a valid weapons carry license.

(4) "Long gun" means a firearm with a barrel length of at least 18 inches and overall length of at least 26 inches designed or made and intended to be fired from the shoulder and designed or made to use the energy of the explosive in a fixed:

(A) Shotgun shell to fire through a smooth bore either a number of ball shot or a single projectile for each single pull of the trigger or from which any shot, bullet, or other missile can be discharged; or

(B) Metallic cartridge to fire only a single projectile through a rifle bore for each single pull of the trigger; provided, however, that the term "long gun" shall not include a gun which discharges a single shot of .46 centimeters or less in diameter.

(5) "Weapon" means a knife or handgun.

(6) "Weapons carry license" or "license" means a license issued pursuant to Code § 16-11-129.

§ 16-11-126. Having or carrying handguns, long guns, or other weapons; license requirement; exceptions for homes, motor vehicles, private property, and other locations and conditions

(a) Any person who is not prohibited by law from possessing a handgun or long gun may have or carry on his or her person a weapon or long gun on his or her property or inside his or her home, motor vehicle, or place of business without a valid weapons carry license.

(b) Any person who is not prohibited by law from possessing a handgun or long gun may have or carry on his or her person a long gun without a valid weapons carry license, provided that if the long gun is loaded, it shall only be carried in an open and fully exposed manner.

(c) Any person who is not prohibited by law from possessing a handgun or long gun may have or carry any handgun provided that it is enclosed in a case and unloaded.

(d) Any person who is not prohibited by law from possessing a handgun or long gun who is eligible for a weapons carry license may transport a handgun or long gun in any private passenger motor vehicle; provided, however, that private property owners or persons in legal control of private property through a lease, rental agreement, licensing agreement, contract, or any other agreement to control access to such private property shall have the right to exclude or eject a person who is in possession of a weapon or long gun on their private property in accordance with paragraph (3) of subsection (b) of Code § 16-7-21, except as provided in Code § 16-11-135.

(e) Any person licensed to carry a handgun or weapon in any other state whose laws recognize and give effect to a license issued pursuant to this part shall be authorized to carry a weapon in this state, but only while the licensee is not a resident of this state; provided, however, that such licensee shall carry the weapon in compliance with the laws of this state.

(f) Any person with a valid hunting or fishing license on his or her person, or any person not required by law to have a hunting or fishing license, who is engaged in legal hunting, fishing, or sport shooting when the person has the permission of the owner of the land on which the activities are being conducted may have or carry on his or her person a handgun or long gun without a valid weapons carry license while hunting, fishing, or engaging in sport shooting.

(g) Notwithstanding Code §§ 12-3-10, 27-3-1.1, 27-3-6, and 16-12-122 through 16-12-127, any person with a valid weapons carry license may carry a weapon in all parks, historic sites, or recreational areas, as such term is defined in Code § 12-3-10, including all publicly owned buildings located in such parks, historic sites, and recreational areas, in wildlife management areas, and on public transportation; provided, however, that a person shall not carry a handgun into a place where it is prohibited by federal law.

(h) (1) No person shall carry a weapon without a valid weapons carry license unless he or she meets one of the exceptions to having such license as provided in subsections (a) through (g) of this Code section.

(2) A person commits the offense of carrying a weapon without a license when he or she violates the provisions of paragraph (1) of this subsection.

(i) Upon conviction of the offense of carrying a weapon without a valid weapons carry license, a person shall be punished as follows:

(1) For the first offense, he or she shall be guilty of a misdemeanor; and

(2) For the second offense within 5 years, as measured from the dates of previous arrests for which convictions were obtained to the date of the current arrest for which a conviction is obtained, and for any subsequent offense, he or she shall be guilty of a felony and, upon conviction thereof, shall be imprisoned for not less than 2 years and not more than 5 years.

(j) Nothing in this Code section shall in any way operate or be construed to affect, repeal, or limit the exemptions provided for under Code § 16-11-130.

§ 16-11-127. Carrying weapons in unauthorized locations

(a) As used in this Code section, the term:

(1) "Courthouse" means a building occupied by judicial courts and containing rooms in which judicial proceedings are held.

(2) "Government building" means:

(A) The building in which a government entity is housed;

(B) The building where a government entity meets in its official capacity; provided, however, that if such building is not a publicly owned building, such building shall be considered a government building for the purposes of this Code section only during the time such government entity is meeting at such building; or

(C) The portion of any building that is not a publicly owned building that is occupied by a government entity.

(3) "Government entity" means an office, agency, authority, department, commission, board, body, division, instrumentality, or institution of the state or any county, municipal corporation, consolidated government, or local board of education within this state.

(4) "Parking facility" means real property owned or leased by a government entity, courthouse, jail, prison, or place of worship that has been designated by such government entity, courthouse, jail, prison, or place of worship for the parking of motor vehicles at a government building or at such courthouse, jail, prison, or place of worship.

(b) Except as provided in Code § 16-11-127.1 and subsection (d) or (e) of this Code section, a person shall be guilty of carrying a weapon or long gun in an unauthorized location and punished as for a misdemeanor when he or she carries a weapon or long gun while:

(1) In a government building as a nonlicense holder;

(2) In a courthouse;

(3) In a jail or prison;

(4) In a place of worship, unless the governing body or authority of the place of worship permits the carrying of weapons or long guns by license holders;

(5) In a state mental health facility as defined in Code § 37-1-1 which admits individuals on an involuntary basis for treatment of mental illness, developmental disability, or addictive disease; provided, however, that carrying a weapon or long gun in such location in a manner in compliance with paragraph (3) of subsection (d) of this Code section shall not constitute a violation of this subsection;

(6) On the premises of a nuclear power facility, except as provided in Code § 16-11-127.2, and the punishment provisions of Code § 16-11-127.2 shall supersede the punishment provisions of this Code section; or

(7) Within 150 feet of any polling place when elections are being conducted and such polling place is being used as a polling place as provided for in paragraph (27) of Code § 21-2-2, except as provided in subsection (i) of Code § 21-2-413.

(c) A license holder or person recognized under subsection (e) of Code § 16-11-126 shall be authorized to carry a weapon as provided in Code § 16-11-135 and in every location in this state not listed in subsection (b) or prohibited by subsection (e) of this Code section; provided, however, that private property owners or persons in legal control of private property through a lease, rental agreement, licensing agreement, contract, or any other agreement to control access to such private property shall have the right to exclude or eject a person who is in possession of a weapon or long gun on their private property in accordance with paragraph (3) of subsection (b) of Code § 16-7-21, except as provided in Code § 16-11-135. A violation of subsection (b) of this Code section shall not create or give rise to a civil action for damages.

(d) Subsection (b) of this Code section shall not apply:

(1) To the use of weapons or long guns as exhibits in a legal proceeding, provided such weapons or long guns are secured and handled as directed by the personnel providing courtroom security or the judge hearing the case;

(2) To a license holder who approaches security or management personnel upon arrival at a location described in subsection (b) of this Code section and notifies such security or management personnel of the presence of the weapon or long gun and explicitly follows the security or management personnel's direction for removing, securing, storing, or temporarily surrendering such weapon or long gun; and

(3) To a weapon or long gun possessed by a license holder which is under the possessor's control in a motor vehicle or is in a locked compartment of a motor vehicle or one which is in a locked container in or a locked firearms rack which is on a motor vehicle and such vehicle is parked in a parking facility.

(e) (1) A license holder shall be authorized to carry a weapon in a government building when the government building is open for business and where ingress into such building is not restricted or screened by security personnel. A license holder who enters or attempts to enter a government building carrying a weapon where ingress is restricted or screened by security personnel shall be guilty of a misdemeanor if at least one member of such security personnel is certified as a peace officer pursuant to Chapter 8 of Title 35; provided, however, that a license holder who immediately exits such building or immediately leaves such location upon notification of his or her failure to clear security due to the carrying of a weapon shall not be guilty of violating this subsection or paragraph (1) of subsection (b) of this Code section. A person who is not a license holder and who attempts to enter a government building carrying a weapon shall be guilty of a misdemeanor.

(2) Any license holder who violates subsection (b) of this Code section in a place of worship shall not be arrested but shall be fined not more than $100. Any person who is not a license holder who violates subsection (b) of this Code section in a place of worship shall be punished as for a misdemeanor.

(f) Nothing in this Code section shall in any way operate or be construed to affect, repeal, or limit the exemptions provided for under Code § 16-11-130.

§ 16-11-127.1. Carrying weapons within school safety zones, at school functions, or on a bus or other transportation furnished by a school

(a) As used in this Code section, the term:

(1) "Bus or other transportation furnished by a school" means a bus or other transportation furnished by a public or private elementary or secondary school.

(2) "School function" means a school function or related activity that occurs outside of a school safety zone and is for a public or private elementary or secondary school.

(3) "School safety zone" means in or on any real property or building owned by or leased to:

(A) Any public or private elementary school, secondary school, or local board of education and used for elementary or secondary education; and

(B) Any public or private technical school, vocational school, college, university, or other institution of postsecondary education.

(4) "Weapon" means and includes any pistol, revolver, or any weapon designed or intended to propel a missile of any kind…. This paragraph excludes any of these instruments used for classroom work authorized by the teacher.

(b) (1) Except as otherwise provided in subsection (c) of this Code section, it shall be unlawful for any person to carry to or to possess or have under such person's control while within a school safety zone, at a school function, or on a bus or other transportation furnished by a school any weapon or explosive compound, other than fireworks or consumer fireworks the possession of which is regulated by Chapter 10 of Title 25.

(2) Any license holder who violates this subsection shall be guilty of a misdemeanor. Any person who is not a license holder who violates this subsection shall be guilty of a felony and, upon conviction thereof, be punished by a fine of not more than $10,000, by imprisonment for not less than 2 nor more than 10 years, or both.

(3) Any person convicted of a violation of this subsection involving a dangerous weapon or machine gun, as such terms are defined in Code § 16-11-121, shall be punished by a fine of not more than $10,000 or by imprisonment for a period of not less than 5 nor more than 10 years, or both.

(4) A child who violates this subsection may be subject to the provisions of Code § 15-11-601.

(c) The provisions of this Code section shall not apply to:

(2) Participants in organized sport shooting events or firearm training courses;

(3) Persons participating in military training programs conducted by or on behalf of the armed forces of the United States or the Georgia Department of Defense;

(4) Persons participating in law enforcement training conducted by a police academy certified by the Georgia Peace Officer Standards and Training Council or by a law enforcement agency of the state or the United States or any political subdivision thereof;

(5) The following persons, when acting in the performance of their official duties or when en route to or from their official duties:

(A) A peace officer as defined by Code § 35-8-2;

(B) A law enforcement officer of the United States government;

(C) A prosecuting attorney of this state or of the United States;

(D) An employee of the Department of Corrections or a correctional facility operated by a political subdivision of this state or the United States who is authorized by the head of such department or correctional agency or facility to carry a firearm;

(E) An employee of the Department of Community Supervision who is authorized by the commissioner of community supervision to carry a firearm;

(F) A person employed as a campus police officer or school security officer who is authorized to carry a weapon in accordance with Chapter 8 of Title 20; and

(G) Medical examiners, coroners, and their investigators who are employed by the state or any political subdivision thereof;

(6) A person who has been authorized in writing by a duly authorized official of a public or private elementary or secondary school or a public or private technical school, vocational school, college, university, or other institution of postsecondary education or a local board of education as provided in Code § 16-11-130.1 to have in such person's possession or use within a school safety zone, at a school function, or on a bus or other transportation furnished by a school a weapon which would otherwise be prohibited by this Code section. Such authorization shall specify the weapon or weapons which have been authorized and the time period during which the authorization is valid;

(7) A person who is licensed in accordance with Code § 16-11-129 or issued a permit pursuant to Code § 43-38-10, when such person carries or picks up a student within a school safety zone, at a school function, or on a bus or other transportation furnished by a school or a person who is licensed in accordance with Code § 16-11-129 or issued a permit pursuant to Code § 43-38-10 when he or she has any weapon legally kept within a vehicle when such vehicle is parked within a school safety zone or is in transit through a designated school safety zone;

(8) A weapon possessed by a license holder which is under the possessor's control in a motor vehicle or which is in a locked compartment of a motor vehicle or one which is in a locked container in or a locked firearms rack which is on a motor vehicle which is being used by an adult over 21 years of age to bring to or pick up a student within a school safety zone, at a school function, or on a bus or other transportation furnished by a school, or when such vehicle is used to transport someone to an activity being conducted within a school safety zone which has been authorized by a duly authorized official or local board of education as provided by paragraph (6) of this subsection; provided, however, that this exception shall not apply to a student attending a public or private elementary or secondary school;

(9) Persons employed in fulfilling defense contracts with the government of the United States or agencies thereof when possession of the weapon is necessary for manufacture, transport, installation, and testing under the requirements of such contract;

(10) Those employees of the State Board of Pardons and Paroles when specifically designated and authorized in writing by the members of the State Board of Pardons and Paroles to carry a weapon;

(11) The Attorney General and those members of his or her staff whom he or she specifically authorizes in writing to carry a weapon;

(12) Community supervision officers employed by and under the authority of the Department of Community Supervision when specifically designated and authorized in writing by the commissioner of community supervision;

(13) Public safety directors of municipal corporations;

(14) State and federal trial and appellate judges;

(15) United States attorneys and assistant United States attorneys;

(16) Clerks of the superior courts;

(17) Teachers and other personnel who are otherwise authorized to possess or carry weapons, provided that any such weapon is in a locked compartment of a motor vehicle or one which is in a locked container in or a locked firearms rack which is on a motor vehicle;

(18) Constables of any county of this state; or

(d) (1) This Code section shall not prohibit any person who resides or works in a business or is in the ordinary course transacting lawful business or any person who is a visitor of such resident located within a school safety zone from carrying, possessing, or having under such person's control a weapon within a school safety zone; provided, however, that it shall be unlawful for any such person to carry, possess, or have under such person's control while at a school building or school function or on school property or a bus or other transportation furnished by a school any weapon or explosive compound, other than fireworks the possession of which is regulated by Chapter 10 of Title 25.

(2) Any person who violates this subsection shall be subject to the penalties specified in subsection (b) of this Code section.

(e) It shall be no defense to a prosecution for a violation of this Code section that:

(1) School was or was not in session at the time of the offense;

(2) The real property was being used for other purposes besides school purposes at the time of the offense; or

(3) The offense took place on a bus or other transportation furnished by a school.

(g) A county school board may adopt regulations requiring the posting of signs designating the areas of school boards and private or public elementary and secondary schools as "Weapon-free and Violence-free School Safety Zones."

(h) Nothing in this Code section shall in any way operate or be construed to affect, repeal, or limit the exemptions provided for under Code § 16-11-130.

§ 16-11-127.2. Weapons on premises of nuclear power facility

(a) Except as provided in subsection (c) of this Code section, it shall be unlawful for any person to carry, possess, or have under such person's control while on the premises of a nuclear power facility a weapon or long gun. Any person who violates this subsection shall be guilty of a misdemeanor.

(b) Any person who violates subsection (a) of this Code section with the intent to do bodily harm on the premises of a nuclear power facility shall be guilty of a felony and, upon conviction thereof, shall be punished by a fine of not more than $10,000, by imprisonment for not less than 2 nor more than 20 years, or both.

(c) This Code section shall not apply to a security officer authorized to carry dangerous weapons pursuant to Code § 16-11-124 who is acting in connection with his or her official duties on the premises of a federally licensed nuclear power facility; nor shall this Code section apply to persons designated in paragraph (2), (3), (4), or (8) of subsection (c) of Code § 16-11-127.1.

(d) Nothing in this Code section shall in any way operate or be construed to affect, repeal, or limit the exemptions provided for under Code § 16-11-130.

§ 16-11-128. Carrying pistol without license. Repealed by Ga. L. 2010, p. 963, § 1-6, effective June 4, 2010.

§ 16-11-129. Weapons carry license; temporary renewal permit; mandamus; verification of license

(a) Application for weapons carry license or renewal license; term. The judge of the probate court of each county shall, on application under oath, on payment of a fee of $30, and on investigation of applicant pursuant to subsections (b) and (d) of this Code section, issue a weapons carry license or renewal license valid for a period of 5 years to any person whose domicile is in that county or who is on active duty with the United States armed forces and who is not a domiciliary of this state but who either resides in that county or on a military reservation located in whole or in part in that county at the time of such application. Such license or renewal license shall authorize that person to carry any weapon in any county of this state notwithstanding any change in that person's county of residence or state of domicile. Applicants shall submit the application for a weapons carry license or renewal license to the judge of the probate court on forms prescribed and furnished free of charge to persons wishing to apply for the license or renewal license. An application shall be considered to be for a renewal license if the applicant has a weapons carry license or renewal license with 90 or fewer days remaining before the expiration of such weapons carry license or renewal license or 30 or fewer days since the expiration of such weapons carry license or renewal license regardless of the county of issuance of the applicant's expired or expiring weapons carry license or renewal license. An applicant who is not a United States citizen shall provide sufficient personal identifying data, including without limitation his or her place of birth and United States issued alien or admission number, as the Georgia Bureau of Investigation may prescribe by rule or regulation. An applicant who is in nonimmigrant status shall provide proof of his or her qualifications for an exception to the federal firearm prohibition pursuant to 18 U.S.C. § 922(y). Forms shall be designed to elicit information from the applicant pertinent to his or her eligibility under this Code section, including citizenship, but shall not require data which is nonpertinent or irrelevant, such as serial numbers or other identification capable of being used as a de facto registration of firearms owned by the applicant. The Department of Public Safety shall furnish application forms and license forms required by this Code section. The forms shall be furnished to each judge of each probate court within this state at no cost.

(b) Licensing exceptions.

(1) As used in this subsection, the term:

(A) "Armed forces" means active duty or a reserve component of the United States Army, United States Navy, United States Marine Corps, United States Coast Guard, United States Air Force, United States National Guard, Georgia Army National Guard, or Georgia Air National Guard.

(B) "Controlled substance" means any drug, substance, or immediate precursor included in the definition of controlled substances in paragraph (4) of Code § 16-13-21.

(C) "Convicted" means an adjudication of guilt. Such term shall not include an order of discharge and exoneration pursuant to Article 3 of Chapter 8 of Title 42.

(D) "Dangerous drug" means any drug defined as such in Code § 16-13-71.

(2) No weapons carry license shall be issued to:

(A) Any person younger than 21 years of age unless he or she:

(i) Is at least 18 years of age;

(ii) Provides proof that he or she has completed basic training in the armed forces of the United States; and

(iii) Provides proof that he or she is actively serving in the armed forces of the United States or has been honorably discharged from such service;

(B) Any person who has been convicted of a felony by a court of this state or any other state; by a court of the United States, including its territories, possessions, and dominions; or by a court of any foreign nation and has not been pardoned for such felony by the President of the United States, the State Board of Pardons and Paroles, or the person or agency empowered to grant pardons under the constitution or laws of such state or nation;

(C) Any person against whom proceedings are pending for any felony;

(D) Any person who is a fugitive from justice;

(E) Any person who is prohibited from possessing or shipping a firearm in interstate commerce pursuant to subsections (g) and (n) of 18 U.S.C. § 922;

(F) Any person who has been convicted of an offense arising out of the unlawful manufacture or distribution of a controlled substance or other dangerous drug;

(G) Any person who has had his or her weapons carry license revoked pursuant to subsection (e) of this Code section within 3 years of the date of his or her application;

(H) Any person who has been convicted of any of the following:

(i) Carrying a weapon without a weapons carry license in violation of Code § 16-11-126; or

(ii) Carrying a weapon or long gun in an unauthorized location in violation of Code § 16-11-127

and has not been free of all restraint or supervision in connection therewith and free of any other conviction for at least 5 years immediately preceding the date of the application;

(I) Any person who has been convicted of any misdemeanor involving the use or possession of a controlled substance and has not been free of all restraint or supervision in connection therewith or free of:

(i) A second conviction of any misdemeanor involving the use or possession of a controlled substance; or

(ii) Any conviction under subparagraphs (E) through (G) of this paragraph

for at least 5 years immediately preceding the date of the application;

(J) Except as provided for in subsection (b.1) of this Code section, any person who has been hospitalized as an inpatient in any mental hospital or alcohol or drug treatment center within the 5 years immediately preceding the application. The judge of the probate court may require any applicant to sign a waiver authorizing any mental hospital or treatment center to inform the judge whether or not the applicant has been an inpatient in any such facility in the last 5 years and authorizing the superintendent of such facility to make to the judge a recommendation regarding whether the applicant is a threat to the safety of others and whether a license to carry a weapon should be issued. When such a waiver is required by the judge, the applicant shall pay a fee of $3 for reimbursement of the cost of making such a report by the mental health hospital, alcohol or drug treatment center, or the Department of Behavioral Health and Developmental Disabilities, which the judge shall remit to the hospital, center, or department. The judge shall keep any such hospitalization or treatment information confidential. It shall be at the discretion of the judge, considering the circumstances surrounding the hospitalization and the recommendation of the superintendent of the hospital or treatment center where the individual was a patient, to issue the weapons carry license or renewal license;

(K) Except as provided for in subsection (b.1) of this Code section, any person who has been adjudicated mentally incompetent to stand trial; or

(L) Except as provided for in subsection (b.1) of this Code section, any person who has been adjudicated not guilty by reason of insanity at the time of the crime pursuant to Part 2 of Article 6 of Chapter 7 of Title 17.

(b.1) Petitions for relief from certain licensing exceptions.

(1) Persons provided for under subparagraphs (b)(2)(J), (b)(2)(K), and (b)(2)(L) of this Code section may petition the court in which such adjudication, hospitalization, or treatment proceedings, if any, under Chapter 3 or 7 of Title 37 occurred for relief. A copy of such petition for relief shall be served as notice upon the opposing civil party or the prosecuting attorney for the state, as the case may be, or their successors, who appeared in the underlying case. Within 30 days of the receipt of such petition, such court shall hold a hearing on such petition for relief. Such prosecuting attorney for the state may represent the interests of the state at such hearing.

(2) At the hearing provided for under paragraph (1) of this subsection, the court shall receive and consider evidence in a closed proceeding concerning:

(A) The circumstances which caused the person to be subject to subparagraph (b)(2)(J), (b)(2)(K), or (b)(2)(L) of this Code section;

(B) The person's mental health and criminal history records, if any. The judge of such court may require any such person to sign a waiver authorizing the superintendent of any mental hospital or treatment center to make to the judge a recommendation regarding whether such person is a threat to the safety of others. When such a waiver is required by the judge, the applicant shall pay a fee of $3 for reimbursement of the cost of making such a report by the mental health hospital, alcohol or drug treatment center, or the Department of Behavioral Health and Developmental Disabilities, which the judge shall remit to the hospital, center, or department;

(C) The person's reputation which shall be established through character witness statements, testimony, or other character evidence; and

(D) Changes in the person's condition or circumstances since such adjudication, hospitalization, or treatment proceedings under Chapter 3 or 7 of Title 37.

The judge shall issue an order of his or her decision no later than 30 days after the hearing.

(3) The court shall grant the petition for relief if such court finds by a preponderance of the evidence that the person will not likely act in a manner dangerous to public safety in carrying a weapon and that granting the relief will not be contrary to the public interest. A record shall be kept of the hearing; provided, however, that such records shall remain confidential and be disclosed only to a court or to the parties in the event of an appeal. Any appeal of the court's ruling on the petition for relief shall be de novo review.

(4) If the court grants such person's petition for relief, the applicable subparagraph (b)(2)(J), (b)(2)(K), or (b)(2)(L) of this Code section shall not apply to such person in his or her application for a weapons carry license or renewal; provided, however, that such person shall comply with all other requirements for the issuance of a weapons carry license or renewal license. The clerk of such court shall report such order to the Georgia Crime Information Center immediately, but in no case later than 10 business days after the date of such order.

(5) A person may petition for relief under this subsection not more than once every 2 years. In the case of a person who has been hospitalized as an inpatient, such person shall not petition for relief prior to being discharged from such treatment.

(c) Fingerprinting. Following completion of the application for a weapons carry license, the judge of the probate court shall require the applicant to proceed to an appropriate law enforcement agency in the county or to any vendor approved by the Georgia Bureau of Investigation for fingerprint submission services with the completed application so that such agency or vendor can capture the fingerprints of the applicant. The law enforcement agency shall be entitled to a fee of $5 from the applicant for its services in connection with fingerprinting and processing of an application. Fingerprinting shall not be required for applicants seeking temporary renewal licenses or renewal licenses.

(d) Investigation of applicant; issuance of weapons carry license; renewal.

(1) (A) For weapons carry license applications, the judge of the probate court shall within 5 business days following the receipt of the application or request direct the law enforcement agency to request a fingerprint based criminal history records check from the Georgia Crime Information Center and Federal Bureau of Investigation for purposes of determining the suitability of the applicant and return an appropriate report to the judge of the probate court. Fingerprints shall be in such form and of such quality as prescribed by the Georgia Crime Information Center and under standards adopted by the Federal Bureau of Investigation. The Georgia Bureau of Investigation may charge such fee as is necessary to cover the cost of the records search.

(B) For requests for license renewals, the presentation of a weapons carry license issued by any probate judge in this state shall be evidence to the judge of the probate court to whom a request for license renewal is made that the fingerprints of the weapons carry license holder are on file with the judge of the probate court who issued the weapons carry license, and the judge of the probate court to whom a request for license renewal is made shall, within 5 business days following the receipt of the request, direct the law enforcement agency to request a nonfingerprint based criminal history records check from the Georgia Crime Information Center and Federal Bureau of Investigation for purposes of determining the suitability of the applicant and return an appropriate report to the judge of the probate court to whom a request for license renewal is made.

(2) For both weapons carry license applications and requests for license renewals, the judge of the probate court shall within 5 business days following the receipt of the application or request also direct the law enforcement agency, in the same manner as provided for in subparagraph (B) of paragraph (1) of this subsection, to conduct a background check using the Federal Bureau of Investigation's National Instant Criminal Background Check System and return an appropriate report to the probate judge.

(3) When a person who is not a United States citizen applies for a weapons carry license or renewal of a license under this Code section, the judge of the probate court shall direct the law enforcement agency to conduct a search of the records maintained by United States Immigration and Customs Enforcement and return an appropriate report to the probate judge. As a condition to the issuance of a license or the renewal of a license, an applicant who is in nonimmigrant status shall provide proof of his or her qualifications for an exception to the federal firearm prohibition pursuant to 18 U.S.C. § 922(y).

(4) The law enforcement agency shall report to the judge of the probate court within 30 days, by telephone and in writing, of any findings relating to the applicant which may bear on his or her eligibility for a weapons carry license or renewal license under the terms of this Code section. When no derogatory information is found on the applicant bearing on his or her eligibility to obtain a license or renewal license, a report shall not be required. The law enforcement agency shall return the application directly to the judge of the probate court within such time period. Not later than 10 days after the judge of the probate court receives the report from the law enforcement agency concerning the suitability of the applicant for a license, the judge of the probate court shall issue such applicant a license or renewal license to carry any weapon unless facts establishing ineligibility have been reported or unless the judge determines such applicant has not met all the qualifications, is not of good moral character, or has failed to comply with any of the requirements contained in this Code section. The judge of the probate court shall date stamp the report from the law enforcement agency to show the date on which the report was received by the judge of the probate court.

(e) Revocation, loss, or damage to license.

(1) If, at any time during the period for which the weapons carry license was issued, the judge of the probate court of the county in which the license was issued shall learn or have brought to his or her attention in any manner any reasonable ground to believe the licensee is not eligible to retain the license, the judge may, after notice and hearing, revoke the license of the person upon a finding that such person is not eligible for a weapons carry license pursuant to subsection (b) of this Code section or an adjudication of falsification of application, mental incompetency, or chronic alcohol or narcotic usage. The judge of the probate court shall report such revocation to the Georgia Crime Information Center immediately but in no case later than 10 days after such revocation. It shall be unlawful for any person to possess a license which has been revoked pursuant to this paragraph, and any person found in possession of any such revoked license, except in the performance of his or her official duties, shall be guilty of a misdemeanor.

(2) If a person is convicted of any crime or involved in any matter which would make the maintenance of a weapons carry license by such person unlawful pursuant to subsection (b) of this Code section, the judge of the superior court or state court hearing such case or presiding over such matter shall inquire whether such person is the holder of a weapons carry license. If such person is the holder of a weapons carry license, then the judge of the superior court or state court shall inquire of such person the county of the probate court which issued such weapons carry license, or if such person has ever had his or her weapons carry license renewed, then of the county of the probate court which most recently issued such person a renewal license. The judge of the superior court or state court shall notify the judge of the probate court of such county of the matter which makes the maintenance of a weapons carry license by such person to be unlawful pursuant to subsection (b) of this Code section. The Council of Superior Court Judges of Georgia and The Council of State Court Judges of Georgia shall provide by rule for the procedures which judges of the superior court and the judges of the state courts, respectively, are to follow for the purposes of this paragraph.

(3) Loss of any license issued in accordance with this Code section or damage to the license in any manner which shall render it illegible shall be reported to the judge of the probate court of the county in which it was issued within 48 hours of the time the loss or damage becomes known to the license holder. The judge of the probate court shall thereupon issue a replacement for and shall take custody of and destroy a damaged license; and in any case in which a license has been lost, he or she shall issue a cancellation order. The judge shall charge the fee specified in subsection (k) of Code § 15-9-60 for such services.

(f) (1) Weapons carry license specifications. Weapons carry licenses issued prior to January 1, 2012, shall be in the format specified by the former provisions of this paragraph as they existed on June 30, 2013.

(2) On and after January 1, 2012, newly issued or renewal weapons carry licenses shall incorporate overt and covert security features which shall be blended with the personal data printed on the license to form a significant barrier to imitation, replication, and duplication. There shall be a minimum of 3 different ultraviolet colors used to enhance the security of the license incorporating variable data, color shifting characteristics, and front edge only perimeter visibility. The weapons carry license shall have a color photograph viewable under ambient light on both the front and back of the license. The license shall incorporate custom optical variable devices featuring the great seal of the State of Georgia as well as matching demetalized optical variable devices viewable under ambient light from the front and back of the license incorporating microtext and unique alphanumeric serialization specific to the license holder. The license shall be of similar material, size, and thickness of a credit card and have a holographic laminate to secure and protect the license for the duration of the license period.

(3) Using the physical characteristics of the license set forth in paragraph (2) of this subsection, The Council of Probate Court Judges of Georgia shall create specifications for the probate courts so that all weapons carry licenses in this state shall be uniform and so that probate courts can petition the Department of Administrative Services to purchase the equipment and supplies necessary for producing such licenses. The department shall follow the competitive bidding procedure set forth in Code § 50-5-102.

(g) Alteration or counterfeiting of license; penalty. A person who deliberately alters or counterfeits a weapons carry license or who possesses an altered or counterfeit weapons carry license with the intent to misrepresent any information contained in such license shall be guilty of a felony and, upon conviction thereof, shall be punished by imprisonment for a period of not less than 1 nor more than 5 years.

(h) Licenses for former law enforcement officers. Except as otherwise provided in Code § 16-11-130, any person who has served as a law enforcement officer for at least ten of the 12 years immediately preceding the retirement of such person as a law enforcement officer shall be entitled to be issued a weapons carry license as provided for in this Code section without the payment of any of the fees provided for in this Code section. Such person shall comply with all the other provisions of this Code section relative to the issuance of such licenses. As used in this subsection, the term "law enforcement officer" means any peace officer who is employed by the United States government or by the State of Georgia or any political subdivision thereof and who is required by the terms of his or her employment, whether by election or appointment, to give his or her full time to the preservation of public order or the protection of life and property or the prevention of crime. Such term shall include conservation rangers.

(i) Temporary renewal licenses.

(1) Any person who holds a weapons carry license under this Code section may, at the time he or she applies for a renewal of the license, also apply for a temporary renewal license if less than 90 days remain before expiration of the license he or she then holds or if the previous license has expired within the last 30 days.

(2) Unless the judge of the probate court knows or is made aware of any fact which would make the applicant ineligible for a 5-year renewal license, the judge shall at the time of application issue a temporary renewal license to the applicant.

(3) Such a temporary renewal license shall be in the form of a paper receipt indicating the date on which the court received the renewal application and shall show the name, address, sex, age, and race of the applicant and that the temporary renewal license expires 90 days from the date of issue.

(4) During its period of validity the temporary renewal license, if carried on or about the holder's person together with the holder's previous license, shall be valid in the same manner and for the same purposes as a 5-year license.

(5) A $1 fee shall be charged by the probate court for issuance of a temporary renewal license.

(6) A temporary renewal license may be revoked in the same manner as a 5-year license.

(j) Applicant may seek relief. When an eligible applicant fails to receive a license, temporary renewal license, or renewal license within the time period required by this Code section and the application or request has been properly filed, the applicant may bring an action in mandamus or other legal proceeding in order to obtain a license, temporary renewal license, or renewal license. When an applicant is otherwise denied a license, temporary renewal license, or renewal license and contends that he or she is qualified to be issued a license, temporary renewal license, or renewal license, the applicant may bring an action in mandamus or other legal proceeding in order to obtain such license. Additionally, the applicant may request a hearing before the judge of the probate court relative to the applicant's fitness to be issued such license. Upon the issuance of a denial, the judge of the probate court shall inform the applicant of his or her rights pursuant to this subsection. If such applicant is the prevailing party, he or she shall be entitled to recover his or her costs in such action, including reasonable attorney's fees.

(k) Data base prohibition. A person or entity shall not create or maintain a multijurisdictional data base of information regarding persons issued weapons carry licenses.

(l) Verification of license. The judge of a probate court or his or her designee shall be authorized to verify the legitimacy and validity of a weapons carry license of a license holder pursuant to a subpoena or court order, for public safety purposes to law enforcement agencies pursuant to paragraph (40) of subsection (a) of Code § 50-18-72, and for licensing to a judge of a probate court or his or her designee pursuant to paragraph (40) of subsection (a) of Code § 50-18-72; provided, however, that the judge of a probate court or his or her designee shall not be authorized to provide any further information regarding license holders

§ 16-11-130. Exemptions from Code Sections 16-11-126 through 16-11-127.2

(a) Code §§ 16-11-126 through 16-11-127.2 shall not apply to or affect any of the following persons if such persons are employed in the offices listed below or when authorized by federal or state law, regulations, or order:

(1) Peace officers, as such term is defined in paragraph (11) of Code § 16-1-3, and retired peace officers so long as they remain certified whether employed by the state or a political subdivision of the state or another state or a political subdivision of another state but only if such other state provides a similar privilege for the peace officers of this state;

(2) Wardens, superintendents, and keepers of correctional institutions, jails, or other institutions for the detention of persons accused or convicted of an offense;

(3) Persons in the military service of the state or of the United States;

(4) Persons employed in fulfilling defense contracts with the government of the United States or agencies thereof when possession of the weapon or long gun is necessary for manufacture, transport, installation, and testing under the requirements of such contract;

(5) District attorneys, investigators employed by and assigned to a district attorney's office, assistant district attorneys, attorneys or investigators employed by the Prosecuting Attorneys' Council of the State of Georgia, and any retired district attorney, assistant district attorney, district attorney's investigator, or attorney or investigator retired from the Prosecuting Attorneys' Council of the State of Georgia, if such employee is retired in good standing and is receiving benefits under Title 47 or is retired in good standing and receiving benefits from a county or municipal retirement system;

(6) State court solicitors-general; investigators employed by and assigned to a state court solicitor-general's office; assistant state court solicitors-general; the corresponding personnel of any city court expressly continued in existence as a city court pursuant to Article VI, § X, Paragraph I, subparagraph (5) of the Constitution; and the corresponding personnel of any civil court expressly continued as a civil court pursuant to said provision of the Constitution;

(7) Those employees of the State Board of Pardons and Paroles when specifically designated and authorized in writing by the members of the State Board of Pardons and Paroles to carry a weapon or long gun;

(8) The Attorney General and those members of his or her staff whom he or she specifically authorizes in writing to carry a weapon or long gun;

(9) Community supervision officers employed by and under the authority of the Department of Community Supervision when specifically designated and authorized in writing by the commissioner of community supervision;

(10) Public safety directors of municipal corporations;

(11) Explosive ordnance disposal technicians, as such term is defined by Code § 16-7-80, and persons certified as provided in Code § 35-8-13 to handle animals trained to detect explosives, while in the performance of their duties;

(12) Federal judges, Justices of the Supreme Court, Judges of the Court of Appeals, judges of superior, state, probate, juvenile, and magistrate courts, full-time judges of municipal and city courts, permanent part-time judges of municipal and city courts, and administrative law judges;

(12.1) Former federal judges, Justices of the Supreme Court, Judges of the Court of Appeals, judges of superior, state, probate, juvenile, and magistrate courts, full-time judges of municipal and city courts, permanent part-time judges of municipal courts, and administrative law judges who are retired from their respective offices, provided that such judge or Justice would otherwise be qualified to be issued a weapons carry license;

(12.2) Former federal judges, Justices of the Supreme Court, Judges of the Court of Appeals, judges of superior, state, probate, juvenile, and magistrate courts, full-time judges of municipal and city courts, permanent part-time judges of municipal courts, and administrative law judges who are no longer serving in their respective office, provided that he or she served as such judge or Justice for more than 24 months; and provided, further, that such judge or Justice would otherwise be qualified to be issued a weapons carry license;

(13) United States Attorneys and Assistant United States Attorneys;

(14) County medical examiners and coroners and their sworn officers employed by county government;

(15) Clerks of the superior courts; and

(16) Constables employed by a magistrate court of this state.

(b) Code §§ 16-11-126 through 16-11-127.2 shall not apply to or affect persons who at the time of their retirement from service with the Department of Community Supervision were community supervision officers, when specifically designated and authorized in writing by the commissioner of community supervision.

(c) Code §§ 16-11-126 through 16-11-127.2 shall not apply to or affect any:

(1) Sheriff, retired sheriff, deputy sheriff, or retired deputy sheriff if such retired sheriff or deputy sheriff is eligible to receive or is receiving benefits under the Peace Officers' Annuity and Benefit Fund provided under Chapter 17 of Title 47, the Sheriffs' Retirement Fund of Georgia provided under Chapter 16 of Title 47, or any other public retirement system established under the laws of this state for service as a law enforcement officer;

(2) Member of the Georgia State Patrol or agent of the Georgia Bureau of Investigation or retired member of the Georgia State Patrol or agent of the Georgia Bureau of Investigation if such retired member or agent is receiving benefits under the Employees' Retirement System;

(3) Full-time law enforcement chief executive engaging in the management of a county, municipal, state, state authority, or federal law enforcement agency in the State of Georgia, including any college or university law enforcement chief executive that is registered or certified by the Georgia Peace Officer Standards and Training Council; or retired law enforcement chief executive that formerly managed a county, municipal, state, state authority, or federal law enforcement agency in the State of Georgia, including any college or university law enforcement chief executive that was registered or certified at the time of his or her retirement by the Georgia Peace Officer Standards and Training Council, if such retired law enforcement chief executive is receiving benefits under the Peace Officers' Annuity and Benefit Fund provided under Chapter 17 of Title 47 or is retired in good standing and receiving benefits from a county, municipal, State of Georgia, state authority, or federal retirement system; or

(4) Police officer of any county, municipal, state, state authority, or federal law enforcement agency in the State of Georgia, including any college or university police officer that is registered or certified by the Georgia Peace Officer Standards and Training Council, or retired police officer of any county, municipal, state, state authority, or federal law enforcement agency in the State of Georgia, including any college or university police officer that was registered or certified at the time of his or her retirement by the Georgia Peace Officer Standards and Training Council, if such retired employee is receiving benefits under the Peace Officers' Annuity and Benefit Fund provided under Chapter 17 of Title 47 or is retired in good standing and receiving benefits from a county, municipal, State of Georgia, state authority, or federal retirement system.

In addition, any such sheriff, retired sheriff, deputy sheriff, retired deputy sheriff, active or retired law enforcement chief executive, or other law enforcement officer referred to in this subsection shall be authorized to carry a handgun on or off duty anywhere within the state and the provisions of Code §§ 16-11-126 through 16-11-127.2 shall not apply to the carrying of such firearms.

(d) A prosecution based upon a violation of Code § 16-11-126 or 16-11-127 need not negative any exemptions.

§ 16-11-130.1. Allowing personnel to carry weapons within certain school safety zones and at school functions

(a) As used in this Code section, the term:

(1) "Bus or other transportation furnished by a school" means a bus or other transportation furnished by a public or private elementary or secondary school.

(2) "School function" means a school function or related activity that occurs outside of a school safety zone for a public or private elementary or secondary school.

(3) "School safety zone" means in or on any real property or building owned by or leased to any public or private elementary or secondary school or local board of education and used for elementary or secondary education.

(4) "Weapon" shall have the same meaning as set forth in Code § 16-11-127.1.

(b) This Code section shall not be construed to require or otherwise mandate that any local board of education or school administrator adopt or implement a practice or program for the approval of personnel to possess or carry weapons within a school safety zone, at a school function, or on a bus or other transportation furnished by a school nor shall this Code section create any liability for adopting or declining to adopt such practice or program. Such decision shall rest with each individual local board of education. If a local board of education adopts a policy to allow certain personnel to possess or carry weapons as provided in paragraph (6) of subsection (c) of Code § 16-11-127.1, such policy shall include approval of personnel to possess or carry weapons and provide for:

(1) Training of approved personnel prior to authorizing such personnel to carry weapons. The training shall at a minimum include training on judgment pistol shooting, marksmanship, and a review of current laws relating to the use of force for the defense of self and others; provided, however, that the local board of education training policy may substitute for certain training requirements the personnel's prior military or law enforcement service if the approved personnel has previously served as a certified law enforcement officer or has had military service which involved similar weapons training;

(2) An approved list of the types of weapons and ammunition and the quantity of weapons and ammunition authorized to be possessed or carried;

(3) The exclusion from approval of any personnel who has had an employment or other history indicating any type of mental or emotional instability as determined by the local board of education; and

(4) A mandatory method of securing weapons which shall include at a minimum a requirement that the weapon, if permitted to be carried concealed by personnel, shall be carried on the person and not in a purse, briefcase, bag, or similar other accessory which is not secured on the body of the person and, if maintained separate from the person, shall be maintained in a secured lock safe or similar lock box that cannot be easily accessed by students.

(c) Any personnel selected to possess or carry weapons within a school safety zone, at a school function, or on a bus or other transportation furnished by a school shall be a license holder, and the local board of education shall be responsible for conducting a criminal history background check of such personnel annually to determine whether such personnel remains qualified to be a license holder.

(d) The selection of approved personnel to possess or carry a weapon within a school safety zone, at a school function, or on a bus or other transportation furnished by a school shall be done strictly on a voluntary basis. No personnel shall be required to possess or carry a weapon within a school safety zone, at a school function, or on a bus or other transportation furnished by a school and shall not be terminated or otherwise retaliated against for refusing to possess or carry a weapon.

(e) The local board of education shall be responsible for any costs associated with approving personnel to carry or possess weapons within a school safety zone, at a school function, or on a bus or other transportation furnished by a school; provided, however, that nothing contained in this Code section shall prohibit any approved personnel from paying for part or all of such costs or using any other funding mechanism available, including donations or grants from private persons or entities.

(f) Documents and meetings pertaining to personnel approved to carry or possess weapons within a school safety zone, at a school function, or on a bus or other transportation furnished by a school shall be considered employment and public safety security records and shall be exempt from disclosure under Article 4 of Chapter 18 of Title 50.

§ 16-11-130.2. Carrying a weapon or long gun at a commercial service airport

(a) No person shall enter the restricted access area of a commercial service airport, in or beyond the airport security screening checkpoint, knowingly possessing or knowingly having under his or her control a weapon or long gun. Such area shall not include an airport drive, general parking area, walkway, or shops and areas of the terminal that are outside the screening checkpoint and that are normally open to unscreened passengers or visitors to the airport. Any restricted access area shall be clearly indicated by prominent signs indicating that weapons are prohibited in such area.

(b) A person who is not a license holder and who violates this Code section shall be guilty of a misdemeanor. A license holder who violates this Code section shall be guilty of a misdemeanor; provided, however, that a license holder who is notified at the screening checkpoint for the restricted access area that he or she is in possession of a weapon or long gun and who immediately leaves the restricted access area following such notification and completion of federally required transportation security screening procedures shall not be guilty of violating this Code section.

(c) Any person who violates this Code section with the intent to commit a separate felony offense shall be guilty of a felony and, upon conviction thereof, shall be punished by a fine of not less than $1,000 nor more than $15,000, imprisonment for not less than 1 nor more than 10 years, or both.

(d) Any ordinance, resolution, regulation, or policy of any county, municipality, or other political subdivision of this state which is in conflict with this Code section shall be null, void, and of no force and effect, and this Code section shall preempt any such ordinance, resolution, regulation, or policy.

§ 16-11-131. Possession of firearms by convicted felons and first offender probationers

(a) As used in this Code section, the term:

 (1) "Felony" means any offense punishable by imprisonment for a term of 1 year or more and includes conviction by a court-martial under the Uniform Code of Military Justice for an offense which would constitute a felony under the laws of the United States.

 (2) "Firearm" includes any handgun, rifle, shotgun, or other weapon which will or can be converted to expel a projectile by the action of an explosive or electrical charge.

(b) Any person who is on probation as a felony first offender pursuant to Article 3 of Chapter 8 of Title 42 or who has been convicted of a felony by a court of this state or any other state; by a court of the United States including its territories, possessions, and dominions; or by a court of any foreign nation and who receives, possesses, or transports any firearm commits a felony and, upon conviction thereof, shall be imprisoned for not less than 1 nor more than 5 years; provided, however, that if the felony as to which the person is on probation or has been previously convicted is a forcible felony, then upon conviction of receiving, possessing, or transporting a firearm, such person shall be imprisoned for a period of 5 years.

(b.1) Any person who is prohibited by this Code section from possessing a firearm because of conviction of a forcible felony or because of being on probation as a first offender for a forcible felony pursuant to this Code section and who attempts to purchase or obtain transfer of a firearm shall be guilty of a felony and shall be punished by imprisonment for not less than 1 nor more than 5 years.

(c) This Code section shall not apply to any person who has been pardoned for the felony by the President of the United States, the State Board of Pardons and Paroles, or the person or agency empowered to grant pardons under the constitutions or laws of the several states or of a foreign nation and, by the terms of the pardon, has expressly been authorized to receive, possess, or transport a firearm.

(d) A person who has been convicted of a felony, but who has been granted relief from the disabilities imposed by the laws of the United States with respect to the acquisition, receipt, transfer, shipment, or possession of firearms by the secretary of the United States Department of the Treasury pursuant to 18 U.S.C. § 925, shall, upon presenting to the Board of Public Safety proof that the relief has been granted and it being established from proof submitted by the applicant to the satisfaction of the Board of Public Safety that the circumstances regarding the conviction and the applicant's record and reputation are such that the acquisition, receipt, transfer, shipment, or possession of firearms by the person would not present a threat to the safety of the citizens of Georgia and that the granting of the relief sought would not be contrary to the public interest, be granted relief from the disabilities imposed by this Code section. A person who has been convicted under federal or state law of a felony pertaining to antitrust violations, unfair trade practices, or restraint of trade shall, upon presenting to the Board of Public Safety proof, and it being established from said proof, submitted by the applicant to the satisfaction of the Board of Public Safety that the circumstances regarding the conviction and the applicant's record and reputation are such that the acquisition, receipt, transfer, shipment, or possession of firearms by the person would not present a threat to the safety of the citizens of Georgia and that the granting of the relief sought would not be contrary to the public interest, be granted relief from the disabilities imposed by this Code section. A record that the relief has been granted by the board shall be entered upon the criminal history of the person maintained by the Georgia Crime Information Center and the board shall maintain a list of the names of such persons which shall be open for public inspection.

(e) As used in this Code section, the term "forcible felony" means any felony which involves the use or threat of physical force or violence against any person and further includes, without limitation, murder; murder in the second degree; burglary in any degree; robbery; armed robbery; home invasion in any degree; kidnapping; hijacking of an aircraft or motor vehicle; aggravated stalking; rape; aggravated child molestation; aggravated sexual battery; arson in the first degree; the manufacturing, transporting, distribution, or possession of explosives with intent to kill, injure, or intimidate individuals or destroy a public building; terroristic threats; or acts of treason or insurrection.

(f) Any person placed on probation as a first offender pursuant to Article 3 of Chapter 8 of Title 42 and subsequently discharged without court adjudication of guilt as a matter of law pursuant to Code § 42-8-60 shall, upon such discharge, be relieved from the disabilities imposed by this Code section.

§ 16-11-132. Possession of handgun by person under the age of 18 years

(a) For the purposes of this Code section, a handgun is considered loaded if there is a cartridge in the chamber or cylinder of the handgun.

(b) Notwithstanding any other provisions of this part and except as otherwise provided in this Code section, it shall be unlawful for any person under the age of 18 years to possess or have under such person's control a handgun. A person convicted of a first violation of this subsection shall be guilty of a misdemeanor and shall be punished by a fine not to exceed $1,000 or by imprisonment for not more than 12 months, or both. A person convicted of a second or subsequent violation of this subsection shall be guilty of a felony and shall be punished by a fine of $5,000 or by imprisonment for a period of 3 years, or both.

(c) Except as otherwise provided in subsection (d) of this Code section, the provisions of subsection (b) of this Code section shall not apply to:

(1) Any person under the age of 18 years who is:

    (A) Attending a hunter education course or a firearms safety course;

    (B) Engaging in practice in the use of a firearm or target shooting at an established range authorized by the governing body of the jurisdiction where such range is located;

    (C) Engaging in an organized competition involving the use of a firearm or participating in or practicing for a performance by an organized group under 26 U.S.C. § 501(c)(3) which uses firearms as a part of such performance;

    (D) Hunting or fishing pursuant to a valid license if such person has in his or her possession such a valid hunting or fishing license if required; is engaged in legal hunting or fishing; has permission of the owner of the land on which the activities are being conducted; and the handgun, whenever loaded, is carried only in an open and fully exposed manner; or

    (E) Traveling to or from any activity described in subparagraphs (A) through (D) of this paragraph if the handgun in such person's possession is not loaded;

    (2) Any person under the age of 18 years who is on real property under the control of such person's parent, legal guardian, or grandparent and who has the permission of such person's parent or legal guardian to possess a handgun; or

    (3) Any person under the age of 18 years who is at such person's residence and who, with the permission of such person's parent or legal guardian, possesses a handgun for the purpose of exercising the rights authorized in Code § 16-3-21 or 16-3-23.

(d) Subsection (c) of this Code section shall not apply to any person under the age of 18 years who has been convicted of a forcible felony or forcible misdemeanor, as defined in Code § 16-1-3, or who has been adjudicated for committing a delinquent act under the provisions of Article 6 of Chapter 11 of Title 15 for an offense which would constitute a forcible felony or forcible misdemeanor, as defined in Code § 16-1-3, if such person were an adult.

§ 16-11-133. Minimum periods of confinement for persons convicted who have prior convictions

(a) As used in this Code section, the term:

    (1) "Felony" means any offense punishable by imprisonment for a term of 1 year or more and includes conviction by a court-martial under the Uniform Code of Military Justice for an offense which would constitute a felony under the laws of the United States.

    (2) "Firearm" includes any handgun, rifle, shotgun, stun gun, taser, or other weapon which will or can be converted to expel a projectile by the action of an explosive or electrical charge.

(b) Any person who has previously been convicted of or who has previously entered a guilty plea to the offense of murder, murder in the second degree, armed robbery, home invasion in any degree, kidnapping, rape, aggravated child molestation, aggravated sodomy, aggravated sexual battery, or any felony involving the use or possession of a firearm and who shall have on or within arm's reach of his or her person a firearm during the commission of, or the attempt to commit:

    (1) Any crime against or involving the person of another;

    (2) The unlawful entry into a building or vehicle;

    (3) A theft from a building or theft of a vehicle;

    (4) Any crime involving the possession, manufacture, delivery, distribution, dispensing, administering, selling, or possession with intent to distribute any controlled substance as provided in Code § 16-13-30; or

    (5) Any crime involving the trafficking of cocaine, marijuana, or illegal drugs as provided in Code § 16-13-31, and which crime is a felony, commits a felony and, upon conviction thereof, shall be punished by confinement for a period of 15 years, such sentence to run consecutively to any other sentence which the person has received.

(c) Upon the second or subsequent conviction of a convicted felon under this Code section, such convicted felon shall be punished by confinement for life. Notwithstanding any other law to the contrary, the sentence of any convicted felon which is imposed for violating this Code section a second or subsequent time shall not be suspended by the court and probationary sentence imposed in lieu thereof.

(d) Any crime committed in violation of subsections (b) and (c) of this Code section shall be considered a separate offense.

§ 16-11-134. Discharging firearm while under the influence of alcohol or drugs

(a) It shall be unlawful for any person to discharge a firearm while:

    (1) Under the influence of alcohol or any drug or any combination of alcohol and any drug to the extent that it is unsafe for the person to discharge such firearm except in the defense of life, health, and property;

    (2) The person's alcohol concentration is 0.08 grams or more at any time while discharging such firearm or within 3 hours after such discharge of such firearm from alcohol consumed before such discharge ended; or

    (3) Subject to the provisions of subsection (b) of this Code section, there is any amount of marijuana or a controlled substance, as defined in Code § 16-13-21, present in the person's blood or urine, or both, including the metabolites and derivatives of each or both without regard to whether or not any alcohol is present in the person's breath or blood.

(b) The fact that any person charged with violating this Code section is or has been legally entitled to use a drug shall not constitute a defense against any charge of violating this Code section; provided, however, that such person shall not be in violation of this Code section unless such person is rendered incapable of possessing or discharging a firearm safely as a result of using a drug other than alcohol which such person is legally entitled to use.

(c) Any person convicted of violating subsection (a) of this Code section shall be guilty of a misdemeanor of a high and aggravated nature.

§ 16-11-137. Required possession of weapons carry license or proof of exemption when carrying a weapon; detention for investigation of carrying permit

(a) Every license holder shall have his or her valid weapons carry license in his or her immediate possession at all times when carrying a weapon, or if such person is exempt from having a weapons carry license pursuant to Code § 16-11-130 or subsection (c) of Code § 16-11-127.1, he or she shall have proof of his or her exemption in his or her immediate possession at all times when carrying a weapon, and his or her failure to do so shall be prima-facie evidence of a violation of the applicable provision of Code §§ 16-11-126 through 16-11-127.2.

(b) A person carrying a weapon shall not be subject to detention for the sole purpose of investigating whether such person has a weapons carry license.

(c) A person convicted of a violation of this Code section shall be fined not more than $10 if he or she produces in court his or her weapons carry license, provided that it was valid at the time of his or her arrest, or produces proof of his or her exemption.

§ 16-11-138. Defense of self or others as absolute defense. Defense of self or others, as contemplated by and provided for under Article 2 of Chapter 3 of this title, shall be an absolute defense to any violation under this part.

Part 5. Brady Law Regulations

§ 16-11-171. Definitions. As used in this part, the term:

(1) "Center" means the Georgia Crime Information Center within the Georgia Bureau of Investigation.

(2) "Dealer" means any person licensed as a dealer pursuant to 18 U.S.C. § 921, et seq.

(3) "Firearm" means any weapon that is designed to or may readily be converted to expel a projectile by the action of an explosive or the frame or receiver of any such weapon, any firearm muffler or firearm silencer, or any destructive device as defined in 18 U.S.C. § 921(a)(3).

(4) "Involuntarily hospitalized" means hospitalized as an inpatient in any mental health facility pursuant to Code § 37-3-81 or hospitalized as an inpatient in any mental health facility as a result of being adjudicated mentally incompetent to stand trial or being adjudicated not guilty by reason of insanity at the time of the crime pursuant to Part 2 of Article 6 of Title 17.

(5) "NICS" means the National Instant Criminal Background Check System created by the federal "Brady Handgun Violence Prevention Act" (P. L. No. 103-159).

§ 16-11-172. Transfers or purchases of firearms subject to the NICS; information concerning persons who have been involuntarily hospitalized to be forwarded to the FBI; penalties for breach of confidentiality; exceptions

(a) All transfers or purchases of firearms conducted by a licensed importer, licensed manufacturer, or licensed dealer shall be subject to the NICS. To the extent possible, the center shall provide to the NICS all necessary criminal history information and wanted person records in order to complete an NICS check.

(b) The center shall forward to the Federal Bureau of Investigation information concerning persons who have been involuntarily hospitalized as defined in this part for the purpose of completing an NICS check.

(c) Any government official who willfully or intentionally compromises the identity, confidentiality, and security of any records and data pursuant to this part shall be guilty of a felony and fined no less than $5,000 and shall be subject to automatic dismissal from his or her employment.

(d) The provisions of this part shall not apply to:

　(1) Any firearm, including any handgun with a matchlock, flintlock, percussion cap, or similar type of ignition system, manufactured in or before 1898;

　(2) Any replica of any firearm described in paragraph (1) of this subsection if such replica is not designed or redesigned to use rimfire or conventional center-fire fixed ammunition or uses rimfire or conventional center-fire fixed ammunition which is no longer manufactured in the United States and which is not readily available in the ordinary channels of commercial trade; and

　(3) Any firearm which is a curio or relic as defined by 27 CFR 178.11.

§ 16-11-173. Legislative findings; preemption of local regulation and lawsuits; exceptions

(a) (1) It is declared by the General Assembly that the regulation of firearms and other weapons is properly an issue of general, state-wide concern.

　(2) The General Assembly further declares that the lawful design, marketing, manufacture, and sale of firearms and ammunition and other weapons to the public is not unreasonably dangerous activity and does not constitute a nuisance per se.

(b) (1) Except as provided in subsection (c) of this Code section, no county or municipal corporation, by zoning, by ordinance or resolution, or by any other means, nor any agency, board, department, commission, political subdivision, school district, or authority of this state, other than the General Assembly, by rule or regulation or by any other means shall regulate in any manner:

　(A) Gun shows;

(B) The possession, ownership, transport, carrying, transfer, sale, purchase, licensing, or registration of firearms or other weapons or components of firearms or other weapons;

(C) Firearms dealers or dealers of other weapons; or

(D) Dealers in components of firearms or other weapons.

(2) The authority to bring suit and right to recover against any weapons, firearms, or ammunition manufacturer, trade association, or dealer by or on behalf of any governmental unit created by or pursuant to an Act of the General Assembly or the Constitution, or any department, agency, or authority thereof, for damages, abatement, or injunctive relief resulting from or relating to the lawful design, manufacture, marketing, or sale of weapons, firearms, or ammunition to the public shall be reserved exclusively to the state. This paragraph shall not prohibit a political subdivision or local government authority from bringing an action against a weapons, firearms, or ammunition manufacturer or dealer for breach of contract or express warranty as to weapons, firearms, or ammunition purchased by the political subdivision or local government authority.

(c) (1) A county or municipal corporation may regulate the transport, carrying, or possession of firearms by employees of the local unit of government, or by unpaid volunteers of such local unit of government, in the course of their employment or volunteer functions with such local unit of government; provided, however, that the sheriff or chief of police shall be solely responsible for regulating and determining the possession, carrying, and transportation of firearms and other weapons by employees under his or her respective supervision so long as such regulations comport with state and federal law.

(2) The commanding officer of any law enforcement agency shall regulate and determine the possession, carrying, and transportation of firearms and other weapons by employees under his or her supervision so long as such regulations comport with state and federal law.

(3) The district attorney, and the solicitor-general in counties where there is a state court, shall regulate and determine the possession, carrying, and transportation of firearms and other weapons by county employees under his or her supervision so long as such regulations comport with state and federal law.

(d) Nothing contained in this Code section shall prohibit municipalities or counties, by ordinance or resolution, from requiring the ownership of guns by heads of households within the political subdivision.

(e) Nothing contained in this Code section shall prohibit municipalities or counties, by ordinance or resolution, from reasonably limiting or prohibiting the discharge of firearms within the boundaries of the municipal corporation or county.

(f) As used in this Code section, the term "weapon" means any device designed or intended to be used, or capable of being used, for offense or defense, including but not limited to firearms, bladed devices, clubs, electric stun devices, and defense sprays.

(g) Any person aggrieved as a result of a violation of this Code section may bring an action against the person who caused such aggrievement. The aggrieved person shall be entitled to reasonable attorney's fees and expenses of litigation and may recover or obtain against the person who caused such damages any of the following:

(1) Actual damages or $100, whichever is greater;

(2) Equitable relief, including, but not limited to, an injunction or restitution of money and property; and

(3) Any other relief which the court deems proper.

TITLE 43. Professions and Businesses
Chapter 16. Firearms Dealers

§§ 43-16-1 through 43-16-12. Repealed by Ga. L. 2014, p. 599, § 1-14/HB 60, effective July 1, 2014.

Kentucky Code

Current through the 2016 Legislative Session

Office of the Attorney General
Capitol Suite 118
700 Capitol Avenue
Frankfort, Kentucky 40601-3449
Voice: (502) 696-5300
attorney.general@ag.ky.gov

Louisville Field Division
600 Dr. Martin Luther King Jr. Place,
Suite 500
Louisville, Kentucky 40202
Voice: (502) 753-3400
https://www.atf.gov/louisville-field-division

PROTECTING THE PUBLIC
SERVING OUR NATION

Table of Contents

237.200. Definitions for KRS 237.210 and 237.220.
237.210. Effect of changed conditions on nuisance actions involving shooting ranges – Standing to sue – Limitation of liability – Prohibition against retroactive application of laws.
237.220. Retroactivity of KRS 237.200 and 237.210.
Penalties
237.990. Penalties.

TITLE L, Chapter 527 Offenses Relating to Firearms and Weapons
527.010. Definitions for chapter.
527.020. Carrying concealed deadly weapon.
527.030. Defacing a firearm.
527.040. Possession of firearm by convicted felon – Exceptions.
527.050. Possession of defaced firearm.
527.060. Forfeiture.
527.070. Unlawful possession of a weapon on school property – Posting of sign – Exemptions.
527.080. Using restricted ammunition during the commission of a crime – Exception.
527.090. Fraudulent firearm transaction.

TITLE XIX Public Safety and Morals
Chapter 237 Firearms and Destructive Devices

237.020. Right of Kentucky residents, out-of-state residents, and residents of other countries to buy firearms.
(1) Residents of the Commonwealth of Kentucky who are citizens of the United States shall have the right to purchase or otherwise acquire rifles, shotguns, handguns, and any other firearms which they are permitted to purchase or otherwise acquire under federal law and the Kentucky Revised Statutes from properly licensed dealers, manufacturers, importers, or collectors, and unlicensed individual persons in Kentucky or in any other state or nation outside of the Commonwealth of Kentucky.
(2) Residents of states other than the Commonwealth of Kentucky who are citizens of the United States shall have the right to purchase or otherwise acquire rifles, shotguns, handguns, and any other firearms which they are permitted to purchase or otherwise acquire under federal law and the Kentucky Revised Statutes from properly licensed dealers, manufacturers, importers, or collectors, and from unlicensed individual persons in the Commonwealth of Kentucky.
(3) Citizens of countries other than the United States shall have the right to purchase or otherwise acquire rifles, shotguns, handguns, and any other firearms which they are permitted to purchase or otherwise acquire under federal law and the Kentucky Revised Statutes from properly licensed dealers, manufacturers, importers, or collectors, and from unlicensed individual persons in the Commonwealth of Kentucky.
(4) All such sales shall conform to the requirements of federal law, the Kentucky Revised Statutes, applicable local ordinances, and the law of the purchaser's state.

237.025. Requirements for local gun buy-back programs.
(1) Each law enforcement agency of state, county, urban-county, charter county, or city government or any other law enforcement agency that participates in a "gun buy-back program" or other program in which firearms or ammunition are purchased or surrendered for the purpose of destruction shall assure that:
  (a) The serial number of each firearm that is purchased or surrendered to the program is checked against local, state, and federal records of stolen firearms and, if it is found that the firearm is a stolen firearm, that the firearm is not destroyed without the written permission of the lawful owner thereof and that if the lawful owner of the firearm does not give written permission for the firearm to be destroyed, that the firearm is returned to its lawful owner;
  (b) If it is determined that a firearm that is purchased by, or surrendered to the "gun buy-back program" is stolen, that the law enforcement makes an effort to arrest the thief or any person who possessed the firearm knowing it was stolen; and
  (c) Prior to the destruction of any firearm that is purchased or surrendered, that a written determination is made as to whether the firearm may have been used in a crime, and that if it is determined that the firearm probably was used in a crime, that it is retained for evidence, and if it is determined that the firearm probably was not used in a crime, if the firearm is a rifled firearm, that a fired bullet and fired cartridge case is retained for possible use as evidence and that if the firearm is a smooth bore firearm, that a fired cartridge case is retained for possible use as evidence.
(2) Prior to returning a stolen firearm to a lawful owner, the law enforcement agency shall determine whether or not the lawful owner is eligible to possess a firearm under federal law. If the lawful owner of the firearm is ineligible to possess a firearm under federal law, the law enforcement agency may destroy the firearm after compliance with subsection (1) (c) of this section.

237.030. Definitions for KRS 237.040 and 237.050.
(1) "Destructive device" means any explosive, incendiary, or poison gas bomb, grenade, mine, rocket, missile, or similar device and includes the unassembled components from which such a device can be made.

237.040. Criminal possession of destructive device or booby trap device. A person is guilty of criminal possession of a destructive device or a booby trap device when he possesses, manufactures, or transports such substance or device with:

(1) Intent to use that device to commit an offense against the laws of this state, a political subdivision thereof, or of the United States; or

(2) Knowledge that some other person intends to use that device to commit an offense against the laws of this state, a political subdivision thereof, or of the United States.

(3) Mere possession without substantial evidence of the requisite intent is insufficient to bring action under KRS 237.030 to 237.050.

237.050. Exemptions. KRS 237.030 to 237.050 shall not apply to:

(1) Destructive devices or booby trap devices which are possessed by the government of the United States, this state, or a political subdivision thereof;

(2) Any device which is lawfully possessed under the Gun Control Act of 1968, the Organized Crime Control Act of 1971, or any other law of the United States or this state, unless a crime is committed therewith;

(3) Nonlethal devices placed on the premises of the owner or the lawful occupant thereof for his own self-protection or the protection of the said property;

(4) The setting of traps suitable and legal for the taking of game by persons licensed or permitted to do so by the game laws of the Commonwealth;

(5) Inert devices which cannot readily be restored to operating condition; or

(6) The acquisition, possession, use, or control of firearms.

237.060. Definitions for KRS 237.060 to 237.090 and certain other sections. The following definitions apply in KRS 237.060 to 237.090 and KRS 197.170, 218A.992, 244.125, 244.990, and 514.110, unless the context otherwise requires:

(1) "Handgun" means any pistol or revolver originally designed to be fired by the use of a single hand, or any other firearm originally designed to be fired by the use of a single hand.

(2) "Firearm" means any weapon which will expel a projectile by the action of an explosive.

(3) "Licensed gun dealer" means a person who has a federal firearms license and any business license required by a state or local government entity.

(4) "Loaded" with respect to a firearm means:

  (a) There is ammunition in the chamber of the firearm; or

  (b) There is ammunition in the cylinder of the firearm; or

  (c) There is ammunition in the magazine of a firearm, if the magazine is attached to the firearm.

(5) "Juvenile" means a person who has not attained his eighteenth birthday.

(6) "Ammunition" means loaded ammunition designed for use in any firearm.

(7) "Armor-piercing ammunition" means a projectile or projectile core which may be used in a handgun and which is constructed entirely (excluding the presence of traces of other substances) from 1 or a combination of tungsten alloys, steel, iron, brass, bronze, beryllium copper, or depleted uranium. "Armor piercing ammunition" does not include shotgun shot required by federal or state environmental or game regulations for hunting purposes, a frangible projectile designed for target shooting, a projectile which the Secretary of the Treasury of the United States finds is primarily intended to be used for sporting purposes, or any other projectile or projectile core which the Secretary of the Treasury of the United States finds is intended to be used for industrial purposes, including a charge used in an oil and gas well perforating device.

(8) "Flanged ammunition" means ammunition with a soft lead core and having sharp flanges which are designed to expand on impact.

237.070. Prohibition against sale or transfer of firearm to convicted felon.

(1) No person shall knowingly sell or transfer a firearm to any person prohibited from possessing it by KRS 527.040.

(2) Any person who violates the provisions of subsection (1) of this section is guilty of a Class A misdemeanor.

(3) Any firearm transferred in violation of this section shall be subject to forfeiture and shall be disposed of pursuant to KRS 237.090.

237.075. Chief Law enforcement officer's certification for transfer or making of a firearm – Immunity from liability – Appeal of denial of certification request.

(1) For purposes of this section:

  (a) "Certification" means the participation and assent of the chief law enforcement officer necessary under federal law for the approval of the application to transfer or make a firearm;

  (b) "Chief law enforcement officer" means the sheriff of the county of the applicant's residence, notwithstanding the provisions of 27 C.F.R. secs. 479.63 and 479.85; and

  (c) "Firearm" has the same meaning as provided in the National Firearms Act, 26 U.S.C. sec. 5845(a).

(2) (a) When a chief law enforcement officer's certification is required by federal law or regulation for the transfer or making of a firearm, the chief law enforcement officer shall, within 15 days of receipt of a request for certification, provide this certification if the applicant is not prohibited by law from receiving or possessing the firearm and is not the subject of a proceeding that could result in the applicant being prohibited by law from receiving or possessing the firearm. If the chief law enforcement officer is unable to make a certification as required by this section, he or she shall provide the applicant a written notification of the denial and the reason for this determination.

(b) A chief law enforcement officer is not required to make any certification under this subsection he or she knows to be untrue, but he or she may not refuse to provide certification based on a generalized objection to private persons or entities making, possessing, or receiving firearms or any certain type of firearm the possession of which is not prohibited by law.

(3) Chief law enforcement officers and their employees who act in good faith are immune from liability arising from any act or omission in making a certification as required by this section.

(4) An applicant whose request for certification is denied may appeal the chief law enforcement officer's decision to the Circuit Court that is located in the county in which the applicant resides. The court shall review the chief law enforcement officer's decision to deny the certification de novo. If the court finds that the applicant is not prohibited by law from receiving or possessing the firearm, is not the subject of a proceeding that could result in such prohibition, and that no substantial evidence supports the chief law enforcement officer's determination that he or she cannot truthfully make the certification, the court shall order the chief law enforcement officer to issue the certification and award court costs and reasonable attorney's fees to the applicant.

237.080. Prohibition against manufacture, sale, delivery, transfer, or importation of armor-piercing ammunition – Exceptions.

(1) It shall be unlawful for any person to knowingly manufacture, sell, deliver, transfer, or import armor-piercing ammunition.

(2) Subsection (1) of this section shall not apply to members of the Armed Forces of the United States or law enforcement officers within the scope of their duties, nor shall it prohibit licensed gun dealers from possessing armor-piercing ammunition for the purpose of receiving and transferring it to members of the Armed Forces of the United States, or law enforcement officers for use within the scope of their duties.

(3) A violation of subsection (1) of this section shall be a Class D felony for the first offense and a Class C felony for each subsequent offense.

(4) Any armor-piercing ammunition transferred, sold, or offered for sale, in violation of this section is contraband and shall be seized and summarily forfeited to the state and shall be disposed of pursuant to KRS 237.090.

237.090. Disposition of forfeited firearm or ammunition.
Any firearm or ammunition forfeited pursuant to KRS 237.060 to 237.090 shall, upon order of a court of competent jurisdiction, be disposed of or retained as provided in KRS 500.090.

237.095. Persons barred by federal law from purchase of firearms – Duty to notify courts and law enforcement agencies of purchase or attempt to purchase – Protocol for providing notice – Duty to notify petitioner – Immunity from liability.

(1) Upon receiving notice that a person barred from purchasing a firearm under 18 U.S.C. sec. 922(g)(8) has purchased or attempted to purchase a firearm, any agency with the responsibility of entering domestic violence records into the Law Information Network of Kentucky shall notify:

   (a) The court in the jurisdiction where the domestic violence order was issued under KRS 403.750; and

   (b) The law enforcement agencies, as designated by the Department of Kentucky State Police, that have jurisdiction in the county where the domestic violence order was issued and in the county of the victim's residence if different from the county where the domestic violence order was issued.

(2) The Department of Kentucky State Police shall develop a protocol for providing notice to the required court and law enforcement agencies under subsection (1) of this section. Within the protocol, the Department of Kentucky State Police shall designate which local law enforcement agencies are to receive notice in each county. A minimum of 1 law enforcement agency shall be designated in each county.

(3) When a designated law enforcement agency for the county where the domestic violence order was issued or where the victim resides receives notice under subsection (1)(b) of this section, that agency shall make reasonable efforts to ensure that the petitioner who obtained the domestic violence order is notified that the respondent has purchased or attempted to purchase a firearm.

(4) Any person carrying out responsibilities under this section shall be immune from civil liability for good faith conduct in carrying out those responsibilities.

(5) This section shall apply only to domestic violence orders issued, or reissued, on or after July 14, 2000, through July 15, 2002.

237.100. Notification of purchase of firearm or attempt to purchase firearm – Immunity.

(1) Upon receipt of notice that a person barred from purchasing a firearm under 18 U.S.C. sec. 922(g)(8) has purchased or attempted to purchase a firearm, the Justice and Public Safety Cabinet shall make a reasonable effort to provide notice to the petitioner who obtained the domestic violence order issued under KRS 403.740 that the respondent to the order has attempted to purchase a firearm. The Justice and Public Safety Cabinet may contract with a private entity in order to provide notification.

(2) The notification shall be limited to a petitioner who has

   (a) Received a domestic violence protective order issued or reissued under KRS 403.740 on or after July 15, 2002;

   (b) Received a domestic violence protective order that involves a respondent who is prohibited by 18 U.S.C. sec. 922(g)(8) from possessing a firearm; and

(c) Provided the Justice and Public Safety Cabinet or the entity with a request for notification.

(3) Any person carrying out responsibilities under this section shall be immune from civil liability for good faith conduct in carrying out those responsibilities. Nothing in this subsection shall limit liability for negligence.

237.102. Suspension, revocation, limitation, or impairment of concealed deadly weapon license permitted only in accordance with KRS 237.110 and 237.138 to 237.142.

(1) No person, unit of government, or governmental organization shall have the authority to suspend, revoke, limit the use of, or impair the validity of a concealed deadly weapon license issued pursuant to KRS 237.110, or a foreign license which is recognized as valid pursuant to KRS 237.110, unless the license is revoked for the reasons specified in KRS 237.110 and the revocation is done in the manner specified in KRS 237.110.

(2) No person, unit of government, or governmental organization shall have the authority to suspend, revoke, limit the use of, or impair the validity of a concealed deadly weapon license which is issued pursuant to KRS 237.138 to 237.142 unless the license is revoked for the reasons specified in KRS 237.110 or 237.138 to 237.142.

(3) No action which may be taken pursuant to KRS Chapter 39A shall apply with regard to a license specified in this section or to a person who is the holder of a license specified in this section.

237.104. Rights to acquire, carry, and use deadly weapons not to be impaired – Seizure of deadly weapons prohibited – Application of section.

(1) No person, unit of government, or governmental organization shall, during a period of disaster or emergency as specified in KRS Chapter 39A or at any other time, have the right to revoke, suspend, limit the use of, or otherwise impair the validity of the right of any person to purchase, transfer, loan, own, possess, carry, or use a firearm, firearm part, ammunition, ammunition component, or any deadly weapon or dangerous instrument.

(2) No person, unit of government, or governmental organization shall, during a period of disaster or emergency as specified in KRS Chapter 39A or at any other time, take, seize, confiscate, or impound a firearm, firearm part, ammunition, ammunition component, or any deadly weapon or dangerous instrument from any person.

(3) The provisions of this section shall not apply to the taking of an item specified in subsection (1) or (2) of this section from a person who is:

    (a) Forbidden to possess a firearm pursuant to KRS 527.040;

    (b) Forbidden to possess a firearm pursuant to federal law;

    (c) Violating KRS 527.020;

    (d) In possession of a stolen firearm;

    (e) Using a firearm in the commission of a separate criminal offense; or

    (f) Using a firearm or other weapon in the commission of an offense under KRS Chapter 150.

237.106. Right of employees and other persons to possess firearms in vehicle – Employer liable for denying right – Exceptions.

(1) No person, including but not limited to an employer, who is the owner, lessee, or occupant of real property shall prohibit any person who is legally entitled to possess a firearm from possessing a firearm, part of a firearm, ammunition, or ammunition component in a vehicle on the property.

(2) A person, including but not limited to an employer, who owns, leases, or otherwise occupies real property may prevent a person who is prohibited by state or federal law from possessing a firearm or ammunition from possessing a firearm or ammunition on the property.

(3) A firearm may be removed from the vehicle or handled in the case of self-defense, defense of another, defense of property, or as authorized by the owner, lessee, or occupant of the property.

(4) An employer that fires, disciplines, demotes, or otherwise punishes an employee who is lawfully exercising a right guaranteed by this section and who is engaging in conduct in compliance with this statute shall be liable in civil damages. An employee may seek and the court shall grant an injunction against an employer who is violating the provisions of this section when it is found that the employee is in compliance with the provisions of this section.

(5) The provisions of this section shall not apply to any real property:

    (a) Owned, leased, or occupied by the United States government, upon which the possession or carrying of firearms is prohibited or controlled;

    (b) Of a detention facility as defined in KRS 520.010; or

    (c) Where a section of the Kentucky Revised Statutes specifically prohibits possession or carrying of firearms on the property.

237.108. Persons adjudicated mentally defective and committed to mental institutions – Identifying information to be forwarded to Department of Kentucky State Police and Federal Bureau of Investigation – Information to be included in National Instant Criminal Background Check System database – Petition to court for relief from prohibition against possession of firearms – Prohibition against allowing improper use of information obtained by Kentucky State Police.

(1) A court that orders a commitment or makes a finding or adjudication under which a person becomes subject to the provisions of 18 U.S.C. sec. 922(d)(4) and (g)(4) shall order the circuit clerk to forward the person's name and nonclinical identifying information, including the person's Social Security number and date of birth, along with a copy of the order of commitment to the Department of Kentucky State Police, which in turn shall forward the information to the Federal Bureau of Investigation, its successor agency, or agency designated by the Federal Bureau of Investigation, for inclusion in the National Instant Criminal Background Check System database. The court shall also notify the person of the prohibitions of 18 U.S.C. sec. 922(d)(4) and (g)(4).

(2) A person who is subject to the provisions of 18 U.S.C. sec. 922(d)(4) and (g)(4) because of a commitment, finding, or adjudication that occurred in this state may petition the court in which such commitment, finding, or adjudication occurred to remove, pursuant to Section 105(a) of Pub. L. No. 110-180, the disabilities imposed under 18 U.S.C. sec. 922(d)(4) and (g)(4). A copy of the petition for relief shall also be served on the director of the Division of Behavioral Health and the county attorney of the county in which the original commitment, finding, or adjudication occurred. The director of the Division of Behavioral Health and the county attorney may, as each deems appropriate, appear, support, object to, or present evidence relevant to the relief sought by the petitioner. The court shall receive and consider evidence in a closed proceeding, including evidence offered by the petitioner concerning:

(a) The circumstances of the original commitment, finding, or adjudication;

(b) The petitioner's mental health and criminal history records, if any;

(c) The petitioner's reputation;

(d) The petitioner's date of birth and Social Security number; and

(e) Changes in the petitioner's condition or circumstances relevant to the relief sought.

The court shall grant the petition for relief if it finds by a preponderance of the evidence that the petitioner will not be likely to act in a manner dangerous to public safety and that granting of the relief would not be contrary to the public interest. A record shall be kept of the proceedings, but it shall remain confidential and be disclosed only to a court in the event of an appeal. The petitioner may appeal a denial of the requested relief, and review on appeal shall be de novo. A person may file a petition for relief under this section no more than once every 2 years.

(3) When the court issues an order granting a petition for relief under subsection (2) of this section, the circuit clerk shall immediately forward a copy of the order to the Department of Kentucky State Police, which in turn shall immediately forward a copy to the Federal Bureau of Investigation, or its successor agency, for updating of the National Instant Criminal Background Check System database and shall remove all information in any database over which the department exercises control relating to the person whose relief from disability is granted and shall immediately destroy all paper copies of the order of commitment and other documents relating to the matter.

(4) If a petition is granted under this section, the order, finding, or adjudication for which relief is granted shall, pursuant to § 105(a) of Pub. L. No. 110-180, be deemed not to have occurred for purposes of 18 U.S.C. sec. 922(d)(4) and (g)(4).

(5) The Department of Kentucky State Police shall not use or permit the use of the records or information obtained or retained pursuant to this section for any purpose not specified in this section.

(6) The provisions of this section shall supersede any other statute to the contrary for the purposes set forth in this section but otherwise shall be held and construed as ancillary and supplemental to any other statute.

Carrying Concealed Deadly Weapon

237.110. License to carry concealed deadly weapon – Criteria – Training – Paper or electronic application – Issuance and denial of licenses – Automated listing of license holders – Suspension or revocation – Renewal – Prohibitions – Reciprocity – Reports – Requirements for training classes.

(1) The Department of Kentucky State Police is authorized to issue and renew licenses to carry concealed firearms or other deadly weapons, or a combination thereof, to persons qualified as provided in this section.

(2) An original or renewal license issued pursuant to this section shall:

(a) Be valid throughout the Commonwealth and, except as provided in this section or other specific section of the Kentucky Revised Statutes or federal law, permit the holder of the license to carry firearms, ammunition, or other deadly weapons, or a combination thereof, at any location in the Commonwealth;

(b) Unless revoked or suspended as provided by law, be valid for a period of 5 years from the date of issuance;

(c) Authorize the holder of the license to carry a concealed firearm or other deadly weapon, or a combination thereof, on or about his or her person; and

(d) Authorize the holder of the license to carry ammunition for a firearm on or about his or her person.

(3) Prior to the issuance of an original or renewal license to carry a concealed deadly weapon, the Department of Kentucky State Police, upon receipt of a completed application, applicable fees, and any documentation required by this section or administrative regulation promulgated by the Department of Kentucky State Police, shall conduct a background check to ascertain whether the applicant is eligible under 18 U.S.C. sec. 922(g) and (n), any other applicable federal law, and state law to purchase, receive, or possess a firearm or ammunition, or both. The background check shall include:

(a) A state records check covering the items specified in this subsection, together with any other requirements of this section;

(b) A federal records check, which shall include a National Instant Criminal Background Check System (NICS) check;

(c) A federal Immigration Alien Query if the person is an alien who has been lawfully admitted to the United States by the United States government or an agency thereof; and

(d) In addition to the Immigration Alien Query, if the applicant has not been lawfully admitted to the United States under permanent resident status, the Department of Kentucky State Police shall, if a doubt exists relating to an alien's eligibility to purchase a firearm, consult with the United States Department of Homeland Security, United States Department of

Justice, United States Department of State, or other federal agency to confirm whether the alien is eligible to purchase a firearm in the United States, bring a firearm into the United States, or possess a firearm in the United States under federal law.

(4) The Department of Kentucky State Police shall issue an original or renewal license if the applicant:

(a) Is not prohibited from the purchase, receipt, or possession of firearms, ammunition, or both pursuant to 18 U.S.C. 922(g), 18 U.S.C. 922(n), or applicable federal or state law;

(b)1. Is a citizen of the United States who is a resident of this Commonwealth;

2. Is a citizen of the United States who is a member of the Armed Forces of the United States who is on active duty, who is at the time of application assigned to a military posting in Kentucky;

3. Is lawfully admitted to the United States by the United States government or an agency thereof, is permitted by federal law to purchase a firearm, and is a resident of this Commonwealth; or

4. Is lawfully admitted to the United States by the United States government or an agency thereof, is permitted by federal law to purchase a firearm, is, at the time of the application, assigned to a military posting in Kentucky, and has been assigned to a posting in the Commonwealth;

(c) Is 21 years of age or older;

(d) Has not been committed to a state or federal facility for the abuse of a controlled substance or been convicted of a misdemeanor violation of KRS Chapter 218A or similar laws of any other state relating to controlled substances, within a 3 year period immediately preceding the date on which the application is submitted;

(e) Does not chronically and habitually use alcoholic beverages as evidenced by the applicant having 2 or more convictions for violating KRS 189A.010 within the 3 years immediately preceding the date on which the application is submitted, or having been committed as an alcoholic pursuant to KRS Chapter 222 or similar laws of another state within the 3 year period immediately preceding the date on which the application is submitted;

(f) Does not owe a child support arrearage which equals or exceeds the cumulative amount which would be owed after 1 year of nonpayment, if the Department of Kentucky State Police has been notified of the arrearage by the Cabinet for Health and Family Services;

(g) Has complied with any subpoena or warrant relating to child support or paternity proceedings. If the Department of Kentucky State Police has not been notified by the Cabinet for Health and Family Services that the applicant has failed to meet this requirement, the Department of Kentucky State Police shall assume that paternity and child support proceedings are not an issue;

(h) Has not been convicted of a violation of KRS 508.030 or 508.080 within the 3 years immediately preceding the date on which the application is submitted. The commissioner of the Department of Kentucky State Police may waive this requirement upon good cause shown and a determination that the applicant is not a danger and that a waiver would not violate federal law;

(i) Demonstrates competence with a firearm by successful completion of a firearms safety or training course that is conducted by a firearms instructor who is certified by a national organization that certifies firearms instructors and includes the use of written tests, in person instruction, and a component of live-fire training or a firearms safety course offered or approved by the Department of Criminal Justice Training. The firearms safety course offered or approved by the Department of Criminal Justice Training shall:

1. Be not more than 8 hours in length;

2. Include instruction on handguns, the safe use of handguns, the care and cleaning of handguns, and handgun marksmanship principles;

3. Include actual range firing of a handgun in a safe manner, and the firing of not more than 20 rounds at a full-size silhouette target, during which firing, not less than 11 rounds must hit the silhouette portion of the target;

4. Include information on and a copy of laws relating to possession and carrying of firearms, as set forth in KRS Chapters 237 and 527, and the laws relating to the use of force, as set forth in KRS Chapter 503; and

(j) Demonstrates knowledge of the law regarding the justifiable use of force by including with the application a copy of the concealed carry deadly weapons legal handout made available by the Department of Criminal Justice Training and a signed statement that indicates that applicant has read and understands the handout.

(5) (a) A legible photocopy or electronic copy of a certificate of completion issued by a firearms instructor certified by a national organization or the Department of Criminal Justice Training shall constitute evidence of qualification under subsection (4)(i) of this section.

(b) Persons qualifying under subsection (6)(d) of this section may submit with their application:

1. At least one (1) of the following paper or electronic forms or their successor forms showing evidence of handgun training or handgun qualifications:

a. Department of Defense Form DD 2586;

b. Department of Defense Form DD 214;

c. Coast Guard Form CG 3029;

d. Department of the Army Form DA 88-R;

e. Department of the Army Form DA 5704-R;

f. Department of the Navy Form OPNAV 3591-1; or

g. Department of the Air Force Form AF 522; or

2. a. Documentary evidence of an honorable discharge; and

b. A notarized affidavit on a form provided by the Department of Kentucky State Police, signed under penalty of perjury, stating the person has met the training requirements of subsection (6)(d) of this section.

(6) (a) Peace officers who are currently certified as peace officers by the Kentucky Law Enforcement Council pursuant to KRS 15.380 to 15.404 and peace officers who are retired and are members of the Kentucky Employees Retirement System, State Police Retirement System, or County Employees Retirement System or other retirement system operated by or for a city, county, or urban-county in Kentucky shall be deemed to have met the training requirement.

(b) Current and retired peace officers of the following federal agencies shall be deemed to have met the training requirement:

1. Any peace officer employed by a federal agency specified in KRS 61.365;

2. Any peace officer employed by a federal civilian law enforcement agency not specified above who has successfully completed the basic law enforcement training course required by that agency;

3. Any military peace officer of the United States Army, Navy, Marine Corps, or Air Force, or a reserve component thereof, or of the Army National Guard or Air National Guard who has successfully completed the military law enforcement training course required by that branch of the military; and

4. Any member of the United States Coast Guard serving in a peace officer role who has successfully completed the law enforcement training course specified by the United States Coast Guard.

(c) Corrections officers who are currently employed by a consolidated local government, an urban-county government, or the Department of Corrections who have successfully completed a basic firearms training course required for their employment, and corrections officers who were formerly employed by a consolidated local government, an urban-county government, or the Department of Corrections who are retired, and who successfully completed a basic firearms training course required for their employment, and are members of a state-administered retirement system or other retirement system operated by or for a city, county, or urban-county government in Kentucky shall be deemed to have met the training requirement.

(d) Active or honorably discharged service members in the United States Army, Navy, Marine Corps, Air Force, or Coast Guard, or a reserve component thereof, or of the Army National Guard or Air National Guard shall be deemed to have met the training requirement if these persons:

1. Successfully completed handgun training which was conducted by the United States Army, Navy, Marine Corps, Air Force, or Coast Guard, or a reserve component thereof, or of the Army National Guard or Air National Guard; or

2. Successfully completed handgun qualification within the United States Army, Navy, Marine Corps, Air Force, or Coast Guard, or a reserve component thereof, or of the Army Guard or Air Force National Guard.

(7) (a) 1. A paper application for a license, or renewal of a license, to carry a concealed deadly weapon shall be obtained from and submitted to the office of the sheriff in the county in which the person resides.

2. An applicant, in lieu of a paper application, may submit an electronic application for a license, or renewal of a license, to carry a concealed deadly weapon to the Department of Kentucky State Police.\

3. Persons qualifying under subsection (6)(d) of this section shall be supplied the information in subsection (4)(i)4. of this section upon obtaining an application.

(b) 1. The completed paper application and any documentation required by this section plus an application fee or renewal fee, as appropriate, of $60 shall be presented to the office of the sheriff of the county in which the applicant resides.

2. The sheriff shall transmit the paper application and accompanying material to the Department of Kentucky State Police within 5 working days.

3. Twenty dollars ($20) of the paper application fee shall be retained by the office of the sheriff for official expenses of the office. Twenty dollars ($20) shall be sent to the Department of Kentucky State Police with the application. Ten dollars ($10) shall be transmitted by the sheriff to the Administrative Office of the Courts to fund background checks for youth leaders, and $10 shall be transmitted to the Administrative Office of the Courts to fund background checks for applicants for concealed weapons.

(c) 1. A completed electronic application submitted in lieu of a paper application, any documentation required by this section, and an application fee or renewal fee, as appropriate, of $70 shall be presented to the Department of Kentucky State Police.

2. If an electronic application is submitted in lieu of a paper application, $30 of the electronic application fee shall be retained by the Department of Kentucky State Police. Twenty dollars ($20) shall be sent to the office of the sheriff of the applicant's county of residence for official expenses of the office. Ten dollars ($10) shall be transmitted to the Administrative Office of the Courts to fund background checks for youth leaders, and $10 shall be transmitted to the Administrative Office of the Courts to fund background checks for applicants for concealed weapon carry permits.

(d) A full-time or part-time peace officer who is currently certified as a peace officer by the Kentucky Law Enforcement Council and who is authorized by his or her employer or government authority to carry a concealed deadly weapon at all times and all locations within the Commonwealth pursuant to KRS 527.020, or a retired peace officer who is a member of the Kentucky Employees Retirement System, State Police Retirement System, County Employees Retirement System, or other retirement system operated by or for a city, county, or urban-county government in Kentucky, shall be exempt from paying the paper or electronic application or renewal fees.

(e) The application, whether paper or electronic, shall be completed, under oath, on a form or in a manner promulgated by the Department of Kentucky State Police by administrative regulation which shall include:

1. a. The name, address, place and date of birth, citizenship, gender, Social Security number of the applicant; and

b. If not a citizen of the United States, alien registration number if applicable, passport number, visa number, mother's maiden name, and other information necessary to determine the immigration status and eligibility to purchase a firearm under federal law of a person who is not a citizen of the United States;

2. A statement that, to the best of his or her knowledge, the applicant is in compliance with criteria contained within subsections (3) and (4) of this section;

3. A statement that the applicant, if qualifying under subsection (6)(c) of this section, has provided:

a. At least 1 of the forms listed in subsection (5) of this section; or

b. i. Documentary evidence of an honorable discharge; and

ii. A notarized affidavit on a form provided by the Department of Kentucky State Police stating the person has met the training requirements of subsection (6)(c) of this section;

4. A statement that the applicant has been furnished a copy of this section and is knowledgeable about its provisions;

5. A statement that the applicant has been furnished a copy of, has read, and understands KRS Chapter 503 as it pertains to the use of deadly force for self-defense in Kentucky; and

6. A conspicuous warning that the application is executed under oath and that a materially false answer to any question, or the submission of any materially false document by the applicant, subjects the applicant to criminal prosecution under KRS 523.030.

(8) The applicant shall submit to the sheriff of the applicant's county of residence or county of military posting if submitting a paper application, or to the Department of Kentucky State Police if submitting an electronic application:

(a) A completed application as described in subsection (7) of this section;

(b) A recent color photograph of the applicant, as prescribed by administrative regulation;

(c) A paper or electronic certificate or an affidavit or document as described in subsection (5) of this section;

(d) A paper or electronic document establishing the training exemption as described in subsection (6) of this section; and

(e) For an applicant who is not a citizen of the United States and has been lawfully admitted to the United States by the United States government or an agency thereof, an affidavit as prescribed by administrative regulation concerning his or her immigration status and his or her United States government issued:

1. Permanent Resident Card I-551 or its equivalent successor identification;

2. Other United States government issued evidence of lawful admission to the United States which includes the category of admission, if admission has not been granted as a permanent resident; and

3. Evidence of compliance with the provisions of 18 U.S.C. sec. 922(g)(5), 18 U.S.C. sec. 922(d)(5), or 18 U.S.C. sec. 922(y)(2), and 27 C.F.R. Part 178, including, as appropriate, but not limited to evidence of 90 day residence in the Commonwealth, a valid current Kentucky hunting license if claiming exemption as a hunter, or other evidence of eligibility to purchase a firearm by an alien which is required by federal law or regulation.

If an applicant presents identification specified in this paragraph, the sheriff shall examine the identification, may record information from the identification presented, and shall return the identification to the applicant.

(9) The Department of Kentucky State Police shall, within 60 days after the date of receipt of the items listed in subsection (8) of this section if the applicant submitted a paper application, or within 15 business days after the date of receipt of the items listed in subsection (8) of this section if the applicant applied electronically, either:

(a) Issue the license; or

(b) Deny the application based solely on the grounds that the applicant fails to qualify under the criteria listed in subsection (3) or (4) of this section. If the Department of Kentucky State Police denies the application, it shall notify the applicant in writing, stating the grounds for denial and informing the applicant of a right to submit, within 30 days, any additional documentation relating to the grounds of denial. Upon receiving any additional documentation, the Department of Kentucky State Police shall reconsider its decision and inform the applicant within 20 days of the result of the reconsideration. The applicant shall further be informed of the right to seek de novo review of the denial in the District Court of his or her place of residence within 90 days from the date of the letter advising the applicant of the denial.

(10) The Department of Kentucky State Police shall maintain an automated listing of license holders and pertinent information, and this information shall be available upon request, at all times to all Kentucky, federal, and other states law enforcement agencies. A request for the entire list of licensees, or for all licensees in a geographic area, shall be denied. Only requests relating to a named licensee shall be honored or available to law enforcement agencies. Information on applications for licenses, names and addresses, or other identifying information relating to license holders shall be confidential and shall not be made available except to law enforcement agencies. No request for lists of local or statewide permit holders shall be made to any state or local law enforcement agency, peace officer, or other agency of government other than the Department of Kentucky State Police, and no state or local law enforcement agency, peace officer, or agency of government, other than the Department of Kentucky State Police, shall provide any information to any requester not entitled to it by law.

(11) Within 30 days after the changing of a permanent address, or within 30 days after the loss, theft, or destruction of a license, the licensee shall notify the Department of Kentucky State Police of the loss, theft, or destruction. Failure to notify the Department of Kentucky State Police shall constitute a noncriminal violation with a penalty of $25 payable to the clerk of the District Court. No court costs shall be assessed for a violation of this subsection. When a licensee makes application to change his or her residence address or other information on the license, neither the sheriff nor the

Department of Kentucky State Police shall require a surrender of the license until a new license is in the office of the applicable sheriff and available for issuance. Upon the issuance of a new license, the old license shall be destroyed by the sheriff.

(12) If a license is lost, stolen, or destroyed, the license shall be automatically invalid, and the person to whom the same was issued may, upon payment of $15 for a paper request, or $25 for an electronic request submitted in lieu of a paper request, to the Department of Kentucky State Police, obtain a duplicate, upon furnishing a notarized statement to the Department of Kentucky State Police that the license has been lost, stolen, or destroyed.

(13) (a) The commissioner of the Department of Kentucky State Police, or his or her designee in writing, shall revoke the license of any person who becomes permanently ineligible to be issued a license or have a license renewed under the criteria set forth in this section.

(b) The commissioner of the Department of Kentucky State Police, or his or her designee in writing, shall suspend the license of any person who becomes temporarily ineligible to be issued a license or have a license renewed under the criteria set forth in this section. The license shall remain suspended until the person is again eligible for the issuance or renewal of a license.

(c) Upon the suspension or revocation of a license, the commissioner of the Department of Kentucky State Police, or his or her designee in writing, shall:

1. Order any peace officer to seize the license from the person whose license was suspended or revoked; or

2. Direct the person whose license was suspended or revoked to surrender the license to the sheriff of the person's county of residence within 2 business days of the receipt of the notice.

(d) If the person whose license was suspended or revoked desires a hearing on the matter, the person shall surrender the license as provided in paragraph (c)2. of this subsection and petition the commissioner of the Department of Kentucky State Police to hold a hearing on the issue of suspension or revocation of the license.

(e) Upon receipt of the petition, the commissioner of the Department of Kentucky State Police shall cause a hearing to be held in accordance with KRS Chapter 13B on the suspension or revocation of the license. If the license has not been surrendered, no hearing shall be scheduled or held.

(f) If the hearing officer determines that the licensee's license was wrongly suspended or revoked, the hearing officer shall order the commissioner of the Department of Kentucky State Police to return the license and abrogate the suspension or revocation of the license.

(g) Any party may appeal a decision pursuant to this subsection to the District Court in the licensee's county of residence in the same manner as for the denial of a license.

(h) If the license is not surrendered as ordered, the commissioner of the Department of Kentucky State Police shall order a peace officer to seize the license and deliver it to the commissioner.

(i) Failure to surrender a suspended or revoked license as ordered is a Class A misdemeanor.

(j) The provisions of this subsection relating to surrender of a license shall not apply if a court of competent jurisdiction has enjoined its surrender.

(k) When a domestic violence order or emergency protective order is issued pursuant to the provisions of KRS Chapter 403 against a person holding a license issued under this section, the holder of the permit shall surrender the license to the court or to the officer serving the order. The officer to whom the license is surrendered shall forthwith transmit the license to the court issuing the order. The license shall be suspended until the order is terminated, or until the judge who issued the order terminates the suspension prior to the termination of the underlying domestic violence order or emergency protective order, in writing and by return of the license, upon proper motion by the license holder. Subject to the same conditions as above, a peace officer against whom an emergency protective order or domestic violence order has been issued shall not be permitted to carry a concealed deadly weapon when not on duty, the provisions of KRS 527.020 to the contrary notwithstanding.

(14) (a) Not less than 120 days prior to the expiration date of the license, the Department of Kentucky State Police shall mail to each licensee a written notice of the expiration and a renewal form prescribed by the Department of Kentucky State Police. The outside of the envelope containing the license renewal notice shall bear only the name and address of the applicant. No other information relating to the applicant shall appear on the outside of the envelope sent to the applicant. The licensee may renew his or her license on or before the expiration date by filing with the sheriff of his or her county of residence the paper renewal form, or by filing with the Department of Kentucky State Police an electronic renewal form in lieu of a paper renewal form, stating that the licensee remains qualified pursuant to the criteria specified in subsections (3) and (4) of this section, and the required renewal fee set forth in subsection (7) of this section. The sheriff shall issue to the applicant a receipt for the paper application for renewal of the license and shall date the receipt. The Department of Kentucky State Police shall issue to the applicant a receipt for an electronic application for renewal of the license submitted in lieu of a paper application for renewal and shall date the receipt.

(b) A license which has expired shall be void and shall not be valid for any purpose other than surrender to the sheriff in exchange for a renewal license.

(c) The license shall be renewed to a qualified applicant upon receipt of the completed renewal application, records check as specified in subsection (3) of this section, determination that the renewal applicant is not ineligible for a license as specified in subsection (4), and appropriate payment of fees. Upon the issuance of a new license, the old license shall be destroyed by the sheriff. A licensee who fails to file a renewal application on or before its expiration date may renew his or her license by paying, in addition to the license fees, a late fee of $15. No license shall be renewed 6 months or more after its expiration date, and the license shall be deemed to be permanently expired 6 months after its expiration date. A person whose license has permanently expired may reapply for licensure pursuant to subsections (7), (8), and (9) of this section.

(15) The licensee shall carry the license at all times the licensee is carrying a concealed firearm or other deadly weapon and shall display the license upon request of a law enforcement officer. Violation of the provisions of this subsection shall constitute a noncriminal violation with a penalty of $25, payable to the clerk of the District Court, but no court costs shall be assessed.

(16) Except as provided in KRS 527.020, no license issued pursuant to this section shall authorize any person to carry a concealed firearm into:

(a) Any police station or sheriff's office;

(b) Any detention facility, prison, or jail;

(c) Any courthouse, solely occupied by the Court of Justice courtroom, or court proceeding;

(d) Any meeting of the governing body of a county, municipality, or special district; or any meeting of the General Assembly or a committee of the General Assembly, except that nothing in this section shall preclude a member of the body, holding a concealed deadly weapon license, from carrying a concealed deadly weapon at a meeting of the body of which he or she is a member;

(e) Any portion of an establishment licensed to dispense beer or alcoholic beverages for consumption on the premises, which portion of the establishment is primarily devoted to that purpose;

(f) Any elementary or secondary school facility without the consent of school authorities as provided in KRS 527.070, any child-caring facility as defined in KRS 199.011, any day-care center as defined in KRS 199.894, or any certified family child-care home as defined in KRS 199.8982, except however, any owner of a certified child-care home may carry a concealed firearm into the owner's residence used as a certified child-care home;

(g) An area of an airport to which access is controlled by the inspection of persons and property; or

(h) Any place where the carrying of firearms is prohibited by federal law.

(17) The owner, business or commercial lessee, or manager of a private business enterprise, day-care center as defined in KRS 199.894 or certified or licensed family child-care home as defined in KRS 199.8982, or a health-care facility licensed under KRS Chapter 216B, except facilities renting or leasing housing, may prohibit persons holding concealed deadly weapon licenses from carrying concealed deadly weapons on the premises and may prohibit employees, not authorized by the employer, holding concealed deadly weapons licenses from carrying concealed deadly weapons on the property of the employer. If the building or the premises are open to the public, the employer or business enterprise shall post signs on or about the premises if carrying concealed weapons is prohibited. Possession of weapons, or ammunition, or both in a vehicle on the premises shall not be a criminal offense so long as the weapons, or ammunition, or both are not removed from the vehicle or brandished while the vehicle is on the premises. A private but not a public employer may prohibit employees or other persons holding a concealed deadly weapons license from carrying concealed deadly weapons, or ammunition, or both in vehicles owned by the employer, but may not prohibit employees or other persons holding a concealed deadly weapons license from carrying concealed deadly weapons, or ammunition, or both in vehicles owned by the employee, except that the Justice and Public Safety Cabinet may prohibit an employee from carrying any weapons, or ammunition, or both other than the weapons, or ammunition, or both issued or authorized to be used by the employee of the cabinet, in a vehicle while transporting persons under the employee's supervision or jurisdiction. Carrying of a concealed weapon, or ammunition, or both in a location specified in this subsection by a license holder shall not be a criminal act but may subject the person to denial from the premises or removal from the premises, and, if an employee of an employer, disciplinary measures by the employer.

(19) ...The General Assembly does not delegate to the Department of Kentucky State Police the authority to regulate or restrict the issuing of licenses provided for in this section beyond those provisions contained in this section. This section shall be liberally construed to carry out the constitutional right to bear arms for self-defense.

(20) (a) A person who is not a resident of Kentucky and who has a valid license issued by another state of the United States to carry a concealed deadly weapon in that state may, subject to provisions of Kentucky law, carry a concealed deadly weapon in Kentucky, and his or her license shall be considered as valid in Kentucky.

(b) If a person with a valid license to carry a concealed deadly weapon issued from another state that has entered into a reciprocity agreement with the Department of Kentucky State Police becomes a resident of Kentucky, the license issued by the other state shall be considered as valid for the first 120 days of the person's residence in Kentucky, if within 60 days of moving to Kentucky, the person completes a form promulgated by the Department of Kentucky State Police which shall include:

1. A signed and notarized statement averring that to the best of his or her knowledge the person's license to carry a concealed deadly weapon is valid and in compliance with applicable out-of-state law, and has not been revoked or suspended for any reason except for valid forfeiture due to departure from the issuing state;

2. The person's name, date of birth, citizenship, gender, Social Security number if applicable, proof that he or she is a citizen of the United States, a permanent resident of the United States, or otherwise lawfully present in the United States, former out-of-state address, current address within the state of Kentucky, date on which Kentucky residence began, state which issued the concealed carry license, the issuing state's concealed carry license number, and the state of issuance of license; and

3. A photocopy of the person's out-of-state license to carry a concealed deadly weapon.

(c) Within 60 days of moving to Kentucky, the person shall deliver the form and accompanying documents by registered or certified mail, return receipt requested, to the address indicated on the form provided by the Department of Kentucky State Police pursuant to this subsection.

(d) The out-of-state concealed carry license shall become invalid in Kentucky upon the earlier of:

1. The out-of-state person having resided in Kentucky for more than 120 days; or

2. The person being issued a Kentucky concealed deadly weapon license pursuant to this section.

(e) The Department of Kentucky State Police shall, not later than 30 days after July 15, 1998, and not less than once every 12 months thereafter, make written inquiry of the concealed deadly weapon carrying licensing authorities in each other state as to whether a Kentucky resident may carry a concealed deadly weapon in their state based upon having a valid Kentucky concealed deadly weapon license, or whether a Kentucky resident may apply for a concealed deadly weapon carrying license in that state based upon having a valid Kentucky concealed deadly weapon license. The Department of Kentucky State Police shall attempt to secure from each other state permission for Kentucky residents who hold a valid Kentucky concealed deadly weapon license to carry concealed deadly weapons in that state, either on the basis of the Kentucky license or on the basis that the Kentucky license is sufficient to permit the issuance of a similar license by the other state. The Department of Kentucky State Police shall enter into a written reciprocity agreement with the appropriate agency in each state that agrees to permit Kentucky residents to carry concealed deadly weapons in the other state on the basis of a Kentucky-issued concealed deadly weapon license or that will issue a license to carry concealed deadly weapons in the other state based upon a Kentucky concealed deadly weapon license. If a reciprocity agreement is reached, the requirement to recontact the other state each 12 months shall be eliminated as long as the reciprocity agreement is in force. The information shall be a public record and shall be available to individual requesters free of charge for the first copy and at the normal rate for open records requests for additional copies.

(22) The following provisions shall apply to concealed deadly weapon training classes conducted by the Department of Criminal Justice Training or any other agency pursuant to this section:

(a) No concealed deadly weapon instructor trainer shall have his or her certification as a concealed deadly weapon instructor trainer reduced to that of instructor or revoked except after a hearing conducted pursuant to KRS Chapter 13B in which the instructor is found to have committed an act in violation of the applicable statutes or administrative regulations;

(b) No concealed deadly weapon instructor shall have his or her certification as a concealed deadly weapon instructor license suspended or revoked except after a hearing conducted pursuant to KRS Chapter 13B in which the instructor is found to have committed an act in violation of the applicable statutes or administrative regulations;

(d) Each concealed deadly weapon instructor or instructor trainer who teaches a concealed deadly weapon applicant or concealed deadly weapon instructor class shall supply the Department of Criminal Justice Training with a class roster indicating which students enrolled and successfully completed the class, and which contains the name and address of each student, within 5 working days of the completion of the class. The information may be sent by mail, facsimile, e-mail, or other method which will result in the receipt of or production of a hard copy of the information. The postmark, facsimile date, or e-mail date shall be considered as the date on which the notice was sent. Concealed deadly weapon class applicant, instructor, and instructor trainer information and records shall be confidential. The department may release to any person or organization the name, address, and telephone number of a concealed deadly weapon instructor or instructor trainer if that instructor or instructor trainer authorizes the release of the information in writing. The department shall include on any application for an instructor or instructor trainer certification a statement that the applicant either does or does not desire the applicant's name, address, and telephone number to be made public;

(g) If the Department of Criminal Justice Training believes that a firearms instructor trainer or certified firearms instructor has not in fact complied with the requirements for teaching a certified firearms instructor or applicant class by not teaching the class as specified in KRS 237.126, or who has taught an insufficient class as specified in KRS 237.128, the department shall send to each person who has been listed as successfully completing the concealed deadly weapon applicant class or concealed deadly weapon instructor class a verification form on which the time, date, date of range firing if different from the date on which the class was conducted, location, and instructor of the class is listed by the department and which requires the person to answer "yes" or "no" to specific questions regarding the conduct of the training class. The form shall be completed under oath and shall be returned to the Department of Criminal Justice Training not later than 45 days after its receipt. A person who fails to complete the form, to sign the form, or to return the form to the Department of Criminal Justice Training within the time frame specified in this section or who, as a result of information on the returned form, is determined by the Department of Criminal Justice Training, following a hearing pursuant to KRS Chapter 13B, to not have received the training required by law shall have his or her concealed deadly weapon license revoked by the Department of Kentucky State Police, following a hearing conducted by the Department of Criminal Justice Training pursuant to KRS Chapter 13B, at which hearing the person is found to have violated the provisions of this section or who has been found not to have received the training required by law;

(i) If a concealed deadly weapon license holder is convicted of, pleads guilty to, or enters an Alford plea to a felony offense, then his or her concealed deadly weapon license shall be forthwith revoked by the Department of Kentucky State Police as a matter of law;

(j) If a concealed deadly weapon instructor or instructor trainer is convicted of, pleads guilty to, or enters an Alford plea to a felony offense, then his or her concealed deadly weapon instructor certification or concealed deadly weapon instructor trainer certification shall be revoked by the Department of Criminal Justice Training as a matter of law; and

(k) The following shall be in effect:

1. Action to eliminate the firearms instructor trainer program is prohibited. The program shall remain in effect, and no firearms instructor trainer shall have his or her certification reduced to that of certified firearms instructor;

2. The Department of Kentucky State Police shall revoke the concealed deadly weapon license of any person who received no firearms training as required by KRS 237.126 and administrative regulations, or who received insufficient training as required by KRS 237.128 and administrative regulations, if the person voluntarily admits nonreceipt of training or admits receipt of insufficient training, or if either nonreceipt of training or receipt of insufficient training is proven following a hearing conducted by the Department of Criminal Justice Training pursuant to KRS Chapter 13B.

237.115. Construction of KRS 237.110 – Prohibition by local government units of carrying concealed deadly weapons in governmental buildings – Restriction on criminal penalties.

(1) Except as provided in KRS 527.020, nothing contained in KRS 237.110 shall be construed to limit, restrict, or prohibit in any manner the right of a college, university, or any postsecondary education facility, including technical schools and community colleges, to control the possession of deadly weapons on any property owned or controlled by them or the right of a unit of state, city, county, urban-county, or charter county government to prohibit the carrying of concealed deadly weapons by licensees in that portion of a building actually owned, leased, or occupied by that unit of government.

(2) Except as provided in KRS 527.020, the legislative body of a state, city, county, or urban-county government may, by statute, administrative regulation, or ordinance, prohibit or limit the carrying of concealed deadly weapons by licensees in that portion of a building owned, leased, or controlled by that unit of government. That portion of a building in which the carrying of concealed deadly weapons is prohibited or limited shall be clearly identified by signs posted at the entrance to the restricted area. The statute or ordinance shall exempt any building used for public housing by private persons, highway rest areas, firing ranges, and private dwellings owned, leased, or controlled by that unit of government from any restriction on the carrying or possession of deadly weapons. The statute, administrative regulation, or ordinance shall not specify any criminal penalty for its violation but may specify that persons violating the statute or ordinance may be denied entrance to the building, ordered to leave the building, and if employees of the unit of government, be subject to employee disciplinary measures for violation of the provisions of the statute or ordinance. The provisions of this section shall not be deemed to be a violation of KRS 65.870 if the requirements of this section are followed. The provisions of this section shall not apply to any other unit of government.

(3) Unless otherwise specifically provided by the Kentucky Revised Statutes or applicable federal law, no criminal penalty shall attach to carrying a concealed firearm or other deadly weapon with a permit at any location at which an unconcealed firearm or other deadly weapon may be constitutionally carried.

237.124. Program for training applicants for concealed deadly weapon license.

(1) The Department of Criminal Justice Training shall operate a program for the training of applicants for a concealed deadly weapon license. Only the General Assembly may eliminate the training program for applicants for a concealed deadly weapon license.

(2) Training pursuant to this section shall be conducted by a firearms instructor trainer or certified firearms instructor in accordance with the provisions of this chapter and administrative regulations promulgated thereunder.

237.126. Misrepresentation of having conducted training courses.

(1) A firearms instructor trainer or certified firearms instructor is guilty of not providing firearms training if he or she represents to the department that he or she has conducted training for a student firearms instructor or for an applicant in an applicant training course and has not, in fact, provided any such training.

(2) Not providing firearms training is a Class D felony.

237.128. Providing incomplete firearms training.

(1) A firearms instructor trainer or firearms instructor is guilty of providing incomplete firearms training if he or she represents to the department that he or she has conducted training for a student firearms instructor or for an applicant in an applicant training course and has not, in fact, provided lecture instruction, showed a required visual aid, conducted hands-on firearm safety and cleaning training, provided range instruction and range firing, or has permitted a student to qualify on a target on which the student has not achieved the marksmanship required by administrative regulation.

(2) Providing incomplete firearms training is a Class D felony.

237.130. Failure to report nonreceipt of firearms training when receiving certification without notice to specified law enforcement or prosecutorial personnel.

(1) A person is guilty of failure to report nonreceipt of firearms training when he or she receives certification that he or she has successfully completed a firearms instructor trainer, certified firearms instructor, or applicant training course and has not, in fact, received any such training and has not reported the matter in writing to the sheriff, Commonwealth's attorney, or county attorney serving the county in which the training was conducted or has not made a written report to the Department of Kentucky State Police and provided a copy of the certification documents to the agency reported to along with the report. The report shall be made not more than 30 working days after receiving documentation of successful completion of training, unless a request for additional time has been made and has been granted by an officer or agency to which the report shall be made.

(2) Failure to report nonreceipt of firearms training is a Class A misdemeanor.

(3) A person who makes a report pursuant to this section within the time frame specified in subsection (1) of this section shall not be prosecuted for a violation of this section and shall be eligible to reenroll in the level of class for which they were originally enrolled.

237.132. Failure to report insufficient firearms training when receiving certification without notice to specified law enforcement or prosecutorial personnel.

(1) A person is guilty of failure to report insufficient firearms training when he or she receives certification that he or she has successfully completed a firearms instructor trainer, certified firearms instructor, or applicant training course and has not, in fact received lecture instruction, the showing of a required visual aid, hands-on firearm safety and cleaning training, range instruction and range firing, or has not successfully completed the marksmanship requirement during range firing and has not reported the matter in writing to the sheriff, Commonwealth's attorney, or county attorney serving the county in which the training was conducted or has not made a written report to the Department of Kentucky State Police and provided a copy of the certification documents to the agency reported to along with the report. The report shall be made not more than 30 working days after receiving documentation of successful completion of training, unless additional time is requested and has been granted by an officer or agency to which a report shall be made.

(2) Failure to report insufficient firearms training is a Class A misdemeanor.

(3) A person who makes a report pursuant to this section within the time frame specified in subsection (1) of this section shall not be prosecuted for a violation of this section and shall be eligible to reenroll in the level of class for which the person was originally enrolled.

237.137. Concealed carry authority for off-duty and certified retired peace officers.
Off-duty peace officers authorized to do so by the government employing the officer and retired peace officers certified under KRS 237.138 to 237.142 may carry concealed firearms on or about their persons at all times and at any location within the Commonwealth where an on-duty peace officer is permitted to carry firearms.

237.138. Application of KRS 237.138 to 237.142 to retired peace officers.
KRS 237.138 to 237.142 shall apply to any elected or appointed peace officer who is honorably retired and who:

(1) Meets the provisions of the federal Law Enforcement Officers Safety Act, 18 U.S.C. sec. 926C;

(2) Meets the provisions of KRS 237.138 to 237.142; and

(3) Desires to carry a concealed deadly weapon in conformity with the provisions of the federal Law Enforcement Officers Safety Act, 18 U.S.C. sec. 926C.

237.140. Certification for retired peace officer to carry concealed deadly weapon – Administrative regulations – Requirements – Firearms instruction.

(1) (a) Certification for a retired peace officer to carry a concealed deadly weapon pursuant to KRS 237.138 to 237.142 shall be administered by the Department of Kentucky State Police.

(b) Costs of certification shall be paid for by moneys generated by the concealed deadly weapon license program under KRS 15.383 and collected by the Department of Kentucky State Police pursuant to that section.

(c) The Department of Kentucky State Police shall promulgate administrative regulations in accordance with KRS Chapter 13A necessary to implement the provisions of KRS 237.138 to 237.142. The regulations shall allow the validity of any license or certifying documentation issued to the retired peace officer under this section to be extended in yearly increments not more than 4 times. To facilitate this objective, the regulations may authorize the material required by subsection (2) of this section to be submitted to the person supervising the firearms qualifications under subsection (4)(b) of this section, with that person then submitting the material to the Department of Kentucky State Police and signing the license or certification in a manner that satisfies the requirements of federal law as to the retiree's passage of the required yearly firearms testing.

(2) Each retired peace officer who desires certification to carry a concealed deadly weapon shall annually submit:

(a) Evidence of retired status to the commissioner of the Department of Kentucky State Police together with all information required by federal law, this section, and administrative regulations promulgated pursuant to this section;

(b) Evidence of successful completion of firearms qualification required under this section; and

(c) A notarized statement that he or she is not prohibited by state or federal law from possessing a firearm.

(3) Each law enforcement agency that employed the retired peace officer, or at which the retired peace officer served in an elected capacity, shall provide to the retired officer and the Department of Kentucky State Police the information required by federal law, this section, and the administrative regulations promulgated pursuant to this section in a prompt and efficient manner, without charge either to the Department of Kentucky State Police or the retiree.

(4) (a) Each retired peace officer shall annually fire 20 rounds at an adult size silhouette target at a range of 21 feet, with a handgun, and shall hit the target not less than 11 times to obtain or maintain certification under KRS 237.138 to 237.142.

(b) The rounds fired pursuant to paragraph (a) of this subsection shall be done under the supervision of:

1. A firearms instructor of the retiree's former employing agency;

2. A currently certified peace officer who has successfully completed a Kentucky Law Enforcement Council approved firearms instructor course;

3. A Department of Criminal Justice Training certified police firearms instructor or instructor trainer; or

4. A Department of Criminal Justice Training certified concealed carry instructor or instructor trainer.

(c) A firearms instructor may, if not compensated pursuant to paragraph (d) of this subsection, charge each participant a fee of not more than $20, which shall include the cost of the range, firearms instructor, range personnel, targets, and all other costs associated therewith, but not the cost of ammunition. Ammunition, or the cost of ammunition, shall be provided by the retiree.

(d) A local or state law enforcement agency that desires to conduct firearms qualification for its retirees shall schedule not less than 2 dates for firearms qualification per year, and those dates shall be approximately 6 months apart. The local or state law enforcement agency may charge each participant a fee of not more than $20, which shall include the cost of use of the range, firearms instructor, range personnel, targets, and all other costs associated therewith, but not the cost of ammunition. Ammunition, or the cost of ammunition, shall be provided by the retiree.

(e) No employer or appointing authority of a firearms instructor who has successfully completed a Kentucky Law Enforcement Council approved firearms instructor course, Department of Criminal Justice Training certified police firearms instructor or instructor trainer, or Department of Criminal Justice Training certified concealed carry instructor or instructor trainer shall prohibit or in any way limit the instructor from qualifying active or retired peace officers in conformity with KRS 237.138 or 237.142 while that instructor is off duty. No employer or appointing authority of an instructor specified in this paragraph shall be liable in civil damages for the actions or omissions of the instructor during qualification of active or retired peace officers when that instructor is off duty.

237.142. Availability of range facilities for retired peace officers.
(1) The following agencies of the Commonwealth shall make range facilities available not less than 4 days per year for firearms qualification by retired peace officers seeking certification pursuant to the provisions of KRS 237.138 to 237.142:
    (a) The Justice and Public Safety Cabinet;
    (b) The Department of Military Affairs; and
    (c) The Department of Fish and Wildlife Resources.
(2) Firearms qualification may be conducted at any location, public or private, at which a handgun may be safely fired. The safety of the location at which firing takes place shall be the responsibility of the instructor conducting the qualification.

Shooting Ranges

237.200. Definitions for KRS 237.210 and 237.220. As used in KRS 237.210 and 237.220:
(1) **"Shooting range"** or **"range"** means an area designated and operated by a person for the shooting of firearms and not available for that use by the general public without payment of a fee, membership contribution, or dues, or by invitation of an authorized person; or any area so designated and operated by a unit of government, regardless of the terms of admission thereto.
(2) **"Unit of government"** means any of the departments of state government or political subdivisions of the state, cities, counties, urban-counties, or charter counties, or any of their respective departments, agencies, or authorities.

237.210. Effect of changed conditions on nuisance actions involving shooting ranges – Standing to sue – Limitation of liability – Prohibition against retroactive application of laws.
(1) No shooting range shall be or shall become a nuisance, either public or private, solely as a result of changed conditions in or around the locality of the range if the range has been in operation for 1 year since the date on which it commenced operation as a shooting range. Subsequent physical expansion of the range or expansion of the types of firearms in use at the range shall not establish a new date of commencement of operations for purposes of this section unless the change triples the amount of the noise produced by the shooting range. The increase in the noise level at the shooting range shall be measured by an independent testing agency or a unit of government and shall compare the highest noise levels during any 1 month during which the range is in full operation with a subsequent month in which the range is in full operation and conducting a comparable level of shooting activities. Only a person who lives adjacent to the shooting range shall have standing to bring an action under this section.
(2) No shooting range or unit of government or person owning, operating, or using a shooting range for the shooting of firearms shall be subject to any action for civil or criminal liability, damages, abatement, or injunctive relief resulting from or relating to noise generated by the operation of the range if the range remains in compliance with noise control or nuisance abatement administrative regulations, statutes, or ordinances applicable to the range on the date on which it commenced operation.
(3) No administrative regulations, statutes, or ordinances relating to noise control, noise pollution, or noise abatement adopted or enacted by a unit of government shall be applied retroactively to prohibit conduct at a shooting range, which conduct was lawful and being engaged in prior to the adoption or enactment of the administrative regulations, statutes, or ordinances.

Penalties

237.990. Penalties.
(1) Any person who violates any of the provisions of KRS 237.030 to 237.050 shall be guilty of a Class D felony.
(2) Any person who violates any of the provisions of KRS 237.030 to 237.050, and in so doing uses any destructive device or booby trap device to avoid detection by law enforcement or other government personnel or to avoid theft or

detection by any other person, of any controlled substance as set forth in KRS Chapter 218A and held in violation of KRS 218A.140, shall be guilty of a Class C felony.

TITLE L Kentucky Penal Code
Chapter 527 Offenses Relating to Firearms and Weapons

527.010. Definitions for chapter. The following definitions apply in this chapter unless the context otherwise requires:

(2) "Deface" means to remove, deface, cover, alter, or destroy the manufacturer's serial number or any other distinguishing number or identification mark.

(3) "Destructive device" shall have the same meaning as set forth in KRS 237.030.

(4) "Firearm" means any weapon which will expel a projectile by the action of an explosive.

(5) "Handgun" means any pistol or revolver originally designed to be fired by the use of a single hand, or any other firearm originally designed to be fired by the use of a single hand.

527.020. Carrying concealed deadly weapon.

(1) A person is guilty of carrying a concealed weapon when he or she carries concealed a firearm or other deadly weapon on or about his or her person.

(2) Peace officers and certified court security officers, when necessary for their protection in the discharge of their official duties; United States mail carriers when actually engaged in their duties; and agents and messengers of express companies, when necessary for their protection in the discharge of their official duties, may carry concealed weapons on or about their person.

(3) The director of the Division of Law Enforcement in the Department of Fish and Wildlife Resources, conservation officers of the Department of Fish and Wildlife Resources, and policemen directly employed by state, county, city, or urban-county governments may carry concealed deadly weapons on or about their person at all times within the Commonwealth of Kentucky, when expressly authorized to do so by law or by the government employing the officer.

(4) Persons, except those specified in subsection (5) of this section, licensed to carry a concealed deadly weapon pursuant to KRS 237.110 may carry a firearm or other concealed deadly weapon on or about their persons at all times within the Commonwealth of Kentucky, if the firearm or concealed deadly weapon is carried in conformity with the requirements of that section. Unless otherwise specifically provided by the Kentucky Revised Statutes or applicable federal law, no criminal penalty shall attach to carrying a concealed firearm or other deadly weapon with a permit at any location at which an unconcealed firearm or other deadly weapon may be constitutionally carried. No person or organization, public or private, shall prohibit a person licensed to carry a concealed deadly weapon from possessing a firearm, ammunition, or both, or other deadly weapon in his or her vehicle in compliance with the provisions of KRS 237.110 and 237.115. Any attempt by a person or organization, public or private, to violate the provisions of this subsection may be the subject of an action for appropriate relief or for damages in a Circuit Court or District Court of competent jurisdiction.

(5) (a) The following persons, if they hold a license to carry a concealed deadly weapon pursuant to KRS 237.110 or 237.138 to 237.142, may carry a firearm or other concealed deadly weapon on or about their persons at all times and at all locations within the Commonwealth of Kentucky, without any limitation other than as provided in this subsection:

    1. A Commonwealth's attorney or assistant Commonwealth's attorney;

    2. A retired Commonwealth's attorney or retired assistant Commonwealth's attorney;

    3. A county attorney or assistant county attorney;

    4. A retired county attorney or retired assistant county attorney;

    5. A justice or judge of the Court of Justice;

    6. A retired or senior status justice or judge of the Court of Justice; and

    7. A retired peace officer who holds a concealed deadly weapon license issued pursuant to the federal Law Enforcement Officers Safety Act, 18 U.S.C. sec. 926C, and KRS 237.138 to 237.142.

  (b) The provisions of this subsection shall not authorize a person specified in this subsection to carry a concealed deadly weapon in a detention facility as defined in KRS 520.010 or on the premises of a detention facility without the permission of the warden, jailer, or other person in charge of the facility, or the permission of a person authorized by the warden, jailer, or other person in charge of the detention facility to give such permission. As used in this section, "detention facility" does not include courtrooms, facilities, or other premises used by the Court of Justice or administered by the Administrative Office of the Courts.

  (c) A person specified in this section who is issued a concealed deadly weapon license shall be issued a license which bears on its face the statement that it is valid at all locations within the Commonwealth of Kentucky and may have such other identifying characteristics as determined by the Department of Kentucky State Police.

(6) (a) Except provided in this subsection, the following persons may carry concealed deadly weapons on or about their person at all times and at all locations within the Commonwealth of Kentucky:

    1. An elected sheriff and full-time and part-time deputy sheriffs certified pursuant to KRS 15.380 to 15.404 when expressly authorized to do so by the unit of government employing the officer;

    2. An elected jailer and a deputy jailer who has successfully completed Department of Corrections basic training and maintains his or her current in-service training when expressly authorized to do so by the jailer; and

3. The department head or any employee of a corrections department in any jurisdiction where the office of elected jailer has been merged with the office of sheriff who has successfully completed Department of Corrections basic training and maintains his or her current in-service training when expressly authorized to do so by the unit of government by which he or she is employed.

(b) The provisions of this subsection shall not authorize a person specified in this subsection to carry a concealed deadly weapon in a detention facility as defined in KRS 520.010 or on the premises of a detention facility without the permission of the warden, jailer, or other person in charge of the facility, or the permission of a person authorized by the warden, jailer, or other person in charge of the detention facility to give such permission. As used in this section, "detention facility" does not include courtrooms, facilities, or other premises used by the Court of Justice or administered by the Administrative Office of the Courts.

(7) (a) A full-time paid peace officer of a government agency from another state or territory of the United States or an elected sheriff from another territory of the United States may carry a concealed deadly weapon in Kentucky, on or off duty, if the other state or territory accords a Kentucky full-time paid peace officer and a Kentucky elected sheriff the same rights by law. If the other state or territory limits a Kentucky full-time paid peace officer or elected sheriff to carrying a concealed deadly weapon while on duty, then that same restriction shall apply to a full-time paid peace officer or elected sheriff from that state or territory.

(b) The provisions of this subsection shall not authorize a person specified in this subsection to carry a concealed deadly weapon in a detention facility as defined in KRS 520.010 or on the premises of a detention facility without the permission of the warden, jailer, or other person in charge of the facility, or the permission of a person authorized by the warden, jailer, or other person in charge of the detention facility to give such permission. As used in this section, "detention facility" does not include courtrooms, facilities, or other premises used by the Court of Justice or administered by the Administrative Office of the Courts.

(8) A loaded or unloaded firearm or other deadly weapon shall not be deemed concealed on or about the person if it is located in any enclosed container, compartment, or storage space installed as original equipment in a motor vehicle by its manufacturer, including but not limited to a glove compartment, center console, or seat pocket, regardless of whether said enclosed container, storage space, or compartment is locked, unlocked, or does not have a locking mechanism. No person or organization, public or private, shall prohibit a person from keeping a loaded or unloaded firearm or ammunition, or both, or other deadly weapon in a vehicle in accordance with the provisions of this subsection. Any attempt by a person or organization, public or private, to violate the provisions of this subsection may be the subject of an action for appropriate relief or for damages in a Circuit Court or District Court of competent jurisdiction. This subsection shall not apply to any person prohibited from possessing a firearm pursuant to KRS 527.040.

(9) The provisions of this section shall not apply to a person who carries a concealed deadly weapon on or about his or her person without a license issued pursuant to KRS 237.110:

(a) If he or she is the owner of the property or has the permission of the owner of the property, on real property which he or she or his or her spouse, parent, grandparent, or child owns;

(b) If he or she is the lessee of the property or has the permission of the lessee of the property, on real property which he or she or his or her spouse, parent, grandparent, or child occupies pursuant to a lease; or

(c) If he or she is the sole proprietor of the business, on real property owned or leased by the business.

(10) Carrying a concealed weapon is a Class A misdemeanor, unless the defendant has been previously convicted of a felony in which a deadly weapon was possessed, used, or displayed, in which case it is a Class D felony.

527.030. Defacing a firearm.
(1) A person is guilty of defacing a firearm when he intentionally defaces a firearm.
(2) Defacing a firearm is a Class A misdemeanor.

527.040. Possession of firearm by convicted felon – Exceptions.
(1) A person is guilty of possession of a firearm by a convicted felon when he possesses, manufactures, or transports a firearm when he has been convicted of a felony, as defined by the laws of the jurisdiction in which he was convicted, in any state or federal court and has not:

(a) Been granted a full pardon by the Governor or by the President of the United States;

(b) Been granted relief by the United States Secretary of the Treasury pursuant to the Federal Gun Control Act of 1968, as amended.

(2) Possession of a firearm by a convicted felon is a Class D felony unless the firearm possessed is a handgun in which case it is a Class C felony.

(3) The provisions of this section shall apply to any youthful offender convicted of a felony offense under the laws of this Commonwealth. The exceptions contained in KRS 527.100 prohibiting possession of a handgun by a minor shall not apply to this section.

(4) The provisions of this section with respect to handguns, shall apply only to persons convicted after January 1, 1975, and with respect to other firearms, to persons convicted after July 15, 1994.

527.050. Possession of defaced firearm.
(1) A person is guilty of possession of a defaced firearm when he knowingly possesses a defaced firearm unless he makes a report to the police or other appropriate government agency of such possession prior to arrest or authorization of

a warrant by a court.

(2) Possession of a defaced firearm is a Class A misdemeanor.

527.060. Forfeiture. Upon the conviction of any person for the violation of any law of this Commonwealth in which a deadly weapon was used, displayed or unlawfully possessed by such person the court shall order the weapon forfeited to the state and sold, destroyed or otherwise disposed of in accordance with KRS 500.090.

527.070. Unlawful possession of a weapon on school property – Posting of sign – Exemptions.

(1) A person is guilty of unlawful possession of a weapon on school property when he knowingly deposits, possesses, or carries, whether openly or concealed, for purposes other than instructional or school-sanctioned ceremonial purposes, or the purposes permitted in subsection (3) of this section, any firearm or other deadly weapon, destructive device, or booby trap device in any public or private school building or bus, on any public or private school campus, grounds, recreation area, athletic field, or any other property owned, used, or operated by any board of education, school, board of trustees, regents, or directors for the administration of any public or private educational institution. The provisions of this section shall not apply to institutions of postsecondary or higher education.

(2) Each chief administrator of a public or private school shall display about the school in prominent locations, including, but not limited to, sports arenas, gymnasiums, stadiums, and cafeterias, a sign at least 6 inches high and 14 inches wide stating:

UNLAWFUL POSSESSION OF A WEAPON ON SCHOOL PROPERTY IN KENTUCKY IS A FELONY PUNISHABLEBY A MAXIMUM OF FIVE (5) YEARS IN PRISON AND ATEN THOUSAND DOLLAR ($ 10,000) FINE.

Failure to post the sign shall not relieve any person of liability under this section.

(3) The provisions of this section prohibiting the unlawful possession of a weapon on school property shall not apply to:

  (a) An adult who possesses a firearm, if the firearm is contained within a vehicle operated by the adult and is not removed from the vehicle, except for a purpose permitted herein, or brandished by the adult, or by any other person acting with expressed or implied consent of the adult, while the vehicle is on school property;

  (b) Any pupils who are members of the reserve officers training corps or pupils enrolled in a course of instruction or members of a school club or team, to the extent they are required to carry arms or weapons in the discharge of their official class or team duties;

  (c) Any peace officer or police officer authorized to carry a concealed weapon pursuant to KRS 527.020;

  (d) Persons employed by the Armed Forces of the United States or members of the National Guard or militia when required in the discharge of their official duties to carry arms or weapons;

  (e) Civil officers of the United States in the discharge of their official duties. Nothing in this section shall be construed as to allow any person to carry a concealed weapon into a public or private elementary or secondary school building;

  (f) Any other persons, including, but not limited to, exhibitors of historical displays, who have been authorized to carry a firearm by the board of education or board of trustees of the public or private institution;

  (g) A person hunting during the lawful hunting season on lands owned by any public or private educational institution and designated as open to hunting by the board of education or board of trustees of the educational institution;

  (h) A person possessing unloaded hunting weapons while traversing the grounds of any public or private educational institution for the purpose of gaining access to public or private lands open to hunting with the intent to hunt on the public or private lands, unless the lands of the educational institution are posted prohibiting the entry; or

  (i) A person possessing guns or knives when conducting or attending a "gun and knife show" when the program has been approved by the board of education or board of trustees of the educational institution.

(4) Unlawful possession of a weapon on school property is a Class D felony.

527.080. Using restricted ammunition during the commission of a crime – Exception.

(1) A person is guilty of using restricted ammunition during the commission of a crime when he commits any felony offense under this code and is armed at the time of the commission of the offense or in the immediate flight therefrom with a firearm loaded, as defined in KRS 237.060, with armor-piercing ammunition as defined in KRS 237.060 or flanged ammunition as defined in KRS 237.060.

(2) Using restricted ammunition during the commission of a crime is:

  (a) A Class D felony if no shot is fired;

  (b) A Class C felony if a shot is fired and no person is killed or wounded thereby;

  (c) A Class B felony if a shot is fired and a person other than the defendant or an accomplice of the defendant is wounded by the shot; and

  (d) A Class A felony if a shot is fired and a person other than the defendant or an accomplice of the defendant is killed by the shot.

(3) The provisions of this section are intended to be a separate offense from the underlying crime, which shall be punished separately. If a person is convicted of this offense, his sentence shall be served consecutively to the sentence for the underlying offense.

(4) The provisions of this section shall not apply to any person who is justified in acting pursuant to the provisions of KRS Chapter 503.

527.090. Fraudulent firearm transaction.

(1) As used in this section:

(a) "Licensed dealer" means a person who is licensed pursuant to 18 U.S.C. sec. 923 and pursuant to any laws of this Commonwealth and engages in the business of dealing in firearms;

(b) "Materially false information" means information that portrays an illegal transaction as legal or a legal transaction as illegal; and

(c) "Private seller" means a person who sells or offers for sale any firearm.

(2) A person is guilty of fraudulent firearm transaction when he or she knowingly:

(a) Solicits, persuades, encourages, or entices a licensed dealer or private seller of firearms to transfer a firearm under circumstances which the person knows would violate the laws of this Commonwealth or the United States;

(b) Provides to a licensed dealer or private seller of firearms what the person knows to be materially false information with intent to deceive the dealer or seller about the legality of a transfer of a firearm; or

(c) Procures another to engage in conduct prohibited by this section.

(3) Fraudulent firearm transaction is a Class D felony.

Louisiana Revised Statutes

Updated through 2016 Regular Session legislation for the Civil Code, Evidence Code, Titles 1, 2, 4-7, 9-10, 13-16, 18-21, 23-24, 26-29, 31, 35, 41-43, 45, 50, and 52-55, with partial updates for the remaining codes and titles. Updated for all 2016 Second Extraordinary Session Legislation except Titles 39 and 47, which are in progress.
Changes and corrections from the Louisiana State Law Institute are in process.

Office of the Attorney General
1885 N. Third Street
Baton Rouge, LA 70802
Voice: (225) 326-6705
admininfo@ag.state.la.us

New Orleans Field Division
One Galleria Boulevard, Suite 1700
Metairie, Louisiana 70001
Voice: (504) 841-7000
https://www.atf.gov/new-orleans-field-division

PROTECTING THE PUBLIC
SERVING OUR NATION

Table of Contents

TITLE 14. Criminal law
Chapter 1. Criminal code
Part 3. Offenses against property
Subpart C. By misappropriation without violence

§ 14:67.15. Theft of a firearm.

A. Theft of a firearm is the misappropriation or taking of a firearm which belongs to another, either without the consent of the other to the misappropriation or taking or by means of fraudulent conduct, practices, or representations. An intent to deprive the other permanently of the firearm is essential.

B. For purposes of this Section, "firearm" means a shotgun or rifle, or a pistol, revolver, or other handgun.

C. (1) For a first offense, the penalty for theft of a firearm shall be imprisonment with or without hard labor for not less than 2 years nor more than 10 years, without the benefit of probation, parole, or suspension of sentence and a fine of $1,000.

(2) For a second offense, the penalty for theft of a firearm shall be imprisonment with or without hard labor for not less than 5 years nor more than 15 years, without the benefit of probation, parole, or suspension of sentence and a fine of $2,000.

(3) For a third and subsequent offense, the penalty for theft of a firearm shall be imprisonment at hard labor for not less than 15 years nor more than 30 years, without the benefit of probation, parole, or suspension of sentence and a fine of $5,000.

§ 14:69.1. Illegal possession of stolen firearms.

A. (1) Illegal possession of stolen firearms is the intentional possessing, procuring, receiving, or concealing of a firearm which has been the subject of any form of misappropriation.

(2) It shall be an affirmative defense to a prosecution for a violation of this Section that the offender had no knowledge that the firearm was the subject of any form of misappropriation.

(3) It shall be an affirmative defense to a prosecution for a violation of this Section that the alleged offender has or had possession of the firearm pursuant to his regular course of business, is in possession of a valid federal firearms license, is routinely in the possession of firearms for sale, pawn, lease, rent, repair, modification, or other legitimate acts as part of his normal scope of business operations, and is enforcing a privilege pursuant to R.S. 9:4502.

B. Whoever commits the crime of illegal possession of firearms shall be punished as follows:

(1) For a first offense, the penalty shall be imprisonment, with or without hard labor, for not less than 1 year nor more than 5 years.

(2) For second and subsequent offenses, the penalty shall be imprisonment, with or without hard labor, for not less than 2 years nor more than 10 years.

Part 5. Offenses affecting the public morals
Subpart B. Offenses affecting general morality
2. Offenses affecting the health and morals of minors

§ 14:91. Unlawful sales of weapons to minors.

A. Unlawful sales of weapons to minors is the selling or otherwise delivering for value of any firearm or other instrumentality customarily used as a dangerous weapon to any person under the age of eighteen. Lack of knowledge of the minor's age shall not be a defense.

B. Whoever commits the crime of unlawful sales of weapons to minors shall be fined not more than $300 or imprisoned for not more than 6 months, or both.

Part 6. Offenses affecting the public generally
Subpart A. Offenses affecting the public safety

§ 14:94. Illegal use of weapons or dangerous instrumentalities.

A. Illegal use of weapons or dangerous instrumentalities is the intentional or criminally negligent discharging of any firearm, or the throwing, placing, or other use of any article, liquid, or substance, where it is foreseeable that it may result in death or great bodily harm to a human being.

B. Except as provided in Subsection E, whoever commits the crime of illegal use of weapons or dangerous instrumentalities shall be fined not more than $1,000, or imprisoned with or without hard labor for not more than 2 years, or both.

C. Except as provided in Subsection E, on a second or subsequent conviction, the offender shall be imprisoned at hard labor for not less than 5 years nor more than 7 years, without benefit of probation or suspension of sentence.

D. The enhanced penalty upon second and subsequent convictions provided for in Subsection C of this Section shall not be applicable in cases where more than 5 years have elapsed since the expiration of the maximum sentence, or sentences, of the previous conviction or convictions, and the time of the commission of the last offense for which he has been convicted. The sentence to be imposed in such event shall be the same as may be imposed upon a first conviction.

E. Whoever commits the crime of illegal use of weapons or dangerous instrumentalities by discharging a firearm from a motor vehicle located upon a public street or highway, where the intent is to injure, harm, or frighten another human being, shall be imprisoned at hard labor for not less than 5 nor more than 10 years without benefit of probation or suspension of sentence.

F. Whoever commits the crime of illegal use of weapons or dangerous instrumentalities by discharging a firearm while committing, attempting to commit, conspiring to commit, or soliciting, coercing, or intimidating another person to commit a crime of violence or violation of the Uniform Controlled Dangerous Substances Law, shall be imprisoned at hard labor for not less than 10 years nor more than 20 years, without benefit of parole, probation, or suspension of sentence. If the firearm used in violation of this Subsection is a machine gun or is equipped with a firearm silencer or muffler, as defined by R.S. 40:1751 and R.S. 40:1781, respectively, the offender shall be sentenced to imprisonment for not less than 20 years nor more than 30 years, without benefit of parole, probation, or suspension of sentence. Upon a second or subsequent conviction, under this Subsection, such offender shall be sentenced to imprisonment for not less than 20 years. If the violation of this Subsection, upon second or subsequent conviction, involves the use of a machine gun or a firearm equipped with a firearm silencer or muffler, such offender shall be sentenced to imprisonment for life without benefit of parole, probation, or suspension of sentence.

§ 14:95. Illegal carrying of weapons.

A. Illegal carrying of weapons is:

(1) The intentional concealment of any firearm, or other instrumentality customarily used or intended for probable use as a dangerous weapon, on one's person; or

(2) The ownership, possession, custody or use of any firearm, or other instrumentality customarily used as a dangerous weapon, at any time by an enemy alien; or

(5) (a) The intentional possession or use by any person of a dangerous weapon on a school campus during regular school hours or on a school bus. "School" means any elementary, secondary, high school, or vo-tech school in this state and "campus" means all facilities and property within the boundary of the school property. "School bus" means any motor bus being used to transport children to and from school or in connection with school activities.

(b) The provisions of this Paragraph shall not apply to:

(i) A peace officer as defined by R.S. 14:30(B) in the performance of his official duties.

(ii) A school official or employee acting during the normal course of his employment or a student acting under the direction of such school official or employee.

(iii) Any person having the written permission of the principal or school board and engaged in competition or in marksmanship or safety instruction.

B. (1) Whoever commits the crime of illegal carrying of weapons shall be fined not more than $500, or imprisoned for not more than 6 months, or both.

(2) Whoever commits the crime of illegal carrying of weapons with any firearm used in the commission of a crime of violence as defined in R.S. 14:2(B), shall be fined not more than $2,000, or imprisoned, with or without hard labor, for not less than 1 year nor more than 2 years, or both. Any sentence issued pursuant to the provisions of this Paragraph and any sentence issued pursuant to a violation of a crime of violence as defined in R.S. 14:2(B) shall be served consecutively.

C. On a second conviction, the offender shall be imprisoned with or without hard labor for not more than 5 years.

D. On third and subsequent convictions, the offender shall be imprisoned with or without hard labor for not more than 10 years without benefit of parole, probation, or suspension of sentence.

E. If the offender uses, possesses, or has under his immediate control any firearm, or other instrumentality customarily used or intended for probable use as a dangerous weapon, while committing or attempting to commit a crime of violence or while unlawfully in the possession of a controlled dangerous substance except the possession of 14 grams or less of marijuana, or during the unlawful sale or distribution of a controlled dangerous substance, the offender shall be fined not more than $10,000 and imprisoned at hard labor for not less than 5 nor more than 10 years without the benefit of probation, parole, or suspension of sentence. Upon a second or subsequent conviction, the offender shall be imprisoned at hard labor for not less than 20 years nor more than 30 years without the benefit of probation, parole, or suspension of sentence

F. (1) For purposes of determining whether a defendant has a prior conviction for a violation of this Section, a conviction pursuant to this Section or a conviction pursuant to an ordinance of a local governmental subdivision of this state which contains the elements provided for in Subsection A of this Section shall constitute a prior conviction.

(2) The enhanced penalty upon second, third, and subsequent convictions shall not be applicable in cases where more than 5 years have elapsed since the expiration of the maximum sentence, or sentences, of the previous conviction or convictions, and the time of the commission of the last offense for which he has been convicted; the sentence to be imposed in such event shall be the same as may be imposed upon a first conviction.

(3) Any ordinance that prohibits the unlawful carrying of firearms enacted by a municipality, town, or similar political subdivision or governing authority of this state shall be subject to the provisions of R.S. 40:1796.

G. (1) The provisions of this Section except Paragraph (4) of Subsection A shall not apply to sheriffs and their deputies, state and city police, constables and town marshals, or persons vested with police power when in the actual discharge of official duties. These provisions shall not apply to sheriffs and their deputies and state and city police who are not actually discharging their official duties, provided that such persons are full time, active, and certified by the Council on Peace

Officer Standards and Training and have on their persons valid identification as duly commissioned law enforcement officers.

(2) The provisions of this Section except Paragraph (4) of Subsection A shall not apply to any law enforcement officer who is retired from full-time active law enforcement service with at least 12 years of service upon retirement, nor shall it apply to any enforcement officer of the office of state parks, in the Department of Culture, Recreation and Tourism who is retired from active duty as an enforcement officer, provided that such retired officers have on their persons valid identification as retired law enforcement officers, which identification shall be provided by the entity which employed the officer prior to his or her public retirement. The retired law enforcement officer must be qualified annually in the use of firearms by the Council on Peace Officer Standards and Training and have proof of such qualification. This exception shall not apply to such officers who are medically retired based upon any mental impairment.

(3) (a) The provisions of this Section except Paragraph (4) of Subsection A shall not apply to active or retired reserve or auxiliary law enforcement officers qualified annually by the Council on Peace Officer Standards and Training and who have on their person valid identification as active or retired reserve law or auxiliary municipal police officers. The active or retired reserve or auxiliary municipal police officer shall be qualified annually in the use of firearms by the Council on Peace Officer Standards and Training and have proof of such certification.

(b) For the purposes of this Paragraph, a reserve or auxiliary municipal police officer shall be defined as a volunteer, non-regular, sworn member of a law enforcement agency who serves with or without compensation and has regular police powers while functioning as such agency's representative, and who participates on a regular basis in agency activities including, but not limited to those pertaining to crime prevention or control, and the preservation of the peace and enforcement of the law.

H. (1) Except as provided in Paragraph (A)(5) of this Section and in Paragraph (2) of this Subsection, the provisions of this Section shall not prohibit active justices or judges of the supreme court, courts of appeal, district courts, parish courts, juvenile courts, family courts, city courts, federal courts domiciled in the state of Louisiana, and traffic courts, members of either house of the legislature, officers of either house of the legislature, the legislative auditor, designated investigative auditors, constables, coroners, designated coroner investigators, district attorneys and designated assistant district attorneys, United States attorneys and assistant United States attorneys and investigators, the attorney general, designated assistant attorneys general, and justices of the peace from possessing and concealing a handgun on their person when such persons are qualified annually in the use of firearms by the Council on Peace Officer Standards and Training.

(2) Nothing in this Subsection shall permit the carrying of a weapon in the state capitol building.

I. The provisions of this Section shall not prohibit the carrying of a concealed handgun by a person who is a college or university police officer under the provisions of R.S. 17:1805 and who is carrying a concealed handgun in accordance with the provisions of that statute.

K. (1) The provisions of this Section shall not prohibit a retired justice or judge of the supreme court, courts of appeal, district courts, parish courts, juvenile courts, family courts, city courts, retired attorney general, retired assistant attorneys general, retired district attorneys, and retired assistant district attorneys, from possessing and concealing a handgun on their person provided that such retired person is qualified annually in the use of firearms by the Council on Peace Officer Standards and Training and has on their person valid identification showing proof of their status as a retired justice, judge, attorney general, assistant attorney general, district attorney, or assistant district attorney.

(2) The retired justice, judge, attorney general, assistant attorney general, district attorney, or assistant district attorney shall be qualified annually in the use of firearms by the Council on Peace Officer Standards and Training and have proof of qualification. However, this Subsection shall not apply to a retired justice, judge, attorney general, assistant attorney general, district attorney, or assistant district attorney who is medically retired based upon any mental impairment, or who has entered a plea of guilty or nolo contendere to or been found guilty of a felony offense. For the purposes of this Subsection, "retired district attorney" or "retired assistant district attorney" shall mean a district attorney or an assistant district attorney receiving retirement benefits from the District Attorneys' Retirement System.

§ 14:95.1. Possession of firearm or carrying concealed weapon by a person convicted of certain felonies.

A. It is unlawful for any person who has been convicted of a crime of violence as defined in R.S. 14:2(B) which is a felony or simple burglary, burglary of a pharmacy, burglary of an inhabited dwelling, unauthorized entry of an inhabited dwelling, felony illegal use of weapons or dangerous instrumentalities, manufacture or possession of a delayed action incendiary device, manufacture or possession of a bomb, or possession of a firearm while in the possession of or during the sale or distribution of a controlled dangerous substance, or any violation of the Uniform Controlled Dangerous Substances Law which is a felony, or any crime which is defined as a sex offense in R.S. 15:541, or any crime defined as an attempt to commit one of the above-enumerated offenses under the laws of this state, or who has been convicted under the laws of any other state or of the United States or of any foreign government or country of a crime which, if committed in this state, would be one of the above-enumerated crimes, to possess a firearm or carry a concealed weapon.

B. Whoever is found guilty of violating the provisions of this Section shall be imprisoned at hard labor for not less than 10 nor more than 20 years without the benefit of probation, parole, or suspension of sentence and be fined not less than $1,000 nor more than $5,000. Notwithstanding the provisions of R.S. 14:27, whoever is found guilty of attempting to violate the provisions of this Section shall be imprisoned at hard labor for not more than 7-1/2 years and fined not less than $500 nor more than $2,500.

C. The provisions of this Section prohibiting the possession of firearms and carrying concealed weapons by persons who have been convicted of certain felonies shall not apply to any person who has not been convicted of any felony for a period of 10 years from the date of completion of sentence, probation, parole, or suspension of sentence.

D. For the purposes of this Section, "firearm" means any pistol, revolver, rifle, shotgun, machine gun, submachine gun, black powder weapon, or assault rifle which is designed to fire or is capable of firing fixed cartridge ammunition or from which a shot or projectile is discharged by an explosive.

§ 14:95.1.1. Illegally supplying a felon with a firearm.

A. Illegally supplying a felon with a firearm is the intentional giving, selling, donating, providing, lending, delivering, or otherwise transferring a firearm to any person known by the offender to be a person convicted of a felony and prohibited from possessing a firearm as provided for in R.S. 14:95.1.

B. Whoever commits the crime of illegally supplying a felon with a firearm shall be imprisoned for not more than 5 years and may be fined not less than $1,000 nor more than $5,000. At least 1 year of the sentence imposed shall be served without benefit of parole, probation, or suspension of sentence.

§ 14:95.1.2. Illegally supplying a felon with ammunition.

A. Illegally supplying a felon with ammunition is the intentional giving, selling, donating, providing, lending, delivering, or otherwise transferring ammunition to any person known by the offender to be a person convicted of a felony and prohibited from possessing a firearm as provided for in R.S. 14:95.1.

B. For the purposes of this Section, the following words shall have the following meanings:

(1) "Ammunition" means any projectiles with their fuses, propelling charges, or primers fired from any firearm.

(2) "Firearm" means any pistol, revolver, rifle, shotgun, machine gun, submachine gun, or assault rifle, which is designed to fire or is capable of firing fixed cartridge ammunition or from which a shot or projectile is discharged by an explosive.

C. Whoever commits the crime of illegally supplying a felon with ammunition shall be imprisoned for not more than 5 years and may be fined not less than $1,000 nor more than $5,000.

§ 14:95.1.3. Fraudulent firearm and ammunition purchase.

A. It is unlawful for any person:

(1) To knowingly solicit, persuade, encourage, or entice a licensed dealer or private seller of firearms or ammunition to sell a firearm or ammunition under circumstances which the person knows would violate the laws of this state or of the United States.

(2) To provide to a licensed dealer or private seller of firearms or ammunition what the person knows to be materially false information with intent to deceive the dealer or seller about the legality of a sale of a firearm or ammunition.

(3) To willfully procure another person to engage in conduct prohibited by this Section.

B. For purposes of this Section:

(1) "Ammunition" means any cartridge, shell, or projectile designed for use in a firearm.

(2) "Licensed dealer" means a person who is licensed pursuant to 18 U.S.C. § 923 to engage in the business of dealing in firearms or ammunition.

(3) "Materially false information" means information that portrays an illegal transaction as legal or a legal transaction as illegal.

(4) "Private seller" means a person who sells or offers for sale any firearm or ammunition.

C. The provisions of this Section shall not apply to a law enforcement officer acting in his official capacity or to a person acting at the direction of such law enforcement officer.

D. Whoever violates the provisions of this Section shall be fined not less than $1,000 or more than $5,000, or imprisoned, with or without hard labor, for not less than 1 year or more than 5 years, or both. At least 1 year of the sentence imposed shall be served without benefit of parole, probation, or suspension of sentence.

§ 14:95.2. Carrying a firearm or dangerous weapon by a student or nonstudent on school property, at school-sponsored functions, or in a firearm-free zone.

A. Carrying a firearm, or dangerous weapon as defined in R.S. 14:2, by a student or nonstudent on school property, at a school sponsored function, or in a firearm-free zone is unlawful and shall be defined as possession of any firearm or dangerous weapon, on one's person, at any time while on a school campus, on school transportation, or at any school sponsored function in a specific designated area including but not limited to athletic competitions, dances, parties, or any extracurricular activities, or within 1,000 feet of any school campus.

B. For purposes of this Section, the following words have the following meanings:

(1) "Campus" means all facilities and property within the boundary of the school property.

(2) "Nonstudent" means any person not registered and enrolled in that school or a suspended student who does not have permission to be on the school campus.

(3)."School" means any elementary, secondary, high school, vocational-technical school, college, or university in this state.

(4) "School bus" means any motor bus being used to transport children to and from school or in connection with school activities

C. The provisions of this Section shall not apply to:

(1) A federal law enforcement officer or a Louisiana-commissioned state or local Post Certified law enforcement officer who is authorized to carry a firearm.

(2) A school official or employee acting during the normal course of his employment or a student acting under the direction of such school official or employee.

(3) Any person having the written permission of the principal or as provided in R.S. 17:3361.1.

(4) The possession of a firearm occurring within one thousand feet of school property and entirely on private property, or entirely within a private residence, or in accordance with a concealed handgun permit issued pursuant to R.S. 40:1379.1 or R.S. 40:1379.3.

(5) Any constitutionally protected activity which cannot be regulated by the state, such as a firearm contained entirely within a motor vehicle.

(6) Any student carrying a firearm to or from a class, in which he is duly enrolled, that requires the use of the firearm in the class.

(7) A student enrolled or participating in an activity requiring the use of a firearm including but not limited to any ROTC function under the authorization of a university.

(8) A student who possesses a firearm in his dormitory room or while going to or from his vehicle or any other person with permission of the administration.

D. (1) Whoever commits the crime of carrying a firearm, or a dangerous weapon as defined in R.S. 14:2, by a student or nonstudent on school property, at a school-sponsored function, or in a firearm-free zone shall be imprisoned at hard labor for not more than 5 years.

(2) Whoever commits the crime of carrying a firearm, or a dangerous weapon as defined in R.S. 14:2, on school property or in a firearm-free zone with the firearm or dangerous weapon being used in the commission of a crime of violence as defined in R.S. 14:2(B) on school property or in a firearm-free zone, shall be fined not more than $2,000, or imprisoned, with or without hard labor, for not less than 1 year nor more than 5 years, or both. Any sentence issued pursuant to the provisions of this Paragraph and any sentence issued pursuant to a violation of a crime of violence as defined in R.S. 14:2(B) shall be served consecutively. Upon commitment to the Department of Public Safety and Corrections after conviction for a crime committed on school property, at a school-sponsored function or in a firearm-free zone, the department shall have the offender evaluated through appropriate examinations or tests conducted under the supervision of the department. Such evaluation shall be made within 30 days of the order of commitment.

E. Lack of knowledge that the prohibited act occurred on or within 1,000 feet of school property shall not be a defense.

F. (1) School officials shall notify all students and parents of the impact of this legislation and shall post notices of the impact of this Section at each major point of entry to the school. These notices shall be maintained as permanent notices.

(2) (a) If a student is detained by the principal or other school official for violation of this Section or the school principal or other school official confiscates or seizes a firearm or concealed weapon from a student while upon school property, at a school function, or on a school bus, the principal or other school official in charge at the time of the detention or seizure shall immediately report the detention or seizure to the police department or sheriff's department where the school is located and shall deliver any firearm or weapon seized to that agency.

(b) The confiscated weapon shall be disposed of or destroyed as provided by law.

(3) If a student is detained pursuant to Paragraph (2) of this Subsection for carrying a concealed weapon on campus, the principal shall immediately notify the student's parents.

(4) If a person is arrested for carrying a concealed weapon on campus by a university or college police officer, the weapon shall be given to the sheriff, chief of police, or other officer to whom custody of the arrested person is transferred as provided by R.S. 17:1805(B).

G. Any principal or school official in charge who fails to report the detention of a student or the seizure of a firearm or concealed weapon to a law enforcement agency as required by Paragraph (F)(2) of this Section within 72 hours of notice of the detention or seizure may be issued a misdemeanor summons for a violation hereof and may be fined not more than $500 or sentenced to not more than 40 hours of community service, or both. Upon successful completion of the community service or payment of the fine, or both, the arrest and conviction shall be set aside as provided for in Code of Criminal Procedure Article 894(B).

§ 14:95.2.1. Illegal carrying of a firearm at a parade with any firearm used in the commission of a crime of violence.

A. Whoever commits the crime of illegal carrying of weapons pursuant to R.S. 14:95 with any firearm used in the commission of a crime of violence as defined in R.S. 14:2(B), within 1,000 feet of any parade or demonstration for which a permit is issued by a governmental entity, shall be fined not more than $2,000, or imprisoned, with or without hard labor, for not less than 1 year nor more than 5 years, or both. Any sentence issued pursuant to the provisions of this Subsection and any sentence issued pursuant to a violation of a crime of violence as defined in R.S. 14:2(B) shall be served consecutively.

B. As used in this Section, the following words mean:

(1) "Firearm" means any pistol, revolver, rifle, shotgun, machine gun, submachine gun, or assault rifle, which is designed to fire or is capable of firing fixed cartridge ammunition or from which a shot or projectile is discharged by an explosive.

(2) "Parade" for the purposes of this Section shall be defined as any celebration of Mardi Gras or directly related pre-Lenten or carnival related festivities, school parades, parish parades, state parades or municipal parades, or any demonstration for which a permit is issued by a governmental entity.

(3) "Parade route" means any public sidewalk, street, highway, bridge, alley, road, or other public passageway upon which a parade travels.

C. Lack of knowledge that the prohibited act occurred on or within 1,000 feet of the parade route shall not be a defense.

§ 14:95.2.2. Reckless discharge of a firearm at a parade or demonstration.

A. Reckless discharge of a firearm at a parade or demonstration is the reckless or criminally negligent discharge of a firearm within one thousand feet of any parade, demonstration, or gathering for which a permit is issued by a governmental entity.

B. For the purposes of this Section:

(1) "Firearm" means any pistol, revolver, rifle, shotgun, machine gun, submachine gun, excluding black powder weapons, or assault rifle which is designed to fire or is capable of firing fixed cartridge ammunition or from which a shot or projectile is discharged by an explosive.

(2) "Parade" for the purposes of this Section shall be defined as any celebration of Mardi Gras or directly related pre-Lenten or carnival-related festivities, school parades, parish parades, state parades, or municipal parades, or any demonstration or gathering for which a permit is issued by a governmental entity.

(3) "Reckless or criminally negligent" means that although neither specific nor general criminal intent is present, there is such disregard of the interest of others that the offender's conduct amounts to a gross deviation below the standard of care expected to be maintained by a reasonably careful man under like circumstances.

C. The provisions of this Section shall not apply to:

(1) A federal, state, or local law enforcement officer in the performance of his official duties.

(2) The possession of a firearm occurring within 1,000 feet of a public gathering entirely within a private residence or in accordance with a concealed handgun permit issued pursuant to R.S. 40:1379.1.

(3) The possession or discharge of a firearm by a person who holds a valid certificate as a living historian in the use, storage, and handling of black powder issued by the Louisiana office of state parks for the purpose of historic reenactments if the firearm is a black powder weapon which is an antique firearm as defined in 18 U.S.C. 921(a)(16), or an antique device exempted from the term "destructive device" in 18 U.S.C. 921(a)(4).

(4) The discharge of a firearm by a person engaged in any lawful hunting or sport shooting activity on public or private property.

D. Whoever commits the crime of reckless or negligent discharge of a firearm at a parade or demonstration shall be sentenced to imprisonment at hard labor for not less than 5 nor more than 15 years, at least 3 years of the sentence imposed shall be served without benefit of parole, probation, or suspension of sentence and shall be fined not more than $5,000.

E. The provisions of this Section shall not apply to the discharge of any firearm which has been authorized as part of the parade itself.

§ 14:95.5. Possession of firearm on premises of alcoholic beverage outlet.

A. No person shall intentionally possess a firearm while on the premises of an alcoholic beverage outlet.

B. "Alcoholic beverage outlet" as used herein means any commercial establishment in which alcoholic beverages of either high or low alcoholic content are sold in individual servings for consumption on the premises, whether or not such sales are a primary or incidental purpose of the business of the establishment.

C. (1) The provisions of this Section shall not apply to the owner or lessee of an alcoholic beverage outlet, an employee of such owner or lessee, or to a law enforcement officer or other person vested with law enforcement authority or listed in R.S. 14:95(G) or (H) .

(2) The provisions of this Section shall not apply to a person possessing a firearm in accordance with a concealed handgun permit issued pursuant to R.S. 40:1379.1 or 1379.3 on the premises of an alcoholic beverage outlet which has been issued a Class A-Restaurant permit, as defined in Part II of Chapter 1 or Part II of Chapter 2 of Title 26 of the Louisiana Revised Statutes of 1950.

(3) The provisions of this Section shall not be construed to limit the ability of a sheriff or chief law enforcement officer to establish policies within his department or office regarding the carrying of a concealed handgun on the premises of an alcoholic beverage outlet by any law enforcement officer under his authority.

D. Whoever violates the provisions of this Section shall be fined not more than $500 or imprisoned for not more than 6 months, or both.

§ 14:95.6. Firearm-free zone; notice; signs; crime; penalties.

A. A "firearm-free zone" is an area inclusive of any school campus and within 1,000 feet of any such school campus, and within a school bus, wherein the possession of firearms is prohibited, except as specifically set forth in Subsection B of this Section and R.S. 14:95.2(C).

B. The provisions of this Section shall not apply to:

(1) A federal, state, or local law enforcement building.

(2) A military base.

(3) A commercial establishment which is permitted by law to have firearms or armed security.

(4) Private premises where a firearm is kept pursuant to law.

(5) Any constitutionally protected activity within the firearm-free zone, such as a firearm contained entirely within a motor vehicle.

C. For purposes of this Section:

(1) "School" means any public or private elementary, secondary, high school, or vocational-technical school, college, or university in this state.

(2) "School campus" means all facilities and property within the boundary of the school property.

(3) "School bus" means any motor bus being used to transport children to and from school or in connection with school activities.

D. The local governing authority which has jurisdiction over zoning matters in which each firearm-free zone is located shall publish a map clearly indicating the boundaries of each firearm-free zone in accordance with the specifications in Subsection A. The firearm-free zone map shall be made an official public document and placed with the clerk of court for the parish or parishes in which the firearm-free zone is located.

E. (1) The state superintendent of education, with the approval of the State Board of Elementary and Secondary Education, and the commissioner of higher education, with the approval of the Board of Regents, shall develop a method by which to mark firearm-free zones, including the use of signs or other markings suitable to the situation. Signs or other markings shall be located in a visible manner on or near each school and on and in each school bus indicating that such area is a firearm-free zone and that such zone extends to 1,000 feet from the boundary of school property. The state Department of Education shall assist each approved school with the posting of notice as required in this Subsection.

(2) Signs or other markings, in addition to the method developed pursuant to Paragraph (1) of this Subsection, shall provide notice that armed law enforcement officers are permitted within the firearm-free zone by including in the signs or other markings the language "Law Enforcement Weapons Permitted" or language substantially similar thereto.

F. (1) It is unlawful for any person to cover, remove, deface, alter, or destroy any sign or other marking identifying a firearm-free zone as provided in this Section.

(2) Whoever violates the provisions of this Subsection shall be fined not more than $1,000 or imprisoned for not more than 6 months, or both.

§ 14:95.7. Possession of or dealing in firearms with obliterated numbers or marks.

A. No person shall intentionally receive, possess, carry, conceal, buy, sell, or transport any firearm from which the serial number or mark of identification has been obliterated.

B. This Section shall not apply to any firearm which is an antique or war relic and is inoperable or for which ammunition is no longer manufactured in the United States and is not readily available in the ordinary channels of commercial trade, or which was originally manufactured without such a number.

C. Whoever violates the provisions of this Section shall be fined not more than $1,000 and imprisoned as follows:

(1) For a first offense, the penalty shall be imprisonment, with or without hard labor, for not less than 1 year nor more than 5 years.

(2) For a second or subsequent offense, the penalty shall be imprisonment, with or without hard labor, for not less than 2 years nor more than 10 years.

§ 14:95.8. Illegal possession of a handgun by a juvenile.

A. It is unlawful for any person who has not attained the age of 17 years knowingly to possess any handgun on his person. Any person possessing any handgun in violation of this Section commits the offense of illegal possession of a handgun by a juvenile.

B. (1) On a first conviction, the offender shall be fined not more than $100 and imprisoned for not less than 90 days and not more than 6 months.

(2) On a second conviction, the offender shall be fined not more than $500 and imprisoned with or without hard labor for not more than 2 years.

(3) On a third or subsequent conviction, the offender shall be fined not more than $1,000 and imprisoned at hard labor for not more than 5 years.

(4) A juvenile adjudicated delinquent under this Section, having been previously found guilty or adjudicated delinquent for any crime of violence as defined by R.S. 14:2(B), or attempt or conspiracy to commit any such offense, shall upon a first or subsequent conviction be fined not less than $500 and not more than $1,000 and shall be imprisoned with or without hard labor for not less than 6 months and not more than 5 years. At least 90 days shall be served without benefit of probation, parole, or suspension of sentence.

C. The provisions of this Section shall not apply to any person under the age of 17 years who is:

(1) Attending a hunter's safety course or a firearms safety course.

(2) Engaging in practice in the use of a firearm or target shooting at an established range.

(3) Hunting or trapping pursuant to a valid license issued to him pursuant to the laws of this state.

(4) Traveling to or from any activity described in Paragraph (1), (2), or (3) of this Subsection while in possession of an unloaded gun.

(5) On real property with the permission of his parent or legal guardian and with the permission of the owner or lessee of the property.

(6) At such person's residence and who, with the permission of such person's parent or legal guardian, possesses a handgun.

(7) Possessing a handgun with the written permission of such person's parent or legal guardian; provided that such person carries on his person a copy of such written permission.

D. For the purposes of this Section "handgun" means a firearm as defined in R.S. 14:37.2, provided however, that the barrel length shall not exceed twelve inches.

§ 14:95.10 Possession of a firearm or carrying of a concealed weapon by a person convicted of domestic abuse battery.

A. It is unlawful for any person who has been convicted of the crime of domestic abuse battery, R.S. 14:35.3, to possess a firearm or carry a concealed weapon.

B. Whoever is found guilty of violating the provisions of this Section shall be imprisoned with or without hard labor for not less than 1 year nor more than 5 years and shall be fined not less than $500 nor more than $1,000.

C. A person shall not be considered to have been convicted of domestic abuse battery for purposes of this Section unless the person was represented by counsel in the case, or knowingly and intelligently waived the right to counsel in the case; and in the case of a prosecution for an offense described in this Section for which a person was entitled to a jury trial in the jurisdiction in which the case was tried, either the case was tried by a jury, or the person knowingly and intelligently waived the right to have the case tried by a jury, by guilty plea or otherwise. A person shall not be considered convicted of R.S. 14:35.3 for the purposes of this Section if the conviction has been expunged, set aside, or is an offense for which the person has been pardoned or had civil rights restored unless the pardon, expungement, or restoration of civil rights expressly provides that the person may not ship, possess, or receive firearms.

D. For the provisions of this Section, "firearm" means any pistol, revolver, rifle, shotgun, machine gun, submachine gun, black powder weapon, or assault rifle which is designed to fire or is capable of firing fixed cartridge ammunition or from which a shot or projectile is discharged by an explosive.

E. The provisions of this Section prohibiting the possession of firearms and carrying concealed weapons by persons who have been convicted of domestic abuse battery shall not apply to any person who has not been convicted of domestic abuse battery for a period of 10 years from the date of completion of sentence, probation, parole, or suspension of sentence.

TITLE 40. Public health and safety
Chapter 9. Weapons
Part 1. Machine guns

§ 40:1751. Definitions. For purposes of this Part, "machine gun" includes all firearms of any calibre, commonly known as machine rifles, machine guns, and sub-machine guns, capable of automatically discharging more than 8 cartridges successively without reloading, in which the ammunition is fed to the gun from or by means of clips, disks, belts, or some other separable mechanical device. "Manufacturer" includes all persons manufacturing machine guns; "Merchant" includes all persons dealing with machine guns as merchandise.

§ 40:1752. Handling of machine guns unlawful; exceptions. No person shall sell, keep or offer for sale, loan or give away, purchase, possess, carry, or transport any machine gun within this state, except that:

(1) All duly appointed peace officers may purchase, possess, carry, and transport machine guns.

(2) This Part does not apply to the Army, Navy, or Marine Corps of the United States, the National Guard, and organizations authorized by law to purchase or receive machine guns from the United States or from this state. The members of such Corps, National Guard, and organizations may possess, carry, and transport machine guns while on duty.

(3) Persons possessing war relics may purchase and possess machine guns which are relics of any war in which the United States was involved, may exhibit and carry the machine guns in the parades of any military organization, and may sell, offer to sell, loan, or give the machine guns to other persons possessing war relics.

(4) Guards or messengers employed by common carriers, banks, and trust companies, and pay-roll guards or messengers may possess and carry machine guns while actually employed in and about the shipment, transportation, or delivery, or in the guarding of any money, treasure, bullion, bonds, or other thing of value. Their employers may purchase or receive machine guns and keep them in their possession when the guns are not being used by their guards or messengers.

(5) Manufacturers and merchants may sell, keep or offer for sale, loan or give away, purchase, possess, and transport machine guns in the same manner as other merchandise except as otherwise provided in this Part. Common carriers may possess and transport unloaded machine guns as other merchandise.

§ 40:1753. Transfers of possessions permitted in certain cases; method. No manufacturer or merchant shall permit any machine gun to pass from his possession to the possession of any person other than:

(1) A manufacturer or a merchant.

(2) A common carrier for shipment to a manufacturer or merchant.

(3) A duly authorized agent of the government of the United States or of this state, acting in his official capacity.

(4) A person authorized to purchase a machine gun under the provisions of paragraphs (1) and (4) of R.S. 40:1752.

Manufacturers or merchants shall not deliver a machine gun to any of the persons authorized to purchase it under the provisions of paragraphs (1) and (4) of R.S. 40:1752 unless the person presents a written permit to purchase and possess a machine gun, signed by the sheriff of the parish in which the manufacturer or merchant has his place of business or delivers the machine gun. The manufacturer or merchant shall retain the written permit and keep it on file in his place of business. Each sheriff shall keep a record of all permits issued by him.

§ 40:1754. Registers to be kept; inspection thereof. Every manufacturer or merchant shall keep a register of all machine guns manufactured or handled by him. This register shall show:
(1) The date of the sale, loan, gift, delivery, or receipt of any machine gun;
(2) The name, address, and occupation of the person to whom the machine gun was sold, loaned, given, or delivered, or from whom it was received; and
(3) The purpose for which the person, to whom the machine gun was sold, loaned, given, or delivered, purchased or obtained it.
Upon demand, every manufacturer or merchant shall permit any sheriff or deputy sheriff or any police officer to inspect his entire stock of machine guns, and parts and supplies therefor, and shall produce the register required in this Section and all written permits to purchase or possess a machine gun, which he has retained and filed in his place of business.

§ 40:1755. Penalty.
A. Any manufacturer who:
(1) Passes possession of or delivers a machine gun to any person in violation of R.S. 40:1753; or
(2) Fails to keep an accurate register, as required in R.S. 40:1754; or
(3) Fails to produce or account for a sheriff's permit for each machine gun sold by him for which a permit is necessary under the provisions of R.S. 40:1753, shall be imprisoned at hard labor for not less than 1 year nor more than 5 years.
B. Any person who violates R.S. 40:1752 shall be imprisoned at hard labor for not less than 1 year nor more than 10 years.
C. Whoever, having been convicted of murder, armed or simple robbery, aggravated or simple burglary, or aggravated battery, or an attempt to commit any one of those crimes, thereafter violates any of the provisions of this Part shall be imprisoned at hard labor for not less than 3 years nor more than 10 years.

Part 2. Registration

§ 40:1781. Definitions. For the purpose of this Part, the following terms have the meanings ascribed to them in this Section:
(1) "Dealer" means any person not a manufacturer or importer engaged in this state in the business of selling any firearm. The term includes wholesalers, pawnbrokers, and other persons dealing in used firearms.
(2) "Department" means the Department of Public Safety.
(3) "Firearm" means a shotgun having a barrel of less than 18 inches in length; a rifle having a barrel of less than 16 inches in length; any weapon made from either a rifle or a shotgun if said weapon has been modified to have an overall length of less than 26 inches; any other firearm, pistol, revolver, or shotgun from which the serial number or mark of identification has been obliterated, from which a shot is discharged by an explosive, if that weapon is capable of being concealed on the person; or a machine gun, grenade launcher, flame thrower, bazooka, rocket launcher, excluding black powder weapons, or gas grenade; and includes a muffler or silencer for any firearm, whether or not the firearm is included within this definition. Pistols and revolvers and those rifles and shotguns which have not previously been defined in this Paragraph as firearms from which serial numbers or marks of identification have not been obliterated are specifically exempt from this definition.
(4) "Importer" means any person who imports or brings into the state any firearm.
(5) "Machine gun" means any weapon, including a submachine gun, which shoots or is designed to shoot automatically more than one shot without manual reloading, by a single function of the trigger.
(6) "Manufacturer" means any person who is engaged in this state in the manufacture, assembling, alteration, or repair of any firearm.
(7) "Muffler" or **"silencer"** includes any device for silencing or diminishing the report of any portable weapon such as a rifle, carbine, pistol, revolver, machine gun, submachine gun, shotgun, fowling piece, or other device from which a shot, bullet, or projectile may be discharged by an explosive and is not limited to mufflers and silencers for firearms as defined in this Section.
(8) "Transfer" includes the sale, assignment, pledge, lease, loan, gift, or other disposition of any firearm.

§ 40:1782. Exemptions from Part. This Part does not apply to the following persons and things:
(1) Sheriffs or equivalent municipal officers in municipalities of over ten thousand, when they are acting in their official capacity.
(2) The arms, accoutrements, and equipment of the military and naval forces of the United States or of other officers of the United States authorized by law to possess weapons of any kind.
(3) The arms, accoutrements, and equipment of the militia.
(4) Any firearm which is unserviceable and which is transferred as a curiosity or ornament.

§ 40:1785. Possession or dealing in unregistered or illegally transferred weapons.
No person shall receive, possess, carry, conceal, buy, sell, or transport any firearm which has not been registered or transferred in accordance with Title 18 or Title 26 of the United States Code as applicable.

§ 40:1788. Identification with number or other mark; obliteration or alteration of number or mark.
A. Each manufacturer, importer, and dealer in any firearm shall identify it with a number or other identification mark approved by the department and shall mark or stamp or otherwise place the number or mark thereon in a manner approved by the department.
B. No one shall obliterate, remove, change, or alter this number or mark.

§ 40:1789. Records of importers, manufacturers, or dealers.
Importers, manufacturers, and dealers shall keep such books and records and render such returns in relation to the transactions in firearms specified in this Part as the department requires.

§ 40:1790. Rules and regulations; importation of firearms.
The department may prescribe such rules and regulations as are necessary for carrying out the provisions of this Part.
Under regulations prescribed by the department, any firearm may be imported or brought into this state or possessed or transferred when the purpose thereof is shown to be lawful.

§ 40:1791. Penalty.
Upon the first violation of any provision of this Part the penalty shall be a fine of not less than $500 nor more than $2,000 and imprisonment with or without hard labor for not less than 1 nor more than 5 years. For any subsequent violation of this Part the penalty shall be a fine of not less than $2,000 nor more than $5,000 and imprisonment at hard labor for not less than 5 years nor more than 10 years.

§ 40:1792. Possession of unidentifiable firearm; particular penalties; identification of source of firearm.
A. No person shall intentionally receive, possess, carry, conceal, buy, sell, transfer, or transport any firearm which has been illegally obtained or from which the serial number or individual identifying mark, as required by R.S. 40:1788, has been intentionally obliterated, altered, removed, or concealed.
B. The provisions of this Section shall not apply to any firearm which is an antique or war relic and is inoperable or for which ammunition is no longer manufactured in the United States and is not readily available in the ordinary channels of commercial trade, or which was originally manufactured without such a number.
C. Except as otherwise provided in this Section, whoever violates the provisions of this Section may be fined not more than $1,000 and shall be imprisoned at hard labor for 5 years without benefit of probation, parole, or suspension of sentence.
D. Prior to sentencing for a conviction under this Section, the defendant shall be given the opportunity to identify the source of the firearm upon which the conviction was based. If the defendant reveals the identity of the source of the weapon and the identity of the source is confirmed by the prosecutor or the court, the defendant shall be fined not more than $1,000 or imprisoned for not more than 6 months, or both.
E. Nothing in this Section shall be construed to prevent the prosecution of an individual who obtained the firearm by theft, robbery, deception, or by other unlawful means from the lawful owner of the firearm.
F. Any illegally obtained firearm or a firearm from which the serial number or identifying mark required by R.S. 40:1788 has been obliterated or altered is hereby declared to be contraband and shall be seized by the law enforcement agency of jurisdiction. If it is determined that a person other than the owner was responsible for removing, altering, or obliterating the serial number or identifying mark, the firearm shall be returned to its lawful owner or may be disposed of according to law but only after a new serial number has been permanently fixed on the firearm. If a new serial number is not so affixed, the firearm shall be destroyed by the law enforcement agency in possession of the firearm.

Part 2-A. Miscellaneous provisions

§ 40:1796. Preemption of state law.
A. No governing authority of a political subdivision shall enact after July 15, 1985, any ordinance or regulation more restrictive than state law concerning in any way the sale, purchase, possession, ownership, transfer, transportation, license, or registration of firearms, ammunition, or components of firearms or ammunition; however, this Section shall not apply to the levy and collection of sales and use taxes, license fees and taxes and permit fees, nor shall it affect the authority of political subdivisions to prohibit the possession of a weapon or firearm in certain commercial establishments and public buildings.
B. Nothing in this Section shall prohibit a local governing authority in a high-risk area from developing a plan with federally licensed firearms manufacturers, dealers, or importers to secure the inventory of firearms and ammunition of those licensees in order to prevent looting of the licensee's premises during a declared state of emergency or disaster. Such plan shall be renewed on a periodic basis. The information contained in the plan shall be deemed security procedures as defined in R.S. 44:3.1 and shall be released only to the sheriffs of the parishes or police chiefs of municipalities in which the declared state of emergency or disaster exists.
C. For the purposes of this Section:
   (1) "Declared emergency or disaster" means an emergency or disaster declared by the governor or parish president pursuant to the provisions of the Louisiana Homeland Security and Emergency Assistance and Disaster Act.

(2) "High-risk area" means the parishes of Assumption, Calcasieu, Cameron, Iberia, Jefferson, Lafourche, Orleans, Plaquemines, St. Bernard, St. Charles, St. James, St. John, St. Martin, St. Mary, St. Tammany, Tangipahoa, Terrebonne, and Vermilion.

§ 40:1797. Law enforcement officers; possession of a firearm in courtroom; prohibition. No state or local law enforcement officer shall carry a firearm, whether concealed or not on his person, into a courtroom while attending any session of state, parish, city, municipal, family, juvenile, drug, or traffic court as a party to a proceeding.

§ 40:1798. Firearms; disposal by law enforcement agencies.
A. Notwithstanding any provision of the law to the contrary, the Louisiana Department of Public Safety and Corrections, office of the state police, the Louisiana Department of Wildlife and Fisheries, and each law enforcement agency of a political subdivision of the state shall dispose of firearms which are lawfully seized by and forfeited to those agencies in the manner provided for in this Section.
B. For the purpose of this Section, the following words shall have the following meanings:
  (1) "Contraband" means any firearm which cannot be lawfully owned or possessed by any state or local law enforcement agency or by any private citizen.
  (2) "Firearm" means any pistol, revolver, rifle, shotgun, machine gun, submachine gun, or assault rifle, which is designed to fire or is capable of firing fixed cartridge ammunition or from which a shot or projectile is discharged by an explosive.
  (3) "Forfeited" means that the ownership of the firearm has been transferred to a law enforcement agency by a court order and that the firearm is not being held as evidence or for any other purpose related to an investigation or prosecution of criminal activity.
  (4) "Law enforcement agency" means the Louisiana Department of Public Safety and Corrections, office of state police, the Louisiana Department of Wildlife and Fisheries, the sheriff of any parish, or the police department of any municipality.
  (5) "Seized" means lawfully taken and held by a law enforcement agency in connection with an investigation or prosecution of criminal activity.
C. If the seized or forfeited firearm is contraband, the law enforcement agency shall destroy the seized or forfeited firearm.
D. If the seized or forfeited firearm is not contraband, and if the law enforcement agency knows the owner of the seized or forfeited firearm, and if the owner did not commit any violation of any federal or state law or local ordinance in which the seized or forfeited firearm was involved, and if the owner may lawfully possess the seized or forfeited firearm, the law enforcement agency shall return the seized or forfeited firearm to the owner.
E. If the provisions of Subsections C and D do not apply, the law enforcement agency shall dispose of the seized or forfeited firearm in accordance with the following provisions:
  (1) If the firearm is of a type which can lawfully be possessed and used by a law enforcement agency, the law enforcement agency may dispose of the firearm in one of the following ways:
    (a) The law enforcement agency may retain and use the firearm.
    (b) The law enforcement agency may sell or donate the firearm to another law enforcement agency or may use the firearm as consideration or partial consideration in an exchange with another law enforcement agency.
    (c) The law enforcement agency may sell the firearm to a firearms dealer or a firearms manufacturer, or may use the firearm as consideration or partial consideration in an exchange with a firearms dealer or a firearms manufacturer, provided the firearms dealer or the firearms manufacturer is licensed to buy, sell, or trade that type of firearm.
    (d) The law enforcement agency may destroy the firearm.
  (2) If the firearm is of a type which can lawfully be possessed and used by a private citizen, the law enforcement agency may dispose of the firearm in one of the following ways:
    (a) The law enforcement agency may retain and use the firearm.
    (b) The law enforcement agency may sell or donate the firearm to another law enforcement agency or may use the firearm as consideration or partial consideration in an exchange with another law enforcement agency.
    (c) The law enforcement agency may sell the firearm to a firearms dealer or a firearms manufacturer, or may use the firearm as consideration or partial consideration in an exchange with a firearms dealer or a firearms manufacturer, provided the firearms dealer or the firearms manufacturer is licensed to buy, sell, or trade that type of firearm.
    (d) The law enforcement agency may sell the firearm to a private citizen. A sale of a firearm to a private citizen shall be at a public auction in the same manner as a sale of surplus property. A sale of a firearm to a private citizen shall comply with all federal laws, state laws, and local ordinances which apply to that sale, and the law enforcement agency shall perform the background checks on the purchaser which are required by state and federal laws for sales of firearms by licensed firearms dealers.
    (e) The law enforcement agency may destroy the firearm.
F. Before a law enforcement agency destroys a seized or forfeited firearm under the provisions of Subsections D and E, the law enforcement agency shall ensure that any security interest attached to the firearm to be destroyed is satisfied in favor of the party holding the security interest in the firearm.

§ 40:1799. Preemption of state law; liability of manufacturer, trade association, or dealer of firearms and ammunition.
A. The governing authority of any political subdivision or local or other governmental authority of the state is precluded and preempted from bringing suit to recover against any firearms or ammunition manufacturer, trade association, or

dealer for damages for injury, death, or loss or to seek other injunctive relief resulting from or relating to the lawful design, manufacture, marketing, or sale of firearms or ammunition. The authority to bring such actions as may be authorized by law shall be reserved exclusively to the state.

B. This Section shall not prohibit the governing authority of a political subdivision or local or other governing authority of the state from bringing an action against a firearms or ammunition manufacturer, trade association, or dealer for breach of contract as to firearms or ammunition purchased by the political subdivision or local authority of the state.

Part 4. Armor-piercing bullets

§ 40:1810. Definitions. As used in this Part, "armor-piercing bullet" shall mean any bullet, except a shotgun shell or ammunition primarily designed for use in rifles, that:

(1) Has a steel inner core or core of equivalent density and hardness, truncated cone, and is designed for use in a pistol or revolver as a body armor or metal piercing bullet; or

(2) Has been primarily manufactured or designed, by virtue of its shape, cross-sectional density, or any coating applied thereto, to breach or penetrate body armor when fired from a handgun.

§ 40:1811. Prohibitions.

A. No person shall import, manufacture, sell, purchase, possess, or transfer armor-piercing bullets.

B. Whoever violates the provisions of this Section shall be fined not more than $1,000 or imprisoned with or without hard labor for not more than 1 year, or both.

§ 40:1812. Exemptions. The provisions of this Part shall not apply to:

(1) Law enforcement officers and employees acting in the lawful performance of their duties.

(2) Law enforcement or other authorized agencies conducting a firearms training course, operating a forensic ballistics laboratory, or specializing in the development of ammunition or explosive ordinance.

(3) Department of Corrections officials and employees authorized to carry firearms while engaged in the performance of their official duties.

(4) Members of the armed services or reserve forces of the United States or Louisiana National Guard while engaged in the performance of their official duties.

(5) Federal officials authorized to carry firearms while engaged in the performance of their official duties.

(6) The lawful manufacture, importation, sale, purchase, possession, or transfer of armor-piercing bullets exclusively to or for persons authorized by law to possess such bullets.

(7) A bonafide collector licensed by the Department of Public Safety.

Mississippi Code

Current through the 2016 Regular and 1st and 2nd Extraordinary Sessions of the Legislature

Office of the Attorney General
Walter Sillers Building
550 High Street, Suite 1200
Jackson, MS 39201
Voice: (601) 359-3680
msag05@ago.state.ms.us

New Orleans Field Division
One Galleria Boulevard, Suite 1700
Metairie, Louisiana 70001
Voice: (504) 841-7000
https://www.atf.gov/new-orleans-field-division

PROTECTING THE PUBLIC
SERVING OUR NATION

Table of Contents

TITLE 45. Public Safety and Good Order
Chapter 9. Weapons
Restrictions upon Local Regulation of Firearms or Ammunition

§ 45-9-51. Prohibition against adoption of certain ordinances

(1) Subject to the provisions of § 45-9-53, no county or municipality may adopt any ordinance that restricts the possession, carrying, transportation, sale, transfer or ownership of firearms or ammunition or their components.

(2) No public housing authority operating in this state may adopt any rule or regulation restricting a lessee or tenant of a dwelling owned and operated by such public housing authority from lawfully possessing firearms or ammunition or their components within individual dwelling units or the transportation of such firearms or ammunition or their components to and from such dwelling.

§ 45-9-53. Exceptions; procedure for challenging ordinances; county or municipal programs to purchase weapons from citizens

(1) This section and § 45-9-51 do not affect the authority that a county or municipality may have under another law:

(a) To require citizens or public employees to be armed for personal or national defense, law enforcement, or another lawful purpose;

(b) To regulate the discharge of firearms within the limits of the county or municipality. A county or municipality may not apply a regulation relating to the discharge of firearms or other weapons in the extraterritorial jurisdiction of the county or municipality or in an area annexed by the county or municipality after September 1, 1981, if the firearm or other weapon is:

(i) A shotgun, air rifle or air pistol, BB gun or bow and arrow discharged:

1. On a tract of land of 10 acres or more and more than 150 feet from a residence or occupied building located on another property; and

2. In a manner not reasonably expected to cause a projectile to cross the boundary of the tract; or

(ii) A center fire or rim fire rifle or pistol or a muzzle-loading rifle or pistol of any caliber discharged:

1. On a tract of land of 50 acres or more and more than 300 feet from a residence or occupied building located on another property; and

2. In a manner not reasonably expected to cause a projectile to cross the boundary of the tract;

(d) To regulate the use of firearms in cases of insurrection, riots and natural disasters in which the city finds such regulation necessary to protect the health and safety of the public. However, the provisions of this section shall not apply to the lawful possession of firearms, ammunition or components of firearms or ammunition;

(e) To regulate the storage or transportation of explosives in order to protect the health and safety of the public, with the exception of black powder which is exempt up to 25 pounds per private residence and 50 pounds per retail dealer;

(f) To regulate the carrying of a firearm at: **(i)** a public park or at a public meeting of a county, municipality or other governmental body; **(ii)** a political rally, parade or official political meeting; or **(iii)** a nonfirearm-related school, college or professional athletic event; or

(2) The exception provided by subsection (1)(f) of this section does not apply if the firearm was in or carried to and from an area designated for use in a lawful hunting, fishing or other sporting event and the firearm is of the type commonly used in the activity.

(4) No county or a municipality may use the written notice provisions of § 45-9-101(13) to prohibit concealed firearms on property under their control except:

(a) At a location listed in § 45-9-101(13) indicating that a license issued under § 45-9-101 does not authorize the holder to carry a firearm into that location, as long as the sign also indicates that carrying a firearm is unauthorized only for license holders without a training endorsement or that it is a location included in § 97-37-7(2) where carrying a firearm is unauthorized for all license holders; and

(b) At any location under the control of the county or municipality aside from a location listed in subsection (1)(f) of this section or § 45-9-101(13) indicating that the possession of a firearm is prohibited on the premises, as long as the sign also indicates that it does not apply to a person properly licensed under § 45-9-101 or § 97-37-7(2) to carry a concealed firearm or to a person lawfully carrying a firearm that is not concealed.

(5) (a) A citizen of this state, or a person licensed to carry a concealed pistol or revolver under § 45-9-101, or a person licensed to carry a concealed pistol or revolver with the endorsement under § 97-37-7, who is adversely affected by an ordinance or posted written notice adopted by a county or municipality in violation of this section may file suit for declarative and injunctive relief against a county or municipality in the circuit court which shall have jurisdiction over the county or municipality where the violation of this section occurs.

(b) Before instituting suit under this subsection, the party adversely impacted by the ordinance or posted written notice shall notify the Attorney General in writing of the violation and include evidence of the violation. The Attorney General shall, within 30 days, investigate whether the county or municipality adopted an ordinance or posted written notice in violation of this section and provide the chief administrative officer of the county or municipality notice of his findings, including, if applicable, a description of the violation and specific language of the ordinance or posted written notice found to be in violation. The county or municipality shall have 30 days from receipt of that notice to cure the violation. If the county or municipality fails to cure the violation within that 30-day time period, a suit under paragraph (a) of this subsection may proceed.

(c) If the circuit court finds that a county or municipality adopted an ordinance or posted written notice in violation of this section and failed to cure that violation in accordance with paragraph (b) of this subsection, the circuit court shall issue a permanent injunction against a county or municipality prohibiting it from enforcing the ordinance or posted written notice. Any elected county or municipal official under whose jurisdiction the violation occurred may be civilly liable in a sum not to exceed $1,000, plus all reasonable attorney's fees and costs incurred by the party bringing the suit. Public funds may not be used to defend or reimburse officials who are found by the court to have violated this section.

(d) It shall be an affirmative defense to any claim brought against an elected county or municipal official under this subsection (5) that the elected official:

(i) Did not vote in the affirmative for the adopted ordinance or posted written notice deemed by the court to be in violation of this section;

(ii) Did attempt to take recorded action to cure the violation as noticed by the Attorney General in paragraph (b) of this subsection; or

(iii) Did attempt to take recorded action to rescind the ordinance or remove the posted written notice deemed by the court to be in violation of this section.

(6) No county or municipality or their officers or employees may participate in any program in which individuals are given a thing of value provided by another individual or other entity in exchange for surrendering a firearm to the county, municipality or other governmental body unless:

(a) The county or municipality has adopted an ordinance authorizing the participation of the county or municipality, or participation by an officer or employee of the county or municipality in such a program; and

(b) Any ordinance enacted pursuant to this section must require that any firearm received shall be offered for sale at auction as provided by §§ 19-3-85 and 21-39-21 to federally licensed firearms dealers, with the proceeds from such sale at auction reverting to the general operating fund of the county, municipality or other governmental body. Any firearm remaining in possession of the county, municipality or other governmental body after attempts to sell at auction may be disposed of in a manner that the body deems appropriate.

§ 45-9-55. Employer not permitted to prohibit transportation or storage of firearms on employer property; exceptions; certain immunity for employer

(1) Except as otherwise provided in subsection (2) of this section, a public or private employer may not establish, maintain, or enforce any policy or rule that has the effect of prohibiting a person from transporting or storing a firearm in a locked vehicle in any parking lot, parking garage, or other designated parking area.

(2) A private employer may prohibit an employee from transporting or storing a firearm in a vehicle in a parking lot, parking garage, or other parking area the employer provides for employees to which access is restricted or limited through the use of a gate, security station or other means of restricting or limiting general public access onto the property.

(3) This section shall not apply to vehicles owned or leased by an employer and used by the employee in the course of his business.

(4) This section does not authorize a person to transport or store a firearm on any premises where the possession of a firearm is prohibited by state or federal law.

(5) A public or private employer shall not be liable in a civil action for damages resulting from or arising out of an occurrence involving the transportation, storage, possession or use of a firearm covered by this section.

§ 45-9-57. Regulation by county of discharge of any firearm within platted subdivision.
A county may regulate the discharge of any firearm or weapon, other than a BB gun, within any platted subdivision. However, no county may prohibit the discharge of any firearm or weapon on land, if such firearm or weapon is discharged in a manner not reasonably expected to cause a projectile from such firearm or weapon to travel across any property line without permission of the property owner.

License to Carry Concealed Pistol or Revolver

§ 45-9-101. License to carry stun gun, concealed pistol or revolver; license fees; exemptions; no license required to carry pistol or revolver in purse, briefcase, fully enclosed case, etc.

(1) (a) Except as otherwise provided, the Department of Public Safety is authorized to issue licenses to carry stun guns, concealed pistols or revolvers to persons qualified as provided in this section. Such licenses shall be valid throughout the state for a period of 5 years from the date of issuance. Any person possessing a valid license issued pursuant to this section may carry a stun gun, concealed pistol or concealed revolver.

(b) The licensee must carry the license, together with valid identification, at all times in which the licensee is carrying a stun gun, concealed pistol or revolver and must display both the license and proper identification upon demand by a law enforcement officer. A violation of the provisions of this paragraph (b) shall constitute a noncriminal violation with a penalty of $25 and shall be enforceable by summons.

(2) The Department of Public Safety shall issue a license if the applicant:

(a) Is a resident of the state. However, this residency requirement may be waived if the applicant possesses a valid permit from another state, is active military personnel stationed in Mississippi, or is a retired law enforcement officer establishing residency in the state;

(b) (i) Is 21 years of age or older; or

(ii) Is at least 18 years of age but not yet 21 years of age and the applicant:
    1. Is a member or veteran of the United States Armed Forces, including National Guard or Reserve; and
    2. Holds a valid Mississippi driver's license or identification card issued by the Department of Public Safety;
(c) Does not suffer from a physical infirmity which prevents the safe handling of a stun gun, pistol or revolver;
(d) Is not ineligible to possess a firearm by virtue of having been convicted of a felony in a court of this state, of any other state, or of the United States without having been pardoned for same;
(e) Does not chronically or habitually abuse controlled substances to the extent that his normal faculties are impaired. It shall be presumed that an applicant chronically and habitually uses controlled substances to the extent that his faculties are impaired if the applicant has been voluntarily or involuntarily committed to a treatment facility for the abuse of a controlled substance or been found guilty of a crime under the provisions of the Uniform Controlled Substances Law or similar laws of any other state or the United States relating to controlled substances within a 3-year period immediately preceding the date on which the application is submitted;
(f) Does not chronically and habitually use alcoholic beverages to the extent that his normal faculties are impaired. It shall be presumed that an applicant chronically and habitually uses alcoholic beverages to the extent that his normal faculties are impaired if the applicant has been voluntarily or involuntarily committed as an alcoholic to a treatment facility or has been convicted of 2 or more offenses related to the use of alcohol under the laws of this state or similar laws of any other state or the United States within the 3-year period immediately preceding the date on which the application is submitted;
(g) Desires a legal means to carry a stun gun, concealed pistol or revolver to defend himself;
(h) Has not been adjudicated mentally incompetent, or has waited 5 years from the date of his restoration to capacity by court order;
(i) Has not been voluntarily or involuntarily committed to a mental institution or mental health treatment facility unless he possesses a certificate from a psychiatrist licensed in this state that he has not suffered from disability for a period of 5 years;
(j) Has not had adjudication of guilt withheld or imposition of sentence suspended on any felony unless 3 years have elapsed since probation or any other conditions set by the court have been fulfilled;
(k) Is not a fugitive from justice; and
(l) Is not disqualified to possess a weapon based on federal law.
(3) The Department of Public Safety may deny a license if the applicant has been found guilty of one or more crimes of violence constituting a misdemeanor unless 3 years have elapsed since probation or any other conditions set by the court have been fulfilled or expunction has occurred prior to the date on which the application is submitted, or may revoke a license if the licensee has been found guilty of one or more crimes of violence within the preceding 3 years. The department shall, upon notification by a law enforcement agency or a court and subsequent written verification, suspend a license or the processing of an application for a license if the licensee or applicant is arrested or formally charged with a crime which would disqualify such person from having a license under this section, until final disposition of the case. The provisions of subsection (7) of this section shall apply to any suspension or revocation of a license pursuant to the provisions of this section.
(4) The application shall be completed, under oath, on a form promulgated by the Department of Public Safety and shall include only:
(a) The name, address, place and date of birth, race, sex and occupation of the applicant;
(b) The driver's license number or social security number of applicant;
(c) Any previous address of the applicant for the 2 years preceding the date of the application;
(d) A statement that the applicant is in compliance with criteria contained within subsections (2) and (3) of this section;
(e) A statement that the applicant has been furnished a copy of this section and is knowledgeable of its provisions;
(f) A conspicuous warning that the application is executed under oath and that a knowingly false answer to any question, or the knowing submission of any false document by the applicant, subjects the applicant to criminal prosecution; and
(g) A statement that the applicant desires a legal means to carry a stun gun, concealed pistol or revolver to defend himself.
(5) The applicant shall submit only the following to the Department of Public Safety:
(a) A completed application as described in subsection (4) of this section;
(b) A full-face photograph of the applicant taken within the preceding 30 days in which the head, including hair, in a size as determined by the Department of Public Safety, except that an applicant who is younger than 21 years of age must submit a photograph in profile of the applicant;
(c) A nonrefundable license fee of $80. Costs for processing the set of fingerprints as required in paragraph (d) of this subsection shall be borne by the applicant. Honorably retired law enforcement officers, disabled veterans and active duty members of the Armed Forces of the United States shall be exempt from the payment of the license fee;
(d) A full set of fingerprints of the applicant administered by the Department of Public Safety; and
(e) A waiver authorizing the Department of Public Safety access to any records concerning commitments of the applicant to any of the treatment facilities or institutions referred to in subsection (2) and permitting access to all the applicant's criminal records.

(6) (a) The Department of Public Safety, upon receipt of the items listed in subsection (5) of this section, shall forward the full set of fingerprints of the applicant to the appropriate agencies for state and federal processing.

(b) The Department of Public Safety shall forward a copy of the applicant's application to the sheriff of the applicant's county of residence and, if applicable, the police chief of the applicant's municipality of residence. The sheriff of the applicant's county of residence and, if applicable, the police chief of the applicant's municipality of residence may, at his discretion, participate in the process by submitting a voluntary report to the Department of Public Safety containing any readily discoverable prior information that he feels may be pertinent to the licensing of any applicant. The reporting shall be made within 30 days after the date he receives the copy of the application. Upon receipt of a response from a sheriff or police chief, such sheriff or police chief shall be reimbursed at a rate set by the department.

(c) The Department of Public Safety shall, within 45 days after the date of receipt of the items listed in subsection (5) of this section:

(i) Issue the license;

(ii) Deny the application based solely on the ground that the applicant fails to qualify under the criteria listed in subsections (2) and (3) of this section. If the Department of Public Safety denies the application, it shall notify the applicant in writing, stating the ground for denial, and the denial shall be subject to the appeal process set forth in subsection (7); or

(iii) Notify the applicant that the department is unable to make a determination regarding the issuance or denial of a license within the 45-day period prescribed by this subsection, and provide an estimate of the amount of time the department will need to make the determination.

(d) In the event a legible set of fingerprints, as determined by the Department of Public Safety and the Federal Bureau of Investigation, cannot be obtained after a minimum of 2 attempts, the Department of Public Safety shall determine eligibility based upon a name check by the Mississippi Highway Safety Patrol and a Federal Bureau of Investigation name check conducted by the Mississippi Highway Safety Patrol at the request of the Department of Public Safety.

(7) (a) If the Department of Public Safety denies the issuance of a license, or suspends or revokes a license, the party aggrieved may appeal such denial, suspension or revocation to the Commissioner of Public Safety, or his authorized agent, within 30 days after the aggrieved party receives written notice of such denial, suspension or revocation. The Commissioner of Public Safety, or his duly authorized agent, shall rule upon such appeal within 30 days after the appeal is filed and failure to rule within this 30-day period shall constitute sustaining such denial, suspension or revocation. Such review shall be conducted pursuant to such reasonable rules and regulations as the Commissioner of Public Safety may adopt.

(b) If the revocation, suspension or denial of issuance is sustained by the Commissioner of Public Safety, or his duly authorized agent pursuant to paragraph (a) of this subsection, the aggrieved party may file within 10 days after the rendition of such decision a petition in the circuit or county court of his residence for review of such decision. A hearing for review shall be held and shall proceed before the court without a jury upon the record made at the hearing before the Commissioner of Public Safety or his duly authorized agent. No such party shall be allowed to carry a stun gun, concealed pistol or revolver pursuant to the provisions of this section while any such appeal is pending.

(8) The Department of Public Safety shall maintain an automated listing of license holders and such information shall be available online, upon request, at all times, to all law enforcement agencies through the Mississippi Crime Information Center. However, the records of the department relating to applications for licenses to carry stun guns, concealed pistols or revolvers and records relating to license holders shall be exempt from the provisions of the Mississippi Public Records Act of 1983, and shall be released only upon order of a court having proper jurisdiction over a petition for release of the record or records.

(9) Within 30 days after the changing of a permanent address, or within 30 days after having a license lost or destroyed, the licensee shall notify the Department of Public Safety in writing of such change or loss. Failure to notify the Department of Public Safety pursuant to the provisions of this subsection shall constitute a noncriminal violation with a penalty of $25 and shall be enforceable by a summons.

(10) In the event that a stun gun, concealed pistol or revolver license is lost or destroyed, the person to whom the license was issued shall comply with the provisions of subsection (9) of this section and may obtain a duplicate, or substitute thereof, upon payment of $15 to the Department of Public Safety, and furnishing a notarized statement to the department that such license has been lost or destroyed.

(11) A license issued under this section shall be revoked if the licensee becomes ineligible under the criteria set forth in subsection (2) of this section.

(12) (a) No less than 90 days prior to the expiration date of the license, the Department of Public Safety shall mail to each licensee a written notice of the expiration and a renewal form prescribed by the department. The licensee must renew his license on or before the expiration date by filing with the department the renewal form, a notarized affidavit stating that the licensee remains qualified pursuant to the criteria specified in subsections (2) and (3) of this section, and a full set of fingerprints administered by the Department of Public Safety or the sheriff of the county of residence of the licensee. The first renewal may be processed by mail and the subsequent renewal must be made in person. Thereafter every other renewal may be processed by mail to assure that the applicant must appear in person every 10 years for the purpose of obtaining a new photograph.

(i) Except as provided in this subsection, a renewal fee of $40 shall also be submitted along with costs for processing the fingerprints;

(ii) Honorably retired law enforcement officers, disabled veterans and active duty members of the Armed Forces of the United States shall be exempt from the renewal fee; and

(iii) The renewal fee for a Mississippi resident aged 65 years of age or older shall be $20.

(b) The Department of Public Safety shall forward the full set of fingerprints of the applicant to the appropriate agencies for state and federal processing. The license shall be renewed upon receipt of the completed renewal application and appropriate payment of fees.

(c) A licensee who fails to file a renewal application on or before its expiration date must renew his license by paying a late fee of $15. No license shall be renewed 6 months or more after its expiration date, and such license shall be deemed to be permanently expired. A person whose license has been permanently expired may reapply for licensure; however, an application for licensure and fees pursuant to subsection (5) of this section must be submitted, and a background investigation shall be conducted pursuant to the provisions of this section.

(13) No license issued pursuant to this section shall authorize any person to carry a stun gun, concealed pistol or revolver into any place of nuisance as defined in § 95-3-1, Mississippi Code of 1972; any police, sheriff or highway patrol station; any detention facility, prison or jail; any courthouse; any courtroom, except that nothing in this section shall preclude a judge from carrying a concealed weapon or determining who will carry a concealed weapon in his courtroom; any polling place; any meeting place of the governing body of any governmental entity; any meeting of the Legislature or a committee thereof; any school, college or professional athletic event not related to firearms; any portion of an establishment, licensed to dispense alcoholic beverages for consumption on the premises, that is primarily devoted to dispensing alcoholic beverages; any portion of an establishment in which beer or light wine is consumed on the premises, that is primarily devoted to such purpose; any elementary or secondary school facility; any junior college, community college, college or university facility unless for the purpose of participating in any authorized firearms-related activity; inside the passenger terminal of any airport, except that no person shall be prohibited from carrying any legal firearm into the terminal if the firearm is encased for shipment, for purposes of checking such firearm as baggage to be lawfully transported on any aircraft; any church or other place of worship, except as provided in § 45-9-171; or any place where the carrying of firearms is prohibited by federal law. In addition to the places enumerated in this subsection, the carrying of a stun gun, concealed pistol or revolver may be disallowed in any place in the discretion of the person or entity exercising control over the physical location of such place by the placing of a written notice clearly readable at a distance of not less than 10 feet that the "carrying of a pistol or revolver is prohibited." No license issued pursuant to this section shall authorize the participants in a parade or demonstration for which a permit is required to carry a stun gun, concealed pistol or revolver.

(14) A law enforcement officer as defined in § 45-6-3, chiefs of police, sheriffs and persons licensed as professional bondsmen pursuant to Chapter 39, Title 83, Mississippi Code of 1972, shall be exempt from the licensing requirements of this section. The licensing requirements of this section do not apply to the carrying by any person of a stun gun, pistol or revolver, knife, or other deadly weapon that is not concealed as defined in § 97-37-1.

(15) Any person who knowingly submits a false answer to any question on an application for a license issued pursuant to this section, or who knowingly submits a false document when applying for a license issued pursuant to this section, shall, upon conviction, be guilty of a misdemeanor and shall be punished as provided in § 99-19-31, Mississippi Code of 1972.

(18) Nothing in this section shall be construed to require or allow the registration, documentation or providing of serial numbers with regard to any stun gun or firearm.

(19) Any person holding a valid unrevoked and unexpired license to carry stun guns, concealed pistols or revolvers issued in another state shall have such license recognized by this state to carry stun guns, concealed pistols or revolvers. The Department of Public Safety is authorized to enter into a reciprocal agreement with another state if that state requires a written agreement in order to recognize licenses to carry stun guns, concealed pistols or revolvers issued by this state.

(20) The provisions of this section shall be under the supervision of the Commissioner of Public Safety. The commissioner is authorized to promulgate reasonable rules and regulations to carry out the provisions of this section.

(21) For the purposes of this section, the term "stun gun" means a portable device or weapon from which an electric current, impulse, wave or beam may be directed, which current, impulse, wave or beam is designed to incapacitate temporarily, injure, momentarily stun, knock out, cause mental disorientation or paralyze.

(22) (a) From and after January 1, 2016, the Commissioner of Public Safety shall promulgate rules and regulations which provide that licenses authorized by this section for honorably retired law enforcement officers and honorably retired correctional officers from the Mississippi Department of Corrections shall **(i)** include the words "retired law enforcement officer" on the front of the license, and **(ii)** that the license itself have a red background to distinguish it from other licenses issued under this section.

(b) An honorably retired law enforcement officer and honorably retired correctional officer shall provide the following information to receive the license described in this section: **(i)** a letter, with the official letterhead of the agency or department from which such officer is retiring, which explains that such officer is honorably retired, and **(ii)** a letter with the official letterhead of the agency or department, which explains that such officer has completed a certified law enforcement training academy.

(23) A disabled veteran who seeks to qualify for an exemption under this section shall be required to provide, as proof of service-connected disability, verification from the United States Department of Veterans Affairs.

(24) A license under this section is not required for a loaded or unloaded pistol or revolver to be carried upon the person in a sheath, belt holster or shoulder holster or in a purse, handbag, satchel, other similar bag or briefcase or fully enclosed case if the person is not engaged in criminal activity other than a misdemeanor traffic offense, is not otherwise prohibited from possessing a pistol or revolver under state or federal law, and is not in a location prohibited under subsection (13) of this section.

§ 45-9-103. Federal firearm reporting

(1) In this section, "federal prohibited-person information" means information that identifies an individual as:

(a) A person who has been judicially determined by a court as a person with mental illness or person with an intellectual disability under Title 41, Chapter 21, Mississippi Code of 1972, whether ordered for inpatient treatment, outpatient treatment, day treatment, night treatment or home health services treatment;

(b) A person acquitted in a criminal case by reason of insanity or on a ground of intellectual disability, without regard to whether the person is ordered by a court to receive inpatient treatment or residential care under § 99-13-7;

(c) An adult individual for whom a court has appointed a guardian or conservator under Title 93, Chapter 13, based on the determination that the person is incapable of managing his own estate due to mental weakness; or

(d) A person determined to be incompetent to stand trial by a court pursuant to Rule 9.06 of the Mississippi Rules of Circuit and County Court Practice.

(2) The Department of Public Safety by rule shall establish a procedure to provide federal prohibited-person information to the Federal Bureau of Investigation for use with the National Instant Criminal Background Check System. Except as otherwise provided by state law, the department may disseminate federal prohibited-person information under this subsection only to the extent necessary to allow the Federal Bureau of Investigation to collect and maintain a list of persons who are prohibited under federal law from engaging in certain activities with respect to a firearm.

(3) The department shall grant access to a person's own federal prohibited-person information to the person who is the subject of the information.

(4) Federal prohibited-person information maintained by the department is confidential information for the use of the department and, except as otherwise provided by this section and other state law, is not a public record and may not be disseminated by the department.

(5) The department by rule shall establish a procedure to correct department records and transmit those corrected records to the Federal Bureau of Investigation when a person provides:

(a) A copy of a judicial order or finding under § 93-13-151 that a person has been restored to reason;

(b) Proof that the person has obtained notice of relief from disabilities under 18 USC, § 925; or

(c) A copy of a judicial order of relief from a firearms disability under § 97-37-5(4).

Purchase of Sidearms by Retiring Law Enforcement Personnel

§ 45-9-131. Purchase of sidearm by retiring law enforcement officer or spouse of law enforcement officer killed in line of duty.
Upon approval of the governing authority of the municipality or county, a member of any municipal or county law enforcement agency who retires under any state retirement system or the spouse of a law enforcement officer who is killed in the line of duty may be allowed to purchase as his or her personal property 1 sidearm which was issued to the law enforcement officer by the law enforcement agency from which he or she retired or by whom he or she was employed at the time of death. The governing authority of the municipality or county shall determine the amount to be paid for the firearm by the retiring member of the law enforcement agency or the spouse of the law enforcement officer.

§ 45-9-133. Retention of sidearm by retiring law enforcement officer of Mississippi Department of Transportation
Each person employed as a law enforcement officer by the Mississippi Department of Transportation who retires for superannuation or for reason of disability under the Public Employees' Retirement System shall be allowed to retain as his personal property, 1 sidearm which was issued to such law enforcement officer.

Docket of Deadly Weapons Seized

§ 45-9-151. Docket of deadly weapons seized

(1) Every law enforcement agency of the state or of any political subdivision thereof shall maintain a docket which shall contain a record of all deadly weapons that are seized by employees of such law enforcement agency. Such docket shall include the name of the arresting officer, the date of the arrest, the charge upon which the seizure was based, the name of the person from whom such deadly weapon was seized, the physical description of the deadly weapon, the serial number, if any, of the deadly weapon, and the chain of custody of the deadly weapon.

TITLE 75. Regulation of Trade, Commerce and Investments
Chapter 67. Loans
Article 7. Mississippi Pawnshop Act

§ 75-67-305. Information required to be recorded on pawn ticket; detailed recording of transactions required

(1) At the time of making the pawn or purchase transaction, the pawnbroker shall enter upon the pawn ticket a record of the following information which shall be typed or written in ink and in the English language:

(a) A clear and accurate description of the property, including the following:

(i) Brand name;

(ii) Model number;

(iii) Serial number;

(iv) Size;

(v) Color, as apparent to the untrained eye;

(vi) Precious metal type, weight and content, if known;

(vii) Gemstone description, including the number of stones;

(viii) In the case of firearms, the type of action, caliber or gauge, number of barrels, barrel length and finish; and

(ix) Any other unique identifying marks, numbers, names or letters;

(b) The name, residence address and date of birth of pledgor or seller;

(c) Date of pawn or purchase transaction;

(d) Driver's license number or social security number or Mississippi identification card number, as defined in § 45-35-1, Mississippi Code of 1972, of the pledgor or seller or identification information verified by at least 2 forms of identification, 1 of which shall be a photographic identification;

(e) Description of the pledgor including approximate height, sex and race;

(f) Amount of cash advanced;

(g) The maturity date of the pawn transaction and the amount due; and

(h) The monthly rate and pawn charge. Such rates and charges shall be disclosed using the requirements prescribed in Regulation Z (Truth in Lending) of the rules and regulations of the Board of Governors of the Federal Reserve.

(2) Each pawn or purchase transaction document shall be consecutively numbered and entered in a corresponding log or record book. Separate logs or record books for pawn and purchase transactions shall be kept.

(3) Records may be in the form of traditional hard copies, computer printouts or magnetic media if readily accessible for viewing on a screen with the capability of being promptly printed upon request.

(4) Every licensee shall maintain a record which indicates the total number of accounts and the total dollar value of all pawn transactions outstanding as of December 31 of each year.

TITLE 97. Crimes
Chapter 37. Weapons and Explosives
General Provisions

§ 97-37-1. Deadly weapons; carrying while concealed; use or attempt to use; penalties; "concealed" defined

(1) Except as otherwise provided in § 45-9-101, any person who carries, concealed on or about one's person, any bowie knife, dirk knife, butcher knife, switchblade knife, metallic knuckles, blackjack, slingshot, pistol, revolver, or any rifle with a barrel of less than 16 inches in length, or any shotgun with a barrel of less than 18 inches in length, machine gun or any fully automatic firearm or deadly weapon, or any muffler or silencer for any firearm, whether or not it is accompanied by a firearm, or uses or attempts to use against another person any imitation firearm, shall, upon conviction, be punished as follows:

(a) By a fine of not less than $100 nor more than $500, or by imprisonment in the county jail for not more than 6 months, or both, in the discretion of the court, for the first conviction under this section.

(b) By a fine of not less than $100 nor more than $500, and imprisonment in the county jail for not less than 30 days nor more than 6 months, for the second conviction under this section.

(c) By confinement in the custody of the Department of Corrections for not less than 1 year nor more than 5 years, for the third or subsequent conviction under this section.

(d) By confinement in the custody of the Department of Corrections for not less than 1 year nor more than 10 years for any person previously convicted of any felony who is convicted under this section.

(2) It shall not be a violation of this section for any person over the age of 18 years to carry a firearm or deadly weapon concealed within the confines of his own home or his place of business, or any real property associated with his home or business or within any motor vehicle.

(3) It shall not be a violation of this section for any person to carry a firearm or deadly weapon concealed if the possessor of the weapon is then engaged in a legitimate weapon-related sports activity or is going to or returning from such activity. For purposes of this subsection, "legitimate weapon-related sports activity" means hunting, fishing, target shooting or any other legal activity which normally involves the use of a firearm or other weapon.

(4) For the purposes of this section, "concealed" means hidden or obscured from common observation and shall not include any weapon listed in subsection (1) of this section, including, but not limited to, a loaded or unloaded pistol carried upon the person in a sheath, belt holster or shoulder holster that is wholly or partially visible, or carried upon the person in a scabbard or case for carrying the weapon that is wholly or partially visible.

§ 97-37-3. Deadly weapons; forfeiture of weapon; return upon dismissal or acquittal; confiscated firearms may be sold at auction; proceeds of sale used to purchase bulletproof vests for seizing law enforcement agency

(1) Any weapon used in violation of § 97-37-1, or used in the commission of any other crime, shall be seized by the arresting officer, may be introduced in evidence, and in the event of a conviction, shall be ordered to be forfeited, and shall be disposed of as ordered by the court having jurisdiction of such offense. In the event of dismissal or acquittal of charges, such weapon shall be returned to the accused from whom it was seized.

(2) (a) If the weapon to be forfeited is merchantable, the court may order the weapon forfeited to the seizing law enforcement agency.

(b) A weapon so forfeited to a law enforcement agency may be sold at auction as provided by §§ 19-3-85 and 21-39-21 to a federally-licensed firearms dealer, with the proceeds from such sale at auction to be used to buy bulletproof vests for the seizing law enforcement agency.

§ 97-37-5. Unlawful for convicted felon to possess any firearms, or other weapons or devices; penalties; exceptions

(1) It shall be unlawful for any person who has been convicted of a felony under the laws of this state, any other state, or of the United States to possess any firearm or any bowie knife, dirk knife, butcher knife, switchblade knife, metallic knuckles, blackjack, or any muffler or silencer for any firearm unless such person has received a pardon for such felony, has received a relief from disability pursuant to § 925(c) of Title 18 of the United States Code, or has received a certificate of rehabilitation pursuant to subsection (3) of this section.

(2) Any person violating this section shall be guilty of a felony and, upon conviction thereof, shall be fined not more than $5,000, or committed to the custody of the State Department of Corrections for not less than 1 year nor more than 10 years, or both.

(3) A person who has been convicted of a felony under the laws of this state may apply to the court in which he was convicted for a certificate of rehabilitation. The court may grant such certificate in its discretion upon a showing to the satisfaction of the court that the applicant has been rehabilitated and has led a useful, productive and law-abiding life since the completion of his sentence and upon the finding of the court that he will not be likely to act in a manner dangerous to public safety.

(4) (a) A person who is discharged from court-ordered mental health treatment may petition the court which entered the commitment order for an order stating that the person qualifies for relief from a firearms disability.

  (b) In determining whether to grant relief, the court must hear and consider evidence about:

    (i) The circumstances that led to imposition of the firearms disability under 18 USC, § 922(d)(4);

    (ii) The person's mental history;

    (iii) The person's criminal history; and

    (iv) The person's reputation.

  (c) A court may not grant relief unless it makes and enters in the record the following affirmative findings:

    (i) That the person is no longer likely to act in a manner dangerous to public safety; and

    (ii) Removing the person's disability to purchase a firearm is not against the public interest.

§ 97-37-7. Deadly weapons; persons permitted to carry weapons; bond; permit to carry weapon; grounds for denying application for permit; required weapons training course; reciprocal agreements

(1) (a) It shall not be a violation of § 97-37-1 or any other statute for pistols, firearms or other suitable and appropriate weapons to be carried by duly constituted bank guards, company guards, watchmen, railroad special agents or duly authorized representatives who are not sworn law enforcement officers, agents or employees of a patrol service, guard service, or a company engaged in the business of transporting money, securities or other valuables, while actually engaged in the performance of their duties as such, provided that such persons have made a written application and paid a nonrefundable permit fee of $100 to the Department of Public Safety.

  (b) No permit shall be issued to any person who has ever been convicted of a felony under the laws of this or any other state or of the United States. To determine an applicant's eligibility for a permit, the person shall be fingerprinted. If no disqualifying record is identified at the state level, the fingerprints shall be forwarded by the Department of Public Safety to the Federal Bureau of Investigation for a national criminal history record check. The department shall charge a fee which includes the amounts required by the Federal Bureau of Investigation and the department for the national and state criminal history record checks and any necessary costs incurred by the department for the handling and administration of the criminal history background checks. In the event a legible set of fingerprints, as determined by the Department of Public Safety and the Federal Bureau of Investigation, cannot be obtained after a minimum of 3 attempts, the Department of Public Safety shall determine eligibility based upon a name check by the Mississippi Highway Safety Patrol and a Federal Bureau of Investigation name check conducted by the Mississippi Highway Safety Patrol at the request of the Department of Public Safety.

  (c) A person may obtain a duplicate of a lost or destroyed permit upon payment of a $15 replacement fee to the Department of Public Safety, if he furnishes a notarized statement to the department that the permit has been lost or destroyed.

  (d) (i) No less than 90 days prior to the expiration date of a permit, the Department of Public Safety shall mail to the permit holder written notice of expiration together with the renewal form prescribed by the department. The permit holder shall renew the permit on or before the expiration date by filing with the department the renewal form, a notarized affidavit stating that the permit holder remains qualified, and the renewal fee of $50; honorably retired law enforcement officers shall be exempt from payment of the renewal fee. A permit holder who fails to file a renewal application on or before its expiration date shall pay a late fee of $15.

    (ii) Renewal of the permit shall be required every 4 years. The permit of a qualified renewal applicant shall be renewed upon receipt of the completed renewal application and appropriate payment of fees.

    (iii) A permit cannot be renewed 6 months or more after its expiration date, and such permit shall be deemed to be permanently expired; the holder may reapply for an original permit as provided in this section.

(2) It shall not be a violation of this or any other statute for pistols, firearms or other suitable and appropriate weapons to be carried by Department of Wildlife, Fisheries and Parks law enforcement officers, railroad special agents who are sworn law enforcement officers, investigators employed by the Attorney General, criminal investigators employed by the district attorneys, all prosecutors, public defenders, investigators or probation officers employed by the Department of Corrections, employees of the State Auditor who are authorized by the State Auditor to perform investigative functions, or any deputy fire marshal or investigator employed by the State Fire Marshal, while engaged in the performance of their duties as such, or by fraud investigators with the Department of Human Services, or by judges of the Mississippi Supreme Court, Court of Appeals, circuit, chancery, county, justice and municipal courts, or by coroners. Before any person shall be authorized under this subsection to carry a weapon, he shall complete a weapons training course approved by the Board of Law Enforcement Officer Standards and Training. Before any criminal investigator employed by a district attorney shall be authorized under this section to carry a pistol, firearm or other weapon, he shall have complied with § 45-6-11 or any training program required for employment as an agent of the Federal Bureau of Investigation. A law enforcement officer, as defined in § 45-6-3, shall be authorized to carry weapons in courthouses in performance of his official duties. A person licensed under § 45-9-101 to carry a concealed pistol, who (a) has voluntarily completed an instructional course in the safe handling and use of firearms offered by an instructor certified by a nationally recognized organization that customarily offers firearms training, or by any other organization approved by the Department of Public Safety, (b) is a member or veteran of any active or reserve component branch of the United States of America Armed Forces having completed law enforcement or combat training with pistols or other handguns as recognized by such branch after submitting an affidavit attesting to have read, understand and agree to comply with all provisions of the enhanced carry law, or (c) is an honorably retired law enforcement officer or honorably retired member or veteran of any active or reserve component branch of the United States of America Armed Forces having completed law enforcement or combat training with pistols or other handguns, after submitting an affidavit attesting to have read, understand and agree to comply with all provisions of Mississippi enhanced carry law shall also be authorized to carry weapons in courthouses except in courtrooms during a judicial proceeding, and any location listed in subsection (13) of § 45-9-101, except any place of nuisance as defined in § 95-3-1, any police, sheriff or highway patrol station or any detention facility, prison or jail. For the purposes of this subsection (2), component branch of the United States Armed Forces includes the Army, Navy, Air Force, Coast Guard or Marine Corps, or the Army National Guard, the Army National Guard of the United States, the Air National Guard or the Air National Guard of the United States, as those terms are defined in § 101, Title 10, United States Code, and any other reserve component of the United States Armed Forces enumerated in § 10101, Title 10, United States Code. The department shall promulgate rules and regulations allowing concealed pistol permit holders to obtain an endorsement on their permit indicating that they have completed the aforementioned course and have the authority to carry in these locations. This section shall in no way interfere with the right of a trial judge to restrict the carrying of firearms in the courtroom.

(3) It shall not be a violation of this or any other statute for pistols, firearms or other suitable and appropriate weapons, to be carried by any out-of-state, full-time commissioned law enforcement officer who holds a valid commission card from the appropriate out-of-state law enforcement agency and a photo identification. The provisions of this subsection shall only apply if the state where the out-of-state officer is employed has entered into a reciprocity agreement with the state that allows full-time commissioned law enforcement officers in Mississippi to lawfully carry or possess a weapon in such other states. The Commissioner of Public Safety is authorized to enter into reciprocal agreements with other states to carry out the provisions of this subsection.

§ 97-37-9. Deadly weapons; defenses against indictment for carrying deadly weapon. Any person indicted or charged for a violation of § 97-37-1 may show as a defense:

(a) That he was threatened, and had good and sufficient reason to apprehend a serious attack from any enemy, and that he did so apprehend; or

(b) That he was traveling and was not a tramp, or was setting out on a journey and was not a tramp; or

(c) That he was a law enforcement or peace officer in the discharge of his duties; or

(d) That he was at the time in the discharge of his duties as a mail carrier; or

(e) That he was at the time engaged in transporting valuables for an express company or bank; or

(f) That he was a member of the Armed Forces of the United States, National Guard, State Militia, Emergency Management Corps, guard or patrolman in a state or municipal institution while in the performance of his official duties; or

(g) That he was in lawful pursuit of a felon; or

(h) That he was lawfully engaged in legitimate sports;

(i) That at the time he was a company guard, bank guard, watchman, or other person enumerated in § 97-37-7, and was then actually engaged in the performance of his duties as such, and then held a valid permit from the sheriff, the commissioner of public safety, or a valid permit issued by the Secretary of State prior to May 1, 1974, to carry the weapon; and the burden of proving either of said defenses shall be on the accused; or

(j) That at the time he or she was a member of a church or place of worship security program, and was then actually engaged in the performance of his or her duties as such and met the requirements of § 45-9-171.

§ 97-37-13. Deadly weapons; weapons and cartridges not to be given to minor or intoxicated person. It shall not be lawful for any person to sell, give or lend to any minor under 18 years of age or person intoxicated, knowing him to be a minor under 18 years of age or in a state of intoxication, any deadly weapon, or other weapon the carrying of which

concealed is prohibited, or pistol cartridge; and, on conviction thereof, he shall be punished by a fine not more than $1,000, or imprisoned in the county jail not exceeding 1 year, or both.

§ 97-37-14. Possession of handgun by minor; act of delinquency; exceptions

(1) Except as otherwise provided in this section, it is an act of delinquency for any person who has not attained the age of 18 years knowingly to have any handgun in such person's possession.

(2) This section shall not apply to:

  (a) Any person who is:

   (i) In attendance at a hunter's safety course or a firearms safety course; or

   (ii) Engaging in practice in the use of a firearm or target shooting at an established range authorized by the governing body of the jurisdiction in which such range is located or any other area where the discharge of a firearm is not prohibited; or

   (iii) Engaging in an organized competition involving the use of a firearm, or participating in or practicing for a performance by an organized group under 501(c)(3) as determined by the federal internal revenue service which uses firearms as a part of such performance; or

   (iv) Hunting or trapping pursuant to a valid license issued to such person by the Department of Wildlife, Fisheries and Parks or as otherwise allowed by law; or

   (v) Traveling with any handgun in such person's possession being unloaded to or from any activity described in subparagraph (i), (ii), (iii) or (iv) of this paragraph (a) and paragraph (b).

  (b) Any person under the age of 18 years who is on real property under the control of an adult and who has the permission of such adult to possess a handgun.

(3) This section shall not apply to any person who uses a handgun or other firearm to lawfully defend himself from imminent danger at his home or place of domicile and any such person shall not be held criminally liable for such use of a handgun or other firearm.

(4) For the purposes of this section, "handgun" means a pistol, revolver or other firearm of any description, loaded or unloaded, from which any shot, bullet or other missile can be discharged, the length of the barrel of which, not including any revolving, detachable or magazine breech, is less than 16 inches.

§ 97-37-15. Parent or guardian not to permit minor son to have or carry weapon; penalty.
Any parent, guardian or custodian who shall knowingly suffer or permit any child under the age of 18 years to have or to own, or to carry, any weapon the carrying of which concealed is prohibited by § 97-37-1, shall be guilty of a misdemeanor, and, on conviction, shall be fined not more than $1,000, and shall be imprisoned not more than 6 months in the county jail. The provisions of this section shall not apply to a minor who is exempt from the provisions of § 97-37-14.

§ 97-37-17. Possession of weapons by students; aiding or encouraging

(1) The following definitions apply to this section:

  (a) "Educational property" shall mean any public or private school building or bus, public or private school campus, grounds, recreational area, athletic field, or other property owned, used or operated by any local school board, school, college or university board of trustees, or directors for the administration of any public or private educational institution or during a school-related activity, and shall include the facility and property of the Oakley Youth Development Center, operated by the Department of Human Services; provided, however, that the term "educational property" shall not include any sixteenth section school land or lieu land on which is not located a school building, school campus, recreational area or athletic field.

  (b) "Student" shall mean a person enrolled in a public or private school, college or university, or a person who has been suspended or expelled within the last 5 years from a public or private school, college or university, or a person in the custody of the Oakley Youth Development Center, operated by the Department of Human Services, whether the person is an adult or a minor.

  (d) "Weapon" shall mean any device enumerated in subsection (2) or (4) of this section.

(2) It shall be a felony for any person to possess or carry, whether openly or concealed, any gun, rifle, pistol or other firearm of any kind, or any dynamite cartridge, bomb, grenade, mine or powerful explosive on educational property. However, this subsection does not apply to a BB gun, air rifle or air pistol. Any person violating this subsection shall be guilty of a felony and, upon conviction thereof, shall be fined not more than $5,000, or committed to the custody of the State Department of Corrections for not more than 3 years, or both.

(3) It shall be a felony for any person to cause, encourage or aid a minor who is less than 18 years old to possess or carry, whether openly or concealed, any gun, rifle, pistol or other firearm of any kind, or any dynamite cartridge, bomb, grenade, mine or powerful explosive on educational property. However, this subsection does not apply to a BB gun, air rifle or air pistol. Any person violating this subsection shall be guilty of a felony and, upon conviction thereof, shall be fined not more than $5,000, or committed to the custody of the State Department of Corrections for not more than 3 years, or both.

(4) It shall be a misdemeanor for any person to possess or carry, whether openly or concealed, any BB gun, air rifle, air pistol, ... on educational property. Any person violating this subsection shall be guilty of a misdemeanor and, upon conviction thereof, shall be fined not more than $1,000, or be imprisoned not exceeding 6 months, or both.

(5) It shall be a misdemeanor for any person to cause, encourage or aid a minor who is less than 18 years old to possess or carry, whether openly or concealed, any BB gun, air rifle, air pistol, ... on educational property. Any person violating this subsection shall be guilty of a misdemeanor and, upon conviction thereof, shall be fined not more than $1,000, or be imprisoned not exceeding 6 months, or both.

(6) It shall not be a violation of this section for any person to possess or carry, whether openly or concealed, any gun, rifle, pistol or other firearm of any kind on educational property if:

(a) The person is not a student attending school on any educational property;

(b) The firearm is within a motor vehicle; and

(c) The person does not brandish, exhibit or display the firearm in any careless, angry or threatening manner.

(7) This section shall not apply to:

(a) A weapon used solely for educational or school-sanctioned ceremonial purposes, or used in a school-approved program conducted under the supervision of an adult whose supervision has been approved by the school authority;

(b) Armed Forces personnel of the United States, officers and soldiers of the militia and National Guard, law enforcement personnel, any private police employed by an educational institution, State Militia or Emergency Management Corps and any guard or patrolman in a state or municipal institution, and any law enforcement personnel or guard at a state juvenile training school, when acting in the discharge of their official duties;

(c) Home schools as defined in the compulsory school attendance law, § 37-13-91;

(d) Competitors while participating in organized shooting events;

(e) Any person as authorized in § 97-37-7 while in the performance of his official duties;

(f) Any mail carrier while in the performance of his official duties; or

(g) Any weapon not prescribed by § 97-37-1 which is in a motor vehicle under the control of a parent, guardian or custodian, as defined in § 43-21-105, which is used to bring or pick up a student at a school building, school property or school function.

(8) All schools shall post in public view a copy of the provisions of this section.

§ 97-37-19. Deadly weapons; exhibiting in threatening manner. If any person, having or carrying any dirk, dirk-knife, sword, sword-cane, or any deadly weapon, or other weapon the carrying of which concealed is prohibited by § 97-37-1, shall, in the presence of another person, brandish or wield the same in a threatening manner, not in necessary self-defense, or shall in any manner unlawfully use the same in any fight or quarrel, the person so offending, upon conviction thereof, shall be fined in a sum not exceeding $500 or be imprisoned in the county jail not exceeding 3 months, or both. In prosecutions under this section it shall not be necessary for the affidavit or indictment to aver, nor for the state to prove on the trial, that any gun, pistol, or other firearm was charged, loaded, or in condition to be discharged.

§ 97-37-29. Shooting into dwelling house. If any person shall willfully and unlawfully shoot or discharge any pistol, shotgun, rifle or firearm of any nature or description into any dwelling house or any other building usually occupied by persons, whether actually occupied or not, he shall be guilty of a felony whether or not anybody be injured thereby and, on conviction thereof, shall be punished by imprisonment in the state penitentiary for a term not to exceed 10 years, or by imprisonment in the county jail for not more than 1 year, or by fine of not more than $5,000, or by both such imprisonment and fine, within the discretion of the court.

§ 97-37-30. Willful discharge of a firearm toward the dwelling of another causing damage to property or domesticated animal or livestock. A person who willfully discharges his firearm toward the dwelling of another, causing property damage to the dwelling or any domesticated animal or livestock, is guilty of a misdemeanor punishable by a fine of not more than $1,000 or imprisonment not exceeding 12 months in the county jail, or both.

§ 97-37-31. Silencers on firearms; manufacture, sale, possession or use unlawful. It shall be unlawful for any person, persons, corporation or manufacturing establishment, not duly authorized under federal law, to make, manufacture, sell or possess any instrument or device which, if used on firearms of any kind, will arrest or muffle the report of the firearm when shot or fired. Any person violating this section shall be guilty of a misdemeanor and, upon conviction, shall be fined not more than $500, or imprisoned in the county jail not more than 30 days, or both.

§ 97-37-33. Toy pistols; sale of pistol or cartridges prohibited; cap pistols excepted. If any person shall sell, or offer, or expose for sale any toy pistol, or cartridges, or other contrivance by which such pistols are fired or made to cause an explosion, he shall be guilty of a misdemeanor, and, upon conviction, shall be punished by a fine of not less than $5 nor more than $25, or by imprisonment in the county jail not less than 3 days nor more than 30 days, or both.

It is expressly provided, however, that nothing herein shall be construed to prohibit the sale, or offering, or exposure for sale of any toy cap pistols, or other devices, in which paper caps manufactured in accordance with United States Interstate Commerce Commission regulations for packing or shipping of toy paper caps are used or exploded, and the sale of such toy cap pistols is hereby declared to be permissible.

§ 97-37-35. Stolen firearms; possession, receipt, acquisition or disposal; offense; punishment

(1) It is unlawful for any person knowingly or intentionally to possess, receive, retain, acquire or obtain possession or dispose of a stolen firearm or attempt to possess, receive, retain, acquire or obtain possession or dispose of a stolen firearm.

(2) It is unlawful for any person knowingly or intentionally to sell, deliver or transfer a stolen firearm or attempt to sell, deliver or transfer a stolen firearm.

(3) Any person convicted of violating this section shall be guilty of a felony and shall be punished as follows:

(a) For the first conviction, punishment by commitment to the Department of Corrections for 5 years;

(b) For the second and subsequent convictions, the offense shall be considered trafficking in stolen firearms punishable by commitment to the Department of Corrections for not less than 15 years.

(c) For a conviction where the offender possesses 2 or more stolen firearms, the offense shall be considered trafficking in stolen firearms punishable by commitment to the Department of Corrections for not less than 15 years.

(4) Any person who commits or attempts to commit any other crime while in possession of a stolen firearm shall be guilty of a separate felony of possession of a stolen firearm under this section and, upon conviction thereof, shall be punished by commitment to the Department of Corrections for 5 years, such term to run consecutively and not concurrently with any other sentence of incarceration.

§ 97-37-37. Enhanced penalty for use of firearm during commission of felony

(1) Except to the extent that a greater minimum sentence is otherwise provided by any other provision of law, any person who uses or displays a firearm during the commission of any felony shall, in addition to the punishment provided for such felony, be sentenced to an additional term of imprisonment in the custody of the Department of Corrections of 5 years, which sentence shall not be reduced or suspended.

(2) Except to the extent that a greater minimum sentence is otherwise provided by any other provision of law, any convicted felon who uses or displays a firearm during the commission of any felony shall, in addition to the punishment provided for such felony, be sentenced to an additional term of imprisonment in the custody of the Department of Corrections of 10 years, to run consecutively, not concurrently, which sentence shall not be reduced or suspended.

Honesty in Purchasing Firearms Act

§ 97-37-101. Short title. §§ 97-37-101 through 97-37-105 shall be known and may be cited as the "Honesty in Purchasing Firearms Act."

§ 97-37-103. Definition. For purposes of §§ 97-37-101 through 97-37-105:

(a) "Licensed dealer" means a person who is licensed pursuant to 18 USCS, § 923, to engage in the business of dealing in firearms.

(b) "Private seller" means a person who sells or offers for sale any firearm or ammunition.

(c) "Ammunition" means any cartridge, shell or projectile designed for use in a firearm.

(d) "Materially false information" means information that portrays an illegal transaction as legal or a legal transaction as illegal.

§ 97-37-105. Crime of soliciting, persuading, encouraging or enticing illegal sale of firearms or ammunition; crime of providing false information to licensed dealer or private seller of firearms or ammunition.

(1) Any person who knowingly solicits, persuades, encourages or entices a licensed dealer or private seller of firearms or ammunition to transfer a firearm or ammunition under circumstances which the person knows would violate the laws of this state or the United States is guilty of a felony.

(2) Any person who provides to a licensed dealer or private seller of firearms or ammunition what the person knows to be materially false information with intent to deceive the dealer or seller about the legality of a transfer of a firearm or ammunition is guilty of a felony.

(3) Any person found guilty of violating the provisions of this section shall be punished by a fine not exceeding $5,000 or imprisoned in the custody of the Department of Corrections for not more than 3 years, or both.

(4) This section does not apply to a law enforcement officer acting in the officer's official capacity or to a person acting at the direction of a law enforcement officer.

Chapter 44. Mississippi Streetgang Act

§ 97-44-17. Forfeiture of firearms, ammunition, and dangerous weapons used by criminal street gangs; disposition of property seized; procedure

(1) Any firearm, ammunition to be used in a firearm, or dangerous weapon in the possession of a member of a criminal street gang may be seized by any law enforcement agency or peace officer when the law enforcement agency or peace officer has probable cause to believe that the firearm, ammunition to be used in a firearm, or dangerous weapon is or has been used by a gang in the commission of illegal activity.

(2) The district attorney or an attorney for the seizing agency shall initiate, in a civil action, forfeiture proceedings by petition in the circuit courts as to any property seized pursuant to the provisions of this section within 30 days of seizure. The district attorney shall provide notice of the filing of the petition to those members of the gang who become known to law enforcement officials as a result of the seizure and any related arrests, and to any person determined by law enforcement officials to be the owner of any of the property involved. After initial notice of the filing of the petition, the court shall assure that all persons so notified continue to receive notice of all subsequent proceedings related to the property.

(3) Any person who claims an interest in any seized property shall, in order to assert a claim that the property should not be forfeited, file a notice with the court, without necessity of paying costs, of the intent to establish either of the following:

    (a) That the persons asserting the claim did not know of, could not have known of, or had no reason to believe in its use by a gang in the commission of illegal activity; or

    (b) That the law enforcement officer lacked the requisite reasonable belief that the property was or had been used by a gang in the commission of illegal activity.

(4) An acquittal or dismissal in a criminal proceeding shall not preclude civil proceedings under this section; however, for good cause shown, on motion by the district attorney, the court may stay civil forfeiture proceedings during the criminal trial for related criminal indictment or information alleging a violation of this section. Such a stay shall not be available pending an appeal.

(5) Except as otherwise provided by this section, all proceedings hereunder shall be governed by the provisions of the Mississippi Rules of Civil Procedure.

(6) The issue shall be determined by the court alone, and the hearing on the claim shall be held within 60 days after service of the petition unless continued for good cause. The district attorney shall have the burden of showing by clear and convincing proof that forfeiture of the property is appropriate.

(7) Any person who asserts a successful claim in accordance with subsection (3) of this section shall be awarded the seized property by the court, together with costs of filing such action. All property as to which no claim is filed, or as to which no successful claim is made, may be destroyed, sold at a public sale, retained for use by the seizing agency or transferred without charge to any law enforcement agency of the state for use by it. Property that is sold shall be sold by the circuit court at a public auction for cash to the highest and best bidder after advertising the sale for at least once each week for 3 consecutive weeks, the last notice to appear not more than 10 days nor less than 5 days prior to such sale in a newspaper having a general circulation in the county. Such notice shall contain a description of the property to be sold and a statement of the time and place of sale. It shall not be necessary to the validity of such sale either to have the property present at the place of sale or to have the name of the owner thereof stated in such notice. The proceeds of the sale, less any expenses of concluding the sale, shall be deposited in the seizing agency's general fund to be used only for approved law enforcement activity affecting the agency's efforts to combat gang activities.

(8) Any action under the provisions of this section may be consolidated with any other action or proceedings pursuant to this section relating to the same property on motion of the district attorney.

New Mexico Annotated Statutes

Current through all legislation for 2016, including 92 chapters of the Second Regular session of the Fifty-Second legislature

Office of the Attorney General
408 Galisteo Street
Villagra Building
Santa Fe, New Mexico 87501
Phone: (505) 827-6000
http://www.nmag.gov/

Phoenix Field Division
201 E. Washington Street, Suite 940
Phoenix, Arizona 85004
Voice: (602) 776-5400 (criminal)
Voice: (602) 776-5480 (industry)
https://www.atf.gov/phoenix-field-division

PROTECTING THE PUBLIC
SERVING OUR NATION

Table of Contents

Chapter 29 Law Enforcement
Article 19 Concealed Handgun Carry

29-19-2. Definitions. As used in the Concealed Handgun Carry Act [29-19-1 NMSA 1978]:
A. "applicant" means a person seeking a license to carry a concealed handgun;
B. "caliber" means the diameter of the bore of a handgun;
C. "category" means whether a handgun is semiautomatic or not semiautomatic;
D. "concealed handgun" means a loaded handgun that is not visible to the ordinary observations of a reasonable person;
E. "department" means the department of public safety;
F. "handgun" means a firearm that will, is designed to or may readily be converted to expel a projectile by the action of an explosion and the barrel length of which, not including a revolving, detachable or magazine breech, does not exceed 12 inches; and
G. "licensee" means a person holding a valid concealed handgun license issued to him by the department.

29-19-3. Date of licensure; period of licensure. Effective January 1, 2004, the department is authorized to issue concealed handgun licenses to qualified applicants. Original and renewed concealed handgun licenses shall be valid for a period of 4 years from the date of issuance, unless the license is suspended or revoked.

29-19-4. Applicant qualifications.
A. The department shall issue a concealed handgun license to an applicant who:
   (1) is a citizen of the United States;

(2) is a resident of New Mexico or is a member of the armed forces whose permanent duty station is located in New Mexico or is a dependent of such a member;

(3) is 21 years of age or older;

(4) is not a fugitive from justice;

(5) has not been convicted of a felony in New Mexico or any other state or pursuant to the laws of the United States or any other jurisdiction;

(6) is not currently under indictment for a felony criminal offense in New Mexico or any other state or pursuant to the laws of the United States or any other jurisdiction;

(7) is not otherwise prohibited by federal law or the law of any other jurisdiction from purchasing or possessing a firearm;

(8) has not been adjudicated mentally incompetent or committed to a mental institution;

(9) is not addicted to alcohol or controlled substances; and

(10) has satisfactorily completed a firearms training course approved by the department for the category and the largest caliber of handgun that the applicant wants to be licensed to carry as a concealed handgun.

B. The department shall deny a concealed handgun license to an applicant who has:

(1) received a conditional discharge, a diversion or a deferment or has been convicted of, pled guilty to or entered a plea of nolo contendere to a misdemeanor offense involving a crime of violence within ten years immediately preceding the application;

(2) been convicted of a misdemeanor offense involving driving while under the influence of intoxicating liquor or drugs within 5 years immediately preceding the application for a concealed handgun license;

(3) been convicted of a misdemeanor offense involving the possession or abuse of a controlled substance within ten years immediately preceding the application; or

(4) been convicted of a misdemeanor offense involving assault, battery or battery against a household member.

C. Firearms training course instructors who are approved by the department shall not be required to complete a firearms training course pursuant to Paragraph (10) of Subsection A of this section.

29-19-5. Application form; screening of applicants; fee; limitations on liability.

A. Effective July 1, 2003, applications for concealed handgun licenses shall be made readily available at locations designated by the department. Applications for concealed handgun licenses shall be completed, under penalty of perjury, on a form designed and provided by the department and shall include:

(1) the applicant's name, current address, date of birth, place of birth, social security number, height, weight, gender, hair color, eye color and driver's license number or other state-issued identification number;

(2) a statement that the applicant is aware of, understands and is in compliance with the requirements for licensure set forth in the Concealed Handgun Carry Act [29-19-1 NMSA 1978];

(3) a statement that the applicant has been furnished a copy of the Concealed Handgun Carry Act [29-19-1 NMSA 1978] and is knowledgeable of its provisions; and

(4) a conspicuous warning that the application form is executed under penalty of perjury and that a materially false answer or the submission of a materially false document to the department may result in denial or revocation of a concealed handgun license and may subject the applicant to criminal prosecution for perjury as provided in § 30-25-1 NMSA 1978.

B. The applicant shall submit to the department:

(1) a completed application form;

(2) a nonrefundable application fee in an amount not to exceed $100;

(3) two full sets of fingerprints;

(4) a certified copy of a certificate of completion for a firearms training course approved by the department;

(5) two color photographs of the applicant;

(6) a certified copy of a birth certificate or proof of United States citizenship, if the applicant was not born in the United States; and

(7) proof of residency in New Mexico.

C. A law enforcement agency may fingerprint an applicant and may charge a reasonable fee.

D. Upon receipt of the items listed in Subsection B of this section, the department shall make a reasonable effort to determine if an applicant is qualified to receive a concealed handgun license. The department shall conduct an appropriate check of available records and shall forward the applicant's fingerprints to the federal bureau of investigation for a national criminal background check. The department shall comply with the license-issuing requirements set forth in § 29-19-7 NMSA 1978. However, the department shall suspend or revoke a license if the department receives information that would disqualify an applicant from receiving a concealed handgun license after the 30-day time period has elapsed.

E. A state or local government agency shall comply with a request from the department pursuant to the Concealed Handgun Carry Act [29-19-1 NMSA 1978] within 30 days of the request.

29-19-6. Appeal; license renewal; refresher firearms training course; suspension or revocation of license.

A. Pursuant to rules adopted by the department, the department, within 30 days after receiving a completed application for a concealed handgun license and the results of a national criminal background check on the applicant, shall:

(1) issue a concealed handgun license to an applicant; or

(2) deny the application on the grounds that the applicant failed to qualify for a concealed handgun license pursuant to the provisions of the Concealed Handgun Carry Act [29-19-1 NMSA 1978].

B. Information relating to an applicant or to a licensee received by the department or any other law enforcement agency is confidential and exempt from public disclosure unless an order to disclose information is issued by a court of competent jurisdiction. The information shall be made available by the department to a state or local law enforcement agency upon request by the agency.

C. A concealed handgun license issued by the department shall include:

(1) a color photograph of the licensee;

(2) the licensee's name, address and date of birth;

(3) the expiration date of the concealed handgun license; and

(4) the category and the largest caliber of handgun that the licensee is licensed to carry, with a statement that the licensee is licensed to carry smaller caliber handguns but shall carry only 1 concealed handgun at any given time.

D. A licensee shall notify the department within 30 days regarding a change of the licensee's name or permanent address. A licensee shall notify the department within 10 days if the licensee's concealed handgun license is lost, stolen or destroyed.

E. If a concealed handgun license is lost, stolen or destroyed, the license is invalid and the licensee may obtain a duplicate license by furnishing the department a notarized statement that the original license was lost, stolen or destroyed and paying a reasonable fee. If the license is lost or stolen, the licensee shall file a police report with a local law enforcement agency and include the police case number in the notarized statement.

F. A licensee may renew a concealed handgun license by submitting to the department:

(1) a completed renewal form, under penalty of perjury, designed and provided by the department;

(2) a payment of a $75 renewal fee; and

(3) a certificate of completion of a 4-hour refresher firearms training course approved by the department.

G. The department shall conduct a national criminal records check of a licensee seeking to renew a license. A concealed handgun license shall not be renewed more than 60 days after it has expired. A licensee who fails to renew a concealed handgun license within 60 days after it has expired may apply for a new concealed handgun license pursuant to the provisions of the Concealed Handgun Carry Act [29-19-1 NMSA 1978].

H. A licensee shall complete a 2-hour refresher firearms training course 2 years after the issuance of an original or renewed license. The refresher course shall be approved by the department and shall be taken 22 to 26 months after the issuance of an original or renewed license. A certificate of completion shall be submitted to the department no later than 30 days after completion of the course.

I. The department shall suspend or revoke a concealed handgun license if:

(1) the licensee provided the department with false information on the application form or renewal form for a concealed handgun license;

(2) the licensee did not satisfy the criteria for issuance of a concealed handgun license at the time the license was issued; or

(3) subsequent to receiving a concealed handgun license, the licensee violated a provision of the Concealed Handgun Carry Act [29-19-1 NMSA 1978].

29-19-7. Demonstration of ability and knowledge; course requirement; proprietary interest; exemptions.

A. The department shall prepare and publish minimum standards for approved firearms training courses that teach competency with handguns. A firearms training course shall include classroom instruction and range instruction and an actual demonstration by the applicant of his ability to safely use a handgun. An applicant shall not be licensed unless he demonstrates, at a minimum, his ability to use a handgun of .32 caliber. An approved firearms training course shall be a course that is certified or sponsored by a federal or state law enforcement agency, a college, a firearms training school or a nationally recognized organization, approved by the department that customarily offers firearms training. The firearms training course shall be not less than 15 hours in length and shall provide instruction regarding:

(1) knowledge of and safe handling of single- and double-action revolvers and semiautomatic handguns;

(2) safe storage of handguns and child safety;

(3) safe handgun shooting fundamentals;

(4) live shooting of a handgun on a firing range;

(5) identification of ways to develop and maintain handgun shooting skills;

(6) federal, state and local criminal and civil laws pertaining to the purchase, ownership, transportation, use and possession of handguns;

(7) techniques for avoiding a criminal attack and how to control a violent confrontation; and

(8) techniques for nonviolent dispute resolution.

B. Every instructor of an approved firearms training course shall annually file a copy of the course description and proof of certification with the department.

29-19-8. Limitation on license.

A. Nothing in the Concealed Handgun Carry Act [29-19-1 NMSA 1978] shall be construed as allowing a licensee in possession of a valid concealed handgun license to carry a concealed handgun into or on premises where to do so would be in violation of state or federal law.

B. Nothing in the Concealed Handgun Carry Act [29-19-1 NMSA 1978] shall be construed as allowing a licensee in possession of a valid concealed handgun license to carry a concealed handgun on school premises, as provided in § 30-7-2.1 NMSA 1978.

C. Nothing in the Concealed Handgun Carry Act [29-19-1 NMSA 1978] shall be construed as allowing a licensee in possession of a valid concealed handgun license to carry a concealed handgun on the premises of a preschool.

29-19-9. Possession of license. A licensee shall have his concealed handgun license in his possession at all times while carrying a concealed handgun.

29-19-10. Validity of license on tribal land. A concealed handgun license shall not be valid on tribal land, unless authorized by the governing body of an Indian nation, tribe or pueblo.

29-19-11. Validity of license in a courthouse or court facility. A concealed handgun license shall not be valid in a courthouse or court facility, unless authorized by the presiding judicial officer for that courthouse or court facility.

29-19-12. Rules; department to administer; reciprocal agreements with other states. The department shall promulgate rules necessary to implement the provisions of the Concealed Handgun Carry Act [29-19-1 NMSA 1978]. The rules shall include:

A. grounds for the suspension and revocation of concealed handgun licenses issued pursuant to the provisions of the Concealed Handgun Carry Act [29-19-1 NMSA 1978];

B. provision of authority for a law enforcement officer to confiscate a concealed handgun license when a licensee violates the provisions of the Concealed Handgun Carry Act [29-19-1 NMSA 1978];

C. provision of authority for a private property owner to disallow the carrying of a concealed handgun on the owner's property;

D. creation of a sequential numbering system for all concealed handgun licenses issued by the department and display of numbers on issued concealed handgun licenses; and

E. provision of discretionary state authority for the transfer, recognition or reciprocity of a concealed handgun license issued by another state if the issuing authority for the other state:

    (1) includes provisions at least as stringent as or substantially similar to the Concealed Handgun Carry Act [29-19-1 NMSA 1978];

    (2) issues a license or permit with an expiration date printed on the license or permit;

    (3) is available to verify the license or permit status for law enforcement purposes within 3 business days of a request for verification;

    (4) has disqualification, suspension and revocation requirements for a concealed handgun license or permit; and

    (5) requires that an applicant for a concealed handgun license or permit:

        (a) submit to a national criminal history record check;

        (b) not be prohibited from possessing firearms pursuant to federal or state law; and

        (c) satisfactorily complete a firearms safety program that covers deadly force issues, weapons care and maintenance, safe handling and storage of firearms and marksmanship.

29-19-14. Current and retired law enforcement officers and New Mexico mounted patrol members.

A. An application fee, a renewal fee and a firearms training course are not required for an applicant or licensee who is:

    (1) a current or retired certified law enforcement officer pursuant to the Law Enforcement Training Act; or

    (2) a current member of the New Mexico mounted patrol who has successfully completed a law enforcement academy basic law enforcement training program for New Mexico mounted patrol members pursuant to § 29-6-4.1 NMSA 1978.

B. A law enforcement officer or New Mexico mounted patrol member shall submit to the department 2 full sets of fingerprints and a color photograph of the law enforcement officer or New Mexico mounted patrol member. The department shall conduct an appropriate check of available records and shall forward the fingerprints to the federal bureau of investigation for a national criminal background check.

C. A retired law enforcement officer is not required to submit an application fee or a renewal fee if:

    (1) the officer was a certified law enforcement officer pursuant to the Law Enforcement Training Act for at least 15 years prior to retirement; and

    (2) the retirement is in good standing as shown by a letter from the agency from which the officer retired.

D. A retired law enforcement officer who has been retired 10 years or less is not required to complete a firearms training course.

E. A retired law enforcement officer who has been retired for more than 10 years shall be required to complete a firearms training course. The officer shall be allowed to attend any local law enforcement agency's firearms qualification course; provided that the officer supplies the officer's own ammunition, handgun, targets and range equipment. A local law enforcement agency shall not be liable under the Tort Claims Act for providing a firearms training course to a retired law enforcement officer pursuant to this subsection.

F. A retired law enforcement officer's concealed handgun license shall have printed on the license "retired police officer" and shall be valid for a period of 5 years.

29-19-15. Military service persons; requirements.

A. For a concealed handgun license applicant or licensee who submits with a concealed handgun license application documentation satisfactory to the department that the applicant is a military service person as defined in Subsection E of this section, an application fee or renewal fee is not required. For a military service person discharged from military service within 20 years of the application for a license or renewal of a license, a firearms training course or refresher firearms training course is not required.

B. A military service person shall submit to the department 2 full sets of fingerprints and a color photograph of the military service person. The department shall conduct an appropriate check of available records and shall forward the fingerprints to the federal bureau of investigation for a national criminal background check.

C. A military service person's concealed handgun carry license shall have printed on the license "military service person" and shall be valid for a period of 5 years.

D. The department shall suspend or revoke a military service person's concealed handgun license if:

(1) the military service person provided the department with false information on the application form or renewal form;

(2) the military service person did not satisfy the criteria for issuance of a concealed handgun license at the time the license was issued; or

(3) subsequent to receiving a concealed handgun license, the military service person violated a provision of the Concealed Handgun Carry Act.

E. As used in this section, "military service person" means a person who was accepted into the United States armed forces and:

(1) is on active duty with the United States armed forces;

(2) is on reserve or guard duty with the United States armed forces; or

(3) is a veteran or a retiree who received an honorable discharge as indicated on a United States department of defense form 214.

Chapter 30 Criminal Offenses
Article 7 Weapons and Explosives

30-7-1. "Carrying a deadly weapon." "Carrying a deadly weapon" means being armed with a deadly weapon by having it on the person, or in close proximity thereto, so that the weapon is readily accessible for use.

30-7-2. Unlawful carrying of a deadly weapon.
A. Unlawful carrying of a deadly weapon consists of carrying a concealed loaded firearm or any other type of deadly weapon anywhere, except in the following cases:

(1) in the person's residence or on real property belonging to him as owner, lessee, tenant or licensee;

(2) in a private automobile or other private means of conveyance, for lawful protection of the person's or another's person or property;

(3) by a peace officer in accordance with the policies of his law enforcement agency who is certified pursuant to the Law Enforcement Training Act [29-7-1 NMSA 1978];

(4) by a peace officer in accordance with the policies of his law enforcement agency who is employed on a temporary basis by that agency and who has successfully completed a course of firearms instruction prescribed by the New Mexico law enforcement academy or provided by a certified firearms instructor who is employed on a permanent basis by a law enforcement agency; or

(5) by a person in possession of a valid concealed handgun license issued to him by the department of public safety pursuant to the provisions of the Concealed Handgun Carry Act [29-19-1 NMSA 1978].

B. Nothing in this section shall be construed to prevent the carrying of any unloaded firearm.

C. Whoever commits unlawful carrying of a deadly weapon is guilty of a petty misdemeanor.

30-7-2.1. Unlawful carrying of a deadly weapon on school premises.
A. Unlawful carrying of a deadly weapon on school premises consists of carrying a deadly weapon on school premises except by:

(1) a peace officer;

(2) school security personnel;

(3) a student, instructor or other school-authorized personnel engaged in army, navy, marine corps or air force reserve officer training corps programs or state-authorized hunter safety training instruction;

(4) a person conducting or participating in a school-approved program, class or other activity involving the carrying of a deadly weapon; or

(5) a person older than 19 years of age on school premises in a private automobile or other private means of conveyance, for lawful protection of the person's or another's person or property.

B. As used in this section, "school premises" means:

(1) the buildings and grounds, including playgrounds, playing fields and parking areas and any school bus of any public elementary, secondary, junior high or high school in or on which school or school-related activities are being operated under the supervision of a local school board; or

(2) any other public buildings or grounds, including playing fields and parking areas that are not public school property, in or on which public school-related and sanctioned activities are being performed.

C. Whoever commits unlawful carrying of a deadly weapon on school premises is guilty of a fourth degree felony.

30-7-2.2. Unlawful possession of a handgun by a person; exceptions; penalty.
A. Unlawful possession of a handgun by a person consists of a person knowingly having a handgun in his possession or knowingly transporting a handgun, except when the person is:
  (1) in attendance at a hunter's safety course or a handgun safety course;
  (2) engaging in the use of a handgun for target shooting at an established range authorized by the governing body of the jurisdiction in which the range is located or in an area where the discharge of a handgun without legal justification is not prohibited by law;
  (3) engaging in an organized competition involving the use of a handgun;
  (4) participating in or practicing for a performance by an organization that has been granted exemption from federal income tax by the United States commissioner of internal revenue as an organization described in § 501(c)(3) of the United States Internal Revenue Code of 1954 [26 USCS § 501(c)(3)], as amended or renumbered;
  (5) legal hunting or trapping activities;
  (6) traveling, with an unloaded handgun in his possession, to or from an activity described in Paragraph (1), (2), (3), (4) or (5) of this subsection; or
  (7) on real property under the control of the person's parent, grandparent or legal guardian and the person is being supervised by his parent, grandparent or legal guardian.
B. A person who commits unlawful possession of a handgun by a person is guilty of a misdemeanor.
C. As used in this section:
  (1) "person" means an individual who is less than 19 years old; and
  (2) "handgun" means a loaded or unloaded pistol, revolver or firearm which will or is designed to or may readily be converted to expel a projectile by the action of an explosion and the barrel length of which, not including a revolving, detachable or magazine breech, does not exceed 12 inches.

30-7-2.3. Seizure and forfeiture of a handgun possessed or transported by a person in violation of unlawful possession of a handgun by a person.
A. A handgun is subject to seizure and forfeiture by a law enforcement agency when the handgun is possessed or transported by a person in violation of the offense of unlawful possession of a handgun by a person.
B. The provisions of the Forfeiture Act [31-27-1 NMSA 1978] apply to the seizure, forfeiture and disposal of a handgun subject to forfeiture pursuant to Subsection A of this section.

30-7-2.4. Unlawful carrying of a firearm on university premises; notice; penalty.
A. Unlawful carrying of a firearm on university premises consists of carrying a firearm on university premises except by:
  (1) a peace officer;
  (2) university security personnel;
  (3) a student, instructor or other university-authorized personnel who are engaged in army, navy, marine corps or air force reserve officer training corps programs or a state-authorized hunter safety training program;
  (4) a person conducting or participating in a university-approved program, class or other activity involving the carrying of a firearm; or
  (5) a person older than 19 years of age on university premises in a private automobile or other private means of conveyance, for lawful protection of the person's or another's person or property.
B. A university shall conspicuously post notices on university premises that state that it is unlawful to carry a firearm on university premises.
C. As used in this section:
  (1) "university" means a baccalaureate degree-granting post-secondary educational institution, a community college, a branch community college, a technical-vocational institute and an area vocational school; and
  (2) "university premises" means:
    (a) the buildings and grounds of a university, including playing fields and parking areas of a university, in or on which university or university-related activities are conducted; or
    (b) any other public buildings or grounds, including playing fields and parking areas that are not university property, in or on which university-related and sanctioned activities are performed.
D. Whoever commits unlawful carrying of a firearm on university premises is guilty of a petty misdemeanor.

30-7-3. Unlawful carrying of a firearm in licensed liquor establishments.
A. Unlawful carrying of a firearm in an establishment licensed to dispense alcoholic beverages consists of carrying a loaded or unloaded firearm on any premises licensed by the regulation and licensing department for the dispensing of alcoholic beverages except:
  (1) by a law enforcement officer in the lawful discharge of the officer's duties;
  (2) by a law enforcement officer who is certified pursuant to the Law Enforcement Training Act [29-7-1 NMSA 1978] acting in accordance with the policies of the officer's law enforcement agency;
  (3) by the owner, lessee, tenant or operator of the licensed premises or the owner's, lessee's, tenant's or operator's agents, including privately employed security personnel during the performance of their duties;
  (4) by a person carrying a concealed handgun who is in possession of a valid concealed handgun license for that gun pursuant to the Concealed Handgun Carry Act [29-19-1 NMSA 1978] on the premises of:
    (a) a licensed establishment that does not sell alcoholic beverages for consumption on the premises; or

(b) a restaurant licensed to sell only beer and wine that derives no less than 60% of its annual gross receipts from the sale of food for consumption on the premises, unless the restaurant has a sign posted, in a conspicuous location at each public entrance, prohibiting the carrying of firearms, or the person is verbally instructed by the owner or manager that the carrying of a firearm is not permitted in the restaurant;

(5) by a person in that area of the licensed premises usually and primarily rented on a daily or short-term basis for sleeping or residential occupancy, including hotel or motel rooms;

(6) by a person on that area of a licensed premises primarily used for vehicular traffic or parking; or

(7) for the purpose of temporary display, provided that the firearm is:

(a) made completely inoperative before it is carried onto the licensed premises and remains inoperative while it is on the licensed premises; and

(b) under the control of the licensee or an agent of the licensee while the firearm is on the licensed premises.

B. Whoever commits unlawful carrying of a firearm in an establishment licensed to dispense alcoholic beverages is guilty of a fourth degree felony.

30-7-4. Negligent use of a deadly weapon.

A. Negligent use of a deadly weapon consists of:

(1) discharging a firearm into any building or vehicle or so as to knowingly endanger a person or his property;

(2) carrying a firearm while under the influence of an intoxicant or narcotic;

(3) endangering the safety of another by handling or using a firearm or other deadly weapon in a negligent manner; or

(4) discharging a firearm within 150 yards of a dwelling or building, not including abandoned or vacated buildings on public lands during hunting seasons, without the permission of the owner or lessees thereof.

B. The provisions of Paragraphs (1), (3) and (4) of Subsection A of this section shall not apply to a peace officer or other public employee who is required or authorized by law to carry or use a firearm in the course of his employment and who carries, handles, uses or discharges a firearm while lawfully engaged in carrying out the duties of his office or employment.

C. The exceptions from criminal liability provided for in Subsection B of this section shall not preclude or affect civil liability for the same conduct.

Whoever commits negligent use of a deadly weapon is guilty of a petty misdemeanor.

30-7-16. Firearms or destructive devices; receipt, transportation or possession by a felon; penalty.

A. It is unlawful for a felon to receive, transport or possess any firearm or destructive device in this state.

B. Any person violating the provisions of this section shall be guilty of a fourth degree felony and shall be sentenced in accordance with the provisions of the Criminal Sentencing Act [31-18-12 NMSA 1978].

C. As used in this section:

(1) "destructive device" means:

(a) any explosive, incendiary or poison gas: **1)** bomb; **2)** grenade; **3)** rocket having a propellant charge of more than 4 ounces; **4)** missile having an explosive or incendiary charge of more than 1/4 ounce; **5)** mine; or **6)** similar device;

(b) any type of weapon by whatever name known that will, or that may be readily converted to, expel a projectile by the action of an explosive or other propellant, the barrel or barrels of which have a bore of more than 1/2 inch in diameter, except a shotgun or shotgun shell that is generally recognized as particularly suitable for sporting purposes; and

(c) any combination of parts either designed or intended for use in converting any device into a destructive device as defined in this paragraph and from which a destructive device may be readily assembled.

The term "destructive device" does not include any device that is neither designed nor redesigned for use as a weapon or any device, although originally designed for use as a weapon, that is redesigned for use as a signaling, pyrotechnic, line throwing, safety or similar device;

(2) "felon" means a person convicted of a felony offense by a court of the United States or of any state or political subdivision thereof and:

(a) less than 10 years have passed since the person completed serving his sentence or period of probation for the felony conviction, whichever is later;

(b) the person has not been pardoned for the felony conviction by the proper authority; and

(c) the person has not received a deferred sentence; and

(3) "firearm" means any weapon that will or is designed to or may readily be converted to expel a projectile by the action of an explosion; the frame or receiver of any such weapon; or any firearm muffler or firearm silencer. "Firearm" includes any handgun, rifle or shotgun.

Constitution of the State of New Mexico
Article II Bill of Rights

Sec. 6 [Right to bear arms.] No law shall abridge the right of the citizen to keep and bear arms for security and defense, for lawful hunting and recreational use and for other lawful purposes, but nothing herein shall be held to permit the carrying of concealed weapons. No municipality or county shall regulate, in any way, an incident of the right to keep and bear arms. (As amended November 2, 1971 and November 2, 1986.)

General Statutes of North Carolina
Current through Session Laws 2016-3, 2016 2nd Extra Session.

Office of the Attorney General
9001 Mail Service Center
Raleigh, NC 27699-9001
Voice: (919) 716-6400
http://www.ncdoj.com/About-
DOJ/The-Attorney-General.aspx

Charlotte Field Division
6701 Carmel Road, Suite 200
Charlotte, North Carolina 28226
Voice: (704) 716-1800
https://www.atf.gov/charlotte-field-
division

PROTECTING THE PUBLIC
SERVING OUR NATION

Table of Contents

Chapter 14. Criminal Law
Article 23. Trespasses to Personal Property

§ 14-160.1. Alteration, destruction or removal of permanent identification marks from personal property

(a) It shall be unlawful for any person to alter, deface, destroy or remove the permanent serial number, manufacturer's identification plate or other permanent, distinguishing number or identification mark from any item of personal property with the intent thereby to conceal or misrepresent the identity of said item.

(b) It shall be unlawful for any person knowingly to sell, buy or be in possession of any item of personal property, not his own, on which the permanent serial number, manufacturer's identification plate or other permanent, distinguishing number or identification mark has been altered, defaced, destroyed or removed for the purpose of concealing or misrepresenting the identity of said item.

(c) Unless the conduct is covered under some other provision of law providing greater punishment, a violation of any of the provisions of this section shall be a Class 1 misdemeanor.

(d) This section shall not in any way affect the provisions of G.S. 20-108, 20-109(a) or 20-109(b).

§ 14-160.2. Alteration, destruction, or removal of serial number from firearm; possession of firearm with serial number removed

(a) It shall be unlawful for any person to alter, deface, destroy, or remove the permanent serial number, manufacturer's identification plate, or other permanent distinguishing number or identification mark from any firearm with the intent thereby to conceal or misrepresent the identity of the firearm.

(b) It shall be unlawful for any person knowingly to sell, buy, or be in possession of any firearm on which the permanent serial number, manufacturer's identification plate, or other permanent distinguishing number or identification mark has been altered, defaced, destroyed, or removed for the purpose of concealing or misrepresenting the identity of the firearm.

(c) A violation of any of the provisions of this section shall be a Class H felony.

Article 35. Offenses Against the Public Peace

§ 14-269. Carrying concealed weapons

(a1) It shall be unlawful for any person willfully and intentionally to carry concealed about his or her person any pistol or gun except in the following circumstances:

   (1) The person is on the person's own premises.

   (2) The deadly weapon is a handgun, the person has a concealed handgun permit issued in accordance with Article 54B of this Chapter or considered valid under G.S. 14-415.24, and the person is carrying the concealed handgun in accordance with the scope of the concealed handgun permit as set out in G.S. 14-415.11(c).

   (3) The deadly weapon is a handgun and the person is a military permittee as defined under G.S. 14-415.10(2a) who provides to the law enforcement officer proof of deployment as required under G.S. 14-415.11(a).

(a2) This prohibition does not apply to a person who has a concealed handgun permit issued in accordance with Article 54B of this Chapter, has a concealed handgun permit considered valid under G.S. 14-415.24, or is exempt from obtaining a permit pursuant to G.S. 14-415.25, provided the weapon is a handgun, is in a closed compartment or container within the person's locked vehicle, and the vehicle is in a parking area that is owned or leased by State government. A person may unlock the vehicle to enter or exit the vehicle, provided the handgun remains in the closed compartment at all times and the vehicle is locked immediately following the entrance or exit.

(b) This prohibition shall not apply to the following persons:

(1) Officers and enlisted personnel of the Armed Forces of the United States when in discharge of their official duties as such and acting under orders requiring them to carry arms and weapons;

(2) Civil and law enforcement officers of the United States;

(3) Officers and soldiers of the militia and the National Guard when called into actual service;

(3a) A member of the North Carolina National Guard who has been designated in writing by the Adjutant General, State of North Carolina, who has a concealed handgun permit issued in accordance with Article 54B of this Chapter or considered valid under G.S. 14-415.24, and is acting in the discharge of his or her official duties, provided that the member does not carry a concealed weapon while consuming alcohol or an unlawful controlled substance or while alcohol or an unlawful controlled substance remains in the member's body.

(4) Officers of the State, or of any county, city, town, or company police agency charged with the execution of the laws of the State, when acting in the discharge of their official duties;

(4a) Any person who is a district attorney, an assistant district attorney, or an investigator employed by the office of a district attorney and who has a concealed handgun permit issued in accordance with Article 54B of this Chapter or considered valid under G.S. 14-415.24; provided that the person shall not carry a concealed weapon at any time while in a courtroom or while consuming alcohol or an unlawful controlled substance or while alcohol or an unlawful controlled substance remains in the person's body. The district attorney, assistant district attorney, or investigator shall secure the weapon in a locked compartment when the weapon is not on the person of the district attorney, assistant district attorney, or investigator. Notwithstanding the provisions of this subsection, a district attorney may carry a concealed weapon while in a courtroom;

(4b) Any person who is a qualified retired law enforcement officer as defined in G.S. 14-415.10 and meets any one of the following conditions:

a. Is the holder of a concealed handgun permit in accordance with Article 54B of this Chapter.

b. Is exempt from obtaining a permit pursuant to G.S. 14-415.25.

c. Is certified by the North Carolina Criminal Justice Education and Training Standards Commission pursuant to G.S. 14-415.26;

(4c) Detention personnel or correctional officers employed by the State or a unit of local government who park a vehicle in a space that is authorized for their use in the course of their duties may transport a firearm to the parking space and store that firearm in the vehicle parked in the parking space, provided that: **(i)** the firearm is in a closed compartment or container within the locked vehicle, or **(ii)** the firearm is in a locked container securely affixed to the vehicle;

(4d) Any person who is a North Carolina district court judge, North Carolina superior court judge, or a North Carolina magistrate and who has a concealed handgun permit issued in accordance with Article 54B of this Chapter or considered valid under G.S. 14-415.24; provided that the person shall not carry a concealed weapon at any time while consuming alcohol or an unlawful controlled substance or while alcohol or an unlawful controlled substance remains in the person's body. The judge or magistrate shall secure the weapon in a locked compartment when the weapon is not on the person of the judge or magistrate;

(4e) Any person who is serving as a clerk of court or as a register of deeds and who has a concealed handgun permit issued in accordance with Article 54B of this Chapter or considered valid under G.S. 14-415.24; provided that the person shall not carry a concealed weapon at any time while consuming alcohol or an unlawful controlled substance or while alcohol or an unlawful controlled substance remains in the person's body. The clerk of court or register of deeds shall secure the weapon in a locked compartment when the weapon is not on the person of the clerk of court or register of deeds. This subdivision does not apply to assistants, deputies, or other employees of the clerk of court or register of deeds;

(5) Sworn law-enforcement officers, when off-duty, provided that an officer does not carry a concealed weapon while consuming alcohol or an unlawful controlled substance or while alcohol or an unlawful controlled substance remains in the officer's body;

(6) State probation or parole certified officers, when off-duty, provided that an officer does not carry a concealed weapon while consuming alcohol or an unlawful controlled substance or while alcohol or an unlawful controlled substance remains in the officer's body.

(7) A person employed by the Department of Public Safety who has been designated in writing by the Secretary of the Department, who has a concealed handgun permit issued in accordance with Article 54B of this Chapter or considered valid under G.S. 14-415.24, and has in the person's possession written proof of the designation by the Secretary of the Department, provided that the person shall not carry a concealed weapon at any time while consuming alcohol or an unlawful controlled substance or while alcohol or an unlawful controlled substance remains in the person's body.

(8) Any person who is an administrative law judge described in Article 60 of Chapter 7A of the General Statutes and who has a concealed handgun permit issued in accordance with Article 54B of this Chapter or considered valid under G.S. 14-415.24, provided that the person shall not carry a concealed weapon at any time while consuming alcohol or an unlawful controlled substance or while alcohol or an unlawful controlled substance remains in the person's body.

(9) State correctional officers, when off-duty, provided that an officer does not carry a concealed weapon while consuming alcohol or an unlawful controlled substance or while alcohol or an unlawful controlled substance remains in the officer's body. If the concealed weapon is a handgun, the correctional officer must meet the firearms training standards of the Division of Adult Correction of the Department of Public Safety.

(b1) It is a defense to a prosecution under this section that:

(1) The weapon was not a firearm;

(2) The defendant was engaged in, or on the way to or from, an activity in which the defendant legitimately used the weapon;

(3) The defendant possessed the weapon for that legitimate use; and

(4) The defendant did not use or attempt to use the weapon for an illegal purpose.

The burden of proving this defense is on the defendant.

(b2) It is a defense to a prosecution under this section that:

(1) The deadly weapon is a handgun;

(2) The defendant is a military permittee as defined under G.S. 14-415.10(2a); and

(3) The defendant provides to the court proof of deployment as defined under G.S. 14-415.10(3a).

(c) Any person violating the provisions of subsection (a) of this section shall be guilty of a Class 2 misdemeanor. Any person violating the provisions of subsection (a1) of this section shall be guilty of a Class 2 misdemeanor for the first offense and a Class H felony for a second or subsequent offense. A violation of subsection (a1) of this section punishable under G.S. 14-415.21(a) is not punishable under this section.

§ 14-269.1. Confiscation and disposition of deadly weapons.

Upon conviction of any person for violation of G.S. 14-269, G.S. 14-269.7, or any other offense involving the use of a deadly weapon of a type referred to in G.S. 14-269, the deadly weapon with reference to which the defendant shall have been convicted shall be ordered confiscated and disposed of by the presiding judge at the trial in one of the following ways in the discretion of the presiding judge.

(1) By ordering the weapon returned to its rightful owner, but only when such owner is a person other than the defendant and has filed a petition for the recovery of such weapon with the presiding judge at the time of the defendant's conviction, and upon a finding by the presiding judge that petitioner is entitled to possession of same and that he was unlawfully deprived of the same without his consent.

(4) By ordering such weapon turned over to the sheriff of the county in which the trial is held or his duly authorized agent to be destroyed if the firearm does not have a legible, unique identification number or is unsafe for use because of wear, damage, age, or modification. The sheriff shall maintain a record of the destruction thereof.

(4b) By ordering the weapon turned over to a law enforcement agency in the county of trial for **(i)** the official use of the agency or **(ii)** sale, trade, or exchange by the agency to a federally licensed firearm dealer in accordance with all applicable State and federal firearm laws. The court may order a disposition of the firearm pursuant to this subdivision only upon the written request of the head or chief of the law enforcement agency and only if the firearm has a legible, unique identification number. If the law enforcement agency sells the firearm, then the proceeds of the sale shall be remitted to the appropriate county finance officer as provided by G.S. 115C-452 to be used to maintain free public schools. The receiving law enforcement agency shall maintain a record and inventory of all firearms received pursuant to this subdivision.

§ 14-269.2. Weapons on campus or other educational property

(a) The following definitions apply to this section:

(1) Educational property. – Any school building or bus, school campus, grounds, recreational area, athletic field, or other property owned, used, or operated by any board of education or school board of trustees, or directors for the administration of any school.

(1a) Employee. – A person employed by a local board of education or school whether the person is an adult or a minor.

(1b) School. – A public or private school, community college, college, or university.

(2) Student. – A person enrolled in a school or a person who has been suspended or expelled within the last 5 years from a school, whether the person is an adult or a minor.

(3a) Volunteer school safety resource officer. – A person who volunteers as a school safety resource officer as provided by G.S. 162-26 or G.S. 160A-288.4.

(4) Weapon. – Any device enumerated in subsection (b), (b1), or (d) of this section.

(b) It shall be a Class I felony for any person knowingly to possess or carry, whether openly or concealed, any gun, rifle, pistol, or other firearm of any kind on educational property or to a curricular or extracurricular activity sponsored by a school. Unless the conduct is covered under some other provision of law providing greater punishment, any person who willfully discharges a firearm of any kind on educational property is guilty of a Class F felony. However, this subsection does not apply to a BB gun, stun gun, air rifle, or air pistol.

(b1) It shall be a Class G felony for any person to possess or carry, whether openly or concealed, any dynamite cartridge, bomb, grenade, mine, or powerful explosive as defined in G.S. 14-284.1, on educational property or to a curricular or extracurricular activity sponsored by a school. This subsection shall not apply to fireworks.

(c) It shall be a Class I felony for any person to cause, encourage, or aid a minor who is less than 18 years old to possess or carry, whether openly or concealed, any gun, rifle, pistol, or other firearm of any kind on educational property. However, this subsection does not apply to a BB gun, stun gun, air rifle, or air pistol.

(c1) It shall be a Class G felony for any person to cause, encourage, or aid a minor who is less than 18 years old to possess or carry, whether openly or concealed, any dynamite cartridge, bomb, grenade, mine, or powerful explosive as defined in G.S. 14-284.1 on educational property. This subsection shall not apply to fireworks.

(d) It shall be a Class 1 misdemeanor for any person to possess or carry, whether openly or concealed, any BB gun, stun gun, air rifle, air pistol, … on educational property.

(e) It shall be a Class 1 misdemeanor for any person to cause, encourage, or aid a minor who is less than 18 years old to possess or carry, whether openly or concealed, any BB gun, stun gun, air rifle, air pistol, … on educational property.

(f) Notwithstanding subsection (b) of this section it shall be a Class 1 misdemeanor rather than a Class I felony for any person to possess or carry, whether openly or concealed, any gun, rifle, pistol, or other firearm of any kind, on educational property or to a curricular or extracurricular activity sponsored by a school if:

  (1) The person is not a student attending school on the educational property or an employee employed by the school working on the educational property; and

  (1a) The person is not a student attending a curricular or extracurricular activity sponsored by the school at which the student is enrolled or an employee attending a curricular or extracurricular activity sponsored by the school at which the employee is employed; and

  (2) Repealed by Session Laws 1999-211, s. 1, effective December 1, 1999, and applicable to offenses committed on or after that date.

  (3) The firearm is not loaded, is in a motor vehicle, and is in a locked container or a locked firearm rack.

  (4) Repealed by Session Laws 1999-211, s. 1, effective December 1, 1999, and applicable to offenses committed on or after that date.

(g) This section shall not apply to any of the following:

  (1) A weapon used solely for educational or school-sanctioned ceremonial purposes, or used in a school-approved program conducted under the supervision of an adult whose supervision has been approved by the school authority.

  (1a) A person exempted by the provisions of G.S. 14-269(b).

  (2) Firefighters, emergency service personnel, North Carolina Forest Service personnel, detention officers employed by and authorized by the sheriff to carry firearms, and any private police employed by a school, when acting in the discharge of their official duties.

  (3) Home schools as defined in G.S. 115C-563(a).

  (4) Weapons used for hunting purposes on the Howell Woods Nature Center property in Johnston County owned by Johnston Community College when used with the written permission of Johnston Community College or for hunting purposes on other educational property when used with the written permission of the governing body of the school that controls the educational property.

  (5) A person registered under Chapter 74C of the General Statutes as an armed armored car service guard or an armed courier service guard when acting in the discharge of the guard's duties and with the permission of the college or university.

  (6) A person registered under Chapter 74C of the General Statutes as an armed security guard while on the premises of a hospital or health care facility located on educational property when acting in the discharge of the guard's duties with the permission of the college or university.

  (7) A volunteer school safety resource officer providing security at a school pursuant to an agreement as provided in G.S. 115C-47(61) and either G.S. 162-26 or G.S. 160A-288.4, provided that the volunteer school safety resource officer is acting in the discharge of the person's official duties and is on the educational property of the school that the officer was assigned to by the head of the appropriate local law enforcement agency.

(h) No person shall be guilty of a criminal violation of this section with regard to the possession or carrying of a weapon so long as both of the following apply:

  (1) The person comes into possession of a weapon by taking or receiving the weapon from another person or by finding the weapon.

  (2) The person delivers the weapon, directly or indirectly, as soon as practical to law enforcement authorities.

(i) The provisions of this section shall not apply to an employee of an institution of higher education as defined in G.S. 116-143.1 or a nonpublic post-secondary educational institution who resides on the campus of the institution at which the person is employed when all of the following criteria are met:

  (1) The employee's residence is a detached, single-family dwelling in which only the employee and the employee's immediate family reside.

  (2) The institution is either:

    a. An institution of higher education as defined by G.S. 116-143.1.

    b. A nonpublic post-secondary educational institution that has not specifically prohibited the possession of a handgun pursuant to this subsection.

  (3) The weapon is a handgun.

  (4) The handgun is possessed in one of the following manners as appropriate:

    a. If the employee has a concealed handgun permit that is valid under Article 54B of this Chapter, or who is exempt from obtaining a permit pursuant to that Article, the handgun may be on the premises of the employee's residence or in a closed compartment or container within the employee's locked vehicle that is located in a parking area of the educational property of the institution at which the person is employed and resides. Except for direct transfer between the residence and the vehicle, the handgun must remain at all times either on the premises of the employee's residence or in the closed compartment of the employee's locked vehicle. The employee may unlock the vehicle to enter or exit, but must lock the vehicle immediately following the entrance or exit if the handgun is in the vehicle.

b. If the employee is not authorized to carry a concealed handgun pursuant to Article 54B of this Chapter, the handgun may be on the premises of the employee's residence, and may only be in the employee's vehicle when the vehicle is occupied by the employee and the employee is immediately leaving the campus or is driving directly to their residence from off campus. The employee may possess the handgun on the employee's person outside the premises of the employee's residence when making a direct transfer of the handgun from the residence to the employee's vehicle when the employee is immediately leaving the campus or from the employee's vehicle to the residence when the employee is arriving at the residence from off campus.

(j) The provisions of this section shall not apply to an employee of a public or nonpublic school who resides on the campus of the school at which the person is employed when all of the following criteria are met:

(1) The employee's residence is a detached, single-family dwelling in which only the employee and the employee's immediate family reside.

(2) The school is either:

a. A public school which provides residential housing for enrolled students.

b. A nonpublic school which provides residential housing for enrolled students and has not specifically prohibited the possession of a handgun pursuant to this subsection.

(3) The weapon is a handgun.

(4) The handgun is possessed in one of the following manners as appropriate:

a. If the employee has a concealed handgun permit that is valid under Article 54B of this Chapter, or who is exempt from obtaining a permit pursuant to that Article, the handgun may be on the premises of the employee's residence or in a closed compartment or container within the employee's locked vehicle that is located in a parking area of the educational property of the school at which the person is employed and resides. Except for direct transfer between the residence and the vehicle, the handgun must remain at all times either on the premises of the employee's residence or in the closed compartment of the employee's locked vehicle. The employee may unlock the vehicle to enter or exit, but must lock the vehicle immediately following the entrance or exit if the handgun is in the vehicle.

b. If the employee is not authorized to carry a concealed handgun pursuant to Article 54B of this Chapter, the handgun may be on the premises of the employee's residence, and may only be in the employee's vehicle when the vehicle is occupied by the employee and the employee is immediately leaving the campus or is driving directly to their residence from off campus. The employee may possess the handgun on the employee's person outside the premises of the employee's residence when making a direct transfer of the handgun from the residence to the employee's vehicle when the employee is immediately leaving the campus or from the employee's vehicle to the residence when the employee is arriving at the residence from off campus.

(k) The provisions of this section shall not apply to a person who has a concealed handgun permit that is valid under Article 54B of this Chapter, or who is exempt from obtaining a permit pursuant to that Article, if any of the following conditions are met:

(1) The person has a handgun in a closed compartment or container within the person's locked vehicle or in a locked container securely affixed to the person's vehicle and only unlocks the vehicle to enter or exit the vehicle while the firearm remains in the closed compartment at all times and immediately locks the vehicle following the entrance or exit.

(2) The person has a handgun concealed on the person and the person remains in the locked vehicle and only unlocks the vehicle to allow the entrance or exit of another person.

(3) The person is within a locked vehicle and removes the handgun from concealment only for the amount of time reasonably necessary to do either of the following:

a. Move the handgun from concealment on the person to a closed compartment or container within the vehicle.

b. Move the handgun from within a closed compartment or container within the vehicle to concealment on the person.

(l) It is an affirmative defense to a prosecution under subsection (b) or (f) of this section that the person was authorized to have a concealed handgun in a locked vehicle pursuant to subsection (k) of this section and removed the handgun from the vehicle only in response to a threatening situation in which deadly force was justified pursuant to G.S. 14-51.3.

§ 14-269.3. Carrying weapons into assemblies and establishments where alcoholic beverages are sold and consumed

(a) It shall be unlawful for any person to carry any gun, rifle, or pistol into any assembly where a fee has been charged for admission thereto, or into any establishment in which alcoholic beverages are sold and consumed. Any person violating the provisions of this section shall be guilty of a Class 1 misdemeanor.

(b) This section shall not apply to any of the following:

(1) A person exempted from the provisions of G.S. 14-269.

(2) The owner or lessee of the premises or business establishment.

(3) A person participating in the event, if the person is carrying a gun, rifle, or pistol with the permission of the owner, lessee, or person or organization sponsoring the event.

(4) A person registered or hired as a security guard by the owner, lessee, or person or organization sponsoring the event.

(5) A person carrying a handgun if the person has a valid concealed handgun permit issued in accordance with Article 54B of this Chapter, has a concealed handgun permit considered valid under G.S. 14-415.24, or is exempt from obtaining a permit pursuant to G.S. 14-415.25. This subdivision shall not be construed to permit a person to carry a handgun on any premises where the person in legal possession or control of the premises has posted a conspicuous notice prohibiting the carrying of a concealed handgun on the premises in accordance with G.S. 14-415.11(c).

§ 14-269.4. Weapons on certain State property and in courthouses. It shall be unlawful for any person to possess, or carry, whether openly or concealed, any deadly weapon, not used solely for instructional or officially sanctioned ceremonial purposes in the State Capitol Building, the Executive Mansion, the Western Residence of the Governor, or on the grounds of any of these buildings, and in any building housing any court of the General Court of Justice. If a court is housed in a building containing nonpublic uses in addition to the court, then this prohibition shall apply only to that portion of the building used for court purposes while the building is being used for court purposes.
This section shall not apply to any of the following:
(1a) A person exempted by the provisions of G.S. 14-269(b).
(4a) Any person in a building housing a court of the General Court of Justice in possession of a weapon for evidentiary purposes, to deliver it to a law-enforcement agency, or for purposes of registration.
(4b) Any district court judge or superior court judge who carries or possesses a concealed handgun in a building housing a court of the General Court of Justice if the judge is in the building to discharge his or her official duties and the judge has a concealed handgun permit issued in accordance with Article 54B of this Chapter or considered valid under G.S. 14-415.24.
(4c) Firearms in a courthouse, carried by detention officers employed by and authorized by the sheriff to carry firearms.
(4d) Any magistrate who carries or possesses a concealed handgun in any portion of a building housing a court of the General Court of Justice other than a courtroom itself unless the magistrate is presiding in that courtroom, if the magistrate **(i)** is in the building to discharge the magistrate's official duties, **(ii)** has a concealed handgun permit issued in accordance with Article 54B of this Chapter or considered valid under G.S. 14-415.24, **(iii)** has successfully completed a one-time weapons retention training substantially similar to that provided to certified law enforcement officers in North Carolina, and **(iv)** secures the weapon in a locked compartment when the weapon is not on the magistrate's person.
(5) State-owned rest areas, rest stops along the highways, and State-owned hunting and fishing reservations.
(6) A person with a permit issued in accordance with Article 54B of this Chapter, with a permit considered valid under G.S. 14-415.24, or who is exempt from obtaining a permit pursuant to G.S. 14-415.25, who has a firearm in a closed compartment or container within the person's locked vehicle or in a locked container securely affixed to the person's vehicle. A person may unlock the vehicle to enter or exit the vehicle provided the firearm remains in the closed compartment at all times and the vehicle is locked immediately following the entrance or exit.
Any person violating the provisions of this section shall be guilty of a Class 1 misdemeanor.

§ 14-269.7. Prohibitions on handguns for minors
(a) Any minor who willfully and intentionally possesses or carries a handgun is guilty of a Class 1 misdemeanor.
(b) This section does not apply:
  (1) To officers and enlisted personnel of the Armed Forces of the United States when in discharge of their official duties or acting under orders requiring them to carry handguns.
  (2) To a minor who possesses a handgun for educational or recreational purposes while the minor is supervised by an adult who is present.
  (3) To an emancipated minor who possesses such handgun inside his or her residence.
  (4) To a minor who possesses a handgun while hunting or trapping outside the limits of an incorporated municipality if he has on his person written permission from a parent, guardian, or other person standing in loco parentis.
(c) The following definitions apply in this section:
  (1) Handgun. – A firearm that has a short stock and is designed to be fired by the use of a single hand, or any combination of parts from which such a firearm can be assembled.
  (2) Minor. – Any person under 18 years of age.

§ 14-269.8. Purchase or possession of firearms by person subject to domestic violence order prohibited
(a) In accordance with G.S. 50B 3.1, it is unlawful for any person to possess, purchase, or receive or attempt to possess, purchase, or receive a firearm, as defined in G.S. 14-409.39(2), machine gun, ammunition, or permits to purchase or carry concealed firearms if ordered by the court for so long as that protective order or any successive protective order entered against that person pursuant to Chapter 50B of the General Statutes is in effect.
(b) Any person violating the provisions of this section shall be guilty of a Class H felony.

Article 36A. Riots, Civil Disorders, and Emergencies

§ 14-288.1. Definitions. Unless the context clearly requires otherwise, the following definitions apply in this Article:
(2) Dangerous weapon or substance. – Any deadly weapon, ammunition, explosive, incendiary device, radioactive material or device, as defined in G.S. 14-288.8(c)(5), or any instrument or substance designed for a use that carries a threat of serious bodily injury or destruction of property; or any instrument or substance that is capable of being used to inflict serious bodily injury, when the circumstances indicate a probability that such instrument or substance will be so used; or any part or ingredient in any instrument or substance included above, when the circumstances indicate a probability that such part or ingredient will be so used.

§ 14-288.8. Manufacture, assembly, possession, storage, transportation, sale, purchase, delivery, or acquisition of weapon of mass death and destruction; exceptions

(a) Except as otherwise provided in this section, it is unlawful for any person to manufacture, assemble, possess, store, transport, sell, offer to sell, purchase, offer to purchase, deliver or give to another, or acquire any weapon of mass death and destruction.

(b) This section does not apply to any of the following:

(1) Persons exempted from the provisions of G.S. 14-269 with respect to any activities lawfully engaged in while carrying out their duties.

(2) Importers, manufacturers, dealers, and collectors of firearms, ammunition, or destructive devices validly licensed under the laws of the United States or the State of North Carolina, while lawfully engaged in activities authorized under their licenses.

(3) Persons under contract with the United States, the State of North Carolina, or any agency of either government, with respect to any activities lawfully engaged in under their contracts.

(4) Inventors, designers, ordnance consultants and researchers, chemists, physicists, and other persons lawfully engaged in pursuits designed to enlarge knowledge or to facilitate the creation, development, or manufacture of weapons of mass death and destruction intended for use in a manner consistent with the laws of the United States and the State of North Carolina.

(5) Persons who lawfully possess or own a weapon as defined in subsection (c) of this section in compliance with 26 U.S.C. Chapter 53, §§ 5801-5871. Nothing in this subdivision shall limit the discretion of the sheriff in executing the paperwork required by the United States Bureau of Alcohol, Tobacco and Firearms for such person to obtain the weapon.

(c) The term "weapon of mass death and destruction" includes:

(1) Any explosive or incendiary:

a. Bomb; or

b. Grenade; or

c. Rocket having a propellant charge of more than four ounces; or

d. Missile having an explosive or incendiary charge of more than one-quarter ounce; or

e. Mine; or

f. Device similar to any of the devices described above; or

(2) Any type of weapon (other than a shotgun or a shotgun shell of a type particularly suitable for sporting purposes) which will, or which may be readily converted to, expel a projectile by the action of an explosive or other propellant, and which has any barrel with a bore of more than 1/2 inch in diameter; or

(3) Any firearm capable of fully automatic fire, any shotgun with a barrel or barrels of less than 18 inches in length or an overall length of less than 26 inches, any rifle with a barrel or barrels of less than 16 inches in length or an overall length of less than 26 inches, any muffler or silencer for any firearm, whether or not such firearm is included within this definition. For the purposes of this section, rifle is defined as a weapon designed or redesigned, made or remade, and intended to be fired from the shoulder; or

(4) Any combination of parts either designed or intended for use in converting any device into any weapon described above and from which a weapon of mass death and destruction may readily be assembled.

The term "weapon of mass death and destruction" does not include any device which is neither designed nor redesigned for use as a weapon; any device, although originally designed for use as a weapon, which is redesigned for use as a signaling, pyrotechnic, line-throwing, safety, or similar device; surplus ordnance sold, loaned, or given by the Secretary of the Army pursuant to the provisions of § 4684(2), 4685, or 4686 of Title 10 of the United States Code; or any other device which the Secretary of the Treasury finds is not likely to be used as a weapon, is an antique, or is a rifle which the owner intends to use solely for sporting purposes, in accordance with Chapter 44 of Title 18 of the United States Code.

(d) Any person who violates any provision of this section is guilty of a Class F felony.

§ 14-288.20. Certain weapons at civil disorders

(a) The definitions in G.S. 14-288.1 do not apply to this section. As used in this section:

(1) The term **"civil disorder"** means any public disturbance involving acts or violence by assemblages of 3 or more persons, which causes an immediate danger of damage or injury to the property or person of any other individual or results in damage or injury to the property or person of any other individual.

(2) The term **"firearm"** means any weapon which is designed to or may readily be converted to expel any projectile by the action of an explosive; or the frame or receiver of such a weapon.

(3) The term **"explosive or incendiary device"** means **(i)** dynamite and all other forms of high explosives, **(ii)** any explosive bomb, grenade, missile, or similar device, and **(iii)** any incendiary bomb or grenade, fire bomb, or similar device, including any device which **(i)** consists of or includes a breakable container including a flammable liquid or compound, and a wick composed of any material which, when ignited, is capable of igniting that flammable liquid or compound, and **(ii)** can be carried or thrown by one individual acting alone.

(4) The term **"law-enforcement officer"** means any officer of the United States, any state, any political subdivision of a state, or the District of Columbia charged with the execution of the laws thereof; civil officers of the United States; officers and soldiers of the organized militia and state guard of any state or territory of the United States, the Commonwealth of Puerto Rico, or the District of Columbia; and members of the Armed Forces of the United States.

(b) A person is guilty of a Class H felony, if he:

(1) Teaches or demonstrates to any other person the use, application, or making of any firearm, explosive or incendiary device, or technique capable of causing injury or death to persons, knowing or having reason to know or intending that the same will be unlawfully employed for use in, or in furtherance of, a civil disorder; or

(2) Assembles with 1 or more persons for the purpose of training with, practicing with, or being instructed in the use of any firearm, explosive or incendiary device, or technique capable of causing injury or death to persons, intending to employ unlawfully the training, practicing, instruction, or technique for use in, or in furtherance of, a civil disorder.

(c) Nothing contained in this section shall make unlawful any act of any law-enforcement officer which is performed in the lawful performance of his official duties.

Article 39. Protection of Minors

§ 14-315. Selling or giving weapons to minors

(a) Sale of Weapons Other Than Handguns. – If a person sells, offers for sale, gives, or in any way transfers to a minor any pistol cartridge, brass knucks, bowie knife, dirk, shurikin, leaded cane, or slungshot, the person is guilty of a Class 1 misdemeanor and, in addition, shall forfeit the proceeds of any sale made in violation of this section.

(a1) Sale of Handguns. – If a person sells, offers for sale, gives, or in any way transfers to a minor any handgun as defined in G.S. 14-269.7, the person is guilty of a Class H felony and, in addition, shall forfeit the proceeds of any sale made in violation of this section. This section does not apply in any of the following circumstances:

(1) The handgun is lent to a minor for temporary use if the minor's possession of the handgun is lawful under G.S. 14-269.7 and G.S. 14-316 and is not otherwise unlawful.

(2) The handgun is transferred to an adult custodian pursuant to Chapter 33A of the General Statutes, and the minor does not take possession of the handgun except that the adult custodian may allow the minor temporary possession of the handgun in circumstances in which the minor's possession of the handgun is lawful under G.S. 14-269.7 and G.S. 14-316 and is not otherwise unlawful.

(3) The handgun is a devise and is distributed to a parent or guardian under G.S. 28A-22-7, and the minor does not take possession of the handgun except that the parent or guardian may allow the minor temporary possession of the handgun in circumstances in which the minor's possession of the handgun is lawful under G.S. 14-269.7 and G.S. 14-316 and is not otherwise unlawful.

(b1) Defense. – It shall be a defense to a violation of this section if all of the following conditions are met:

(1) The person shows that the minor produced an apparently valid permit to receive the weapon, if such a permit would be required under G.S. 14-402 for transfer of the weapon to an adult.

(2) The person reasonably believed that the minor was not a minor.

(3) The person either:

a. Shows that the minor produced a drivers license, a special identification card issued under G.S. 20-37.7, a military identification card, or a passport, showing the minor's age to be at least the required age for purchase and bearing a physical description of the person named on the card reasonably describing the minor; or

b. Produces evidence of other facts that reasonably indicated at the time of sale that the minor was at least the required age.

§ 14-315.1. Storage of firearms to protect minors

(a) Any person who resides in the same premises as a minor, owns or possesses a firearm, and stores or leaves the firearm **(i)** in a condition that the firearm can be discharged and **(ii)** in a manner that the person knew or should have known that an unsupervised minor would be able to gain access to the firearm, is guilty of a Class 1 misdemeanor if a minor gains access to the firearm without the lawful permission of the minor's parents or a person having charge of the minor and the minor:

(1) Possesses it in violation of G.S. 14-269.2(b);

(2) Exhibits it in a public place in a careless, angry, or threatening manner;

(3) Causes personal injury or death with it not in self defense; or

(4) Uses it in the commission of a crime.

(b) Nothing in this section shall prohibit a person from carrying a firearm on his or her body, or placed in such close proximity that it can be used as easily and quickly as if carried on the body.

(c) This section shall not apply if the minor obtained the firearm as a result of an unlawful entry by any person.

(d) "Minor" as used in this section means a person under 18 years of age who is not emancipated.

§ 14-315.2. Warning upon sale or transfer of firearm to protect minor

(a) Upon the retail commercial sale or transfer of any firearm, the seller or transferor shall deliver a written copy of G.S. 14-315.1 to the purchaser or transferee.

(b) Any retail or wholesale store, shop, or sales outlet that sells firearms shall conspicuously post at each purchase counter the following warning in block letters not less than 1 inch in height the phrase: "IT IS UNLAWFUL TO STORE OR LEAVE A FIREARM THAT CAN BE DISCHARGED IN A MANNER THAT A REASONABLE PERSON SHOULD KNOW IS ACCESSIBLE TO A MINOR."

(c) A violation of subsection (a) or (b) of this section is a Class 1 misdemeanor.

§ 14-316. Permitting young children to use dangerous firearms

(a) It shall be unlawful for any person to knowingly permit a child under the age of 12 years to have access to, or possession, custody or use in any manner whatever, of any gun, pistol or other dangerous firearm, whether such weapon be loaded or unloaded, unless the person has the permission of the child's parent or guardian, and the child is under the supervision of an adult. Any person violating the provisions of this section shall be guilty of a Class 2 misdemeanor.

(b) Air rifles, air pistols, and BB guns shall not be deemed "dangerous firearms" within the meaning of subsection (a) of this section except in the following counties: Caldwell, Durham, Forsyth, Gaston, Haywood, Mecklenburg, Stokes, Union, Vance.

Article 52A. Sale of Weapons in Certain Counties

§ 14-402. Sale of certain weapons without permit forbidden

(a) It is unlawful for any person, firm, or corporation in this State to sell, give away, or transfer, or to purchase or receive, at any place within this State from any other place within or without the State any pistol unless: **(i)** a license or permit is first obtained under this Article by the purchaser or receiver from the sheriff of the county in which the purchaser or receiver resides; or **(ii)** a valid North Carolina concealed handgun permit is held under Article 54B of this Chapter by the purchaser or receiver who must be a resident of the State at the time of the purchase.

It is unlawful for any person or persons to receive from any postmaster, postal clerk, employee in the parcel post department, rural mail carrier, express agent or employee, railroad agent or employee within the State of North Carolina any pistol without having in his or their possession and without exhibiting at the time of the delivery of the same and to the person delivering the same the permit from the sheriff as provided in G.S. 14-403. Any person violating the provisions of this section is guilty of a Class 2 misdemeanor.

(b) This section does not apply to an antique firearm or an historic edged weapon.

(c) The following definitions apply in this Article:

   (1) Antique firearm. – Defined in G.S. 14-409.11.

   (4) Historic edged weapon. – Defined in G.S. 14-409.12.

§ 14-403. Permit issued by sheriff; form of permit; expiration of permit.
The sheriffs of any and all counties of this State shall issue to any person, firm, or corporation in any county a permit to purchase or receive any weapon mentioned in this Article from any person, firm, or corporation offering to sell or dispose of the weapon. The permit shall expire 5 years from the date of issuance. The permit shall be a standard form created by the State Bureau of Investigation in consultation with the North Carolina Sheriffs' Association, shall be of a uniform size and material, and shall be designed with security features intended to minimize the ability to counterfeit or replicate the permit and shall be set forth as follows: North Carolina, _____ County.

I, _____, Sheriff of said County, do hereby certify that I have conducted a criminal background check of the applicant, _____ whose place of residence is _____ in _____ (or) in _____ Township, _____ County, North Carolina, and have received no information to indicate that it would be a violation of State or federal law for the applicant to purchase, transfer, receive, or possess a handgun. The applicant has further satisfied me as to his, her (or) their good moral character. Therefore, a permit is issued to _____ to purchase one pistol from any person, firm or corporation authorized to dispose of the same. This permit expires five years from its date of issuance.

This ___ day of _____, _____.

_____, Sheriff.

The standard permit created by this section shall be used statewide by the sheriffs of any and all counties and, when issued by a sheriff, shall also contain an embossed seal unique to the office of the issuing sheriff.

§ 14-404. Issuance or refusal of permit; appeal from refusal; grounds for refusal; sheriff's fee

(a) Upon application, and such application must be provided by the sheriff electronically, the sheriff shall issue the permit to a resident of that county, unless the purpose of the permit is for collecting, in which case a sheriff can issue a permit to a nonresident, when the sheriff has done all of the following:

   (1) Verified, before the issuance of a permit, by a criminal history background investigation that it is not a violation of State or federal law for the applicant to purchase, transfer, receive, or possess a handgun. The sheriff shall determine the criminal and background history of any applicant by accessing computerized criminal history records as maintained by the State Bureau of Investigation and the Federal Bureau of Investigation, by conducting a national criminal history records check, by conducting a check through the National Instant Criminal Background Check System (NICS), and by conducting a criminal history check through the Administrative Office of the Courts.

   (2) Fully satisfied himself or herself by affidavits, oral evidence, or otherwise, as to the good moral character of the applicant. For purposes of determining an applicant's good moral character to receive a permit, the sheriff shall only consider an applicant's conduct and criminal history for the 5-year period immediately preceding the date of the application.

   (3) Fully satisfied himself or herself that the applicant desires the possession of the weapon mentioned for **(i)** the protection of the home, business, person, family or property, **(ii)** target shooting, **(iii)** collecting, or **(iv)** hunting.

(b) If the sheriff is not fully satisfied, the sheriff may, for good cause shown, decline to issue the permit and shall provide to the applicant within 7 days of the refusal a written statement of the reason(s) for the refusal. The statement shall cite the specific facts upon which the sheriff concluded that the applicant was not qualified for the issuance of a permit and list, by statute number, the applicable law upon which the denial is based. An appeal from the refusal shall lie by way of petition to the superior court in the district in which the application was filed. The determination by the court, on appeal, shall be upon the facts, the law, and the reasonableness of the sheriff's refusal, and shall be final.

(b1) The sheriff shall keep a list of all permit denials, with the specific reasons for the denials noted. The list shall not include any information that would identify the applicant whose application was denied. The list, as described in this subsection, shall be a public record, and the sheriff shall make the list available upon request to any member of the public. The list shall be organized by the quarters of the year, showing the number of denials and the reasons in each 3-month period, and the list shall only be released for past, completed quarters.

(c) A permit may not be issued to the following persons:

(1) One who is under an indictment or information for or has been convicted in any state, or in any court of the United States, of a felony (other than an offense pertaining to antitrust violations, unfair trade practices, or restraints of trade). However, a person who has been convicted of a felony in a court of any state or in a court of the United States and **(i)** who is later pardoned, or **(ii)** whose firearms rights have been restored pursuant to G.S. 14-415.4, may obtain a permit, if the purchase or receipt of a pistol permitted in this Article does not violate a condition of the pardon or restoration of firearms rights.

(2) One who is a fugitive from justice.

(3) One who is an unlawful user of or addicted to marijuana or any depressant, stimulant, or narcotic drug (as defined in 21 U.S.C. § 802).

(4) One who has been adjudicated mentally incompetent or has been committed to any mental institution.

(5) One who is an alien illegally or unlawfully in the United States.

(6) One who has been discharged from the Armed Forces of the United States under dishonorable conditions.

(7) One who, having been a citizen of the United States, has renounced his or her citizenship.

(8) One who is subject to a court order that:

a. Was issued after a hearing of which the person received actual notice, and at which the person had an opportunity to participate;

b. Restrains the person from harassing, stalking, or threatening an intimate partner of the person or child of the intimate partner of the person, or engaging in other conduct that would place an intimate partner in reasonable fear of bodily injury to the partner or child; and

c. Includes a finding that the person represents a credible threat to the physical safety of the intimate partner or child; or by its terms explicitly prohibits the use, attempted use, or threatened use of physical force against the intimate partner or child that would reasonably be expected to cause bodily injury.

(c1) Repealed by Session Laws 2015-195, s. 11(c), effective August 5, 2015.

(d) Nothing in this Article shall apply to officers authorized by law to carry firearms if the officers identify themselves to the vendor or donor as being officers authorized by law to carry firearms and provide any of the following:

(1) A letter signed by the officer's supervisor or superior officer stating that the officer is authorized by law to carry a firearm.

(2) A current photographic identification card issued by the officer's employer.

(3) A current photographic identification card issued by a State agency that identifies the individual as a law enforcement officer certified by the State of North Carolina.

(4) A current identification card issued by the officer's employer and another form of current photographic identification.

(e) The sheriff shall charge for the sheriff's services upon receipt of an application a fee of $5 for each permit requested. There shall be no limit as to the number or frequency of permit applications and no other costs or fees other than provided in this subsection shall be charged for the permit, including, but not limited to, any costs for investigation, processing, or medical background checks by the sheriff or others providing records to the sheriff.

(e1) The application for a permit shall be on a form created by the State Bureau of Investigation in consultation with the North Carolina Sheriffs' Association. This application shall be used by all sheriffs and must be provided by the sheriff both electronically and in paper form. Only the following shall be required to be submitted by an applicant for a permit:

(1) The permit application developed pursuant to this subsection.

(2) Five dollars for each permit requested pursuant to subsection (e) of this section.

(3) A government issued identification confirming the identity of the applicant.

(4) Proof of residency.

(5) A signed release, in a form to be prescribed by the Administrative Office of the Court, that authorizes and requires disclosure to the sheriff of any court orders concerning the mental health or capacity of the applicant to be used for the sole purpose of determining whether the applicant is disqualified to receive a permit pursuant to this section. No additional document or evidence shall be required from any applicant.

(f) Each applicant for a license or permit shall be informed by the sheriff within 14 days of the date of the application whether the license or permit will be granted or denied and, if granted, the license or permit shall be immediately issued to the applicant.

(g) An applicant shall not be ineligible to receive a permit under subdivision (c)(4) of this section because of involuntary commitment to mental health services if the individual's rights have been restored under G.S. 14-409.42.

(h) The sheriff shall revoke any permit upon the occurrence of any event or condition subsequent to the issuance of the permit, or the applicant's subsequent inability to meet a requirement under this Article, which would have resulted in a denial of the application submitted to obtain the permit if the event, condition, or the applicant's current inability to meet a statutory requirement had existed at the time of the application and prior to the issuance of the permit. The following procedures apply to a revocation:

(1) The sheriff shall provide written notice to the permittee, pursuant to the provisions of G.S. 1A-1, Rule 4(j), that the permit is revoked upon the service of the notice. The notice shall provide the permittee with information on the process to appeal the revocation.

(2) Upon receipt of the written notice of revocation, the permittee shall surrender the permit to the sheriff. Any law enforcement officer serving the notice is authorized to take immediate possession of the permit from the permittee. If the notice is served by means other than by a law enforcement officer, the permittee shall surrender the permit to the sheriff no later than 48 hours after service of the notice.

(3) The sheriff shall insure that the list of permits which have been revoked is immediately updated so that any potential transferor calling to check the validity of the permit will be informed of the revocation.

(4) A permittee may appeal the revocation of a permit pursuant to this subsection by petitioning a district court judge of the district in which the permittee resides.

(5) Any person who willfully fails to surrender a permit upon notice of revocation shall be guilty of a Class 2 misdemeanor.

(i) A person or entity shall promptly disclose to the sheriff, upon presentation by the applicant or sheriff of an original or photocopied release form described in subdivision (5) of subsection (e1) of this section, any court orders concerning the mental health or capacity of the applicant who signed the release form

§ 14-405. Record of permits kept by sheriff; confidentiality of permit information

(a) The sheriff shall keep a record of all permits issued under this article, including the name, date, place of residence, age, former place of residence, etc., of each such person, firm, or corporation to whom or which a permit is issued. The record shall include the date that a permit was revoked, the date that the permittee received notice of the revocation, whether the permit was surrendered, and the reason for the revocation.

(b) The records maintained by the sheriff pursuant to this section are confidential and are not a public record under G.S. 132-1; provided, however, that the sheriff shall make the records available upon request to any federal, State, and local law enforcement agencies and shall also make the records available to the court if the records are required to be released pursuant to a court order. Any application to a court for release of the list of permit holders and permit application information shall be by a petition to the chief judge of the district court for the district in which the person seeking the information resides.

§ 14-406. Dealer to keep record of sales; confidentiality of records

(a) Every dealer in pistols and other weapons mentioned in this Article shall keep an accurate record of all sales thereof, including the name, place of residence, date of sale, etc., of each person, firm, or corporation to whom or which such sales are made. The records maintained by a dealer pursuant to this section are confidential and are not a public record under G.S. 132-1; provided, however, that the dealer shall make the records available upon request to all State and local law enforcement agencies.

§ 14-407.1. Sale of blank cartridge pistols

The provisions of G.S. 14-402, 14-405, and 14-406 shall apply to the sale of pistols suitable for firing blank cartridges. The sheriffs of all the counties of this State are authorized and may in their discretion issue to any person, firm or corporation, in any such county, a license or permit to purchase or receive any pistol suitable for firing blank cartridges from any person, firm or corporation offering to sell or dispose of the same, which said permit shall be in substantially the following form:

North Carolina, _____ County

I, _____, sheriff of said county, do hereby certify that _____, whose place of residence is _____ Street in _____ (or) in _____ Township in _____ County, North Carolina, having this day satisfied me that the possession of a pistol suitable for firing blank cartridges will be used only for lawful purposes, a permit is therefore given said _____ to purchas e said pistol from any person, firm or corporation authorized to dispose of the same, this ____ day of _____, _____.

_____, Sheriff

The sheriff shall charge for the sheriff's services, upon issuing such permit, a fee of $0.50.

§ 14-408. Violation of § 14-406 a misdemeanor.
Any person, firm, or corporation violating any of the provisions of G.S. 14-406 shall be guilty of a Class 2 misdemeanor.

§ 14-408.1. Solicit unlawful purchase of firearm; unlawful to provide materially false information regarding legality of firearm or ammunition transfer

(a) The following definitions apply in this section:

(1) Ammunition. – Any cartridge, shell, or projectile designed for use in a firearm.

(2) Firearm. – A handgun, shotgun, or rifle which expels a projectile by action of an explosion.

(3) Handgun. – A pistol, revolver, or other gun that has a short stock and is designed to be held and fired by the use of a single hand.

(4) Licensed dealer. – A person who is licensed pursuant to 18 U.S.C. § 923 to engage in the business of dealing in firearms.

(5) Materially false information. – Information that portrays an illegal transaction as legal or a legal transaction as illegal.

(6) Private seller. – A person who sells or offers for sale any firearm, as defined in G.S. 14-409.39, or ammunition.

(b) Any person who knowingly solicits, persuades, encourages, or entices a licensed dealer or private seller of firearms or ammunition to transfer a firearm or ammunition under circumstances that the person knows would violate the laws of this State or the United States is guilty of a Class F felony.

(c) Any person who provides to a licensed dealer or private seller of firearms or ammunition information that the person knows to be materially false information with the intent to deceive the dealer or seller about the legality of a transfer of a firearm or ammunition is guilty of a Class F felony.

(d) Any person who willfully procures another to engage in conduct prohibited by this section shall be held accountable as a principal.

(e) This section does not apply to a law enforcement officer acting in his or her official capacity or to a person acting at the direction of the law enforcement officer.

§ 14-409. Machine guns and other like weapons

(a) As used in this section, "machine gun" or "submachine gun" means any weapon which shoots, is designed to shoot, or can be readily restored to shoot, automatically more than 1 shot, without manual reloading, by a single function of the trigger. The term shall also include the frame or receiver of any such weapon, any combination of parts designed and intended for use in converting a weapon into a machine gun, and any combination of parts from which a machine gun can be assembled if such parts are in the possession or under the control of a person.

(b) It shall be unlawful for any person, firm or corporation to manufacture, sell, give away, dispose of, use or possess machine guns, submachine guns, or other like weapons as defined by subsection (a) of this section: Provided, however, that this subsection shall not apply to the following:

Banks, merchants, and recognized business establishments for use in their respective places of business, who shall first apply to and receive from the sheriff of the county in which said business is located, a permit to possess the said weapons for the purpose of defending the said business; officers and soldiers of the United States Army, when in discharge of their official duties, officers and soldiers of the militia when called into actual service, officers of the State, or of any county, city or town, charged with the execution of the laws of the State, when acting in the discharge of their official duties; the manufacture, use or possession of such weapons for scientific or experimental purposes when such manufacture, use or possession is lawful under federal laws and the weapon is registered with a federal agency, and when a permit to manufacture, use or possess the weapon is issued by the sheriff of the county in which the weapon is located; a person who lawfully possesses or owns a weapon as defined by subsection (a) of this section in compliance with 26 U.S.C. Chapter 53, §§ 5801-5871. Nothing in this subdivision shall limit the discretion of the sheriff in executing the paperwork required by the United States Bureau of Alcohol, Tobacco and Firearms for such person to obtain the weapon. Provided, further, that any bona fide resident of this State who now owns a machine gun used in former wars, as a relic or souvenir, may retain and keep same as his or her property without violating the provisions of this section upon his reporting said ownership to the sheriff of the county in which said person lives.

(c) Any person violating any of the provisions of this section shall be guilty of a Class I felony.

Article 53A. Other Firearms

§ 14-409.10. Purchase of rifles and shotguns out of State. Unless otherwise prohibited by law, a citizen of this State may purchase a firearm in another state if the citizen undergoes a background check that satisfies the law of the state of purchase and that includes an inquiry of the National Instant Background Check System.

§ 14-409.11. "Antique firearm" defined

(a) The term "antique firearm" means any of the following:

(1) Any firearm (including any firearm with a matchlock, flintlock, percussion cap, or similar type of ignition system) manufactured on or before 1898.

(2) Any replica of any firearm described in subdivision (1) of this subsection if the replica is not designed or redesigned for using rimfire or conventional centerfire fixed ammunition.

(3) Any muzzle loading rifle, muzzle loading shotgun, or muzzle loading pistol, which is designed to use black powder substitute, and which cannot use fixed ammunition.

(b) For purposes of this section, the term "antique firearm" shall not include any weapon which:

(1) Incorporates a firearm frame or receiver.

(2) Is converted into a muzzle loading weapon.

(3) Is a muzzle loading weapon that can be readily converted to fire fixed ammunition by replacing the barrel, bolt, breechblock, or any combination thereof.

Article 53B. Firearm Regulation

§ 14-409.39. Definitions. The following definitions apply in this Article:

(1) Dealer. – Any person licensed as a dealer pursuant to 18 U.S.C. § 921, et seq., or G.S. 105-80.

(2) Firearm. – A handgun, shotgun, or rifle which expels a projectile by action of an explosion.

(3) Handgun. – A pistol, revolver, or other gun that has a short stock and is designed to be held and fired by the use of a single hand.

§ 14-409.40. Statewide uniformity of local regulation

(a) It is declared by the General Assembly that the regulation of firearms is properly an issue of general, statewide concern, and that the entire field of regulation of firearms is preempted from regulation by local governments except as provided by this section.

(a1) .... This subsection applies only to causes of action brought under subsection (g) of this section.

(b) Unless otherwise permitted by statute, no county or municipality, by ordinance, resolution, or other enactment, shall regulate in any manner the possession, ownership, storage, transfer, sale, purchase, licensing, taxation, manufacture, transportation, or registration of firearms, firearms ammunition, components of firearms, dealers in firearms, or dealers in handgun components or parts.

(c) Notwithstanding subsection (b) of this section, a county or municipality, by zoning or other ordinance, may regulate or prohibit the sale of firearms at a location only if there is a lawful, general, similar regulation or prohibition of commercial activities at that location. Nothing in this subsection shall restrict the right of a county or municipality to adopt a general zoning plan that prohibits any commercial activity within a fixed distance of a school or other educational institution except with a special use permit issued for a commercial activity found not to pose a danger to the health, safety, or general welfare of persons attending the school or educational institution within the fixed distance.

(d) No county or municipality, by zoning or other ordinance, shall regulate in any manner firearms shows with regulations more stringent than those applying to shows of other types of items.

(e) A county or municipality may regulate the transport, carrying, or possession of firearms by employees of the local unit of government in the course of their employment with that local unit of government.

(f) Nothing contained in this section prohibits municipalities or counties from application of their authority under G.S. 153A-129, 160A-189, 14-269, 14-269.2, 14-269.3, 14-269.4, 14-277.2, 14-415.11, 14-415.23, including prohibiting the possession of firearms in public-owned buildings, on the grounds or parking areas of those buildings, or in public parks or recreation areas, except nothing in this subsection shall prohibit a person from storing a firearm within a motor vehicle while the vehicle is on these grounds or areas. Nothing contained in this section prohibits municipalities or counties from exercising powers provided by law in states of emergency declared under Article 1A of Chapter 166A of the General Statutes.

(g) The authority to bring suit and the right to recover against any firearms or ammunition marketer, manufacturer, distributor, dealer, seller, or trade association by or on behalf of any governmental unit, created by or pursuant to an act of the General Assembly or the Constitution, or any department, agency, or authority thereof, for damages, abatement, injunctive relief, or any other remedy resulting from or relating to the lawful design, marketing, manufacture, distribution, sale, or transfer of firearms or ammunition to the public is reserved exclusively to the State. Any action brought by the State pursuant to this section shall be brought by the Attorney General on behalf of the State. This section shall not prohibit a political subdivision or local governmental unit from bringing an action against a firearms or ammunition marketer, manufacturer, distributor, dealer, seller, or trade association for breach of contract or warranty for defect of materials or workmanship as to firearms or ammunition purchased by the political subdivision or local governmental unit.

(h) A person adversely affected by any ordinance, rule, or regulation promulgated or caused to be enforced by any county or municipality in violation of this section may bring an action for declaratory and injunctive relief and for actual damages arising from the violation. The court shall award the prevailing party in an action brought under this subsection reasonable attorneys' fees and court costs as authorized by law.

§ 14-409.41. Chief law enforcement officer certification; certain firearms

(a) Definitions. – The following definitions apply in this section:

(1) Certification. – The participation and assent of the chief law enforcement officer necessary under federal law for the approval of the application to transfer or make a firearm.

(2) Chief law enforcement officer. – Any official that the United States Bureau of Alcohol, Tobacco, Firearms, and Explosives, or any successor agency, has identified by regulation or otherwise as eligible to provide any required certification for the transfer or making of a firearm.

(3) Firearm. – Any firearm that meets the definition of firearm in 26 U.S.C. § 5845.

(b) When a chief law enforcement officer's certification is required by federal law or regulation for the transfer or making of a firearm, the chief law enforcement officer shall, within 15 days of receipt of a request for certification, provide the certification if the applicant is not prohibited by State or federal law from receiving or possessing the firearm and is not the subject of a proceeding that could result in the applicant being prohibited by State or federal law from receiving or possessing the firearm. If the chief law enforcement officer is unable to make a certification as required by this section, the chief law enforcement officer shall provide the applicant with a written notification of the denial and the reason for the denial.

Nothing in this section shall require a chief law enforcement officer to make a certification the chief law enforcement officer knows to be untrue, but the chief law enforcement officer may not refuse to provide certification based on a generalized objection to private persons or entities making, possessing, or receiving firearms or any certain type of firearm the possession of which is not prohibited by law.

(c) An applicant whose request for certification is denied may appeal the decision of the chief law enforcement officer to the district court of the district in which the request for certification was made. The court shall make a de novo review of the chief law enforcement officer's decision to deny the certification. If the court finds that the applicant is not prohibited by State or federal law from receiving or possessing the firearm, is not the subject of a proceeding that could result in the applicant being prohibited by State or federal law from receiving or possessing the firearm, and that no substantial evidence supports the chief law enforcement officer's determination that the chief law enforcement officer cannot truthfully make the certification, the court shall order the chief law enforcement officer to issue the certification and award court costs and reasonable attorneys' fees to the applicant.

(d) Chief law enforcement officers and their employees who act in good faith are immune from liability arising from any act or omission in making a certification as required by this section.

§ 14-409.42. Restoration process to remove mental commitment bar

(a) Any individual over the age of 18 may petition for the removal of the disabilities pursuant to 18 U.S.C. § 922(d)(4) and (g)(4), G.S. 14-415.3, and G.S. 14-415.12 arising out of a determination or finding required to be transmitted to the National Instant Criminal Background Check System by subdivisions (1) through (6) of subsection (a) of G.S. 14-409.43. The individual may file the petition with a district court judge upon the expiration of any current inpatient or outpatient commitment.

(b) The petition must be filed in the district court of the county where the respondent was the subject of the most recent judicial determination or finding or in the district court of the county of the petitioner's residence. The clerk of court upon receipt of the petition shall schedule a hearing using the regularly scheduled commitment court time and provide notice of the hearing to the petitioner and the attorney who represented the State in the underlying case, or that attorney's successor. Copies of the petition must be served on the director of the relevant inpatient or outpatient treatment facility and the district attorney in the petitioner's current county of residence.

(c) The burden is on the petitioner to establish by a preponderance of the evidence that the petitioner will not be likely to act in a manner dangerous to public safety and that the granting of the relief would not be contrary to the public interest. The district attorney shall present any and all relevant information to the contrary. For these purposes, the district attorney may access and use any and all mental health records, juvenile records, and criminal history of the petitioner wherever maintained. The applicant must sign a release for the district attorney to receive any mental health records of the applicant. This hearing shall be closed to the public, unless the court finds that the public interest would be better served by conducting the hearing in public. If the court determines the hearing should be open to the public, upon motion by the petitioner, the court may allow for the in camera inspection of any mental health records. The court may allow the use of the record but shall restrict it from public disclosure, unless it finds that the public interest would be better served by making the record public. The district court shall enter an order that the petitioner is or is not likely to act in a manner dangerous to public safety and that the granting of the relief would or would not be contrary to the public interest. The court shall include in its order the specific findings of fact on which it bases its decision. In making its determination, the court shall consider the circumstances regarding the firearm disabilities from which relief is sought, the petitioner's mental health and criminal history records, the petitioner's reputation, developed at a minimum through character witness statements, testimony, or other character evidence, and any changes in the petitioner's condition or circumstances since the original determination or finding relevant to the relief sought. The decision of the district court may be appealed to the superior court for a hearing de novo. After a denial by the superior court, the applicant must wait a minimum of 1 year before reapplying. Attorneys designated by the Attorney General shall be available to represent the State, or assist in the representation of the State, in a restoration proceeding when requested to do so by a district attorney and approved by the Attorney General. An attorney so designated shall have all the powers of the district attorney under this section.

(d) Upon a judicial determination to grant a petition under this section, the clerk of superior court in the county where the petition was granted shall forward the order to the National Instant Criminal Background Check System (NICS) for updating of the respondent's record.

§ 14-409.43. Reporting of certain disqualifiers to the National Instant Criminal Background Check System (NICS)

(a) Excluding Saturdays, Sundays, and holidays, not later than 48 hours after receiving notice of any of the following judicial determinations or findings, the clerk of superior court in the county where the determination or finding was made shall work through the Administrative Office of the Courts to cause a record of the determination or finding to be transmitted to the National Instant Criminal Background Check System (NICS):

(1) A determination that an individual shall be involuntarily committed to a facility for inpatient mental health treatment upon a finding that the individual is mentally ill and a danger to self or others.

(2) A determination that an individual shall be involuntarily committed to a facility for outpatient mental health treatment upon a finding that the individual is mentally ill and, based on the individual's treatment history, in need of treatment in order to prevent further disability or deterioration that would predictably result in a danger to self or others.

(3) A determination that an individual shall be involuntarily committed to a facility for substance abuse treatment upon a finding that the individual is a substance abuser and a danger to self or others.

(4) A finding that an individual is not guilty by reason of insanity.

(5) A finding that an individual is mentally incompetent to proceed to criminal trial.

(6) A finding that an individual lacks the capacity to manage the individual's own affairs due to marked subnormal intelligence or mental illness, incompetency, condition, or disease.

(7) A determination to grant a petition to an individual for the removal of disabilities pursuant to G.S. 14-409.42 or any applicable federal law.

The 48-hour period for transmitting a record of a judicial determination or finding to the NICS under subsection (a) of this section begins upon receipt by the clerk of a copy of the judicial determination or finding. The Administrative Office of the Courts shall adopt rules to require clerks of court to transmit information to the NICS in a uniform manner.

(b) Excluding Saturdays, Sundays, and holidays, not later than 48 hours after receiving notice of the issuance of a felony warrant, indictment, criminal summons, or order for arrest, the Administrative Office of the Courts shall transmit any unserved felony warrants, indictments, criminal summons, or order for arrests to the NCIC (or National Instant Criminal Background Check System (NICS)).

(c) Excluding Saturdays, Sundays, and holidays, not later than 48 hours after service by the sheriff of an order issued by a judge pursuant to Chapter 50B of the General Statutes and pursuant to G.S. 50B-3(d) the sheriff shall cause a record of the order to be transmitted to the National Instant Criminal Information System.

Article 54A. The Felony Firearms Act

§ 14-415.1. Possession of firearms, etc., by felon prohibited

(a) It shall be unlawful for any person who has been convicted of a felony to purchase, own, possess, or have in his custody, care, or control any firearm or any weapon of mass death and destruction as defined in G.S. 14-288.8(c). For the purposes of this section, a firearm is **(i)** any weapon, including a starter gun, which will or is designed to or may readily be converted to expel a projectile by the action of an explosive, or its frame or receiver, or **(ii)** any firearm muffler or firearm silencer. This section does not apply to an antique firearm, as defined in G.S. 14-409.11.

Every person violating the provisions of this section shall be punished as a Class G felon.

(b) Prior convictions which cause disentitlement under this section shall only include:

(1) Felony convictions in North Carolina that occur before, on, or after December 1, 1995; and

(2) Repealed by Session Laws 1995, c. 487, s. 3, effective December 1, 1995.

(3) Violations of criminal laws of other states or of the United States that occur before, on, or after December 1, 1995, and that are substantially similar to the crimes covered in subdivision (1) which are punishable where committed by imprisonment for a term exceeding one year.

When a person is charged under this section, records of prior convictions of any offense, whether in the courts of this State, or in the courts of any other state or of the United States, shall be admissible in evidence for the purpose of proving a violation of this section. The term "conviction" is defined as a final judgment in any case in which felony punishment, or imprisonment for a term exceeding 1 year, as the case may be, is authorized, without regard to the plea entered or to the sentence imposed. A judgment of a conviction of the defendant or a plea of guilty by the defendant to such an offense certified to a superior court of this State from the custodian of records of any state or federal court shall be prima facie evidence of the facts so certified.

(c) The indictment charging the defendant under the terms of this section shall be separate from any indictment charging him with other offenses related to or giving rise to a charge under this section. An indictment which charges the person with violation of this section must set forth the date that the prior offense was committed, the type of offense and the penalty therefor, and the date that the defendant was convicted or plead guilty to such offense, the identity of the court in which the conviction or plea of guilty took place and the verdict and judgment rendered therein.

(d) This section does not apply to a person who, pursuant to the law of the jurisdiction in which the conviction occurred, has been pardoned or has had his or her firearms rights restored if such restoration of rights could also be granted under North Carolina law.

(e) This section does not apply and there is no disentitlement under this section if the felony conviction is a violation under the laws of North Carolina, another state, or the United States that pertains to antitrust violations, unfair trade practices, or restraints of trade.

§ 14-415.3. Possession of a firearm or weapon of mass destruction by persons acquitted of certain crimes by reason of insanity or persons determined to be incapable to proceed prohibited

(a) It is unlawful for the following persons to purchase, own, possess, or have in the person's custody, care, or control, any firearm or any weapon of mass death and destruction as defined by G.S. 14-288.8(c):

(1) A person who has been acquitted by reason of insanity of any crime set out in G.S. 14-415.1(b) or any violation of G.S. 14-33(b)(1), 14-33(b)(8), or 14-34.

(2) A person who has been determined to lack capacity to proceed as provided in G.S. 15A-1002 for any crime set out in G.S. 14-415.1(b) or any violation of G.S. 14-33(b)(1), 14-33(b)(8), or 14-34.

(b) A violation of this section is a Class H felony. Any firearm or weapon of mass death and destruction lawfully seized for a violation of this section shall be forfeited to the State and disposed of as provided in G.S. 15-11.1.

(c) The provisions of this section shall not apply to a person whose rights have been restored pursuant to G.S. 14-409.42.

§ 14-415.4. Restoration of firearms rights

(a) Definitions. – The following definitions apply in this section:

(1) Firearms rights. – The legal right in this State of a person to purchase, own, possess, or have in the person's custody, care, or control any firearm or any weapon of mass death and destruction as those terms are defined in G.S. 14-415.1 and G.S. 14-288.8(c).

(2) Nonviolent felony. – The term nonviolent felony does not include any felony that is a Class A, Class B1, or Class B2 felony. Also, the term nonviolent felony does not include any Class C through Class I felony that is one of the following:

    a. An offense that includes assault as an essential element of the offense.

    b. An offense that includes the possession or use of a firearm or other deadly weapon as an essential or nonessential element of the offense, or the offender was in possession of a firearm or other deadly weapon at the time of the commission of the offense.

    c. An offense for which the offender was armed with or used a firearm or other deadly weapon.

    d. An offense for which the offender must register under Article 27A of Chapter 14 of the General Statutes.

(b) Purpose. – It is the purpose of this section to establish a procedure that allows a North Carolina resident who was convicted of a single nonviolent felony and whose citizenship rights have been restored pursuant to Chapter 13 of the General Statutes to petition the court to remove the petitioner's disentitlement under G.S. 14-415.1 and to restore the person's firearms rights in this State. If the single nonviolent felony conviction was an out-of-state conviction or a federal conviction, then the North Carolina resident shall show proof of the restoration of his or her civil rights and the right to possess a firearm in the jurisdiction where the conviction occurred. Restoration of a person's firearms rights under this section means that the person may purchase, own, possess, or have in the person's custody, care, or control any firearm or any weapon of mass death and destruction as those terms are defined in G.S. 14-415.1 and G.S. 14-288.8(c) without being in violation of G.S. 14-415.1, if otherwise qualified.

(c) Petition for Restoration of Firearms Rights. – A person who was convicted of a nonviolent felony in North Carolina but whose civil rights have been restored pursuant to Chapter 13 of the General Statutes for a period of at least 20 years may petition the district court in the district where the person resides to restore the person's firearms rights pursuant to this section. A person who was convicted of a nonviolent felony in a jurisdiction other than North Carolina may petition the district court in the district where the person resides to restore the person's firearms rights pursuant to this section only if the person's civil rights, including the right to possess a firearm, have been restored, pursuant to the law of the jurisdiction where the conviction occurred, for a period of at least 20 years. The court may restore a petitioner's firearms rights after a hearing in court if the court determines that the petitioner meets the criteria set out in this section and is not otherwise disqualified to have that right restored.

(d) Criteria. – The court may grant a petition to restore a person's firearms rights under this section if the petitioner satisfies all of the following criteria and is not otherwise disqualified to have that right restored:

(1) The petitioner is a resident of North Carolina and has been a resident of the State for 1 year or longer immediately preceding the filing of the petition.

(2) The petitioner has only 1 felony conviction and that conviction is for a nonviolent felony. For purposes of this subdivision, multiple felony convictions arising out of the same event and consolidated for sentencing shall count as 1 felony only.

(3) The petitioner's rights of citizenship have been restored pursuant to Chapter 13 of the General Statutes or, if the conviction was in a jurisdiction other than North Carolina, have been restored, pursuant to the laws of the jurisdiction where the conviction occurred, for a period of at least 20 years before the date of the filing of the petition.

(4) The petitioner has not been convicted under the laws of the United States, the laws of this State, or the laws of any other state of any misdemeanor as described in subdivision (6) of subsection (e) of this section since the conviction of the nonviolent felony.

(5) The petitioner submits his or her fingerprints to the sheriff of the county in which the petitioner resides for a criminal background check pursuant to G.S. 143B-959.

(6) The petitioner is not disqualified under subsection (e) of this section.

(e) Disqualifiers Requiring Denial of Petition. – The court shall deny the petition to restore the firearms rights of any petitioner if the court finds any of the following:

(1) The petitioner is ineligible to purchase, own, possess, or have in the person's custody, care, or control a firearm under the provisions of any law in North Carolina other than G.S. 14-415.1.

(2) The petitioner is under indictment for a felony or a finding of probable cause exists against the petitioner for a felony.

(3) The petitioner is a fugitive from justice.

(4) The petitioner is an unlawful user of, or addicted to, marijuana, alcohol, or any depressant, stimulant, or narcotic drug, or any other controlled substance as defined in 21 U.S.C. § 802.

(5) The petitioner is or has been dishonorably discharged from the Armed Forces of the United States.

(6) The petitioner is or has been adjudicated guilty of or received a prayer for judgment continued or suspended sentence for 1 or more crimes of violence constituting a misdemeanor, including a misdemeanor under Article 8 of Chapter 14 of the General Statutes, or a misdemeanor under G.S. 14-225.2, 14-226.1, 14-258.1, 14-269.2, 14-269.3, 14-269.4, 14-269.6, 14-276.1, 14-277, 14-277.1, 14-277.2, 14-277.3, 14-281.1, 14-283, 14-288.2, 14-288.4(a)(1) or (2), 14-288.6, 14-288.9, former 14-288.12, former 14-288.13, former 14-288.14, 14-288.20A, 14-318.2, 14-415.21(b), or 14-415.26(d), or a substantially similar out-of-state or federal offense.

(7) The petitioner has had entry of a prayer for judgment continued for a felony, in addition to the nonviolent felony conviction.

(8) The petitioner is free on bond or personal recognizance pending trial, appeal, or sentencing for a crime which would prohibit the person from having his or her firearms rights restored under this section.

(9) An emergency order, ex parte order, or protective order has been issued pursuant to Chapter 50B of the General Statutes or a similar out-of-state or federal order has been issued against the petitioner and the court order issued is still in effect.

(10) A civil no-contact order has been issued pursuant to Chapter 50C of the General Statutes or a similar out-of-state or federal order has been issued against the petitioner and the court order issued is still in effect.

(f) Notice of Hearing and Hearing Procedure. – The clerk of court shall provide notice of the hearing to the district attorney in the district in which the petition is filed at least 4 weeks before the hearing on the matter. The petitioner may present evidence in support of the petition, and the district attorney may present evidence in opposition to the requested restoration of firearms rights or may otherwise demonstrate the reasons why the petition should be denied. The burden is on the petitioner to establish by a preponderance of the evidence that the petitioner is qualified to receive the restoration under subsection (d) of this section and that the petitioner is not disqualified under subsection (e) of this section.

(g) Right to Petition Again Upon Denial of Petition. – If the court denies the petition, the person may again petition the court for restoration of his or her firearms rights in accordance with this section 1 year from the date of the denial of the original petition. However, if the sole basis for the denial of the petition are the grounds set out under G.S. 14-415.4(e)(9) or (10), then the person does not have to wait for 1 year from the date of denial of the original petition but may petition again upon the expiration of the order.

(h) Certified Copies of Order Granting Petition to Sheriff, Department of Justice, and National Instant Background Check System Index. – If the court grants the petition to restore the petitioner's firearms rights, the clerk of court shall forward within 10 days of the entry of the order a certified copy of the order to the sheriff of the county in which the petitioner resides, the North Carolina Department of Justice, and the denied person's file of the national instant criminal background check system index.

(i) Restoration is Not an Expunction or Pardon. – A restoration of firearms rights under this section does not result in the expunction of any criminal history record information nor does it constitute a pardon.

(j) Automatic Revocation Upon Conviction of a Subsequent Felony. – If a person's firearms rights are restored under this section and the person is convicted of a second or subsequent felony, then the person's firearms rights are automatically revoked and shall not be restored under this section.

(k) Fee. – A person who files a petition for restoration of firearms rights under this section shall pay the clerk of court a fee of $200 at the time the petition is filed. Fees collected under this subsection shall be deposited in the General Fund. This subsection does not apply to petitions filed by an indigent.

(l) Criminal Offense to Submit False Information. – A person who knowingly and willfully submits false information under this section is guilty of a Class 1 misdemeanor. In addition, a person who is convicted of an offense under this subsection is permanently prohibited from petitioning to restore his or her firearms rights under this section.

Article 54B. Concealed Handgun Permit

§ 14-415.10. Definitions. The following definitions apply to this Article:

(1) Carry a concealed handgun. – The term includes possession of a concealed handgun.

(1a) Deployed or deployment. – Any military duty that removes a military permittee from the permittee's county of residence during which time the permittee's permit expires or will expire.

(2) Handgun. – A firearm that has a short stock and is designed to be held and fired by the use of a single hand.

(2a) Military permittee. – A person who holds a permit who is also a member of the Armed Forces of the United States, the reserve components of the Armed Forces of the United States, the North Carolina Army National Guard, or the North Carolina Air National Guard.

(3) Permit. – A concealed handgun permit issued in accordance with the provisions of this Article.

(3a) Proof of deployment. – A copy of the military permittee's deployment orders or other written notification from the permittee's command indicating the start and end date of deployment and that orders the permittee to travel outside the permittee's county of residence.

(4) Qualified former sworn law enforcement officer. – An individual who retired from service as a law enforcement officer with a local, State, campus police, or company police agency in North Carolina, other than for reasons of mental disability, who has been retired as a sworn law enforcement officer 2 years or less from the date of the permit application, and who satisfies all of the following:

a. Immediately before retirement, the individual was a qualified law enforcement officer with a local, State, or company police agency in North Carolina.

b. The individual has a nonforfeitable right to benefits under the retirement plan of the local, State, or company police agency as a law enforcement officer; or has 20 or more aggregate years of law enforcement service and has retired from a company police agency that does not have a retirement plan; or has 20 or more aggregate years of part-time or auxiliary law enforcement service.

c. The individual is not prohibited by State or federal law from receiving a firearm.

(4a) Qualified retired correctional officer. – An individual who retired from service as a State correctional officer, other than for reasons of mental disability, who has been retired as a correctional officer 2 years or less from the date of the permit application and who meets all of the following criteria:

    a. Immediately before retirement, the individual met firearms training standards of the Division of Adult Correction of the Department of Public Safety and was authorized by the Division of Adult Correction of the Department of Public Safety to carry a handgun in the course of assigned duties.

    b. The individual retired in good standing and was never a subject of a disciplinary action by the Division of Adult Correction of the Department of Public Safety that would have prevented the individual from carrying a handgun.

    c. The individual has a vested right to benefits under the Teachers' and State Employees' Retirement System of North Carolina established under Article 1 of Chapter 135 of the General Statutes.

    d. The individual is not prohibited by State or federal law from receiving a firearm.

(4b) Qualified retired law enforcement officer. – An individual who meets the definition of "qualified retired law enforcement officer" contained in § 926C of Title 18 of the United States Code.

(4c) Qualified retired probation or parole certified officer. – An individual who retired from service as a State probation or parole certified officer, other than for reasons of mental disability, who has been retired as a probation or parole certified officer 2 years or less from the date of the permit application and who meets all of the following criteria:

    a. Immediately before retirement, the individual met firearms training standards of the Division of Adult Correction of the Department of Public Safety and was authorized by the Division of Adult Correction of the Department of Public Safety to carry a handgun in the course of duty.

    b. The individual retired in good standing and was never a subject of a disciplinary action by the Division of Adult Correction of the Department of Public Safety that would have prevented the individual from carrying a handgun.

    c. The individual has a vested right to benefits under the Teachers' and State Employees' Retirement System of North Carolina established under Article 1 of Chapter 135 of the General Statutes.

    d. The individual is not prohibited by State or federal law from receiving a firearm.

(5) Qualified sworn law enforcement officer. – A law enforcement officer employed by a local, State, campus police, or company police agency in North Carolina who satisfies all of the following:

    a. The individual is authorized by the agency to carry a handgun in the course of duty.

    b. The individual is not the subject of a disciplinary action by the agency that prevents the carrying of a handgun.

    c. The individual meets the requirements established by the agency regarding handguns.

§ 14-415.11. Permit to carry concealed handgun; scope of permit

(a) Any person who has a concealed handgun permit may carry a concealed handgun unless otherwise specifically prohibited by law. The person shall carry the permit together with valid identification whenever the person is carrying a concealed handgun, shall disclose to any law enforcement officer that the person holds a valid permit and is carrying a concealed handgun when approached or addressed by the officer, and shall display both the permit and the proper identification upon the request of a law enforcement officer. In addition to these requirements, a military permittee whose permit has expired during deployment may carry a concealed handgun during the 90 days following the end of deployment and before the permit is renewed provided the permittee also displays proof of deployment to any law enforcement officer.

(b) The sheriff shall issue a permit to carry a concealed handgun to a person who qualifies for a permit under G.S. 14-415.12. The permit shall be valid throughout the State for a period of 5 years from the date of issuance.

(c) Except as provided in G.S. 14-415.27, a permit does not authorize a person to carry a concealed handgun in any of the following:

    (1) Areas prohibited by G.S. 14-269.2, 14-269.3, and 14-277.2.

    (2) Areas prohibited by G.S. 14-269.4, except as allowed under G.S. 14-269.4(6).

    (3) In an area prohibited by rule adopted under G.S. 120-32.1.

    (4) In any area prohibited by 18 U.S.C. § 922 or any other federal law.

    (5) In a law enforcement or correctional facility.

    (6) In a building housing only State or federal offices.

    (7) In an office of the State or federal government that is not located in a building exclusively occupied by the State or federal government.

    (8) On any private premises where notice that carrying a concealed handgun is prohibited by the posting of a conspicuous notice or statement by the person in legal possession or control of the premises.

(c1) Any person who has a concealed handgun permit may carry a concealed handgun on the grounds or waters of a park within the State Parks System as defined in G.S. 143B-135.44.

(c2) It shall be unlawful for a person, with or without a permit, to carry a concealed handgun while consuming alcohol or at any time while the person has remaining in the person's body any alcohol or in the person's blood a controlled substance previously consumed, but a person does not violate this condition if a controlled substance in the person's blood was lawfully obtained and taken in therapeutically appropriate amounts or if the person is on the person's own property.

(c3) As provided in G.S. 14-269.4(5), it shall be lawful for a person to carry any firearm openly, or to carry a concealed handgun with a concealed carry permit, at any State-owned rest area, at any State-owned rest stop along the highways, and at any State-owned hunting and fishing reservation.

(d) A person who is issued a permit shall notify the sheriff who issued the permit of any change in the person's permanent address within 30 days after the change of address. If a permit is lost or destroyed, the person to whom the permit was issued shall notify the sheriff who issued the permit of the loss or destruction of the permit. A person may obtain a duplicate permit by submitting to the sheriff a notarized statement that the permit was lost or destroyed and paying the required duplicate permit fee.

§ 14-415.12. Criteria to qualify for the issuance of a permit

(a) The sheriff shall issue a permit to an applicant if the applicant qualifies under the following criteria:

(1) The applicant is a citizen of the United States or has been lawfully admitted for permanent residence as defined in 8 U.S.C. § 1101(a)(20), and has been a resident of the State 30 days or longer immediately preceding the filing of the application.

(2) The applicant is 21 years of age or older.

(3) The applicant does not suffer from a physical or mental infirmity that prevents the safe handling of a handgun.

(4) The applicant has successfully completed an approved firearms safety and training course which involves the actual firing of handguns and instruction in the laws of this State governing the carrying of a concealed handgun and the use of deadly force. The North Carolina Criminal Justice Education and Training Standards Commission shall prepare and publish general guidelines for courses and qualifications of instructors which would satisfy the requirements of this subdivision. An approved course shall be any course which satisfies the requirements of this subdivision and is certified or sponsored by:

a. The North Carolina Criminal Justice Education and Training Standards Commission,

b. The National Rifle Association, or

c. A law enforcement agency, college, private or public institution or organization, or firearms training school, taught by instructors certified by the North Carolina Criminal Justice Education and Training Standards Commission or the National Rifle Association.

Every instructor of an approved course shall file a copy of the firearms course description, outline, and proof of certification annually, or upon modification of the course if more frequently, with the North Carolina Criminal Justice Education and Training Standards Commission.

(5) The applicant is not disqualified under subsection (b) of this section.

(b) The sheriff shall deny a permit to an applicant who:

(1) Is ineligible to own, possess, or receive a firearm under the provisions of State or federal law.

(2) Is under indictment or against whom a finding of probable cause exists for a felony.

(3) Has been adjudicated guilty in any court of a felony, unless: **(i)** the felony is an offense that pertains to antitrust violations, unfair trade practices, or restraints of trade, or **(ii)** the person's firearms rights have been restored pursuant to G.S. 14-415.4.

(4) Is a fugitive from justice.

(5) Is an unlawful user of, or addicted to marijuana, alcohol, or any depressant, stimulant, or narcotic drug, or any other controlled substance as defined in 21 U.S.C. § 802.

(6) Is currently, or has been previously adjudicated by a court or administratively determined by a governmental agency whose decisions are subject to judicial review to be, lacking mental capacity or mentally ill. Receipt of previous consultative services or outpatient treatment alone shall not disqualify an applicant under this subdivision.

(7) Is or has been discharged from the Armed Forces of the United States under conditions other than honorable.

(8) Except as provided in subdivision (8a), (8b), or (8c) of this section, is or has been adjudicated guilty of or received a prayer for judgment continued or suspended sentence for 1 or more crimes of violence constituting a misdemeanor, including but not limited to, a violation of a misdemeanor under Article 8 of Chapter 14 of the General Statutes except for a violation of G.S. 14-33(a), or a violation of a misdemeanor under G.S. 14-226.1, 4-258.1, 14-269.2, 14-269.3, 14-269.4, 14-269.6, 14-277, 14-277.1, 14-277.2, 14-283 except for a violation involving fireworks exempted under G.S. 14-414, 14-288.2, 14-288.4(a)(1), 14-288.6, 14-288.9, former 14-288.12, former 14-288.13, former 14-288.14, 14-415.21(b), or 14-415.26(d) within 3 years prior to the date on which the application is submitted.

(8a) Is or has been adjudicated guilty of or received a prayer for judgment continued or suspended sentence for 1 or more crimes of violence constituting a misdemeanor under G.S. 14-33(c)(1), 14-33(c)(2), 14-33(c)(3), 14-33(d), 14-277.3A, 14-318.2, 14-134.3, 50B-4.1, or former G.S. 14-277.3.

(8b) Is prohibited from possessing a firearm pursuant to 18 U.S.C. § 922(g) as a result of a conviction of a misdemeanor crime of domestic violence.

(8c) Has been adjudicated guilty of or received a prayer for judgment continued or suspended sentence for 1 or more crimes involving an assault or a threat to assault a law enforcement officer, probation or parole officer, person employed at a State or local detention facility, firefighter, emergency medical technician, medical responder, or emergency department personnel.

(9) Has had entry of a prayer for judgment continued for a criminal offense which would disqualify the person from obtaining a concealed handgun permit.

(10) Is free on bond or personal recognizance pending trial, appeal, or sentencing for a crime which would disqualify him from obtaining a concealed handgun permit.

(11) Has been convicted of an impaired driving offense under G.S. 20-138.1, 20-138.2, or 20-138.3 within 3 years prior to the date on which the application is submitted.

(c) An applicant shall not be ineligible to receive a concealed carry permit under subdivision (6) of subsection (b) of this section because of an adjudication of mental incapacity or illness or an involuntary commitment to mental health services if the individual's rights have been restored under G.S. 14-409.42.

§ 14-415.12A. Firearms safety and training course exemption for qualified sworn law enforcement officers and certain other persons

(a) A person who is a qualified sworn law enforcement officer, a qualified former sworn law enforcement officer, a qualified retired correctional officer, or a qualified retired probation or parole certified officer is deemed to have satisfied the requirement under G.S. 14-415.12(a)(4) that an applicant successfully complete an approved firearms safety and training course.

(a1) An individual who is a qualified retired law enforcement officer and has met the standards, as approved by the North Carolina Criminal Justice Education and Training Standards Commission, for handgun qualification for active law enforcement officers within the last 12 months is deemed to have satisfied the requirement under G.S. 14-415.12(a)(4) that an applicant successfully complete an approved firearms safety and training course.

(b) A person who is licensed or registered by the North Carolina Private Protective Services Board under Article 1 of Chapter 74C of the General Statutes as an armed security guard, who also has a firearm registration permit issued by the Board in compliance with G.S. 74C-13, is deemed to have satisfied the requirement under G.S. 14-415.12(a)(4) that an applicant successfully complete an approved firearms safety and training course.

§ 14-415.13. Application for a permit; fingerprints

(a) A person shall apply to the sheriff of the county in which the person resides to obtain a concealed handgun permit. The applicant shall submit to the sheriff all of the following:

    (1) An application, completed under oath, on a form provided by the sheriff, and such application form must be provided by the sheriff electronically. The sheriff shall not request employment information, character affidavits, additional background checks, photographs, or other information unless specifically permitted by this Article.

    (2) A nonrefundable permit fee.

    (3) A full set of fingerprints of the applicant administered by the sheriff.

    (4) An original certificate of completion of an approved course, adopted and distributed by the North Carolina Criminal Justice Education and Training Standards Commission, signed by the certified instructor of the course attesting to the successful completion of the course by the applicant which shall verify that the applicant is competent with a handgun and knowledgeable about the laws governing the carrying of a concealed handgun and the use of deadly force.

    (5) A release, in a form to be prescribed by the Administrative Office of the Courts, that authorizes and requires disclosure to the sheriff of any records concerning the mental health or capacity of the applicant to be used for the sole purpose of determining whether the applicant is disqualified for a permit under the provisions of G.S. 14-415.12. This provision does not prohibit submitting information related to involuntary commitment to the National Instant Criminal Background Check System (NICS).

(b) The sheriff shall submit the fingerprints to the State Bureau of Investigation for a records check of State and national databases. The State Bureau of Investigation shall submit the fingerprints to the Federal Bureau of Investigation as necessary. The sheriff shall determine the criminal and background history of an applicant also by conducting a check through the National Instant Criminal Background Check System (NICS). The cost of processing the set of fingerprints shall be charged to an applicant as provided by G.S. 14-415.19.

§ 14-415.14. Application form to be provided by sheriff; information to be included in application form

(a) The sheriff shall make permit applications readily available at the office of the sheriff or at other public offices in the sheriff's jurisdiction. The permit application shall be in triplicate, in a form to be prescribed by the State Bureau of Investigation, and shall include the following information with regard to the applicant: name, address, physical description, signature, date of birth, social security number, military status, law enforcement status, and the drivers license number or State identification card number of the applicant if used for identification in applying for the permit.

(b) The permit application shall also contain a warning substantially as follows:
"CAUTION: Federal law and State law on the possession of handguns and firearms may differ. If you are prohibited by federal law from possessing a handgun or a firearm, you may be prosecuted in federal court. A State permit is not a defense to a federal prosecution."

(c) Any person or entity who is presented by the applicant or by the sheriff with an original or photocopied release form as described in G.S. 14-415.13(a)(5) shall promptly disclose to the sheriff any records concerning the mental health or capacity of the applicant who signed the form and authorized the release of the records.

§ 14-415.15. Issuance or denial of permit

(a) Except as permitted under subsection (b) of this section, within 45 days after receipt of the items listed in G.S. 14-415.13 from an applicant, and receipt of the required records concerning the mental health or capacity of the applicant, the sheriff shall either issue or deny the permit. The sheriff may conduct any investigation necessary to determine the qualification or competency of the person applying for the permit, including record checks. The sheriff shall make the request for any records concerning the mental health or capacity of the applicant within 10 days of receipt of the items listed in G.S. 14-415.13. No person, company, mental health provider, or governmental entity may charge additional fees to the applicant for background checks conducted under this subsection. A permit shall not be denied unless the applicant is determined to be ineligible pursuant to G.S. 14-415.12.

(b) Upon presentment to the sheriff of the items required under G.S. 14-415.13 (a)(1), (2), and (3), the sheriff may issue a temporary permit for a period not to exceed 45 days to a person who the sheriff reasonably believes is in an emergency situation that may constitute a risk of safety to the person, the person's family or property. The applicant may submit proof of a protective order issued under G.S. 50B-3 for the protection of the applicant as evidence of an emergency situation. The temporary permit may not be renewed and may be revoked by the sheriff without a hearing.

(c) A person's application for a permit shall be denied only if the applicant fails to qualify under the criteria listed in this Article. If the sheriff denies the application for a permit, the sheriff shall, within 45 days, notify the applicant in writing, stating the grounds for denial. An applicant may appeal the denial, revocation, or nonrenewal of a permit by petitioning a district court judge of the district in which the application was filed. The determination by the court, on appeal, shall be upon the facts, the law, and the reasonableness of the sheriff's refusal. The determination by the court shall be final.

§ 14-415.16. Renewal of permit

(a) At least 45 days prior to the expiration date of a permit, the sheriff of the county where the permit was issued shall send a written notice to the permittee explaining that the permit is about to expire and including information about the requirements for renewal of the permit. The notice shall be sent by first class mail to the last known address of the permittee. Failure to receive a renewal notice shall not relieve a permittee of requirements imposed in this section for renewal of the permit.

(b) The holder of a permit shall apply to renew the permit within the 90-day period prior to its expiration date by filing with the sheriff of the county in which the person resides a renewal form provided by the sheriff's office, an affidavit stating that the permittee remains qualified under the criteria provided in this Article, a newly administered full set of the permittee's fingerprints, and a renewal fee.

(c) Upon receipt of the completed renewal application and the appropriate payment of fees, the sheriff shall determine if the permittee remains qualified to hold a permit in accordance with the provisions of G.S. 14-415.12. The permittee's criminal history shall be updated, including with another inquiry of the National Instant Criminal Background Check System (NICS), and the sheriff may waive the requirement of taking another firearms safety and training course. If the permittee applies for a renewal of the permit within the 90-day period prior to its expiration date and if the permittee remains qualified to have a permit under G.S. 14-415.12, the sheriff shall renew the permit. The permit of a permittee who complies with this section shall remain valid beyond the expiration date of the permit until the permittee either receives a renewal permit or is denied a renewal permit by the sheriff.

(d) No fingerprints shall be required for a renewal permit if the applicant's fingerprints were submitted to the State Bureau of Investigation after June 30, 2001, on the Automated Fingerprint Information System (AFIS) as prescribed by the State Bureau of Investigation.

(e) If the permittee does not apply to renew the permit prior to its expiration date, but does apply to renew the permit within 60 days after the permit expires, the sheriff may waive the requirement of taking another firearms safety and training course. This subsection does not extend the expiration date of the permit.

§ 14-415.16A. Permit extensions and renewals for deployed military permittees

(a) A deployed military permittee whose permit will expire during the permittee's deployment, or the permittee's agent, may apply to the sheriff for an extension of the military permittee's permit by providing the sheriff with a copy of the permittee's proof of deployment. Upon receipt of the proof, the sheriff shall extend the permit for a period to end 90 days after the permittee's deployment is scheduled to end. A permit that has been extended under this section shall be valid throughout the State during the period of its extension.

(b) A military permittee's permit that is not extended under subsection (a) of this section and that expires during deployment shall remain valid during the deployment and for 90 days after the end of the deployment as if the permit had not expired. The military permittee may carry a concealed handgun during this period provided the permittee meets all the requirements of G.S. 14-415.11(a).

(c) A military permittee under subsection (a) or subsection (b) of this section shall have 90 days after the end of the permittee's deployment to renew the permit. In addition to the requirements of G.S. 14-415.16, the permittee shall provide to the sheriff proof of deployment. The sheriff shall renew the permit upon receipt of this documentation provided the permittee otherwise remains qualified to hold a concealed handgun permit.

§ 14-415.17. Permit; sheriff to retain a list of permittees; confidentiality of list and permit application information; availability to law enforcement agencies

(a) The permit shall be in a certificate form, as prescribed by the State Bureau of Investigation, that is approximately the size of a North Carolina drivers license. It shall bear the signature, name, address, date of birth, and the drivers license identification number used in applying for the permit.

(b) The sheriff shall maintain a listing, including the identifying information, of those persons who are issued a permit. Within 5 days of the date a permit is issued, the sheriff shall send a copy of the permit to the State Bureau of Investigation.

(c) Except as provided otherwise by this subsection, the list of permit holders and the information collected by the sheriff to process an application for a permit are confidential and are not a public record under G.S. 132-1. The sheriff shall make the list of permit holders and the permit information available upon request to all State and local law enforcement agencies. The State Bureau of Investigation shall make the list of permit holders and the information collected by the sheriff to process an application for a permit available to law enforcement officers and clerks of court on a statewide system.

§ 14-415.18. Revocation or suspension of permit
(a) The sheriff of the county where the permit was issued or the sheriff of the county where the person resides may revoke a permit subsequent to a hearing for any of the following reasons:

(1) Fraud or intentional and material misrepresentation in the obtaining of a permit.

(2) Misuse of a permit, including lending or giving a permit or a duplicate permit to another person, materially altering a permit, or using a permit with the intent to unlawfully cause harm to a person or property. It shall not be considered misuse of a permit to provide a duplicate of the permit to a vender for record-keeping purposes.

(3) The doing of an act or existence of a condition which would have been grounds for the denial of the permit by the sheriff.

(4) The violation of any of the terms of this Article.

(5) Repealed by Session Laws 2013-369, s. 20, effective October 1, 2013.

A permittee may appeal the revocation, or nonrenewal of a permit by petitioning a district court judge of the district in which the applicant resides. The determination by the court, on appeal, shall be upon the facts, the law, and the reasonableness of the sheriff's refusal.

(a1) The sheriff of the county where the permit was issued or the sheriff of the county where the person resides shall revoke a permit of any permittee who is adjudicated guilty of or receives a prayer for judgment continued for a crime which would have disqualified the permittee from initially receiving a permit. Upon determining that a permit should be revoked pursuant to this subsection, the sheriff shall provide written notice to the permittee, pursuant to the provisions of G.S. 1A-1, Rule 4(j), that the permit is revoked upon the service of the notice. The notice shall provide the permittee with information on the process to appeal the revocation.

Upon receipt of the written notice of revocation, the permittee shall surrender the permit to the sheriff. Any law enforcement officer serving the notice is authorized to take immediate possession of the permit from the permittee. If the notice is served by means other than by a law enforcement officer, the permittee shall surrender the permit to the sheriff no later than 48 hours after service of the notice.

A permittee may appeal the revocation of a permit pursuant to this subsection by petitioning a district court judge of the district in which the permittee resides. The determination by the court, on appeal, shall be limited to whether the permittee was adjudicated guilty of or received a prayer for judgment continued for a crime which would have disqualified the permittee from initially receiving a permit. Revocation of the permit is not stayed pending appeal.

(b) The court may suspend a permit as part of and for the duration of any orders permitted under Chapter 50B of the General Statutes.

§ 14-415.19. Fees
(a) The permit fees assessed under this Article are payable to the sheriff. The sheriff shall transmit the proceeds of these fees to the county finance officer to be remitted or credited by the county finance officer in accordance with the provisions of this section. Except as otherwise provided by this section, the permit fees are as follows:

Application fee. $80
Renewal fee. $75
Duplicate permit fee. $15

(a1) The permit fees for a retired sworn law enforcement officer who provides the information required by subdivisions (1) and (2) of this subsection to the sheriff, in addition to any other information required under this Article, are as follows:

Application fee. $45
Renewal fee. $40

(1) A copy of the officer's letter of retirement from either the North Carolina Teachers' and State Employees' Retirement System or the North Carolina Local Governmental Employees' Retirement System.

(2) Written documentation from the head of the agency where the person was previously employed indicating that the person was neither involuntarily terminated nor under administrative or criminal investigation within 6 months of retirement.

(b) An additional fee, not to exceed $10, shall be collected by the sheriff from an applicant for a permit to pay for the costs of processing the applicant's fingerprints, if fingerprints were required to be taken. This fee shall be retained by the sheriff.

§ 14-415.21. Violations of this Article punishable as an infraction
(a) A person who has been issued a valid permit who is found to be carrying a concealed handgun without the permit in the person's possession or who fails to disclose to any law enforcement officer that the person holds a valid permit and is carrying a concealed handgun, as required by G.S. 14-415.11, shall be guilty of an infraction and shall be punished in accordance with G.S. 14-3.1. Any person who has been issued a valid permit who is found to be carrying a concealed handgun in violation of G.S. 14-415.11(c)(8) shall be guilty of an infraction and may be required to pay a fine of up to $500. In lieu of paying a fine the person may surrender the permit.

(a1) A person who has been issued a valid permit who is found to be carrying a concealed handgun in violation of subsection (c2) of G.S. 14-415.11 shall be guilty of a Class 1 misdemeanor.

(b) A person who violates the provisions of this Article other than as set forth in subsection (a) or (a1) of this section is guilty of a Class 2 misdemeanor.

§ **14-415.22. Construction of Article.** This Article shall not be construed to require a person who may carry a concealed handgun under the provisions of G.S. 14-269(b) to obtain a concealed handgun permit. The provisions of this Article shall not apply to a person who may lawfully carry a concealed weapon or handgun pursuant to G.S. 14-269(b). A person who may lawfully carry a concealed weapon or handgun pursuant to G.S. 14-269(b) shall not be prohibited from carrying the concealed weapon or handgun on property on which a notice is posted prohibiting the carrying of a concealed handgun, unless otherwise prohibited by statute.

§ 14-415.23. Statewide uniformity

(a) It is the intent of the General Assembly to prescribe a uniform system for the regulation of legally carrying a concealed handgun. To insure uniformity, no political subdivisions, boards, or agencies of the State nor any county, city, municipality, municipal corporation, town, township, village, nor any department or agency thereof, may enact ordinances, rules, or regulations concerning legally carrying a concealed handgun. A unit of local government may adopt an ordinance to permit the posting of a prohibition against carrying a concealed handgun, in accordance with G.S. 14-415.11(c), on local government buildings and their appurtenant premises.

(b) A unit of local government may adopt an ordinance to prohibit, by posting, the carrying of a concealed handgun on municipal and county recreational facilities that are specifically identified by the unit of local government. If a unit of local government adopts such an ordinance with regard to recreational facilities, then the concealed handgun permittee may, nevertheless, secure the handgun in a locked vehicle within the trunk, glove box, or other enclosed compartment or area within or on the motor vehicle.

(c) For purposes of this section, the term "recreational facilities" includes only the following:

(1) An athletic field, including any appurtenant facilities such as restrooms, during an organized athletic event if the field had been scheduled for use with the municipality or county office responsible for operation of the park or recreational area.

(2) A swimming pool, including any appurtenant facilities used for dressing, storage of personal items, or other uses relating to the swimming pool.

(3) A facility used for athletic events, including, but not limited to, a gymnasium.

(d) For the purposes of this section, the term "recreational facilities" does not include any greenway, designated biking or walking path, an area that is customarily used as a walkway or bike path although not specifically designated for such use, open areas or fields where athletic events may occur unless the area qualifies as an "athletic field" pursuant to subdivision (1) of subsection (c) of this section, and any other area that is not specifically described in subsection (c) of this section.

(e) A person adversely affected by any ordinance, rule, or regulation promulgated or caused to be enforced by any unit of local government in violation of this section may bring an action for declaratory and injunctive relief and for actual damages arising from the violation. The court shall award the prevailing party in an action brought under this subsection reasonable attorneys' fees and court costs as authorized by law.

§ 14-415.24. Reciprocity; out-of-state handgun permits

(a) A valid concealed handgun permit or license issued by another state is valid in North Carolina.

(c) Every 12 months after the effective date of this subsection, the Department of Justice shall make written inquiry of the concealed handgun permitting authorities in each other state as to: **(i)** whether a North Carolina resident may carry a concealed handgun in their state based upon having a valid North Carolina concealed handgun permit and **(ii)** whether a North Carolina resident may apply for a concealed handgun permit in that state based upon having a valid North Carolina concealed handgun permit. The Department of Justice shall attempt to secure from each state permission for North Carolina residents who hold a valid North Carolina concealed handgun permit to carry a concealed handgun in that state, either on the basis of the North Carolina permit or on the basis that the North Carolina permit is sufficient to permit the issuance of a similar license or permit by the other state.

§ 14-415.25. Exemption from permit requirement.
Law enforcement officers and qualified retired law enforcement officers authorized by federal law to carry a concealed handgun pursuant to § 926B or 926C of Title 18 of the United States Code, who are in compliance with the requirements of those sections, are exempt from obtaining the permit described in G.S. 14-415.11.

§ 14-415.26. Certification of qualified retired law enforcement officers

(a) In lieu of obtaining a permit under this Article, a qualified retired law enforcement officer may apply to the North Carolina Criminal Justice Education and Training Standards Commission for certification. The application shall include all of the following:

(1) Verification of completion of the firearms qualification criteria established by the Commission.

(2) Photographic identification indicating retirement status issued by the agency from which the applicant retired from service.

(3) Any other application information required by the Commission.

(b) The Commission shall include with the certification a notice of the limitations applicable under federal or State law to the concealed carry of firearms in this State. The failure to receive a notification under this subsection shall not be a defense to any offense or violation of applicable State or federal laws.

(b1) The Commission shall coordinate with local and State law enforcement officers and with the community college system to provide multiple firearms qualification sites throughout the State where a qualified retired law enforcement officer may satisfy the firearms qualification criteria required for certification under this section.

(c) The Commission shall not incur any civil or criminal liability as the result of the performance of its duties under this section.

(d) It shall be unlawful for an applicant, or any person assisting an applicant, to make a willful and intentional misrepresentation on any form or application submitted to the Commission. A violation of this subsection shall be a Class 2 misdemeanor, and shall result in the immediate revocation of any certification issued by the Commission. A person convicted under this subsection shall be ineligible for certification under this section, or from obtaining a concealed carry permit under State law.

(e) This section shall not exempt any individual engaged in the private protective services profession in this State from fulfilling the registration and training requirements in Chapter 74C of the General Statutes.

§ 14-415.27. Expanded permit scope for certain persons

Notwithstanding G.S. 14-415.11(c), any of the following persons who has a concealed handgun permit issued pursuant to this Article or that is considered valid under G.S. 14-415.24 is not subject to the area prohibitions set out in G.S. 14-415.11(c) and may carry a concealed handgun in the areas listed in G.S. 14-415.11(c) unless otherwise prohibited by federal law:

(1) A district attorney.

(2) An assistant district attorney.

(3) An investigator employed by the office of a district attorney.

(4) A North Carolina district or superior court judge.

(5) A magistrate.

(6) A person who is elected and serving as a clerk of court.

(7) A person who is elected and serving as a register of deeds.

(8) A person employed by the Department of Public Safety who has been designated in writing by the Secretary of the Department and who has in the person's possession written proof of the designation.

(9) A North Carolina administrative law judge.

Oklahoma Annotated Statutes

Current through Acts 1-201, 203-243, 245-297, 299-348, 350-352, 354-365, 367-395 of the Second Regular Session of the 55th Legislature (2016).

Office of the Attorney General
313 Northeast 21st Street
Oklahoma City, OK 73105
Voice: (405) 521-3921
https://www.ok.gov/oag/

Dallas Field Division
1114 Commerce Street, Room 303
Dallas, Texas 75242
Voice: (469) 227-4300
https://www.atf.gov/dallas-field-division

PROTECTING THE PUBLIC
SERVING OUR NATION

Table of Contents

Oklahoma Self-Defense Act

Chapter 55. Other Crimes against Public Peace–Miscellaneous Provisions

TITLE 21. Crimes and Punishments
Part VI. Crimes against Public Peace
Chapter 53. Manufacturing, Selling and Wearing Weapons

§ 1271.1. Confiscation and Forfeiture of Weapons Upon Arrest of Person Under 18–Disposition

A. Whenever a person under 18 years of age is detained or arrested by a law enforcement officer and is carrying any weapon or firearm prohibited by § 1272 of this title, each such prohibited weapon and firearm may be confiscated and forfeited to the State of Oklahoma by the law enforcement authority. Such confiscation and forfeiture shall not require that criminal charges be filed against the minor.

B. However, when a weapon or firearm confiscated pursuant to the provisions of this section has been taken by a minor without the permission of the owner, the weapon or firearm shall be returned to the owner pursuant to the procedures provided in § 1321 of Title 22 of the Oklahoma Statutes, provided the possession of such weapon or firearm by the owner is not otherwise prohibited by law.

C. Any weapon or firearm confiscated and forfeited by any law enforcement authority may be sold at public auction, or when no longer needed as evidence in the criminal proceeding the confiscating authority may lease any firearm confiscated and forfeited by law pursuant to this section to any law enforcement agency for a period of 1 year. Such lease may be renewed each year thereafter at the discretion of such authority to assist in the enforcement of the laws of this state or its political subdivisions. Any weapon or firearm deemed by the confiscating authority to be inappropriate for lease or sale shall be destroyed.

D. For purposes of this section, the term "confiscate" shall not be construed to prohibit any parent, guardian or other adult person from removing or otherwise seizing from any minor any weapon or firearm in the minor's possession. Provided however, no school authority shall return any weapon or firearm removed or otherwise seized from any minor to any person, and shall immediately deliver such weapon or firearm to a law enforcement authority for prosecution and forfeiture.

§ 1272. Unlawful carry [Effective November 1, 2016]

A. It shall be unlawful for any person to carry upon or about his or her person, or in a purse or other container belonging to the person, any pistol, revolver, shotgun or rifle whether loaded or unloaded, … or any other offensive weapon, whether such weapon be concealed or unconcealed, except this section shall not prohibit:

    1. The proper use of guns and knives for hunting, fishing, educational or recreational purposes;

    2. The carrying or use of weapons in a manner otherwise permitted by statute or authorized by the Oklahoma Self-Defense Act;

3. The carrying, possession and use of any weapon by a peace officer or other person authorized by law to carry a weapon in the performance of official duties and in compliance with the rules of the employing agency;

4. The carrying or use of weapons in a courthouse by a district judge, associate district judge or special district judge within this state, who is in possession of a valid handgun license issued pursuant to the provisions of the Oklahoma Self-Defense Act and whose name appears on a list maintained by the Administrative Director of the Courts; or

5. The carrying and use of firearms and other weapons provided in this subsection when used for the purpose of living history reenactment. For purposes of this paragraph, "living history reenactment" means depiction of historical characters, scenes, historical life or events for entertainment, education, or historical documentation through the wearing or use of period, historical, antique or vintage clothing, accessories, firearms, weapons, and other implements of the historical period.

B. Any person convicted of violating the foregoing provision shall be guilty of a misdemeanor punishable as provided in § 1276 of this title.

§ 1272.1. Carrying Firearms Where Liquor Is Consumed

A. It shall be unlawful for any person to carry or possess any weapon designated in § 1272 of this title in any establishment where low-point beer, as defined by § 163.2 of Title 37 of the Oklahoma Statutes, or alcoholic beverages, as defined by § 506 of Title 37 of the Oklahoma Statutes, are consumed. This provision shall not apply to a peace officer, as defined in § 99 of this title, or to private investigators with a firearms authorization when acting in the scope and course of employment, and shall not apply to an owner or proprietor of the establishment having a pistol, rifle, or shotgun on the premises. Provided however, a person possessing a valid handgun license pursuant to the provisions of the Oklahoma Self-Defense Act may carry the concealed or unconcealed handgun into any restaurant or other establishment licensed to dispense low-point beer or alcoholic beverages where the sale of low-point beer or alcoholic beverages does not constitute the primary purpose of the business.

Provided further, nothing in this section shall be interpreted to authorize any peace officer in actual physical possession of a weapon to consume low-point beer or alcoholic beverages, except in the authorized line of duty as an undercover officer.

Nothing in this section shall be interpreted to authorize any private investigator with a firearms authorization in actual physical possession of a weapon to consume low-point beer or alcoholic beverages in any establishment where low-point beer or alcoholic beverages are cons

B. Any person violating the provisions of this section shall be punished as provided in § 1272.2 of this title.

§ 1272.2. Penalty for Firearm in Liquor Establishment.
Any person who intentionally or knowingly carries on his or her person any weapon in violation of § 1272.1 of this title, shall, upon conviction, be guilty of a felony punishable by a fine not to exceed $1,000, or imprisonment in the custody of the Department of Corrections for a period not to exceed 2 years, or by both such fine and imprisonment.

Any person convicted of violating the provisions of this section after having been issued a handgun license pursuant to the provisions of the Oklahoma Self-Defense Act shall have the license revoked by the Oklahoma State Bureau of Investigation after a hearing and determination that the person is in violation of § 1272.1 of this title.

§ 1273. Allowing Minors to Possess Firearms

A. It shall be unlawful for any person within this state to sell or give to any child any of the arms or weapons designated in § 1272 of this title; provided, the provisions of this section shall not prohibit a parent of a child or legal guardian of a child, or a person acting with the permission of the parent of the child or legal guardian of the child, from giving the child a firearm for participation in hunting animals or fowl, hunter safety classes, education and training in the safe use and handling of firearms, target shooting, skeet, trap or other sporting events or competitions, except as provided in subsection B of this section.

B. It shall be unlawful for any parent or guardian to intentionally, knowingly, or recklessly permit his or her child to possess any of the arms or weapons designated in § 1272 of this title, including any firearm, if such parent is aware of a substantial risk that the child will use the weapon to commit a criminal offense or if the child has either been adjudicated a delinquent or has been convicted as an adult for any criminal offense that contains as an element the threat or use of physical force against the person of another.

C. It shall be unlawful for any child to possess any of the arms or weapons designated in § 1272 of this title, except firearms used for participation in hunting animals or fowl, hunter safety classes, education and training in the safe use and handling of firearms, target shooting, skeet, trap or other sporting events or competitions. Provided, this section shall not authorize the possession of such weapons by any person who is subject to the provisions of § 1283 of this title.

D. Any person violating the provisions of this section shall, upon conviction, be punished as provided in § 1276 of this title, and, any child violating the provisions of this section shall be subject to adjudication as a delinquent. In addition, any person violating the provisions of subsection A or B of this section shall be liable for civil damages for any injury or death to any person and for any damage to property, as provided in § 10 of Title 23 of the Oklahoma Statutes, resulting from any discharge of a firearm by the child or use of any other weapon that the person had given to the child or permitted the child to possess. Any person convicted of violating the provisions of this section after having been issued a handgun license pursuant to the provisions of the Oklahoma Self-Defense Act may be liable for an administrative violation as provided in § 1276 of this title.

E. As used in this section, "child" means a person under 18 years of age.

§ 1276. Penalty for 1272 and 1273. Any person violating the provisions of § 1272 or 1273 of this title shall, upon a first conviction, be adjudged guilty of a misdemeanor and the party offending shall be punished by a fine of not less than $100 nor more than $250, or by imprisonment in the county jail for a period not to exceed 30 days or both such fine and imprisonment. On the second and every subsequent violation, the party offending shall, upon conviction, be punished by a fine of not less than $250 nor more than $500, or by imprisonment in the county jail for a period not less than 30 days nor more than 3 months, or by both such fine and imprisonment.

Any person convicted of violating the provisions of § 1272 or 1273 of this title after having been issued a handgun license pursuant to the provisions of the Oklahoma Self-Defense Act shall have the license suspended for a period of 6 months and shall be liable for an administrative fine of $50 upon a hearing and determination by the Oklahoma State Bureau of Investigation that the person is in violation of the provisions of this section.

§ 1277. Unlawful Carry in Certain Places. [Effective November 1, 2016]
A. It shall be unlawful for any person in possession of a valid handgun license issued pursuant to the provisions of the Oklahoma Self-Defense Act to carry any concealed or unconcealed handgun into any of the following places:
  1. Any structure, building, or office space which is owned or leased by a city, town, county, state or federal governmental authority for the purpose of conducting business with the public;
  2. Any courthouse, courtroom, prison, jail, detention facility or any facility used to process, hold or house arrested persons, prisoners or persons alleged delinquent or adjudicated delinquent, except as provided in § 21 of Title 57 of the Oklahoma Statutes;
  3. Any public or private elementary or public or private secondary school, except as provided in subsection C of this section;
  4. Any publicly owned or operated sports arena or venue during a professional sporting event, unless allowed by the event holder;
  5. Any place where gambling is authorized by law, unless allowed by the property owner; and
  6. Any other place specifically prohibited by law.
B. For purposes of subsection A of this section, the prohibited place does not include and specifically excludes the following property:
  1. Any property set aside for the use or parking of any vehicle, whether attended or unattended, by a city, town, county, state or federal governmental authority;
  2. Any property set aside for the use or parking of any vehicle, whether attended or unattended, which is open to the public, or by any entity engaged in gambling authorized by law;
  3. Any property adjacent to a structure, building or office space in which concealed or unconcealed weapons are prohibited by the provisions of this section;
  4. Any property designated by a city, town, county or state governmental authority as a park, recreational area, or fairgrounds; provided, nothing in this paragraph shall be construed to authorize any entry by a person in possession of a concealed or unconcealed handgun into any structure, building or office space which is specifically prohibited by the provisions of subsection A of this section; and
  5. Any property set aside by a public or private elementary or secondary school for the use or parking of any vehicle, whether attended or unattended; provided, however, said handgun shall be stored and hidden from view in a locked motor vehicle when the motor vehicle is left unattended on school property.

Nothing contained in any provision of this subsection or subsection C of this section shall be construed to authorize or allow any person in control of any place described in subsection A of this section to establish any policy or rule that has the effect of prohibiting any person in lawful possession of a handgun license from possession of a handgun allowable under such license in places described in this subsection.
C. A concealed or unconcealed weapon may be carried onto private school property or in any school bus or vehicle used by any private school for transportation of students or teachers by a person who is licensed pursuant to the Oklahoma Self-Defense Act, provided a policy has been adopted by the governing entity of the private school that authorizes the carrying and possession of a weapon on private school property or in any school bus or vehicle used by a private school. Except for acts of gross negligence or willful or wanton misconduct, a governing entity of a private school that adopts a policy which authorizes the possession of a weapon on private school property, a school bus or vehicle used by the private school shall be immune from liability for any injuries arising from the adoption of the policy. The provisions of this subsection shall not apply to claims pursuant to the Administrative Workers' Compensation Act.
D. Any person violating the provisions paragraph 2 or 3 of subsection A of this section shall, upon conviction, be guilty of a misdemeanor punishable by a fine not to exceed $250. A person violating any other provision of subsection A may be denied entrance onto the property or removed from the property. If the person refuses to leave the property and a peace officer is summoned, the person may be issued a citation for an amount not to exceed $250.
E. No person in possession of a valid handgun license issued pursuant to the provisions of the Oklahoma Self-Defense Act shall be authorized to carry the handgun into or upon any college, university or technology center school property, except as provided in this subsection. For purposes of this subsection, the following property shall not be construed as prohibited for persons having a valid handgun license:
  1. Any property set aside for the use or parking of any vehicle, whether attended or unattended, provided the handgun is carried or stored as required by law and the handgun is not removed from the vehicle without the prior consent of the

college or university president or technology center school administrator while the vehicle is on any college, university or technology center school property;

2. Any property authorized for possession or use of handguns by college, university or technology center school policy; and

3. Any property authorized by the written consent of the college or university president or technology center school administrator, provided the written consent is carried with the handgun and the valid handgun license while on college, university or technology center school property.

The college, university or technology center school may notify the Oklahoma State Bureau of Investigation within 10 days of a violation of any provision of this subsection by a licensee. Upon receipt of a written notification of violation, the Bureau shall give a reasonable notice to the licensee and hold a hearing. At the hearing, upon a determination that the licensee has violated any provision of this subsection, the licensee may be subject to an administrative fine of $250 and may have the handgun license suspended for 3 months.

Nothing contained in any provision of this subsection shall be construed to authorize or allow any college, university or technology center school to establish any policy or rule that has the effect of prohibiting any person in lawful possession of a handgun license from possession of a handgun allowable under such license in places described in paragraphs 1, 2, and 3 of this subsection. Nothing contained in any provision of this subsection shall be construed to limit the authority of any college, university or technology center school in this state from taking administrative action against any student for any violation of any provision of this subsection.

F. The provisions of this section shall not apply to any peace officer or to any person authorized by law to carry a pistol in the course of employment. District judges, associate district judges, and special district judges, who are in possession of a valid handgun license issued pursuant to the provisions of the Oklahoma Self-Defense Act and whose names appear on a list maintained by the Administrative Director of the Courts, shall be exempt from this section when acting in the course and scope of employment within the courthouses of this state. Private investigators with a firearms authorization shall be exempt from this section when acting in the course and scope of employment.

G. For the purposes of this section, "motor vehicle" means any automobile, truck, minivan or sports utility vehicle.

§ 1278. Unlawful Intent to Carry.
Any person in this state who carries or wears any deadly weapons or dangerous instrument whatsoever with the intent or for the avowed purpose of unlawfully injuring another person, upon conviction, shall be guilty of a felony punishable by a fine not exceeding $5,000, by imprisonment in the custody of the Department of Corrections for a period not exceeding 2 years, or by both such fine and imprisonment. The mere possession of such a weapon or dangerous instrument, without more, however, shall not be sufficient to establish intent as required by this section.

Any person convicted of violating the provisions of this section after having been issued a handgun license pursuant to the provisions of the Oklahoma Self-Defense Act shall have the license permanently revoked and shall be liable for an administrative fine of $1,000 upon a hearing and determination by the Oklahoma State Bureau of Investigation that the person is in violation of the provisions of this section.

§ 1279. Pointing Weapons at Others–Exception–Penalty.
Except for an act of self-defense, it shall be unlawful for any person to point any pistol or any other deadly weapon whether loaded or not, at any other person or persons. Any person violating the provisions of this section shall, upon conviction, be guilty of a misdemeanor punishable as provided in § 1280 of this title.

Any person convicted of violating the provisions of this section after having been issued a handgun license pursuant to the provisions of the Oklahoma Self-Defense Act may be subject to an administrative violation as provided in § 1280 of this title.

§ 1280. Punishment for Violation – Penalty for 1279.
Any person violating the provisions of § 1279 of this title, upon conviction, shall be guilty of a misdemeanor. The person offending shall be punished by a fine of not less than $100 nor more than $1,000 and shall be imprisoned in the county jail for a period not less than 3 nor more than 12 months. Any person convicted of violating the provisions of § 1279 of this title after having been issued a handgun license pursuant to the provisions of the Oklahoma Self-Defense Act, §§ 1 through 25 of this act, shall have the handgun license permanently revoked and shall be liable for an administrative fine of $50 upon a hearing and determination by the Oklahoma State Bureau of Investigation that the person is in violation of the provisions of this section.

§ 1280.1. Possession of firearm on school property
A. It shall be unlawful for any person to have in his or her possession on any public or private school property or while in any school bus or vehicle used by any school for transportation of students or teachers any firearm or weapon designated in § 1272 of this title, except as provided in subsection C of this section or as otherwise authorized by law.

B. For purposes of this section:

1. "School property" means any publicly owned property held for purposes of elementary, secondary or vocational-technical education, and shall not include property owned by public school districts or where such property is leased or rented to an individual or corporation and used for purposes other than educational;

2. "Private school" means a school that offers a course of instruction for students in one or more grades from prekindergarten through grade 12 and is not operated by a governmental entity; and

3. "Motor vehicle" means any automobile, truck, minivan or sports utility vehicle.

C. Firearms and weapons are allowed on school property and deemed not in violation of subsection A of this section as follows:

1. A gun or knife designed for hunting or fishing purposes kept in a privately owned vehicle and properly displayed or stored as required by law, provided such vehicle containing said gun or knife is driven onto school property only to transport a student to and from school and such vehicle does not remain unattended on school property;

2. A gun or knife used for the purposes of participating in the Oklahoma Department of Wildlife Conservation certified hunter training education course or any other hunting, fishing, safety or firearms training courses, or a recognized firearms sports event, team shooting program or competition, or living history reenactment, provided the course or event is approved by the principal or chief administrator of the school where the course or event is offered, and provided the weapon is properly displayed or stored as required by law pending participation in the course, event, program or competition;

3. Weapons in the possession of any peace officer or other person authorized by law to possess a weapon in the performance of his or her duties and responsibilities;

4. A concealed or unconcealed weapon carried onto private school property or in any school bus or vehicle used by any private school for transportation of students or teachers by a person who is licensed pursuant to the Oklahoma Self-Defense Act, provided a policy has been adopted by the governing entity of the private school that authorizes the possession of a weapon on private school property or in any school bus or vehicle used by a private school. Except for acts of gross negligence or willful or wanton misconduct, a governing entity of a private school that adopts a policy which authorizes the possession of a weapon on private school property, a school bus or vehicle used by the private school shall be immune from liability for any injuries arising from the adoption of the policy. The provisions of this paragraph shall not apply to claims pursuant to the Workers" Compensation Code;

5. A gun, knife, bayonet or other weapon in the possession of a member of a veterans group, the national guard, active military, the Reserve Officers" Training Corps (ROTC) or Junior ROTC, in order to participate in a ceremony, assembly or educational program approved by the principal or chief administrator of a school or school district where the ceremony, assembly or educational program is being held; provided, however, the gun or other weapon that uses projectiles is not loaded and is inoperable at all times while on school property;

6. A handgun carried in a motor vehicle pursuant to a valid handgun license authorized by the Oklahoma Self-Defense Act onto property set aside by a public or private elementary or secondary school for the use or parking of any vehicle; provided, however, said handgun shall be stored and hidden from view in a locked motor vehicle when the motor vehicle is left unattended on school property; and

7. A handgun carried onto public school property by school personnel who have been designated by the board of education, provided such personnel either:

a. possess a valid armed security guard license as provided for in § 1750.1 et seq. of Title 59 of the Oklahoma Statutes, or

b. hold a valid reserve peace officer certification as provided for in § 3311 of Title 70 of the Oklahoma Statutes, if a policy has been adopted by the board of education of the school district that authorizes the carrying of a handgun onto public school property by such personnel. Nothing in this subsection shall be construed to restrict authority granted elsewhere in law to carry firearms.

D. Any person violating the provisions of this section shall, upon conviction, be guilty of a misdemeanor punishable by a fine of not to exceed $250.

§ 1283. Convicted Felons and Delinquents

A. Except as provided in subsection B of this section, it shall be unlawful for any person convicted of any felony in any court of this state or of another state or of the United States to have in his or her possession or under his or her immediate control, or in any vehicle which the person is operating, or in which the person is riding as a passenger, or at the residence where the convicted person resides, any pistol, imitation or homemade pistol, altered air or toy pistol, machine gun, sawed-off shotgun or rifle, or any other dangerous or deadly firearm.

B. Any person who has previously been convicted of a nonviolent felony in any court of this state or of another state or of the United States, and who has received a full and complete pardon from the proper authority and has not been convicted of any other felony offense which has not been pardoned, shall have restored the right to possess any firearm or other weapon prohibited by subsection A of this section, the right to apply for and carry a handgun, concealed or unconcealed, pursuant to the Oklahoma Self-Defense Act and the right to perform the duties of a peace officer, gunsmith, or for firearms repair.

C. It shall be unlawful for any person serving a term of probation for any felony in any court of this state or of another state or of the United States or under the jurisdiction of any alternative court program to have in his or her possession or under his or her immediate control, or at his or her residence, or in any passenger vehicle which the person is operating or is riding as a passenger, any pistol, shotgun or rifle, including any imitation or homemade pistol, altered air or toy pistol, shotgun or rifle, while such person is subject to supervision, probation, parole or inmate status.

D. It shall be unlawful for any person previously adjudicated as a delinquent child or a youthful offender for the commission of an offense, which would have constituted a felony offense if committed by an adult, to have in the possession of the person or under the immediate control of the person, or have in any vehicle which he or she is driving or in which the person is riding as a passenger, or at the residence of the person, any pistol, imitation or homemade pistol, altered air or toy pistol, machine gun, sawed-off shotgun or rifle, or any other dangerous or deadly firearm within 10 years after such adjudication; provided, that nothing in this subsection shall be construed to prohibit the placement of the person in a home with a full-time duly appointed peace officer who is certified by the Council on Law Enforcement Education and Training (CLEET) pursuant to the provisions of § 3311 of Title 70 of the Oklahoma Statutes.

E. Any person having been issued a handgun license pursuant to the provisions of the Oklahoma Self-Defense Act and who thereafter knowingly or intentionally allows a convicted felon or adjudicated delinquent or a youthful offender as prohibited by the provisions of subsection A, C, or D of this section to possess or have control of any pistol authorized by the Oklahoma Self-Defense Act shall, upon conviction, be guilty of a felony punishable by a fine not to exceed $5,000. In addition, the person shall have the handgun license revoked by the Oklahoma State Bureau of Investigation after a hearing and determination that the person has violated the provisions of this section.

F. Any convicted or adjudicated person violating the provisions of this section shall, upon conviction, be guilty of a felony punishable as provided in § 1284 of this title.

G. For purposes of this section, "sawed-off shotgun or rifle" shall mean any shotgun or rifle which has been shortened to any length.

H. For purposes of this section, "altered toy pistol" shall mean any toy weapon which has been altered from its original manufactured state to resemble a real weapon.

I. For purposes of this section, "altered air pistol" shall mean any air pistol manufactured to propel projectiles by air pressure which has been altered from its original manufactured state.

J. For purposes of this section, "alternative court program" shall mean any drug court, Anna McBride or mental health court, DUI court or veterans court.

§ 1284. Penalty for 1283. Any previously convicted or adjudicated person who violates any provision of § 1283 of this title shall be guilty of a felony and, upon conviction thereof, shall be punished by imprisonment in the State Penitentiary for a period not less than 1 year nor more than 10 years.

§ 1287. Use of Firearm While Committing a Felony

A. Any person who, while committing or attempting to commit a felony, possesses a pistol, shotgun or rifle or any other offensive weapon in such commission or attempt, whether the pistol, shotgun or rifle is loaded or not, or who possesses a blank or imitation pistol, altered air or toy pistol, shotgun or rifle capable of raising in the mind of one threatened with such device a fear that it is a real pistol, shotgun or rifle, … in addition to the penalty provided by statute for the felony committed or attempted, upon conviction shall be guilty of a felony for possessing such weapon or device, which shall be a separate offense from the felony committed or attempted and shall be punishable by imprisonment in the custody of the Department of Corrections for a period of not less than 2 years nor for more than 10 years for the first offense, and for a period of not less than 10 years nor more than 30 years for any second or subsequent offense.

B. Any person convicted of violating the provisions of this section after having been issued a handgun license pursuant to the provisions of the Oklahoma Self-Defense Act shall have the license permanently revoked and shall be liable for an administrative fine of $1,000 upon a hearing and determination by the Oklahoma State Bureau of Investigation that the person is in violation of the provisions of this section.

C. As used in this section, "altered toy pistol" shall mean any toy weapon which has been altered from its original manufactured state to resemble a real weapon.

D. As used in this section, "altered air pistol" shall mean any air pistol manufactured to propel projectiles by air pressure which has been altered from its original manufactured state.

§ 1287.1. Penalty Enhancement for Weapon Possession.
Any person who, while committing or attempting to commit a crime of violence, discharges a firearm, in addition to the penalty provided by statute for the crime of violence committed or attempted, upon conviction, may be charged, in the discretion of the district attorney, with an additional felony for possessing such weapon, which shall be a separate offense punishable, upon conviction, by not less than 10 years in the custody of the Department of Corrections which may be served concurrently with the sentence for the crime of violence. For purposes of this section, "crime of violence" means an offense that is a felony and has as an element of the offense, the use, attempted use, or threatened use of physical force against the person of another or that by its nature involves a substantial risk that physical force against the person of another may be used in the course of committing the offense. For purposes of this section, "firearm" means a rifle, pistol or shotgun.

§ 1288. Purchases of Firearms, Ammunition and Equipment in Other States by Oklahoma Residents–Purchases in Oklahoma by Residents of Other States

A. Residents of the State of Oklahoma may purchase rifles, shotguns, ammunition, cartridge and shotgun shell handloading components and equipment from a dealer licensed in a state other than Oklahoma. This authorization is enacted in conformance with the provisions of § 922(b)(3) of Title 18 of the United States Code and provided further that such residents conform to the provisions of law applicable to such purchase in the State of Oklahoma and the state in which the purchase is made.

B. Residents of a state other than Oklahoma may purchase rifles, shotguns, ammunition, cartridge and shotgun shell handloading components and equipment from a dealer licensed in the State of Oklahoma. This authorization is enacted in conformance with the provisions of § 922(b)(3) of Title 18 of the United States Code and provided further that such residents conform to the provisions of law applicable to such purchase in the State of Oklahoma and in the state in which such persons reside.

Firearms Act of 1971

§ 1289.1. Short Title. Sections 1289.1 through 1289.17 of this title may be known and cited as the "Oklahoma Firearms Act of 1971".

§ 1289.3. Definition of Pistols. "Pistols" as used in the Oklahoma Firearms Act of 1971, §§ 1289.1 through 1289.17 of this title, shall mean any firearm capable of discharging a projectile composed of any material which may reasonably be expected to be able to cause lethal injury, with a barrel or barrels less than 16 inches in length, and using either gunpowder, gas or any means of rocket propulsion, but not to include flare guns, underwater fishing guns or blank pistols.

§ 1289.4. Definition of Rifles. "Rifles" as used in the Oklahoma Firearms Act of 1971, §§ 1289.1 through 1289.17 of this title, shall mean any firearm capable of discharging a projectile composed of any material which may reasonably be expected to be able to cause lethal injury, with a barrel or barrels more than 16 inches in length, and using either gunpowder, gas or any means of rocket propulsion, but not to include archery equipment, flare guns or underwater fishing guns. In addition, any rifle capable of firing "shot" but primarily designed to fire single projectiles will be regarded as a "rifle".

§ 1289.5. Definition of Shotguns. "Shotguns" as used in the Oklahoma Firearms Act of 1971, §§ 1289.1 through 1289.17 of this title, shall mean any firearm capable of discharging a series of projectiles of any material which may reasonably be expected to be able to cause lethal injury, with a barrel or barrels more than 18 inches in length, and using either gunpowder, gas or any means of rocket propulsion, but not to include any weapon so designed with a barrel less than 18 inches in length. In addition, any "shotgun" capable of firing single projectiles but primarily designed to fire multiple projectiles such as "shot" will be regarded as a "shotgun".

§ 1289.6. Conditions under Which Firearms May be Carried [Effective November 1, 2016]
A. A person shall be permitted to carry loaded and unloaded shotguns, rifles and pistols, open and not concealed and without a handgun license as authorized by the Oklahoma Self-Defense Act pursuant to the following conditions:
   1. When hunting animals or fowl;
   2. During competition in or practicing in a safety or hunter safety class, target shooting, skeet, trap or other recognized sporting events;
   3. During participation in or in preparation for a military function of the state military forces to be defined as the Oklahoma Army or Air National Guard, Federal Military Reserve and active military forces. It is further provided that Oklahoma Army or Air National Guard personnel with proper authorization and performing a military function may carry loaded or unloaded and concealed weapons on Oklahoma Military Department facilities in accordance with rules promulgated by the Adjutant General;
   4. During participation in or in preparation for a recognized police function of either a municipal, county or state government as functioning police officials;
   5. During a practice for or a performance for entertainment purposes;
   6. For lawful self-defense and self-protection or any other legitimate purpose in or on property that is owned, leased, rented, or otherwise legally controlled by the person; or
   7. For any legitimate purpose not in violation of the Oklahoma Firearms Act of 1971 or any legislative enactment regarding the use, ownership and control of firearms.
B. A person shall be permitted to carry unloaded shotguns, rifles and pistols, open and not concealed and without a handgun license as authorized by the Oklahoma Self-Defense Act pursuant to the following conditions:
   1. When going to or from the person's private residence or vehicle or a vehicle in which the person is riding as a passenger to a place designated or authorized for firearms repairs or reconditioning, or for firearms trade, sale, or barter, or gunsmith, or hunting animals or fowl, or hunter safety course, or target shooting, or skeet or trap shooting or any recognized firearms activity or event and while in such places; or
   2. For any legitimate purpose not in violation of the Oklahoma Firearms Act of 1971.
C. The provisions of this section shall not be construed to prohibit educational or recreational activities, exhibitions, displays or shows involving the use or display of rifles, shotguns or pistols or other weapons if the activity is approved by the property owner and sponsor of the activity.

§ 1289.7. Firearms in Vehicles. Any person, except a convicted felon, may transport in a motor vehicle a rifle, shotgun or pistol, open and unloaded, at any time. For purposes of this section "open" means the firearm is transported in plain view, in a case designed for carrying firearms, which case is wholly or partially visible, in a gun rack mounted in the vehicle, in an exterior locked compartment or a trunk of a vehicle.
Any person, except a convicted felon, may transport in a motor vehicle a rifle or shotgun concealed behind a seat of the vehicle or within the interior of the vehicle provided the rifle or shotgun is not clip, magazine or chamber loaded. The authority to transport a clip or magazine loaded rifle or shotgun shall be pursuant to § 1289.13 of this title.
Any person who is the operator of a vehicle or is a passenger in any vehicle wherein another person who is licensed pursuant to the Oklahoma Self-Defense Act to carry a handgun, concealed or unconcealed, and is carrying a handgun or

has the handgun in such vehicle, shall not be deemed in violation of the provisions of this section provided the licensee is in or near the vehicle.

§ 1289.7a. Liability for Prohibiting Persons from Transporting, Storing Firearms or Ammunition in Locked Vehicle

A. No person, property owner, tenant, employer, or business entity shall maintain, establish, or enforce any policy or rule that has the effect of prohibiting any person, except a convicted felon, from transporting and storing firearms or ammunition in a locked motor vehicle, or from transporting and storing firearms or ammunition locked in or locked to a motor vehicle on any property set aside for any motor vehicle.

B. No person, property owner, tenant, employer, or business entity shall be liable in any civil action for occurrences which result from the storing of firearms or ammunition in a locked motor vehicle on any property set aside for any motor vehicle, unless the person, property owner, tenant, employer, or owner of the business entity commits a criminal act involving the use of the firearms or ammunition. The provisions of this subsection shall not apply to claims pursuant to the Workers' Compensation Act.

C. An individual may bring a civil action to enforce this section. If a plaintiff prevails in a civil action related to the personnel manual against a person, property owner, tenant, employer or business for a violation of this section, the court shall award actual damages, enjoin further violations of this section, and award court costs and attorney fees to the prevailing plaintiff.

D. As used in this section, "motor vehicle" means any automobile, truck, minivan, sports utility vehicle, motorcycle, motor scooter, and any other vehicle required to be registered under the Oklahoma Vehicle License and Registration Act.

§ 1289.8. Carrying weapon [Effective November 1, 2016]

A. Any fire marshal inspector who is retired, state, county or municipal peace officer of this state who is retired, or any state, county or municipal peace officer classified as a reserve who is retired, or any federal law enforcement officer who is retired may retain their status as a peace officer, retired, in the State of Oklahoma, and as such may carry a firearm pursuant to the provisions of subsection B of this section. A retired state, county or municipal peace officer may in times of great emergency or danger serve to enforce the law, keep the peace or to protect the public in keeping with their availability and ability at the request of the Governor, the sheriff or the mayor of their retirement jurisdiction. If a retired fire marshal is activated for duty, the peace officer powers of the retired fire marshal are limited to the duties granted prior to retirement.

B. The Council on Law Enforcement Education and Training (CLEET) shall issue an identification card to eligible retired federal, state, county, and municipal peace officers which authorizes the retired peace officer to carry a firearm anywhere in the State of Oklahoma. The identification card shall bear the full name of the retired officer, the signature of the retired officer, the date of issuance, and such other information as may be deemed appropriate by CLEET. The card shall expire every 10 years and may be denied, suspended or revoked as provided by the rules promulgated by CLEET or upon the discovery of any preclusion prescribed in § 1290.10 or 1290.11 of this title. In order to renew the permit, the Council on Law Enforcement Education and Training shall request, pursuant to § 150.9 of Title 74 of the Oklahoma Statutes, the Oklahoma State Bureau of Investigation to conduct a state and national criminal history records search on each retired peace officer authorized to carry a firearm pursuant to the provisions of this section; and unless a preclusion prescribed in § 1290.10 or 1290.11 of this title is found to exist, no action shall be necessary. A retired peace officer requesting a renewal of his or her permit shall submit to the Council a nonrefundable fee for a national criminal history record with fingerprint analysis, as provided in § 150.9 of Title 74 of the Oklahoma Statutes. When a preclusion is discovered, the Council shall notify the retired peace officer and shall hold a hearing before taking any action to suspend or revoke the authority to carry a firearm.

C. The retired peace officer shall be required to submit the following information to the Council on Law Enforcement Education and Training (CLEET) and any other information requested by CLEET:

   1. A statement from the appropriate law enforcement agency verifying the status of the person as a retired peace officer of that jurisdiction; and

   2. A notarized statement, signed by the retired peace officer, stating that the officer:

      a. has not been convicted of and is currently not subject to any pending criminal prosecution for any preclusion prescribed in § 1290.10 or 1290.11 of this title,

      b. has not been forced into retirement due to any mental disorder, and

      c. has not suffered any injury or any physical or mental impairment which would render the person unsafe to carry a firearm.

D. A retired peace officer, who has made application for the CLEET identification card authorized in subsection B of this section, shall be authorized to carry a firearm as an off-duty peace officer, pursuant to § 1289.23 of this title, until the authority to carry a firearm as a retired officer is finally approved or denied by CLEET.

E. The Council on Law Enforcement Education and Training shall promulgate rules and procedures necessary to implement the provisions of this section.

F. Any peace officer, retired, who carries any firearm in violation of the provisions of this section shall be deemed to be in violation of § 1272 of this title and may be prosecuted as provided by law for a violation of that section.

§ 1289.9. Carrying Weapon Under the Influence of Alcohol.
It shall be unlawful for any person to carry or use shotguns, rifles or pistols in any circumstances while under the influence of beer, intoxicating liquors or any

hallucinogenic, or any unlawful or unprescribed drug, and it shall be unlawful for any person to carry or use shotguns, rifles or pistols when under the influence of any drug prescribed by a licensed physician if the aftereffects of such consumption affect mental, emotional or physical processes to a degree that would result in abnormal behavior. Any person convicted of a violation of the provisions of this section shall be punished as provided in § 1289.15 of this title. Any person convicted of a violation of the provisions of this section after having been issued a handgun license pursuant to the provisions of the Oklahoma Self-Defense Act shall have the license suspended for a term of 6 months and shall be subject to an administrative fine of $50, upon a hearing and determination by the Oklahoma State Bureau of Investigation that the person is in violation of the provisions of this section.

§ 1289.10. Furnishing Firearms to Incompetent Persons. It shall be unlawful for any person to knowingly transmit, transfer, sell, lend or furnish any shotgun, rifle or pistol to any person who is under an adjudication of mental incompetency, or to any person who is mentally deficient or of unsound mind. Any person convicted of a violation of the provisions of this section shall be punished as provided in § 1289.15 of this title.

Any person convicted of a violation of the provisions of this section after having been issued a handgun license pursuant to the provisions of the Oklahoma Self-Defense Act shall have the license suspended for a term of 6 months and shall be subject to an administrative fine of $50, upon a hearing and determination by the Oklahoma State Bureau of Investigation that the person is in violation of the provisions of this section.### § 1289.11. Reckless Conduct. It shall be unlawful for any person to engage in reckless conduct while having in his or her possession any shotgun, rifle or pistol, such actions consisting of creating a situation of unreasonable risk and probability of death or great bodily harm to another, and demonstrating a conscious disregard for the safety of another person. Any person convicted of violating the provisions of this section shall be punished as provided in § 1289.15 of this title.

Any person convicted of a violation of the provisions of this section after having been issued a handgun license pursuant to the Oklahoma Self-Defense Act shall have the license revoked and shall be subject to an administrative fine of $1,000, upon a hearing and determination by the Oklahoma State Bureau of Investigation that the person is in violation of the provisions of this section.

§ 1289.12. Giving Firearms to Convicted Persons. It shall be unlawful for any person within this state to knowingly sell, trade, give, transmit or otherwise cause the transfer of rifles, shotguns or pistols to any convicted felon or an adjudicated delinquent, and it shall be unlawful for any person within this state to knowingly sell, trade, give, transmit or otherwise cause the transfer of any shotgun, rifle or pistol to any individual who is under the influence of alcohol or drugs or is mentally or emotionally unbalanced or disturbed. All persons who engage in selling, trading or otherwise transferring firearms will display this section prominently in full view at or near the point of normal firearms sale, trade or transfer. Any person convicted of violating the provisions of this section shall be punished as provided in § 1289.15 of this title.

Any person convicted of a violation of this section after having been issued a handgun license pursuant to the Oklahoma Self-Defense Act shall have the license suspended for 6 months and shall be liable for an administrative fine of $50, upon a hearing and determination by the Oklahoma State Bureau of Investigation that the person is in violation of the provisions of this section.

§ 1289.13. Transporting a Loaded Firearm. Except as otherwise provided by the provisions of the Oklahoma Self-Defense Act or another provision of law, it shall be unlawful to transport a loaded pistol, rifle or shotgun in a landborne motor vehicle over a public highway or roadway. However, a rifle or shotgun may be transported clip or magazine loaded and not chamber loaded when transported in an exterior locked compartment of the vehicle or trunk of the vehicle or in the interior compartment of the vehicle notwithstanding the provisions of § 1289.7 of this title when the person is in possession of a valid handgun license pursuant to the Oklahoma Self-Defense Act.

Any person convicted of a violation of this section shall be punished as provided in § 1289.15 of this title.

Any person who is the operator of a vehicle or is a passenger in any vehicle wherein another person who is licensed pursuant to the Oklahoma Self-Defense Act to carry a handgun, concealed or unconcealed, and is carrying a handgun or has a handgun or rifle or shotgun in such vehicle shall not be deemed in violation of the provisions of this section provided the licensee is in or near the vehicle.

§ 1289.13A. Improper Transportation of Firearms
A. Notwithstanding the provisions of § 1272 or 1289.13 of this title, any person stopped pursuant to a moving traffic violation who is transporting a loaded pistol in the motor vehicle without a valid handgun license authorized by the Oklahoma Self-Defense Act or valid license from another state, whether the loaded firearm is concealed or unconcealed in the vehicle, shall be issued a traffic citation in the amount of $70, plus court costs for transporting a firearm improperly. In addition to the traffic citation provided in this section, the person may also be arrested for any other violation of law.
B. When the arresting officer determines that a valid handgun license exists, pursuant to the Oklahoma Self-Defense Act or any provision of law from another state, for any person in the stopped vehicle, any firearms permitted to be carried pursuant to that license shall not be confiscated, unless:
   1. The person is arrested for violating another provision of law other than a violation of subsection A of this section; provided, however, if the person is never charged with an offense pursuant to this paragraph or if the charges are dismissed or the person is acquitted, the weapon shall be returned to the person; or
   2. The officer has probable cause to believe the weapon is:
      a. contraband, or

b. a firearm used in the commission of a crime other than a violation of subsection A of this section.
C. Nothing in this section shall be construed to require confiscation of any firearm.

§ 1289.15. Penalty for Firearms Act of 1971. Any person adjudged guilty of violating any provision of § 1289.9, 1289.10, 1289.11, 1289.12 or 1289.13 of this title shall, upon conviction, be punished by a fine of not less than $50 nor more than $500, or imprisonment in the county jail for not less than 10 days nor more than 6 months, or by both such fine and imprisonment.

§ 1289.16. Felony Pointing Firearms. It shall be unlawful for any person to willfully or without lawful cause point a shotgun, rifle or pistol, or any deadly weapon, whether loaded or not, at any person or persons for the purpose of threatening or with the intention of discharging the firearm or with any malice or for any purpose of injuring, either through physical injury or mental or emotional intimidation or for purposes of whimsy, humor or prank, or in anger or otherwise, but not to include the pointing of shotguns, rifles or pistols by law enforcement authorities in the performance of their duties, members of the state military forces in the performance of their duties, members of the federal military reserve and active military components in the performance of their duties, or any federal government law enforcement officer in the performance of any duty, or in the performance of a play on stage, rodeo, television or on film, or in defense of any person, one's home or property. Any person convicted of a violation of the provisions of this section shall be punished as provided in § 1289.17 of this title.

Any person convicted of a violation of the provisions of this section after having been issued a handgun license pursuant to the Oklahoma Self-Defense Act shall have the license revoked and shall be subject to an administrative fine of $1,000, upon a hearing and determination by the Oklahoma State Bureau of Investigation that the person is in violation of the provisions of this section.**§ 1289.17. Penalties for 1289.16.** Any violation of § 1289.16 of this title shall constitute a felony, for which a person convicted thereof shall be sentenced to imprisonment in the State Penitentiary for not less than 1 year nor more than 10 years.

§ 1289.17A. Felony Discharging Firearms. It shall be unlawful for any person to willfully or intentionally discharge any firearm or other deadly weapon at or into any dwelling, or at or into any building used for public or business purposes. Any violation of the provisions of this section shall be a felony punishable by imprisonment in the custody of the Department of Corrections for a term not less than 2 years nor more than 20 years. The provisions of this section shall not apply to any law enforcement officer in the performance of any lawful duty.

§ 1289.18. Definitions–Possession of Sawed-off Shotgun or Sawed-off Rifle–Penalties
A. "Sawed-off shotgun" shall mean any firearm capable of discharging a series of projectiles of any material which may reasonably be expected to be able to cause lethal injury, with a barrel or barrels less than 18 inches in length, and using either gunpowder, gas or any means of rocket propulsion.
B. "Sawed-off rifle" shall mean any rifle having a barrel or barrels of less than 16 inches in length or any weapon made from a rifle (whether by alteration, modification, or otherwise) if such a weapon as modified has an overall length of less than 26 inches in length, including the stock portion.
C. Every person who has in his possession or under his immediate control a sawed-off shotgun or a sawed-off rifle, whether concealed or not, shall upon conviction be guilty of a felony for the possession of such device, and shall be punishable by a fine not to exceed $1,000, or imprisonment in the State Penitentiary for a period not to exceed 2 years, or both such fine and imprisonment.
D. It is a defense to prosecution under this section, if the approved application form that authorized the making or transfer of the particular firearm to the defendant, which indicates the registration of the firearm to said defendant pursuant to the National Firearm's Act, is introduced.

§ 1289.19. Restricted Bullet and Body Armor Defined. As used in §§ 1289.20 through 1289.22 of this title and § 2 of this act:
1. "Restricted bullet" means a round or elongated missile with a core of less than 60% lead and having a fluorocarbon coating, which is designed to travel at a high velocity and is capable of penetrating body armor....

§ 1289.20. Manufacture of Restricted Bullets
A. Except for the purpose of public safety or national security, it shall be unlawful to manufacture, cause to be manufactured, import, advertise for sale or sell within this state any restricted bullet as defined in § 1289.19 of this title.
B. Any person convicted of violating subsection A of this section shall be guilty of a felony and shall be punished by a fine of not less than $500 nor more than $10,000, or by imprisonment in the State Penitentiary for not more than 10 years, or by both such fine and imprisonment.

§ 1289.21. Possession or Use of Restricted Bullets
A. It shall be unlawful for any person to possess, carry upon his person, use or attempt to use against another person any restricted bullet as defined in § 1289.19 of this title.
B. Any person convicted of violating subsection A of this section shall be guilty of a felony and shall be punished by imprisonment in the State Penitentiary for not less than 2 years nor more than 10 years. The sentence so imposed shall not be suspended.

§ 1289.22. Exemptions. The prohibition of possessing or using a restricted bullet shall not apply to law enforcement agencies when such bullet is used for testing, training or demonstration.

§ 1289.23. Concealed Firearm for Off-Duty Police Officer
A. Notwithstanding any provision of law to the contrary, a full-time duly appointed peace officer who is certified by the Council on Law Enforcement Education and Training (CLEET), pursuant to the provisions of § 3311 of Title 70 of the Oklahoma Statutes, is hereby authorized to carry a weapon approved by the employing agency anywhere in the state of Oklahoma, both while on active duty and during periods when the officer is not on active duty as provided by the provisions of subsection B of this section.
B. When a full-time duly appointed officer carries an approved weapon, the officer shall be wearing the law enforcement uniform prescribed by the employing agency or plainclothes. When not wearing the prescribed law enforcement uniform, the officer shall be required:
  1. To have the official peace officers badge, Commission Card and CLEET Certification Card on his or her person at all times when carrying a weapon approved by the employing agency; and
  2. To keep the approved weapon concealed or unconcealed at all times, except when the weapon is used within the guidelines established by the employing agency.
C. Nothing in this section shall be construed to alter or amend the provisions of § 1272.1 of this title or expand the duties, authority or jurisdiction of any peace officer.
D. A reserve peace officer who has satisfactorily completed a basic police course of not less than 120 hours of accredited instruction for reserve police officers and reserve deputies from the Council on Law Enforcement Education and Training or a course of study approved by CLEET may carry an approved weapon when such officer is off duty as provided by subsection E of this section, provided:
  1. The officer has been granted written authorization signed by the director of the employing agency; and
  2. The employing agency shall maintain a current list of any officers authorized to carry an approved weapon while the officers are off duty, and shall provide a copy of such list to the Council on Law Enforcement Education and Training. Any change to the list shall be made in writing and mailed to the Council on Law Enforcement Education and Training within 5 days.
E. When an off-duty reserve peace officer carries an approved weapon, the officer shall be wearing the law enforcement uniform prescribed by the employing agency or when not wearing the prescribed law enforcement uniform, the officer shall be required:
  1. To have his or her official peace officer's badge, Commission Card, CLEET Certification Card; and
  2. To keep the approved weapon concealed or unconcealed at all times, except when the weapon is used within the guidelines established by the employing agency.
F. Nothing in subsection D of this section shall be construed to alter or amend the provisions of § 1750.2 of Title 59 of the Oklahoma Statutes or expand the duties, jurisdiction or authority of any reserve peace officer.
G. Nothing in this section shall be construed to limit or restrict any peace officer or reserve peace officer from carrying a handgun, concealed or unconcealed, as allowed by the Oklahoma Self-Defense Act after issuance of a valid license. An off-duty, full-time peace officer or reserve peace officer shall be deemed to have elected to carry a handgun under the authority of the Oklahoma Self-Defense Act when the officer:
  1. Has been issued a valid handgun license and is carrying a handgun not authorized by the employing agency; or
  2. Is carrying a handgun in a manner or in a place not specifically authorized for off-duty carry by the employing agency.
H. Any off-duty peace officer who carries any weapon in violation of the provisions of this section shall be deemed to be in violation of § 1272 of this title and may be prosecuted as provided by law for a violation of that section.
I. On or after November 1, 2004, a reserve or full-time commissioned peace officer may apply to carry a weapon pursuant to the Oklahoma Self-Defense Act as follows:
  1. The officer shall apply in writing to the Council on Law Enforcement Education and Training (CLEET) stating that the officer desires to have a handgun license pursuant to the Oklahoma Self-Defense Act and certifying that he or she has no preclusions to having such handgun license. The officer shall submit with the application:
    a. an official letter from his or her employing agency confirming the officer's employment and status as a full-time commissioned peace officer or an active reserve peace officer,
    b. a fee of $25 for the handgun license, and
    c. two passport-size photographs of the peace officer applicant;
  2. Upon receiving the required information, CLEET shall determine whether the peace officer is in good standing, has CLEET certification and training, and is otherwise eligible for a handgun license. Upon verification of the officer's eligibility, CLEET shall send the information to the Oklahoma State Bureau of Investigation (OSBI) and OSBI shall issue a handgun license in the same or similar form as other handgun licenses. All other requirements in § 1290.12 of this title concerning application for a handgun license shall be waived for active duty peace officers except as provided in this subsection including, but not limited to, training, fingerprints and criminal history records checks unless the officer does not have fingerprints on file or a criminal history records background check conducted prior to employment as a peace officer. The OSBI shall not be required to conduct any further investigation into the eligibility of the peace officer applicant and shall not deny a handgun license except when preclusions are found to exist;
  3. The term of the handgun license for an active duty reserve or full-time commissioned peace officer pursuant to this section shall be as provided in § 1290.5 of this title, renewable in the same manner provided in this subsection for an

original application by a peace officer. The handgun license shall be valid when the peace officer is in possession of a valid driver license and law enforcement commission card;

4. If the commission card of a law enforcement officer is terminated, revoked or suspended, the handgun license shall be immediately returned to CLEET. When a peace officer in possession of a handgun license pursuant to this subsection changes employment, the person must notify CLEET within 90 days and send a new letter verifying employment and status as a full-time commissioned or reserve peace officer;

5. There shall be no refund of any fee for any unexpired term of any handgun license that is suspended, revoked or voluntarily returned to CLEET, or that is denied, suspended or revoked by the OSBI;

6. CLEET may promulgate any rules, forms or procedures necessary to implement the provisions of this section; and

7. Nothing in this subsection shall be construed to change or amend the application process, eligibility, effective date or fees of any handgun license pending issuance on November 1, 2004, or previously issued to any peace officer prior to November 1, 2004.§ 1289.24. Firearm Regulation–State Preemption

A. 1. The State Legislature hereby occupies and preempts the entire field of legislation in this state touching in any way firearms, knives, components, ammunition, and supplies to the complete exclusion of any order, ordinance, or regulation by any municipality or other political subdivision of this state. Any existing or future orders, ordinances, or regulations in this field, except as provided for in paragraph 2 of this subsection and subsection C of this section, are null and void.

2. A municipality may adopt any ordinance:

a. relating to the discharge of firearms within the jurisdiction of the municipality, and

b. allowing the municipality to issue a traffic citation for transporting a firearm improperly as provided for in § 1289.13A of this title, provided however, that penalties contained for violation of any ordinance enacted pursuant to the provisions of this subparagraph shall not exceed the penalties established in the Oklahoma Self-Defense Act.

3. As provided in the preemption provisions of this section, the otherwise lawful open carrying of a handgun under the provisions of the Oklahoma Self-Defense Act shall not be punishable by any municipality or other political subdivision of this state as disorderly conduct, disturbing the peace or similar offense against public order.

B. No municipality or other political subdivision of this state shall adopt any order, ordinance, or regulation concerning in any way the sale, purchase, purchase delay, transfer, ownership, use, keeping, possession, carrying, bearing, transportation, licensing, permit, registration, taxation other than sales and compensating use taxes, or other controls on firearms, knives, components, ammunition, and supplies.

C. Except as hereinafter provided, this section shall not prohibit any order, ordinance, or regulation by any municipality concerning the confiscation of property used in violation of the ordinances of the municipality as provided for in § 28-121 of Title 11 of the Oklahoma Statutes. Provided, however, no municipal ordinance relating to transporting a firearm or knife improperly may include a provision for confiscation of property.

D. When a person's rights pursuant to the protection of the preemption provisions of this section have been violated, the person shall have the right to bring a civil action against the persons, municipality, and political subdivision jointly and severally for injunctive relief or monetary damages or both.

§ 1289.24a. Lawsuits Against Gun Manufacturers

2. The authority to bring suit and right to recover against any firearms or ammunition manufacturer, trade association, or dealer by or on behalf of any governmental unit created by or pursuant to an act of the Legislature or the Constitution, or any department, agency, or authority thereof, for damages, abatement, or injunctive relief resulting from or relating to the lawful design, manufacturing, marketing, or sale of firearms or ammunition to the public shall be reserved exclusively to the state. This paragraph shall not prohibit a political subdivision or local government authority from bringing an action against a firearms or ammunition manufacturer or dealer for breach of contract or warranty as to firearms or ammunition purchased by the political subdivision or local government authority. This bill shall not be construed to prohibit an individual from bringing a cause of action based upon an existing recognized theory of law.

§ 1289.25. Physical or Deadly Force Against Intruder

A. The Legislature hereby recognizes that the citizens of the State of Oklahoma have a right to expect absolute safety within their own homes or places of business.

B. A person or an owner, manager or employee of a business is presumed to have held a reasonable fear of imminent peril of death or great bodily harm to himself or herself or another when using defensive force that is intended or likely to cause death or great bodily harm to another if:

1. The person against whom the defensive force was used was in the process of unlawfully and forcefully entering, or had unlawfully and forcibly entered, a dwelling, residence, occupied vehicle, or a place of business, or if that person had removed or was attempting to remove another against the will of that person from the dwelling, residence, occupied vehicle, or place of business; and

2. The person who uses defensive force knew or had reason to believe that an unlawful and forcible entry or unlawful and forcible act was occurring or had occurred.

C. The presumption set forth in subsection B of this section does not apply if:

1. The person against whom the defensive force is used has the right to be in or is a lawful resident of the dwelling, residence, or vehicle, such as an owner, lessee, or titleholder, and there is not a protective order from domestic violence in effect or a written pretrial supervision order of no contact against that person;

2. The person or persons sought to be removed are children or grandchildren, or are otherwise in the lawful custody or under the lawful guardianship of, the person against whom the defensive force is used; or

3. The person who uses defensive force is engaged in an unlawful activity or is using the dwelling, residence, occupied vehicle, or place of business to further an unlawful activity.

D. A person who is not engaged in an unlawful activity and who is attacked in any other place where he or she has a right to be has no duty to retreat and has the right to stand his or her ground and meet force with force, including deadly force, if he or she reasonably believes it is necessary to do so to prevent death or great bodily harm to himself or herself or another or to prevent the commission of a forcible felony.

E. A person who unlawfully and by force enters or attempts to enter the dwelling, residence, occupied vehicle of another person, or a place of business is presumed to be doing so with the intent to commit an unlawful act involving force or violence.

F. A person who uses force, as permitted pursuant to the provisions of subsections B and D of this section, is justified in using such force and is immune from criminal prosecution and civil action for the use of such force. As used in this subsection, the term "criminal prosecution" includes charging or prosecuting the defendant.

G. A law enforcement agency may use standard procedures for investigating the use of force, but the law enforcement agency may not arrest the person for using force unless it determines that there is probable cause that the force that was used was unlawful.

H. The court shall award reasonable attorney fees, court costs, compensation for loss of income, and all expenses incurred by the defendant in defense of any civil action brought by a plaintiff if the court finds that the defendant is immune from prosecution as provided in subsection F of this section.

I. The provisions of this section and the provisions of the Oklahoma Self-Defense Act shall not be construed to require any person using a pistol pursuant to the provisions of this section to be licensed in any manner.

J. As used in this section:

1. "Dwelling" means a building or conveyance of any kind, including any attached porch, whether the building or conveyance is temporary or permanent, mobile or immobile, which has a roof over it, including a tent, and is designed to be occupied by people;

2. "Residence" means a dwelling in which a person resides either temporarily or permanently or is visiting as an invited guest; and

3. "Vehicle" means a conveyance of any kind, whether or not motorized, which is designed to transport people or property.

§ 1289.27. Prohibiting Firearm Inquiry by Employer

A. It shall be unlawful for any private employer doing business in this state to ask any applicant for employment information about whether the applicant owns or possesses a firearm. Any private employer who violates the provisions of this section shall, upon conviction, be guilty of a misdemeanor punishable by a fine of not more than $1,000.

B. All public employers and public officials within this state shall be prohibited from asking any applicant for employment information about whether the applicant owns or possesses a firearm. Any public employer or public official who violates the provisions of this subsection shall be deemed to be acting outside the scope of their employment and shall be barred from seeking statutory immunity from any exemption or provision of The Governmental Tort Claims Act.

C. As used in this section:

1. "Private employer" means any individual, partnership, firm, association, corporation or nonprofit organization that employs or offers to employ one or more persons in this state;

2. "Public employer" means the State of Oklahoma or any political subdivision thereof, including any department, agency, board, commission, institution, authority, public trust, municipality, county, district or instrumentalities thereof; and

3. "Public official" means any elected or appointed official in the executive, legislative or judicial branch of a political subdivision of the state.

§ 1289.28. Unlawful Actions Related to Licensed Dealers and Private Sellers of Firearms–Penalty

A. For purposes of this section:

1. "Licensed dealer" means a person who is licensed pursuant to 18 U.S.C., § 923 and pursuant to any laws of this state and engages in the business of dealing in firearms;

2. "Private seller" means a person who sells or offers for sale any firearm, as defined by the laws of this state, or ammunition;

3. "Ammunition" means any cartridge, shell, or projectile designed for use in a firearm; and

4. "Materially false information" means information that portrays an illegal transaction as legal or a legal transaction as illegal.

B. Any person, who knowingly solicits, persuades, encourages or entices a licensed dealer or private seller of firearms or ammunition to transfer a firearm or ammunition under circumstances which the person knows would violate the laws of this state or the United States is guilty of a felony.

C. Any person who provides to a licensed dealer or private seller of firearms or ammunition what the person knows to be materially false information with intent to deceive the dealer or seller about the legality of a transfer of a firearm or ammunition is guilty of a felony.

D. Any person who willfully procures another to engage in conduct prohibited by this section shall be held accountable as a principal.

E. This section does not apply to a law enforcement officer acting in his or her official capacity or to a person acting at the direction of such law enforcement officer.

F. A violation of this section is punishable by a fine not to exceed $5,000, a term of imprisonment in the custody of the Department of Corrections not to exceed 5 years, or by both fine and imprisonment.

§ 1289.29. US Attorney or Assistant US Attorney–Carrying Firearms. Any United States Attorney or Assistant United States Attorney may carry a firearm on his or her person anywhere in the State of Oklahoma if the person has successfully completed a handgun qualification course for court officials developed by the Council on Law Enforcement Education and Training. The Council on Law Enforcement Education and Training may provide for an identification card to be issued to the United States Attorney or Assistant United States Attorney and may provide application forms. If the person issued an identification card is no longer eligible, that person shall immediately return the identification card to the Council on Law Enforcement Education and Training.

§ 1289.30. Certification of Transfer or Making of Firearm–Appeal

A. When certification by a chief law enforcement officer is required by federal law or regulation for the transfer or making of a firearm, the chief law enforcement officer shall, within 15 days of receipt of a request for certification, provide such certification if the applicant is not prohibited by law from receiving the firearm or the applicant is not the subject of a proceeding that could result in the applicant being prohibited by law from receiving the firearm. If the applicant is prohibited by law from receiving the firearm or the applicant is the subject of a proceeding that could result in such prohibition, the chief law enforcement officer shall provide written notification to the applicant that certification has been denied and state the reasons for such findings.

B. An applicant whose request for certification is denied may appeal the decision of the chief law enforcement officer to the district court that is located in the county in which the applicant resides. The court shall review the decision of the chief law enforcement officer to deny the certification de novo. If the court finds that the applicant is not prohibited by law from receiving the firearm or the applicant is not the subject of a proceeding that could result in such prohibition, the court shall order the chief law enforcement officer to issue the certification and shall award court costs and reasonable attorney fees to the applicant.

C. For purposes of this section:

1. "Certification" means the participation and assent of the chief law enforcement officer necessary under federal law for the approval of the application to transfer or make a firearm;

2. "Chief law enforcement officer" means any official that the Bureau of Alcohol, Tobacco, Firearms and Explosives, or any successor agency, identifies by regulation or otherwise as eligible to provide any required certification for applications to transfer or make a firearm; and

3. "Firearm" shall have the same meaning as provided for in the National Firearms Act, subsection a. of § 5845 of Title 26 of the United States Code.

Oklahoma Self-Defense Act

§ 1290.2. Definitions

A. As used in the Oklahoma Self-Defense Act:

1. "Concealed handgun" means a loaded or unloaded pistol, the presence of which is not openly discernible to the ordinary observation of a reasonable person;

2. "Unconcealed handgun" means a loaded or unloaded pistol carried upon the person in a belt holster or shoulder holster that is wholly or partially visible, or carried upon the person in a scabbard or case designed for carrying firearms that is wholly or partially visible; and

3. "Pistol" means any derringer, revolver or semiautomatic firearm which:

    a. has an overall length of less than 16 inches,

    b. is capable of discharging a projectile composed of any material which may reasonably be expected to be able to cause lethal injury,

    c. is designed to be held and fired by the use of a single hand, and

    d. uses either gunpowder, gas or any means of rocket propulsion to discharge the projectile.

B. The definition of pistol for purposes of the Oklahoma Self-Defense Act shall not apply to homemade or imitation pistols, flare guns, underwater fishing guns or blank pistols.

§ 1290.3. Authority to Issue License. The Oklahoma State Bureau of Investigation is hereby authorized to license an eligible person to carry a concealed or unconcealed handgun as provided by the provisions of the Oklahoma Self-Defense Act. The authority of the Bureau shall be limited to the provisions specifically provided in the Oklahoma Self-Defense Act. The Bureau shall promulgate rules, forms and procedures necessary to implement the provisions of the Oklahoma Self-Defense Act.

§ 1290.4. Unlawful Carry. As provided by § 1272 of this title, it is unlawful for any person to carry a concealed or unconcealed handgun in this state, except as hereby authorized by the provisions of the Oklahoma Self-Defense Act or as may otherwise be provided by law.

§ 1290.5. Term of License and Renewal

A. A handgun license when issued shall authorize the person to whom the license is issued to carry a loaded or unloaded handgun, concealed or unconcealed, as authorized by the provisions of the Oklahoma Self-Defense Act, and any future modifications thereto. The license shall be valid in this state for a period of 5 or 10 years, unless subsequently surrendered, suspended or revoked as provided by law. The person shall have no authority to continue to carry a concealed or unconcealed handgun in this state pursuant to the Oklahoma Self-Defense Act when a license is expired or when a license has been voluntarily surrendered or suspended or revoked for any reason.

B. A license may be renewed any time within 90 days prior to the expiration date as provided in this subsection. The Bureau shall send a renewal application to each eligible licensee with a return address requested. There shall be a 90-day grace period on license renewals beginning on the date of expiration, thereafter the license is considered expired. However, any applicant shall have 3 years from the expiration of the license to comply with the renewal requirements of this section.

    1. To renew a handgun license, the licensee must first obtain a renewal form from the Oklahoma State Bureau of Investigation.

    2. The applicant must complete the renewal form, attach 2 current passport size photographs of the applicant, and submit a renewal fee in the amount of $85 to the Bureau. The renewal fee may be paid with a nationally recognized credit card as provided in subparagraph b of paragraph 4 of subsection A of § 1290.12 of this title, by electronic funds transfer, or by a cashier's check or money order made payable to the Oklahoma State Bureau of Investigation.

    3. Upon receipt of the renewal application, photographs and fee, the Bureau will conduct a criminal history records name search, an investigation of medical records or other records or information deemed by the Bureau to be relevant to the renewal application. If the applicant appears not to have any prohibition to renewing the handgun license, the Bureau shall issue the renewed license for a period of 5 or 10 years.

C. Any person making application for a handgun license or any licensee seeking to renew a handgun license shall have the option to request that said license be valid for a period of 10 years. The fee for any handgun license issued for a period of 10 years shall be double the amount of the fee provided for in paragraph 4 of subsection A of § 1290.12 of this title. The renewal fee for a handgun license issued for a period of 10 years shall be double the amount of the fee provided for in paragraph 2 of subsection B of this section.

§ 1290.6. Prohibited Ammunition.
Any concealed or unconcealed handgun when carried in a manner authorized by the provisions of the Oklahoma Self-Defense Act and when loaded with any ammunition which is either a restricted bullet as defined by § 1289.19 of this title or is larger than .45 caliber or is otherwise prohibited by law shall be deemed a prohibited weapon for purposes of the Oklahoma Self-Defense Act. Any person violating the provisions of this section shall be punished for a criminal offense as provided by § 1272 of this title or any other applicable provision of law. In addition to any criminal prosecution for a violation of the provisions of this section, the licensee shall be subject to an administrative fine of $500, upon a hearing and determination by the Oklahoma State Bureau of Investigation that the person is in violation of the provisions of this section.

§ 1290.7. Construing Authority of License.
The authority to carry a concealed or unconcealed handgun pursuant to a valid handgun license as authorized by the provisions of the Oklahoma Self-Defense Act shall not be construed to authorize any person to:

1. Carry or possess any weapon other than an authorized pistol as defined by the provisions of § 1290.2 of this title;

2. Carry or possess any pistol in any manner or in any place otherwise prohibited by law;

3. Carry or possess any prohibited ammunition or any illegal, imitation or homemade pistol;

4. Carry or possess any pistol when the person is prohibited by state or federal law from carrying or possessing any firearm; or

5. Point, discharge or use the pistol in any manner not otherwise authorized by law.

§ 1290.8. Possession of License Required–Notification to Police of Gun

A. Except as otherwise prohibited by law, an eligible person shall have authority to carry a concealed or unconcealed handgun in this state when the person has been issued a handgun license from the Oklahoma State Bureau of Investigation pursuant to the provisions of the Oklahoma Self-Defense Act, provided the person is in compliance with the provisions of the Oklahoma Self-Defense Act, and the license has not expired or been subsequently suspended or revoked. A person in possession of a valid handgun license and in compliance with the provisions of the Oklahoma Self-Defense Act shall be authorized to carry such concealed or unconcealed handgun while bow hunting or fishing.

B. The person shall be required to have possession of his or her valid handgun license and a valid Oklahoma driver license or an Oklahoma State photo identification at all times when in possession of an authorized pistol. The person shall display the handgun license on demand of a law enforcement officer; provided, however, that in the absence of reasonable and articulable suspicion of other criminal activity, an individual carrying an unconcealed or concealed handgun shall not be disarmed or physically restrained unless the individual fails to display a valid handgun license in response to that demand. Any violation of the provisions of this subsection may be punishable as a criminal offense as authorized by § 1272 of this title or pursuant to any other applicable provision of law. Any second or subsequent violation of the provisions of this subsection shall be grounds for the Bureau to suspend the handgun license for a period of 6 months, in addition to any other penalty imposed.

    Upon the arrest of any person for a violation of the provisions of this subsection, the person may show proof to the court that a valid handgun license and the other required identification has been issued to such person and the person may state any reason why the handgun license or the other required identification was not carried by the person as required by the Oklahoma Self-Defense Act. The court shall dismiss an alleged violation of § 1272 of this title upon payment of court costs, if proof of a valid handgun license and other required identification is shown to the court within 10 days of the arrest of the person. The court shall report a dismissal of a charge to the Bureau for consideration of administrative proceedings against the licensee.

C. It shall be unlawful for any person to fail or refuse to identify the fact that the person is in actual possession of a concealed or unconcealed handgun pursuant to the authority of the Oklahoma Self-Defense Act when the person comes into contact with any law enforcement officer of this state or its political subdivisions or a federal law enforcement officer during the course of any arrest, detainment, or routine traffic stop. Said identification to the law enforcement officer shall be made at the first opportunity. No person shall be required to identify himself or herself as a handgun licensee when no handgun is in the possession of the person or in any vehicle in which the person is driving or is a passenger. Any violation of the provisions of this subsection shall, upon conviction, be a misdemeanor punishable by a fine not exceeding $100.

D. Any law enforcement officer coming in contact with a person whose handgun license is suspended, revoked, or expired, or who is in possession of a handgun license which has not been lawfully issued to that person, shall confiscate the license and return it to the Oklahoma State Bureau of Investigation for appropriate administrative proceedings against the licensee when the license is no longer needed as evidence in any criminal proceeding.

E. Nothing in this section shall be construed to authorize a law enforcement officer to inspect any weapon properly concealed or unconcealed without probable cause that a crime has been committed.

§ 1290.9. Eligibility.
The following requirements shall apply to any person making application to the Oklahoma State Bureau of Investigation for a handgun license pursuant to the provisions of the Oklahoma Self-Defense Act. The person must:

1. Be a citizen of the United States;

2. Establish a residency in the State of Oklahoma. For purposes of the Oklahoma Self-Defense Act, the term "residency" shall apply to any person who either possesses a valid Oklahoma driver license or state photo identification card, and physically maintains a residence in this state or to any person, including the spouse of such person, who has permanent military orders within this state and possesses a valid driver license from another state where such person and spouse of such person claim residency;

3. Be at least 21 years of age;

4. Complete a firearms safety and training course and demonstrate competence and qualifications with the type of pistol to be carried by the person as provided in § 1290.14 of this title, and submit proof of training and qualification or an exemption for training and qualification as authorized by § 1290.14 of this title;

5. Submit the required fee and complete the application process as provided in § 1290.12 of this title; and

6. Comply in good faith with the provisions of the Oklahoma Self-Defense Act.

§ 1290.10. Mandatory Preclusions.
In addition to the requirements stated in § 1290.9 of this title, the conditions stated in this section shall preclude a person from eligibility for a handgun license pursuant to the provisions of the Oklahoma Self-Defense Act. The occurrence of any one of the following conditions shall deny the person the right to have a handgun license pursuant to the provisions of the Oklahoma Self-Defense Act. Prohibited conditions are:

1. Ineligible to possess a pistol due to any felony conviction or adjudication as a delinquent as provided by § 1283 of this title, except as provided in subsection B of § 1283 of this title;

2. Any felony conviction pursuant to any law of another state, a felony conviction pursuant to any provision of the United States Code, or any conviction pursuant to the laws of any foreign country, provided such foreign conviction would constitute a felony offense in this state if the offense had been committed in this state, except as provided in subsection B of § 1283 of this title;

3. Adjudication as a mentally incompetent person pursuant to the provisions of the Oklahoma Mental Health Law, or an adjudication of incompetency entered in another state pursuant to any provision of law of that state, unless the person has been granted relief from the disqualifying disability pursuant to § 1290.27 of this title;

4. Any false or misleading statement on the application for a handgun license as provided by paragraph 5 of subsection A of § 1290.12 of this title;

5. Conviction of any one of the following misdemeanor offenses in this state or in any other state:

  a. any assault and battery which caused serious physical injury to the victim, or any second or subsequent assault and battery conviction,

  b. any aggravated assault and battery,

  c. any stalking pursuant to § 1173 of this title, or a similar law of another state,

  d. a violation relating to the Protection from Domestic Abuse Act or any violation of a victim protection order of another state,

  e. any conviction relating to illegal drug use or possession, or

  f. an act of domestic abuse as defined by § 644 of this title or an act of domestic assault and battery or any comparable acts under the laws of another state.

The preclusive period for a misdemeanor conviction related to illegal drug use or possession shall be 10 years from the date of completion of a sentence. For purposes of this subsection, "date of completion of a sentence" shall mean the day an offender completes all incarceration, probation, and parole pertaining to such sentence;

6. An attempted suicide or other condition relating to or indicating mental instability or an unsound mind which occurred within the preceding 10-year period from the date of the application for a license to carry a concealed firearm or that occurs during the period of licensure;

7. Currently undergoing treatment for a mental illness, condition, or disorder. For purposes of this paragraph, "currently undergoing treatment for a mental illness, condition, or disorder" means the person has been diagnosed by a licensed physician as being afflicted with a substantial disorder of thought, mood, perception, psychological orientation, or memory that significantly impairs judgment, behavior, capacity to recognize reality, or ability to meet the ordinary demands of life;

8. Significant character defects of the applicant as evidenced by a misdemeanor criminal record indicating habitual criminal activity;

9. Ineligible to possess a pistol due to any provision of law of this state or the United States Code, except as provided in subsection B of § 1283 of this title;

10. Failure to pay an assessed fine or surrender the handgun license as required by a decision by the administrative hearing examiner pursuant to authority of the Oklahoma Self-Defense Act;

11. Being subject to an outstanding felony warrant issued in this state or another state or the United States; or

12. Adjudication as a delinquent as provided by § 1283 of this title, except as provided in subsection B of § 1283 of this title.

§ 1290.11. Other Preclusions

A. The following conditions shall preclude a person from being eligible for a handgun license pursuant to the provisions of the Oklahoma Self-Defense Act for a period of time as prescribed in each of the following paragraphs:

1. An arrest for an alleged commission of a felony offense or a felony charge pending in this state, another state or pursuant to the United States Code. The preclusive period shall be until the final determination of the matter;

2. The person is subject to the provisions of a deferred sentence or deferred prosecution in this state or another state or pursuant to federal authority for the commission of a felony offense. The preclusive period shall be 3 years and shall begin upon the final determination of the matter;

3. Any involuntary commitment for a mental illness, condition, or disorder pursuant to the provisions of § 5-410 of Title 43A of the Oklahoma Statutes or any involuntary commitment in another state pursuant to any provisions of law of that state. The preclusive period shall be permanent as provided by Title 18 of the United States Code § 922(g)(4) unless the person has been granted relief from the disqualifying disability pursuant to § 3 of this act;

4. The person has previously undergone treatment for a mental illness, condition, or disorder which required medication or supervision as defined by paragraph 7 of § 1290.10 of this title. The preclusive period shall be 3 years from the last date of treatment or upon presentation of a certified statement from a licensed physician stating that the person is either no longer disabled by any mental or psychiatric illness, condition, or disorder or that the person has been stabilized on medication for 10 years or more;

5. Inpatient treatment for substance abuse. The preclusive period shall be 3 years from the last date of treatment or upon presentation of a certified statement from a licensed physician stating that the person has been free from substance use for 12 months or more preceding the filing of an application for a handgun license;

6. Two or more convictions of public intoxication pursuant to § 8 of Title 37 of the Oklahoma Statutes, or a similar law of another state. The preclusive period shall be 3 years from the date of the completion of the last sentence;

7. Two or more misdemeanor convictions relating to intoxication or driving under the influence of an intoxicating substance or alcohol. The preclusive period shall be 3 years from the date of the completion of the last sentence or shall require a certified statement from a licensed physician stating that the person is not in need of substance abuse treatment;

8. A court order for a final Victim Protection Order against the applicant, as authorized by the Protection from Domestic Abuse Act, or any court order granting a final victim protection order against the applicant from another state. The preclusive period shall be 3 years from the date of the entry of the final court order, or 60 days from the date an order was vacated, canceled or withdrawn;

9. An adjudicated delinquent or convicted felon residing in the residence of the applicant which may be a violation of § 1283 of this title. The preclusive period shall be 30 days from the date the person no longer resides in the same residence as the applicant; or

10. An arrest for an alleged commission of, a charge pending for, or the person is subject to the provisions of a deferred prosecution for any one or more of the following misdemeanor offenses in this state or another state:

    a. any assault and battery which caused serious physical injury to the victim or any second or subsequent assault and battery,

    b. any aggravated assault and battery,

    c. any stalking pursuant to § 1173 of this title, or a similar law of another state,

    d. any violation of the Protection from Domestic Abuse Act or any violation of a victim protection order of another state,

    e. any violation relating to illegal drug use or possession, or

    f. an act of domestic abuse as defined by § 644 of this title or an act of domestic assault and battery or any comparable acts under the law of another state.

The preclusive period shall be until the final determination of the matter. The preclusive period for a person subject to the provisions of a deferred sentence for the offenses mentioned in this paragraph shall be 3 years and shall begin upon the final determination of the matter.

B. Nothing in this section shall be construed to require a full investigation of the applicant by the Oklahoma State Bureau of Investigation.

§ 1290.12. Procedure for Application [Effective November 1, 2016]

A. Except as provided in paragraph 11 of this subsection, the procedure for applying for a handgun license and processing the application shall be as follows:

1. An eligible person may request an application packet for a handgun license from the Oklahoma State Bureau of Investigation or the county sheriff's office either in person or by mail. The Bureau may provide application packets to each sheriff not exceeding 200 packets per request. The Bureau shall provide the following information in the application packet:

a. an application form,

b. procedures to follow to process the application form, and

c. a copy of the Oklahoma Self-Defense Act with any modifications thereto;

2. The person shall be required to successfully complete a firearms safety and training course from a firearms instructor who is approved and registered in this state as provided in § 1290.14 of this title or from an interactive online firearms safety and training course available electronically via the Internet which has been approved as to curriculum by the Council on Law Enforcement Education and Training, and the person shall be required to demonstrate competency and qualification with a pistol authorized for concealed or unconcealed carry by the Oklahoma Self-Defense Act. The original certificate of successful completion of a firearms safety and training course and an original certificate of successful demonstration of competency and qualification to carry and handle a pistol shall be submitted with the application for a handgun license. No duplicate, copy, facsimile or other reproduction of the certificate of training, certificate of competency and qualification or exemption from training shall be acceptable as proof of training as required by the provisions of the Oklahoma Self-Defense Act. A person exempt from the training requirements as provided in § 1290.15 of this title must show the required proof of such exemption to the firearms instructor to receive an exemption certificate. The original exemption certificate must be submitted with the application for a handgun license when the person claims an exemption from training and qualification;

3. The application form shall be completed and delivered by the applicant, in person, to the sheriff of the county wherein the applicant resides;

4. The person shall deliver to the sheriff at the time of delivery of the completed application form a fee of $100 for processing the application through the Oklahoma State Bureau of Investigation and processing the required fingerprints through the Federal Bureau of Investigation. The processing fee shall be in the form of:

a. a money order or a cashier's check made payable to the Oklahoma State Bureau of Investigation,

b. a nationally recognized credit card issued to the applicant. For purposes of this paragraph, "nationally recognized credit card" means any instrument or device, whether known as a credit card, credit plate, charge plate, or by any other name, issued with or without fee by the issuer for the use of the cardholder in obtaining goods, services, or anything else of value on credit which is accepted by over one thousand merchants in the state. The Oklahoma State Bureau of Investigation shall determine which nationally recognized credit cards will be accepted by the Bureau, or

c. electronic funds transfer.

Any person paying application fees to the Oklahoma State Bureau of Investigation by means of a nationally recognized credit card or by means of an electronic funds transfer shall be required to complete and submit his or her application through the online application process of the Bureau.

The processing fee shall not be refundable in the event of a denial of a handgun license or any suspension or revocation subsequent to the issuance of a license. Persons making application for a firearms instructor shall not be required to pay the application fee as provided in this section, but shall be required to pay the costs provided in paragraphs 6 and 8 of this subsection;

5. The completed application form shall be signed by the applicant in person before the sheriff. The signature shall be given voluntarily upon a sworn oath that the person knows the contents of the application and that the information contained in the application is true and correct. Any person making any false or misleading statement on an application for a handgun license shall, upon conviction, be guilty of perjury as defined by § 491 of this title. Any conviction shall be punished as provided in § 500 of this title. In addition to a criminal conviction, the person shall be denied the right to have a handgun license pursuant to the provisions of § 1290.10 of this title and the Oklahoma State Bureau of Investigation shall revoke the handgun license, if issued;

6. Two passport size photographs of the applicant shall be submitted with the completed application. The cost of the photographs shall be the responsibility of the applicant. The sheriff is authorized to take the photograph of the applicant for purposes of the Oklahoma Self-Defense Act and, if such photographs are taken by the sheriff the cost of the photographs shall not exceed $10 for the 2 photos. All money received by the sheriff from photographing applicants pursuant to the provisions of this paragraph shall be retained by the sheriff and deposited into the Sheriff's Service Fee Account;

7. The sheriff shall witness the signature of the applicant and review or take the photographs of the applicant and shall verify that the person making application for a handgun license is the same person in the photographs submitted and the same person who signed the application form. Proof of a valid Oklahoma driver license with a photograph of the applicant or an Oklahoma State photo identification for the applicant shall be required to be presented by the applicant to the sheriff for verification of the person's identity;

8. Upon verification of the identity of the applicant, the sheriff shall take 2 complete sets of fingerprints of the applicant. Both sets of fingerprints shall be submitted by the sheriff with the completed application, certificate of training or an exemption certificate, photographs and processing fee to the Oklahoma State Bureau of Investigation within 14 days of taking the fingerprints. The cost of the fingerprints shall be paid by the applicant and shall not exceed $25 for the 2 sets. All fees collected by the sheriff from taking fingerprints pursuant to the provisions of this paragraph shall be retained by the sheriff and deposited into the Sheriff's Service Fee Account;

9. The sheriff shall submit to the Oklahoma State Bureau of Investigation within the 14-day period, together with the completed application, including the certificate of training or exemption certificate, photographs, processing fee and legible fingerprints meeting the Oklahoma State Bureau of Investigation's Automated Fingerprint Identification System (AFIS) submission standards, and a report of information deemed pertinent to an investigation of the applicant for a handgun license. The sheriff shall make a preliminary investigation of pertinent information about the applicant and the court clerk shall assist the sheriff in locating pertinent information in court records for this purpose. If no pertinent information is found to exist either for or against the applicant, the sheriff shall so indicate in the report;

10. The Oklahoma State Bureau of Investigation, upon receipt of the application and required information from the sheriff, shall forward 1 full set of fingerprints of the applicant to the Federal Bureau of Investigation for a national criminal history records search. The cost of processing the fingerprints nationally shall be paid from the processing fee collected by the Oklahoma State Bureau of Investigation;

11. Notwithstanding the provisions of the Oklahoma Self-Defense Act, or any other provisions of law, any person who has been granted a permanent victim protective order by the court, as provided for in the Protection from Domestic Abuse Act, may be issued a temporary handgun license for a period not to exceed 6 months. A temporary handgun license may be issued if the person has successfully passed the required weapons course, completed the application process for the handgun license, passed the preliminary investigation of the person by the sheriff and court clerk, and provided the sheriff proof of a certified permanent victim protective order and a valid Oklahoma state photo identification card or driver license. The sheriff shall issue a temporary handgun license on a form approved by the Oklahoma State Bureau of Investigation, at no cost. Any person who has been issued a temporary license shall carry the temporary handgun license and a valid Oklahoma state photo identification on his or her person at all times, and shall be subject to all the requirements of the Oklahoma Self-Defense Act when carrying a handgun. The person may proceed with the handgun licensing process. In the event the victim protective order is no longer enforceable, the temporary handgun license shall cease to be valid;

12. The Oklahoma State Bureau of Investigation shall make a reasonable effort to investigate the information submitted by the applicant and the sheriff, to ascertain whether or not the issuance of a handgun license would be in violation of the provisions of the Oklahoma Self-Defense Act. The investigation by the Bureau of an applicant shall include, but shall not be limited to: a statewide criminal history records search, a national criminal history records search, a Federal Bureau of Investigation fingerprint search, and if applicable, an investigation of medical records or other records or information deemed by the Bureau to be relevant to the application.

a. In the course of the investigation by the Bureau, it shall present the name of the applicant along with any known aliases, the address of the applicant and the social security number of the applicant to the Department of Mental Health and Substance Abuse Services. The Department of Mental Health and Substance Abuse Services shall respond within 10 days of receiving such information to the Bureau as follows:

(1) with a "Yes" answer, if the records of the Department indicate that the person was involuntarily committed to a mental institution in Oklahoma,

(2) with a "No" answer, if there are no records indicating the name of the person as a person involuntarily committed to a mental institution in Oklahoma, or

(3) with an "Inconclusive" answer if the records of the Department suggest the applicant may be a formerly committed person. In the case of an inconclusive answer, the Bureau shall ask the applicant whether he or she was involuntarily committed. If the applicant states under penalty of perjury that he or she has not been involuntarily committed, the Bureau shall continue processing the application for a license.

b. In the course of the investigation by the Bureau, it shall check the name of any applicant who is 28 years of age or younger along with any known aliases, the address of the applicant and the social security number of the applicant against the records in the Juvenile Online Tracking System (JOLTS) of the Office of Juvenile Affairs. The Office of Juvenile Affairs shall provide the Bureau direct access to check the applicant against the records available on JOLTS:

(1) if the Bureau finds a record on the JOLTS that indicates the person was adjudicated a delinquent for an offense that would constitute a felony offense if committed by an adult within the last 10 years the Bureau shall deny the license,

(2) if the Bureau finds no record on the JOLTS indicating the named person was adjudicated delinquent for an offense that would constitute a felony offense if committed by an adult within the last 10 years, or

(3) if the records suggest the applicant may have been adjudicated delinquent for an offense that would constitute a felony offense if committed by an adult but such record is inconclusive, the Bureau shall ask the applicant whether he or she was adjudicated a delinquent for an offense that would constitute a felony offense if committed by an adult within the last 10 years. If the applicant states under penalty of perjury that he or she was not adjudicated a delinquent within 10 years, the Bureau shall continue processing the application for a license; and

13. If the background check set forth in paragraph 12 of this subsection reveals no records pertaining to the applicant, the Oklahoma State Bureau of Investigation shall either issue a handgun license or deny the application within 60 days of the date of receipt of the applicant's completed application and the required information from the sheriff. In all other cases, the Oklahoma State Bureau of Investigation shall either issue a handgun license or deny the application within 90 days of the date of the receipt of the applicant's completed application and the required information from the sheriff. The Bureau shall approve an applicant who appears to be in full compliance with the provisions of the Oklahoma Self-Defense Act, if completion of the federal fingerprint search is the only reason for delay of the issuance of the handgun license to that applicant. Upon receipt of the federal fingerprint search information, if the Bureau receives information which precludes the person from having a handgun license, the Bureau shall revoke the handgun license previously issued to the applicant. The Bureau shall deny a license when the applicant fails to properly complete the application form or application process or is determined not to be eligible as specified by the provisions of § 1290.9, 1290.10 or 1290.11 of this title. The Bureau shall approve an application in all other cases. If an application is denied, the Bureau shall notify the applicant in writing of its decision. The notification shall state the grounds for the denial and inform the applicant of the right to an appeal as may be provided by the provisions of the Administrative Procedures Act. All notices of denial shall be mailed by first-class mail to the address of the applicant listed in the application. Within 60 calendar days from the date of mailing a denial of application to an applicant, the applicant shall notify the Bureau in writing of the intent to appeal the decision of denial or the right of the applicant to appeal shall be deemed waived. Any administrative hearing on a denial which may be provided shall be conducted by a hearing examiner appointed by the Bureau. The decision of the hearing examiner shall be a final decision appealable to a district court in accordance with the Administrative Procedures Act. When an application is approved, the Bureau shall issue the license and shall mail the license by first-class mail to the address of the applicant listed in the application.

B. Nothing contained in any provision of the Oklahoma Self-Defense Act shall be construed to require or authorize the registration, documentation or providing of serial numbers with regard to any firearm. For purposes of the Oklahoma Self-Defense Act, the sheriff may designate a person to receive, fingerprint, photograph or otherwise process applications for handgun licenses.

§ 1290.13. Automatic Listing of Licenses. The Oklahoma State Bureau of Investigation shall maintain an automated listing of all persons issued a handgun license in this state pursuant to the provisions of the Oklahoma Self-Defense Act and all subsequent suspended or revoked licenses. Information from the automated listing shall only be available to a law enforcement officer or law enforcement agency upon request for law enforcement purposes. The Bureau shall also maintain for each applicant the original application or a copy of the original application form and any subsequent renewal application forms together with the photographs, fingerprints and other pertinent information on the applicant which shall be confidential, except to law enforcement officers or law enforcement agencies in the performance of their duties. The Bureau may release a copy of fingerprints of a deceased applicant maintained by the Bureau due to an application for a handgun license pursuant to the Oklahoma Self-Defense Act. Provided, however, the Bureau may release a copy of fingerprints of a deceased applicant only to an immediate family member upon written request. Such request shall be accompanied by a payment of $15, which shall be deposited into the OSBI Revolving Fund. For purposes of this section, "immediate family member" shall mean the spouse, a child by birth or adoption, a stepchild, a parent by birth or adoption, a stepparent, a grandparent, a grandchild, a sibling, a stepsibling or the spouse of any immediate family member. To facilitate the Bureau's administration of the Oklahoma Self-Defense Act, all licensees shall maintain a current mailing address where the licensee may receive certified mail. The licensee shall within 30 days of a change of name or address inform the Bureau of such change.

§ 1290.14. Safety and Training Course

A. Each applicant for a license to carry a concealed or unconcealed handgun pursuant to the Oklahoma Self-Defense Act must successfully complete a firearms safety and training course in this state conducted by a registered and approved firearms instructor as provided by the provisions of this section or from an interactive online firearms safety and training course available electronically via the Internet approved and certified by the Council on Law Enforcement Education and Training. The applicant must further demonstrate competence and qualification with an authorized pistol of the type or types that the applicant desires to carry as a concealed or unconcealed handgun pursuant to the provisions of the Oklahoma Self-Defense Act, except certain persons may be exempt from such training requirement as provided by the provisions of § 1290.15 of this title.

B. The Council on Law Enforcement Education and Training (CLEET) shall establish criteria for approving firearms instructors and interactive online firearms safety and training courses available electronically via the Internet for purposes of training and qualifying individuals for a handgun license pursuant to the provisions of the Oklahoma Self-Defense Act. Prior to submitting an application for CLEET approval as a firearms instructor, applicants shall attend a firearms instructor school, meeting the following minimum requirements:

  1. Firearms instructor training conducted by one of the following entities:

  a. Council on Law Enforcement Education and Training,

  b. National Rifle Association,

  c. Oklahoma Rifle Association,

  d. federal law enforcement agencies, or

  e. other professionally recognized organizations;

2. The course shall be at least 16 hours in length;

3. Upon completion of the course, the applicant shall be qualified to provide instruction on revolvers, semiautomatic pistols, or both; and

4. Receive a course completion certificate.

All firearms instructors shall be required to meet the eligibility requirements for a handgun license as provided in §§ 1290.9, 1290.10, and 1290.11 of this title and the application shall be processed as provided for applicants in § 1290.12 of this title, including the state and national criminal history records search and fingerprint search. A firearms instructor shall be required to pay a fee of $100 to the Council on Law Enforcement Education and Training (CLEET) each time the person makes application for CLEET approval as a firearms instructor pursuant to the provisions of the Oklahoma Self-Defense Act. … CLEET shall periodically review each approved instructor during a training and qualification course to assure compliance with the rules and course contents. Any violation of the rules may result in the revocation or suspension of CLEET and Oklahoma State Bureau of Investigation approval. Unless the approval has been revoked or suspended, a firearms instructor's CLEET approval shall be for a term of 5 years. Beginning on July 1, 2003, any firearms instructor who has been issued a 4-year CLEET approval shall not be eligible for the 5-year approval until the expiration of the approval previously issued. CLEET shall be responsible for notifying all approved firearms instructors of statutory and policy changes related to the Oklahoma Self-Defense Act. A firearms instructor shall not be required to submit his or her fingerprints for a fingerprint search when renewing a firearms instructor's CLEET approval.

C. 1. All firearms instructors approved by CLEET to train and qualify individuals for a handgun license shall be required to apply for registration with the Oklahoma State Bureau of Investigation after receiving CLEET approval. All firearms instructors teaching the approved course for a handgun license must display their registration certificate during each training and qualification course. Each approved firearms instructor shall complete a registration form provided by the Bureau and shall have the option to pay a registration fee of either $100 for a 5-year registration certificate or $200 for a 10-year registration certificate to the Bureau at the time of each application for registration, except as provided in paragraph 2 of this subsection. Registration certificates issued by the Bureau shall be valid for a period of 5 years or 10 years from the date of issuance. The Bureau shall issue a 5-year or 10-year handgun license to an approved firearms instructor at the time of issuance of a registration certificate and no additional fee shall be required or charged. The Bureau shall maintain a current listing of all registered firearms instructors in this state. Nothing in this paragraph shall be construed to eliminate the requirement for registration and training with CLEET as provided in subsection B of this section. Failure to register or be trained as required shall result in a revocation or suspension of the instructor certificate by the Bureau.

2. On or after July 1, 2003, the registered instructors listed in subparagraphs a and b of this paragraph shall not be required to renew the firearms instructor registration certificate with the Oklahoma State Bureau of Investigation at the expiration of the registration term, provided the instructor is not subject to any suspension or revocation of the firearms instructor certificate. The firearms instructor registration with the Oklahoma State Bureau of Investigation shall automatically renew together with the handgun license authorized in paragraph 1 of this subsection for an additional 5-year term and no additional cost or fee may be charged for the following individuals:

a. an active duty law enforcement officer of this state or any of its political subdivisions or of the federal government who has a valid CLEET approval as a firearms instructor pursuant to the Oklahoma Self-Defense Act, and

b. a retired law enforcement officer authorized to carry a firearm pursuant to § 1289.8 of this title who has a valid CLEET approval as a firearms instructor pursuant to the Oklahoma Self-Defense Act.

D. The Oklahoma State Bureau of Investigation shall approve registration for a firearms instructor applicant who is in full compliance with CLEET rules regarding firearms instructors and the provisions of subsection B of this section, if completion of the federal fingerprint search is the only reason for delay of registration of that firearms instructor applicant. Upon receipt of the federal fingerprint search information, if the Bureau receives information which precludes the person from having a handgun license, the Bureau shall revoke both the registration and the handgun license previously issued to the firearms instructor.

E. The required firearms safety and training course and the actual demonstration of competency and qualification required of the applicant shall be designed and conducted in such a manner that the course can be reasonably completed by the applicant within an 8-hour period. CLEET shall establish the course content and promulgate rules, procedures and forms necessary to implement the provisions of this subsection. For the training and qualification course, an applicant may be charged a fee which shall be determined by the instructor or entity that is conducting the course. The maximum class size shall be determined by the instructor conducting the course; provided, however, practice shooting sessions shall not have more than 10 participating students at one time. CLEET may establish criteria for assistant instructors and any other requirements deemed necessary to conduct a safe and effective training and qualification course. The course content shall include a safety inspection of the firearm to be used by the applicant in the training course; instruction on pistol handling, safety and storage; dynamics of ammunition and firing; methods or positions for firing a pistol; information about the criminal provisions of the Oklahoma law relating to firearms; the requirements of the Oklahoma Self-Defense Act as it relates to the applicant; self-defense and the use of appropriate force; a practice shooting session; and a familiarization course. The firearms instructor shall refuse to train or qualify any person when the pistol to be used or carried by the person is either deemed unsafe or unfit for firing or is a weapon not authorized by the Oklahoma Self-Defense Act. The course shall provide an opportunity for the applicant to qualify himself or herself on either a derringer, a revolver, a semiautomatic pistol or any combination of a derringer, a revolver and a semiautomatic pistol, provided no pistol shall be capable of firing larger than .45 caliber ammunition. Any applicant who successfully trains and qualifies himself or herself with a semiautomatic pistol may be approved by the firearms instructor on the training certificate for a semiautomatic pistol, a revolver and a derringer upon request of the applicant. Any person who qualifies on a derringer or revolver shall not be eligible for a semiautomatic rating until the person has demonstrated competence and qualifications on a semiautomatic pistol. Upon successful completion of the training and qualification course, a certificate of training and a certificate of competency and qualification shall be issued to each applicant who successfully completes the course. The certificate of training and certificate of competency and qualification shall comply with the forms established by CLEET and shall be submitted with an application for a handgun license pursuant to the provisions of paragraph 2 of subsection A of § 1290.12 of this title. The certificate of training and certificate of competency and qualification issued to an applicant shall be valid for a period of 3 years.

G. Firearms instructors shall keep on file for a period of not less than 3 years a roster of each training class, the safety test score of each individual, the caliber and type of weapon each individual used when qualifying and whether or not each individual successfully completed the training course. Firearms instructors shall be authorized to destroy all training documents and records upon expiration of the three-year time period.

§ 1290.15. Persons Exempt from Training Courses

A. The following individuals may be exempt from all or part of the required training and qualification course established pursuant to the provisions of § 1290.14 of this title:

1. A firearms instructor registered with the Oklahoma State Bureau of Investigation for purposes of the Oklahoma Self-Defense Act;

2. An active duty law enforcement officer of this state or any of its political subdivisions or of the federal government;

3. A retired law enforcement officer authorized by this state pursuant to § 1289.8 of this title to carry a firearm;

4. A CLEET-certified armed security officer, armed guard, correctional officer, or any other person having a CLEET certification to carry a firearm in the course of their employment;

5. A person on active military duty, National Guard duty or regular military reserve duty who is a legal resident of this state and who is trained and qualified in the use of handguns;

6. A person honorably discharged from active military duty, National Guard duty or military reserves within 20 years preceding the date of the application for a handgun license pursuant to the provisions of the Oklahoma Self-Defense Act, who is a legal resident of this state, and who has been trained and qualified in the use of handguns;

7. A person retired as a peace officer in good standing from a law enforcement agency located in another state, who is a legal resident of this state, and who has received training equivalent to the training required for CLEET certification in this state; and

8. Any person who is otherwise deemed qualified for a training exemption by CLEET.

Provided, however, persons applying for an exemption pursuant to paragraph 3, 4, 5, 6 or 7 of this subsection may be required to successfully complete the classroom portion of the training course. The fee for the classroom portion of the training course shall be determined by the instructor or entity that is conducting the course.

B. CLEET shall establish criteria for providing proof of an exemption. Before any person shall be considered exempt from all or part of the required training and qualification pursuant to the provisions of the Oklahoma Self-Defense Act, the person shall present the required proof of exemption to a registered firearms instructor. Each person determined to be exempt from training or qualification as provided in this subsection shall receive an exemption certificate from the registered firearms instructor. The rules promulgated by CLEET to implement the provisions of this section and § 1290.14 of this title may require that a fee not to exceed $5 be charged for processing an exemption certificate. The original exemption certificate must be submitted with an application for a handgun license as provided in paragraph 2 of § 1290.12 of this title. No person who is determined to be exempt from training or qualification may carry a concealed or unconcealed firearm pursuant to the authority of the Oklahoma Self-Defense Act until issued a valid handgun license.

C. Nothing contained in any provision of the Oklahoma Self-Defense Act shall be construed to alter, amend, or modify the authority of any active duty law enforcement officer, or any person certified by the Council on Law Enforcement Education and Training to carry a pistol during the course of their employment, to carry any pistol in any manner authorized by law or authorized by the employing agency.

§ 1290.17. Suspension and Revocation of License

A. The Oklahoma State Bureau of Investigation shall have authority pursuant to the provisions of the Oklahoma Self-Defense Act and any other provision of law to suspend or revoke any handgun license issued pursuant to the provisions of the Oklahoma Self-Defense Act. A person whose license has been suspended or revoked or against whom a fine has been assessed shall be entitled to an appeal through a hearing in accordance with the Administrative Procedures Act. Any administrative hearing on suspensions, revocations or fines shall be conducted by a hearing examiner appointed by the Bureau. The hearing examiner's decision shall be a final decision appealable to a district court in accordance with the Administrative Procedures Act. After a handgun license has been issued, the discovery of or the occurrence of any condition which directly affects a person's eligibility for a handgun license as provided by the provisions of § 1290.9 or 1290.10 of this title shall require a revocation of the license by the Bureau. The discovery of or the occurrence of any condition pursuant to § 1290.11 of this title, after a license has been issued, shall cause a suspension of the handgun license for a period of time as prescribed for the condition. Any provision of law that requires a revocation of a handgun license upon a conviction shall cause the Bureau to suspend the handgun license upon the discovery of the arrest of the person for such offense until a determination of the criminal case at which time the Bureau shall proceed with the appropriate administrative action. A licensee may voluntarily surrender a license to the Oklahoma State Bureau of Investigation at any time. Such surrender of a handgun license will render the license invalid. Nothing in this section may be interpreted to prevent a subsequent new application for a license. The licensee shall be informed and acknowledge in writing as follows:

1. The licensee understands that the voluntary surrender of the license will not be deemed a suspension or revocation by the Bureau;

2. A voluntary surrender of a license will not be reviewable by a hearing examiner or subject to judicial review under the Administrative Procedures Act; and

3. By surrendering the license, the licensee shall forfeit all fees paid to date.

B. Any handgun license which is subsequently suspended or revoked shall be immediately returned to the Oklahoma State Bureau of Investigation upon notification. Any person refusing or failing to return a license after notification of its suspension or revocation shall, upon conviction, be guilty of a misdemeanor punishable by a fine of not exceeding $500, by imprisonment in the county jail for not exceeding 6 months, or by both such fine and imprisonment. In addition, the person shall be subject to an administrative fine of $500, upon a hearing and determination by the Bureau that the person is in violation of the provisions of this subsection.

C. Any law enforcement officer of this state shall confiscate a handgun license in the possession of any person and return it to the Oklahoma State Bureau of Investigation for appropriate administrative proceedings against the licensee when the license is no longer needed as evidence in any criminal proceeding, as follows:

1. Upon the arrest of the person for any felony offense;

2. Upon the arrest of the person for any misdemeanor offense enumerated as a preclusion to a handgun license;

3. For any violation of the provisions of the Oklahoma Self-Defense Act;

4. When the officer has been called to assist or is investigating any situation which would be a preclusion to having a handgun license; or

5. As provided in subsection D of § 1290.8 of this title.

D. Any administrative fine assessed in accordance with the provisions of the Oklahoma Self-Defense Act shall be paid in full within 30 days of assessment. The Oklahoma State Bureau of Investigation shall, without a hearing, suspend the handgun license of any person who fails to pay in full any administrative fine assessed against the person in accordance with the provisions of this subsection. The suspension of any handgun license shall be automatic and shall begin 30 days from the date of the assessment of the administrative fine. The suspension shall be removed and the handgun license returned to its prior standing upon payment of the administrative fine being paid in full to the Bureau.

E. Whenever a handgun license has been suspended in accordance with the provisions of this act or the administrative rules of the Bureau promulgated for purposes of this act, the license shall remain under suspension and shall not be reinstated until:

1. The person whose license has been suspended applies for reinstatement in accordance with the administrative rules of the Bureau. The Bureau shall not charge any fee in conjunction with an application for a license reinstatement. The person whose license has been suspended must demonstrate that the condition or preclusion which was the basis for the suspension has lapsed and is no longer in effect; and

2. Any and all administrative fines assessed against the person have been paid in full.

In the event a handgun license expires during the term of the suspension, the person shall be required to apply for renewal of the license in accordance with § 1290.5 of this title.

§ 1290.18. Application Form Contents. The application shall be completed upon the sworn oath of the applicant as provided in paragraph 5 of § 1290.12 of this title. The application form shall be provided by the Oklahoma State Bureau of Investigation and shall contain the following information in addition to any other information deemed relevant by the Bureau:

1. Applicant's full legal name;

2. Applicant's birth name, alias names or nicknames;

3. Maiden name, if applicable;

4. County of residence;

5. Length of residency at the current address;

6. Previous addresses for the preceding 3 years;

7. Place of birth;

8. Date of birth;

9. Declaration of citizenship and date United States citizenship was acquired, if applicable;

10. Race;

11. Weight;

12. Height;

13. Sex;

14. Color of eyes;

15. Current driver license number;

16. Military service number, if applicable;

17. Law enforcement identification numbers, if applicable;

18. Current occupation;

19. Authorized type or types of pistol for which the applicant qualified as stated on the certificate of training or exemption of training which shall be stated as either derringer, revolver, semiautomatic pistol, or some combination of derringer, revolver and semiautomatic pistol and the maximum ammunition capacity of the firearm shall be .45 caliber;

20. An acknowledgment that the applicant desires a handgun license as a means of lawful self-defense and self-protection and for no other intent or purpose;

21. A statement that the applicant has never been convicted of any felony offense in this state, another state or pursuant to any federal offense;

22. A statement that the applicant has none of the conditions which would preclude the issuing of a handgun license pursuant to any of the provisions of §§ 1290.10 and 1290.11 of this title and that the applicant further meets all of the eligibility criteria required by § 1290.9 of this title;

23. An authorization for the Oklahoma State Bureau of Investigation to investigate the applicant and any or all records relating to the applicant for purposes of approving or denying a handgun license pursuant to the provisions of the Oklahoma Self-Defense Act;

24. An acknowledgment that the applicant has been furnished a copy of the Oklahoma Self-Defense Act and is knowledgeable about its provisions;

25. A statement that the applicant is the identical person who completed the firearms training course for which the original training certificate is submitted as part of the application or a statement that the applicant is the identical person who is exempt from firearms training for which the original exemption certificate is submitted as part of the application, whichever is applicable to the applicant;

26. A conspicuous warning that the application is executed upon the sworn oath of the applicant and that any false or misleading answer to any question or the submission of any false information or documentation by the applicant is punishable by criminal penalty as provided in paragraph 5 of § 1290.12 of this title;

27. A signed verification that the contents of the application are known to the applicant and are true and correct;

28. Two separate places for the original signature of the applicant;

29. A place for attachment of a passport size photograph of the applicant; and

30. A place for the signature and verification of the identity of the applicant by the sheriff or the sheriff's designee. Information provided by the person on an application for a handgun license shall be confidential except to law enforcement officers or law enforcement agencies.

§ 1290.19. License Form. The handgun license shall be on a form prescribed by the Oklahoma State Bureau of Investigation and shall contain the following information in addition to any other information deemed relevant by the Bureau:

1. The full name of the person;

2. Current address;

3. County of residence;

4. Date of birth;

5. Weight;

6. Height;

7. Sex;

8. Race;

9. Color of eyes;

10. Handgun license identification number;

11. Expiration date of the handgun license; and

12. Authorized pistol to be either: (D) derringer, (R) revolver, (S) semiautomatic pistol, or some combination of derringer, revolver and semiautomatic pistol as may be authorized by the Oklahoma Self-Defense Act for which the person demonstrated qualification pursuant to the certificate of training or an exemption certificate.

§ 1290.20. Penalty for Refusal to Submit or Falsification. It shall be unlawful for any sheriff or designee to fail or refuse to accept an application for a handgun license as authorized by the provisions of the Oklahoma Self-Defense Act or to fail or refuse to process or submit the completed application to the Oklahoma State Bureau of Investigation within the time prescribed by paragraph 8 of § 1290.12 of this title, or to falsify or knowingly allow any person to falsify any information, documentation, fingerprint or photograph submitted with a handgun application. Any violation shall, upon conviction, be a misdemeanor. There is a presumption that the sheriff has acted in good faith to comply with the provisions of the Oklahoma Self-Defense Act and any alleged violation of the provisions of this section shall require proof beyond a reasonable doubt.

§ 1290.21. Replacement License

A. In the event a handgun license becomes missing, lost, stolen or destroyed, the license shall be invalid, and the person to whom the license was issued shall notify the Oklahoma State Bureau of Investigation within 30 days of the discovery of the fact that the license is not in the possession of the licensee. The person may obtain a substitute license upon furnishing a notarized statement to the Bureau that the license is missing, lost, stolen or destroyed and paying a fifteen-dollar replacement fee. During any period when a license is missing, lost, stolen or destroyed, the person shall have no authority to carry a concealed or unconcealed handgun pursuant to the provisions of the Oklahoma Self-Defense Act. The

Bureau shall, upon receipt of the notarized statement and fee from the licensee, issue a substitute license with the same expiration date within 10 days of the receipt of the notarized statement and fee.

B. Any person who knowingly or intentionally carries a concealed or unconcealed handgun pursuant to a handgun license authorized and issued pursuant to the provisions of the Oklahoma Self-Defense Act which is stolen shall, upon conviction, be guilty of a felony punishable by a fine of $5,000.

C. Any person having a valid handgun license pursuant to the Oklahoma Self-Defense Act may carry any make or model of an authorized pistol listed on the license, provided the type of pistol shall not be other than the type or types listed on the license. A person may complete additional firearms training for an additional type of pistol during any license period and upon successful completion of the training may request the additional type of pistol be included on the license. The person shall submit to the Bureau a $15 replacement fee, the original certificate of training and qualification for the additional type of firearm, and a statement requesting the license be updated to include the additional type of pistol. The Bureau shall issue an updated license with the same expiration date within 10 days of the receipt of the request. The person shall have no authority to carry any additional type of pistol pursuant to the provisions of the Oklahoma Self-Defense Act until the updated license has been received by the licensee. The original license shall be destroyed upon receipt of an updated handgun license.

D. A person may request during any license period an update for a change of address or change of name by submitting to the Bureau a $15 replacement fee, and a notarized statement that the address or name of the licensee has changed. The Bureau shall issue an updated license with the same expiration date within 10 days of receipt of the request. The original license shall be destroyed upon the receipt of the updated handgun license.

§ 1290.22. Business Owner's Rights [Effective November 1, 2016]

A. Except as provided in subsections B, C and D of this section, nothing contained in any provision of the Oklahoma Self-Defense Act shall be construed to limit, restrict or prohibit in any manner the existing rights of any person, property owner, tenant, employer, place of worship or business entity to control the possession of weapons on any property owned or controlled by the person or business entity.

B. No person, property owner, tenant, employer, holder of an event permit, place of worship or business entity shall be permitted to establish any policy or rule that has the effect of prohibiting any person, except a convicted felon, from transporting and storing firearms in a locked vehicle on any property set aside for any vehicle.

C. A property owner, tenant, employer, place of worship or business entity may prohibit any person from carrying a concealed or unconcealed firearm on the property. If the building or property is open to the public, the property owner, tenant, employer, place of worship or business entity shall post signs on or about the property stating such prohibition.

D. No person, property owner, tenant, employer, holder of an event permit, place of worship or business entity shall be permitted to establish any policy or rule that has the effect of prohibiting any person from carrying a concealed or unconcealed firearm on property within the specific exclusion provided for in paragraph 4 of subsection B of § 1277 of this title; provided that carrying a concealed or unconcealed firearm may be prohibited in the following places:

   1. The portion of a public property structure or building during an event authorized by the city, town, county, state or federal governmental authority owning or controlling such building or structure;

   2. Any public property sports field, including any adjacent seating or adjacent area set aside for viewing a sporting event, where an elementary or secondary school, collegiate, or professional sporting event or an International Olympic Committee or organization or any committee subordinate to the International Olympic Committee event is being held;

   3. The fairgrounds during the Oklahoma State Fair or the Tulsa State Fair; and

   4. The portion of a public property structure or building that is leased or under contract to a business or not-for-profit entity or group for offices.

E. The carrying of a concealed or unconcealed firearm by a person who has been issued a handgun license on property that has signs prohibiting the carrying of firearms shall not be deemed a criminal act but may subject the person to being denied entrance onto the property or removed from the property. If the person refuses to leave the property and a peace officer is summoned, the person may be issued a citation for an amount not to exceed $250.

F. A person, property owner, tenant, employer, holder of an event permit, place of worship or business entity that does or does not prohibit any individual except a convicted felon from carrying a loaded or unloaded, concealed or unconcealed weapon on property that the person, property owner, tenant, employer, holder of an event permit, place of worship or business entity owns, or has legal control of, is immune from any liability arising from that decision. Except for acts of gross negligence or willful or wanton misconduct, an employer who does or does not prohibit their employees from carrying a concealed or unconcealed weapon is immune from any liability arising from that decision. A person, property owner, tenant, employer, holder of an event permit, place of worship or business entity that does not prohibit persons from carrying a concealed or unconcealed weapon pursuant to subsection D of this section shall be immune from any liability arising from the carrying of a concealed or unconcealed weapon on the property. The provisions of this subsection shall not apply to claims pursuant to the Administrative Workers' Compensation Act.

G. It shall not be considered part of an employee's job description or within the employee's scope of employment if an employee is allowed to carry or discharge a weapon pursuant to this section.

H. Nothing in subsections F and G shall prevent an employer, employee or person who has suffered loss resulting from the discharge of a weapon to seek redress or damages of the person who discharged the weapon or used the weapon outside the provisions of the Oklahoma Self-Defense Act.

§ 1290.24. Immunity [Effective November 1, 2016]

A. The state or any political subdivision of the state as defined in § 152 of Title 51 of the Oklahoma Statutes, and its officers, agents and employees shall be immune from liability resulting or arising from:

1. Failure to prevent the licensing of an individual for whom the receipt of the license is unlawful pursuant to the provisions of the Oklahoma Self-Defense Act or any other provision of law of this state;

2. Any action or misconduct with a pistol committed by a person to whom a license to carry a concealed or unconcealed handgun has been issued pursuant to the provisions of the Oklahoma Self-Defense Act or by any person who obtains a pistol from a licensee;

3. Any injury to any person during a handgun training course conducted by a firearms instructor certified by the Council on Law Enforcement Education and Training to conduct training under the Oklahoma Self-Defense Act, or injury from any misfire or malfunction of any handgun on a training course firing range supervised by a certified firearms instructor under the provisions of the Oklahoma Self-Defense Act, or any injury resulting from carrying a concealed or unconcealed handgun pursuant to a handgun license; and

4. Any action or finding pursuant to a hearing conducted in accordance with the Administrative Procedures Act as required in the Oklahoma Self-Defense Act.

B. Firearms instructors certified by the Council on Law Enforcement Education and Training to conduct training for the Oklahoma Self-Defense Act shall be immune from liability to third persons resulting or arising from any claim based on an act or omission of a trainee.

C. The provisions of this subsection shall not apply to claims pursuant to the Administrative Workers' Compensation Act.

§ 1290.25. Legislative Intent.

The Legislature does not delegate to the Oklahoma State Bureau of Investigation any authority to regulate or restrict the issuing of handgun licenses except as provided by the provisions of this act. Subjective or arbitrary actions or rules which encumber the issuing process by placing burdens on the applicant beyond those requirements detailed in the provisions of the Oklahoma Self-Defense Act or which create restrictions beyond those specified in this act are deemed to be in conflict with the intent of this act and are hereby prohibited. The Oklahoma Self-Defense Act shall be liberally construed to carry out the constitutional right to bear arms for self-defense and self-protection. The provisions of the Oklahoma Self-Defense Act are cumulative to existing rights to bear arms and nothing in the Oklahoma Self-Defense Act shall impair or diminish those rights.

§ 1290.26. Reciprocal Agreement Authority.

The State of Oklahoma hereby recognizes any valid concealed or unconcealed carry weapons permit or license issued by another state, or if the state is a nonpermitting carry state, this state shall reciprocate under the permitting law of that state.

A. Any person entering this state in possession of a firearm authorized for concealed or unconcealed carry upon the authority and license of another state is authorized to continue to carry a concealed or unconcealed firearm and license in this state; provided the license from the other state remains valid. The firearm must either be carried unconcealed or concealed from detection and view, and upon coming in contact with any peace officer of this state, the person must disclose the fact that he or she is in possession of a concealed or unconcealed firearm pursuant to a valid concealed or unconcealed carry weapons permit or license issued in another state.

B. Any person entering this state in possession of a firearm authorized for concealed carry upon the authority of a state that is a nonpermitted carry state and the person is in compliance with the Oklahoma Self-Defense Act, the person is authorized to carry a concealed firearm in this state. The firearm must be carried fully concealed from detection and view, and upon coming in contact with any peace officer of this state, the person must disclose the fact that he or she is in possession of a concealed firearm pursuant to the nonpermitting laws of the state in which he or she is a legal resident. The person shall present proper identification by a valid photo ID as proof that he or she is a legal resident in such a non-permitting state. The Department of Public Safety shall keep a current list of non-permitting states for law enforcement officers to confirm that a state is nonpermitting.

C. Any person who is 21 years of age or older having a valid firearm license from another state may apply for a handgun license in this state immediately upon establishing a residence in this state.

§ 1290.27. Court Orders Regarding Involuntary Commitment and Mental Incompetence–Inclusion in National Instant Background Check System–Petition to Remove Disability

A. When a court adjudicates a person mentally incompetent or orders the involuntary commitment of a person due to a mental illness, condition or disorder under the laws of this state by which a person becomes subject to the provisions of § 922(d)(4) and (g)(4) of Title 18 of the United States Code, the clerk of the court shall forward a certified copy of the order or adjudication to the Federal Bureau of Investigation or its successor agency for the sole purpose of inclusion in the National Instant Criminal Background Check System database and to the Oklahoma State Bureau of Investigation. The clerk of the court shall also notify the person of the prohibitions contained within the provisions of § 922(d)(4) and (g)(4) of Title 18 of the United States Code, paragraph 3 of § 1290.10 or paragraph 3 of subsection A of § 1290.11 of Title 21 of the Oklahoma Statutes.

B. When a court adjudicates a person mentally incompetent or orders the involuntary commitment of a person due to a mental illness, condition or disorder under the laws of this state by which a person becomes subject to the provisions of § 922(d)(4) and (g)(4) of Title 18 of the United States Code, paragraph 3 of § 1290.10 or paragraph 3 of subsection A of § 1290.11 of Title 21 of the Oklahoma Statutes, or when a person is otherwise disqualified from eligibility for a handgun license under paragraph 6 or 7 of § 1290.10 of Title 21 of the Oklahoma Statutes or paragraph 4 of subsection A of §

1290.11 of Title 21 of the Oklahoma Statutes, the person may petition the court in which the adjudication or commitment proceedings occurred or the district court of the county in which the person currently resides to remove the disability.

C. On filing of the petition, the court shall set a hearing. Not less than 30 days prior to a hearing on the matter, a copy of the petition for relief shall be served upon the district attorney for that county. The court shall receive and consider evidence in a closed hearing.

D. The court shall receive evidence on and consider the following before granting or denying the petition:

    1. Psychological or psychiatric evidence from the petitioner and in support of the petition;

    2. The circumstances that resulted in the firearm disabilities;

    3. The petitioner's criminal history records provided by the state, if any;

    4. The petitioner's mental health records;

    5. The reputation of the petitioner based on character witness statements, testimony or other character evidence;

    6. Whether the petitioner is a danger to self or others;

    7. Changes in the condition or circumstances of the petitioner since the original adjudication of mental incompetency or involuntary commitment for a mental illness, condition or disorder relevant to the relief sought; and

    8. Any other evidence deemed admissible by the court.

E. The court shall grant the relief requested if the petitioner proves by clear and convincing evidence that:

    1. The petitioner is not likely to act in a manner that is dangerous to the public safety; and

    2. Granting the relief requested is not contrary to the public interest.

F. At the conclusion of the hearing, the court shall issue findings of fact and conclusions of law. A record shall be kept of the proceedings, but shall remain confidential and be disclosed only to a court or the parties. No records of the proceedings pursuant to this subsection shall be open to public inspection except by order of the court or to a person's attorney of record. The petitioner may appeal a denial of the requested relief, and review on appeal shall be de novo.

G. If the court grants the petition for relief, the original adjudication of mental incompetency or order of involuntary commitment due to a mental illness, condition or disorder of the petitioner is deemed not to have occurred for purposes of applying § 922(d)(4) and (g)(4) of Title 18 of the United States Code, paragraph 3, 6 or 7 of § 1290.10, or paragraph 3 or 4 of subsection A of § 1290.11 of Title 21 of the Oklahoma Statutes.

H. The clerk of the court shall promptly forward to the Federal Bureau of Investigation or its successor agency for the sole purpose of inclusion in the National Instant Criminal Background Check System database and the Department of Mental Health and Substance Abuse Services and the Oklahoma State Bureau of Investigation, a certified copy of the order granting relief under this section. The Department of Mental Health and Substance Abuse Services and the Oklahoma State Bureau of Investigation shall as soon thereafter as is practicable, but in no case later than 10 business days, update, correct, modify, or remove the record of the person in any databases that these agencies use or refer to for the purposes of handgun licensing, or make available to the National Instant Criminal Background Check System and notify the United States Attorney that the basis for such record being made available no longer applies.

Chapter 55. Other Crimes against Public Peace
Miscellaneous Provisions

§ 1364. Discharging Firearm. Every person who willfully discharges any pistol, rifle, shotgun, airgun or other weapon, or throws any other missile in any public place, or in any place where there is any person to be endangered thereby, although no injury to any person shall ensue, is guilty of a misdemeanor. Any person convicted of a violation of the provisions of this section after having been issued a handgun license pursuant to the provisions of the Oklahoma Self-Defense Act shall have the license suspended for a period of 6 months and shall be subject to an administrative fine of $50, upon a hearing and determination by the Oklahoma State Bureau of Investigation that the person is in violation of the provisions of this section.

Office of the Attorney General
Rembert Dennis Building
1000 Assembly Street, Room 519
Columbia, S.C. 29201
Voice: (803) 734-3970
info@scattorneygeneral.com

Charlotte Field Division
6701 Carmel Road, Suite 200
Charlotte, North Carolina 28226
Voice: (704) 716-1800
https://www.atf.gov/charlotte-field-division

PROTECTING THE PUBLIC
SERVING OUR NATION

Table of Contents

TITLE 16. Crimes and Offenses
Chapter 23. Offenses Involving Weapons
Article 1. Handguns

§ 16-23-10. Definitions. When used in this article:
(1) "**Handgun**" means any firearm designed to expel a projectile and designed to be fired from the hand, but shall not include any firearm generally recognized or classified as an antique, curiosity, or collector's item, or any that does not fire fixed cartridges.
(2) "**Dealer**" means any person engaged in the business of selling firearms at retail or any person who is a pawnbroker.
(3) "**Crime of violence**" means murder, manslaughter (except negligent manslaughter arising out of traffic accidents), rape, mayhem, kidnapping, burglary, robbery, housebreaking, assault with intent to kill, commit rape, or rob, assault with a dangerous weapon, or assault with intent to commit any offense punishable by imprisonment for more than one year.
(4) "**Fugitive from justice**" means any person who has fled from or is fleeing from any law enforcement officer to avoid prosecution or imprisonment for a crime of violence.
(5) "**Subversive organization**" means any group, committee, club, league, society, association, or combination of individuals the purpose of which, or one of the purposes of which, is the establishment, control, conduct, seizure, or overthrow of the government of the United States or any state or political subdivision thereof, by the use of force, violence, espionage, sabotage, or threats or attempts of any of the foregoing.
(6) "**Conviction**'" as used herein shall include pleas of guilty, pleas of nolo contendere, and forfeiture of bail.
(7) "**Division**" means the State Law Enforcement Division.
(8) "**Purchase**" or "sell" means to knowingly buy, offer to buy, receive, lease, rent, barter, exchange, pawn or accept in pawn.
(9) "**Person**" means any individual, corporation, company, association, firm, partnership, society, or joint stock company.
(10) "**Luggage compartment**" means the trunk of a motor vehicle which has a trunk; however, with respect to a motor vehicle which does not have a trunk, the term "luggage compartment" refers to the area of the motor vehicle in which the manufacturer designed that luggage be carried or to the area of the motor vehicle in which luggage is customarily carried.

In a station wagon, van, hatchback vehicle, truck, or sport utility vehicle, the term "luggage compartment" refers to the area behind the rearmost seat.

§ 16-23-20. Unlawful carrying of handgun; exceptions. It is unlawful for anyone to carry about the person any handgun, whether concealed or not, except as follows, unless otherwise specifically prohibited by law:

(1) regular, salaried law enforcement officers, and reserve police officers of a state agency, municipality, or county of the State, uncompensated Governor's constables, law enforcement officers of the federal government or other states when they are carrying out official duties while in this State, deputy enforcement officers of the Natural Resources Enforcement Division of the Department of Natural Resources, and retired commissioned law enforcement officers employed as private detectives or private investigators;

(2) members of the Armed Forces of the United States, the National Guard, organized reserves, or the State Militia when on duty;

(3) members, or their invited guests, of organizations authorized by law to purchase or receive firearms from the United States or this State or regularly enrolled members, or their invited guests, of clubs organized for the purpose of target shooting or collecting modern and antique firearms while these members, or their invited guests, are at or going to or from their places of target practice or their shows and exhibits;

(4) licensed hunters or fishermen who are engaged in hunting or fishing or going to or from their places of hunting or fishing while in a vehicle or on foot;

(5) a person regularly engaged in the business of manufacturing, repairing, repossessing, or dealing in firearms, or the agent or representative of this person, while possessing, using, or carrying a handgun in the usual or ordinary course of the business;

(6) guards authorized by law to possess handguns and engaged in protection of property of the United States or any agency of the United States;

(7) members of authorized military or civil organizations while parading or when going to and from the places of meeting of their respective organizations;

(8) a person in his home or upon his real property or a person who has the permission of the owner or the person in legal possession or the person in legal control of the home or real property;

(9) a person in a vehicle if the handgun is:

   (a) secured in a closed glove compartment, closed console, closed trunk, or in a closed container secured by an integral fastener and transported in the luggage compartment of the vehicle; however, this item is not violated if the glove compartment, console, or trunk is opened in the presence of a law enforcement officer for the sole purpose of retrieving a driver's license, registration, or proof of insurance. If the person has been issued a concealed weapon permit pursuant to Article 4, Chapter 31, Title 23, then the person also may secure his weapon under a seat in a vehicle, or in any open or closed storage compartment within the vehicle's passenger compartment; or

   (b) concealed on or about his person, and he has a valid concealed weapons permit pursuant to the provisions of Article 4, Chapter 31, Title 23;

(10) a person carrying a handgun unloaded and in a secure wrapper from the place of purchase to his home or fixed place of business or while in the process of changing or moving one's residence or changing or moving one's fixed place of business;

(11) a prison guard while engaged in his official duties;

(12) a person who is granted a permit under provision of law by the State Law Enforcement Division to carry a handgun about his person, under conditions set forth in the permit, and while transferring the handgun between the permittee's person and a location specified in item (9);

(13) the owner or the person in legal possession or the person in legal control of a fixed place of business, while at the fixed place of business, and the employee of a fixed place of business, other than a business subject to § 16-23-465, while at the place of business; however, the employee may exercise this privilege only after: (a) acquiring a permit pursuant to item (12), and (b) obtaining the permission of the owner or person in legal control or legal possession of the premises;

(14) a person engaged in firearms-related activities while on the premises of a fixed place of business which conducts, as a regular course of its business, activities related to sale, repair, pawn, firearms training, or use of firearms, unless the premises is posted with a sign limiting possession of firearms to holders of permits issued pursuant to item (12);

(15) a person while transferring a handgun directly from or to a vehicle and a location specified in this section where one may legally possess the handgun.

(16) Any person on a motorcycle when the pistol is secured in a closed saddlebag or other similar closed accessory container attached, whether permanently or temporarily, to the motorcycle.

§ 16-23-30. Sale or delivery of handgun to and possession by certain persons unlawful; stolen handguns.
(A) It is unlawful for a person to knowingly sell, offer to sell, deliver, lease, rent, barter, exchange, or transport for sale into this State any handgun to:

   (1) a person who has been convicted of a crime of violence in any court of the United States, the several states, commonwealths, territories, possessions, or the District of Columbia or who is a fugitive from justice or a habitual drunkard or a drug addict or who has been adjudicated mentally incompetent;

   (2) a person who is a member of a subversive organization;

(3) a person under the age of eighteen, but this shall not apply to the issue of handguns to members of the Armed Forces of the United States, active or reserve, National Guard, State Militia, or R. O. T. C., when on duty or training or the temporary loan of handguns for instructions under the immediate supervision of a parent or adult instructor; or

(4) a person who by order of a circuit judge or county court judge of this State has been adjudged unfit to carry or possess a firearm, such adjudication to be made upon application by any police officer, or by any prosecuting officer of this State, or sua sponte, by the court, but a person who is the subject of such an application is entitled to reasonable notice and a proper hearing prior to any such adjudication.

(B) It is unlawful for a person enumerated in subsection (A) to possess or acquire handguns within this State.

(C) A person shall not knowingly buy, sell, transport, pawn, receive, or possess any stolen handgun or one from which the original serial number has been removed or obliterated.

§ 16-23-50. Penalties; disposition of fines; forfeiture and disposition of handguns.

(A) (1) A person, including a dealer, who violates the provisions of this article, except § 16-23-20, is guilty of a felony and, upon conviction, must be fined not more than $2,000 or imprisoned not more than 5 years, or both.

(2) A person violating the provisions of § 16-23-20 is guilty of a misdemeanor and, upon conviction, must be fined not more than $1,000 or imprisoned not more than 1 year, or both.

(B) In addition to the penalty provided in this section, the handgun involved in the violation of this article must be confiscated. The handgun must be delivered to the chief of police of the municipality or to the sheriff of the county if the violation occurred outside the corporate limits of a municipality. The law enforcement agency that receives the confiscated handgun may use it within the agency, transfer it to another law enforcement agency for the lawful use of that agency, trade it with a retail dealer licensed to sell handguns in this State for a handgun or any other equipment approved by the agency, or destroy it. A weapon must not be disposed of in any manner until the results of any legal proceeding in which it may be involved are finally determined. If the State Law Enforcement Division seized the handgun, the division may keep the handgun for use by its forensic laboratory. Records must be kept of all confiscated handguns received by the law enforcement agencies under the provisions of this article.

§ 16-23-55. Procedure for returning found handgun.

(A) A handgun that is found and turned over to a law enforcement agency must be held for a period of 90 days. During that period, the agency shall make a diligent effort to determine:

(1) if the handgun is stolen;

(2) if the handgun has been used in the commission of a crime; and (3) the true owner of the handgun.

(B) At least twice during the 90-day holding period, the agency shall advertise the handgun with its full description in a newspaper having general circulation in the county where the handgun was found.

(C) After the 90 days have elapsed from publication of the first advertisement, and upon request of the individual who found and turned over the handgun, the agency shall return the handgun to this person if the individual fully completes the application process as described in § 23-31-140 and in federal law, and pays all advertising and other costs incidental to returning the handgun. No handgun may be returned until the individual fully completes the application.

(D) Upon proper completion of the application, the law enforcement agency shall provide copies of the application in compliance with § 23-31-140.

§ 16-23-60. Construction. Provisions of this article must not be construed to grant any additional police powers not authorized by law, and do not in any manner affect the powers of constables commissioned by the Governor.

Article 3. Machine Guns, Sawed-Off Shotguns and Rifles

§ 16-23-210. Definitions. When used in this article:

(a) "Machine gun" applies to and includes any weapon which shoots, is designed to shoot, or can be readily restored to shoot, automatically more than 1 shot, without manual reloading, by a single function of the trigger. The term shall also include the frame or receiver of any such weapon, any combination or parts designed and intended for use in converting a weapon into a machine gun, and any combination of parts from which a machine gun can be assembled if such parts are in the possession or under the control of a person.

(b) "Sawed-off shotgun" means a shotgun having a barrel or barrels of less than 18 inches in length or a weapon made from a shotgun which as modified has an overall length of less than 26 inches or a barrel or barrels of less than 18 inches in length.

(c) "Shotgun" means a weapon designed or redesigned, made or remade, and intended to be fired from the shoulder and designed or redesigned and made or remade to use the energy of the explosive in a fixed shotgun shell to fire through a smooth bore either a number of ball shot or a single projectile for each pull of the trigger. The term includes any such weapon which may be readily restored to fire a fixed shotgun shell but does not include an antique firearm as defined in this section.

(d) "Sawed-off rifle" means a rifle having a barrel or barrels of less than 16 inches in length or a weapon made from a rifle which as modified has an overall length of less than 26 inches or a barrel or barrels of less than 16 inches in length.

(e) "Rifle" means a weapon designed or redesigned, made or remade, and intended to be fired from the shoulder and designed or redesigned and made or remade to use the energy of the explosive in a fixed cartridge to fire only a single projectile through a rifled bore for each single pull of the trigger. The term includes any such weapon which may be readily restored to fire a fixed cartridge but does not include an antique firearm as described in this section.

(f) "Antique firearm" means any firearm not designed or redesigned for using rim fire or conventional center fire ignition with fixed ammunition and manufactured in or before 1898 (including any matchlock, flintlock, percussion cap, or similar type of ignition system or replica thereof, whether actually manufactured before or after the year 1898) and also any firearm using fixed ammunition manufactured in or before 1898, for which ammunition is no longer manufactured in the United States and is not readily available in the ordinary channels of commercial trade.

(g) "Military firearm" means any military weapon, firearm, or destructive device, other than a machine gun, that is manufactured for military use by a firm licensed by the federal government pursuant to a contract with the federal government and does not include a pistol, rifle, or shotgun which fires only one shot for each pull of the trigger.

§ 16-23-220. Unlawful transportation of machine gun, military firearm, or sawed-off shotgun or rifle within State. It is unlawful for a person to transport from one place to another in this State or for any railroad company, express company, or other common carrier or any officer, agent, or employee of any of them or other person acting in their behalf knowingly to ship or to transport from one place to another in this State a machine gun or firearm commonly known as a machine gun, military firearm, sawed-off shotgun, or sawed-off rifle, except as provided in §§ 16-23-250 and 23-31-330. A person who violates the provisions of this section, upon conviction, must be punished pursuant to § 16-23-260.

§ 16-23-230. Unlawful storing, keeping, or possessing of machine gun, military firearm, or sawed-off shotgun or rifle. It is unlawful for a person to store, keep, possess, or have in possession or permit another to store, keep, possess, or have in possession a machine gun or firearm commonly known as a machine gun, military firearm, sawed-off shotgun, or sawed-off rifle, except as provided in §§ 16-23-250 and 23-31-330. A person who violates the provisions of this section, upon conviction, must be punished pursuant to § 16-23-260.

§ 16-23-240. Unlawful sale, rental, or giving away of machine gun, military firearm, or sawed-off shotgun or rifle; exceptions. It is unlawful for a person to sell, rent, give away, or participate in any manner, directly or indirectly, in the sale, renting, giving away, or otherwise disposing of a machine gun, or firearm commonly known as a machine gun, military firearm, sawed-off shotgun, or sawed-off rifle, except as provided in §§ 16-23-250 and 23-31-330. A person who violates the provisions of this section, upon conviction, must be punished pursuant to § 16-23-260.

§ 16-23-250. Exceptions to application of article. The provisions of this article do not apply to the Army, Navy, or Air Force of the United States, the National Guard, and organizations authorized by law to purchase or receive machine guns, military firearms, or sawed-off shotguns or sawed-off rifles, from the United States or from this State and the members of these organizations. Any peace officer of the State or of a county or other political subdivision, state constable, member of the highway patrol, railway policeman or warden, superintendent, head keeper or deputy of a state prison, correction facility, workhouse, county jail, city jail, or other institution for the detention of persons convicted or accused of crime or held as witnesses in criminal cases or persons on duty in the postal service of the United States or a common carrier while transporting direct to a police department, military, or naval organization or person authorized by law to possess or use a machine gun, or sawed-off shotgun, or sawed-off rifle, may possess machine guns, or sawed-off shotguns, or sawed-off rifles, when required in the performance of their duties. The provisions of this section must not be construed to apply to machine guns, or sawed-off shotguns, or sawed-off rifles kept for display as relics and which are rendered harmless and not usable.

The provisions of this article do not apply to any manufacturer of machine guns or military firearms licensed pursuant to the provisions of 18 U. S. C. § 921 et seq., any person authorized to possess these weapons by the United States Department of the Treasury, the Bureau of Alcohol, Tobacco and Firearms, or any other federal agency empowered to grant this authorization, any common or contract carrier transporting or shipping any machine gun or military firearm to or from the manufacturer if the transportation or shipment is not prohibited by federal law, or persons licensed pursuant to § 23-31-370.

§ 16-23-260. Penalties. A person violating the provisions of this article is guilty of a felony and, upon conviction, must be fined not more than $10,000 or imprisoned not more than 10 years, or both.

§ 16-23-270. Article not applicable to antique firearms. The provisions of this article shall not apply to antique firearms.

§ 16-23-280. Manufacture and sale of machine guns by licensed manufacturer. Notwithstanding the provisions of this article, machine guns or military firearms manufactured by a firm licensed by the federal government and subject to the Federal Gun Control Act may be legally manufactured, transported, possessed, and sold within the State by the manufacturer thereof.

Article 5. Miscellaneous Offenses

§ 16-23-405. Definition of "weapon"; confiscation and disposition of weapons used in commission or in furtherance of crime.
(A) Except for the provisions relating to rifles and shotguns in § 16-23-460, as used in this chapter, "weapon" means firearm (rifle, shotgun, pistol, or similar device that propels a projectile through the energy of an explosive), a blackjack, a metal pipe or pole, or any other type of device, or object which may be used to inflict bodily injury or death.

(B) A person convicted of a crime, in addition to a penalty, shall have a weapon used in the commission or in furtherance of the crime confiscated. Each weapon must be delivered to the chief of police of the municipality or to the sheriff of the county if the violation occurred outside the corporate limits of a municipality. The law enforcement agency that receives the confiscated weapon may use it within the agency, transfer it to another law enforcement agency for the lawful use of that agency, trade it with a retail dealer licensed to sell pistols in this State for a pistol or other equipment approved by the agency, or destroy it. A weapon may not be disposed of until the results of all legal proceedings in which it may be involved are finally determined. A firearm seized by the State Law Enforcement Division may be kept by the division for use by its forensic laboratory.

§ 16-23-410. Pointing firearm at another person.
It is unlawful for a person to present or point at another person a loaded or unloaded firearm.

A person who violates the provisions of this section is guilty of a felony and, upon conviction, must be fined in the discretion of the court or imprisoned not more than 5 years. This section must not be construed to abridge the right of self-defense or to apply to theatricals or like performances.

§ 16-23-415. Taking firearm or other weapon from law enforcement officer.
An individual who takes a firearm, stun gun, or taser device from the person of a law enforcement officer or a corrections officer is guilty of a felony and, upon conviction, must be imprisoned for not more than 5 years, or fined not more than $5,000, or both, if all of the following circumstances exist at the time the firearm is taken:

(1) the individual knows or has reason to believe the person from whom the weapon is taken is a law enforcement officer or a corrections officer;

(2) the law enforcement officer or corrections officer is performing his duties as a law enforcement officer or a corrections officer, or the individual's taking of the weapon is directly related to the law enforcement officer's or corrections officer's professional responsibilities;

(3) the individual takes the weapon without consent of the law enforcement officer or corrections officer;

(4) the law enforcement officer is authorized by his employer to carry the weapon in the line of duty; and

(5) the law enforcement officer or corrections officer is authorized by his employer to carry the weapon while off duty and has identified himself as a law enforcement officer.

§ 16-23-420. Possession of firearm on school property; concealed weapons.
(A) It is unlawful for a person to possess a firearm of any kind on any premises or property owned, operated, or controlled by a private or public school, college, university, technical college, other post-secondary institution, or in any publicly owned building, without the express permission of the authorities in charge of the premises or property. The provisions of this subsection related to any premises or property owned, operated, or controlled by a private or public school, college, university, technical college, or other post-secondary institution, do not apply to a person who is authorized to carry a concealed weapon pursuant to Article 4, Chapter 31, Title 23 when the weapon remains inside an attended or locked motor vehicle and is secured in a closed glove compartment, closed console, closed trunk, or in a closed container secured by an integral fastener and transported in the luggage compartment of the vehicle.

(B) It is unlawful for a person to enter the premises or property described in subsection (A) and to display, brandish, or threaten others with a firearm.

(C) A person who violates the provisions of this section is guilty of a felony and, upon conviction, must be fined not more than $5,000 or imprisoned not more than 5 years, or both.

(D) This section does not apply to a guard, law enforcement officer, or member of the armed forces, or student of military science. A married student residing in an apartment provided by the private or public school whose presence with a weapon in or around a particular building is authorized by persons legally responsible for the security of the buildings is also exempted from the provisions of this section.

(E) For purposes of this section, the terms "premises" and "property" do not include state or locally owned or maintained roads, streets, or rights-of-way of them, running through or adjacent to premises or property owned, operated, or controlled by a private or public school, college, university, technical college, or other post-secondary institution, which are open full time to public vehicular traffic.

(F) This section does not apply to a person who is authorized to carry concealed weapons pursuant to Article 4, Chapter 31 of Title 23 when upon any premises, property, or building that is part of an interstate highway rest area facility.

§ 16-23-430. Carrying weapon on school property; concealed weapons.
(A) It shall be unlawful for any person, except state, county, or municipal law enforcement officers or personnel authorized by school officials, to carry on his person, while on any elementary or secondary school property, … firearms, or any other type of weapon, device, or object which may be used to inflict bodily injury or death.

(B) This section does not apply to a person who is authorized to carry a concealed weapon pursuant to Article 4, Chapter 31, Title 23 when the weapon remains inside an attended or locked motor vehicle and is secured in a closed glove compartment, closed console, closed trunk, or in a closed container secured by an integral fastener and transported in the luggage compartment of the vehicle.

(C) A person who violates the provisions of this section is guilty of a felony and, upon conviction, must be fined not more than $1,000 or imprisoned not more than 5 years, or both. Any weapon or object used in violation of this section may be confiscated by the law enforcement division making the arrest.

§ 16-23-440. Discharging firearms at or into dwellings, structures, enclosures, vehicles or equipment; penalties.

(A) It is unlawful for a person to discharge or cause to be discharged unlawfully firearms at or into a dwelling house, other building, structure, or enclosure regularly occupied by persons. A person who violates the provisions of this subsection is guilty of a felony and, upon conviction, must be fined not more than $1,000 or imprisoned not more than 10 years, or both.

(B) It is unlawful for a person to discharge or cause to be discharged unlawfully firearms at or into any vehicle, aircraft, watercraft, or other conveyance, device, or equipment while it is occupied. A person who violates the provisions of this subsection is guilty of a felony and, upon conviction, must be fined not more than $1,000 or imprisoned not more than 10 years, or both.

§ 16-23-450. Placing loaded trap gun, spring gun or like device.

It shall be unlawful for any person to construct, set or place a loaded trap gun, spring gun or any like device in any manner in any building or in any place within this State, and any violation of the provisions of this section shall constitute a misdemeanor and be punished by a fine of not less than $100 nor more than $500 or by imprisonment of not less than 30 days nor more than 1 year or by both fine and imprisonment, in the discretion of the court.

§ 16-23-460. Carrying concealed weapons; forfeiture of weapons.

(A) A person carrying a deadly weapon usually used for the infliction of personal injury concealed about his person is guilty of a misdemeanor, must forfeit to the county, or, if convicted in a municipal court, to the municipality, the concealed weapon, and must be fined not less than $200 nor more than $500 or imprisoned not less than 30 days nor more than 90 days.

(B) The provisions of this section do not apply to:

 (1) A person carrying a concealed weapon upon his own premises or pursuant to and in compliance with Article 4, Chapter 31 of Title 23; or

 (2) peace officers in the actual discharge of their duties.

(C) The provisions of this section also do not apply to rifles, shotguns, dirks, slingshots, metal knuckles, knives, or razors unless they are used with the intent to commit a crime or in furtherance of a crime.

§ 16-23-465. Additional penalty for unlawfully carrying pistol or firearm onto premises of business selling alcoholic liquor, beer or wine for on-premises consumption; exceptions.

(A) In addition to the penalties provided for by §§ 16-11-330, 16-11-620, 16-23-460, 23-31-220, and Article 1, Chapter 23, Title 16, a person convicted of carrying a firearm into a business which sells alcoholic liquor, beer, or wine for consumption on the premises is guilty of a misdemeanor, and, upon conviction, must be fined not more than $2,000 or imprisoned not more than 2 years, or both.

In addition to the penalties described above, a person who violates this section while carrying a concealable weapon pursuant to Article 4, Chapter 31, Title 23 must have his concealed weapon permit revoked for a period of 5 years.

(B) (1) This section does not apply to a person carrying a concealable weapon pursuant to and in compliance with Article 4, Chapter 31, Title 23; however, the person shall not consume alcoholic liquor, beer, or wine while carrying the concealable weapon on the business' premises. A person who violates this item may be charged with a violation of subsection (A).

 (2) A property owner, holder of a lease interest, or operator of a business may prohibit the carrying of concealable weapons into the business by posting a "NO CONCEALABLE WEAPONS ALLOWED" sign in compliance with § 23-31-235. A person who carries a concealable weapon into a business with a sign posted in compliance with § 23-31-235 may be charged with a violation of subsection (A).

 (3) A property owner, holder of a lease interest, or operator of a business may request that a person carrying a concealable weapon leave the business' premises, or any portion of the premises, or request that a person carrying a concealable weapon remove the concealable weapon from the business' premises, or any portion of the premises. A person carrying a concealable weapon who refuses to leave a business' premises or portion of the premises when requested or refuses to remove the concealable weapon from a business' premises or portion of the premises when requested may be charged with a violation of subsection (A).

§ 16-23-470. Illegal possession of tear-gas gun or ammunition.

(A) It is unlawful for anyone except an authorized law enforcement officer to possess, use, transport, sell, or buy a tear-gas machine or gun, or its parts, or any ammunition, shells, or equipment that may be used in a tear-gas gun or machine. It is lawful for a person for self-defense purposes only to possess, use, transport, sell, or buy a tear-gas machine or gun, or its parts, or ammunition, shells, or equipment for a tear-gas machine or gun, but the capacity of a tear-gas cartridge, shell, or container shall not exceed 50 cubic centimeters nor shall a tear-gas machine or gun have the capability of shooting a cartridge, shell, or container of more than 50 cubic centimeters.

(B) A person who violates the provisions of this section is guilty of a misdemeanor and, upon conviction, must be imprisoned not more than 3 years or fined not more than $5,000, or both.

(C) Except as permitted above, nothing in this section prohibits the purchase, sale, transportation, or use of tear gas for the destruction of insects or rodents if tear gas is not in containers or shells suitable for use in a tear-gas gun, equipment, or machine and if the purchaser has written authority for the purchase and use of tear gas from the county agent of the county in which he resides.

§ 16-23-480. Manufacture or possession of article designed to cause damage by fire or other means. It is unlawful for a person to manufacture, cause to be manufactured, or possess any object or article which is designed to cause damage by fire or any other means to person or property either by ignition, detonation, or other means. It is unlawful for a person to possess any object or article solely for the purpose of causing damage by fire or other means to person or property either by ignition, detonation, or other means.

A person who violates the provisions of this section is guilty of a felony and, upon conviction, must be fined in the discretion of the court or imprisoned not more than 5 years, or both.

§ 16-23-490. Additional punishment for possession of firearm or knife during commission of, or attempt to commit, violent crime.

(A) If a person is in possession of a firearm or visibly displays what appears to be a firearm or visibly displays a knife during the commission of a violent crime and is convicted of committing or attempting to commit a violent crime as defined in § 16-1-60, he must be imprisoned 5 years, in addition to the punishment provided for the principal crime. This 5-year sentence does not apply in cases where the death penalty or a life sentence without parole is imposed for the violent crime.

(B) Service of the 5-year sentence is mandatory unless a longer mandatory minimum term of imprisonment is provided by law for the violent crime. The court may impose this mandatory 5-year sentence to run consecutively or concurrently.

(C) Except as provided in this subsection, the person sentenced under this section is not eligible during this 5-year period for parole, work release, or extended work release. The 5 years may not be suspended and the person may not complete his term of imprisonment in less than 5 years pursuant to good-time credits or work credits, but may earn credits during this period. The person is eligible for work release, if the person is sentenced for voluntary manslaughter (§ 16-3-50), kidnapping (§ 16-3-910), carjacking (§ 16-3-1075), burglary in the second degree (§ 16-11-312(B)), armed robbery (§ 16-11-330(A)), or attempted armed robbery (§ 16-11-330(B)), the crime did not involve any criminal sexual conduct or an additional violent crime as defined in § 16-1-60, and the person is within 3 years of release from imprisonment.

(D) As used in this section, "firearm" means any machine gun, automatic rifle, revolver, pistol, or any weapon which will, or is designed to, or may readily be converted to expel a projectile; "knife" means an instrument or tool consisting of a sharp cutting blade whether or not fastened to a handle which is capable of being used to inflict a cut, slash, or wound.

(E) The additional punishment may not be imposed unless the indictment alleged as a separate count that the person was in possession of a firearm or visibly displayed what appeared to be a firearm or visibly displays a knife during the commission of the violent crime and conviction was had upon this count in the indictment. The penalties prescribed in this section may not be imposed unless the person convicted was at the same time indicted and convicted of a violent crime as defined in § 16-1-60.

§ 16-23-500. Unlawful possession of a firearm by a person convicted of violent offense; confiscation.

(A) It is unlawful for a person who has been convicted of a violent crime, as defined by § 16-1-60, that is classified as a felony offense, to possess a firearm or ammunition within this State.

(B) A person who violates the provisions of this section is guilty of a felony and, upon conviction, must be fined not more than $2,000 or imprisoned not more than 5 years, or both.

(C) (1) In addition to the penalty provided in this section, the firearm or ammunition involved in the violation of this section must be confiscated. The firearm or ammunition must be delivered to the chief of police of the municipality or to the sheriff of the county if the violation occurred outside the corporate limits of a municipality. The law enforcement agency that receives the confiscated firearm or ammunition may use it within the agency, transfer it to another law enforcement agency for the lawful use of that agency, trade it with a retail dealer licensed to sell firearms or ammunition in this State for a firearm, ammunition, or any other equipment approved by the agency, or destroy it. A firearm or ammunition must not be disposed of in any manner until the results of any legal proceeding in which it may be involved are finally determined. If the State Law Enforcement Division seized the firearm or ammunition, the division may keep the firearm or ammunition for use by its forensic laboratory. Records must be kept of all confiscated firearms or ammunition received by the law enforcement agencies under the provisions of this section.

(2) A law enforcement agency that receives a firearm or ammunition pursuant to this section shall administratively release the firearm or ammunition to an innocent owner. The firearm or ammunition must not be released to the innocent owner until the results of any legal proceedings in which the firearm or ammunition may be involved are finally determined. Before the firearm or ammunition may be released, the innocent owner shall provide the law enforcement agency with proof of ownership and shall certify that the innocent owner will not release the firearm or ammunition to the person who has been charged with a violation of this section which resulted in the confiscation of the firearm or ammunition. The law enforcement agency shall notify the innocent owner when the firearm or ammunition is available for release. If the innocent owner fails to recover the firearm or ammunition within thirty days after notification of the release, the law enforcement agency may maintain or dispose of the firearm or ammunition as otherwise provided in this section.

(D) The judge that hears the case involving the violent offense, as defined by § 16-1-60, that is classified as a felony offense, shall make a specific finding on the record that the offense is a violent offense, as defined by § 16-1-60, and is classified as a felony offense. A judge's failure to make a specific finding on the record does not bar or otherwise affect prosecution pursuant to this subsection and does not constitute a defense to prosecution pursuant to this subsection.

§ 16-23-520. Use, transportation, manufacture, possession, purchase, or sale of teflon-coated ammunition. It is unlawful for a person to use, transport, manufacture, possess, distribute, sell, or buy any ammunition or shells that are coated with polytetrafluoroethylene (teflon).

A person who violates the provisions of this section is guilty of a felony and, upon conviction, must be imprisoned not more than 5 years or fined not more than $5,000, or both.

§ 16-23-530. Firearms; possession by or sale to unlawful alien; penalties.

(A) It is unlawful for an alien unlawfully present in the United States to possess, purchase, offer to purchase, sell, lease, rent, barter, exchange, or transport into this State a firearm.

(B) It is unlawful for a person to knowingly sell, offer to sell, deliver, lease, rent, barter, exchange, or transport for sale into this State a firearm to a person knowing that such person is not lawfully present in the United States.

(C) A person violating the provisions of subsection (A) of this section is guilty of a felony and, upon conviction, must be fined not more than $10,000 or imprisoned not more than 10 years, or both.

(D) A person violating the provisions of subsection (B) of this section is guilty of a misdemeanor and, upon conviction, must be fined not more than $2,000 or imprisoned not more than 3 years, or both.

Article 7. Bombs, Destructive Devices, and Weapons of Mass Destruction

§ 16-23-710. Definitions. For purposes of this article:

(2) "**Bomb**" includes a destructive device capable of being detonated, triggered, or set off to release any substance or material that is destructive, irritating, odoriferous, or otherwise harmful to one or more organisms including, but not limited to, human beings, livestock, animals, crops or vegetation, or to earth, air, water, or any other material or substance necessary or required to sustain human or any other individual form of life, or to real or personal property.

(4) "**Building**" means any structure, vehicle, watercraft, or aircraft:

(a) where any person lodges or lives; or

(b) where people assemble for purposes of business, government, education, religion, entertainment, public transportation, or public use or where goods are stored. Where a building consists of 2 or more units separately occupied or secured, each unit is considered both a separate building in itself and a part of the main building.

(5) "**Device**" means an object, contrivance, instrument, technique, or any thing that is designed, manufactured, assembled, or capable of serving any purpose in a bomb, destructive device, explosive, incendiary, or weapon of mass destruction.

(6) "**Detonate**" means to explode or cause to explode.

(7) "**Destructive device**" means:

(a) a bomb, incendiary device, or any thing that can detonate, explode, be released, or burn by mechanical, chemical, or nuclear means, or that contains an explosive, incendiary, poisonous gas, or toxic substance (chemical, biological, or nuclear materials) including, but not limited to, an incendiary or over-pressure device, or any other device capable of causing damage, injury, or death;

(c) a combination of any parts, components, chemical compounds, or other substances, either designed or intended for use in converting any device into a destructive device which has been or can be assembled to cause damage, injury, or death.

(8) "**Detonator**" means a device containing a detonating charge used to initiate detonation in an explosive or any device capable of triggering or setting off an explosion or explosive charge including, but not limited to, impact or an impact device, a timing mechanism, electricity, a primer, primer or detonating cord, a detonating cap or device of any kind, detonating waves, electric blasting caps, blasting caps for use with safety fuses, shock tube initiator, and detonating cord delay connectors, or any other device capable of detonating or exploding a bomb, weapon of mass destruction, or destructive device.

(9) "**Distribute**" means the actual or constructive delivery or the attempted transfer from one person to another.

(10) "**Explosive**" means a chemical compound or other substance or a mechanical system intended for the purpose of producing an explosion capable of causing injury, death, or damage to property or an explosive containing oxidizing and combustible units or other ingredients in such proportions or quantities that ignition, fire, friction, concussion, percussion, or detonation may produce an explosion capable of causing injury, death, or damage to property. Explosives include, but are not limited to, the list of explosive materials published and periodically updated by the Bureau of Alcohol, Tobacco and Firearms.

(11) "**Hoax device**" or "**replica**" means a device or object which has the appearance of a destructive device.

(13) "**Incendiary device**" means a destructive device, however possessed or delivered, and by whatever name called, containing or holding a flammable liquid or compound, which is capable of being ignited by any means possible. Incendiary device includes, but is not limited to, any form of explosive, explosive bomb, grenade, missile, or similar device, whether capable of being carried or thrown by a person acting alone or with one or more persons, but does not include a device manufactured or produced for the primary purpose of illumination or for marking detours, obstructions, defective paving, or other hazards on streets, roads, highways, or bridges, when used in a lawful manner.

(14) "**Over-pressure device**" means a container filled with an explosive gas or expanding gas or liquid which is designed or constructed so as to cause the container to break, fracture, or rupture in a manner capable of causing death, injury, or property damage, and includes, but is not limited to, a chemical reaction bomb, an acid bomb, a caustic bomb, or a dry ice bomb.

(15) "**Parts**" mean a combination of parts, components, chemical compounds, or other substances, designed or intended for use in converting any device into a destructive device.

(17) "**Property**" means real or personal property of any kind including money, choses in action, and other similar interest in property.

(18) "**Terrorism**" includes activities that:
   (a) involve acts dangerous to human life that are a violation of the criminal laws of this State;
   (b) appear to be intended to:
      (i) intimidate or coerce a civilian population;
      (ii) influence the policy of a government by intimidation or coercion; or
      (iii) affect the conduct of a government by mass destruction, assassination, or kidnapping; and
   (c) occur primarily within the territorial jurisdiction of this State.

(19) "**Weapon of mass destruction**" means :
   (a) any destructive device as defined in item (7);

§ 16-23-715. Possession, threatened or attempted use of weapon of mass destruction for act of terrorism; penalty.
A person who, without lawful authority, possesses, uses, threatens, or attempts or conspires to possess or use a weapon of mass destruction in furtherance of an act of terrorism is guilty of a felony and upon conviction:

(1) in cases resulting in the death of another person, must be punished by death or by imprisonment for life; or

(2) in cases which do not result in the death of another person, must be punished by imprisonment for not less than 25 years nor more than life.

§ 16-23-720. Use, counseling or soliciting others to use, possessing, or threatening to use destructive device; harboring terrorist.

(A) It is unlawful for a person intentionally to use a destructive device or cause an explosion, or intentionally to aid, counsel, solicit another, or procure the use of a destructive device. A person who violates this subsection is guilty of a felony and, upon conviction:

   (1) in cases resulting in the death of another person where there was malice aforethought, must be punished by death, by imprisonment for life, or by a mandatory minimum term of imprisonment for 30 years;

   (2) in cases resulting in the death of another person where there was not malice aforethought, must be imprisoned not less than 10 years nor more than 30 years; and

   (3) in cases resulting in injury to a person, must be imprisoned for not less than 10 years nor more than 25 years.

(B) A person who intentionally causes an explosion by means of a destructive device or aids, counsels, solicits another, or procures an explosion by means of a destructive device, which results in damage to a building or other real or personal property, or a person who attempts to injure another or damage or destroy a building or other real or personal property by means of a destructive device, is guilty of a felony and, upon conviction, must be imprisoned for not less than 10 years nor more than 25 years.

(C) A person who knowingly possesses, manufactures, transports, distributes, or possesses with the intent to distribute a destructive device or any explosive, incendiary device, or over-pressure device or toxic substance or material which has been configured to cause damage, injury, or death, or a person who possesses parts, components, or materials which when assembled constitute a destructive device is guilty of a felony and, upon conviction, must be imprisoned for not less than 2 years nor more than 15 years.

(D) A person who threatens, solicits another to threaten, or conspires to threaten to cause damage, injury, or death or to cause damage to or destroy a building or other real or personal property by means of destructive device is guilty of a felony and, upon conviction, must be imprisoned for not more than 15 years.

(E) A person who knowingly protects, harbors, or conceals another who is known by the person to have planned, executed, or committed any violation of the provisions of this article is guilty of a felony and, upon conviction, must be imprisoned for not more than 15 years.

§ 16-23-730. Hoax device or replica of destructive device or detonator; manufacture, possession or transport; threat to use; penalties.
A person who knowingly manufactures, possesses, transports, distributes, uses or aids, or counsels, solicits another, or conspires with another in the use of a hoax device or replica of a destructive device or detonator which causes any person reasonably to believe that the hoax device or replica is a destructive device or detonator is guilty of a misdemeanor and, upon conviction, must be imprisoned for not more than 1 year or fined not more than $10,000, or both. A person who communicates or transmits to another person that a hoax device or replica is a destructive device or detonator with the intent to intimidate or threaten injury, to obtain property of another, or to interfere with the ability of another person to conduct or carry on his life, business, trade, education, religious worship, or to interfere with the operations and functions of any government entity is guilty of a felony and, upon conviction, must be imprisoned for not less than 2 years nor more than 15 years.

§ 16-23-750. Conveying false information regarding attempted use of a destructive device; aiding or conspiring; penalty.
A person who conveys or causes to be conveyed false information, knowing the information to be false, concerning an attempt or alleged attempt being made or to be made to kill, injure, or intimidate any person or to damage or destroy any building or other real or personal property by means of an explosive, incendiary, or destructive device or who aids, employs, or conspires with any person to do or cause to be done any of the acts in this section, is guilty of a

felony and, upon conviction, for a first offense must be imprisoned for not less than 1 year nor more than 10 years. For a second or subsequent offense, the person must be imprisoned for not less than 5 years nor more than 15 years. A sentence imposed for a violation of this section must not be suspended and probation must not be granted.

Chapter 25. Criminal Domestic Violence
Article 1. General Provisions

§ 16-25-30. Firearms and ammunition prohibitions; penalties.

(A) Notwithstanding the provisions of § 16-23-30, it is unlawful for a person to ship, transport, receive, or possess a firearm or ammunition, if the person:

(1) has been convicted of a violation of § 16-25-20(B) or 16-25-65, or has been convicted of domestic violence in another state, tribe, or territory containing among its elements those elements enumerated in § 16-25-20(B) or § 16-25-65;

(2) has been convicted of a violation of § 16-25-20(C) and the court made specific findings and concluded that the person caused moderate bodily injury to their own household member, or has been convicted of domestic violence in another state, tribe, or territory containing among its elements those elements enumerated in § 16-25-20(C) and the court made specific findings and concluded that the person caused moderate bodily injury to their own household member;

(3) has been convicted of a violation of § 16-25-20(C) or (D) and the judge at the time of sentencing ordered that the person is prohibited from shipping, transporting, receiving, or possessing a firearm or ammunition, or has been convicted of domestic violence in another state, tribe, or territory containing among its elements those elements enumerated in § 16-25-20(C) or (D) and the judge at the time of sentencing ordered that the person is prohibited from shipping, transporting, receiving, or possessing a firearm or ammunition;

(4) is subject to a valid order of protection issued by the family court pursuant to Chapter 4, Title 20, and the family court judge at the time of the hearing made specific findings of physical harm, bodily injury, assault, or that the person offered or attempted to cause physical harm or injury to a person's own household member with apparent and present ability under the circumstances reasonably creating fear of imminent peril and the family court judge ordered that the person is prohibited from shipping, transporting, receiving, or possessing a firearm or ammunition. The standard applied in this subsection applies only to the determination of whether to prohibit a person from possessing a firearm or ammunition and does not apply to the issuance of the order pursuant to Chapter 4, Title 20; or

(5) is subject to a valid order of protection related to domestic or family violence issued by a court of another state, tribe, or territory in compliance with the Uniform Interstate Enforcement of Domestic Violence Protection Orders Act, and the judge at the time of the hearing made specific findings of physical harm, bodily injury, assault, or that the person offered or attempted to cause physical harm or injury to a person's own household member with apparent and present ability under the circumstances reasonably creating fear of imminent peril and the judge ordered that the person is prohibited from shipping, transporting, receiving, or possessing a firearm or ammunition. The standard applied in this subsection applies only to the determination of whether to prohibit a person from possessing a firearm or ammunition and does not apply to the issuance of the order pursuant to Chapter 4, Title 20.

(B) A person who violates subsection (A)(1) is guilty of a felony and, upon conviction, must be fined not more than $2,000 or imprisoned for not more than 5 years, or both. A person who violates subsection (A)(2) or (A)(3) is guilty of a misdemeanor and, upon conviction, must be fined not more than $1,000 or imprisoned not more than 3 years, or both. A person who violates subsection (A)(4) or (A)(5) is guilty of a misdemeanor and, upon conviction, must be fined not more than $500 or imprisoned not more than 30 days, or both.

(C) A person must not be considered to have been convicted of domestic violence for purposes of this section unless the person was represented by counsel in the case, or knowingly and intelligently waived the right to counsel in the case; and in the case of a prosecution for an offense described in this section for which a person was entitled to a jury trial in the jurisdiction in which the case was tried, either the case was tried by a jury, or the person knowingly and intelligently waived the right to have the case tried by a jury, by guilty plea or otherwise. A person must not be considered to have been convicted of domestic violence for purposes of this section if the conviction has been expunged, set aside, or is an offense for which the person has been pardoned.

(D) At the time a person is convicted of violating the provisions of § 16-25-20 or 16-25-65, or upon the issuance of an order of protection pursuant to Chapter 4, Title 20, the court must deliver to the person a written form that conspicuously bears the following language: "Pursuant to 18 U.S.C. § 922, it is unlawful for a person convicted of a violation of § 16-25-20 or 16-25-65, or a person who is subject to a valid order of protection pursuant to Chapter 4, Title 20, to ship, transport, possess, or receive a firearm or ammunition."

(E) The provisions of this section prohibiting the possession of firearms and ammunition by persons who have been convicted of domestic violence shall apply to a person who has been convicted of domestic violence for:

(1) life, if the person has been convicted of a violation of § 16-25-65, or has been convicted of domestic violence in another state, tribe, or territory containing among its elements those elements enumerated in § 16-25-65;

(2) ten years from the date of conviction or the date the person is released from confinement for the conviction, whichever is later, if the person has been convicted of a violation of § 16-25-20(B), or has been convicted of domestic violence in another state, tribe, or territory containing among its elements those elements enumerated in § 16-25-20(B);

(3) three years from the date of conviction or the date the person is released from confinement for the conviction, whichever is later, if the person has been convicted of a violation of § 16-25-20(C) or (D) and the judge at the time of sentencing ordered that the person is prohibited from shipping, transporting, receiving, or possessing a firearm or ammunition, or has been convicted of domestic violence in another state, tribe, or territory containing among its elements those elements enumerated in § 16-25-20(C) or (D) and the judge at the time of sentencing ordered that the person is prohibited from shipping, transporting, receiving, or possessing a firearm or ammunition; or

(4) the duration of the order of protection, if the person is subject to a valid order of protection issued by the family court pursuant to Chapter 4, Title 20, and the family court judge at the time of the hearing made specific findings of physical harm, bodily injury, assault, or that the person offered or attempted to cause physical harm or injury to a person's own household member with apparent and present ability under the circumstances reasonably creating fear of imminent peril and the family court judge ordered that the person is prohibited from shipping, transporting, receiving, or possessing a firearm or ammunition, or is subject to a valid order of protection related to domestic or family violence issued by a court of another state, tribe, or territory in compliance with the Uniform Interstate Enforcement of Domestic Violence Protection Orders Act and the judge at the time of the hearing made specific findings of physical harm, bodily injury, assault, or that the person offered or attempted to cause physical harm or injury to a person's own household member with apparent and present ability under the circumstances reasonably creating fear of imminent peril and the judge ordered that the person is prohibited from shipping, transporting, receiving, or possessing a firearm or ammunition.

(F) (1) Following the period of time established in subsection (E), if the person has not been convicted of any other domestic violence offenses pursuant to this article or similar offenses in another jurisdiction, no domestic violence charges are currently pending against the person, and the person is not otherwise prohibited from shipping, transporting, receiving, or possessing a firearm or ammunition pursuant to any other State law, the person's right to ship, transport, receive, or possess a firearm or ammunition shall be restored.

(2) Following the period of time established in subsection (E), if the person requests in writing to the South Carolina Law Enforcement Division (SLED), SLED shall notify the National Instant Criminal Background Check System (NICS) that the State has restored the person's right to ship, transport, receive, or possess a firearm or ammunition, and shall request immediate removal of the person's name to whom the restrictions contained in this section apply.

TITLE 23. Law Enforcement and Public Safety
Chapter 31. Firearms
Article 1. Purchase of Rifles and Shotguns

§ 23-31-10. Purchase of rifle or shotgun in another state. A resident of this State including a corporation or other business entity maintaining a place of business in this State, who may lawfully purchase and receive delivery of a rifle or shotgun in this State, may purchase a rifle or shotgun in another state and transport or receive it in this State; provided, that the sale meets the lawful requirements of each state, meets all lawful requirements of any federal statute, and is made by a licensed importer, licensed manufacturer, licensed dealer, or licensed collector.

§ 23-31-20. Purchase of rifle or shotgun in this State by resident of any state. A resident of any state may purchase rifles and shotguns in this State if the resident conforms to applicable provisions of statutes and regulations of this State, the United States, and of the state in which the person resides.

Article 4. Concealed Weapon Permits

§ 23-31-210. Definitions. As used in this article:
(1) "**Resident**" means an individual who is present in South Carolina with the intention of making a permanent home in South Carolina or military personnel on permanent change of station orders.
(2) "**Qualified nonresident**" means an individual who owns real property in South Carolina, but who resides in another state.
(3) "**Picture identification**" means:
  (a) a valid driver's license or photographic identification card issued by the state in which the applicant resides; or
  (b) an official photographic identification card issued by the Department of Revenue, a federal or state law enforcement agency, an agency of the United States Department of Defense, or the United States Department of State.
(4) "**Proof of training**" means an original document or certified copy of the document supplied by an applicant that certifies that he is either:
  (a) a person who, within 3 years before filing an application, successfully has completed a basic or advanced handgun education course offered by a state, county, or municipal law enforcement agency or a nationally recognized organization that promotes gun safety. This education course must include, but is not limited to:
    (i) information on the statutory and case law of this State relating to handguns and to the use of deadly force;
    (ii) information on handgun use and safety;
    (iii) information on the proper storage practice for handguns with an emphasis on storage practices that reduces the possibility of accidental injury to a child; and
    (iv) the actual firing of the handgun in the presence of the instructor;
  (b) a person who demonstrates any of the following must comply with the provisions of subitem (a)(i) only:
    (i) a person who demonstrates the completion of basic military training provided by any branch of the United States military who produces proof of his military service through the submission of a DD214 form;

(ii) a retired law enforcement officer who produces proof that he is a graduate of the Criminal Justice Academy or that he was a law enforcement officer prior to the requirement for graduation from the Criminal Justice Academy; or

(iii) a retired state or federal law enforcement officer who produces proof of graduation from a federal or state academy that includes firearms training as a graduation requirement;

(c) an instructor certified by the National Rifle Association or another SLED-approved competent national organization that promotes the safe use of handguns;

(d) a person who can demonstrate to the Director of SLED or his designee that he has a proficiency in both the use of handguns and state laws pertaining to handguns;

(e) an active duty police handgun instructor;

(f) a person who has a SLED-certified or approved competitive handgun shooting classification; or

(g) a member of the active or reserve military, or a member of the National Guard.

SLED shall promulgate regulations containing general guidelines for courses and qualifications for instructors which would satisfy the requirements of this item. For purposes of subitems (a) and (c), "proof of training" is not satisfied unless the organization and its instructors meet or exceed the guidelines and qualifications contained in the regulations promulgated by SLED pursuant to this item.

(5) "**Concealable weapon**" means a firearm having a length of less than 12 inches measured along its greatest dimension that must be carried in a manner that is hidden from public view in normal wear of clothing except when needed for self-defense, defense of others, and the protection of real or personal property.

(6) "**Proof of ownership of real property**" means a certified current document from the county assessor of the county in which the property is located verifying ownership of the real property. SLED must determine the appropriate document that fulfills this requirement.

§ 23-31-215. Issuance of permits.

(A) Notwithstanding any other provision of law, except subject to subsection (B), SLED must issue a permit, which is no larger than 3-1/2 inches by 3 inches in size, to carry a concealable weapon to a resident or qualified nonresident who is at least 21 years of age and who is not prohibited by state law from possessing the weapon upon submission of:

(1) a completed application signed by the person;

(2) a photocopy of a driver's license or photographic identification card;

(3) proof of residence or if the person is a qualified nonresident, proof of ownership of real property in this State;

(4) proof of actual or corrected vision rated at 20/40 within 6 months of the date of application or, in the case of a person licensed to operate a motor vehicle in this State, presentation of a valid driver's license;

(5) proof of training;

(6) payment of a $50 application fee. This fee must be waived for disabled veterans and retired law enforcement officers; and

(7) a complete set of fingerprints unless, because of a medical condition verified in writing by a licensed medical doctor, a complete set of fingerprints is impossible to submit. In lieu of the submission of fingerprints, the applicant must submit the written statement from a licensed medical doctor specifying the reason or reasons why the applicant's fingerprints may not be taken. If all other qualifications are met, the Chief of SLED may waive the fingerprint requirements of this item. The statement of medical limitation must be attached to the copy of the application retained by SLED. A law enforcement agency may charge a fee not to exceed $5 for fingerprinting an applicant.

(B) Upon submission of the items required by subsection (A), SLED must conduct or facilitate a local, state, and federal fingerprint review of the applicant. SLED also must conduct a background check of the applicant through notification to and input from the sheriff of the county where the applicant resides or if the applicant is a qualified nonresident, where the applicant owns real property in this State. The sheriff within 10 working days after notification by SLED, may submit a recommendation on an application. Before making a determination whether or not to issue a permit under this article, SLED must consider the recommendation provided pursuant to this subsection. If the fingerprint review and background check are favorable, SLED must issue the permit.

(C) SLED shall issue a written statement to an unqualified applicant specifying its reasons for denying the application within 90 days from the date the application was received; otherwise, SLED shall issue a concealable weapon permit. If an applicant is unable to comply with the provisions of § 23-31-210(4), SLED shall offer the applicant a handgun training course that satisfies the requirements of § 23-31-210(4). The course shall cost $50. If a permit is granted by operation of law because an applicant was not notified of a denial within the 90-day notification period, the permit may be revoked upon written notification from SLED that sufficient grounds exist for revocation or initial denial.

(D) Denial of an application may be appealed. The appeal must be in writing and state the basis for the appeal. The appeal must be submitted to the Chief of SLED within 30 days from the date the denial notice is received. The chief shall issue a written decision within 10 days from the date the appeal is received. An adverse decision shall specify the reasons for upholding the denial and may be reviewed by the Administrative Law Court pursuant to Article 5, Chapter 23, Title 1, upon a petition filed by an applicant within 30 days from the date of delivery of the division's decision.

(E) SLED must make permit application forms available to the public. A permit application form shall require an applicant to supply:

(1) name, including maiden name if applicable;

(2) date and place of birth;

(3) sex;

(4) race;

(5) height;

(6) weight;

(7) eye and hair color;

(8) current residence address; and

(9) all residence addresses for the 3 years preceding the application date.

(F) The permit application form shall require the applicant to certify that:

(1) he is not a person prohibited under state law from possessing a weapon;

(2) he understands the permit is revoked and must be surrendered immediately to SLED if the permit holder becomes a person prohibited under state law from possessing a weapon; and

(3) all information contained in his application is true and correct to the best of his knowledge.

(G) Medical personnel, law enforcement agencies, organizations offering handgun education courses pursuant to § 23-31-210(4), and their personnel, who in good faith provide information regarding a person's application, must be exempt from liability that may arise from issuance of a permit; provided, however, a weapons instructor must meet the requirements established in § 23-31-210(4) in order to be exempt from liability under this subsection.

(H) A permit application must be submitted in person, by mail, or online to SLED headquarters which shall verify the legibility and accuracy of the required documents. If an applicant submits his application online, SLED may continue to make all contact with that applicant through online communications.

(I) SLED must maintain a list of all permit holders and the current status of each permit. SLED may release the list of permit holders or verify an individual's permit status only if the request is made by a law enforcement agency to aid in an official investigation, or if the list is required to be released pursuant to a subpoena or court order. SLED may charge a fee not to exceed its costs in releasing the information under this subsection. Except as otherwise provided in this subsection, a person in possession of a list of permit holders obtained from SLED must destroy the list.

(J) A permit is valid statewide unless revoked because the person has:

(1) become a person prohibited under state law from possessing a weapon;

(2) moved his permanent residence to another state and no longer owns real property in this State;

(3) voluntarily surrendered the permit; or

(4) been charged with an offense that, upon conviction, would prohibit the person from possessing a firearm. However, if the person subsequently is found not guilty of the offense, then his permit must be reinstated at no charge.

Once a permit is revoked, it must be surrendered to a sheriff, police department, a SLED agent, or by certified mail to the Chief of SLED. A person who fails to surrender his permit in accordance with this subsection is guilty of a misdemeanor and, upon conviction, must be fined $25.

(K) A permit holder must have his permit identification card in his possession whenever he carries a concealable weapon. When carrying a concealable weapon pursuant to Article 4, Chapter 31, Title 23, a permit holder must inform a law enforcement officer of the fact that he is a permit holder and present the permit identification card when an officer:

(1) identifies himself as a law enforcement officer; and

(2) requests identification or a driver's license from a permit holder.

A permit holder immediately must report the loss or theft of a permit identification card to SLED headquarters. A person who violates the provisions of this subsection is guilty of a misdemeanor and, upon conviction, must be fined $25.

(L) SLED shall issue a replacement for lost, stolen, damaged, or destroyed permit identification cards after the permit holder has updated all information required in the original application and the payment of a $5 replacement fee. Any change of permanent address must be communicated in writing to SLED within 10 days of the change accompanied by the payment of a fee of $5 to defray the cost of issuance of a new permit. SLED shall then issue a new permit with the new address. A permit holder's failure to notify SLED in accordance with this subsection constitutes a misdemeanor punishable by a $25 fine. The original permit shall remain in force until receipt of the corrected permit identification card by the permit holder, at which time the original permit must be returned to SLED.

(M) A permit issued pursuant to this section does not authorize a permit holder to carry a concealable weapon into a:

(1) law enforcement, correctional, or detention facility;

(2) courthouse or courtroom;

(3) polling place on election days;

(4) office of or the business meeting of the governing body of a county, public school district, municipality, or special purpose district;

(5) school or college athletic event not related to firearms;

(6) daycare facility or preschool facility;

(7) place where the carrying of firearms is prohibited by federal law;

(8) church or other established religious sanctuary unless express permission is given by the appropriate church official or governing body;

(9) hospital, medical clinic, doctor's office, or any other facility where medical services or procedures are performed unless expressly authorized by the employer; or

(10) place clearly marked with a sign prohibiting the carrying of a concealable weapon on the premises pursuant to §§ 23-31-220 and 23-31-235. Except that a property owner or an agent acting on his behalf, by express written consent, may allow individuals of his choosing to enter onto property regardless of any posted sign to the contrary. A person who violates a provision of this item, whether the violation is wilful or not, only may be charged with a violation of § 16-11-620 and must not be charged with or penalized for a violation of this subsection.

Except as provided for in item (10), a person who wilfully violates a provision of this subsection is guilty of a misdemeanor and, upon conviction, must be fined not less than $1,000 or imprisoned not more than 1 year, or both, at the discretion of the court and have his permit revoked for 5 years.

Nothing contained in this subsection may be construed to alter or affect the provisions of §§ 10-11-320, 16-23-420, 16-23-430, 16-23-465, 44-23-1080, 44-52-165, 50-9-830, and 51-3-145.

(N)(1) Valid out-of-state permits to carry concealable weapons held by a resident of a reciprocal state must be honored by this State, provided, that the reciprocal state requires an applicant to successfully pass a criminal background check and a course in firearm training and safety. A resident of a reciprocal state carrying a concealable weapon in South Carolina is subject to and must abide by the laws of South Carolina regarding concealable weapons. SLED shall maintain and publish a list of those states as the states with which South Carolina has reciprocity.

   (2) Notwithstanding the reciprocity requirements of subitem (1), South Carolina shall automatically recognize concealed weapon permits issued by Georgia and North Carolina.

   (3) The reciprocity provisions of this section shall not be construed to authorize the holder of any out-of-state permit or license to carry, in this State, any firearm or weapon other than a handgun.

(O) A permit issued pursuant to this article is not required for a person:

   (1) specified in § 16-23-20, items (1) through (5) and items (7) through (11);

   (2) carrying a self-defense device generally considered to be nonlethal including the substance commonly referred to as "pepper gas"; or

   (3) carrying a concealable weapon in a manner not prohibited by law.

(P) Upon renewal, a permit issued pursuant to this article is valid for 5 years. Subject to subsection (Q), SLED shall renew a currently valid permit upon:

   (1) payment of a $50 renewal fee by the applicant. This fee must be waived for disabled veterans and retired law enforcement officers;

   (2) completion of the renewal application; and

   (3) picture identification or facsimile copy thereof.

(Q) Upon submission of the items required by subsection (P), SLED must conduct or facilitate a state and federal background check of the applicant. If the background check is favorable, SLED must renew the permit.

(R) No provision contained within this article shall expand, diminish, or affect the duty of care owed by and liability accruing to, as may exist at law immediately before the effective date of this article, the owner of or individual in legal possession of real property for the injury or death of an invitee, licensee, or trespasser caused by the use or misuse by a third party of a concealable weapon. Absence of a sign prohibiting concealable weapons shall not constitute negligence or establish a lack of duty of care.

(S) At least 30 days before a permit issued pursuant to this article expires, SLED shall notify the permit holder by mail or online if permitted by subsection (H) at the permit holder's address of record that the permit is set to expire along with notification of the permit holder's opportunity to renew the permit pursuant to the provisions of subsections (P) and (Q).

(T) During the first quarter of each calendar year, SLED must publish a report of the following information regarding the previous calendar year:

   (1) the number of permits;

   (2) the number of permits that were issued;

   (3) the number of permit applications that were denied;

   (4) the number of permits that were renewed;

   (5) the number of permit renewals that were denied;

   (6) the number of permits that were suspended or revoked; and

   (7) the name, address, and county of a person whose permit was revoked, including the reason for the revocation pursuant to subsection (J)(1).

The report must include a breakdown of such information by county.

(U) A concealable weapon permit holder whose permit has been expired for no more than 1 year may not be charged with a violation of § 16-23-20 but must be fined not more than $100.

§ 23-31-216. Collection and retention of fees. The State Law Enforcement Division shall collect, retain, expend, and carry forward all fees associated with the concealable weapon application, renewal, and replacement of the permit, as provided pursuant to this article.

§ 23-31-217. Effect on Section 16-23-20. Nothing in this article shall affect the provisions of § 16-23-20.

§ 23-31-220. Right to allow or permit concealed weapons upon premises; signs. Nothing contained in this article shall in any way be construed to limit, diminish, or otherwise infringe upon:

(1) the right of a public or private employer to prohibit a person who is licensed under this article from carrying a concealable weapon upon the premises of the business or work place or while using any machinery, vehicle, or equipment owned or operated by the business;

(2) the right of a private property owner or person in legal possession or control to allow or prohibit the carrying of a concealable weapon upon his premises.

The posting by the employer, owner, or person in legal possession or control of a sign stating "No Concealable Weapons Allowed" shall constitute notice to a person holding a permit issued pursuant to this article that the employer, owner, or person in legal possession or control requests that concealable weapons not be brought upon the premises or into the work place. A person who brings a concealable weapon onto the premises or work place in violation of the provisions of this paragraph may be charged with a violation of § 16-11-620. In addition to the penalties provided in § 16-11-620, a person convicted of a second or subsequent violation of the provisions of this paragraph must have his permit revoked for a period of 1 year. The prohibition contained in this section does not apply to persons specified in § 16-23-20, item (1).

§ 23-31-225. Carrying concealed weapons into residences or dwellings. No person who holds a permit issued pursuant to Article 4, Chapter 31, Title 23 may carry a concealable weapon into the residence or dwelling place of another person without the express permission of the owner or person in legal control or possession, as appropriate. A person who violates this provision is guilty of a misdemeanor and, upon conviction, must be fined not less than $1,000 or imprisoned for not more than 1 year, or both, at the discretion of the court and have his permit revoked for 5 years.

§ 23-31-230. Carrying concealed weapons between automobile and accommodation. Notwithstanding any provision of law, any person may carry a concealable weapon from an automobile or other motorized conveyance to a room or other accommodation he has rented and upon which an accommodations tax has been paid.

§ 23-31-235. Sign requirements.
(A) Notwithstanding any other provision of this article, any requirement of or allowance for the posting of signs prohibiting the carrying of a concealable weapon upon any premises shall only be satisfied by a sign expressing the prohibition in both written language interdict and universal sign language.
(B) All signs must be posted at each entrance into a building where a concealable weapon permit holder is prohibited from carrying a concealable weapon and must be:
(1) clearly visible from outside the building;
(2) eight inches wide by twelve inches tall in size;
(3) contain the words "NO CONCEALABLE WEAPONS ALLOWED" in black 1-inch tall uppercase type at the bottom of the sign and centered between the lateral edges of the sign;
(4) contain a black silhouette of a handgun inside a circle 7 inches in diameter with a diagonal line that runs from the lower left to the upper right at a 45 degree angle from the horizontal;
(5) a diameter of a circle; and
(6) placed not less than 40 inches and not more than 60 inches from the bottom of the building's entrance door.
(C) If the premises where concealable weapons are prohibited does not have doors, then the signs contained in subsection (A) must be:
(1) thirty-six inches wide by 48 inches tall in size;
(2) contain the words "NO CONCEALABLE WEAPONS ALLOWED" in black 3-inch tall uppercase type at the bottom of the sign and centered between the lateral edges of the sign;
(3) contain a black silhouette of a handgun inside a circle 34 inches in diameter with a diagonal line that is 2 inches wide and runs from the lower left to the upper right at a 45 degree angle from the horizontal and must be a diameter of a circle whose circumference is 2 inches wide;
(4) placed not less than 40 inches and not more than 96 inches above the ground;
(5) posted in sufficient quantities to be clearly visible from any point of entry onto the premises.

§ 23-31-240. Persons allowed to carry concealed weapon while on duty. Notwithstanding any other provision contained in this article, the following persons who possess a valid permit pursuant to this article may carry a concealable weapon anywhere within this State, when carrying out the duties of their office:
(1) active Supreme Court justices;
(2) active judges of the court of appeals;
(3) active circuit court judges;
(4) active family court judges;
(5) active masters-in-equity;
(6) active probate court judges;
(7) active magistrates;
(8) active municipal court judges;
(9) active federal judges;
(10) active administrative law judges;
(11) active solicitors and assistant solicitors; and
(12) active workers' compensation commissioners.

Article 5. Use and Possession of Machine Guns, Sawed-Off Shotguns and Rifles

§ 23-31-310. Definitions. When used in this article:
(a) "**Machine gun**" applies to and includes any weapon which shoots, is designed to shoot, or can be readily restored to shoot, automatically more than 1 shot, without manual reloading, by a single function of the trigger. The term shall also

include the frame or receiver of any such weapon, any combination or parts designed and intended for use in converting a weapon into a machine gun, and any combination of parts from which a machine gun can be assembled if such parts are in the possession or under the control of a person.

(b) "Sawed-off shotgun" means a shotgun having a barrel or barrels of less than 18 inches in length or a weapon made from a shotgun which as modified has an overall length of less than 26 inches or a barrel or barrels of less than 18 inches in length.

(c) "Shotgun" means a weapon designed or redesigned, made or remade, and intended to be fired from the shoulder and designed or redesigned and made or remade to use the energy of the explosive in a fixed shotgun shell to fire through a smooth bore either a number of ball shot or a single projectile for each pull of the trigger. The term includes any such weapon which may be readily restored to fire a fixed shotgun shell but does not include an antique firearm as defined in this section.

(d) "Sawed-off rifle" means a rifle having a barrel or barrels of less than 16 inches in length or a weapon made from a rifle which as modified has an overall length of less than 26 inches or a barrel or barrels of less than 16 inches in length.

(e) "Rifle" means a weapon designed or redesigned, made or remade, and intended to be fired from the shoulder and designed or redesigned and made or remade to use the energy of the explosive in a fixed cartridge to fire only a single projectile through a rifled bore for each single pull of the trigger. The term includes any such weapon which may be readily restored to fire a fixed cartridge but does not include an antique firearm as described in this section.

(f) "Antique firearm" means any firearm not designed or redesigned for using rim fire or conventional center fire ignition with fixed ammunition and manufactured in or before 1898 (including any matchlock, flintlock, percussion cap, or similar type of ignition system or replica thereof, whether actually manufactured before or after the year 1898) and also any firearm using fixed ammunition manufactured in or before 1898, for which ammunition is no longer manufactured in the United States and is not readily available in the ordinary channels of commercial trade.

(g) "Military firearm" means any military weapon, firearm, or destructive device, other than a machine gun, that is manufactured for military use by a firm licensed by the federal government pursuant to a contract with the federal government and does not include a pistol, rifle, or shotgun which fires only one shot for each pull of the trigger.

§ 23-31-320. Exceptions to application of article. The provisions of this article shall not apply to the Army, Navy, or Air Force of the United States, the National Guard, and organizations authorized by law to purchase or receive machine guns, military firearms, or sawed-off shotguns or sawed-off rifles, from the United States or from this State and the members of such organizations. Any peace officer of the State or of any county or other political subdivision thereof, state constable, member of the highway patrol, railway policeman or warden, superintendent, head keeper or deputy of any state prison, penitentiary, workhouse, county jail, city jail, or other institution for the detention of persons convicted or accused of crime or held as witnesses in criminal cases or person on duty in the postal service of the United States or any common carrier while transporting direct to any police department, military, or naval organization or person authorized by law to possess or use a machine gun, or sawed-off shotgun or sawed-off rifle, may possess machine guns, or sawed-off shotguns or sawed-off rifles, when required in the performance of their duties. Nor shall the provisions hereof be construed to apply to machine guns, or sawed-off shotguns or sawed-off rifles, kept for display as relics and which are rendered harmless and not usable.

The provisions of this article shall not apply to any manufacturer of machine guns or military firearms licensed pursuant to the provisions of 18 U. S. C. § 921 et seq., nor to any common or contract carrier transporting or shipping any machine guns or military firearms to or from such manufacturer if the transportation or shipment is not prohibited by federal law. Any such manufacturer shall furnish to the South Carolina Law Enforcement Division the serial numbers of all machine guns or military firearms manufactured by it within 30 days of such manufacture and shall be subject to the penalties provided in § 23-31-340 for noncompliance.

§ 23-31-330. Application and registration of person allowed to possess machine gun or sawed-off shotgun or rifle.

(A) Every person permitted by § 23-31-320 to possess a machine gun or sawed-off shotgun or sawed-off rifle, and any person elected or appointed to any office or position which entitles the person to possess a machine gun or sawed-off shotgun or sawed-off rifle, upon taking office, shall file with the State Law Enforcement Division on a blank to be supplied by the division on request an application which is properly sworn. The application must be approved by the sheriff of the county in which the applicant resides or has his principal place of business and include the applicant's name, residence and business address, physical description, whether or not ever charged or convicted of any crime, municipal, state, or otherwise, and where, if charged, and when it was disposed of. The applicant shall also give a description including the serial number and make of the machine gun or sawed-off shotgun or sawed-off rifle which he possesses or desires to possess. The State Law Enforcement Division shall file the application in its office. The division shall register the applicant together with the information required in the application in a book or index to be kept for that purpose, assign to him a number, and issue to him a card which shall bear the signature of the applicant and which he shall keep with him while he has the machine gun or sawed-off shotgun or sawed-off rifle in his possession. This registration must be made on the date application is received and filed with the division. The registration expires on December thirty-first of the year in which the license is issued.

(B) No permit or registration required by the provisions of this section is required where weapons are possessed by a governmental entity which has a significant public safety responsibility for the protection of life or property.

§ 23-31-340. Penalties. A person who violates the provisions of this article is guilty of a felony and, upon conviction, must be fined not more than $10,000 or imprisoned not more than 10 years, or both.

§ 23-31-350. Article not applicable to antique firearms. The provisions of this article shall not apply to antique firearms.

§ 23-31-360. Unregistered possession of machine guns or military firearms by licensed manufacturer. Machine guns or military firearms manufactured by a firm licensed by the federal government and subject to the Federal Gun Control Act may be legally possessed by the manufacturer without being registered with the State Law Enforcement Division. The manufacturing firm shall furnish to SLED the serial numbers of all machine guns or military firearms manufactured by it within 30 days of their manufacture and it is subject to the penalties provided in § 23-31-340 for noncompliance.

§ 23-31-370. Special limited license for possession, transportation, and sale of machine guns; violations and penalties.
(a) The South Carolina Law Enforcement Division may issue a special limited license for the possession, transportation, and sale of machine guns in this State to persons: **(1)** who are authorized representatives of a machine gun manufacturer or dealer engaged in demonstrating and selling them to agencies authorized by law to possess them, or **(2)** who are engaged in professional movie-making or providing services to professional movie-makers who use machine guns as regulated by this article in the course of creating movie "special effects".
(b) Applications for the special license authorized by this section must be on a form prescribed by the division, duly sworn to, containing the applicant's name, business and residence address, a record of any criminal charges filed against the applicant in the United States for other than traffic law violations and the disposition of the charges, a description of the machine guns to be possessed, transported, or sold in this State, including their make and serial numbers, the sites within the State to which the machine guns will be transported, and such other information the division considers necessary to implement this section.
(c) The division may issue a special license pursuant to this section if it determines that the applicant has not been convicted of any offense other than traffic violations and the applicant clearly qualifies under item (1) or (2) of subsection (a). The special license is valid for a specified period not to exceed 6 months which must be stated on the license.
(d) Any person who knowingly and wilfully makes any false statement for the purpose of obtaining the special license or who violates its terms, in addition to any other penalty provided by law, is guilty of a misdemeanor and, upon conviction, must be fined not more than $5,000 or imprisoned for not more than 2 years, or both.

Article 6. Using a Firearm While Under the Influence of Alcohol or a Controlled Substance

§ 23-31-400. Definitions; unlawful use of firearm; violations.
(A) As used in this article:
　(1) "Use a firearm" means to discharge a firearm.
　(2) "Serious bodily injury" means a physical condition which creates a substantial risk of death, serious personal disfigurement, or protracted loss or impairment of the function of a bodily member or organ.
(B) It is unlawful for a person who is under the influence of alcohol or a controlled substance to use a firearm in this State.
(C) A person who violates the provisions of subsection (B) is guilty of a misdemeanor and, upon conviction, must be fined not less than $2,000 or imprisoned not more than 2 years.
(D) This article does not apply to persons lawfully defending themselves or their property.

Article 7. Local Regulations

§ 23-31-510. Regulation of ownership, transfer, or possession of firearm or ammunition; discharge on landowner's own property. No governing body of any county, municipality, or other political subdivision in the State may enact or promulgate any regulation or ordinance that regulates or attempts to regulate:
(1) the transfer, ownership, possession, carrying, or transportation of firearms, ammunition, components of firearms, or any combination of these things; or
(2) a landowner discharging a firearm on the landowner's property to protect the landowner's family, employees, the general public, or the landowner's property from animals that the landowner reasonably believes pose a direct threat or danger to the landowner's property, people on the landowner's property, or the general public. For purposes of this item, the landowner's property must be a parcel of land comprised of at least 25 contiguous acres. Any ordinance regulating the discharge of firearms that does not specifically provide for an exclusion pursuant to this item is unenforceable as it pertains to an incident described in this item; otherwise, the ordinance is enforceable.

§ 23-31-520. Power to regulate public use of firearms; confiscation of firearms or ammunition. This article does not affect the authority of any county, municipality, or political subdivision to regulate the careless or negligent discharge or public brandishment of firearms, nor does it prevent the regulation of public brandishment of firearms during the times of or a demonstrated potential for insurrection, invasions, riots, or natural disasters. This article denies any county, municipality, or political subdivision the power to confiscate a firearm or ammunition unless incident to an arrest.

Article 8. Identification Cards Issued to and Firearm Qualification Provided for Retired Law Enforcement Personnel

§ 23-31-600. Retired personnel; identification cards; qualification for carrying concealed weapon.
(A) For purposes of this section:
(1) "Identification card" is a photographic identification card complying with 18 U.S.C. § 926C.
(2) "Qualified retired law enforcement officer" shall have the same meaning as in 18 U.S.C. § 926C.
(B) An agency or department within this State may comply with 18 U.S.C. § 926C, by issuing an identification card to any qualified retired law enforcement officer. If the agency or department currently issues credentials to active law enforcement officers, the agency or department may comply with the requirements of this section by issuing the same credentials to qualified retired law enforcement officers. If the same credentials are issued, then the agency or department must stamp the credentials with the word "RETIRED".
(C) (1) Subject to the limitations of subsection (E), a qualified retired law enforcement officer may carry a concealed weapon in this State if the qualified retired law enforcement officer possesses an identification card along with a certification that the qualified retired law enforcement officer has, not less recently than 1 year before the date the individual is carrying the firearm, met the standards established by the agency for training and qualification for active law enforcement officers to carry a firearm of the same type as the concealed firearm.
(2) The firearms certification required by this subsection may be reflected on the identification card or may be in a separate document carried with the identification card.
(D) The restrictions contained in §§ 23-31-220 and 23-31-225 are applicable to a person carrying a concealed weapon pursuant to this section.
(E) The agency or department must provide the qualified retired law enforcement officer with the opportunity to qualify to carry a firearm under the same standards for training and qualification for active law enforcement officers to carry firearms. However, the agency or department, as provided in 18 U.S.C. § 926C, may require the qualified retired law enforcement officer to pay the actual expenses of the training and qualification.

Article 10. Nics: Mental Health Adjudication and Commitment Reporting

Article 10. Nics: Mental Health Adjudication and Commitment Reporting Notes
Editor's Note: 2013 Act No. 22, § 3, provides as follows:
"SECTION 3. A court required to submit information to SLED pursuant to this act concerning individuals who have been adjudicated as a mental defective or who have been committed to a mental institution shall, from the effective date of this act forward, submit information by court order within 5 days from the filing of each order and in accordance with procedures developed as required by this act and have 1 year from this act's effective date to submit retroactive information by court order on such individuals going back a minimum of 10 years or, if records are not available as far back as 10 years, as far back as records exist."

§ 23-31-1010. Definitions. As used in this article:
(1) "Adjudicated as a mental defective" means a determination by a court of competent jurisdiction that a person, as a result of marked subnormal intelligence, mental illness, mental incompetency, mental condition, or mental disease:
(a) is a danger to himself or to others; or
(b) lacks the mental capacity to contract or manage the person's own affairs.
The term includes:
(a) a finding of insanity by a court in a criminal case; and
(b) those persons found incompetent to stand trial or found not guilty by reason of lack of mental responsibility pursuant to Articles 50a and 72b of the Uniform Code of Military Justice, 10 U.S.C. §§ 850(a) and 876(b).
(2) "Committed to a mental institution" means a formal commitment of a person to a mental institution by a court of competent jurisdiction. The term includes a commitment to a mental institution involuntarily, and a commitment to a mental institution for mental defectiveness, mental illness, and other reasons, such as drug use. The term does not include a person in a mental institution for observation or a voluntary admission to a mental institution.
(3) "Mental institution" includes mental health facilities, mental hospitals, sanitariums, psychiatric facilities, and other facilities that provide diagnoses by licensed professionals of mental retardation or mental illness, including a psychiatric ward in a general hospital.

§ 23-31-1020. Collection and submission of information of persons adjudicated as a mental defective or committed to a mental institution.
(A) The Judicial Department and the Chief of SLED, or the chief's designee, shall work in conjunction with a court of competent jurisdiction in developing procedures for the collection and submission of information of persons who have been adjudicated as a mental defective or who have been committed to a mental institution.
(B) When a court submits this information to SLED by court order, SLED shall transmit the information to the National Instant Criminal Background Check System (NICS) established pursuant to the Brady Handgun Violence Protection Act of 1993, Pub. L. (pg.79) 103-159.
(C) The court shall submit the information to SLED by court order within 5 days from the filing of each order related to adjudications and commitments. Under no circumstances may the court or SLED submit information pursuant to this

section relating to a person's diagnosis or treatment.

(D) SLED shall keep information submitted by the court confidential, and that information only may be disclosed to NICS pursuant to this section, for purposes directly related to the Brady Act, or as provided in subsection (E).

(E) If the court, by court order, has submitted a person's name and other identifying information to SLED to be transmitted to NICS, SLED shall review the state concealed weapons permit holders list, and if the review reveals that the person possesses a current concealed weapons permit, the permit must be revoked and surrendered to a sheriff, police department, SLED agent, or by certified mail to the Chief of SLED. If the permit holder fails to return the permit within 10 days of being notified of the permit's revocation, SLED shall retrieve the permit from the permit holder.

(F) Information submitted by the court pursuant to this section, which is also contained in court orders or in other state or local agency records, is not affected by this section, and such court orders or other state or local agency records may be disclosed in accordance with existing laws and procedures.

§ 23-31-1030. Petition to remove prohibition from shipping, transporting, possessing, or receiving a firearm or ammunition.

(A) If a person is prohibited from shipping, transporting, possessing, or receiving a firearm or ammunition pursuant to 18 U.S.C. § 922(g)(4) or § 23-31-1040 as a result of adjudication as a mental defective or commitment to a mental institution, the person may petition the court that issued the original order to remove the prohibitions. The person may file the petition upon the expiration of any current commitment order; however, the court only may consider petitions for relief due to adjudications and commitments that occurred in this State.

(B) The petition must be accompanied by an authorization and release signed by the petitioner authorizing disclosure of the petitioner's current and past medical records, including mental health records.

(C) If the petition is filed pro se, the court shall provide notice to all parties of record. If the petitioner is represented by counsel, counsel shall provide notice to all parties of record.

(D) Notwithstanding the exclusive jurisdiction of the court to preside over hearings initiated pursuant to this section, the case may be removed to the circuit court upon motion of the petitioner or on motion of the court, made not later than 10 days following the date the petition is filed. Upon such motion, the case must be removed to the circuit court where the court shall proceed with the case de novo.

(E)(1) Within 90 days of receiving the petition, unless the court grants an extension upon request of the petitioner, the court shall conduct a hearing which must be presided over by a person other than the person who gathered evidence for use by the court in the hearing.

(2) At the hearing on the petition, the petitioner shall have the opportunity to submit evidence, and a record of the hearing must be made and maintained for review. The court shall consider information and records, which otherwise are confidential or privileged, relevant to the criteria for removing firearm and ammunition prohibitions and shall receive and consider evidence concerning the following:

(a) the circumstances regarding the firearm and ammunitions prohibitions imposed by 18 U.S.C. § 922(g)(4) and § 23-31-1040;

(b) the petitioner's record, which must include, at a minimum, the petitioner's mental health and criminal history records;

(c) evidence of the petitioner's reputation developed through character witness statements, testimony, or other character evidence; and

(d) a current evaluation presented by the petitioner conducted by the Department of Mental Health or a physician licensed in this State specializing in mental health specifically addressing whether due to mental defectiveness or mental illness the petitioner poses a threat to the safety of the public or himself or herself.

(F) The hearing must be closed to the public, and the petitioner's mental health records must be restricted from public disclosure. However, upon motion by the petitioner, the hearing may be open to the public, and the court may allow for the in camera inspection of the petitioner's mental health records and for the use of these records, but these records must be restricted from public disclosure.

(G) (1) The court shall make findings of fact regarding the following and shall remove the firearm and ammunition prohibitions if the petitioner proves by a preponderance of the evidence that:

(a) the petitioner is no longer required to participate in court-ordered psychiatric treatment;

(b) the petitioner is determined by the Department of Mental Health or by a physician licensed in this State specializing in mental health to be not likely to act in a manner dangerous to public safety; and

(c) granting the petitioner relief will not be contrary to the public interest.

(2) Notwithstanding item (1), the court must not remove the firearm and ammunition prohibitions if, by a preponderance of the evidence, it is proven that the petitioner has engaged in acts of violence subsequent to the petitioner's last adjudication as a mental defective or last commitment to a mental institution, unless the petitioner, by clear and convincing evidence, proves that he is not likely to act in a manner dangerous to public safety.

(H) If the petitioner is denied relief and the firearm and ammunition prohibitions are not removed, the petitioner may appeal to the circuit court for de novo review. In conducting its review, the circuit court:

(1) shall review the record;

(2) may give deference to the decision of the court denying the petitioner relief; and

(3) may receive additional evidence as necessary to conduct an adequate review.

(I) Medical records, psychological reports, and other treatment records which have been submitted to the court or admitted into evidence under this section must be part of the record, but must be sealed and opened only on order of the court.

(J) If a court issues an order pursuant to this section that removes the firearm and ammunition prohibitions that prohibited the petitioner from shipping, transporting, possessing, or receiving a firearm or ammunition pursuant to 18 U.S.C. § 922(g)(4) or § 23-31-1040, arising from adjudication as a mental defective or commitment to a mental institution, the court shall provide SLED with a certified copy of the order that may be transmitted through electronic means. SLED promptly shall inform the NICS of the court action removing these firearm and ammunition prohibitions.

§ 23-31-1040. Unlawful for a person adjudicated as a mental defective or committed to a mental institution to ship, transport, possess, or receive a firearm or ammunition; penalty; confiscation.

(A) It is unlawful for a person who has been adjudicated as a mental defective or who has been committed to a mental institution to ship, transport, possess, or receive a firearm or ammunition.

(B) A person who violates this section is guilty of a felony, and, upon conviction, must be fined not more than $2,000 or imprisoned not more than 5 years, or both.

(C) In addition to the penalty provided in this section, the firearm or ammunition involved in the violation of this section must be confiscated. The firearm or ammunition must be delivered to the chief of police of the municipality or to the sheriff of the county if the violation occurred outside the corporate limits of a municipality. The law enforcement agency that receives the confiscated firearm or ammunition may use the firearm or ammunition within the agency, transfer the firearm or ammunition to another law enforcement agency for the lawful use of that agency, trade the firearm or ammunition with a retail dealer licensed to sell firearms or ammunition in this State for a firearm, ammunition, or any other equipment approved by the agency, or destroy the firearm or ammunition. A firearm or ammunition must not be disposed of in any manner until the results of any legal proceeding in which the firearm or ammunition may be involved are finally determined. If SLED seized the firearm or ammunition, SLED may keep the firearm or ammunition for use by SLED's forensic laboratory. Records must be kept of all confiscated firearms or ammunition received by the law enforcement agencies pursuant to this section. A law enforcement agency that receives a firearm or ammunition pursuant to this subsection may administratively release the firearm or ammunition to an innocent owner. If possession of the firearm or ammunition is necessary for legal proceedings, the firearm or ammunition must not be released to the innocent owner until the results of any legal proceedings in which the firearm or ammunition may be involved are finally concluded. Before the firearm or ammunition may be released, the innocent owner shall provide the law enforcement agency with proof of ownership and shall certify that the innocent owner will not release the firearm or ammunition to the person who has been charged with a violation of this subsection which resulted in the firearm's or ammunition's confiscation. The law enforcement agency shall notify the innocent owner when the firearm or ammunition is available for release. If the innocent owner fails to recover the firearm or ammunition within 30 days after notification of the release, the law enforcement agency may maintain or dispose of the firearm or ammunition as otherwise provided in this subsection.

(D) At the time the person is adjudicated as a mental defective or is committed to a mental institution, the court shall provide to the person or the person's representative, as appropriate, a written form that conspicuously informs the person or the person's representative, as appropriate, of the provisions of this section.

§ 23-31-1060. Hearing on fitness to stand trial. Nothing in this article affects a court's duty to conduct a hearing on the issue of a person's fitness to stand trial pursuant to § 44-23-430. A solicitor shall not dismiss charges against a person prior to such hearing based solely on the person's fitness to stand trial.

Tennessee Code
Current through the 2016 Session

Office of the Attorney General
P.O. Box 20207
Nashville, TN 37202-0207
Voice: (615) 741-3491
https://www.tn.gov/attorneygeneral

Nashville Field Division
5300 Maryland Way, Suite 200
Brentwood, Tennessee 37027
Voice: (615) 565-1400
https://www.atf.gov/nashville-field-division

PROTECTING THE PUBLIC
SERVING OUR NATION

Table of Contents

TITLE 39 Criminal Offenses
Chapter 17 Offenses Against Public Health, Safety and Welfare
Part 13 Weapons

39-17-1301. Part definitions. As used in this part, unless the context otherwise requires:
(1) "Adjudication as a mental defective or adjudicated as a mental defective" means:

(A) A determination by a court in this state that a person, as a result of marked subnormal intelligence, mental illness, incompetency, condition or disease:

    (i) Is a danger to such person or to others; or

    (ii) Lacks the ability to contract or manage such person's own affairs due to mental defect;

(B) A finding of insanity by a court in a criminal proceeding; or

(C) A finding that a person is incompetent to stand trial or is found not guilty by reason of insanity pursuant to Article 50a and 76b of the Uniform Code of Military Justice, codified in 10 U.S.C. §§ 850a and 876b respectively;

(3) **"Crime of violence"** includes any degree of murder, voluntary manslaughter, aggravated rape, rape, especially aggravated robbery, aggravated robbery, burglary, aggravated assault or aggravated kidnapping;

(4) (A) **"Explosive weapon"** means any explosive, incendiary or poisonous gas:

    (i) Bomb;

    (ii) Grenade;

    (iii) Rocket;

    (iv) Mine; or

    (v) Shell, missile or projectile that is designed, made or adapted for the purpose of inflicting serious bodily injury, death or substantial property damage;

(B) "Explosive weapon" also means:

    (i) Any breakable container which contains a flammable liquid with a flashpoint of 150 degrees Fahrenheit and has a wick or similar device capable of being ignited, other than a device which is commercially manufactured primarily for purposes of illumination; or

    (ii) Any sealed device containing dry ice or other chemically reactive substances for the purposes of causing an explosion by a chemical reaction;

(5) **"Firearm silencer"** means any device designed, made or adapted to muffle the report of a firearm;

(6) **"Hoax device"** means any device that reasonably appears to be or is purported to be an explosive or incendiary device and is intended to cause alarm or reaction of any type by an official of a public safety agency or a volunteer agency organized to deal with emergencies;

(7) **"Immediate vicinity"** refers to the area within the person's immediate control within which the person has ready access to the ammunition;

(8) **"Judicial commitment to a mental institution"** means a judicially ordered involuntary admission to a private or state hospital or treatment resource in proceedings conducted pursuant to title 33, chapter 6 or 7;

(11) **"Machine gun"** means any firearm that is capable of shooting more than 2 shots automatically, without manual reloading, by a single function of the trigger;

(12) **"Mental institution"** means a mental health facility, mental hospital, sanitarium, psychiatric facility and any other facility that provides diagnoses by a licensed professional of an intellectual disability or mental illness, including, but not limited to, a psychiatric ward in a general hospital;

(13) **"Restricted firearm ammunition"** means any cartridge containing a bullet coated with a plastic substance with other than a lead or lead alloy core or a jacketed bullet with other than a lead or lead alloy core or a cartridge of which the bullet itself is wholly composed of a metal or metal alloy other than lead. "Restricted firearm ammunition" does not include shotgun shells or solid plastic bullets;

(14) **"Rifle"** means any firearm designed, made or adapted to be fired from the shoulder and to use the energy of the explosive in a fixed metallic cartridge to fire a projectile through a rifled bore by a single function of the trigger;

(15) **"Short barrel"** means a barrel length of less than 16 inches for a rifle and 18 inches for a shotgun, or an overall firearm length of less than 26 inches;

(16) **"Shotgun"** means any firearm designed, made or adapted to be fired from the shoulder and to use the energy of the explosive in a fixed shotgun shell to fire through a smooth-bore barrel either a number of ball shot or a single projectile by a single function of the trigger;

(18) **"Unloaded"** means the rifle, shotgun or handgun does not have ammunition in the chamber, cylinder, clip or magazine, and no clip or magazine is in the immediate vicinity of the weapon.

39-17-1302. Prohibited weapons.

(a) A person commits an offense who intentionally or knowingly possesses, manufactures, transports, repairs or sells:

    (1) An explosive or an explosive weapon;

    (2) A device principally designed, made or adapted for delivering or shooting an explosive weapon;

    (3) A machine gun;

    (4) A short-barrel rifle or shotgun;

    (5) A firearm silencer;

    (6) Hoax device;

    (8) Any other implement for infliction of serious bodily injury or death that has no common lawful purpose.

(b) It is a defense to prosecution under this section that the person's conduct:

    (1) Was incident to the performance of official duty and pursuant to military regulations in the army, navy, air force, coast guard or marine service of the United States or the Tennessee national guard, or was incident to the performance of official duty in a governmental law enforcement agency or a penal institution;

(2) Was incident to engaging in a lawful commercial or business transaction with an organization identified in subdivision (b)(1);

(3) Was incident to using an explosive or an explosive weapon in a manner reasonably related to a lawful industrial or commercial enterprise;

(4) Was incident to using the weapon in a manner reasonably related to a lawful dramatic performance or scientific research;

(5) Was incident to displaying the weapon in a public museum or exhibition;

(6) Was licensed by the state of Tennessee as a manufacturer, importer or dealer in weapons; provided, that the manufacture, import, purchase, possession, sale or disposition of weapons is authorized and incident to carrying on the business for which licensed and is for scientific or research purposes or sale or disposition to an organization designated in subdivision (b)(1); or

(7) [Deleted by 2015 amendment.]

(8) [Deleted by 2014 amendment.]

(c) It is an affirmative defense to prosecution under this section that the person must prove by a preponderance of the evidence that:

(1) The person's conduct was relative to dealing with the weapon solely as a curio, ornament or keepsake, and if the weapon is a type described in subdivisions (a)(1)-(5), that it was in a nonfunctioning condition and could not readily be made operable; or

(2) The possession was brief and occurred as a consequence of having found the weapon or taken it from an aggressor.

(d) It is an exception to the application of subsection (a) that the person acquiring or possessing a weapon described in subdivisions (a)(3), (a)(4), or (a)(5) is in full compliance with the requirements of the National Firearms Act (26 U.S.C. §§ 5841-5862).

(e) Subsection (a) shall not apply to the possession, manufacture, transportation, repair, or sale of an explosive if:

(1) The person in question is 18 years of age or older; and

(2) The possession, manufacture, transport, repair, or sale was incident to creating or using an exploding target for lawful sporting activity, as solely intended by the commercial manufacturer.

(f)(1) An offense under subdivision (a)(1) is a Class B felony.

(2) An offense under subdivisions (a)(2)-(5) is a Class E felony.

(3) An offense under subdivision (a)(6) is a Class C felony.

(4) An offense under subdivisions (a)(7)-(8) is a Class A misdemeanor.

39-17-1303. Unlawful sale, loan or gift of firearm.

(a) A person commits an offense who:

(1) Intentionally, knowingly, or recklessly sells, loans or makes a gift of a firearm to a minor;

(2) Intentionally, knowingly or recklessly sells a firearm or ammunition for a firearm to a person who is intoxicated; or

(3) Intentionally, knowingly, recklessly or with criminal negligence violates § 39-17-1316.

(b) It is a defense to prosecution under subdivision (a)(1) that:

(1) A firearm was loaned or given to a minor for the purposes of hunting, trapping, fishing, camping, sport shooting or any other lawful sporting activity; and

(2) The person is not required to obtain a license under § 39-17-1316.

(c) For purposes of this section, "intoxicated" means substantial impairment of mental or physical capacity resulting from introduction of any substance into the body.

(d) An offense under this section is a Class A misdemeanor.

39-17-1304. Restrictions on firearm ammunition.

(a) It is an offense for any person to possess, use or attempt to use restricted firearm ammunition while committing or attempting to commit a crime of violence. A violation of this section constitutes a separate and distinct felony.

(b) It is an offense for any person or corporation to manufacture, sell, offer for sale, display for sale or use in this state any ammunition cartridge, metallic or otherwise, containing a bullet with a hollow-nose cavity that is filled with an explosive material and designed to detonate upon impact; provided, that this section shall not apply to any state or federal military unit or personnel for use in the performance of its duties.

(c)(1) A violation of subsection (a) by possession of restricted firearm ammunition is a Class E felony.

(2) A violation of subsection (a) by use or attempted use of restricted firearm ammunition is a Class D felony.

(3) A violation of subsection (b) is a Class E felony.

39-17-1306. Carrying weapons during judicial proceedings.

(a) No person shall intentionally, knowingly, or recklessly carry on or about the person while inside any room in which judicial proceedings are in progress any weapon prohibited by § 39-17-1302(a), for the purpose of going armed; provided, that if the weapon carried is a firearm, the person is in violation of this section regardless of whether the weapon is carried for the purpose of going armed.

(b) Any person violating subsection (a) commits a Class E felony.

(c) Subsection (a) shall not apply to any person who:

(1) Is in the actual discharge of official duties as a law enforcement officer, or is employed in the army, air force, navy, coast guard or marine service of the United States or any member of the Tennessee national guard in the line of duty and pursuant to military regulations, or is in the actual discharge of official duties as a guard employed by a penal institution, or as a bailiff, marshal or other court officer who has responsibility for protecting persons or property or providing security;

(2) Has been directed by a court to bring the firearm for purposes of providing evidence; or

(3) Is in the actual discharge of official duties as a judge, and:

(A) Is authorized to carry a handgun pursuant to § 39-17-1351;

(B) Keeps the handgun concealed at all times when in the discharge of such duties; and

(C) Is vested with judicial powers under § 16-1-101.

39-17-1307. Unlawful carrying or possession of a weapon.

(a) (1) A person commits an offense who carries, with the intent to go armed, a firearm or a club.

(2) (A) The first violation of subdivision (a)(1) is a Class C misdemeanor, and, in addition to possible imprisonment as provided by law, may be punished by a fine not to exceed $500.

(B) A second or subsequent violation of subdivision (a)(1) is a Class B misdemeanor.

(C) A violation of subdivision (a)(1) is a Class A misdemeanor if the person's carrying of a handgun occurred at a place open to the public where 1 or more persons were present.

(b)(1) A person commits an offense who unlawfully possesses a firearm, as defined in § 39-11-106, and:

(A) Has been convicted of a felony involving the use or attempted use of force, violence, or a deadly weapon; or

(B) Has been convicted of a felony drug offense.

(2) An offense under subdivision (b)(1)(A) is a Class C felony.

(3) An offense under subdivision (b)(1)(B) is a Class D felony.

(c)(1) A person commits an offense who possesses a handgun and has been convicted of a felony.

(2) An offense under subdivision (c)(1) is a Class E felony.

(d)(1) A person commits an offense who possesses a deadly weapon other than a firearm with the intent to employ it during the commission of, attempt to commit, or escape from a dangerous offense as defined in § 39-17-1324.

(2) A person commits an offense who possesses any deadly weapon with the intent to employ it during the commission of, attempt to commit, or escape from any offense not defined as a dangerous offense by § 39-17-1324.

(3)(A) Except as provided in subdivision (d)(3)(B), a violation of this subsection (d) is a Class E felony.

(e)(1) It is an exception to the application of subsection (a) that a person is carrying or possessing a firearm or firearm ammunition in a motor vehicle if the person:

(A) Is not prohibited from possessing or receiving a firearm by 18 U.S.C. § 922(g) or purchasing a firearm by § 39-17-1316; and

(B) Is in lawful possession of the motor vehicle.

(2) As used in this subsection (e):

(A) "Motor vehicle" has the same meaning as defined in § 55-1-103;

(B) "Motor vehicle" does not include any motor vehicle that is:

(i) Owned or leased by a governmental or private entity that has adopted a written policy prohibiting firearms or ammunition not required for employment within such a motor vehicle; and

(ii) Provided by such entity to an employee for use during the course of employment.

(f)(1) A person commits an offense who possesses a firearm, as defined in § 39-11-106(a), and:

(A) Has been convicted of a misdemeanor crime of domestic violence as defined in 18 U.S.C. § 921, and is still subject to the disabilities of such a conviction;

(B) Is, at the time of the possession, subject to an order of protection that fully complies with 18 U.S.C. § 922(g)(8); or

(C) Is prohibited from possessing a firearm under any other state or federal law.

(2) If the person is licensed as a federal firearms dealer or a responsible party under a federal firearms license, the determination of whether such an individual possesses firearms that constitute the business inventory under the federal license shall be determined based upon the applicable federal statutes or the rules, regulations and official letters, rulings and publications of the bureau of alcohol, tobacco, firearms and explosives.

(3) For purposes of this section, a person does not possess a firearm, including, but not limited to, firearms registered under the National Firearms Act, compiled in 26 U.S.C. § 5801 et seq., if the firearm is in a safe or similar container that is securely locked and to which the respondent does not have the combination, keys or other means of normal access.

(4) A violation of subdivision (f)(1) is a Class A misdemeanor and each violation constitutes a separate offense.

(5) If a violation of subdivision (f)(1) also constitutes a violation of § 36-3-625(h) or § 39-13-113(h), the respondent may be charged and convicted under any or all such sections.

39-17-1308. Defenses to unlawful possession or carrying of a weapon.

(a) It is a defense to the application of § 39-17-1307 if the possession or carrying was:

(1) Of an unloaded rifle, shotgun or handgun not concealed on or about the person and the ammunition for the weapon was not in the immediate vicinity of the person or weapon;

(2) By a person authorized to possess or carry a firearm pursuant to § 39-17-1315 or § 39-17-1351;

(3) At the person's:

(A) Place of residence;

(B) Place of business; or

(C) Premises;

(4) Incident to lawful hunting, trapping, fishing, camping, sport shooting or other lawful activity;

(5) By a person possessing a rifle or shotgun while engaged in the lawful protection of livestock from predatory animals;

(6) By a Tennessee valley authority officer who holds a valid commission from the commissioner of safety pursuant to this part while the officer is in the performance of the officer's official duties;

(7) By a state, county or municipal judge or any federal judge or any federal or county magistrate;

(10) By any out-of-state, full-time, commissioned law enforcement officer who holds a valid commission card from the appropriate out-of-state law enforcement agency and a photo identification; provided, that if no valid commission card and photo identification are retained, then it shall be unlawful for that officer to carry firearms in this state and this section shall not apply. The defense provided by this subdivision (a)(10) shall only be applicable if the state where the out-of-state officer is employed has entered into a reciprocity agreement with this state that allows a full-time, commissioned law enforcement officer in Tennessee to lawfully carry or possess a weapon in the other state.

(b) The defenses described in this section are not available to persons described in § 39-17-1307(b)(1).

39-17-1309. Carrying weapons on school property.

(b)(1) It is an offense for any person to possess or carry, whether openly or concealed, with the intent to go armed, any firearm, explosive, explosive weapon, ... or any other weapon of like kind, not used solely for instructional or school-sanctioned ceremonial purposes, in any public or private school building or bus, on any public or private school campus, grounds, recreation area, athletic field or any other property owned, operated, or while in use by any board of education, school, college or university board of trustees, regents or directors for the administration of any public or private educational institution.

(2) A violation of this subsection (b) is a Class E felony.

(c)(1)(A) It is an offense for any person to possess or carry, whether openly or concealed, any firearm, not used solely for instructional or school-sanctioned ceremonial purposes, in any public or private school building or bus, on any public or private school campus, grounds, recreation area, athletic field or any other property owned, operated, or while in use by any board of education, school, college or university board of trustees, regents or directors for the administration of any public or private educational institution.

(B) It is not an offense under this subsection (c) for a nonstudent adult to possess a firearm, if the firearm is contained within a private vehicle operated by the adult and is not handled by the adult, or by any other person acting with the expressed or implied consent of the adult, while the vehicle is on school property.

(2) A violation of this subsection (c) is a Class B misdemeanor.

(d)(1) Each chief administrator of a public or private school shall display in prominent locations about the school a sign, at least 6 inches high and 14 inches wide, stating: FELONY. STATE LAW PRESCRIBES A MAXIMUM PENALTY OF SIX (6) YEARS IMPRISONMENT AND A FINE NOT TO EXCEED THREE THOUSAND DOLLARS ($3,000) FOR CARRYING WEAPONS ON SCHOOL PROPERTY.

(2) As used in this subsection (d), "prominent locations about a school" includes, but is not limited to, sports arenas, gymnasiums, stadiums and cafeterias.

(e) Subsections (b) and (c) do not apply to the following persons:

(1) Persons employed in the army, air force, navy, coast guard or marine service of the United States or any member of the Tennessee national guard when in discharge of their official duties and acting under orders requiring them to carry arms or weapons;

(2) Civil officers of the United States in the discharge of their official duties;

(3) Officers and soldiers of the militia and the national guard when called into actual service;

(4) Officers of the state, or of any county, city or town, charged with the enforcement of the laws of the state, when in the discharge of their official duties;

(5) Any pupils who are members of the reserve officers training corps or pupils enrolled in a course of instruction or members of a club or team, and who are required to carry arms or weapons in the discharge of their official class or team duties;

(6) Any private police employed by the administration or board of trustees of any public or private institution of higher education in the discharge of their duties;

(7) Any registered security guard/officer who meets the requirements of title 62, chapter 35, and who is discharging the officer's official duties;

(8)(A) Persons possessing a handgun, who are authorized to carry the handgun pursuant to § 39-17-1351, while within or on a public park, natural area, historic park, nature trail, campground, forest, greenway, waterway, or other similar public place;

(B) Subdivision (e)(8)(A) shall not apply if the permit holder:

(i) Possessed a handgun on property described in subdivision (e)(8)(A) that is owned or operated by a board of education, school, college, or university board of trustees, regents, or directors unless the permit holder's possession is otherwise excepted by this subsection (e); or

(ii) Possessed a handgun in the immediate vicinity of property that was, at the time of possession, in use by any board of education, school, college or university board of trustees, regents, or directors for the administration of any public or private educational institution for the purpose of conducting an athletic event or other school-related activity on an athletic field, permanent or temporary, including but not limited to, a football or soccer field, tennis court, basketball court, track, running trail, Frisbee field, or any similar multi-use field; and

(iii) Knew or should have known that:

(a) An athletic event or school-related activity described in subdivision (e)(8)(B)(ii) was taking place on the property at the time of the possession; or

(b) The property on which the possession occurred was owned or operated by a school entity described in subdivision (e)(8)(B)(ii); or

(iv) Failed to take reasonable steps to leave the area of the athletic field or school-related activity or the property after being informed or becoming aware of:

(a) Its use for athletic or school-related purposes; or

(b) That it was, at the time of the possession, owned or operated by a school entity described in (e)(8)(B)(ii);

(9) Persons permitted to carry a handgun on the property of private K-12 schools by § 49-50-803, and persons permitted to carry a handgun on the property of private for-profit or nonprofit institutions of higher education pursuant to § 49-7-161; provided, that this subdivision (e)(9) shall apply only:

(A) To the school or institution where the person is located, when that school or institution has adopted a handgun carry policy pursuant to § 49-50-803 or § 49-7-161;

(B) While the person is on the property or grounds covered by the private school or institution's policy; and

(C) When the person is otherwise in compliance with the policy adopted by the private school or institution;

(10) Persons carrying a handgun pursuant to § 49-6-815 or § 49-6-816; provided, that this subdivision (e)(10) shall apply only within and on the grounds of the school for which the person is authorized;

(11)(A) Employees authorized to carry a handgun pursuant to § 39-17-1351 on property owned, operated, or controlled by the public institution of higher education at which the employee is employed;

(B)(i) Any authorized employee who elects to carry a handgun pursuant to this subdivision (e)(11) shall provide written notification to the law enforcement agency or agencies with jurisdiction over the property owned, operated, or controlled by the public institution of higher education that employs the employee;

(ii) The employee's name and any other information that might identify the employee as a person who has elected to carry a handgun pursuant to this subdivision (e)(11) shall be confidential, not open for public inspection, and shall not be disclosed by any law enforcement agency with which an employee registers; except that the employee's name and other information may be disclosed to an administrative officer of the institution who is responsible for school facility security; provided, however, that the administrative officer is not the employee's immediate supervisor or a supervisor responsible for evaluation of the employee. An administrative officer to whom such information is disclosed shall not disclose the information to another person. Identifying information about the employee collected pursuant to this subdivision (e)(11) shall not be disclosed to any person or entity other than another law enforcement agency and only for law enforcement purposes; and

(iii) Law enforcement agencies are authorized to develop and implement:

(a) Policies and procedures designed to implement the notification and confidentiality requirements of this subdivision (e)(11)(B); and

(b) A voluntary course or courses of special or supplemental firearm training to be offered to the employees electing to carry a handgun pursuant to this subdivision (e)(11). Firearm safety shall be a component of any firearm course;

(C) Unless carrying a handgun is a requirement of the employee's job description, the carrying of a handgun pursuant to this subdivision (e)(11) is a personal choice of the employee and not a requirement of the employer. Consequently, an employee who carries a handgun on property owned, operated, or controlled by the public institution of higher education at which the employee is employed is not:

(i) Acting in the course of or scope of their employment when carrying or using the handgun;

(ii) Entitled to workers' compensation benefits under § 9-8-307(a)(1)(K) for injuries arising from the carrying or use of a handgun;

(iii) Immune from personal liability with respect to use or carrying of a handgun under § 9-8-307(h);

(iv) Permitted to carry a handgun openly, or in any other manner in which the handgun is visible to ordinary observation; or

(v) Permitted to carry a handgun at the following times and at the following locations:

(a) Stadiums, gymnasiums, and auditoriums when school-sponsored events are in progress;

(b) In meetings regarding disciplinary matters;

(c) In meetings regarding tenure issues;

(d) A hospital, or an office where medical or mental health services are the primary services provided; and

(e) Any location where a provision of state or federal law, except the posting provisions of § 39-17-1359, prohibits the carrying of a handgun on that property;

(D) Notwithstanding any other law to the contrary, a public institution of higher education shall be absolutely immune from claims for monetary damages arising solely from or related to an employee's use of, or failure to use, a handgun; provided the employee is employed by the institution against whom the claim is filed and the employee elects to carry the handgun pursuant to this subdivision (e)(11). Nothing in this section shall expand the existing conditions under which sovereign immunity is waived pursuant to § 9-8-307; and

(E) As used in subdivisions (e)(11)-(13):

    (i) "Employee" includes all faculty, staff, and other persons who are employed on a full-time basis by a public institution of higher education; and

    (ii) "Employee" does not include a person who is enrolled as a student at a public institution of higher education, regardless of whether the person is also an employee;

(12)(A) Any employee of the University of Tennessee institute of agriculture or a college or department of agriculture at a campus in the University of Tennessee system when in the discharge of the employee's official duties and with prior authorization from the chancellor of the University of Tennessee institute of agriculture; or

    (B) Any employee of the University of Tennessee institute of agriculture or a college or department of agriculture at a campus in the University of Tennessee system, and any member of the employee's household, living in a residence owned, used, or operated by the University of Tennessee, if the employee has prior authorization from the chancellor of the University of Tennessee institute of agriculture and the employee and household members are permitted to possess firearms in their residence under Tennessee and federal law; and

(13)(A) Any employee of the university's college or department of agriculture when in the discharge of the employee's official duties and with prior authorization from the president of a university in the board of regents system;

    (B) Any employee of the university's college or department of agriculture, and any member of the employee's household, living in a residence owned, used, or operated by the university, if the employee has prior authorization from the president of a university in the board of regents system and the employee and household members are permitted to possess firearms in their residence under Tennessee and federal law; or

    (C) Any employee, with prior authorization of the president of a university in the board of regents system, who is engaged in wildlife biology or ecology research and education for the purpose of capture or collection of specimens.

39-17-1310. Affirmative defense to carrying weapons on school property. It is an affirmative defense to prosecution under § 39-17-1309(a)-(d) that the person's behavior was in strict compliance with the requirements of 1 of the following classifications:

(1) A person hunting during the lawful hunting season on lands owned by any public or private educational institution and designated as open to hunting by the administrator of the educational institution;

(2) A person possessing unloaded hunting weapons while transversing the grounds of any public or private educational institution for the purpose of gaining access to public or private lands open to hunting with the intent to hunt on the public or private lands unless the lands of the educational institution are posted prohibiting entry;

(3) A person possessing guns or knives when conducting or attending "gun and knife shows" and the program has been approved by the administrator of the educational institution; or

(4) A person entering the property for the sole purpose of delivering or picking up passengers and who does not remove, utilize or allow to be removed or utilized any weapon from the vehicle.

39-17-1311. Carrying weapons on public parks, playgrounds, civic centers and other public recreational buildings and grounds.

(a) It is an offense for any person to possess or carry, whether openly or concealed, with the intent to go armed, any weapon prohibited by § 39-17-1302(a), not used solely for instructional, display or sanctioned ceremonial purposes, in or on the grounds of any public park, playground, civic center or other building facility, area or property owned, used or operated by any municipal, county or state government, or instrumentality thereof, for recreational purposes.

(b)(1) Subsection (a) shall not apply to the following persons:

    (A) Persons employed in the army, air force, navy, coast guard or marine service of the United States or any member of the Tennessee national guard when in discharge of their official duties and acting under orders requiring them to carry arms or weapons;

    (B) Civil officers of the United States in the discharge of their official duties;

    (C) Officers and soldiers of the militia and the national guard when called into actual service;

    (D) Officers of the state, or of any county, city or town, charged with the enforcement of the laws of the state, in the discharge of their official duties;

    (E) Any pupils who are members of the reserve officers training corps or pupils enrolled in a course of instruction or members of a club or team, and who are required to carry arms or weapons in the discharge of their official class or team duties;

    (F) Any private police employed by the municipality, county, state or instrumentality thereof in the discharge of their duties;

    (G) A registered security guard/officer, who meets the requirements of title 62, chapter 35, while in the performance of the officer's duties;

    (H)(i) Persons possessing a handgun, who are authorized to carry the handgun pursuant to § 39-17-1351, while within or on a public park, natural area, historic park, nature trail, campground, forest, greenway, waterway, or other similar public place that is owned or operated by the state, a county, a municipality, or instrumentality of the state, a county, or municipality;

        (ii) Subdivision (b)(1)(H)(i) shall not apply if the permit holder:

            (a) Possessed a handgun in the immediate vicinity of property that was, at the time of possession, in use by any board of education, school, college or university board of trustees, regents, or directors for the administration of any public or private educational institution for the purpose of conducting an athletic event or other school-related activity on an athletic field, permanent or temporary, including but not limited to, a football or soccer field, tennis court, basketball court, track, running trail, Frisbee field, or similar multi-use field; and

(*b*) Knew or should have known the athletic activity or school-related activity described in subdivision (b)(1)(H)(ii)(*a*) was taking place on the property; or

(*c*) Failed to take reasonable steps to leave the area of the athletic event or school-related activity after being informed of or becoming aware of its use;

(I) Persons possessing a handgun, who are authorized to carry the handgun pursuant to § 39-17-1351, while within or on property designated by the federal government as a national park, forest, preserve, historic park, military park, trail or recreation area, to the extent permitted by federal law; and

(J) Also, only to the extent a person strictly conforms the person's behavior to the requirements of one (1) of the following classifications:

(i) A person hunting during the lawful hunting season on lands owned by any municipality, county, state or instrumentality thereof and designated as open to hunting by law or by the appropriate official;

(ii) A person possessing unloaded hunting weapons while traversing the grounds of any public recreational building or property for the purpose of gaining access to public or private lands open to hunting with the intent to hunt on the public or private lands unless the public recreational building or property is posted prohibiting entry;

(iii) A person possessing guns or knives when conducting or attending "gun and knife shows" when the program has been approved by the administrator of the recreational building or property;

(iv) A person entering the property for the sole purpose of delivering or picking up passengers and who does not remove any weapon from the vehicle or utilize it in any manner; or

(v) A person who possesses or carries a firearm for the purpose of sport or target shooting and sport or target shooting is permitted in the park or recreational area.

(2) At any time the person's behavior no longer strictly conforms to one (1) of the classifications in subdivision (b)(1), the person shall be subject to subsection (a).

(c) [Deleted by 2015 amendment]

(d) [Deleted by 2015 amendment]

(e) [Deleted by 2015 amendment]

(f) A violation of subsection (a) is a Class A misdemeanor.

(g) For the purposes of this section, a "greenway" means an open-space area following a natural or man-made linear feature designed to be used for recreation, transportation, conservation, and to link services and facilities. A greenway is a paved, gravel-covered, woodchip covered, or wood-covered path that connects one greenway entrance with another greenway entrance. In the event a greenway traverses a park that is owned or operated by a county, municipality or instrumentality thereof, the greenway shall be considered a portion of that park unless designated otherwise by the local legislative body. Except as provided in this part, the definition of a greenway in this section shall not be applicable to any other provision of law.

39-17-1312. Inaction by persons eighteen (18) years of age or older, including parents or guardians, knowing a minor or student illegally possesses a firearm.

(a) It is an offense if a person 18 years of age or older, including a parent or other legal guardian, knows that a minor or student is in illegal possession of a firearm in or upon the premises of a public or private school, in or on the school's athletic stadium or other facility or building where school sponsored athletic events are conducted, or public park, playground or civic center, and the person, parent or guardian fails to prevent the possession or fails to report it to the appropriate school or law enforcement officials.

(b) A violation of this section is a Class A misdemeanor.

39-17-1313. Transporting and storing a firearm or firearm ammunition in permit holder's motor vehicle.

(a) Notwithstanding any provision of law or any ordinance or resolution adopted by the governing body of a city, county or metropolitan government, including any ordinance or resolution enacted before April 8, 1986, that prohibits or regulates the possession, transportation or storage of a firearm or firearm ammunition by a handgun carry permit holder, the holder of a valid handgun carry permit recognized in Tennessee may, unless expressly prohibited by federal law, transport and store a firearm or firearm ammunition in the permit holder's motor vehicle, as defined in § 55-1-103, while on or utilizing any public or private parking area if:

(1) The permit holder's motor vehicle is parked in a location where it is permitted to be; and

(2) The firearm or ammunition being transported or stored in the motor vehicle:

(A) Is kept from ordinary observation if the permit holder is in the motor vehicle; or

(B) Is kept from ordinary observation and locked within the trunk, glove box, or interior of the person's motor vehicle or a container securely affixed to such motor vehicle if the permit holder is not in the motor vehicle.

(b) No business entity, public or private employer, or the owner, manager, or legal possessor of the property shall be held liable in any civil action for damages, injuries or death resulting from or arising out of another's actions involving a firearm or ammunition transported or stored by the holder of a valid handgun carry permit in the permit holder's motor vehicle unless the business entity, public or private employer, or the owner, manager, or legal possessor of the property commits an offense involving the use of the stored firearm or ammunition or intentionally solicits or procures the conduct resulting in the damage, injury or death. Nor shall a business entity, public or private employer, or the owner, manager, or legal possessor of the property be responsible for the theft of a firearm or ammunition stored by the holder of a valid handgun carry permit in the permit holder's motor vehicle.

(c) For purposes of this section:

(1) "Motor vehicle" means any motor vehicle as defined in § 55-1-103, which is in the lawful possession of the permit holder, but does not include any motor vehicle which is owned or leased by a governmental or business entity and that is provided by such entity to an employee for use during the course of employment if the entity has adopted a written policy prohibiting firearms or ammunition not required for employment within the entity's motor vehicles; and

(2)(A) "Parking area" means any property provided by a business entity, public or private employer, or the owner, manager, or legal possessor of the property for the purpose of permitting its invitees, customers, clients or employees to park privately owned motor vehicles; and

(B) "Parking area" does not include the grounds or property of an owner-occupied, single-family detached residence, or a tenant-occupied single-family detached residence.

(d) A handgun carry permit holder transporting, storing or both transporting and storing a firearm or firearm ammunition in accordance with this section does not violate this section if the firearm or firearm ammunition is observed by another person or security device during the ordinary course of the handgun carry permit holder securing the firearm or firearm ammunition from observation in or on a motor vehicle.

39-17-1314. Local regulation of firearms and ammunition and knives preempted by state regulation – Actions against firearms or ammunition manufacturers, trade associations or dealers.

(a) Except as otherwise provided by state law or as specifically provided in subsection (b), the general assembly preempts the whole field of the regulation of firearms, ammunition, or components of firearms or ammunition, or combinations thereof including, but not limited to, the use, purchase, transfer, taxation, manufacture, ownership, possession, carrying, sale, acquisition, gift, devise, licensing, registration, storage, and transportation thereof, to the exclusion of all county, city, town, municipality, or metropolitan government law, ordinances, resolutions, enactments or regulation. No county, city, town, municipality, or metropolitan government nor any local agency, department, or official shall occupy any part of the field regulation of firearms, ammunition or components of firearms or ammunition, or combinations thereof.

(b) A city, county, town, municipality or metropolitan government is expressly authorized to regulate by ordinance, resolution, policy, rule or other enactment the following:

(1) The carrying of firearms by employees or independent contractors of the city, county, town municipality or metropolitan government when acting in the course and scope of their employment or contract, except as otherwise provided in § 39-17-1313;

(2) The discharge of firearms within the boundaries of the applicable city, county, town, municipality or metropolitan government, except when and where the discharge of a firearm is expressly authorized or permitted by state law;

(3) The location of a sport shooting range, except as otherwise provided in §§ 39-17-316 and 13-3-412; and

(4) The enforcement of any state or federal law pertaining to firearms, ammunition, or components of firearms or ammunition, or combinations thereof.

(c) The general assembly declares that the lawful design, marketing, manufacture and sale of firearms and ammunition to the public are not unreasonably dangerous activities and do not constitute a nuisance per se.

(d)(1) The authority to bring suit and right to recover against any firearms or ammunition manufacturer, trade association or dealer by or on behalf of any state entity, county, municipality or metropolitan government for damages, abatement or injunctive relief resulting from or relating to the lawful design, manufacture, marketing or sale of firearms or ammunition to the public shall be reserved exclusively to the state.

(2) Nothing in this subsection (d) shall be construed to prohibit a county, municipality, or metropolitan government from bringing an action against a firearms or ammunition manufacturer or dealer for breach of contract or warranty as to firearms or ammunition purchased by such county, municipality, or metropolitan government.

(3) Nothing in this subsection (d) shall preclude an individual from bringing a cause of action for breach of a written contract, breach of an express warranty, or for injuries resulting from defects in the materials or workmanship in the manufacture of the firearm.

(e) Subsections (c) and (d) shall not apply in any litigation brought by an individual against a firearms or ammunition manufacturer, trade association or dealer.

39-17-1315. Written directive and permit to carry handguns.

(a)(1)(A) The following persons may carry handguns at all times pursuant to a written directive by the executive supervisor of the organization to which the person is or was attached or employed, regardless of the person's regular duty hours or assignments:

(i) Any law enforcement officer, police officer, bonded and sworn deputy sheriff, director, commissioner, county magistrate or retired law enforcement officer who is bonded and who, at the time of receiving the written directive, has successfully completed and, except for a law enforcement officer who has retired in good standing as certified by the chief law enforcement officer of the organization from which the officer retired, continues to successfully complete on an annual basis a firearm training program of at least 8 hours duration;

(ii) Any director or full-time employee of the Tennessee emergency management agency in the performance of the director's or employee's duty;

(iii) Any duly authorized representative or full-time employee of the department of correction who has been specifically designated by the commissioner of the department to execute warrants issued pursuant to § 40-28-121 or § 40-35-311 or to perform such other duties as specifically designated by the commissioner; or

(iv) Any other officer or person authorized to carry handguns by this, or any other law of this state.

(B) A copy of the written directive shall be retained as a portion of the records of the particular law enforcement agency that shall issue the directive. Nothing in this subdivision (a)(1) shall prevent federal officers from carrying firearms as prescribed by federal law.

(2)(A) Any duly elected and sworn constable in any county having a population of not less than 11,100 nor more than 11,200, according to the 1970 federal census or any subsequent federal census, and being a county in which constables retain law enforcement powers and duties under §§ 8-10-108, 40-6-210, 55-8-152, 57-5-202 and 57-9-101, are authorized to and may carry handguns at all times and may equip their vehicles with blue and red lights and sirens. The sheriff of such county shall issue a written directive or permit authorizing the constables to carry a handgun; provided, that each constable has completed the same 8-hour annual firearm training program as is required by this subsection (a).

(B) The county commission may, by a 2/3 vote, require the constable to have in effect a liability policy or a corporate surety bond in an amount of not less than $50,000.

(b)(1) An individual, corporation or business entity is authorized to prohibit the possession of weapons by employees otherwise authorized by this subsection (b) on premises owned, operated or managed by the individual, corporation or business entity. Notice of the prohibition shall be posted or otherwise noticed to all affected employees.

(2) An individual, corporation, business entity or governmental entity or agent thereof is authorized to prohibit possession of weapons by any person otherwise authorized by this subsection (b), at meetings conducted by, or on premises owned, operated, managed or under control of the individual, corporation, business entity or governmental entity. Notice of the prohibition shall be posted or announced.

39-17-1316. Sales of dangerous weapons – Certification of purchaser – Exceptions – Licensing of dealers – Definitions.

(a)(1) Any person appropriately licensed by the federal government may stock and sell firearms to persons desiring firearms; however, sales to persons who have been convicted of the offense of stalking, as prohibited by § 39-17-315, who are addicted to alcohol, who are ineligible to receive firearms under 18 U.S.C. § 922, or who have been judicially committed to a mental institution pursuant to title 33 or adjudicated as a mental defective are prohibited. For purposes of this subdivision (a)(1), the offense of violation of a protective order as prohibited by § 39-13-113 shall be considered a "misdemeanor crime of domestic violence" for purposes of 18 U.S.C. § 921.

(2) The provisions of this subsection (a) prohibiting the sale of a firearm to a person convicted of a felony shall not apply if:

(A) The person was pardoned for the offense;

(B) The conviction has been expunged or set aside; or

(C) The person's civil rights have been restored pursuant to title 40, chapter 29; and

(D) The person is not prohibited from possessing a firearm by § 39-17-1307.

(b)(1) As used in this section, "firearm" has the meaning as defined in § 39-11-106, including handguns, long guns, and all other weapons that meet the definition except "antique firearms" as defined in 18 U.S.C. § 921.

(2) As used in this section, "gun dealer" means a person engaged in the business, as defined in 18 U.S.C. § 921, of selling, leasing, or otherwise transferring a firearm, whether the person is a retail dealer, pawnbroker, or otherwise.

(c) Except with respect to transactions between persons licensed as dealers under 18 U.S.C. § 923, a gun dealer shall comply with the following before a firearm is delivered to a purchaser:

(1) The purchaser shall present to the dealer current identification meeting the requirements of subsection (f);

(2) The gun dealer shall complete a firearms transaction record as required by 18 U.S.C. §§ 921-929, and obtain the signature of the purchaser on the record;

(3) The gun dealer shall request by means designated by the bureau that the Tennessee bureau of investigation conduct a criminal history record check on the purchaser and shall provide the following information to the bureau:

(A) The federal firearms license number of the gun dealer;

(B) The business name of the gun dealer;

(C) The place of transfer;

(D) The name of the person making the transfer;

(E) The make, model, caliber and manufacturer's number of the firearm being transferred;

(F) The name, gender, race, and date of birth of the purchaser;

(G) The social security number of the purchaser, if one has been assigned; and

(H) The type, issuer and identification number of the identification presented by the purchaser; and

(4) The gun dealer shall receive a unique approval number for the transfer from the bureau and record the approval number on the firearms transaction record.

(d) Upon receipt of a request of the gun dealer for a criminal history record check, the Tennessee bureau of investigation shall immediately, during the gun dealer's telephone call or by return call:

(1) Determine, from criminal records and other information available to it, whether the purchaser is disqualified under subdivision (a)(1) from completing the purchase; and

(2) Notify the dealer when a purchaser is disqualified from completing the transfer or provide the dealer with a unique approval number indicating that the purchaser is qualified to complete the transfer.

(e)(1) The Tennessee bureau of investigation may charge a reasonable fee, not to exceed $10, for conducting background checks and other costs incurred under this section, and shall be empowered to bill gun dealers for checks run.

(f)(1) Identification required of the purchaser under subsection (c) shall include 1 piece of current, valid identification bearing a photograph and the date of birth of the purchaser that:

    (A) Is issued under the authority of the United States government, a state, a political subdivision of a state, a foreign government, a political subdivision of a foreign government, an international governmental organization or an international quasi-governmental organization; and

    (B) Is intended to be used for identification of an individual or is commonly accepted for the purpose of identification of an individual.

    (2) If the identification presented by the purchaser under subdivision (f)(1)(A) does not include the current address of the purchaser, the purchaser shall present a second piece of current identification that contains the current address of the purchaser.

(g) The Tennessee bureau of investigation may require that the dealer verify the identification of the purchaser if that identity is in question by sending the thumbprints of the purchaser to the bureau.

(h) The Tennessee bureau of investigation shall establish a telephone number that shall be operational 7 days a week between the hours of 8:00 a.m. and 10:00 p.m. Central Standard Time, except Christmas Day, Thanksgiving Day, and Independence Day, for the purpose of responding to inquiries from dealers for a criminal history record check under this section.

(i) No public employee, official or agency shall be held criminally or civilly liable for performing the investigations required by this section; provided the employee, official or agency acts in good faith and without malice.

(j) Upon the determination that receipt of a firearm by a particular individual would not violate this section, and after the issuance of a unique identifying number for the transaction, the Tennessee bureau of investigation shall destroy all records (except the unique identifying number and the date that it was assigned) associating a particular individual with a particular purchase of firearms.

(k) A law enforcement agency may inspect the records of a gun dealer relating to transfers of firearms in the course of a reasonable inquiry during a criminal investigation or under the authority of a properly authorized subpoena or search warrant.

(l)(1) The background check does not apply to transactions between licensed importers, licensed manufacturers, licensed dealers, or licensed collectors who meet the requirements of subsection (b) and certify prior to the transaction the legal and licensed status of both parties. The burden shall fall upon the transferor to determine the legality of the transaction in progress.

    (2) The background check does not apply to transactions or transfers between a licensed importer, licensed manufacturer, or licensed dealer and a bona fide law enforcement agency or such agency's personnel. However, all other provisions and requirements of subsection (b) must be observed. The burden of proof of the legality of the transactions or transfers shall rest upon the transferor.

    (3) The background check does not apply to any person eligible to purchase a firearm as set out in this section who wishes to make an occasional sale of a used or second-hand firearm legally purchased by the seller.

(m) The director of the Tennessee bureau of investigation is authorized to make and issue all rules and regulations necessary to carry out the provisions of this section.

(n) In addition to the other grounds for denial, the bureau shall deny the transfer of a firearm if the background check reveals information indicating that the purchaser has been charged with a crime for which the purchaser, if convicted, would be prohibited under state or federal law from purchasing, receiving, or possessing a firearm; and, either there has been no final disposition of the case, or the final disposition is not noted.

(o) Upon receipt of the criminal history challenge form indicating a purchaser's request for review of the denial, the bureau shall proceed with efforts to obtain the final disposition information. The purchaser may attempt to assist the bureau in obtaining the final disposition information. If neither the purchaser nor the bureau is able to obtain the final disposition information within 15 calendar days of the bureau's receipt of the criminal history challenge form, the bureau shall immediately notify the federal firearms licensee that the transaction that was initially denied is now a "conditional proceed." A "conditional proceed" means that the federal firearms licensee may lawfully transfer the firearm to the purchaser.

(p) In any case in which the transfer has been denied pursuant to subsection (n), the inability of the bureau to obtain the final disposition of a case shall not constitute the basis for the continued denial of the transfer as long as the bureau receives written notice, signed and verified by the clerk of the court or the clerk's designee, that indicates that no final disposition information is available. Upon receipt of the letter by the bureau, the bureau shall immediately reverse the denial.

(q)(1) It is an offense for a person to purchase or attempt to purchase a firearm knowing that the person is prohibited by state or federal law from owning, possessing or purchasing a firearm.

    (2) It is an offense to sell or offer to sell a firearm to a person knowing that the person is prohibited by state or federal law from owning, possessing or purchasing a firearm.

(3) A violation of this subsection (q) is a Class A misdemeanor.

39-17-1317. Confiscation and disposition of confiscated weapons.

(a) (1) Any weapon that is possessed, used, or sold in violation of the law shall be confiscated by a law enforcement officer and declared to be contraband by a court of record exercising criminal jurisdiction.

(2) (A) The sheriff or chief of police for the jurisdiction where the weapon was confiscated may petition the court for permission to dispose of the weapon in accordance with this section.

(B) If the weapon was confiscated by a judicial district drug task force, then the director of the task force where the weapon was confiscated may petition the court for disposal of the weapon in accordance with this section.

(C) If the weapon was confiscated by the department of safety, then the commissioner of safety may petition the court for disposal of the weapon in accordance with this section.

(D) If the weapon was confiscated by the Tennessee bureau of investigation, then the director may petition the court for disposal of the weapon in accordance with this section.

(b) Any weapon declared contraband, secured by a law enforcement officer or agency after being abandoned, voluntarily surrendered to a law enforcement officer or agency, or obtained by a law enforcement agency, including through a buyback program, shall be, pursuant to a written order of the court:

(1) Sold in a public sale;

(2) Used for legitimate law enforcement purposes, at the discretion of the court; or

(3) Relinquished in accordance with subsection (i).

(c) If the weapon was confiscated, or obtained after being abandoned and secured, after being voluntarily surrendered, or through a buyback program, by a local law enforcement agency or a judicial district drug task force and if the court orders the weapon to be sold, then:

(1) It shall be sold at a public auction not later than 6 months from the date of the court order. The sale shall be conducted by the sheriff of the county or the chief of police of the municipality in which it was seized or obtained;

(3) The sale shall be advertised:

(A) In a daily or weekly newspaper circulated within the county. The advertisement shall run for not less than 3 editions and not less than 30 days prior to the sale; or

(B) By posting the sale on a web site maintained by the state or a political subdivision of the state not less than 30 days prior to the sale; and

(4) If required by federal or state law, then the sale can be conducted under contract with a licensed firearm dealer, whose commission shall not exceed 20% of the gross sales price. However, the dealer shall not hold any elective or appointed position within the federal, state, or local government in this state during any stage of the sales contract.

(d) If the weapon was confiscated, or obtained after being abandoned and secured, after being voluntarily surrendered, or through a buyback program, by the department of safety or the Tennessee bureau of investigation and if the court orders it to be sold, then it shall be turned over to the department of general services, which shall sell the weapon and dispose of the proceeds of the sale in the same manner as it currently does for other confiscated weapons.

(e) If the court orders the weapon to be retained and used for legitimate law enforcement purposes, then:

(1) Title to the weapon shall be placed in the law enforcement agency or judicial district drug task force retaining the weapon; and

(2) When the weapon is no longer needed for legitimate law enforcement purposes, it shall be sold in accordance with this section.

(f) If the weapon is sold, then the commissioner of safety or the director of the Tennessee bureau of investigation, the sheriff, chief of police, or director of the judicial district drug task force shall file an affidavit with the court issuing the sale order. The affidavit shall:

(1) Be filed within 30 days after the sale;

(2) Identify the weapon, including any serial number, and shall state the time, date, and circumstances of the sale; and

(3) List the name and address of the purchaser and the price paid for the weapon.

(g) Notwithstanding any other provisions of this section:

(1) A weapon that may be evidence in an official proceeding shall be retained or otherwise preserved in accordance with the rules or practices regulating the preservation of evidence. The weapon shall be sold or retained for legitimate law enforcement purposes not less than 60 days nor more than 180 days after the last legal proceeding involving the weapon; provided, that the requirements of subdivision (g)(2) have been met; and

(2) A law enforcement agency possessing a weapon declared contraband, retained as evidence in an official proceeding, secured after being abandoned, or surrendered by someone other than the owner shall use best efforts to determine whether the weapon has been lost by or stolen or borrowed from an innocent owner, and if so, the agency shall return the weapon to the owner, if ascertainable, unless that person is ineligible to possess, receive, or purchase such weapon under state or federal law.

(h) (1) Except in accordance with this section, no weapon seized by law enforcement officials or judicial district drug task force members shall be used for law enforcement purposes, sold, or destroyed.

(2) No weapon seized by law enforcement officials or judicial district drug task force members shall be used for any personal use.

(i) Notwithstanding this section, if the chief of police, sheriff, director of the judicial district drug task force, commissioner of safety, or director of the Tennessee bureau of investigation, depending upon who confiscated or obtained the weapon, certifies to the court that a weapon is inoperable or unsafe, then the court shall order the weapon:

(1) Destroyed or recycled; or

(2) Transferred to a museum or historical society that displays such items to the public and is lawfully eligible to receive the weapon.

(j) A violation of this section is a Class B misdemeanor.

(k) Nothing in this section shall authorize the purchase of any weapon, the possession of which is otherwise prohibited by law.

(l) (1) The commissioner of safety, the director of the Tennessee bureau of investigation, the executive director of the Tennessee alcoholic beverage commission, the executive head of any local law enforcement agency, or the director of a judicial district drug task force may petition the criminal court or the court in the official's county having criminal jurisdiction for permission to exchange firearms that have previously been properly titled, as specified by this section, to the law enforcement agency or the drug task force for other firearms, ammunition, or body armor suitable for use by the law enforcement agency or drug task force.

(2) The exchange of firearms for the specified items used for legitimate law enforcement purposes is permitted only between the department of safety, the director of the Tennessee bureau of investigation, the executive director of the Tennessee alcoholic beverage commission, a local law enforcement agency, a judicial district drug task force, and a licensed and qualified law enforcement firearms dealer.

(3) No firearm obtained by a law enforcement agency through a buyback program shall be eligible to be exchanged under this subsection (l).

39-17-1318. New serial numbers for confiscated firearms.

(a) If any firearm confiscated and adjudicated as contraband pursuant to this part or any other law could be sold at public auction or retained by a law enforcement agency for law enforcement as provided in § 39-17-1317, but for the fact that the serial number of the firearm has been defaced or destroyed, the commissioner of safety or the sheriff or chief of police, as appropriate, of the county in which the firearm was confiscated may send the firearm to the director of the Tennessee bureau of investigation. The director shall assign the firearm a new serial number, permanently affix the number to the firearm, record the number in the bureau's computer system, and send the firearm back to the commissioner of safety, the sheriff or chief of police for disposition in accordance with this part.

(b) If any firearm assigned a new serial number pursuant to subsection (a) is later sold at public auction, 10% of the proceeds of the sale shall be returned to the general fund of the state to defray the costs incurred by the director in administering this section.

39-17-1319. Handgun possession prohibited – Exceptions.

(a) As used in this section and § 39-17-1320, unless the context otherwise requires:

(1) "Handgun" means a pistol, revolver, or other firearm of any description, loaded or unloaded, from which any shot, bullet, or other missile can be discharged, the length of the barrel of which, not including any revolving, detachable, or magazine breech, does not exceed 12 inches; and

(2) "Juvenile" means any person less than 18 years of age.

(b) Except as provided in this section, it is an offense for a juvenile to knowingly possess a handgun.

(c) (1) Illegal possession of a handgun by a juvenile is a delinquent act and, in addition to any other disposition authorized by law, the juvenile may be required to perform not more than 100 hours of community service work to be specified by the judge, and the juvenile's driving privileges shall be suspended for a period of 1 year in accordance with the procedure set out in title 55, chapter 10, part 7.

(2) A second or subsequent violation of this section is a delinquent act and, in addition to any other disposition authorized by law, the juvenile may be required to perform not less than 100 nor more than 200 hours of community service work to be specified by the judge, and the juvenile's driving privileges shall be suspended for a period of 2 years in accordance with the procedure set out in title 55, chapter 10, part 7.

(3) Any handgun illegally possessed in violation of this section shall be confiscated and disposed of in accordance with § 39-17-1317.

(d) (1) It is a defense to prosecution under this section that the juvenile is:

(A) In attendance at a hunter's safety course or a firearms safety course;

(B) Engaging in practice in the use of a firearm or target shooting at an established range authorized by the governing body of the jurisdiction in which such range is located or any other area where the discharge of a firearm is not prohibited;

(C) Engaging in an organized competition involving the use of a firearm, or participating in or practicing for a performance by an organized group which is exempt from federal income taxation under § 501(c)(3) of the Internal Revenue Code of 1986 (26 U.S.C. § 501(c)(3)), as amended, and which uses firearms as part of the performance;

(D) Hunting or trapping pursuant to a valid license issued to the juvenile pursuant to title 70;

(E) Accompanied by the juvenile's parent or guardian and is being instructed by the adult or guardian in the use of the handgun possessed by the juvenile;

(F) On real property which is under the control of an adult and has the permission of that adult and the juvenile's parent or legal guardian to possess a handgun;

(G) Traveling to or from any activity described in subdivision (d)(1) with an unloaded gun; or

(H) At the juvenile's residence and with the permission of the juvenile's parent or legal guardian, possesses a handgun and is justified in using physical force or deadly force.

(2) For purposes of subdivision (d)(1)(G), a handgun is "unloaded" if:

(A) There is not a cartridge in the chamber of the handgun;

(B) There is not a cartridge in the cylinder of the handgun if the handgun is a revolver; or

(C) The handgun, and the ammunition for the handgun, are not carried on the person of a juvenile or are not in such close proximity to the juvenile that the juvenile could readily gain access to the handgun and the ammunition and load the handgun.

(e) Notwithstanding any other provision of this part to the contrary, this section shall govern a juvenile who possesses a handgun.

39-17-1320. Providing handguns to juveniles – Penalties.

(a) It is an offense for a person intentionally, knowingly or recklessly to provide a handgun with or without remuneration to any person that the person providing the handgun knows or has reason to believe is a juvenile in violation of § 39-17-1319.

(b) It is an offense for a parent or guardian intentionally, knowingly or recklessly to provide a handgun to a juvenile or permit a juvenile to possess a handgun, if the parent or guardian knows of a substantial risk that the juvenile will use a handgun to commit a felony.

(c) Unlawfully providing or permitting a juvenile to possess a handgun in violation of subsection (a) is a Class A misdemeanor and in violation of subsection (b) is a Class D felony.

39-17-1321. Possession of handgun while under influence – Penalty.

(a) Notwithstanding whether a person has a permit issued pursuant to § 39-17-1315 or § 39-17-1351, it is an offense for a person to possess a handgun while under the influence of alcohol or any controlled substance or controlled substance analogue.

(b) It is an offense for a person to possess a firearm if the person is both:

(1) Within the confines of an establishment open to the public where liquor, wine or other alcoholic beverages, as defined in § 57-3-101(a)(1)(A), or beer, as defined in § 57-6-102, are served for consumption on the premises; and

(2) Consuming any alcoholic beverage listed in subdivision (b)(1).

(c)(1) A violation of this section is a Class A misdemeanor.

(2) In addition to the punishment authorized by subdivision (c)(1), if the violation is of subsection (a), occurs in an establishment described in subdivision (b)(1), and the person has a handgun permit issued pursuant to § 39-17-1351, such permit shall be suspended in accordance with § 39-17-1352 for a period of 3 years.

39-17-1322. Defenses.
A person shall not be charged with or convicted of a violation under this part if the person possessed, displayed or employed a handgun in justifiable self-defense or in justifiable defense of another during the commission of a crime in which that person or the other person defended was a victim.

39-17-1324. Offense of possessing a firearm during commission or attempt to commit dangerous felony.

(a) It is an offense to possess a firearm with the intent to go armed during the commission of or attempt to commit a dangerous felony.

(b) It is an offense to employ a firearm during the:

(1) Commission of a dangerous felony;

(2) Attempt to commit a dangerous felony;

(3) Flight or escape from the commission of a dangerous felony; or

(4) Flight or escape from the attempt to commit a dangerous felony.

(c) A person may not be charged with a violation of subsection (a) or (b) if possessing or employing a firearm is an essential element of the underlying dangerous felony as charged. In cases where possession or employing a firearm are elements of the charged offense, the state may elect to prosecute under a lesser offense wherein possession or employing a firearm is not an element of the offense.

(d) A violation of subsection (a) or (b) is a specific and separate offense, which shall be pled in a separate count of the indictment or presentment and tried before the same jury and at the same time as the dangerous felony. The jury shall determine the innocence or guilt of the defendant unless the defendant and the state waive the jury.

(e)(1) A sentence imposed for a violation of subsection (a) or (b) shall be served consecutive to any other sentence the person is serving at the time of the offense or is sentenced to serve for conviction of the underlying dangerous felony.

(2) A person sentenced for a violation of subsection (a) or (b) shall not be eligible for pretrial diversion pursuant to title 40, chapter 15, judicial diversion pursuant to § 40-35-313, probation pursuant to § 40-35-303, community correction pursuant to title 40, chapter 36, participation in a drug court program or any other program whereby the person is permitted supervised or unsupervised release into the community prior to service of the entire mandatory minimum sentence imposed less allowable sentence credits earned and retained as provided in § 40-35-501(j).

(f) In a trial for a violation of subsection (a) or (b), where the state is also seeking to have the person sentenced under subdivision (g)(2) or (h)(2), the trier of fact shall first determine whether the person possessed or employed a firearm. If the trier of fact finds in the affirmative, proof of a qualifying prior felony conviction pursuant to this section shall then be presented to the trier of fact.

(g)(1) A violation of subsection (a) is a Class D felony, punishable by a mandatory minimum 3-year sentence to the department of correction.

(2) A violation of subsection (a) is a Class D felony, punishable by a mandatory minimum 5-year sentence to the department of correction, if the defendant, at the time of the offense, had a prior felony conviction.

(h)(1) A violation of subsection (b) is a Class C felony, punishable by a mandatory minimum 6-year sentence to the department of correction.

(2) A violation of subsection (b) is a Class C felony, punishable by a mandatory minimum 10-year sentence to the department of correction, if the defendant, at the time of the offense, had a prior felony conviction.

(i) As used in this section, unless the context otherwise requires:

  (1) "Dangerous felony" means:

    (A) Attempt to commit first degree murder, as defined in §§ 39-12-101 and 39-13-202;

    (B) Attempt to commit second degree murder, as defined in §§ 39-13-210 and 39-12-101;

    (C) Voluntary manslaughter, as defined in § 39-13-211;

    (D) Carjacking, as defined in § 39-13-404;

    (E) Especially aggravated kidnapping, as defined in § 39-13-305;

    (F) Aggravated kidnapping, as defined in § 39-13-304;

    (G) Especially aggravated burglary, as defined in § 39-14-404;

    (H) Aggravated burglary, as defined in § 39-14-403;

    (I) Especially aggravated stalking, as defined in § 39-17-315(d);

    (J) Aggravated stalking, as defined in § 39-17-315(c);

    (K) Initiating the process to manufacture methamphetamine, as defined in § 39-17-435;

    (L) A felony involving the sale, manufacture, distribution or possession with intent to sell, manufacture or distribute a controlled substance or controlled substance analogue defined in part 4 of this chapter; or

    (M) Any attempt, as defined in § 39-12-101, to commit a dangerous felony;

  (2)(A) "Prior conviction" means that the person serves and is released or discharged from, or is serving, a separate period of incarceration or supervision for the commission of a dangerous felony prior to or at the time of committing a dangerous felony on or after January 1, 2008;

    (B) "Prior conviction" includes convictions under the laws of any other state, government or country that, if committed in this state, would constitute a dangerous felony. If a felony offense in a jurisdiction other than Tennessee is not identified as a dangerous felony in this state, it shall be considered a prior conviction if the elements of the felony are the same as the elements for a dangerous felony; and

  (3) "Separate period of incarceration or supervision" includes a sentence to any of the sentencing alternatives set out in § 40-35-104(c)(3)-(9). A dangerous felony shall be considered as having been committed after a separate period of incarceration or supervision if the dangerous felony is committed while the person was:

    (A) On probation, parole or community correction supervision for a dangerous felony;

    (B) Incarcerated for a dangerous felony;

    (C) Assigned to a program whereby the person enjoys the privilege of supervised release into the community, including, but not limited to, work release, educational release, restitution release or medical furlough for a dangerous felony; or

    (D) On escape status from any correctional institution when incarcerated for a dangerous felony.

(j) Any person convicted under this section who has a prior conviction under this section shall be sentenced to incarceration with the department of correction for not less than 15 years. A person sentenced under this subsection (j) shall serve 100% of the sentence imposed.

39-17-1325. Immunity for failure to adopt policy that prohibits weapons on premises.

(a) A person, business, or other entity that owns, controls, or manages property and has the authority to prohibit weapons on that property by posting, pursuant to § 39-17-1359, shall be immune from civil liability with respect to any claim based on such person's, business's, or other entity's failure to adopt a policy that prohibits weapons on the property by posting pursuant to § 39-17-1359.

(b) Immunity under subsection (a) does not apply to a person, business, or other entity whose conduct or failure to act is the result of gross negligence or willful or wanton misconduct.

39-17-1350. Law enforcement officers permitted to carry firearms – Exceptions – Restrictions – Identification card for corrections officers.

(a) Notwithstanding any law to the contrary, any law enforcement officer may carry firearms at all times and in all places within Tennessee, on-duty or off-duty, regardless of the officer's regular duty hours or assignments, except as provided by subsection (c), federal law, lawful orders of court or the written directives of the executive supervisor of the employing agency.

(b) The authority conferred by this section is expressly intended to and shall supersede restrictions placed upon law enforcement officers' authority to carry firearms by other sections within this part.

(c) The authority conferred by this section shall not extend to a law enforcement officer:

  (1) Who is not engaged in the actual discharge of official duties as a law enforcement officer and carries a firearm onto school grounds or inside a school building during regular school hours unless the officer immediately informs the principal that the officer will be present on school grounds or inside the school building and in possession of a firearm. If the principal is unavailable, the notice may be given to an appropriate administrative staff person in the principal's office;

(2) Who is consuming beer or an alcoholic beverage or who is under the influence of beer, an alcoholic beverage, or a controlled substance or controlled substance analogue; or

(3) Who is not engaged in the actual discharge of official duties as a law enforcement officer while attending a judicial proceeding.

(d)(1) For purposes of this section, "law enforcement officer" means a person who is a full-time employee of the state in a position authorized by the laws of this state to carry a firearm and to make arrests for violations of some or all of the laws of this state, or a full-time police officer who has been certified by the peace officer standards and training commission, or a commissioned reserve deputy sheriff as authorized in writing by the sheriff, or a commissioned reserve or auxiliary police officer as authorized in writing by the chief of police, or a sheriff who has been certified by the peace officer standards and training commission, or a deputy sheriff employed by a county as a court officer or corrections officer as authorized in writing by the sheriff.

(2) For purposes of this section, "law enforcement officer" also means a vested inmate relations coordinator employed by the department of correction, or a vested correctional officer employed by the department of correction, a person employed by the department of correction as a warden, deputy warden, associate warden, correctional administrator, assistant or deputy commissioner, or commissioner who has successfully completed firearms training in accordance with department of correction standards, which standards shall include, at a minimum, 40 hours initial training and 8 hours annual in-service training in firearms qualification administered by an instructor with certification from the Tennessee Correction Academy's firearms instructor program or from a police firearms instructor training program conducted or sanctioned by the federal bureau of investigation or the National Rifle Association.

(3) For purposes of this section, "law enforcement officer" also means a duly elected and sworn constable in a county where constables retain law enforcement powers and duties under § 8-10-108; provided, that the constable receives, at a minimum, 40 hours initial training, within 1 year of election, and 8 hours annual in-service training in firearms qualification administered by a certified law enforcement firearms instructor.

(e) In counties having a population of not less than 30,200 nor more than 30,475 or not less than 118,400 nor more than 118,700, according to the 1990 federal census or any subsequent federal census, the authority conferred by this section shall only apply to law enforcement officers who are law enforcement officers for those counties or law enforcement officers for municipalities located therein.

(f)(1) The secretary of state shall, in consultation with the commissioner of correction, design and issue to each requesting inmate relations coordinator or correctional officer who is vested and employed by the department of correction, a state identification card certifying that the inmate relations coordinator or correctional officer is authorized to carry a firearm pursuant to this section.

(2) Any inmate relations coordinator or correctional officer desiring an identification card shall notify the secretary of state and shall provide the inmate relations coordinator's or correctional officer's full name and residential address. Upon receipt of the request, the secretary of state shall notify the commissioner of correction of the request. The commissioner of correction shall verify to the secretary of state whether the requesting inmate relations coordinator or correctional officer is vested and employed by the department of correction and shall so certify in a letter to be maintained by the secretary.

(3) If the secretary of state receives certification that a requesting inmate relations coordinator or correctional officer is vested and employed by the department, the secretary shall issue the inmate relations coordinator or correctional officer an identification card so certifying. The card shall be valid for as long as the inmate relations coordinator or correctional officer remains vested and in the employment of the department of correction.

(4) An inmate relations coordinator or correctional officer issued a card pursuant to this subsection (f) shall carry the card at all times the inmate relations coordinator or correctional officer is carrying a firearm. The card shall be sufficient proof that the inmate relations coordinator or correctional officer is authorized to carry a firearm pursuant to this section.

(5) If a vested inmate relations coordinator or correctional officer employed by the department resigns, is terminated, or is otherwise no longer employed by the department, the commissioner shall, within 10 days, so notify the secretary of state. Upon receiving the notice, the secretary of state shall revoke the identification card and send a letter of revocation to the inmate relations coordinator or correctional officer at the coordinator's or officer's last known address.

(6)(A) A person who is no longer a vested inmate relations coordinator or correctional officer employed by the department of correction but who still has an identification card issued by the secretary of state shall have 10 days from receipt of the letter of revocation from the secretary of state to return the card to the secretary.

(B) It is a Class C misdemeanor punishable by fine only of $50 for a person to knowingly fail to return an identification card as required by subdivision (f)(6)(A).

39-17-1351. Handgun carry permits. [Contingent expiration date. See Compiler's Notes. See version effective the earlier of January 1, 2017 or upon notice of program implementation and version effective on January 1, 2017.]

(a) The citizens of this state have a right to keep and bear arms for their common defense; but the general assembly has the power, by law, to regulate the wearing of arms with a view to prevent crime.

(b) Except as provided in subsection (r), any resident of Tennessee who is a United States citizen or lawful permanent resident, as defined by § 55-50-102, who has reached 21 years of age, may apply to the department of safety for a handgun carry permit. If the applicant is not prohibited from purchasing or possessing a firearm in this state pursuant to § 39-17-1316 or § 39-17-1307(b), 18 U.S.C. § 922(g), or any other state or federal law, and the applicant otherwise meets all of the requirements of this section, the department shall issue a permit to the applicant.

(c) The application for a permit shall be on a standard form developed by the department. The application shall clearly state in bold face type directly above the signature line that an applicant who, with intent to deceive, makes any false statement on the application commits the felony offense of perjury pursuant to § 39-16-702. The following are eligibility requirements for obtaining a handgun carry permit and the application shall require the applicant to disclose and confirm compliance with, under oath, the following information concerning the applicant and the eligibility requirements:

(1) Full legal name and any aliases;

(2) Addresses for the last 5 years;

(3) Date of birth;

(4) Social security number;

(5) Physical description (height, weight, race, sex, hair color and eye color);

(6) That the applicant has not been convicted of a criminal offense that is designated as a felony, or that is one of the disqualifying misdemeanors set out in subdivisions (c)(11), (c)(16), or (c)(18), with the exception of any federal or state offenses pertaining to antitrust violations, unfair trade practices, restraints of trade or other similar offenses relating to the regulations of business practices;

(7) That the applicant is not currently under indictment or information for any criminal offense that is designated as a felony, or that is one of the disqualifying misdemeanors set out in subdivisions (c)(11), (c)(16), or (c)(18), with the exception of any federal or state offenses pertaining to antitrust violations, unfair trade practices, restraints of trade or other similar offenses relating to the regulations of business practices;

(8) That the applicant is not currently subject to any order of protection and, if so, the applicant shall provide a copy of the order;

(9) That the applicant is not a fugitive from justice;

(10) That the applicant is not an unlawful user of or addicted to alcohol, any controlled substance or controlled substance analogue, and the applicant has not been either:

(A) A patient in a rehabilitation program pursuant to a court order or hospitalized for alcohol, controlled substance or controlled substance analogue abuse or addiction pursuant to a court order within 10 years from the date of application; or

(B) A voluntary patient in a rehabilitation program or voluntarily hospitalized for alcohol, controlled substance or controlled substance analogue abuse or addiction within 3 years from the date of application;

(11) That the applicant has not been convicted of the offense of driving under the influence of an intoxicant in this or any other state 2 or more times within 10 years from the date of the application and that none of the convictions has occurred within 5 years from the date of application or renewal;

(12) That the applicant has not been adjudicated as a mental defective, has not been judicially committed to or hospitalized in a mental institution pursuant to title 33, has not had a court appoint a conservator for the applicant by reason of a mental defect, has not been judicially determined to be disabled by reason of mental illness, developmental disability or other mental incapacity, and has not, within 7 years from the date of application, been found by a court to pose an immediate substantial likelihood of serious harm, as defined in title 33, chapter 6, part 5, because of mental illness;

(13) That the applicant is not an alien and is not illegally or unlawfully in the United States;

(14) That the applicant has not been discharged from the armed forces under dishonorable conditions;

(15) That the applicant has not renounced the applicant's United States citizenship;

(16) That the applicant has not been convicted of a misdemeanor crime of domestic violence as defined in 18 U.S.C. § 921;

(17) That the applicant is not receiving social security disability benefits by reason of alcohol dependence, drug dependence or mental disability; and

(18) That the applicant has not been convicted of the offense of stalking.

(d)(1) In addition to the information required under subsection (c), the applicant shall be required to provide 2 full sets of classifiable fingerprints at the time the application is filed with the department. The applicant's fingerprints may be taken by the department at the time the application is submitted or the applicant may have the fingerprints taken at any sheriff's office and submit the fingerprints to the department along with the application and other supporting documents. The sheriff may charge a fee not to exceed $5 for taking the applicant's fingerprints. At the time an applicant's fingerprints are taken either by the department or a sheriff's office, the applicant shall be required to present a photo identification. If the person requesting fingerprinting is not the same person as the person whose picture appears on the photo identification, the department or sheriff shall refuse to take the fingerprints. The department shall also be required to photograph the applicant in a manner that is suitable for use on the permit.

(2) An applicant shall also be required to present a photo identification to the department at the time of filing the application. If the name on the photo identification, name on the application and name on the fingerprint card, if taken by a sheriff, are not the same, the department shall refuse to accept the application. If the person whose picture appears on the photo identification is not the same as the applicant, the department shall refuse to accept the application.

(e) The department shall also require an applicant to submit proof of the successful completion of a department approved handgun safety course. Any form created by the department to show proof of the successful completion of a department approved handgun safety course shall not require the applicant to provide the applicant's social security number. Any instructor of a department approved handgun safety course shall not withhold proof of the successful completion of the course solely on the fact the applicant did not disclose the applicant's social security number. The course shall include both classroom hours and firing range hours. Beginning September 1, 2010, and thereafter, a component of the classroom portion of all department-approved handgun safety courses shall be instruction on alcohol and drugs, the effects of those substances on a person's reflexes, judgment and ability to safely handle a firearm, and § 39-17-1321. An applicant shall not be required to comply with the firing range and classroom hours requirements of this subsection (e) if the applicant submits proof to the department that within 5 years from the date the application for a handgun carry permit is filed the applicant has:

(1) Been certified by the peace officer standards and training commission;

(2) Successfully completed training at the law enforcement training academy;

(3) Successfully completed the firearms training course required for armed security guard/officer registration, pursuant to § 62-35-118(b); or

(4) Successfully completed all handgun training of not less than 4 hours as required by any branch of the military; provided, however, that an applicant who seeks waiver of the training course pursuant to this subdivision (e)(4) may have completed the military handgun training at any time prior to submission of proof.

(f) The department shall make applications for permits available for distribution at any location where the department conducts driver license examinations.

(g) (1) Upon receipt of a permit application, the department shall:

(A) Forward 2 full sets of fingerprints of the applicant to the Tennessee bureau of investigation; and

(B) Send a copy of the application to the sheriff of the county in which the applicant resides.

(2) Within 30 days of receiving an application, the sheriff shall provide the department with any information concerning the truthfulness of the applicant's answers to the eligibility requirements of subsection (c) that is within the knowledge of the sheriff.

(h) Upon receipt of the fingerprints from the department, the Tennessee bureau of investigation shall:

(1) Within 30 days from receipt of the fingerprints, conduct computer searches to determine the applicant's eligibility for a permit under subsection (c) as are available to the bureau based solely upon the applicant's name, date of birth and social security number and send the results of the searches to the department;

(2) Conduct a criminal history record check based upon 1 set of the fingerprints received and send the results to the department; and

(3) Send 1 set of the fingerprints received from the department to the federal bureau of investigation, request a federal criminal history record check based upon the fingerprints, as long as the service is available, and send the results of the check to the department.

(i) The department shall deny a permit application if it determines from information contained in the criminal history record checks conducted by the Tennessee and federal bureaus of investigation pursuant to subsection (h), from information received from the clerks of court regarding individuals adjudicated as a mental defective or judicially committed to a mental institution pursuant to title 33, or from other information that comes to the attention of the department, that the applicant does not meet the eligibility requirements of this section. The department shall not be required to confirm the applicant's eligibility for a permit beyond the information received from the Tennessee and federal bureaus of investigation, the clerks of court and the sheriffs, if any.

(j) The department shall not deny a permit application if:

(1) The existence of any arrest or other records concerning the applicant for any indictment, charge or warrant have been judicially or administratively expunged;

(2) An applicant's conviction has been set aside by a court of competent jurisdiction;

(3) The applicant, who was rendered infamous or deprived of the rights of citizenship by judgment of any state or federal court, has had the applicant's full rights of citizenship duly restored pursuant to procedures set forth within title 40, chapter 29, or other federal or state law; provided, however, that this subdivision (j)(3) shall not apply to any person who has been convicted of burglary, any felony offense involving violence or use of a firearm or any felony drug offense involving a Schedule I, II, III, IV or V controlled substance or a controlled substance analogue. If the applicant has been convicted of a felony drug offense involving a Schedule VI controlled substance, this subdivision (j)(3) shall not apply if the offense occurred within 10 years of the date of application or renewal; or

(4) The applicant, who was adjudicated as a mental defective or judicially committed to a mental institution, as defined in § 39-17-1301, has had the applicant's firearm disability removed by an order of the court pursuant to title 16, and either a copy of that order has been provided to the department by the TBI or a certified copy of that court order has been provided to the department by the applicant.

(k) If the department denies an application, the department shall notify the applicant in writing within 10 days of the denial. The written notice shall state the specific factual basis for the denial. It shall include a copy of any reports, records or inquiries reviewed or relied upon by the department.

(l) The department shall issue a permit to an applicant not prohibited from obtaining a permit under this section no later than 90 days after the date the department receives the application. A permit issued prior to the department's receipt of the Tennessee and federal bureaus of investigation's criminal history record checks based upon the applicant's fingerprints shall be subject to immediate revocation if either record check reveals that the applicant is not eligible for a permit pursuant to this section.

(m) A permit holder shall not be required to complete a handgun safety course to maintain or renew a handgun carry permit. No permit holder shall be required to complete any additional handgun safety course after obtaining a handgun carry permit. No person shall be required to complete any additional handgun safety course if the person applies for a renewal of a handgun carry permit within 6 months from the date of expiration.

(n) (1) Except as provided in subdivision (n)(2) and subsection (x), a permit issued pursuant to this section shall be good for 4 years and shall entitle the permit holder to carry any handgun or handguns that the permit holder legally owns or possesses. The permit holder shall have the permit in the holder's immediate possession at all times when carrying a handgun and shall display the permit on demand of a law enforcement officer.

(2) A Tennessee permit issued pursuant to this section to a person who is in or who enters into the United States armed forces shall continue in effect for so long as the person's service continues and the person is stationed outside this state, notwithstanding the fact that the person may be temporarily in this state on furlough, leave, or delay en route, and for a period not to exceed 60 days following the date on which the person is honorably discharged or separated from service or returns to this state on reassignment to a duty station in this state, unless the permit is sooner suspended, cancelled or revoked for cause as provided by law. The permit is valid only when in the immediate possession of the permit holder and the permit holder has in the holder's immediate possession the holder's discharge or separation papers, if the permit holder has been discharged or separated from the service.

(3) Notwithstanding this subsection (n), every handgun carry permit issued or renewed by the department on or after April 17, 2015, shall be issued for a period of 5 years and shall expire on the permit holder's birth date. The commissioner shall issue an initial permit or permit renewal for 3 to 7 years, whichever number is necessary to ensure that the permit will expire on each subsequent birth date of the permit holder that is divisible by 5. It is the intent of this subdivision (n)(3) that after the initial renewal, the renewal date for persons who have both a handgun carry permit and a driver license be the same date. The fee for any original permit and any permit renewal due under this section for a permit issued or renewed on or after the implementation of this act shall be prorated to reflect the appropriate fee for a renewal cycle of greater or lesser length than 5 years.

(o) The permit shall be issued on a wallet-sized laminated card of the same approximate size as is used by the state of Tennessee for driver licenses and shall contain only the following information concerning the permit holder:

(1) The permit holder's name, address and date of birth;

(2) A description of the permit holder by sex, height, weight and eye color;

(3) A color photograph of the permit holder; and

(4) The permit number and expiration date.

(p) (1) Except as provided in subsection (x), the department shall charge an application and processing fee of $115. The fee shall cover all aspects of processing the application and issuing a permit. … Any person, who has been honorably discharged from any branch of the United States armed forces or who is on active duty in any branch of the armed forces or who is currently serving in the national guard or armed forces reserve, and who makes initial application for a handgun carry permit shall be required to pay only that portion of the initial application fee that is necessary to conduct the required criminal history record checks.

(2) The provisions of subdivision (p)(1) increasing each permit application fee by $15 for the purpose of fingerprint data base updating and maintenance shall not take effect if the general appropriation act provides a specific appropriation in the amount of $250,000, to defray the expenses contemplated in subdivision (p)(1). If the appropriation is not included in the general appropriations act, the $15 permit fee increase imposed by subdivision (p)(1) shall take effect on July 1, 1997, the public welfare requiring it.

(3) Beginning July 1, 2008, $15 of the fee established in subdivision (p)(1) shall be submitted to the sheriff of the county where the applicant resides for the purpose of verifying the truthfulness of the applicant's answers as provided in subdivision (g)(1).

(q) (1) Prior to the expiration of a permit, a permit holder may apply to the department for the renewal of the permit by submitting, under oath, a renewal application with a renewal fee of $50. The renewal application shall be on a standard form developed by the department of safety and shall require the applicant to disclose, under oath, the information concerning the applicant as set forth in subsection (c), and shall require the applicant to certify that the applicant still satisfies all the eligibility requirements of this section for the issuance of a permit. In the event the permit expires prior to the department's approval or issuance of notice of denial regarding the renewal application, the permit holder shall be entitled to continue to use the expired permit; provided, however, that the permit holder shall also be required to prove by displaying a receipt for the renewal application fee that the renewal application was delivered to the department prior to the expiration date of the permit.

(2) Any person whose handgun carry permit expires and who applies for a renewal of the handgun carry permit within 6 months from the date of expiration shall only be required to comply with the renewal provisions of subdivision (q)(1). If the renewal application is filed 6 months or more from the date of expiration, the person shall, for all purposes, be considered a new applicant.

(3) If a person whose handgun carry permit remained valid pursuant to subdivision (n)(2) because the person was in the United States armed forces applies for a renewal of the permit within 6 months of the expiration of the 60 day period following discharge, separation, or return to this state on reassignment to a duty station in this state as provided in subdivision (n)(2), the person shall only be required to comply with the renewal provisions of subdivision (q)(1). If the renewal application is filed 6 months or more from expiration of the 60 day period following the date of honorable discharge, separation, or return to this state on reassignment to a duty station in this state, the person shall, for all purposes, be considered a new applicant.

(r) (1) A facially valid handgun permit, firearms permit, weapons permit or license issued by another state shall be valid in this state according to its terms and shall be treated as if it is a handgun permit issued by this state; provided, however, this subsection (r) shall not be construed to authorize the holder of any out-of-state permit or license to carry, in this state, any firearm or weapon other than a handgun.

(2) For a person to lawfully carry a handgun in this state based upon a permit or license issued in another state, the person must be in possession of the permit or license at all times the person carries a handgun in this state.

(3) (A) The commissioner of safety shall enter into written reciprocity agreements with other states that require the execution of the agreements. The commissioner of safety shall prepare and publicly publish a current list of states honoring permits issued by the state of Tennessee and shall make the list available to anyone upon request. The commissioner of safety shall also prepare and publicly publish a current list of states who, after inquiry by the commissioner, refuse to enter into a reciprocity agreement with this state or honor handgun carry permits issued by this state. To the extent that any state may impose conditions in the reciprocity agreements, the commissioner of safety shall publish those conditions as part of the list. If another state imposes conditions on Tennessee permit holders in a reciprocity agreement, the conditions shall also become a part of the agreement and apply to the other state's permit holders when they carry a handgun in this state.

(B) If a person with a handgun permit from another state decides to become a resident of Tennessee, the person must obtain a Tennessee handgun permit within 6 months of establishing residency in Tennessee. The permit may be issued based on the person having a permit from another state provided the other state has substantially similar permit eligibility requirements as this state. However, if during the 6-month period the person applies for a handgun permit in this state and the application is denied, the person shall not be allowed to carry a handgun in this state based upon the other state's permit.

(C) (i) If a person who is a resident of and handgun permit holder in another state is employed in this state on a regular basis and desires to carry a handgun in this state, the person shall have 6 months from the last day of the sixth month of regular employment in this state to obtain a Tennessee handgun carry permit. The permit may be issued based on the person having a permit from another state provided the other state has substantially similar permit eligibility requirements as this state. However, if during the 6-month period the person applies for a handgun permit in this state and the application is denied, the person shall not be allowed to carry a handgun in this state based upon the other state's permit.

(ii) This subdivision (r)(3)(C) shall not apply if the state of residence of the person employed in Tennessee has entered into a handgun permit reciprocity agreement with this state pursuant to this subsection (r).

(iii) As used in this subdivision (r)(3)(C), "employed in this state on a regular basis" means a person has been gainfully employed in this state for at least 30 hours a week for 6 consecutive months not counting any absence from employment caused by the employee's use of sick leave, annual leave, administrative leave or compensatory time.

(t) Any law enforcement officer of this state or of any county or municipality may, within the realm of the officer's lawful jurisdiction and when the officer is acting in the lawful discharge of the officer's official duties, disarm a permit holder at any time when the officer reasonably believes it is necessary for the protection of the permit holder, officer or other individual or individuals. The officer shall return the handgun to the permit holder before discharging the permit holder from the scene when the officer has determined that the permit holder is not a threat to the officer, to the permit holder, or other individual or individuals provided that the permit holder has not violated any provision of this section and provided the permit holder has not committed any other violation that results in the arrest of the permit holder.

(u) Substantial compliance with the requirements of this section shall provide the department and any political subdivision thereof with immunity from civil liability alleging liability for issuance of the permit.

(v) Any permit issued pursuant to this section shall be deemed a "license" within the meaning of title 36, chapter 5, part 7, dealing with the enforcement of child support obligations through license denial and revocation.

(w) (1) Notwithstanding any other law or rule to the contrary, neither the department nor an instructor or employee of a department approved handgun safety course is authorized to require any applicant for a handgun carry permit to furnish or reveal identifying information concerning any handgun the applicant owns, possesses or uses during the safety course in order to apply for or be issued the permit.

(2) For purposes of subdivision (w)(1), "identifying information concerning any handgun" includes, but is not limited to, the serial number, model number, make of gun or manufacturer, type of gun, such as revolver or semi-automatic, caliber or whether the applicant owns the handgun used for the safety course.

(x) (1) Any resident of Tennessee who is a United States citizen or lawful permanent resident, as defined by § 55-50-102, who has reached 21 years of age, may apply to the department of safety for a lifetime handgun carry permit. If the applicant is not prohibited from purchasing or possessing a firearm in this state pursuant to § 39-17-1316 or § 39-17-1307(b), 18 U.S.C. § 922(g), or any other state or federal law, and the applicant otherwise meets all of the requirements of this section, the department shall issue a permit to the applicant. The lifetime handgun carry permit shall entitle the permit holder to carry any handgun or handguns the permit holder legally owns or possesses and shall entitle the permit holder to any privilege granted to handgun carry permit holders. The requirements imposed on handgun carry permit holders by this section shall also apply to lifetime handgun carry permit holders.

(2) The department shall charge an application and processing fee of $500 for a lifetime handgun carry permit. The application process shall otherwise be the same as the application process for a handgun carry permit as set out in this section. Any funds from the fees paid pursuant to this subdivision (x)(2) that are not used for processing applications and issuing permits shall be retained by the department to fund any necessary system modifications required to create a lifetime handgun carry permit and monitor the eligibility of lifetime handgun carry permit holders as required by subdivision (x)(3).

(3) A lifetime handgun carry permit shall not expire and shall continue to be valid for the life of the permit holder unless the permit holder no longer meets the requirements of this section. A lifetime handgun carry permit shall not be subject to renewal; provided, however, that every 5 years after issuance of the lifetime handgun carry permit, the department shall conduct a criminal history record check in the same manner as required for handgun carry permit renewals. Upon discovery that a lifetime handgun carry permit holder no longer satisfies the requirements of this section, the department shall suspend or revoke the permit pursuant to § 39-17-1352.

(4) (A) If the lifetime handgun carry permit holder's permit is suspended or revoked, the permit holder shall deliver, in person or by mail, the permit to the department within 30 days of the suspension or revocation.

(B) If the department does not receive the lifetime handgun carry permit holder's suspended or revoked permit within 30 days of the suspension or revocation, the department shall send notice to the permit holder that:

(i) The permit holder has 30 days from the date of the notice to deliver the permit, in person or by mail, to the department; and

(ii) If the permit holder fails to deliver the suspended or revoked permit to the department within 30 days of the date of the notice, the department will suspend the permit holder's driver license.

(C) If the department does not receive the lifetime handgun carry permit holder's suspended or revoked permit within 30 days of the date of the notice provided by the department, the department shall suspend the permit holder's driver license in the same manner as provided in § 55-50-502.

39-17-1352. Suspension or revocation of license.

(a) The department shall suspend or revoke a handgun permit upon a showing by its records or other sufficient evidence that the permit holder:

(1) Is prohibited from purchasing a handgun under applicable state or federal law;

(2) Has not accurately disclosed any material information required by § 39-17-1351;

(3) Poses a material likelihood of risk of harm to the public;

(4) Has been arrested for a felony involving the use or attempted use of force, violence or a deadly weapon or a felony drug offense;

(5) Has been convicted of a felony;

(6) Has violated any other provision of §§ 39-17-1351 – 39-17-1360;

(7) Has at any time committed an act or omission or engaged in a pattern of conduct that would render the permit holder ineligible to apply for or obtain a permit under the eligibility requirements of § 39-17-1351;

(8) Has been convicted of domestic assault as defined in § 39-13-111, or any other misdemeanor crime of domestic violence and is still subject to the disabilities of such a conviction;

(9) Is subject to a current order of protection that fully complies with 18 U.S.C. § 922(g)(8); or

(10) Has been judicially committed to a mental institution pursuant to title 33, chapter 6 or title 33, chapter 7 or has been adjudicated as a mental defective.

(b) (1) It is an offense for a permit holder to knowingly fail or refuse to surrender to the department a suspended or revoked handgun permit within 10 days from the date appearing on the notice of suspension or revocation sent to such permit holder by the department.

(2) A violation of this subsection (b) is a Class A misdemeanor.

(c) (1) Upon the suspension or revocation of a permit, the department shall send notice of the suspension or revocation to the permit holder and the appropriate local law enforcement officers. The notice shall state the following:

(A) That the permit has been immediately suspended or revoked;

(B) That the permit holder must surrender the permit to the department within 10 days of the date appearing on the notice;

(C) That it is a Class A misdemeanor punishable by up to 1 year in jail for the permit holder to knowingly fail or refuse to surrender the permit to the department within the 10-day period;

(D) That if the permit holder does not surrender the suspended or revoked permit within the 10-day period, a law enforcement officer will be directed to take possession of the permit; and

(E) That the permit holder has 30 days from the date appearing on the notice of suspension or revocation to request a hearing on the suspension or revocation.

(2) If the permit holder fails to surrender the suspended or revoked permit as required by this section, the department shall issue authorization to the appropriate local law enforcement officials to take possession of the suspended or revoked permit and send it to the department.

(d) The applicant shall have a right to petition the general sessions court of the applicant's county of residence for judicial review of departmental denial, suspension or revocation of a permit. At the review by the general sessions court, the department shall be represented by the district attorney general.

(e) (1) If a permit holder is arrested and charged with burglary, a felony drug offense or a felony offense involving violence or the use of a firearm, then the court first having jurisdiction over the permit holder with respect to the felony charge shall inquire as to whether the person has been issued a Tennessee handgun carry permit, order the permit holder to surrender the permit and send the permit to the department with a copy of the court's order that required the surrender of the permit. The department shall suspend the permit pending a final disposition on the felony charge against the permit holder.

(2) If a permit holder is arrested and charged with any felony offense other than an offense subject to subdivision (e)(1), then the court first having jurisdiction over the permit holder with respect to the felony charge shall inquire as to whether the person has been issued a Tennessee handgun carry permit, order the permit holder to surrender the permit and send the permit to the department with a copy of the court's order that required the surrender of the permit, unless the permit holder petitions the court for a hearing on the surrender. If the permit holder does petition the court, the court shall determine whether the permit holder will present a material risk of physical harm to the public if released and allowed to retain the permit. If the court determines that the permit holder will present a material risk of physical harm to the public, it shall condition any release of the permit holder, whether on bond or otherwise, upon the permit holder's surrender of the permit to the court. Upon surrender of the permit, the court shall send the permit to the department with a copy of the court's order that required the surrender of the permit and the department shall suspend the permit pending a final disposition of the felony charges against the permit holder.

(3) If the permit holder is acquitted on the charge or charges, the permit shall be restored to the holder and the temporary prohibition against the carrying of a handgun shall be lifted.

(4) If the permit holder is convicted of the charge or charges, the permit shall be revoked by the court and the revocation shall be noted in the judgment and minutes of the court. The court shall send the surrendered permit to the department.

(5) If the permit holder is placed on pre-trial diversion or judicial diversion, the permit holder's privilege to lawfully carry a handgun shall be suspended for the length of time the permit holder is subject to the jurisdiction of the court. The court shall send the surrendered permit to the department.

(f) (1) If a permit holder is convicted of a Class A misdemeanor offense, the permit holder shall surrender the permit to the court having jurisdiction of the case for transmission to the department.

(2) The permit holder shall not be permitted to lawfully carry a handgun or exercise the privileges conferred by the permit for the term of the sentence imposed by the court for the offense or offenses for which the permit holder was convicted.

(g) In order to reinstate a permit suspended pursuant to subsection (e) or (f), the permit holder shall pay a reinstatement fee of $25 with 1/2 of the fee payable to the department of safety and 1/2 payable to the court that suspended the permit.

(1) Prior to the reinstatement of the permit, the permit holder shall have paid in full all fines, court costs and restitution, if any, required by the sentencing court.

(2) Failure to complete any terms of probation imposed by the court shall be a bar to reinstatement of the permit.

(3) Prior to reissuance of the permit, the department shall verify that the permit holder has complied with all reinstatement requirements of this subsection (g).

39-17-1353. Review of revocation or suspension.

(a) Any person who has received a notice of suspension or revocation may make a written request for a review of the department's determination by the department at a hearing. The request shall be made on a form available from the department. If the person's permit has not been previously surrendered, it must be surrendered at the time the request for a hearing is made. A request for a hearing does not stay the permit suspension or revocation.

(b) Within 30 days from the date the request for a hearing is filed, the department shall establish a hearing date and set the case on a docket. Nothing in this section shall be construed as requiring the hearing to be conducted within such 30-day period. The hearing shall be held at a place designated by the department. The department shall provide written notice of the time and place of the hearing to the party requesting the hearing at least 10 days prior to the scheduled hearing, unless the party agrees to waive this requirement.

(d) The sole issue at the hearing shall be whether by a preponderance of the evidence the person has violated any provision of §§ 39-17-1351 – 39-17-1360. If the presiding hearing officer finds the affirmative of this issue, the suspension or revocation order shall be sustained. If the presiding hearing officer finds the negative of this issue, the suspension or revocation order shall be rescinded.

(e) The hearing shall be recorded. The decision of the presiding hearing officer shall be rendered in writing, and a copy will be provided to the person who requested the hearing.

(f) If the person who requested the hearing fails to appear without just cause, the right to a hearing shall be waived, and the department's earlier determination shall be final.

(g) Witnesses under subpoena shall be entitled to the same fees as are now or may hereafter be provided for witnesses in civil actions in the circuit court and, unless otherwise provided by law or by action of the agency, the party requesting the subpoenas shall bear the cost of paying fees to the witnesses subpoenaed.

39-17-1354. Judicial review of department determination.

(a) Within 30 days of the issuance of the final determination of the department following a hearing under § 39-17-1353, a person aggrieved by the determination shall have the right to file a petition in the chancery court of the county of the person's residence for judicial review. The filing of a petition for judicial review shall not stay the revocation order.

(b) The review shall be on the record, without taking additional testimony. If the court finds that the department exceeded its constitutional or statutory authority, made an erroneous interpretation of the law, acted in an arbitrary and capricious manner, or made a determination that is unsupported by the evidence in the record, the court may reverse the department's determination.

39-17-1356. Duplicate permits. The department shall issue a duplicate permit to a permit holder upon the payment by the permit holder of a fee of $5.

39-17-1357. Notice of address change.
(a) Within 60 days of any change in a permit holder's principal place of residence, the permit holder shall notify the department in writing of the permit holder's new address.
(b) On or after January 1, 2015, the department shall provide a method for permit holders to notify the department electronically on the department's web site.

39-17-1358. Retention of records – Violations.
(a) The sheriff or chief law enforcement officer may retain applications and files related to the approval or denial of any application submitted from October 1, 1994, to October 1, 1996, if the applications and files are relevant to any pending litigation. After the pending litigation is concluded, the applications and files shall be destroyed.
(b) Except as otherwise specifically provided in §§ 39-17-1351 and 39-17-1352, a violation of §§ 39-17-1351 – 39-17-1360 is a Class B misdemeanor punishable only by a fine not to exceed $500.
(c) Any party aggrieved under the terms of §§ 39-17-1351 – 39-17-1360 by the denial, suspension or revocation of a permit, or otherwise, may file a writ of mandamus, as provided by law. The action shall also allow the recovery of any actual damages sustained by the party. The aggrieved party, if prevailing in action, shall also be entitled to recover those costs and attorney's fees reasonably incurred or relating to the action.
(d) Nothing contained in this section shall be construed to alter, reduce or eliminate any personal civil or criminal liability that an applicant may have for the intentional or negligent use of a firearm.

39-17-1359. Prohibition at certain meetings – Posting notice.
(a) (1) Except as provided in § 39-17-1313, an individual, corporation, business entity or local, state or federal government entity or agent thereof is authorized to prohibit the possession of weapons by any person who is at a meeting conducted by, or on property owned, operated, or managed or under the control of the individual, corporation, business entity or government entity.
   (2) The prohibition in subdivision (a)(1) shall apply to any person who is authorized to carry a firearm by authority of § 39-17-1351.
(b) (1) Notice of the prohibition permitted by subsection (a) shall be accomplished by displaying the notice described in subdivision (b)(3) in prominent locations, including all entrances primarily used by persons entering the property, building, or portion of the property or building where weapon possession is prohibited. The notice shall be plainly visible to the average person entering the building, property, or portion of the building or property, posted.
   (2) The notice required by this section shall be in English, but a duplicate notice may also be posted in any language used by patrons, customers, or persons who frequent the place where weapon possession is prohibited.
   (3) (A) A sign shall be used as the method of posting. The sign shall include the phrase "NO FIREARMS ALLOWED", and the phrase shall measure at least one inch (1") high and eight inches (8") wide. The sign shall also include the phrase "As authorized by T.C.A. § 39-17-1359".
      (B) The sign shall include a pictorial representation of the phrase "NO FIREARMS ALLOWED" that shall include a circle with a diagonal line through the circle and an image of a firearm inside the circle under the diagonal line. The entire pictorial representation shall be at least 4 inches high and 4 inches wide. The diagonal line shall be at a 45 degree angle from the upper left to the lower right side of the circle.
   (4) An individual, corporation, business entity, or government entity that, as of January 1, 2015, used signs to provide notice of the prohibition permitted by subsection (a) shall have until January 1, 2018, to replace existing signs with signs that meet the requirements of subdivision (b)(3).
(c) (1) It is an offense to possess a weapon in a building or on property that is properly posted in accordance with this section.
   (2) Possession of a weapon on posted property in violation of this section is a Class B misdemeanor punishable by fine only of $500.
(d) Nothing in this section shall be construed to alter, reduce or eliminate any civil or criminal liability that a property owner or manager may have for injuries arising on their property.
(e) This section shall not apply to title 70 regarding wildlife laws, rules and regulations.
(f) This section shall not apply to the grounds of any public park, natural area, historic park, nature trail, campground, forest, greenway, waterway or other similar public place that is owned or operated by the state, a county, a municipality or instrumentality thereof. The carrying of firearms in those areas shall be governed by § 39-17-1311.

39-17-1360. Rules and regulations. The department of safety is authorized to promulgate rules and regulations pursuant to the Uniform Administrative Procedures Act, compiled in title 4, chapter 5, to implement §§ 39-17-1351 – 39-17-1360.

39-17-1361. Chief law enforcement officer's certification for transfer or making of firearm.
(a) As used in this section:
   (1) "Certification" means the participation and assent of the chief law enforcement officer necessary under federal law for the approval of the application to transfer or make a firearm;

(2) "Chief law enforcement officer" or "officer" means any official, or the official's designee, that the federal bureau of alcohol, tobacco, firearms and explosives, or any successor agency, identifies by regulation or otherwise as eligible to provide any required certification for the making or transfer of a firearm; and

(3) "Firearm" has the same meaning as provided in the National Firearms Act (26 U.S.C. § 5845(a)).

(b) When a chief law enforcement officer's certification is required by federal law or regulation for the transfer or making of a firearm, the officer shall, within 15 days of receipt of a request for certification, provide such certification if the applicant is not prohibited by law from receiving or possessing the firearm, including pursuant to § 39-17-1316, and is not the subject of a proceeding that could result in the applicant being prohibited by law from receiving or possessing the firearm. If the officer is unable to make a certification as required by this section, the officer shall provide the applicant a written notification of the denial and the reason for this determination.

(c) An officer shall not be required by this section to make any certification the officer knows to be untrue, but the officer may not refuse to provide certification based on a generalized objection to private persons or entities making, possessing, or receiving firearms or any certain type of firearm the possession of which is not prohibited by law.

(d) An officer and the officer's employees who act in good faith are immune from civil liability arising from any act or omission in making a certification as required by this section.

(e) An applicant whose request for certification is denied may appeal the officer's decision to the circuit court or chancery court that is located in the jurisdiction in which the applicant resides or maintains its address of record. The court shall review the officer's decision to deny the certification de novo. If the court finds that the applicant is not prohibited by law from receiving or possessing the firearm and is not the subject of a proceeding that could result in such prohibition and that no substantial evidence supports the officer's determination that the officer cannot truthfully make the certification, the court shall order the officer to issue the certification.

(f) In making the determination required by subsection (b), an officer may conduct a criminal background check and may require of the applicant only the information that is necessary to identify the applicant for that purpose or to determine the disposition of an arrest or proceeding relevant to the applicant's eligibility to lawfully possess or receive a firearm. An officer may not require access to or inspection of any private residential premises as a condition of granting an application under this section.

39-17-1362. Imitation firearm – Defined – Offense to display in threatening manner in public place.

(a) As used in this section, unless the context otherwise requires:

(1) "Imitation firearm" means an object or device substantially similar in coloration and overall appearance to a firearm, as defined in § 39-11-106(a), as to lead a reasonable person to perceive that the object or device is a firearm; and

(2) "Public place" means a place to which the public or a group of persons has access and includes, but is not limited to, highways, transportation facilities, schools, places of amusement, parks, places of business, playgrounds, and hallways, lobbies and other portions of apartment houses and hotels not constituting rooms or apartments designed for actual residence. An act is deemed to occur in a public place if it produces its proscribed consequences in a public place, even if the person engaging in the prohibited conduct is not in a public place.

(b) A person commits an offense who intentionally displays in a threatening manner an imitation firearm in a public place in a way that would cause a reasonable person to fear bodily injury to themselves or another.

(c) It is a defense to a violation of subsection (b) if the imitation firearm is displayed in connection with, or as a part of, any justifiable defense as set forth in chapter 11, part 6 of this title.

(d) A violation of this section is a Class B misdemeanor.

(e) Nothing in this section shall be construed to prohibit prosecution under any other law.

39-17-1364. Purchase and shipment of antique firearms and certain edged weapons. Notwithstanding § 39-17-1307, or any other law, it is lawful in this state for a person to purchase, and have shipped directly to such person's residence, the following:

(1) A black powder weapon; provided, that it meets the definition of 18 U.S.C. § 921;

Texas Statutes and Codes
Current through the 2015 regular session, 84th Legislature.

Office of the Attorney General
Post Office Box 12548
Austin, TX 78711-2548
Voice: (512) 463-2100
ken.paxton@oag.state.tx.us

Dallas Field Division
1114 Commerce Street, Room 303
Dallas, Texas 75242
Voice: (469) 227-4300
https://www.atf.gov/dallas-field-division

PROTECTING THE PUBLIC
SERVING OUR NATION

Houston Field Division
5825 N. Sam Houston Pkwy West
Suite 300
Houston, Texas 77086
Voice: (281) 716-8200
https://www.atf.gov/houston-field-division

Table of Contents

Local Government Code, TITLE 7, Subtitle A, Chapter 229, Subchapter A Regulation of Firearms, Knives, and Explosives

Penal Code, TITLE 10, Chapter 46 Weapons

Texas Family Code
TITLE 4 Protective Orders and Family Violence, Subtitle B Protective Orders
Chapter 85 Issuance of Protective Order, Subchapter B Contents of Protective Order

Sec. 85.026. Warning on Protective Order.
(a) Each protective order issued under this subtitle, including a temporary ex parte order, must contain the following prominently displayed statements in boldfaced type, capital letters, or underlined:...
(a) "IT IS UNLAWFUL FOR ANY PERSON, OTHER THAN A PEACE OFFICER, AS DEFINED BY § 1.07, PENAL CODE, ACTIVELY ENGAGED IN EMPLOYMENT AS A SWORN, FULL-TIME PAID EMPLOYEE OF A STATE AGENCY OR POLITICAL SUBDIVISION, WHO IS SUBJECT TO A PROTECTIVE ORDER TO POSSESS A FIREARM OR AMMUNITION."

Chapter 86 Law Enforcement Duties Relating to Protective Orders

Sec. 86.002. Duty to Provide Information to Firearms Dealers.
(a) On receipt of a request for a law enforcement information system record check of a prospective transferee by a licensed firearms dealer under the Brady Handgun Violence Prevention Act, 18 U.S.C. § 922, the chief law enforcement officer shall determine whether the Department of Public Safety has in the department's law enforcement information system a record indicating the existence of an active protective order directed to the prospective transferee.
(b) If the department's law enforcement information system indicates the existence of an active protective order directed to the prospective transferee, the chief law enforcement officer shall immediately advise the dealer that the transfer is prohibited.

Sec. 411.171. Definitions. In this subchapter:

(2) "Chemically dependent person" means a person who frequently or repeatedly becomes intoxicated by excessive indulgence in alcohol or uses controlled substances or dangerous drugs so as to acquire a fixed habit and an involuntary tendency to become intoxicated or use those substances as often as the opportunity is presented.

(3) [Repealed by Acts 2015, 84th Leg., ch. 437 (H.B. 910), §50, effective January 1, 2016.]

(4) "Convicted" means an adjudication of guilt or, except as provided in § 411.1711, an order of deferred adjudication entered against a person by a court of competent jurisdiction whether or not the imposition of the sentence is subsequently probated and the person is discharged from community supervision. The term does not include an adjudication of guilt or an order of deferred adjudication that has been subsequently:

  (A) expunged;

  (B) pardoned under the authority of a state or federal official; or

  (C) otherwise vacated, set aside, annulled, invalidated, voided, or sealed under any state or federal law.

(5) "Handgun" has the meaning assigned by § 46.01, Penal Code.

(6) "Intoxicated" has the meaning assigned by § 49.01, Penal Code.

(7) "Qualified handgun instructor" means a person who is certified to instruct in the use of handguns by the department.

Sec. 411.1711. Certain Exemptions from Convictions. A person is not convicted, as that term is defined by § 411.171, if an order of deferred adjudication was entered against the person on a date not less than 10 years preceding the date of the person's application for a license under this subchapter unless the order of deferred adjudication was entered against the person for:

(1) a felony offense under:

  (A) Title 5, Penal Code;

  (B) Chapter 29, Penal Code;

  (C) Section 25.07 or 25.072, Penal Code; or

  (D) Section 30.02, Penal Code, if the offense is punishable under Subsection (c)(2) or (d) of that section; or

(2) an offense under the laws of another state if the offense contains elements that are substantially similar to the elements of an offense listed in Subdivision (1).

Sec. 411.172. Eligibility.

(a) A person is eligible for a license to carry a handgun if the person:

  (1) is a legal resident of this state for the 6-month period preceding the date of application under this subchapter or is otherwise eligible for a license under § 411.173(a);

  (2) is at least 21 years of age;

  (3) has not been convicted of a felony;

  (4) is not charged with the commission of a Class A or Class B misdemeanor or equivalent offense, or of an offense under § 42.01, Penal Code, or equivalent offense, or of a felony under an information or indictment;

  (5) is not a fugitive from justice for a felony or a Class A or Class B misdemeanor or equivalent offense;

  (6) is not a chemically dependent person;

  (7) is not incapable of exercising sound judgment with respect to the proper use and storage of a handgun;

  (8) has not, in the 5 years preceding the date of application, been convicted of a Class A or Class B misdemeanor or equivalent offense or of an offense under § 42.01, Penal Code, or equivalent offense;

  (9) is fully qualified under applicable federal and state law to purchase a handgun;

  (10) has not been finally determined to be delinquent in making a child support payment administered or collected by the attorney general;

  (11) has not been finally determined to be delinquent in the payment of a tax or other money collected by the comptroller, the tax collector of a political subdivision of the state, or any agency or subdivision of the state;

  (12) is not currently restricted under a court protective order or subject to a restraining order affecting the spousal relationship, other than a restraining order solely affecting property interests;

  (13) has not, in the 10 years preceding the date of application, been adjudicated as having engaged in delinquent conduct violating a penal law of the grade of felony; and

  (14) has not made any material misrepresentation, or failed to disclose any material fact, in an application submitted pursuant to § 411.174.

(b) For the purposes of this section, an offense under the laws of this state, another state, or the United States is:

  (1) except as provided by Subsection (b-1), a felony if the offense, at the time the offense is committed:

    (A) is designated by a law of this state as a felony;

    (B) contains all the elements of an offense designated by a law of this state as a felony; or

    (C) is punishable by confinement for one year or more in a penitentiary; and

  (2) a Class A misdemeanor if the offense is not a felony and confinement in a jail other than a state jail felony facility is affixed as a possible punishment.

(b-1) An offense is not considered a felony for purposes of Subsection (b) if, at the time of a person's application for a license to carry a handgun, the offense:

(1) is not designated by a law of this state as a felony; and

(2) does not contain all the elements of any offense designated by a law of this state as a felony.

(c) An individual who has been convicted two times within the 10-year period preceding the date on which the person applies for a license of an offense of the grade of Class B misdemeanor or greater that involves the use of alcohol or a controlled substance as a statutory element of the offense is a chemically dependent person for purposes of this section and is not qualified to receive a license under this subchapter. This subsection does not preclude the disqualification of an individual for being a chemically dependent person if other evidence exists to show that the person is a chemically dependent person.

(d) For purposes of Subsection (a)(7), a person is incapable of exercising sound judgment with respect to the proper use and storage of a handgun if the person:

(1) has been diagnosed by a licensed physician as suffering from a psychiatric disorder or condition that causes or is likely to cause substantial impairment in judgment, mood, perception, impulse control, or intellectual ability;

(2) suffers from a psychiatric disorder or condition described by Subdivision (1) that:

(A) is in remission but is reasonably likely to redevelop at a future time; or

(B) requires continuous medical treatment to avoid redevelopment;

(3) has been diagnosed by a licensed physician, determined by a review board or similar authority, or declared by a court to be incompetent to manage the person's own affairs; or

(4) has entered in a criminal proceeding a plea of not guilty by reason of insanity.

(e) The following constitutes evidence that a person has a psychiatric disorder or condition described by Subsection (d)(1):

(1) involuntary psychiatric hospitalization;

(2) psychiatric hospitalization;

(3) inpatient or residential substance abuse treatment in the preceding 5-year period;

(4) diagnosis in the preceding 5-year period by a licensed physician that the person is dependent on alcohol, a controlled substance, or a similar substance; or

(5) diagnosis at any time by a licensed physician that the person suffers or has suffered from a psychiatric disorder or condition consisting of or relating to:

(A) schizophrenia or delusional disorder;

(B) bipolar disorder;

(C) chronic dementia, whether caused by illness, brain defect, or brain injury;

(D) dissociative identity disorder;

(E) intermittent explosive disorder; or

(F) antisocial personality disorder.

(f) Notwithstanding Subsection (d), a person who has previously been diagnosed as suffering from a psychiatric disorder or condition described by Subsection (d) or listed in Subsection (e) is not because of that disorder or condition incapable of exercising sound judgment with respect to the proper use and storage of a handgun if the person provides the department with a certificate from a licensed physician whose primary practice is in the field of psychiatry stating that the psychiatric disorder or condition is in remission and is not reasonably likely to develop at a future time.

(g) Notwithstanding Subsection (a)(2), a person who is at least 18 years of age but not yet 21 years of age is eligible for a license to carry a handgun if the person:

(1) is a member or veteran of the United States armed forces, including a member or veteran of the reserves or national guard;

(2) was discharged under honorable conditions, if discharged from the United States armed forces, reserves, or national guard; and

(3) meets the other eligibility requirements of Subsection (a) except for the minimum age required by federal law to purchase a handgun.

(h) The issuance of a license to carry a handgun to a person eligible under Subsection (g) does not affect the person's ability to purchase a handgun or ammunition under federal law.

Sec. 411.173. Nonresident License.

(a) The department by rule shall establish a procedure for a person who meets the eligibility requirements of this subchapter other than the residency requirement established by § 411.172(a) (1) to obtain a license under this subchapter if the person is a legal resident of another state or if the person relocates to this state with the intent to establish residency in this state. The procedure must include payment of a fee in an amount sufficient to recover the average cost to the department of obtaining a criminal history record check and investigation on a nonresident applicant. A license issued in accordance with the procedure established under this subsection:

(1) remains in effect until the license expires under § 411.183; and

(2) may be renewed under § 411.185.

(b) The governor shall negotiate an agreement with any other state that provides for the issuance of a license to carry a handgun under which a license issued by the other state is recognized in this state or shall issue a proclamation that a license issued by the other state is recognized in this state if the attorney general of the State of Texas determines that a background check of each applicant for a license issued by that state is initiated by state or local authorities or an agent of the state or local authorities before the license is issued. For purposes of this subsection, "background check" means a search of the National Crime Information Center database and the Interstate Identification Index maintained by the Federal Bureau of Investigation.

Sec. 411.174. Application.
(a) An applicant for a license to carry a handgun must submit to the director's designee described by § 411.176:
(1) a completed application on a form provided by the department that requires only the information listed in Subsection (b);
(2) one or more photographs of the applicant that meet the requirements of the department;
(3) a certified copy of the applicant's birth certificate or certified proof of age;
(4) proof of residency in this state;
(5) two complete sets of legible and classifiable fingerprints of the applicant taken by a person appropriately trained in recording fingerprints who is employed by a law enforcement agency or by a private entity designated by a law enforcement agency as an entity qualified to take fingerprints of an applicant for a license under this subchapter;
(6) a nonrefundable application and license fee of $140 paid to the department;
(7) evidence of handgun proficiency, in the form and manner required by the department;
(8) an affidavit signed by the applicant stating that the applicant:
  (A) has read and understands each provision of this subchapter that creates an offense under the laws of this state and each provision of the laws of this state related to use of deadly force; and
  (B) fulfills all the eligibility requirements listed under § 411.172; and
(9) a form executed by the applicant that authorizes the director to make an inquiry into any noncriminal history records that are necessary to determine the applicant's eligibility for a license under § 411.172(a).
(b) An applicant must provide on the application a statement of the applicant's:
(1) full name and place and date of birth;
(2) race and sex;
(3) residence and business addresses for the preceding 5 years;
(4) hair and eye color;
(5) height and weight;
(6) driver's license number or identification certificate number issued by the department;
(7) criminal history record information of the type maintained by the department under this chapter, including a list of offenses for which the applicant was arrested, charged, or under an information or indictment and the disposition of the offenses; and
(8) history, if any, of treatment received by, commitment to, or residence in:
  (A) a drug or alcohol treatment center licensed to provide drug or alcohol treatment under the laws of this state or another state, but only if the treatment, commitment, or residence occurred during the preceding 5 years; or
  (B) a psychiatric hospital.
(b-1) The application must provide space for the applicant to:
(1) list any military service that may qualify the applicant to receive a license with a veteran's designation under § 411.179(e); and
(2) include proof required by the department to determine the applicant's eligibility to receive that designation.
(c) The department shall distribute on request a copy of this subchapter and application materials.
(d) The department may not request or require an applicant to provide the applicant's social security number as part of an application under this section.

Sec. 411.1741. Voluntary Contribution to Fund for Veterans' Assistance.
(a) When a person applies for an original or renewal license to carry a concealed handgun under this subchapter, the person may make a voluntary contribution in any amount to the fund for veterans" assistance established by § 434.017....

Sec. 411.175. Procedures for Submitting Fingerprints.
The department shall establish procedures for the submission of legible and classifiable fingerprints by an applicant for a license under this subchapter who:
(1) is required to submit those fingerprints to the department, including an applicant under § 411.199, 411.1991, or 411.201; and
(2) resides in a county having a population of 46,000 or less and does not reside within a 25-mile radius of a facility with the capability to process digital or electronic fingerprints.

Sec. 411.176. Review of Application Materials.
(a) On receipt of application materials by the department at its Austin headquarters, the department shall conduct the appropriate criminal history record check of the applicant through its computerized criminal history system. Not later than the 30th day after the date the department receives the application materials, the department shall forward the materials to the director's designee in the geographical area of the applicant's residence so that the designee may conduct the investigation described by Subsection (b). For purposes of this section, the director's designee may be a noncommissioned employee of the department.
(b) The director's designee as needed shall conduct an additional criminal history record check of the applicant and an

investigation of the applicant's local official records to verify the accuracy of the application materials. The director's designee may access any records necessary for purposes of this subsection. The scope of the record check and the investigation are at the sole discretion of the department, except that the director's designee shall complete the record check and investigation not later than the 60th day after the date the department receives the application materials. The department shall send a fingerprint card to the Federal Bureau of Investigation for a national criminal history check of the applicant. On completion of the investigation, the director's designee shall return all materials and the result of the investigation to the appropriate division of the department at its Austin headquarters.

(c) The director's designee may submit to the appropriate division of the department, at the department's Austin headquarters, along with the application materials a written recommendation for disapproval of the application, accompanied by an affidavit stating personal knowledge or naming persons with personal knowledge of a ground for denial under § 411.172. The director's designee may also submit the application and the recommendation that the license be issued.

(d) On receipt at the department's Austin headquarters of the application materials and the result of the investigation by the director's designee, the department shall conduct any further record check or investigation the department determines is necessary if a question exists with respect to the accuracy of the application materials or the eligibility of the applicant, except that the department shall complete the record check and investigation not later than the 180th day after the date the department receives the application materials from the applicant.

Sec. 411.177. Issuance or Denial of License.

(a) The department shall issue a license to carry a handgun to an applicant if the applicant meets all the eligibility requirements and submits all the application materials. The department shall administer the licensing procedures in good faith so that any applicant who meets all the eligibility requirements and submits all the application materials shall receive a license. The department may not deny an application on the basis of a capricious or arbitrary decision by the department.

(b) The department shall, not later than the 60th day after the date of the receipt by the director's designee of the completed application materials:

(1) issue the license;

(2) notify the applicant in writing that the application was denied:

(A) on the grounds that the applicant failed to qualify under the criteria listed in § 411.172;

(B) based on the affidavit of the director's designee submitted to the department under § 411.176(c); or

(C) based on the affidavit of the qualified handgun instructor submitted to the department under § 411.188(k); or

(3) notify the applicant in writing that the department is unable to make a determination regarding the issuance or denial of a license to the applicant within the 60-day period prescribed by this subsection and include in that notification an explanation of the reason for the inability and an estimation of the amount of time the department will need to make the determination.

(c) Failure of the department to issue or deny a license for a period of more than 30 days after the department is required to act under Subsection (b) constitutes denial.

(d) A license issued under this subchapter is effective from the date of issuance.

Sec. 411.178. Notice to Local Law Enforcement.
On request of a local law enforcement agency, the department shall notify the agency of the licenses that have been issued to license holders who reside in the county in which the agency is located.

Sec. 411.179. Form of License.

(a) The department by rule shall adopt the form of the license. A license must include:

(1) a number assigned to the license holder by the department;

(2) a statement of the period for which the license is effective;

(3) a color photograph of the license holder;

(4) the license holder's full name, date of birth, hair and eye color, height, weight, and signature;

(5) the license holder's residence address or, as provided by Subsection (d), the street address of the courthouse in which the license holder or license holder's spouse serves as a federal judge or the license holder serves as a state judge;

(6) the number of a driver's license or an identification certificate issued to the license holder by the department; and

(7) the designation "VETERAN" if required under Subsection (e).

(b) [Repealed by Acts 2013, 83rd Leg., ch. 1302 (H.B. 3142), § 14(2), effective June 14, 2013.]

(c) In adopting the form of the license under Subsection (a), the department shall establish a procedure for the license of a qualified handgun instructor or of a judge, justice, prosecuting attorney, or assistant prosecuting attorney, as described by § 46.15(a)(4) or (6), Penal Code, to indicate on the license the license holder's status as a qualified handgun instructor or as a judge, justice, district attorney, criminal district attorney, or county attorney. In establishing the procedure, the department shall require sufficient documentary evidence to establish the license holder's status under this subsection.

(d) In adopting the form of the license under Subsection (a), the department shall establish a procedure for the license of a federal judge, a state judge, or the spouse of a federal judge or state judge to omit the license holder's residence address and to include, in lieu of that address, the street address of the courthouse in which the license holder or license holder's spouse serves as a federal judge or state judge. In establishing the procedure, the department shall require sufficient documentary evidence to establish the license holder's status as a federal judge, a state judge, or the spouse of a federal judge or state judge.

(e) In this subsection, "veteran" has the meaning assigned by § 411.1951. The department shall include the designation "VETERAN" on the face of any original, duplicate, modified, or renewed license under this subchapter or on the reverse side of the license, as determined by the department, if the license is issued to a veteran who:

(1) requests the designation; and

(2) provides proof sufficient to the department of the veteran's military service and honorable discharge.

Sec. 411.180. Notification of Denial, Revocation, or Suspension of License; Review.

(a) The department shall give written notice to each applicant for a handgun license of any denial, revocation, or suspension of that license. Not later than the 30th day after the notice is received by the applicant, according to the records of the department, the applicant or license holder may request a hearing on the denial, revocation, or suspension. The applicant must make a written request for a hearing addressed to the department at its Austin address. The request for hearing must reach the department in Austin prior to the 30th day after the date of receipt of the written notice. On receipt of a request for hearing from a license holder or applicant, the department shall promptly schedule a hearing in the appropriate justice court in the county of residence of the applicant or license holder. The justice court shall conduct a hearing to review the denial, revocation, or suspension of the license. In a proceeding under this section, a justice of the peace shall act as an administrative hearing officer. A hearing under this section is not subject to Chapter 2001 (Administrative Procedure Act). A district attorney or county attorney, the attorney general, or a designated member of the department may represent the department.

(b) The department, on receipt of a request for hearing, shall file the appropriate petition in the justice court selected for the hearing and send a copy of that petition to the applicant or license holder at the address contained in departmental records. A hearing under this section must be scheduled within 30 days of receipt of the request for a hearing. The hearing shall be held expeditiously but in no event more than 60 days after the date that the applicant or license holder requested the hearing. The date of the hearing may be reset on the motion of either party, by agreement of the parties, or by the court as necessary to accommodate the court's docket.

(c) The justice court shall determine if the denial, revocation, or suspension is supported by a preponderance of the evidence. Both the applicant or license holder and the department may present evidence. The court shall affirm the denial, revocation, or suspension if the court determines that denial, revocation, or suspension is supported by a preponderance of the evidence. If the court determines that the denial, revocation, or suspension is not supported by a preponderance of the evidence, the court shall order the department to immediately issue or return the license to the applicant or license holder.

(d) A proceeding under this section is subject to Chapter 105, Civil Practice and Remedies Code, relating to fees, expenses, and attorney's fees.

(e) A party adversely affected by the court's ruling following a hearing under this section may appeal the ruling by filing within 30 days after the ruling a petition in a county court at law in the county in which the applicant or license holder resides or, if there is no county court at law in the county, in the county court of the county. A person who appeals under this section must send by certified mail a copy of the person's petition, certified by the clerk of the court in which the petition is filed, to the appropriate division of the department at its Austin headquarters. The trial on appeal shall be a trial de novo without a jury. A district or county attorney or the attorney general may represent the department.

(f) A suspension of a license may not be probated.

(g) If an applicant or a license holder does not petition the justice court, a denial becomes final and a revocation or suspension takes effect on the 30th day after receipt of written notice.

(h) The department may use and introduce into evidence certified copies of governmental records to establish the existence of certain events that could result in the denial, revocation, or suspension of a license under this subchapter, including records regarding convictions, judicial findings regarding mental competency, judicial findings regarding chemical dependency, or other matters that may be established by governmental records that have been properly authenticated.

(i) This section does not apply to a suspension of a license under § 85.022, Family Code, or Article 17.292, Code of Criminal Procedure.

Sec. 411.181. Notice of Change of Address or Name.

(a) If a person who is a current license holder moves from any residence address stated on the license, if the name of the person is changed by marriage or otherwise, or if the person's status becomes inapplicable for purposes of the information required to be displayed on the license under § 411.179, the person shall, not later than the 30th day after the date of the address, name, or status change, notify the department and provide the department with the number of the person's license and, as applicable, the person's:

(1) former and new addresses;

(2) former and new names; or

(3) former and new status.

(b) If the name of the license holder is changed by marriage or otherwise, or if the person's status becomes inapplicable as described by Subsection (a), the person shall apply for a duplicate license. The duplicate license must reflect the person's current name, residence address, and status.

(c) If a license holder moves from the address stated on the license, the person shall apply for a duplicate license.

(d) The department shall charge a license holder a fee of $25 for a duplicate license.

(e) The department shall make the forms available on request.

(f) On request of a local law enforcement agency, the department shall notify the agency of changes made under Subsection (a) by license holders who reside in the county in which the agency is located.

(g) If a license is lost, stolen, or destroyed, the license holder shall apply for a duplicate license not later than the 30th day after the date of the loss, theft, or destruction of the license.

(h) If a license holder is required under this section to apply for a duplicate license and the license expires not later than the 60th day after the date of the loss, theft, or destruction of the license, the applicant may renew the license with the modified information included on the new license. The applicant must pay only the nonrefundable renewal fee.

(i) A license holder whose application fee for a duplicate license under this section is dishonored or reversed may reapply for a duplicate license at any time, provided the application fee and a dishonored payment charge of $25 is paid by cashier's check or money order made payable to the "Texas Department of Public Safety."

Sec. 411.182. Notice.

(a) For the purpose of a notice required by this subchapter, the department may assume that the address currently reported to the department by the applicant or license holder is the correct address.

(b) A written notice meets the requirements under this subchapter if the notice is sent by certified mail to the current address reported by the applicant or license holder to the department.

(c) If a notice is returned to the department because the notice is not deliverable, the department may give notice by publication once in a newspaper of general interest in the county of the applicant's or license holder's last reported address. On the 31st day after the date the notice is published, the department may take the action proposed in the notice.

Sec. 411.183. Expiration.

(a) A license issued under this subchapter expires on the first birthday of the license holder occurring after the fourth anniversary of the date of issuance.

(b) A renewed license expires on the license holder's birthdate, 5 years after the date of the expiration of the previous license.

(c) A duplicate license expires on the date the license that was duplicated would have expired.

(d) A modified license expires on the date the license that was modified would have expired.

Sec. 411.185. License Renewal Procedure.

(a) To renew a license, a license holder must, on or before the date the license expires, submit to the department by mail or, in accordance with the procedure adopted under Subsection (f), on the Internet:

  (1) a renewal application on a form provided by the department;

  (2) payment of a nonrefundable renewal fee as set by the department; and

  (3) the informational form described by Subsection (c) signed or electronically acknowledged by the applicant.

(b) The director by rule shall adopt a renewal application form requiring an update of the information on the original completed application. The director by rule shall set the renewal fee in an amount that is sufficient to cover the actual cost to the department to:

  (1) verify the information contained in the renewal application form;

  (2) conduct any necessary investigation concerning the license holder's continued eligibility to hold a license; and

  (3) issue the renewed license.

(c) The director by rule shall adopt an informational form that describes state law regarding the use of deadly force and the places where it is unlawful for the holder of a license issued under this subchapter to carry a handgun. An applicant for a renewed license must sign and return the informational form to the department by mail or acknowledge the form electronically on the Internet according to the procedure adopted under Subsection (f).

(d) Not later than the 60th day before the expiration date of the license, the department shall mail to each license holder a written notice of the expiration of the license, a renewal application form, and the informational form described by Subsection (c).

(e) The department shall renew the license of a license holder who meets all the eligibility requirements to continue to hold a license and submits all the renewal materials described by Subsection (a). Not later than the 45th day after receipt of the renewal materials, the department shall issue the renewed license or notify the license holder in writing that the department denied the license holder's renewal application.

(f) The director by rule shall adopt a procedure by which a license holder who satisfies the eligibility requirements to continue to hold a license may submit the renewal materials described by Subsection (a) by mail or on the Internet.

(g) The department may not request or require a license holder to provide the license holder's social security number to renew a license under this section.

Sec. 411.186. Revocation.

(a) The department shall revoke a license under this section if the license holder:

  (1) was not entitled to the license at the time it was issued;

(2) made a material misrepresentation or failed to disclose a material fact in an application submitted under this subchapter;

(3) subsequently becomes ineligible for a license under § 411.172, unless the sole basis for the ineligibility is that the license holder is charged with the commission of a Class A or Class B misdemeanor or equivalent offense, or of an offense under § 42.01, Penal Code, or equivalent offense, or of a felony under an information or indictment;

(4) is convicted of an offense under § 46.035, Penal Code;

(5) is determined by the department to have engaged in conduct constituting a reason to suspend a license listed in § 411.187(a) after the person's license has been previously suspended twice for the same reason; or

(6) submits an application fee that is dishonored or reversed if the applicant fails to submit a cashier's check or money order made payable to the "Department of Public Safety of the State of Texas" in the amount of the dishonored or reversed fee, plus $25, within 30 days of being notified by the department that the fee was dishonored or reversed.

(b) If a peace officer believes a reason listed in Subsection (a) to revoke a license exists, the officer shall prepare an affidavit on a form provided by the department stating the reason for the revocation of the license and giving the department all of the information available to the officer at the time of the preparation of the form. The officer shall attach the officer's reports relating to the license holder to the form and send the form and attachments to the appropriate division of the department at its Austin headquarters not later than the fifth working day after the date the form is prepared. The officer shall send a copy of the form and the attachments to the license holder. If the license holder has not surrendered the license or the license was not seized as evidence, the license holder shall surrender the license to the appropriate division of the department not later than the 10th day after the date the license holder receives the notice of revocation from the department, unless the license holder requests a hearing from the department. The license holder may request that the justice court in the justice court precinct in which the license holder resides review the revocation as provided by § 411.180. If a request is made for the justice court to review the revocation and hold a hearing, the license holder shall surrender the license on the date an order of revocation is entered by the justice court.

(c) A license holder whose license is revoked for a reason listed in Subsections (a)(1)--(5) may reapply as a new applicant for the issuance of a license under this subchapter after the second anniversary of the date of the revocation if the cause for revocation does not exist on the date of the second anniversary. If the cause for revocation exists on the date of the second anniversary after the date of revocation, the license holder may not apply for a new license until the cause for revocation no longer exists and has not existed for a period of two years.

(d) A license holder whose license is revoked under Subsection (a)(6) may reapply for an original or renewed license at any time, provided the application fee and a dishonored payment charge of $25 is paid by cashier's check or money order made payable to the "Texas Department of Public Safety."

Sec. 411.187. Suspension of License.

(a) The department shall suspend a license under this section if the license holder:

(1) is charged with the commission of a Class A or Class B misdemeanor or equivalent offense, or of an offense under § 42.01, Penal Code, or equivalent offense, or of a felony under an information or indictment;

(2) fails to notify the department of a change of address, name, or status as required by § 411.181;

(3) commits an act of family violence and is the subject of an active protective order rendered under Title 4, Family Code; or

(4) is arrested for an offense involving family violence or an offense under § 42.072, Penal Code, and is the subject of an order for emergency protection issued under Article 17.292, Code of Criminal Procedure.

(b) If a peace officer believes a reason listed in Subsection (a) to suspend a license exists, the officer shall prepare an affidavit on a form provided by the department stating the reason for the suspension of the license and giving the department all of the information available to the officer at the time of the preparation of the form. The officer shall attach the officer's reports relating to the license holder to the form and send the form and the attachments to the appropriate division of the department at its Austin headquarters not later than the fifth working day after the date the form is prepared. The officer shall send a copy of the form and the attachments to the license holder. If the license holder has not surrendered the license or the license was not seized as evidence, the license holder shall surrender the license to the appropriate division of the department not later than the 10th day after the date the license holder receives the notice of suspension from the department unless the license holder requests a hearing from the department. The license holder may request that the justice court in the justice court precinct in which the license holder resides review the suspension as provided by § 411.180. If a request is made for the justice court to review the suspension and hold a hearing, the license holder shall surrender the license on the date an order of suspension is entered by the justice court.

(c) The department shall suspend a license under this section:

(1) for 30 days, if the person's license is subject to suspension for a reason listed in Subsection (a)(2), (3), or (4), except as provided by Subdivision (2);

(2) for not less than 1 year and not more than 3 years, if the person's license:

(A) is subject to suspension for a reason listed in Subsection (a), other than the reason listed in Subsection (a)(1); and

(B) has been previously suspended for the same reason;

(3) until dismissal of the charges, if the person's license is subject to suspension for the reason listed in Subsection (a)(1); or

(4) for the duration of or the period specified by:

(A) the protective order issued under Title 4, Family Code, if the person's license is subject to suspension for the reason listed in Subsection (a)(5); or

(B) the order for emergency protection issued under Article 17.292, Code of Criminal Procedure, if the person's license is subject to suspension for the reason listed in Subsection (a)(6).

Sec. 411.1871. Notice of Suspension or Revocation of Certain Licenses. The department shall notify the Texas Commission on Law Enforcement Officer Standards and Education if the department takes any action against the license of a person identified by the commission as a person certified under § 1701.260, Occupations Code, including suspension or revocation.

Sec. 411.188. Handgun Proficiency Requirement.

(a) The director by rule shall establish minimum standards for handgun proficiency and shall develop a course to teach handgun proficiency and examinations to measure handgun proficiency. The course to teach handgun proficiency is required for each person who seeks to obtain a license and must contain training sessions divided into 2 parts. One part of the course must be classroom instruction and the other part must be range instruction and an actual demonstration by the applicant of the applicant's ability to safely and proficiently use a handgun. An applicant must be able to demonstrate, at a minimum, the degree of proficiency that is required to effectively operate a handgun of .32 caliber or above. The department shall distribute the standards, course requirements, and examinations on request to any qualified handgun instructor.

(b) Only qualified handgun instructors may administer the classroom instruction part or the range instruction part of the handgun proficiency course. The classroom instruction part of the course must include not less than 4 hours and not more than 6 hours of instruction on:

(1) the laws that relate to weapons and to the use of deadly force;

(2) handgun use and safety, including use of restraint holsters and methods to ensure the secure carrying of openly carried handguns;

(3) nonviolent dispute resolution; and

(4) proper storage practices for handguns with an emphasis on storage practices that eliminate the possibility of accidental injury to a child.

(c) [Repealed by Acts 2013, 83rd Leg., ch. 156 (S.B. 864), § 3, and by Acts 2013, 83rd Leg., ch. 1387 (H.B. 48), § 5, effective September 1, 2013.]

(d) Only a qualified handgun instructor may administer the proficiency examination to obtain a license. The proficiency examination must include:

(1) a written section on the subjects listed in Subsection (b); and

(2) a physical demonstration of proficiency in the use of 1 or more handguns and in handgun safety procedures.

(g) A person who wishes to obtain a license to carry a handgun must apply in person to a qualified handgun instructor to take the appropriate course in handgun proficiency and demonstrate handgun proficiency as required by the department.

(i) A certified firearms instructor of the department may monitor any class or training presented by a qualified handgun instructor. A qualified handgun instructor shall cooperate with the department in the department's efforts to monitor the presentation of training by the qualified handgun instructor. A qualified handgun instructor shall make available for inspection to the department any and all records maintained by a qualified handgun instructor under this subchapter. The qualified handgun instructor shall keep a record of all information required by department rule.

(j) [Repealed by Acts 2015, 84th Leg., ch. 1236 (S.B. 1296), § 9.006, effective September 1, 2015.]

(k) A qualified handgun instructor may submit to the department a written recommendation for disapproval of the application for a license or modification of a license, accompanied by an affidavit stating personal knowledge or naming persons with personal knowledge of facts that lead the instructor to believe that an applicant does not possess the required handgun proficiency. The department may use a written recommendation submitted under this subsection as the basis for denial of a license only if the department determines that the recommendation is made in good faith and is supported by a preponderance of the evidence. The department shall make a determination under this subsection not later than the 45th day after the date the department receives the written recommendation. The 60-day period in which the department must take action under § 411.177(b) is extended 1 day for each day a determination is pending under this subsection.

Sec. 411.1881. Exemption from Instruction for Certain Persons.

(a) Notwithstanding any other provision of this subchapter, a person may not be required to complete the range instruction portion of a handgun proficiency course to obtain a license issued under this subchapter if the person:

(1) is currently serving in or is honorably discharged from:

(A) the army, navy, air force, coast guard, or marine corps of the United States or an auxiliary service or reserve unit of one of those branches of the armed forces; or

(B) the Texas military forces, as defined by § 437.001; and

(2) has, within the 5 years preceding the date of the person's application for the license, completed a course of training in handgun proficiency or familiarization as part of the person's service with the armed forces or Texas military forces.

(b) The director by rule shall adopt a procedure by which a license holder who is exempt under Subsection (a) from the range instruction portion of the handgun proficiency requirement may submit a form demonstrating the license holder's qualification for an exemption under that subsection. The form must provide sufficient information to allow the department to verify whether the license holder qualifies for the exemption.

Sec. 411.1882. Evidence of Handgun Proficiency for Certain Persons.

(a) A person who is serving in this state as a judge or justice of a federal court, as an active judicial officer as defined by § 411.201, as a district attorney, assistant district attorney, criminal district attorney, assistant criminal district attorney, county attorney, or assistant county attorney, as a supervision officer as defined by § 2, Article 42.12, Code of Criminal Procedure, or as a juvenile probation officer may establish handgun proficiency for the purposes of this subchapter by obtaining from a handgun proficiency instructor approved by the Texas Commission on Law Enforcement for purposes of § 1702.1675, Occupations Code, a sworn statement that indicates that the person, during the 12-month period preceding the date of the person's application to the department, demonstrated to the instructor proficiency in the use of handguns.

(b) The director by rule shall adopt a procedure by which a person described under Subsection (a) may submit a form demonstrating the person's qualification for an exemption under that subsection. The form must provide sufficient information to allow the department to verify whether the person qualifies for the exemption.

(c) A license issued under this section automatically expires on the 6-month anniversary of the date the person's status under Subsection (a) becomes inapplicable. A license that expires under this subsection may be renewed under § 411.185.

Sec. 411.190. Qualified Handgun Instructors.

(a) The director may certify as a qualified handgun instructor a person who:

(1) is certified by the Texas Commission on Law Enforcement or under Chapter 1702, Occupations Code, to instruct others in the use of handguns;

(2) regularly instructs others in the use of handguns and has graduated from a handgun instructor school that uses a nationally accepted course designed to train persons as handgun instructors; or

(3) is certified by the National Rifle Association of America as a handgun instructor.

(b) In addition to the qualifications described by Subsection (a), a qualified handgun instructor must be qualified to instruct persons in:

(1) the laws that relate to weapons and to the use of deadly force;

(2) handgun use, proficiency, and safety, including use of restraint holsters and methods to ensure the secure carrying of openly carried handguns;

(3) nonviolent dispute resolution; and

(4) proper storage practices for handguns, including storage practices that eliminate the possibility of accidental injury to a child.

(c) In the manner applicable to a person who applies for a license to carry a handgun, the department shall conduct a background check of a person who applies for certification as a qualified handgun instructor. If the background check indicates that the applicant for certification would not qualify to receive a handgun license, the department may not certify the applicant as a qualified handgun instructor. If the background check indicates that the applicant for certification would qualify to receive a handgun license, the department shall provide handgun instructor training to the applicant. The applicant shall pay a fee of $100 to the department for the training. The applicant must take and successfully complete the training offered by the department and pay the training fee before the department may certify the applicant as a qualified handgun instructor. The department shall issue a license to carry a handgun under the authority of this subchapter to any person who is certified as a qualified handgun instructor and who pays to the department a fee of $100 in addition to the training fee. The department by rule may prorate or waive the training fee for an employee of another governmental entity.

(d) The certification of a qualified handgun instructor expires on the second anniversary after the date of certification. To renew a certification, the qualified handgun instructor must pay a fee of $100 and take and successfully complete the retraining courses required by department rule.

(d-1) The department shall ensure that an applicant may renew certification under Subsection (d) from any county in this state by using an online format to complete the required retraining courses if:

(1) the applicant is renewing certification for the first time; or

(2) the applicant completed the required retraining courses in person the previous time the applicant renewed certification.

(e) After certification, a qualified handgun instructor may conduct training for applicants for a license under this subchapter.

(f) If the department determines that a reason exists to revoke, suspend, or deny a license to carry a handgun with respect to a person who is a qualified handgun instructor or an applicant for certification as a qualified handgun instructor, the department shall take that action against the person's:

(1) license to carry a handgun if the person is an applicant for or the holder of a license issued under this subchapter; and

(2) certification as a qualified handgun instructor.

Sec. 411.1901. School Safety Certification for Qualified Handgun Instructors.

(a) The department shall establish a process to enable qualified handgun instructors certified under § 411.190 to obtain an additional certification in school safety. The process must include a school safety certification course that provides training in the following:

(1) the protection of students;

(2) interaction of license holders with first responders;

(3) tactics for denying an intruder entry into a classroom or school facility; and

(4) methods for increasing a license holder's accuracy with a handgun while under duress.

(b) The school safety certification course under Subsection (a) must include not less than 15 hours and not more than 20 hours of instruction.

(c) A qualified handgun instructor certified in school safety under this section may provide school safety training, including instruction in the subjects listed under Subsection (a), to employees of a school district or an open-enrollment charter school who hold a license to carry a handgun issued under this subchapter.

(d) The department shall establish a fee in an amount that is sufficient to cover the costs of the school safety certification under this section.

(e) The department may adopt rules to administer this section.

Sec. 411.191. Review of Denial, Revocation, or Suspension of Certification As Qualified Handgun Instructor.
The procedures for the review of a denial, revocation, or suspension of a license under § 411.180 apply to the review of a denial, revocation, or suspension of certification as a qualified handgun instructor. The notice provisions of this subchapter relating to denial, revocation, or suspension of handgun licenses apply to the proposed denial, revocation, or suspension of a certification of a qualified handgun instructor or an applicant for certification as a qualified handgun instructor.

Sec. 411.192. Confidentiality of Records.
(a) The department shall disclose to a criminal justice agency information contained in its files and records regarding whether a named individual or any individual named in a specified list is licensed under this subchapter. Information on an individual subject to disclosure under this section includes the individual's name, date of birth, gender, race, zip code, telephone number, e-mail address, and Internet website address. Except as otherwise provided by this section and by § 411.193, all other records maintained under this subchapter are confidential and are not subject to mandatory disclosure under the open records law, Chapter 552.

(b) An applicant or license holder may be furnished a copy of disclosable records regarding the applicant or license holder on request and the payment of a reasonable fee.

(c) The department shall notify a license holder of any request that is made for information relating to the license holder under this section and provide the name of the agency making the request.

(d) The department shall make public and distribute to the public at no cost lists of individuals who are certified as qualified handgun instructors by the department and who request to be included as provided by Subsection (e). The department shall include on the lists each individual's name, telephone number, e-mail address, and Internet website address. The department shall make the list available on the department's Internet website.

(e) An individual who is certified as a qualified handgun instructor may request in writing that the department disclose all or part of the information described by Subsection (d) regarding the individual. The department shall include all or part of the individual's information on the list as requested.

Sec. 411.193. Statistical Report.
The department shall make available, on request and payment of a reasonable fee to cover costs of copying, a statistical report that includes the number of licenses issued, denied, revoked, or suspended by the department during the preceding month, listed by age, gender, race, and zip code of the applicant or license holder.

Sec. 411.194. Reduction of Fees Due to Indigency.
(a) Notwithstanding any other provision of this subchapter, the department shall reduce by 50% any fee required for the issuance of an original, duplicate, modified, or renewed license under this subchapter if the department determines that the applicant is indigent.

(b) The department shall require an applicant requesting a reduction of a fee to submit proof of indigency with the application materials.

(c) For purposes of this section, an applicant is indigent if the applicant's income is not more than 100% of the applicable income level established by the federal poverty guidelines.

Sec. 411.195. Reduction of Fees for Senior Citizens.
Notwithstanding any other provision of this subchapter, the department shall reduce by 50% any fee required for the issuance of an original, duplicate, modified, or renewed license under this subchapter if the applicant for the license is 60 years of age or older.

Sec. 411.1951. Waiver or Reduction of Fees for Members or Veterans of United States Armed Forces.
(a) In this section, "veteran" means a person who:

(1) has served in:

(A) the army, navy, air force, coast guard, or marine corps of the United States;

(B) the Texas military forces as defined by § 437.001; or

(C) an auxiliary service of one of those branches of the armed forces; and

(2) has been honorably discharged from the branch of the service in which the person served.

(b) Notwithstanding any other provision of this subchapter, the department shall waive any fee required for the issuance of an original, duplicate, modified, or renewed license under this subchapter if the applicant for the license is:

(1) a member of the United States armed forces, including a member of the reserves, national guard, or state guard; or

(2) a veteran who, within 365 days preceding the date of the application, was honorably discharged from the branch of service in which the person served.

(c) Notwithstanding any other provision of this subchapter, if the applicant is a veteran who, more than 365 days preceding the date of the application, was honorably discharged from the branch of the service in which the applicant served:

(1) the applicant must pay a fee of $25 for the issuance of an original or renewed license under this subchapter; and

(2) the department shall reduce by 50% any fee required of the applicant for a duplicate or modified license under this subchapter.

Sec. 411.1952. Reduction of Fees for Employees of Texas Department of Criminal Justice. Notwithstanding any other provision of this subchapter, an applicant who is a correctional officer of the Texas Department of Criminal Justice shall pay a fee of $ 25 for the issuance of an original or renewed license under this subchapter.

Sec. 411.1953. Reduction of Fees for Community Supervision and Corrections Department Officers and Juvenile Probation Officers. Notwithstanding any other provision of this subchapter, an applicant who is serving in this state as a supervision officer, as defined by § 2, Article 42.12, Code of Criminal Procedure, or as a juvenile probation officer shall pay a fee of $25 for the issuance of an original or renewed license under this subchapter.

Sec. 411.196. Method of Payment. A person may pay a fee required by this subchapter by cash, credit card, personal check, cashier's check, or money order. A person who pays a fee required by this subchapter by cash must pay the fee in person. Checks or money orders must be made payable to the "Texas Department of Public Safety." A person whose payment for a fee required by this subchapter is dishonored or reversed must pay any future fees required by this subchapter by cashier's check or money order made payable to the "Texas Department of Public Safety." A fee received by the department under this subchapter is nonrefundabie.

Sec. 411.197. Rules. The director shall adopt rules to administer this subchapter.

Sec. 411.198. Law Enforcement Officer Alias Handgun License.
(a) On written approval of the director, the department may issue to a law enforcement officer an alias license to carry a handgun to be used in supervised activities involving criminal investigations.
(b) It is a defense to prosecution under § 46.035, Penal Code, that the actor, at the time of the commission of the offense, was the holder of an alias license issued under this section.

Sec. 411.199. Honorably Retired Peace Officers.
(a) A person who is licensed as a peace officer under Chapter 1701, Occupations Code, and who has been employed full-time as a peace officer by a law enforcement agency may apply for a license under this subchapter at any time after retirement.
(b) The person shall submit 2 complete sets of legible and classifiable fingerprints and a sworn statement from the head of the law enforcement agency employing the applicant. A head of a law enforcement agency may not refuse to issue a statement under this subsection. If the applicant alleges that the statement is untrue, the department shall investigate the validity of the statement. The statement must include:

(1) the name and rank of the applicant;
(2) the status of the applicant before retirement;
(3) whether or not the applicant was accused of misconduct at the time of the retirement;
(4) the physical and mental condition of the applicant;
(5) the type of weapons the applicant had demonstrated proficiency with during the last year of employment;
(6) whether the applicant would be eligible for reemployment with the agency, and if not, the reasons the applicant is not eligible; and
(7) a recommendation from the agency head regarding the issuance of a license under this subchapter.

(c) The department may issue a license under this subchapter to an applicant under this section if the applicant is honorably retired and physically and emotionally fit to possess a handgun. In this subsection, "honorably retired" means the applicant:

(1) did not retire in lieu of any disciplinary action;
(2) was eligible to retire from the law enforcement agency or was ineligible to retire only as a result of an injury received in the course of the applicant's employment with the agency; and
(3) is entitled to receive a pension or annuity for service as a law enforcement officer or is not entitled to receive a pension or annuity only because the law enforcement agency that employed the applicant does not offer a pension or annuity to its employees.

(d) An applicant under this section must pay a fee of $25 for a license issued under this subchapter.
(e) [Repealed by Acts 2015, 84th Leg., ch. 1236 (S.B. 1296), § 9.007, effective September 1, 2015.]
(f) A license issued under this section expires as provided by § 411.183.
(g) A retired officer of the United States who was eligible to carry a firearm in the discharge of the officer's official duties is eligible for a license under this section. An applicant described by this subsection may submit the application at any time after retirement. The applicant shall submit with the application proper proof of retired status by presenting the following documents prepared by the agency from which the applicant retired:

(1) retirement credentials; and

(2) a letter from the agency head stating the applicant retired in good standing.

Sec. 411.1991. Peace Officers.

(a) A person who is licensed as a peace officer under Chapter 1701, Occupations Code, and employed as a peace officer by a law enforcement agency, or who is a member of the Texas military forces, excluding Texas State Guard members who are serving in the Texas Legislature, may apply for a license under this subchapter.

(a-1) An applicant who is a peace officer shall submit to the department:

(1) the name and rank of the applicant; and

(2) a current copy of the applicant's peace officer license and evidence of employment as a peace officer.

(a-2) The department shall adopt rules regarding the information required to be included in an application submitted by a member of the Texas military forces under this section.

(b) The department may issue a license under this subchapter to an applicant under this section if the applicant complies with Subsection (a-1) or rules adopted under Subsection (a-2), as applicable.

(c) An applicant under this section shall pay a fee of $25 for a license issued under this subchapter.

(d) A license issued under this section expires as provided by § 411.183.

Sec. 411.1992. Former Reserve Law Enforcement Officers.

(a) A person who served as a reserve law enforcement officer, as defined by § 1701.001, Occupations Code, not less than a total of 15 years with one or more state or local law enforcement agencies may apply for a license under this subchapter at any time.

(b) The applicant shall submit to the department 2 complete sets of legible and classifiable fingerprints and a sworn statement from the head of the law enforcement agency at which the applicant last served as a reserve law enforcement officer. A head of a law enforcement agency may not refuse to issue a statement under this subsection. If the applicant alleges that the statement is untrue, the department shall investigate the validity of the statement. The statement must include:

(1) the name and rank of the applicant;

(2) the status of the applicant;

(3) whether the applicant was accused of misconduct at any time during the applicant's term of service and the disposition of that accusation;

(4) a description of the physical and mental condition of the applicant;

(5) a list of the types of weapons the applicant demonstrated proficiency with during the applicant's term of service; and

(6) a recommendation from the agency head regarding the issuance of a license under this subchapter.

(c) The department may issue a license under this subchapter to an applicant under this section if the applicant was a reserve law enforcement officer for not less than a total of 15 years with one or more state or local law enforcement agencies and is physically and emotionally fit to possess a handgun.

(d) An applicant under this section must pay a fee of $25 for a license issued under this subchapter.

(e) A former reserve law enforcement officer who obtains a license as provided by this section must maintain, for the category of weapon licensed, the proficiency required for the person under § 1701.357, Occupations Code. The department or the local law enforcement agency at which the person last served as a reserve law enforcement officer shall allow the person an opportunity to annually demonstrate the required proficiency. The proficiency shall be reported to the department on application and renewal.

(f) A license issued under this section expires as provided by § 411.183.

Sec. 411.200. Application to Licensed Security Officers.
This subchapter does not exempt a license holder who is also employed as a security officer and licensed under Chapter 1702, Occupations Code, from the duty to comply with Chapter 1702, Occupations Code, or § 46.02, Penal Code.

Sec. 411.201. Active and Retired Judicial Officers.

(a) In this section:

(1) "Active judicial officer" means:

(A) a person serving as a judge or justice of the supreme court, the court of criminal appeals, a court of appeals, a district court, a criminal district court, a constitutional county court, a statutory county court, a justice court, or a municipal court;

(B) a federal judge who is a resident of this state; or

(C) a person appointed and serving as an associate judge under Chapter 201, Family Code.

(2) "Federal judge" means:

(A) a judge of a United States court of appeals;

(B) a judge of a United States district court;

(C) a judge of a United States bankruptcy court; or

(D) a magistrate judge of a United States district court.

(3) "Retired judicial officer" means:

(A) a visiting judge appointed under § 26.023 or 26.024;

(B) a senior judge designated under § 75.001 or a judicial officer as designated or defined by § 75.001, 831.001, or 836.001; or

(C) a retired federal judge who is a resident of this state.

(b) Notwithstanding any other provision of this subchapter, the department shall issue a license under this subchapter to an active or retired judicial officer who meets the requirements of this section.

(c) An active judicial officer is eligible for a license to carry a handgun under the authority of this subchapter. A retired judicial officer is eligible for a license to carry a handgun under the authority of this subchapter if the officer:

(1) has not been convicted of a felony;

(2) has not, in the 5 years preceding the date of application, been convicted of a Class A or Class B misdemeanor or equivalent offense;

(3) is not charged with the commission of a Class A or Class B misdemeanor or equivalent offense or of a felony under an information or indictment;

(4) is not a chemically dependent person; and

(5) is not a person of unsound mind.

(d) An applicant for a license who is an active or retired judicial officer must submit to the department:

(1) a completed application, including all required affidavits, on a form prescribed by the department;

(2) one or more photographs of the applicant that meet the requirements of the department;

(3) two complete sets of legible and classifiable fingerprints of the applicant, including one set taken by a person employed by a law enforcement agency who is appropriately trained in recording fingerprints;

(4) evidence of handgun proficiency, in the form and manner required by the department for an applicant under this section;

(5) a nonrefundable application and license fee set by the department in an amount reasonably designed to cover the administrative costs associated with issuance of a license to carry a handgun under this subchapter; and

(6) if the applicant is a retired judicial officer, a form executed by the applicant that authorizes the department to make an inquiry into any noncriminal history records that are necessary to determine the applicant's eligibility for a license under this subchapter.

(e) On receipt of all the application materials required by this section, the department shall:

(1) if the applicant is an active judicial officer, issue a license to carry a handgun under the authority of this subchapter; or

(2) if the applicant is a retired judicial officer, conduct an appropriate background investigation to determine the applicant's eligibility for the license and, if the applicant is eligible, issue a license to carry a handgun under the authority of this subchapter.

(f) Except as otherwise provided by this subsection, an applicant for a license under this section must satisfy the handgun proficiency requirements of § 411.188. The classroom instruction part of the proficiency course for an active judicial officer is not subject to a minimum hour requirement. The instruction must include instruction only on:

(1) handgun use, proficiency, and safety; and

(2) proper storage practices for handguns with an emphasis on storage practices that eliminate the possibility of accidental injury to a child.

(g) A license issued under this section expires as provided by § 411.183 and may be renewed in accordance with § 411.185.

(h) The department shall issue a license to carry a handgun under the authority of this subchapter to an elected attorney representing the state in the prosecution of felony cases who meets the requirements of this section for an active judicial officer. The department shall waive any fee required for the issuance of an original, duplicate, or renewed license under this subchapter for an applicant who is an attorney elected or employed to represent the state in the prosecution of felony cases.

Sec. 411.202. License a Benefit. The issuance of a license under this subchapter is a benefit to the license holder for purposes of those sections of the Penal Code to which the definition of "benefit" under § 1.07, Penal Code, applies.

Sec. 411.203. Rights of Employers. This subchapter does not prevent or otherwise limit the right of a public or private employer to prohibit persons who are licensed under this subchapter from carrying a handgun on the premises of the business. In this section, "premises" has the meaning assigned by § 46.035(f)(3), Penal Code.

Sec. 411.2031. Carrying of Handguns by License Holders on Certain Campuses. [Effective August 1, 2016]

(a) For purposes of this section:

(1) "Campus" means all land and buildings owned or leased by an institution of higher education or private or independent institution of higher education.

(2) "Institution of higher education" and "private or independent institution of higher education" have the meanings assigned by § 61.003, Education Code.

(3) "Premises" has the meaning assigned by § 46.035, Penal Code.

(b) A license holder may carry a concealed handgun on or about the license holder's person while the license holder is on the campus of an institution of higher education or private or independent institution of higher education in this state.

(c) Except as provided by Subsection (d), (d-1), or (e), an institution of higher education or private or independent institution of higher education in this state may not adopt any rule, regulation, or other provision prohibiting license holders from carrying handguns on the campus of the institution.

(d) An institution of higher education or private or independent institution of higher education in this state may establish rules, regulations, or other provisions concerning the storage of handguns in dormitories or other residential facilities that are owned or leased and operated by the institution and located on the campus of the institution.

(d-1) After consulting with students, staff, and faculty of the institution regarding the nature of the student population, specific safety considerations, and the uniqueness of the campus environment, the president or other chief executive officer of an institution of higher education in this state shall establish reasonable rules, regulations, or other provisions regarding the carrying of concealed handguns by license holders on the campus of the institution or on premises located on the campus of the institution. The president or officer may not establish provisions that generally prohibit or have the effect of generally prohibiting license holders from carrying concealed handguns on the campus of the institution. The president or officer may amend the provisions as necessary for campus safety. The provisions take effect as determined by the president or officer unless subsequently amended by the board of regents or other governing board under Subsection (d-2). The institution must give effective notice under § 30.06, Penal Code, with respect to any portion of a premises on which license holders may not carry.

(d-2) Not later than the 90th day after the date that the rules, regulations, or other provisions are established as described by Subsection (d-1), the board of regents or other governing board of the institution of higher education shall review the provisions. The board of regents or other governing board may, by a vote of not less than 2/3 of the board, amend wholly or partly the provisions established under Subsection (d-1). If amended under this subsection, the provisions are considered to be those of the institution as established under Subsection (d-1).

(d-3) An institution of higher education shall widely distribute the rules, regulations, or other provisions described by Subsection (d-1) to the institution's students, staff, and faculty, including by prominently publishing the provisions on the institution's Internet website.

(e) A private or independent institution of higher education in this state, after consulting with students, staff, and faculty of the institution, may establish rules, regulations, or other provisions prohibiting license holders from carrying handguns on the campus of the institution, any grounds or building on which an activity sponsored by the institution is being conducted, or a passenger transportation vehicle owned by the institution.

Sec. 411.2032. Transportation and Storage of Firearms and Ammunition by License Holders in Private Vehicles on Certain Campuses.

(a) For purposes of this section:

(1) "Campus" means all land and buildings owned or leased by an institution of higher education or private or independent institution of higher education.

(2) "Institution of higher education" and "private or independent institution of higher education" have the meanings assigned by § 61.003, Education Code.

(b) An institution of higher education or private or independent institution of higher education in this state may not adopt or enforce any rule, regulation, or other provision or take any other action, including posting notice under § 30.06 or 30.07, Penal Code, prohibiting or placing restrictions on the storage or transportation of a firearm or ammunition in a locked, privately owned or leased motor vehicle by a person, including a student enrolled at that institution, who holds a license to carry a handgun under this subchapter and lawfully possesses the firearm or ammunition:

(1) on a street or driveway located on the campus of the institution; or

(2) in a parking lot, parking garage, or other parking area located on the campus of the institution

Sec. 411.204. Notice Required on Certain Premises.

(a) A business that has a permit or license issued under Chapter 25, 28, 32, 69, or 74, Alcoholic Beverage Code, and that derives 51% or more of its income from the sale of alcoholic beverages for on-premises consumption as determined by the Texas Alcoholic Beverage Commission under § 104.06, Alcoholic Beverage Code, shall prominently display at each entrance to the business premises a sign that complies with the requirements of Subsection (c).

(b) A hospital licensed under Chapter 241, Health and Safety Code, or a nursing home licensed under Chapter 242, Health and Safety Code, shall prominently display at each entrance to the hospital or nursing home, as appropriate, a sign that complies with the requirements of Subsection (c) other than the requirement that the sign include on its face the number "51".

(c) The sign required under Subsections (a) and (b) must give notice in both English and Spanish that it is unlawful for a person licensed under this subchapter to carry a handgun on the premises. The sign must appear in contrasting colors with block letters at least one inch in height and must include on its face the number "51" printed in solid red at least 5 inches in height. The sign shall be displayed in a conspicuous manner clearly visible to the public.

(d) A business that has a permit or license issued under the Alcoholic Beverage Code and that is not required to display a sign under this section may be required to display a sign under § 11.041 or 61.11, Alcoholic Beverage Code.

(e) This section does not apply to a business that has a food and beverage certificate issued under the Alcoholic Beverage Code.

Sec. 411.205. Requirement to Display License.
If a license holder is carrying a handgun on or about the license holder's person when a magistrate or a peace officer demands that the license holder display identification, the license holder shall display both the license holder's driver's license or identification certificate issued by the department and the license holder's handgun license.

Sec. 411.206. Seizure of Handgun and License.

(a) If a peace officer arrests and takes into custody a license holder who is carrying a handgun under the authority of this subchapter, the officer shall seize the license holder's handgun and license as evidence.

(b) The provisions of Article 18.19, Code of Criminal Procedure, relating to the disposition of weapons seized in connection with criminal offenses, apply to a handgun seized under this subsection.

(c) Any judgment of conviction entered by any court for an offense under § 46.035, Penal Code, must contain the handgun license number of the convicted license holder. A certified copy of the judgment is conclusive and sufficient evidence to justify revocation of a license under § 411.186(a)(4).

Sec. 411.207. Authority of Peace Officer to Disarm.

(a) A peace officer who is acting in the lawful discharge of the officer's official duties may disarm a license holder at any time the officer reasonably believes it is necessary for the protection of the license holder, officer, or another individual. The peace officer shall return the handgun to the license holder before discharging the license holder from the scene if the officer determines that the license holder is not a threat to the officer, license holder, or another individual and if the license holder has not violated any provision of this subchapter or committed any other violation that results in the arrest of the license holder.

(b) A peace officer who is acting in the lawful discharge of the officer's official duties may temporarily disarm a license holder when a license holder enters a nonpublic, secure portion of a law enforcement facility, if the law enforcement agency provides a gun locker where the peace officer can secure the license holder's handgun. The peace officer shall secure the handgun in the locker and shall return the handgun to the license holder immediately after the license holder leaves the nonpublic, secure portion of the law enforcement facility.

(c) A law enforcement facility shall prominently display at each entrance to a nonpublic, secure portion of the facility a sign that gives notice in both English and Spanish that, under this section, a peace officer may temporarily disarm a license holder when the license holder enters the nonpublic, secure portion of the facility. The sign must appear in contrasting colors with block letters at least one inch in height. The sign shall be displayed in a clearly visible and conspicuous manner.

(d) In this section:

(1) "Law enforcement facility" means a building or a portion of a building used exclusively by a law enforcement agency that employs peace officers as described by Articles 2.12(1) and (3), Code of Criminal Procedure, and support personnel to conduct the official business of the agency. The term does not include:

(A) any portion of a building not actively used exclusively to conduct the official business of the agency; or

(B) any public or private driveway, street, sidewalk, walkway, parking lot, parking garage, or other parking area.

(2) "Nonpublic, secure portion of a law enforcement facility" means that portion of a law enforcement facility to which the general public is denied access without express permission and to which access is granted solely to conduct the official business of the law enforcement agency.

Sec. 411.208. Limitation of Liability. [Effective August 1, 2016]

(a) A court may not hold the state, an agency or subdivision of the state, an officer or employee of the state, an institution of higher education, an officer or employee of an institution of higher education, a private or independent institution of higher education that has not adopted rules under § 411.2031(e), an officer or employee of a private or independent institution of higher education that has not adopted rules under § 411.2031(e), a peace officer, or a qualified handgun instructor liable for damages caused by:

(1) an action authorized under this subchapter or a failure to perform a duty imposed by this subchapter; or

(2) the actions of an applicant or license holder that occur after the applicant has received a license or been denied a license under this subchapter.

(b) A cause of action in damages may not be brought against the state, an agency or subdivision of the state, an officer or employee of the state, an institution of higher education, an officer or employee of an institution of higher education, a private or independent institution of higher education that has not adopted rules under § 411.2031(e), an officer or employee of a private or independent institution of higher education that has not adopted rules under § 411.2031(e), a peace officer, or a qualified handgun instructor for any damage caused by the actions of an applicant or license holder under this subchapter.

(c) The department is not responsible for any injury or damage inflicted on any person by an applicant or license holder arising or alleged to have arisen from an action taken by the department under this subchapter.

(d) The immunities granted under Subsections (a), (b), and (c) do not apply to:

(1) an act or a failure to act by the state, an agency or subdivision of the state, an officer of the state, an institution of higher education, an officer or employee of an institution of higher education, a private or independent institution of higher education that has not adopted rules under § 411.2031(e), an officer or employee of a private or independent institution of higher education that has not adopted rules under § 411.2031(e), or a peace officer if the act or failure to act was capricious or arbitrary; or

(2) any officer or employee of an institution of higher education or private or independent institution of higher education described by Subdivision (1) who possesses a handgun on the campus of that institution and whose conduct with regard to the handgun is made the basis of a claim for personal injury or property damage.

(e) The immunities granted under Subsection (a) to a qualified handgun instructor do not apply to a cause of action for fraud or a deceptive trade practice.

(f) [Added effective August 01, 2016] For purposes of this section:

(1) "Campus" has the meaning assigned by § 411.2031.

(2) "Institution of higher education" and "private or independent institution of higher education" have the meanings assigned by § 61.003, Education Code.

Sec. 411.209. Wrongful Exclusion of Concealed Handgun License Holder.

(a) A state agency or a political subdivision of the state may not provide notice by a communication described by § 30.06, Penal Code, or by any sign expressly referring to that law or to a concealed handgun license, that a license holder carrying a handgun under the authority of this subchapter is prohibited from entering or remaining on a premises or other place owned or leased by the governmental entity unless license holders are prohibited from carrying a handgun on the premises or other place by § 46.03 or 46.035, Penal Code.

(b) A state agency or a political subdivision of the state that violates Subsection (a) is liable for a civil penalty of:

(1) not less than $1,000 and not more than $1,500 for the first violation; and

(2) not less than $10,000 and not more than $10,500 for the second or a subsequent violation.

(c) Each day of a continuing violation of Subsection (a) constitutes a separate violation.

(d) A citizen of this state or a person licensed to carry a concealed handgun under this subchapter may file a complaint with the attorney general that a state agency or political subdivision is in violation of Subsection (a) if the citizen or person provides the agency or subdivision a written notice that describes the violation and specific location of the sign found to be in violation and the agency or subdivision does not cure the violation before the end of the third business day after the date of receiving the written notice. A complaint filed under this subsection must include evidence of the violation and a copy of the written notice.

(e) A civil penalty collected by the attorney general under this section shall be deposited to the credit of the compensation to victims of crime fund established under Subchapter B, Chapter 56, Code of Criminal Procedure.

(f) Before a suit may be brought against a state agency or a political subdivision of the state for a violation of Subsection (a), the attorney general must investigate the complaint to determine whether legal action is warranted. If legal action is warranted, the attorney general must give the chief administrative officer of the agency or political subdivision charged with the violation a written notice that:

(1) describes the violation and specific location of the sign found to be in violation;

(2) states the amount of the proposed penalty for the violation; and

(3) gives the agency or political subdivision 15 days from receipt of the notice to remove the sign and cure the violation to avoid the penalty, unless the agency or political subdivision was found liable by a court for previously violating Subsection (a).

(g) If the attorney general determines that legal action is warranted and that the state agency or political subdivision has not cured the violation within the 15-day period provided by Subsection (f)(3), the attorney general or the appropriate county or district attorney may sue to collect the civil penalty provided by Subsection (b). The attorney general may also file a petition for a writ of mandamus or apply for other appropriate equitable relief. A suit or petition under this subsection may be filed in a district court in Travis County or in a county in which the principal office of the state agency or political subdivision is located. The attorney general may recover reasonable expenses incurred in obtaining relief under this subsection, including court costs, reasonable attorney's fees, investigative costs, witness fees, and deposition costs.

(h) Sovereign immunity to suit is waived and abolished to the extent of liability created by this section.

Local Government Code, TITLE 7 Regulation of Land Use, Structures, Businesses, and Related Activities
Subtitle A Municipal Regulatory Authority
Chapter 229 Misc. Regulatory Authority of Municipalities
Subchapter A Regulation of Firearms, Knives, and Explosives

Sec. 229.001. Firearms; Air Guns; Knives; Explosives.

(a) Notwithstanding any other law, including § 43.002 of this code and Chapter 251, Agriculture Code, a municipality may not adopt regulations relating to:

(1) the transfer, private ownership, keeping, transportation, licensing, or registration of firearms, air guns, knives, ammunition, or firearm or air gun supplies; or

(2) the discharge of a firearm or air gun at a sport shooting range.

(b) Subsection (a) does not affect the authority a municipality has under another law to:

(1) require residents or public employees to be armed for personal or national defense, law enforcement, or another lawful purpose;

(2) regulate the discharge of firearms or air guns within the limits of the municipality, other than at a sport shooting range;

(3) regulate the use of property, the location of a business, or uses at a business under the municipality's fire code, zoning ordinance, or land-use regulations as long as the code, ordinance, or regulations are not used to circumvent the intent of Subsection (a) or Subdivision (5) of this subsection;

(4) regulate the use of firearms, air guns, or knives in the case of an insurrection, riot, or natural disaster if the municipality finds the regulations necessary to protect public health and safety;

(5) regulate the storage or transportation of explosives to protect public health and safety, except that 25 pounds or less of black powder for each private residence and 50 pounds or less of black powder for each retail dealer are not subject to regulation;

(6) regulate the carrying of a firearm or air gun by a person other than a person licensed to carry a handgun under Subchapter H, Chapter 411, Government Code, at a:

(A) public park;

(B) public meeting of a municipality, county, or other governmental body;

(C) political rally, parade, or official political meeting; or

(D) nonfirearms-related school, college, or professional athletic event;

(7) regulate the hours of operation of a sport shooting range, except that the hours of operation may not be more limited than the least limited hours of operation of any other business in the municipality other than a business permitted or licensed to sell or serve alcoholic beverages for on-premises consumption; or

(8) regulate the carrying of an air gun by a minor on:

(A) public property; or

(B) private property without consent of the property owner.

(c) The exception provided by Subsection (b)(6) does not apply if the firearm or air gun is in or is carried to or from an area designated for use in a lawful hunting, fishing, or other sporting event and the firearm or air gun is of the type commonly used in the activity.

(d) The exception provided by Subsection (b)(4) does not authorize the seizure or confiscation of any firearm, air gun, knife, or ammunition from an individual who is lawfully carrying or possessing the firearm, air gun, knife, or ammunition.

(e) In this section:

(1) "Air gun" means any gun that discharges a pellet, BB, or paintball by means of compressed air, gas propellant, or a spring.

(3) "Sport shooting range" has the meaning assigned by § 250.001.

(f) The attorney general may bring an action in the name of the state to obtain a temporary or permanent injunction against a municipality adopting a regulation in violation of this section.

Sec. 229.002. Regulation of Discharge of Weapon. A municipality may not apply a regulation relating to the discharge of firearms or other weapons in the extraterritorial jurisdiction of the municipality or in an area annexed by the municipality after September 1, 1981, if the firearm or other weapon is:

(1) a shotgun, air rifle or pistol, BB gun, or bow and arrow discharged:

(A) on a tract of land of 10 acres or more and more than 150 feet from a residence or occupied building located on another property; and

(B) in a manner not reasonably expected to cause a projectile to cross the boundary of the tract; or

(2) a center fire or rim fire rifle or pistol of any caliber discharged:

(A) on a tract of land of 50 acres or more and more than 300 feet from a residence or occupied building located on another property; and

(B) in a manner not reasonably expected to cause a projectile to cross the boundary of the tract.

Sec. 229.003. Regulation of Discharge of Weapon by Certain Municipalities.

(a) This section applies only to a municipality located wholly or partly in a county:

(1) with a population of 750,000 or more;

(2) in which all or part of a municipality with a population of one million or more is located; and

(3) that is located adjacent to a county with a population of two million or more.

(b) Notwithstanding § 229.002, a municipality may not apply a regulation relating to the discharge of firearms or other weapons in the extraterritorial jurisdiction of the municipality or in an area annexed by the municipality after September 1, 1981, if the firearm or other weapon is:

(1) a shotgun, air rifle or pistol, BB gun, or bow and arrow discharged:

(A) on a tract of land of 10 acres or more and:

(i) more than 1,000 feet from:

(a) the property line of a public tract of land, generally accessible by the public, that is routinely used for organized sporting or recreational activities or that has permanent recreational facilities or equipment; and

(b) the property line of a school, hospital, or commercial day-care facility;

(ii) more than 600 feet from:

(a) the property line of a residential subdivision; and

(b) the property line of a multifamily residential complex; and

(iii) more than 150 feet from a residence or occupied building located on another property; and

(B) in a manner not reasonably expected to cause a projectile to cross the boundary of the tract;

(2) a center fire or rim fire rifle or pistol of any caliber discharged:

(A) on a tract of land of 50 acres or more and:

(i) more than 1,000 feet from:

(a) the property line of a public tract of land, generally accessible by the public, that is routinely used for organized sporting or recreational activities or that has permanent recreational facilities or equipment; and

(b) the property line of a school, hospital, or commercial day-care facility;
  (ii) more than 600 feet from:
    (a) the property line of a residential subdivision; and
    (b) the property line of a multifamily residential complex; and
  (iii) more than 300 feet from a residence or occupied building located on another property; and
  (B) in a manner not reasonably expected to cause a projectile to cross the boundary of the tract; or
 (3) discharged at a sport shooting range, as defined by § 250.001, in a manner not reasonably expected to cause a projectile to cross the boundary of a tract of land.

Sec. 229.004. Regulation of Discharge of Weapon by Certain Municipalities.

(a) This section applies only to a municipality located in a county in which the majority of the population of 2 or more municipalities with a population of 300,000 or more are located.
(b) Notwithstanding § 229.002, a municipality may not apply a regulation relating to the discharge of firearms or other weapons in the extraterritorial jurisdiction of the municipality or in an area annexed by the municipality on or before September 1, 1981, if the firearm or other weapon is:
 (1) a shotgun, air rifle or pistol, BB gun, or bow and arrow discharged:
  (A) on a tract of land of 100 acres or more and more than 150 feet from a residence or occupied building located on another property; and
  (B) in a manner not reasonably expected to cause a projectile to cross the boundary of the tract; or
 (2) a center fire or rim fire rifle or pistol of any caliber discharged:
  (A) on a tract of land of 100 acres or more and more than 300 feet from a residence or occupied building located on another property; and
  (B) in a manner not reasonably expected to cause a projectile to cross the boundary of the tract.

Penal Code
TITLE 10 Offenses Against Public Health, Safety, and Morals
Chapter 46 Weapons

Sec. 46.01. Definitions. In this chapter:
(2) "Explosive weapon" means any explosive or incendiary bomb, grenade, rocket, or mine, that is designed, made, or adapted for the purpose of inflicting serious bodily injury, death, or substantial property damage, or for the principal purpose of causing such a loud report as to cause undue public alarm or terror, and includes a device designed, made, or adapted for delivery or shooting an explosive weapon.
(3) "Firearm" means any device designed, made, or adapted to expel a projectile through a barrel by using the energy generated by an explosion or burning substance or any device readily convertible to that use. Firearm does not include a firearm that may have, as an integral part, a folding knife blade or other characteristics of weapons made illegal by this chapter and that is:
 (A) an antique or curio firearm manufactured before 1899; or
 (B) a replica of an antique or curio firearm manufactured before 1899, but only if the replica does not use rim fire or center fire ammunition.
(4) "Firearm silencer" means any device designed, made, or adapted to muffle the report of a firearm.
(5) "Handgun" means any firearm that is designed, made, or adapted to be fired with one hand.
(9) "Machine gun" means any firearm that is capable of shooting more than two shots automatically, without manual reloading, by a single function of the trigger.
(10) "Short-barrel firearm" means a rifle with a barrel length of less than 16 inches or a shotgun with a barrel length of less than 18 inches, or any weapon made from a shotgun or rifle if, as altered, it has an overall length of less than 26 inches.
(12) "Armor-piercing ammunition" means handgun ammunition that is designed primarily for the purpose of penetrating metal or body armor and to be used principally in pistols and revolvers.

Sec. 46.02. Unlawful Carrying Weapons.

(a) A person commits an offense if the person intentionally, knowingly, or recklessly carries on or about his or her person a handgun, illegal knife, or club if the person is not:
 (1) on the person's own premises or premises under the person's control; or
 (2) inside of or directly en route to a motor vehicle or watercraft that is owned by the person or under the person's control.
(a-1) A person commits an offense if the person intentionally, knowingly, or recklessly carries on or about his or her person a handgun in a motor vehicle or watercraft that is owned by the person or under the person's control at any time in which:
 (1) the handgun is in plain view, unless the person is licensed to carry a handgun under Subchapter H, Chapter 411, Government Code, and the handgun is carried in a shoulder or belt holster; or
 (2) the person is:

(A) engaged in criminal activity, other than a Class C misdemeanor that is a violation of a law or ordinance regulating traffic or boating;

(B) prohibited by law from possessing a firearm; or

(C) a member of a criminal street gang, as defined by § 71.01.

(a-2) For purposes of this section, "premises" includes real property and a recreational vehicle that is being used as living quarters, regardless of whether that use is temporary or permanent. In this subsection, "recreational vehicle" means a motor vehicle primarily designed as temporary living quarters or a vehicle that contains temporary living quarters and is designed to be towed by a motor vehicle. The term includes a travel trailer, camping trailer, truck camper, motor home, and horse trailer with living quarters.

(a-3) For purposes of this section, "watercraft" means any boat, motorboat, vessel, or personal watercraft, other than a seaplane on water, used or capable of being used for transportation on water.

(b) Except as provided by Subsection (c), an offense under this section is a Class A misdemeanor.

(c) An offense under this section is a felony of the third degree if the offense is committed on any premises licensed or issued a permit by this state for the sale of alcoholic beverages.

Sec. 46.03. Places Weapons Prohibited. [Effective August 1, 2016]

(a) A person commits an offense if the person intentionally, knowingly, or recklessly possesses or goes with a firearm, illegal knife, club, or prohibited weapon listed in § 46.05(a):

(1) on the physical premises of a school or educational institution, any grounds or building on which an activity sponsored by a school or educational institution is being conducted, or a passenger transportation vehicle of a school or educational institution, whether the school or educational institution is public or private, unless:

(A) pursuant to written regulations or written authorization of the institution; or

(B) the person possesses or goes with a concealed handgun that the person is licensed to carry under Subchapter H, Chapter 411, Government Code, and no other weapon to which this section applies, on the premises of an institution of higher education or private or independent institution of higher education, on any grounds or building on which an activity sponsored by the institution is being conducted, or in a passenger transportation vehicle of the institution;

(2) on the premises of a polling place on the day of an election or while early voting is in progress;

(3) on the premises of any government court or offices utilized by the court, unless pursuant to written regulations or written authorization of the court;

(4) on the premises of a racetrack;

(5) in or into a secured area of an airport; or

(6) within 1,000 feet of premises the location of which is designated by the Texas Department of Criminal Justice as a place of execution under Article 43.19, Code of Criminal Procedure, on a day that a sentence of death is set to be imposed on the designated premises and the person received notice that:

(A) going within 1,000 feet of the premises with a weapon listed under this subsection was prohibited; or

(B) possessing a weapon listed under this subsection within 1,000 feet of the premises was prohibited.

(b) It is a defense to prosecution under Subsections (a)(1)--(4) that the actor possessed a firearm while in the actual discharge of his official duties as a member of the armed forces or national guard or a guard employed by a penal institution, or an officer of the court.

(c) In this section:

(1) "Institution of higher education" and "private or independent institution of higher education" have the meanings assigned by § 61.003, Education Code.

(2) "Premises" has the meaning assigned by § 46.035.

(3) "Secured area" means an area of an airport terminal building to which access is controlled by the inspection of persons and property under federal law.

(d) It is a defense to prosecution under Subsection (a)(5) that the actor possessed a firearm or club while traveling to or from the actor's place of assignment or in the actual discharge of duties as:

(1) a member of the armed forces or national guard;

(2) a guard employed by a penal institution; or

(3) a security officer commissioned by the Texas Private Security Board if:

(A) the actor is wearing a distinctive uniform; and

(B) the firearm or club is in plain view; or

(4) a security officer who holds a personal protection authorization under Chapter 1702, Occupations Code, provided that the officer is either:

(A) wearing the uniform of a security officer, including any uniform or apparel described by § 1702.323(d), Occupations Code, and carrying the officer's firearm in plain view; or

(B) not wearing the uniform of a security officer and carrying the officer's firearm in a concealed manner.

(e) It is a defense to prosecution under Subsection (a)(5) that the actor checked all firearms as baggage in accordance with federal or state law or regulations before entering a secured area.

(e-1) It is a defense to prosecution under Subsection (a)(5) that the actor:

(1) possessed, at the screening checkpoint for the secured area, a concealed handgun that the actor was licensed to carry under Subchapter H, Chapter 411, Government Code; and

(2) exited the screening checkpoint for the secured area immediately upon completion of the required screening processes and notification that the actor possessed the handgun.

(e-2) A peace officer investigating conduct that may constitute an offense under Subsection (a)(5) and that consists only of an actor's possession of a concealed handgun that the actor is licensed to carry under Subchapter H, Chapter 411, Government Code, may not arrest the actor for the offense unless:

    (1) the officer advises the actor of the defense available under Subsection (e-1) and gives the actor an opportunity to exit the screening checkpoint for the secured area; and

    (2) the actor does not immediately exit the checkpoint upon completion of the required screening processes.

(f) Except as provided by Subsection (e-1), it is not a defense to prosecution under this section that the actor possessed a handgun and was licensed to carry a handgun under Subchapter H, Chapter 411, Government Code.

(g) An offense under this section is a third degree felony.

(h) It is a defense to prosecution under Subsection (a)(4) that the actor possessed a firearm or club while traveling to or from the actor's place of assignment or in the actual discharge of duties as a security officer commissioned by the Texas Board of Private Investigators and Private Security Agencies, if:

    (1) the actor is wearing a distinctive uniform; and

    (2) the firearm or club is in plain view.

(i) It is an exception to the application of Subsection (a)(6) that the actor possessed a firearm or club:

    (1) while in a vehicle being driven on a public road; or

    (2) at the actor's residence or place of employment.

Sec. 46.035. Unlawful Carrying of Handgun by License Holder.

(a) A license holder commits an offense if the license holder carries a handgun on or about the license holder's person under the authority of Subchapter H, Chapter 411, Government Code, and intentionally displays the handgun in plain view of another person in a public place. It is an exception to the application of this subsection that the handgun was partially or wholly visible but was carried in a shoulder or belt holster by the license holder.

(a-1) Notwithstanding Subsection (a), a license holder commits an offense if the license holder carries a partially or wholly visible handgun, regardless of whether the handgun is holstered, on or about the license holder's person under the authority of Subchapter H, Chapter 411, Government Code, and intentionally or knowingly displays the handgun in plain view of another person:

    (1) on the premises of an institution of higher education or private or independent institution of higher education; or

    (2) on any public or private driveway, street, sidewalk or walkway, parking lot, parking garage, or other parking area of an institution of higher education or private or independent institution of higher education.

(a-2) Notwithstanding Subsection (a) or § 46.03(a), a license holder commits an offense if the license holder carries a handgun on the campus of a private or independent institution of higher education in this state that has established rules, regulations, or other provisions prohibiting license holders from carrying handguns pursuant to § 411.2031(e), Government Code, or on the grounds or building on which an activity sponsored by such an institution is being conducted, or in a passenger transportation vehicle of such an institution, regardless of whether the handgun is concealed, provided the institution gives effective notice under § 30.06.

(a-3) Notwithstanding Subsection (a) or § 46.03(a), a license holder commits an offense if the license holder intentionally carries a concealed handgun on a portion of a premises located on the campus of an institution of higher education in this state on which the carrying of a concealed handgun is prohibited by rules, regulations, or other provisions established under § 411.2031(d-1), Government Code, provided the institution gives effective notice under § 30.06 with respect to that portion.

(b) A license holder commits an offense if the license holder intentionally, knowingly, or recklessly carries a handgun under the authority of Subchapter H, Chapter 411, Government Code, regardless of whether the handgun is concealed or carried in a shoulder or belt holster, on or about the license holder's person:

    (1) on the premises of a business that has a permit or license issued under Chapter 25, 28, 32, 69, or 74, Alcoholic Beverage Code, if the business derives 51 percent or more of its income from the sale or service of alcoholic beverages for on-premises consumption, as determined by the Texas Alcoholic Beverage Commission under § 104.06, Alcoholic Beverage Code;

    (2) on the premises where a high school, collegiate, or professional sporting event or interscholastic event is taking place, unless the license holder is a participant in the event and a handgun is used in the event;

    (3) on the premises of a correctional facility;

    (4) on the premises of a hospital licensed under Chapter 241, Health and Safety Code, or on the premises of a nursing facility licensed under Chapter 242, Health and Safety Code, unless the license holder has written authorization of the hospital or nursing facility administration, as appropriate;

    (5) in an amusement park; or

    (6) on the premises of a church, synagogue, or other established place of religious worship.

(c) A license holder commits an offense if the license holder intentionally, knowingly, or recklessly carries a handgun under the authority of Subchapter H, Chapter 411, Government Code, regardless of whether the handgun is concealed or carried in a shoulder or belt holster, in the room or rooms where a meeting of a governmental entity is held and if the meeting is an open meeting subject to Chapter 551, Government Code, and the entity provided notice as required by that chapter.

(d) A license holder commits an offense if, while intoxicated, the license holder carries a handgun under the authority of Subchapter H, Chapter 411, Government Code, regardless of whether the handgun is concealed or carried in a shoulder or belt holster.

(e) A license holder who is licensed as a security officer under Chapter 1702, Occupations Code, and employed as a security officer commits an offense if, while in the course and scope of the security officer's employment, the security officer violates a provision of Subchapter H, Chapter 411, Government Code.

(f) In this section:

(1) "Amusement park" means a permanent indoor or outdoor facility or park where amusement rides are available for use by the public that is located in a county with a population of more than one million, encompasses at least 75 acres in surface area, is enclosed with access only through controlled entries, is open for operation more than 120 days in each calendar year, and has security guards on the premises at all times. The term does not include any public or private driveway, street, sidewalk or walkway, parking lot, parking garage, or other parking area.

(1-a) "Institution of higher education" and "private or independent institution of higher education" have the meanings assigned by § 61.003, Education Code.

(2) "License holder" means a person licensed to carry a handgun under Subchapter H, Chapter 411, Government Code.

(3) "Premises" means a building or a portion of a building. The term does not include any public or private driveway, street, sidewalk or walkway, parking lot, parking garage, or other parking area.

(g) An offense under Subsection (a), (a-1), (a-2), (a-3), (b), (c), (d), or (e) is a Class A misdemeanor, unless the offense is committed under Subsection (b)(1) or (b)(3), in which event the offense is a felony of the third degree.

(h) It is a defense to prosecution under Subsection (a) or (a-1) that the actor, at the time of the commission of the offense, displayed the handgun under circumstances in which the actor would have been justified in the use of force or deadly force under Chapter 9.

(h-1) It is a defense to prosecution under Subsections (b)(1), (2), and (4)--(6), and (c) that at the time of the commission of the offense, the actor was:

(1) a judge or justice of a federal court;

(2) an active judicial officer, as defined by § 411.201, Government Code; or

(3) a district attorney, assistant district attorney, criminal district attorney, assistant criminal district attorney, county attorney, or assistant county attorney.

(i) Subsections (b)(4), (b)(5), (b)(6), and (c) do not apply if the actor was not given effective notice under § 30.06 or 30.07.

(j) Subsections (a), (a-1), (a-2), (a-3), and (b)(1) do not apply to a historical reenactment performed in compliance with the rules of the Texas Alcoholic Beverage Commission.

(k) It is a defense to prosecution under Subsection (b)(1) that the actor was not given effective notice under § 411.204, Government Code.

(l) Subsection (b)(2) does not apply on the premises where a collegiate sporting event is taking place if the actor was not given effective notice under § 30.06

Sec. 46.04. Unlawful Possession of Firearm.

(a) A person who has been convicted of a felony commits an offense if he possesses a firearm:

(1) after conviction and before the fifth anniversary of the person's release from confinement following conviction of the felony or the person's release from supervision under community supervision, parole, or mandatory supervision, whichever date is later; or

(2) after the period described by Subdivision (1), at any location other than the premises at which the person lives.

(b) A person who has been convicted of an offense under § 22.01, punishable as a Class A misdemeanor and involving a member of the person's family or household, commits an offense if the person possesses a firearm before the fifth anniversary of the later of:

(1) the date of the person's release from confinement following conviction of the misdemeanor; or

(2) the date of the person's release from community supervision following conviction of the misdemeanor.

(c) A person, other than a peace officer, as defined by § 1.07, actively engaged in employment as a sworn, full-time paid employee of a state agency or political subdivision, who is subject to an order issued under § 6.504 or Chapter 85, Family Code, under Article 17.292 or Chapter 7A, Code of Criminal Procedure, or by another jurisdiction as provided by Chapter 88, Family Code, commits an offense if the person possesses a firearm after receiving notice of the order and before expiration of the order.

(d) In this section, "family," "household," and "member of a household" have the meanings assigned by Chapter 71, Family Code.

(e) An offense under Subsection (a) is a felony of the third degree. An offense under Subsection (b) or (c) is a Class A misdemeanor.

(f) For the purposes of this section, an offense under the laws of this state, another state, or the United States is, except as provided by Subsection (g), a felony if, at the time it is committed, the offense:

(1) is designated by a law of this state as a felony;

(2) contains all the elements of an offense designated by a law of this state as a felony; or

(3) is punishable by confinement for 1 year or more in a penitentiary.

(g) An offense is not considered a felony for purposes of Subsection (f) if, at the time the person possesses a firearm, the offense:

(1) is not designated by a law of this state as a felony; and

(2) does not contain all the elements of any offense designated by a law of this state as a felony.

Sec. 46.05. Prohibited Weapons.

(a) A person commits an offense if the person intentionally or knowingly possesses, manufactures, transports, repairs, or sells:

(1) any of the following items, unless the item is registered in the National Firearms Registration and Transfer Record maintained by the Bureau of Alcohol, Tobacco, Firearms and Explosives or classified as a curio or relic by the United States Department of Justice:

    (A) an explosive weapon;

    (B) a machine gun;

    (C) a short-barrel firearm; or

    (D) a firearm silencer;

(3) armor-piercing ammunition;

(b) It is a defense to prosecution under this section that the actor's conduct was incidental to the performance of official duty by the armed forces or national guard, a governmental law enforcement agency, or a correctional facility.

(c) [Repealed by Acts 2015, 84th Leg., ch. 69 (S.B. 473), § 2, effective September 1, 2015.]

(d) It is an affirmative defense to prosecution under this section that the actor's conduct:

(1) was incidental to dealing with a short-barrel firearm or tire deflation device solely as an antique or curio;

(2) was incidental to dealing with armor-piercing ammunition solely for the purpose of making the ammunition available to an organization, agency, or institution listed in Subsection (b); or

(3) was incidental to dealing with a tire deflation device solely for the purpose of making the device available to an organization, agency, or institution listed in Subsection (b).

(e) An offense under Subsection (a)(1), (3), (4), or (5) is a felony of the third degree. An offense under Subsection (a)(6) is a state jail felony. An offense under Subsection (a)(2) is a Class A misdemeanor.

(f) It is a defense to prosecution under this section for the possession of a chemical dispensing device that the actor is a security officer and has received training on the use of the chemical dispensing device by a training program that is:

(1) provided by the Texas Commission on Law Enforcement; or

(2) approved for the purposes described by this subsection by the Texas Private Security Board of the Department of Public Safety.

(g) In Subsection (f), "security officer" means a commissioned security officer as defined by § 1702.002, Occupations Code, or a noncommissioned security officer registered under § 1702.221, Occupations Code.

Sec. 46.06. Unlawful Transfer of Certain Weapons.

(a) A person commits an offense if the person:

(1) sells, rents, leases, loans, or gives a handgun to any person knowing that the person to whom the handgun is to be delivered intends to use it unlawfully or in the commission of an unlawful act;

(2) intentionally or knowingly sells, rents, leases, or gives or offers to sell, rent, lease, or give to any child younger than 18 years any firearm, club, or illegal knife;

(3) intentionally, knowingly, or recklessly sells a firearm or ammunition for a firearm to any person who is intoxicated;

(4) knowingly sells a firearm or ammunition for a firearm to any person who has been convicted of a felony before the fifth anniversary of the later of the following dates:

    (A) the person's release from confinement following conviction of the felony; or

    (B) the person's release from supervision under community supervision, parole, or mandatory supervision following conviction of the felony;

(5) sells, rents, leases, loans, or gives a handgun to any person knowing that an active protective order is directed to the person to whom the handgun is to be delivered; or

(6) knowingly purchases, rents, leases, or receives as a loan or gift from another a handgun while an active protective order is directed to the actor.

(b) In this section:

(1) "Intoxicated" means substantial impairment of mental or physical capacity resulting from introduction of any substance into the body.

(2) "Active protective order" means a protective order issued under Title 4, Family Code, that is in effect. The term does not include a temporary protective order issued before the court holds a hearing on the matter.

(c) It is an affirmative defense to prosecution under Subsection (a)(2) that the transfer was to a minor whose parent or the person having legal custody of the minor had given written permission for the sale or, if the transfer was other than a sale, the parent or person having legal custody had given effective consent.

(d) An offense under this section is a Class A misdemeanor, except that an offense under Subsection (a)(2) is a state jail felony if the weapon that is the subject of the offense is a handgun.

Sec. 46.07. Interstate Purchase.

A resident of this state may, if not otherwise precluded by law, purchase firearms, ammunition, reloading components, or firearm accessories in another state. This authorization is enacted in conformance with 18 U.S.C. § 922(b)(3)(A).

Sec. 46.10. Deadly Weapon in Penal Institution.

(a) A person commits an offense if, while confined in a penal institution, he intentionally, knowingly, or recklessly:

(1) carries on or about his person a deadly weapon; or

(2) possesses or conceals a deadly weapon in the penal institution.

(b) It is an affirmative defense to prosecution under this section that at the time of the offense the actor was engaged in conduct authorized by an employee of the penal institution.

(c) A person who is subject to prosecution under both this section and another section under this chapter may be prosecuted under either section.

(d) An offense under this section is a felony of the third degree.

Sec. 46.11. Penalty If Offense Committed Within Weapon-Free School Zone.

(a) Except as provided by Subsection (b), the punishment prescribed for an offense under this chapter is increased to the punishment prescribed for the next highest category of offense if it is shown beyond a reasonable doubt on the trial of the offense that the actor committed the offense in a place that the actor knew was:

(1) within 300 feet of the premises of a school; or

(2) on premises where:

(A) an official school function is taking place; or

(B) an event sponsored or sanctioned by the University Interscholastic League is taking place.

(b) This section does not apply to an offense under § 46.03(a)(1).

(c) In this section:

(1) "Premises" has the meaning assigned by § 481.134, Health and Safety Code.

(2) "School" means a private or public elementary or secondary school.

Sec. 46.13. Making a Firearm Accessible to a Child.

(a) In this section:

(1) "Child" means a person younger than 17 years of age.

(2) "Readily dischargeable firearm" means a firearm that is loaded with ammunition, whether or not a round is in the chamber.

(3) "Secure" means to take steps that a reasonable person would take to prevent the access to a readily dischargeable firearm by a child, including but not limited to placing a firearm in a locked container or temporarily rendering the firearm inoperable by a trigger lock or other means.

(b) A person commits an offense if a child gains access to a readily dischargeable firearm and the person with criminal negligence:

(1) failed to secure the firearm; or

(2) left the firearm in a place to which the person knew or should have known the child would gain access.

(c) It is an affirmative defense to prosecution under this section that the child's access to the firearm:

(1) was supervised by a person older than 18 years of age and was for hunting, sporting, or other lawful purposes;

(2) consisted of lawful defense by the child of people or property;

(3) was gained by entering property in violation of this code; or

(4) occurred during a time when the actor was engaged in an agricultural enterprise.

(d) Except as provided by Subsection (e), an offense under this section is a Class C misdemeanor.

(e) An offense under this section is a Class A misdemeanor if the child discharges the firearm and causes death or serious bodily injury to himself or another person.

(f) A peace officer or other person may not arrest the actor before the seventh day after the date on which the offense is committed if:

(1) the actor is a member of the family, as defined by § 71.003, Family Code, of the child who discharged the firearm; and

(2) the child in discharging the firearm caused the death of or serious injury to the child.

(g) A dealer of firearms shall post in a conspicuous position on the premises where the dealer conducts business a sign that contains the following warning in block letters not less than 1 inch in height:

"IT IS UNLAWFUL TO STORE, TRANSPORT, OR ABANDON AN UNSECURED FIREARM IN A PLACE WHERE CHILDREN ARE LIKELY TO BE AND CAN OBTAIN ACCESS TO THE FIREARM."

Sec. 46.14. Firearm Smuggling.

(a) A person commits an offense if the person knowingly engages in the business of transporting or transferring a firearm that the person knows was acquired in violation of the laws of any state or of the United States. For purposes of this subsection, a person is considered to engage in the business of transporting or transferring a firearm if the person engages in that conduct:

(1) on more than 1 occasion; or

(2) for profit or any other form of remuneration.

(b) An offense under this section is a felony of the third degree, unless it is shown on the trial of the offense that the offense was committed with respect to 3 or more firearms in a single criminal episode, in which event the offense is a felony of the second degree.

(c) This section does not apply to a peace officer who is engaged in the actual discharge of an official duty.

(d) If conduct that constitutes an offense under this section also constitutes an offense under any other law, the actor may be prosecuted under this section, the other law, or both

Sec. 46.15. Nonapplicability.

(a) Sections 46.02 and 46.03 do not apply to:

(1) peace officers or special investigators under Article 2.122, Code of Criminal Procedure, and neither section prohibits a peace officer or special investigator from carrying a weapon in this state, including in an establishment in this state serving the public, regardless of whether the peace officer or special investigator is engaged in the actual discharge of the officer's or investigator's duties while carrying the weapon;

(2) parole officers and neither section prohibits an officer from carrying a weapon in this state if the officer is:

(A) engaged in the actual discharge of the officer's duties while carrying the weapon; and

(B) in compliance with policies and procedures adopted by the Texas Department of Criminal Justice regarding the possession of a weapon by an officer while on duty;

(3) community supervision and corrections department officers appointed or employed under § 76.004, Government Code, and neither section prohibits an officer from carrying a weapon in this state if the officer is:

(A) engaged in the actual discharge of the officer's duties while carrying the weapon; and

(B) authorized to carry a weapon under § 76.0051, Government Code;

(4) an active judicial officer as defined by § 411.201, Government Code, who is licensed to carry a handgun under Subchapter H, Chapter 411, Government Code;

(5) an honorably retired peace officer, qualified retired law enforcement officer, federal criminal investigator, or former reserve law enforcement officer who holds a certificate of proficiency issued under § 1701.357, Occupations Code, and is carrying a photo identification that is issued by a federal, state, or local law enforcement agency, as applicable, and that verifies that the officer is:

(A) an honorably retired peace officer;

(B) a qualified retired law enforcement officer;

(C) a federal criminal investigator; or

(D) a former reserve law enforcement officer who has served in that capacity not less than a total of 15 years with one or more state or local law enforcement agencies;

(6) a district attorney, criminal district attorney, county attorney, or municipal attorney who is licensed to carry a handgun under Subchapter H, Chapter 411, Government Code;

(7) an assistant district attorney, assistant criminal district attorney, or assistant county attorney who is licensed to carry a handgun under Subchapter H, Chapter 411, Government Code;

(8) a bailiff designated by an active judicial officer as defined by § 411.201, Government Code, who is:

(A) licensed to carry a handgun under Subchapter H, Chapter 411, Government Code; and

(B) engaged in escorting the judicial officer; or

(9) a juvenile probation officer who is authorized to carry a firearm under § 142.006, Human Resources Code.

(b) Section 46.02 does not apply to a person who:

(1) is in the actual discharge of official duties as a member of the armed forces or state military forces as defined by § 437.001, Government Code, or as a guard employed by a penal institution;

(2) is traveling;

(3) is engaging in lawful hunting, fishing, or other sporting activity on the immediate premises where the activity is conducted, or is en route between the premises and the actor's residence, motor vehicle, or watercraft, if the weapon is a type commonly used in the activity;

(4) holds a security officer commission issued by the Texas Private Security Board, if the person is engaged in the performance of the person's duties as an officer commissioned under Chapter 1702, Occupations Code, or is traveling to or from the person's place of assignment and is wearing the officer's uniform and carrying the officer's weapon in plain view;

(5) acts as a personal protection officer and carries the person's security officer commission and personal protection officer authorization, if the person:

(A) is engaged in the performance of the person's duties as a personal protection officer under Chapter 1702, Occupations Code, or is traveling to or from the person's place of assignment; and

(B) is either:

(i) wearing the uniform of a security officer, including any uniform or apparel described by § 1702.323(d), Occupations Code, and carrying the officer's weapon in plain view; or

(ii) not wearing the uniform of a security officer and carrying the officer's weapon in a concealed manner;

(6) is carrying:

(A) a license issued under Subchapter H, Chapter 411, Government Code, to carry a handgun; and

(B) a handgun:

(i) in a concealed manner; or

(ii) in a shoulder or belt holster;

(7) holds an alcoholic beverage permit or license or is an employee of a holder of an alcoholic beverage permit or license if the person is supervising the operation of the permitted or licensed premises; or

(8) is a student in a law enforcement class engaging in an activity required as part of the class, if the weapon is a type commonly used in the activity and the person is:

    (A) on the immediate premises where the activity is conducted; or

    (B) en route between those premises and the person's residence and is carrying the weapon unloaded.

(d) The provisions of § 46.02 prohibiting the carrying of a firearm or carrying of a club do not apply to a public security officer employed by the adjutant general under § 437.053, Government Code, in performance of official duties or while traveling to or from a place of duty.

(f) Section 46.03(a)(6) does not apply to a person who possesses a firearm or club while in the actual discharge of official duties as:

    (1) a member of the armed forces or state military forces, as defined by § 437.001, Government Code; or

    (2) an employee of a penal institution.

(j) The provisions of § 46.02 prohibiting the carrying of a handgun do not apply to an individual who carries a handgun as a participant in a historical reenactment performed in accordance with the rules of the Texas Alcoholic Beverage Commission.

Virginia Code
Includes all acts adopted at the 2016 Regular Session of the General Assembly.

Office of the Attorney General
900 East Main Street
Richmond, VA 23219
Voice: (804) 786-2071
http://www.oag.state.va.us/

Washington Field Division
1401 H Street NW, Suite 900
Washington, DC 20226
Voice: (202) 648-8010
https://www.atf.gov/washington-field-division

PROTECTING THE PUBLIC
SERVING OUR NATION

Table of Contents

§ 15.2-915. Control of firearms; applicability to authorities and local governmental agencies

A. No locality shall adopt or enforce any ordinance, resolution or motion, as permitted by § 15.2-1425, and no agent of such locality shall take any administrative action, governing the purchase, possession, transfer, ownership, carrying, storage or transporting of firearms, ammunition, or components or combination thereof other than those expressly authorized by statute. For purposes of this section, a statute that does not refer to firearms, ammunition, or components or combination thereof, shall not be construed to provide express authorization.

Nothing in this section shall prohibit a locality from adopting workplace rules relating to terms and conditions of employment of the workforce. However, no locality shall adopt any workplace rule, other than for the purposes of a community services board or behavioral health authority as defined in § 37.2-100, that prevents an employee of that locality from storing at that locality's workplace a lawfully possessed firearm and ammunition in a locked private motor vehicle. Nothing in this section shall prohibit a law-enforcement officer, as defined in § 9.1-101, from acting within the scope of his duties.

The provisions of this section applicable to a locality shall also apply to any authority or to a local governmental entity, including a department or agency, but not including any local or regional jail, juvenile detention facility, or state-governed entity, department, or agency.

B. Any local ordinance, resolution or motion adopted prior to the effective date of this act governing the purchase, possession, transfer, ownership, carrying or transporting of firearms, ammunition, or components or combination thereof, other than those expressly authorized by statute, is invalid.

C. In addition to any other relief provided, the court may award reasonable attorney fees, expenses, and court costs to any person, group, or entity that prevails in an action challenging **(i)** an ordinance, resolution, or motion as being in conflict with this section or **(ii)** an administrative action taken in bad faith as being in conflict with this section.

D. For purposes of this section, "workplace" means "workplace of the locality."

§ 15.2-915.2. Regulation of transportation of a loaded rifle or shotgun.

The governing body of any county or city may by ordinance make it unlawful for any person to transport, possess or carry a loaded shotgun or loaded rifle in any vehicle on any public street, road, or highway within such locality. Any violation of such ordinance shall be punishable by a fine of not more than $100. Conservation police officers, sheriffs and all other law-enforcement officers shall enforce the provisions of this section. No ordinance adopted pursuant to this section shall be enforceable unless the governing body adopting such ordinance so notifies the Director of the Department of Game and Inland Fisheries by registered mail prior to May 1 of the year in which such ordinance is to take effect.

The provisions of this section shall not apply to duly authorized law-enforcement officers or military personnel in the performance of their lawful duties, nor to any person who reasonably believes that a loaded rifle or shotgun is necessary for his personal safety in the course of his employment or business.

§ 15.2-915.5. Disposition of firearms acquired by localities

A. No locality or agent of such locality may participate in any program in which individuals are given a thing of value provided by another individual or other entity in exchange for surrendering a firearm to the locality or agent of such locality unless the governing body of the locality has enacted an ordinance, pursuant to § 15.2-1425, authorizing the participation of the locality or agent of such locality in such program.

B. Any ordinance enacted pursuant to this section shall require that any firearm received, except a firearm of the type defined in § 18.2-288 or 18.2-299 or a firearm the transfer for which is prohibited by federal law, shall be offered for sale by public auction or sealed bids to a person licensed as a dealer pursuant to 18 U.S.C. § 921 et seq. Notice of the date, time, and place of sale shall be given by advertisement in at least 2 newspapers published and having general circulation in the Commonwealth, at least one of which shall have general circulation in the locality in which the property to be sold is located. At least 30 days shall elapse between publication of the notice and the auction or the date on which sealed bids will be opened. Any firearm remaining in possession of the locality or agent of the locality after attempts to sell at public auction or by sealed bids shall be disposed of in a manner the locality deems proper, which may include destruction of the firearm or, subject to any registration requirements of federal law, sale of the firearm to a licensed dealer.

§ 15.2-917. Applicability of local noise ordinances to certain sport shooting ranges

A. No local ordinance regulating any noise shall subject a sport shooting range to noise control standards more stringent than those in effect at its effective date. The operation or use of a sport shooting range shall not be enjoined on the basis of noise, nor shall any person be subject to action for nuisance or criminal prosecution in any matter relating to noise resulting from the operation of the range, if the range is in compliance with all ordinances relating to noise in effect at the time construction or operation of the range was approved, or at the time any application was submitted for the construction or operation of the range.

B. Any sport shooting range operating or approved for construction within the Commonwealth, which has been condemned through an eminent domain proceeding by any condemning entity, and which relocates to another site within the same locality within 2 years of the final condemnation order, shall not be subjected to any noise control standard more stringent than those in effect at the effective date of such sport shooting range.

C. For purposes of this section, "sport shooting range" means an area or structure designed for the use of rifles, shotguns, pistols, silhouettes, skeet, trap, black powder, or any other similar sport shooting.

For purposes of this section, "effective date" means the time the construction or operation of the sports shooting range initially was approved, or at the time any application was submitted for the construction or operation of the sports shooting range, whichever is earliest.

Chapter 12. General Powers and Procedures of Counties
Article 1. Miscellaneous Powers

§ 15.2-1207. Pistols and revolvers; reports of sales. The power of any governing body of any county to require sellers of pistols and revolvers to furnish the clerk of the circuit court of the county, after sale of any such weapon, with the name and address of the purchaser, the date of purchase, and the number, make and caliber of the weapon sold is hereby repealed. The clerk shall destroy every record of the reports previously received.

§ 15.2-1208. Same; in certain counties. Chapter 297 of the Acts of Assembly of 1944, approved March 29, 1944, requiring permits to sell or purchase pistols or revolvers in any county having a density of population of more than 1,000 a square mile, is repealed. Any records or copies thereof that were created pursuant to this section that are in the custody of any county shall be destroyed no later than July 31, 2004. Upon destroying the records, the county shall certify to the circuit court that such destruction has been completed.

§ 15.2-1209. Prohibiting outdoor shooting of firearms or arrows from bows in certain areas. Any county may prohibit the outdoor shooting of firearms or arrows from bows in any areas of the county which are in the opinion of the governing body so heavily populated as to make such conduct dangerous to the inhabitants thereof.

Any county that prohibits the outdoor shooting of firearms or arrows from bows shall provide an exemption for the killing of deer pursuant to § 29.1-529. Such exemption for the shooting of firearms shall apply on land of at least 5 acres that is zoned for agricultural use. Such exemption for the shooting of arrows from bows shall apply on land of at least 2 acres that is zoned for agricultural use.

§ 15.2-1209.1. Counties may regulate carrying of loaded firearms on public highways. The governing body of any county is hereby empowered to adopt ordinances making it unlawful for any person to carry or have in his possession, for the purpose of hunting, while on any part of a public highway within such county a loaded firearm when such person is not authorized to hunt on the private property on both sides of the highway along which he is standing or walking; and to provide a penalty for violation of such ordinance not to exceed a fine of $100. The provisions of this section shall not apply to persons carrying loaded firearms in moving vehicles or for purposes other than hunting, or to persons acting at the time in defense of persons or property.

TITLE 18.2. Crimes and Offenses Generally
Chapter 7. Crimes Involving Health and Safety
Article 4. Dangerous Use of Firearms or Other Weapons

§ 18.2-279. Discharging firearms or missiles within or at building or dwelling house; penalty. If any person maliciously discharges a firearm within any building when occupied by 1 or more persons in such a manner as to endanger the life or lives of such person or persons, or maliciously shoots at, or maliciously throws any missile at or against any dwelling house or other building when occupied by 1 or more persons, whereby the life or lives of any such person or persons may be put in peril, the person so offending is guilty of a Class 4 felony. In the event of the death of any person, resulting from such malicious shooting or throwing, the person so offending is guilty of murder in the second degree. However, if the homicide is willful, deliberate and premeditated, he is guilty of murder in the first degree.

If any such act be done unlawfully, but not maliciously, the person so offending is guilty of a Class 6 felony; and, in the event of the death of any person resulting from such unlawful shooting or throwing, the person so offending is guilty of involuntary manslaughter. If any person willfully discharges a firearm within or shoots at any school building whether occupied or not, he is guilty of a Class 4 felony.

§ 18.2-280. Willfully discharging firearms in public places
A. If any person willfully discharges or causes to be discharged any firearm in any street in a city or town, or in any place of public business or place of public gathering, and such conduct results in bodily injury to another person, he shall be guilty of a Class 6 felony. If such conduct does not result in bodily injury to another person, he shall be guilty of a Class 1 misdemeanor.

B. If any person willfully discharges or causes to be discharged any firearm upon the buildings and grounds of any public, private or religious elementary, middle or high school, he shall be guilty of a Class 4 felony, unless he is engaged in a program or curriculum sponsored by or conducted with permission of a public, private or religious school.

C. If any person willfully discharges or causes to be discharged any firearm upon any public property within 1,000 feet of the property line of any public, private or religious elementary, middle or high school property he shall be guilty of a Class 4 felony, unless he is engaged in lawful hunting.

D. This section shall not apply to any law-enforcement officer in the performance of his official duties nor to any other person whose said willful act is otherwise justifiable or excusable at law in the protection of his life or property, or is otherwise specifically authorized by law.

E. Nothing in this statute shall preclude the Commonwealth from electing to prosecute under any other applicable provision of law instead of this section.

§ 18.2-281. Setting spring gun or other deadly weapon. It shall be unlawful for any person to set or fix in any manner any firearm or other deadly weapon so that it may be discharged or activated by a person coming in contact therewith or with any string, wire, spring, or any other contrivance attached thereto or designed to activate such weapon remotely. Any person violating this section shall be guilty of a Class 6 felony.

§ 18.2-282. Pointing, holding, or brandishing firearm, air or gas operated weapon or object similar in appearance; penalty

A. It shall be unlawful for any person to point, hold or brandish any firearm or any air or gas operated weapon or any object similar in appearance, whether capable of being fired or not, in such manner as to reasonably induce fear in the mind of another or hold a firearm or any air or gas operated weapon in a public place in such a manner as to reasonably induce fear in the mind of another of being shot or injured. However, this section shall not apply to any person engaged in excusable or justifiable self-defense. Persons violating the provisions of this section shall be guilty of a Class 1 misdemeanor or, if the violation occurs upon any public, private or religious elementary, middle or high school, including buildings and grounds or upon public property within 1,000 feet of such school property, he shall be guilty of a Class 6 felony.

B. Any police officer in the performance of his duty, in making an arrest under the provisions of this section, shall not be civilly liable in damages for injuries or death resulting to the person being arrested if he had reason to believe that the person being arrested was pointing, holding, or brandishing such firearm or air or gas operated weapon, or object that was similar in appearance, with intent to induce fear in the mind of another.

C. For purposes of this section, the word *"firearm"* means any weapon that will or is designed to or may readily be converted to expel single or multiple projectiles by the action of an explosion of a combustible material. The word *"ammunition,"* as used herein, shall mean a cartridge, pellet, ball, missile or projectile adapted for use in a firearm.

§ 18.2-283. Carrying dangerous weapon to place of religious worship. If any person carry any gun, pistol, bowie knife, dagger or other dangerous weapon, without good and sufficient reason, to a place of worship while a meeting for religious purposes is being held at such place he shall be guilty of a Class 4 misdemeanor.

§ 18.2-283.1. Carrying weapon into courthouse. It shall be unlawful for any person to possess in or transport into any courthouse in this Commonwealth any **(i)** gun or other weapon designed or intended to propel a missile or projectile of any kind, **(ii)** frame, receiver, muffler, silencer, missile, projectile or ammunition designed for use with a dangerous weapon and **(iii)** any other dangerous weapon, including explosives, stun weapons as defined in § 18.2-308.1, and those weapons specified in subsection A of § 18.2-308. Any such weapon shall be subject to seizure by a law-enforcement officer. A violation of this section is punishable as a Class 1 misdemeanor.

The provisions of this section shall not apply to any police officer, sheriff, law-enforcement agent or official, conservation police officer, conservator of the peace, magistrate, court officer, judge, or city or county treasurer while in the conduct of such person's official duties.

§ 18.2-284. Selling or giving toy firearms. No person shall sell, barter, exchange, furnish, or dispose of by purchase, gift or in any other manner any toy gun, pistol, rifle or other toy firearm, if the same shall, by action of an explosion of a combustible material, discharge blank or ball charges. Any person violating the provisions of this section shall be guilty of a Class 4 misdemeanor. Each sale of any of the articles hereinbefore specified to any person shall constitute a separate offense.

Nothing in this section shall be construed as preventing the sale of what are commonly known as cap pistols.

§ 18.2-285. Hunting with firearms while under influence of intoxicant or narcotic drug; penalty. It shall be unlawful for any person to hunt wildlife with a firearm, bow and arrow, or crossbow in the Commonwealth of Virginia while he is **(i)** under the influence of alcohol; **(ii)** under the influence of any narcotic drug or any other self-administered intoxicant or drug of whatsoever nature, or any combination of such drugs, to a degree that impairs his ability to hunt with a firearm, bow and arrow, or crossbow safely; or **(iii)** under the combined influence of alcohol and any drug or drugs to a degree that impairs his ability to hunt with a firearm, bow and arrow, or crossbow safely. Any person who violates the provisions of this section is guilty of a Class 1 misdemeanor. Conservation police officers, sheriffs and all other law-enforcement officers shall enforce the provisions of this section.

§ 18.2-286. Shooting in or across road or in street. If any person discharges a firearm, crossbow or bow and arrow in or across any road, or within the right-of-way thereof, or in a street of any city or town, he shall, for each offense, be guilty of a Class 4 misdemeanor.

The provisions of this section shall not apply to firing ranges or shooting matches maintained, and supervised or approved, by law-enforcement officers and military personnel in performance of their lawful duties.

§ 18.2-286.1. Shooting from vehicles so as to endanger persons; penalty. Any person who, while in or on a motor vehicle, intentionally discharges a firearm so as to create the risk of injury or death to another person or thereby cause another person to have a reasonable apprehension of injury or death shall be guilty of a Class 5 felony. Nothing in this section shall apply to a law-enforcement officer in the performance of his duties.

§ 18.2-287.01. Carrying weapon in air carrier airport terminal. It shall be unlawful for any person to possess or transport into any air carrier airport terminal in the Commonwealth any **(i)** gun or other weapon designed or intended to propel a missile or projectile of any kind, **(ii)** frame, receiver, muffler, silencer, missile, projectile or ammunition designed for use with a dangerous weapon, and **(iii)** any other dangerous weapon, including explosives, stun weapons as defined in § 18.2-308.1, and those weapons specified in subsection A of § 18.2-308. Any such weapon shall be subject to seizure by a law-enforcement officer. A violation of this section is punishable as a Class 1 misdemeanor. Any weapon possessed or transported in violation of this section shall be forfeited to the Commonwealth and disposed of as provided in § 19.2-386.28.

The provisions of this section shall not apply to any police officer, sheriff, law-enforcement agent or official, conservation police officer, conservator of the peace employed by the air carrier airport, or retired law-enforcement officer qualified pursuant to subsection C of § 18.2-308.016, nor shall the provisions of this section apply to any passenger of an airline who, to the extent otherwise permitted by law, transports a lawful firearm, weapon, or ammunition into or out of an air carrier airport terminal for the sole purposes, respectively, of **(i)** presenting such firearm, weapon, or ammunition to U.S. Customs agents in advance of an international flight, in order to comply with federal law, **(ii)** checking such firearm, weapon, or ammunition with his luggage, or **(iii)** retrieving such firearm, weapon, or ammunition from the baggage claim area.

Any other statute, rule, regulation, or ordinance specifically addressing the possession or transportation of weapons in any airport in the Commonwealth shall be invalid, and this section shall control.

§ 18.2-287.4. Carrying loaded firearms in public areas prohibited; penalty. It shall be unlawful for any person to carry a loaded **(a)** semi-automatic center-fire rifle or pistol that expels single or multiple projectiles by action of an explosion of a combustible material and is equipped at the time of the offense with a magazine that will hold more than 20 rounds of ammunition or designed by the manufacturer to accommodate a silencer or equipped with a folding stock or **(b)** shotgun with a magazine that will hold more than 7 rounds of the longest ammunition for which it is chambered on or about his person on any public street, road, alley, sidewalk, public right-of-way, or in any public park or any other place of whatever nature that is open to the public in the Cities of Alexandria, Chesapeake, Fairfax, Falls Church, Newport News, Norfolk, Richmond, or Virginia Beach or in the Counties of Arlington, Fairfax, Henrico, Loudoun, or Prince William.

The provisions of this section shall not apply to law-enforcement officers, licensed security guards, military personnel in the performance of their lawful duties, or any person having a valid concealed handgun permit or to any person actually engaged in lawful hunting or lawful recreational shooting activities at an established shooting range or shooting contest. Any person violating the provisions of this section shall be guilty of a Class 1 misdemeanor.

The exemptions set forth in §§ 18.2-308 and 18.2-308.016 shall apply, mutatis mutandis, to the provisions of this section.

Article 5. Uniform Machine Gun Act

§ 18.2-288. Definitions. When used in this article:
(1) *"Machine gun"* applies to any weapon which shoots or is designed to shoot automatically more than 1 shot, without manual reloading, by a single function of the trigger.
(2) *"Crime of violence"* applies to and includes any of the following crimes or an attempt to commit any of the same, namely, murder, manslaughter, kidnapping, rape, mayhem, assault with intent to maim, disable, disfigure or kill, robbery, burglary, housebreaking, breaking and entering and larceny.
(3) *"Person"* applies to and includes firm, partnership, association or corporation.

§ 18.2-289. Use of machine gun for crime of violence. Possession or use of a machine gun in the perpetration or attempted perpetration of a crime of violence is hereby declared to be a Class 2 felony.

§ 18.2-290. Use of machine gun for aggressive purpose. Unlawful possession or use of a machine gun for an offensive or aggressive purpose is hereby declared to be a Class 4 felony.

§ 18.2-291. What constitutes aggressive purpose. Possession or use of a machine gun shall be presumed to be for an offensive or aggressive purpose:
(1) When the machine gun is on premises not owned or rented for bona fide permanent residence or business occupancy by the person in whose possession the machine gun may be found;
(2) When the machine gun is in the possession of, or used by, a person who has been convicted of a crime of violence in any court of record, state or federal, of the United States of America, its territories or insular possessions;
(3) When the machine gun has not been registered as required in § 18.2-295; or
(4) When empty or loaded shells which have been or are susceptible of use in the machine gun are found in the immediate vicinity thereof.

§ 18.2-292. Presence prima facie evidence of use. The presence of a machine gun in any room, boat or vehicle shall be prima facie evidence of the possession or use of the machine gun by each person occupying the room, boat, or vehicle where the weapon is found.

§ 18.2-293. What article does not apply to. The provisions of this article shall not be applicable to:

(1) The manufacture for, and sale of, machine guns to the armed forces or law-enforcement officers of the United States or of any state or of any political subdivision thereof, or the transportation required for that purpose; and

(2) Machine guns and automatic arms issued to the national guard of Virginia by the United States or such arms used by the United States army or navy or in the hands of troops of the national guards of other states or territories of the United States passing through Virginia, or such arms as may be provided for the officers of the State Police or officers of penal institutions.

§ 18.2-293.1. What article does not prohibit. Nothing contained in this article shall prohibit or interfere with:

(1) The possession of a machine gun for scientific purposes, or the possession of a machine gun not usable as a weapon and possessed as a curiosity, ornament, or keepsake; and

(2) The possession of a machine gun for a purpose manifestly not aggressive or offensive.

Provided, however, that possession of such machine guns shall be subject to the provisions of § 18.2-295.

§ 18.2-294. Manufacturer's and dealer's register; inspection of stock. Every manufacturer or dealer shall keep a register of all machine guns manufactured or handled by him. This register shall show the model and serial number, date of manufacture, sale, loan, gift, delivery or receipt of every machine gun, the name, address, and occupation of the person to whom the machine gun was sold, loaned, given or delivered, or from whom it was received. Upon demand every manufacturer or dealer shall permit any marshal, sheriff or police officer to inspect his entire stock of machine guns, parts, and supplies therefor, and shall produce the register, herein required, for inspection. A violation of any provisions of this section shall be punishable as a Class 3 misdemeanor.

§ 18.2-295. Registration of machine guns. Every machine gun in this Commonwealth shall be registered with the Department of State Police within 24 hours after its acquisition or, in the case of semi-automatic weapons which are converted, modified or otherwise altered to become machine guns, within 24 hours of the conversion, modification or alteration. Blanks for registration shall be prepared by the Superintendent of State Police, and furnished upon application. To comply with this section the application as filed shall be notarized and shall show the model and serial number of the gun, the name, address and occupation of the person in possession, and from whom and the purpose for which, the gun was acquired or altered. The Superintendent of State Police shall upon registration required in this section forthwith furnish the registrant with a certificate of registration, which shall be valid as long as the registrant remains the same. Certificates of registration shall be retained by the registrant and produced by him upon demand by any peace officer. Failure to keep or produce such certificate for inspection shall be a Class 3 misdemeanor, and any peace officer, may without warrant, seize the machine gun and apply for its confiscation as provided in § 18.2-296. Upon transferring a registered machine gun, the transferor shall forthwith notify the Superintendent in writing, setting forth the date of transfer and name and address of the transferee. Failure to give the required notification shall constitute a Class 3 misdemeanor. Registration data shall not be subject to inspection by the public.

§ 18.2-296. Search warrants for machine guns. Warrant to search any house or place and seize any machine gun possessed in violation of this article may issue in the same manner and under the same restrictions as provided by law for stolen property, and any court of record, upon application of the attorney for the Commonwealth, a police officer or conservator of the peace, may order any machine gun, thus or otherwise legally seized, to be confiscated and either destroyed or delivered to a peace officer of the Commonwealth or a political subdivision thereof.

§ 18.2-297. How article construed. This article shall be so interpreted and construed as to effectuate its general purpose to make uniform the law of those states which enact it.

§ 18.2-298. Short title of article. This article may be cited as the "Uniform Machine Gun Act."

Article 6. "Sawed-Off" Shotgun and "Sawed-Off" Rifle Act

§ 18.2-299. Definitions. When used in this article:

"Sawed-off shotgun" means any weapon, loaded or unloaded, originally designed as a shoulder weapon, utilizing a self-contained cartridge from which a number of ball shot pellets or projectiles may be fired simultaneously from a smooth or rifled bore by a single function of the firing device and which has a barrel length of less than 18 inches for smooth bore weapons and 16 inches for rifled weapons. Weapons of less than .225 caliber shall not be included.

"Sawed-off rifle" means a rifle of any caliber, loaded or unloaded, which expels a projectile by action of an explosion of a combustible material and is designed as a shoulder weapon with a barrel or barrels length of less than 16 inches or which has been modified to an overall length of less than 26 inches.

"Crime of violence" applies to and includes any of the following crimes or an attempt to commit any of the same, namely, murder, manslaughter, kidnapping, rape, mayhem, assault with intent to maim, disable, disfigure or kill, robbery, burglary, housebreaking, breaking and entering and larceny.

"Person" applies to and includes firm, partnership, association or corporation.

§ 18.2-300. Possession or use of "sawed-off" shotgun or rifle

A. Possession or use of a "sawed-off" shotgun or "sawed-off" rifle in the perpetration or attempted perpetration of a crime of violence is a Class 2 felony.

B. Possession or use of a "sawed-off" shotgun or "sawed-off" rifle for any other purpose, except as permitted by this article and official use by those persons permitted possession by § 18.2-303, is a Class 4 felony.

§ 18.2-303. What article does not apply to. The provisions of this article shall not be applicable to:
(1) The manufacture for, and sale of, "sawed-off" shotguns or "sawed-off" rifles to the armed forces or law-enforcement officers of the United States or of any state or of any political subdivision thereof, or the transportation required for that purpose; and
(2) "Sawed-off" shotguns, "sawed-off" rifles and automatic arms issued to the National Guard of Virginia by the United States or such arms used by the United States Army or Navy or in the hands of troops of the national guards of other states or territories of the United States passing through Virginia, or such arms as may be provided for the officers of the State Police or officers of penal institutions.

§ 18.2-303.1. What article does not prohibit. Nothing contained in this article shall prohibit or interfere with the possession of a "sawed-off" shotgun or "sawed-off" rifle for scientific purposes, the possession of a "sawed-off" shotgun or "sawed-off" rifle possessed in compliance with federal law or the possession of a "sawed-off" shotgun or "sawed-off" rifle not usable as a firing weapon and possessed as a curiosity, ornament, or keepsake.

§ 18.2-304. Manufacturer's and dealer's register; inspection of stock. Every manufacturer or dealer shall keep a register of all "sawed-off" shotguns and "sawed-off" rifles manufactured or handled by him. This register shall show the model and serial number, date of manufacture, sale, loan, gift, delivery or receipt of every "sawed-off" shotgun and "sawed-off" rifle, the name, address, and occupation of the person to whom the "sawed-off" shotgun or "sawed-off" rifle was sold, loaned, given or delivered, or from whom it was received. Upon demand every manufacturer or dealer shall permit any marshal, sheriff or police officer to inspect his entire stock of "sawed-off" shotguns and "sawed-off" rifles, and "sawed-off" shotgun or "sawed-off" rifle barrels, and shall produce the register, herein required, for inspection. A violation of any provision of this section shall be punishable as a Class 3 misdemeanor.

§ 18.2-306. Search warrants for "sawed-off" shotguns and rifles; confiscation and destruction. Warrant to search any house or place and seize any "sawed-off" shotgun or "sawed-off" rifle possessed in violation of this article may issue in the same manner and under the same restrictions as provided by law for stolen property, and any court of record, upon application of the attorney for the Commonwealth, a police officer or conservator of the peace, may order any "sawed-off" shotgun or "sawed-off" rifle thus or otherwise legally seized, to be confiscated and either destroyed or delivered to a peace officer of the Commonwealth or a political subdivision thereof.

§ 18.2-307. Short title of article. This article may be cited as the "Sawed-Off Shotgun and Sawed-Off Rifle Act."

Article 6.1. Concealed Weapons and Concealed Handgun Permits

§ 18.2-307.1. Definitions. As used in this article, unless the context requires a different meaning:
"Handgun" means any pistol or revolver or other firearm, except a machine gun, originally designed, made, and intended to fire a projectile by means of an explosion of a combustible material from 1 or more barrels when held in one hand.
"Law-enforcement officer" means those individuals defined as a law-enforcement officer in § 9.1-101, law-enforcement agents of the armed forces of the United States and the Naval Criminal Investigative Service, and federal agents who are otherwise authorized to carry weapons by federal law. "Law-enforcement officer" also means any sworn full-time law-enforcement officer employed by a law-enforcement agency of the United States or any state or political subdivision thereof, whose duties are substantially similar to those set forth in § 9.1-101.
"Lawfully admitted for permanent residence" means the status of having been lawfully accorded the privilege of residing permanently in the United States as an immigrant in accordance with the immigration laws, such status not having changed.
"Personal knowledge" means knowledge of a fact that a person has himself gained through his own senses, or knowledge that was gained by a law-enforcement officer or prosecutor through the performance of his official duties.

§ 18.2-308. Carrying concealed weapons; exceptions; penalty
A. If any person carries about his person, hidden from common observation, **(i)** any pistol, revolver, or other weapon designed or intended to propel a missile of any kind by action of an explosion of any combustible material; ... or **(v)** any weapon of like kind as those enumerated in this subsection, he is guilty of a Class 1 misdemeanor. A second violation of this section or a conviction under this section subsequent to any conviction under any substantially similar ordinance of any county, city, or town shall be punishable as a Class 6 felony, and a third or subsequent such violation shall be punishable as a Class 5 felony. For the purpose of this section, a weapon shall be deemed to be hidden from common observation when it is observable but is of such deceptive appearance as to disguise the weapon's true nature. It shall be an affirmative defense to a violation of clause (i) regarding a handgun that a person had been issued, at the time of the offense, a valid concealed handgun permit.
B. This section shall not apply to any person while in his own place of abode or the curtilage thereof.
C. Except as provided in subsection A of § 18.2-308.012, this section shall not apply to:
1. Any person while in his own place of business;

2. Any law-enforcement officer, or retired law-enforcement officer pursuant to § 18.2-308.016, wherever such law-enforcement officer may travel in the Commonwealth;

3. Any person who is at, or going to or from, an established shooting range, provided that the weapons are unloaded and securely wrapped while being transported;

4. Any regularly enrolled member of a weapons collecting organization who is at, or going to or from, a bona fide weapons exhibition, provided that the weapons are unloaded and securely wrapped while being transported;

5. Any person carrying such weapons between his place of abode and a place of purchase or repair, provided the weapons are unloaded and securely wrapped while being transported;

6. Any person actually engaged in lawful hunting, as authorized by the Board of Game and Inland Fisheries, under inclement weather conditions necessitating temporary protection of his firearm from those conditions, provided that possession of a handgun while engaged in lawful hunting shall not be construed as hunting with a handgun if the person hunting is carrying a valid concealed handgun permit;

7. Any attorney for the Commonwealth or assistant attorney for the Commonwealth, wherever such attorney may travel in the Commonwealth;

8. Any person who may lawfully possess a firearm and is carrying a handgun while in a personal, private motor vehicle or vessel and such handgun is secured in a container or compartment in the vehicle or vessel;

9. Any enrolled participant of a firearms training course who is at, or going to or from, a training location, provided that the weapons are unloaded and securely wrapped while being transported; and

10. Any judge or justice of the Commonwealth, wherever such judge or justice may travel in the Commonwealth.

D. This section shall also not apply to any of the following individuals while in the discharge of their official duties, or while in transit to or from such duties:

1. Carriers of the United States mail;

2. Officers or guards of any state correctional institution;

3. Conservators of the peace, except that a judge or justice of the Commonwealth, an attorney for the Commonwealth, or an assistant attorney for the Commonwealth may carry a concealed handgun pursuant to subdivisions C 7 and 10. However, the following conservators of the peace shall not be permitted to carry a concealed handgun without obtaining a permit as provided in this article: **(i)** notaries public; **(ii)** registrars; **(iii)** drivers, operators, or other persons in charge of any motor vehicle carrier of passengers for hire; or **(iv)** commissioners in chancery;

4. Noncustodial employees of the Department of Corrections designated to carry weapons by the Director of the Department of Corrections pursuant to § 53.1-29; and

5. Harbormaster of the City of Hopewell.

§ 18.2-308.01. Carrying a concealed handgun with a permit

A. The prohibition against carrying a concealed handgun in clause (i) of subsection A of § 18.2-308 shall not apply to a person who has a valid concealed handgun permit issued pursuant to this article. The person issued the permit shall have such permit on his person at all times during which he is carrying a concealed handgun and shall display the permit and a photo identification issued by a government agency of the Commonwealth or by the U.S. Department of Defense or U.S. State Department (passport) upon demand by a law-enforcement officer. A person to whom a nonresident permit is issued shall have such permit on his person at all times when he is carrying a concealed handgun in the Commonwealth and shall display the permit on demand by a law-enforcement officer. A person whose permit is extended due to deployment shall carry with him and display, upon request of a law-enforcement officer, a copy of the documents required by subsection B of § 18.2-308.010.

B. Failure to display the permit and a photo identification upon demand by a law-enforcement officer shall be punishable by a $25 civil penalty, which shall be paid into the state treasury. Any attorney for the Commonwealth of the county or city in which the alleged violation occurred may bring an action to recover the civil penalty. A court may waive such penalty upon presentation to the court of a valid permit and a government-issued photo identification. Any law-enforcement officer may issue a summons for the civil violation of failure to display the concealed handgun permit and photo identification upon demand.

C. The granting of a concealed handgun permit pursuant to this article shall not thereby authorize the possession of any handgun or other weapon on property or in places where such possession is otherwise prohibited by law or is prohibited by the owner of private property.

§ 18.2-308.02. Application for a concealed handgun permit; Virginia resident or domiciliary

A. Any person 21 years of age or older may apply in writing to the clerk of the circuit court of the county or city in which he resides, or if he is a member of the United States armed forces, the county or city in which he is domiciled, for a 5-year permit to carry a concealed handgun. There shall be no requirement regarding the length of time an applicant has been a resident or domiciliary of the county or city. The application shall be made under oath before a notary or other person qualified to take oaths and shall be made only on a form prescribed by the Department of State Police, in consultation with the Supreme Court, requiring only that information necessary to determine eligibility for the permit. No information or documentation other than that which is allowed on the application in accordance with this section may be requested or required by the clerk or the court.

B. The court shall require proof that the applicant has demonstrated competence with a handgun and the applicant may demonstrate such competence by one of the following, but no applicant shall be required to submit to any additional demonstration of competence, nor shall any proof of demonstrated competence expire:

1. Completing any hunter education or hunter safety course approved by the Department of Game and Inland Fisheries or a similar agency of another state;

2. Completing any National Rifle Association firearms safety or training course;

3. Completing any firearms safety or training course or class available to the general public offered by a law-enforcement agency, junior college, college, or private or public institution or organization or firearms training school utilizing instructors certified by the National Rifle Association or the Department of Criminal Justice Services;

4. Completing any law-enforcement firearms safety or training course or class offered for security guards, investigators, special deputies, or any division or subdivision of law enforcement or security enforcement;

5. Presenting evidence of equivalent experience with a firearm through participation in organized shooting competition or current military service or proof of an honorable discharge from any branch of the armed services;

6. Obtaining or previously having held a license to carry a firearm in the Commonwealth or a locality thereof, unless such license has been revoked for cause;

7. Completing any firearms training or safety course or class, including an electronic, video, or online course, conducted by a state-certified or National Rifle Association-certified firearms instructor;

8. Completing any governmental police agency firearms training course and qualifying to carry a firearm in the course of normal police duties; or

9. Completing any other firearms training which the court deems adequate.

A photocopy of a certificate of completion of any of the courses or classes; an affidavit from the instructor, school, club, organization, or group that conducted or taught such course or class attesting to the completion of the course or class by the applicant; or a copy of any document that shows completion of the course or class or evidences participation in firearms competition shall constitute evidence of qualification under this subsection.

C. The making of a materially false statement in an application under this article shall constitute perjury, punishable as provided in § 18.2-434.

D. The clerk of court shall withhold from public disclosure the applicant's name and any other information contained in a permit application or any order issuing a concealed handgun permit, except that such information shall not be withheld from any law-enforcement officer acting in the performance of his official duties or from the applicant with respect to his own information. The prohibition on public disclosure of information under this subsection shall not apply to any reference to the issuance of a concealed handgun permit in any order book before July 1, 2008; however, any other concealed handgun records maintained by the clerk shall be withheld from public disclosure.

E. An application is deemed complete when all information required to be furnished by the applicant, including the fee for a concealed handgun permit as set forth in § 18.2-308.03, is delivered to and received by the clerk of court before or concomitant with the conduct of a state or national criminal history records check.

§ 18.2-308.03. Fees for concealed handgun permits

A. The clerk shall charge a fee of $10 for the processing of an application or issuing of a permit, including his costs associated with the consultation with law-enforcement agencies. The local law-enforcement agency conducting the background investigation may charge a fee not to exceed $35 to cover the cost of conducting an investigation pursuant to this article. The $35 fee shall include any amount assessed by the U.S. Federal Bureau of Investigation for providing criminal history record information, and the local law-enforcement agency shall forward the amount assessed by the U.S. Federal Bureau of Investigation to the State Police with the fingerprints taken from any nonresident applicant. The State Police may charge a fee not to exceed $ 5to cover its costs associated with processing the application. The total amount assessed for processing an application for a permit shall not exceed $50, with such fees to be paid in one sum to the person who receives the application. Payment may be made by any method accepted by that court for payment of other fees or penalties. No payment shall be required until the application is received by the court as a complete application.

B. *(Effective until July 1, 2018)* No fee shall be charged for the issuance of such permit to a person who has retired from service (i) as a magistrate in the Commonwealth; (ii) as a special agent with the Alcoholic Beverage Control Board or as a law-enforcement officer with the Department of State Police, the Department of Game and Inland Fisheries, or a sheriff or police department, bureau, or force of any political subdivision of the Commonwealth, after completing 15 years of service or after reaching age 55; (iii) as a law-enforcement officer with the U.S. Federal Bureau of Investigation, Bureau of Alcohol, Tobacco and Firearms, Secret Service Agency, Drug Enforcement Administration, United States Citizenship and Immigration Services, U.S. Customs and Border Protection, Department of State Diplomatic Security Service, U.S. Marshals Service, or Naval Criminal Investigative Service, after completing 15 years of service or after reaching age 55; (iv) as a law-enforcement officer with any police or sheriff's department within the United States, the District of Columbia, or any of the territories of the United States, after completing 15 years of service; (v) as a law-enforcement officer with any combination of the agencies listed in clauses (ii) through (iv), after completing 15 years of service; (vi) as a designated boarding team member or boarding officer of the United States Coast Guard, after completing 15 years of service or after reaching age 55; or (vii) as a correctional officer as defined in § 53.1-1 after completing 15 years of service.

B. *(Effective July 1, 2018)* No fee shall be charged for the issuance of such permit to a person who has retired from service (i) as a magistrate in the Commonwealth; (ii) as a special agent with the Virginia Alcoholic Beverage Control Authority or as a law-enforcement officer with the Department of State Police, the Department of Game and Inland Fisheries, or a sheriff or police department, bureau, or force of any political subdivision of the Commonwealth, after completing 15 years of service or after reaching age 55; **(iii)** as a law-enforcement officer with the U.S. Federal Bureau of Investigation, Bureau of Alcohol, Tobacco and Firearms, Secret Service Agency, Drug Enforcement Administration, United States Citizenship and Immigration Services, U.S. Customs and Border Protection, Department of State Diplomatic Security Service, U.S. Marshals Service, or Naval Criminal Investigative Service, after completing 15 years of service or after reaching age 55; **(iv)** as a law-enforcement officer with any police or sheriff's department within the United States, the District of Columbia, or any of the territories of the United States, after completing 15 years of service; **(v)** as a law-enforcement officer with any combination of the agencies listed in clauses (ii) through (iv), after completing 15 years of service; **(vi)** as a designated boarding team member or boarding officer of the United States Coast Guard, after completing 15 years of service or after reaching age 55; or **(vii)** as a correctional officer as defined in § 53.1-1 after completing 15 years of service.

§ 18.2-308.04. Processing of the application and issuance of a concealed handgun permit
A. The clerk of court shall enter on the application the date on which the application and all other information required to be submitted by the applicant is received.
B. Upon receipt of the completed application, the court shall consult with either the sheriff or police department of the county or city and receive a report from the Central Criminal Records Exchange.
C. The court shall issue the permit via United States mail and notify the State Police of the issuance of the permit within 45 days of receipt of the completed application unless it is determined that the applicant is disqualified. Any order denying issuance of the permit shall be in accordance with § 18.2-308.08. If the applicant is later found by the court to be disqualified after a 5-year permit has been issued, the permit shall be revoked.
D. A court may authorize the clerk to issue concealed handgun permits, without judicial review, to applicants who have submitted complete applications, for whom the criminal history records check does not indicate a disqualification and, after consulting with either the sheriff or police department of the county or city, about which application there are no outstanding questions or issues. The court clerk shall be immune from suit arising from any acts or omissions relating to the issuance of concealed handgun permits without judicial review pursuant to this section unless the clerk was grossly negligent or engaged in willful misconduct. This section shall not be construed to limit, withdraw, or overturn any defense or immunity already existing in statutory or common law, or to affect any cause of action accruing prior to July 1, 2010.
E. The permit to carry a concealed handgun shall specify only the following information: name, address, date of birth, gender, height, weight, color of hair, color of eyes, and signature of the permittee; the signature of the judge issuing the permit, of the clerk of court who has been authorized to sign such permits by the issuing judge, or of the clerk of court who has been authorized to issue such permits pursuant to subsection D; the date of issuance; and the expiration date. The permit to carry a concealed handgun shall be no larger than 2 inches wide by 3-1/4 inches long and shall be of a uniform style prescribed by the Department of State Police.

§ 18.2-308.05. Issuance of a de facto permit.
If the court has not issued the permit or determined that the applicant is disqualified within 45 days of the date of receipt noted on the application, the clerk shall certify on the application that the 45-day period has expired, and mail or send via electronic mail a copy of the certified application to the applicant within 5 business days of the expiration of the 45-day period. The certified application shall serve as a de facto permit, which shall expire 90 days after issuance, and shall be recognized as a valid concealed handgun permit when presented with a valid government-issued photo identification pursuant to subsection A of § 18.2-308.01, until the court issues a 5-year permit or finds the applicant to be disqualified. If the applicant is found to be disqualified after the de facto permit is issued, the applicant shall surrender the de facto permit to the court and the disqualification shall be deemed a denial of the permit and a revocation of the de facto permit.

§ 18.2-308.06. Nonresident concealed handgun permits
A. Nonresidents of the Commonwealth 21 years of age or older may apply in writing to the Virginia Department of State Police for a 5-year permit to carry a concealed handgun. Every applicant for a nonresident concealed handgun permit shall submit 2 photographs of a type and kind specified by the Department of State Police for inclusion on the permit and shall submit fingerprints on a card provided by the Department of State Police for the purpose of obtaining the applicant's state or national criminal history record. As a condition for issuance of a concealed handgun permit, the applicant shall submit to fingerprinting by his local or state law-enforcement agency and provide personal descriptive information to be forwarded with the fingerprints through the Central Criminal Records Exchange to the U.S. Federal Bureau of Investigation for the purpose of obtaining criminal history record information regarding the applicant and obtaining fingerprint identification information from federal records pursuant to criminal investigations by state and local law-enforcement agencies. The application shall be made under oath before a notary or other person qualified to take eligibility for the permit. If the permittee is later found by the Department of State Police to be disqualified, the permit shall be revoked and the person shall return the permit after being so notified by the Department of State Police. The permit requirement and restriction provisions of subsection C of § 18.2-308.02 and § 18.2-308.09 shall apply, mutatis mutandis, to the provisions of this subsection.
B. The applicant shall demonstrate competence with a handgun by one of the following:
  1. Completing a hunter education or hunter safety course approved by the Virginia Department of Game and Inland Fisheries or a similar agency of another state;
  2. Completing any National Rifle Association firearms safety or training course;

3. Completing any firearms safety or training course or class available to the general public offered by a law-enforcement agency, junior college, college, or private or public institution or organization or firearms training school utilizing instructors certified by the National Rifle Association or the Department of Criminal Justice Services or a similar agency of another state;

4. Completing any law-enforcement firearms safety or training course or class offered for security guards, investigators, special deputies, or any division or subdivision of law enforcement or security enforcement;

5. Presenting evidence of equivalent experience with a firearm through participation in organized shooting competition approved by the Department of State Police or current military service or proof of an honorable discharge from any branch of the armed services;

6. Obtaining or previously having held a license to carry a firearm in the Commonwealth or a locality thereof, unless such license has been revoked for cause;

7. Completing any firearms training or safety course or class, including an electronic, video, or on-line course, conducted by a state-certified or National Rifle Association-certified firearms instructor;

8. Completing any governmental police agency firearms training course and qualifying to carry a firearm in the course of normal police duties; or

9. Completing any other firearms training that the Virginia Department of State Police deems adequate.

A photocopy of a certificate of completion of any such course or class; an affidavit from the instructor, school, club, organization, or group that conducted or taught such course or class attesting to the completion of the course or class by the applicant; or a copy of any document that shows completion of the course or class or evidences participation in firearms competition shall satisfy the requirement for demonstration of competence with a handgun.

C. The Department of State Police may charge a fee not to exceed $100 to cover the cost of the background check and issuance of the permit. Any fees collected shall be deposited in a special account to be used to offset the costs of administering the nonresident concealed handgun permit program.

D. The permit to carry a concealed handgun shall contain only the following information: name, address, date of birth, gender, height, weight, color of hair, color of eyes, and photograph of the permittee; the signature of the Superintendent of the Virginia Department of State Police or his designee; the date of issuance; and the expiration date.

E. The Superintendent of the State Police shall promulgate regulations, pursuant to the Administrative Process Act (§ 2.2-4000 et seq.), for the implementation of an application process for obtaining a nonresident concealed handgun permit.

§ 18.2-308.07. Entry of information into the Virginia Criminal Information Network

A. An order issuing a concealed handgun permit pursuant to § 18.2-308.04, or the copy of the permit application certified by the clerk as a de facto permit pursuant to § 18.2-308.05, shall be provided to the State Police and the law-enforcement agencies of the county or city by the clerk of the court. The State Police shall enter the permittee's name and description in the Virginia Criminal Information Network so that the permit's existence and current status will be made known to law-enforcement personnel accessing the Network for investigative purposes.

B. The Department of State Police shall enter the name and description of a person issued a nonresident permit pursuant to § 18.2-308.06 in the Virginia Criminal Information Network so that the permit's existence and current status are known to law-enforcement personnel accessing the Network for investigative purposes.

C. The State Police shall withhold from public disclosure permittee information submitted to the State Police for purposes of entry into the Virginia Criminal Information Network, except that such information shall not be withheld from any law-enforcement agency, officer, or authorized agent thereof acting in the performance of official law-enforcement duties, nor shall such information be withheld from an entity that has a valid contract with any local, state, or federal law-enforcement agency for the purpose of performing official duties of the law-enforcement agency. However, nothing in this subsection shall be construed to prohibit the release of **(i)** records by the State Police concerning permits issued to nonresidents of the Commonwealth pursuant to § 18.2-308.06 or **(ii)** statistical summaries, abstracts, or other records containing information in an aggregate form that does not identify any individual permittees.

§ 18.2-308.08. Denial of a concealed handgun permit; appeal

A. Only a circuit court judge may deny issuance of a concealed handgun permit to a Virginia resident or domiciliary who has applied for a permit pursuant to § 18.2-308.04. Any order denying issuance of a concealed handgun permit shall state the basis for the denial of the permit, including, if applicable, any reason under § 18.2-308.09 that is the basis of the denial, and the clerk shall provide notice, in writing, upon denial of the application, of the applicant's right to an ore tenus hearing and the requirements for perfecting an appeal of such order.

B. Upon request of the applicant made within 21 days, the court shall place the matter on the docket for an ore tenus hearing. The applicant may be represented by counsel, but counsel shall not be appointed, and the rules of evidence shall apply. The final order of the court shall include the court's findings of fact and conclusions of law.

C. Any person denied a permit to carry a concealed handgun by the circuit court may present a petition for review to the Court of Appeals. The petition for review shall be filed within 60 days of the expiration of the time for requesting an ore tenus hearing, or if an ore tenus hearing is requested, within 60 days of the entry of the final order of the circuit court following the hearing. The petition shall be accompanied by a copy of the original papers filed in the circuit court, including a copy of the order of the circuit court denying the permit. Subject to the provisions of subsection B of § 17.1-410, the decision of the Court of Appeals or judge shall be final. Notwithstanding any other provision of law, if the decision to deny the permit is reversed upon appeal, taxable costs incurred by the person shall be paid by the Commonwealth.

§ 18.2-308.09. Disqualifications for a concealed handgun permit. The following persons shall be deemed disqualified from obtaining a permit:

1. An individual who is ineligible to possess a firearm pursuant to § 18.2-308.1:1, 18.2-308.1:2, or 18.2-308.1:3 or the substantially similar law of any other state or of the United States.

2. An individual who was ineligible to possess a firearm pursuant to § 18.2-308.1:1 and who was discharged from the custody of the Commissioner pursuant to § 19.2-182.7 less than 5 years before the date of his application for a concealed handgun permit.

3. An individual who was ineligible to possess a firearm pursuant to § 18.2-308.1:2 and whose competency or capacity was restored pursuant to § 64.2-2012 less than 5 years before the date of his application for a concealed handgun permit.

4. An individual who was ineligible to possess a firearm under § 18.2-308.1:3 and who was released from commitment less than 5 years before the date of this application for a concealed handgun permit.

5. An individual who is subject to a restraining order, or to a protective order and prohibited by § 18.2-308.1:4 from purchasing, possessing, or transporting a firearm.

6. An individual who is prohibited by § 18.2-308.2 from possessing or transporting a firearm, except that a permit may be obtained in accordance with subsection C of that section.

7. An individual who has been convicted of 2 or more misdemeanors within the 5-year period immediately preceding the application, if one of the misdemeanors was a Class 1 misdemeanor, but the judge shall have the discretion to deny a permit for 2 or more misdemeanors that are not Class 1. Traffic infractions and misdemeanors set forth in Title 46.2 shall not be considered for purposes of this disqualification.

8. An individual who is addicted to, or is an unlawful user or distributor of, marijuana, synthetic cannabinoids, or any controlled substance.

9. An individual who has been convicted of a violation of § 18.2-266 or a substantially similar local ordinance, or of public drunkenness, or of a substantially similar offense under the laws of any other state, the District of Columbia, the United States, or its territories within the 3-year period immediately preceding the application, or who is a habitual drunkard as determined pursuant to § 4.1-333.

10. An alien other than an alien lawfully admitted for permanent residence in the United States.

11. An individual who has been discharged from the armed forces of the United States under dishonorable conditions.

12. An individual who is a fugitive from justice.

13. An individual who the court finds, by a preponderance of the evidence, based on specific acts by the applicant, is likely to use a weapon unlawfully or negligently to endanger others. The sheriff, chief of police, or attorney for the Commonwealth may submit to the court a sworn, written statement indicating that, in the opinion of such sheriff, chief of police, or attorney for the Commonwealth, based upon a disqualifying conviction or upon the specific acts set forth in the statement, the applicant is likely to use a weapon unlawfully or negligently to endanger others. The statement of the sheriff, chief of police, or the attorney for the Commonwealth shall be based upon personal knowledge of such individual or of a deputy sheriff, police officer, or assistant attorney for the Commonwealth of the specific acts, or upon a written statement made under oath before a notary public of a competent person having personal knowledge of the specific acts.

14. An individual who has been convicted of any assault, assault and battery, sexual battery, discharging of a firearm in violation of § 18.2-280 or 18.2-286.1 or brandishing of a firearm in violation of § 18.2-282 within the 3-year period immediately preceding the application.

15. An individual who has been convicted of stalking.

16. An individual whose previous convictions or adjudications of delinquency were based on an offense that would have been at the time of conviction a felony if committed by an adult under the laws of any state, the District of Columbia, the United States or its territories. For purposes of this disqualifier, only convictions occurring within 16 years following the later of the date of **(i)** the conviction or adjudication or **(ii)** release from any incarceration imposed upon such conviction or adjudication shall be deemed to be "previous convictions." Disqualification under this subdivision shall not apply to an individual with previous adjudications of delinquency who has completed a term of service of no less than 2 years in the Armed Forces of the United States and, if such person has been discharged from the Armed Forces of the United States, received an honorable discharge.

17. An individual who has a felony charge pending or a charge pending for an offense listed in subdivision 14 or 15.

18. An individual who has received mental health treatment or substance abuse treatment in a residential setting within 5 years prior to the date of his application for a concealed handgun permit.

19. An individual not otherwise ineligible pursuant to this article, who, within the 3-year period immediately preceding the application for the permit, was found guilty of any criminal offense set forth in Article 1 (§ 18.2-247 et seq.) or former § 18.2-248.1:1 or of a criminal offense of illegal possession or distribution of marijuana, synthetic cannabinoids, or any controlled substance, under the laws of any state, the District of Columbia, or the United States or its territories.

20. An individual, not otherwise ineligible pursuant to this article, with respect to whom, within the 3-year period immediately preceding the application, upon a charge of any criminal offense set forth in Article 1 (§ 18.2-247 et seq.) or former § 18.2-248.1:1 or upon a charge of illegal possession or distribution of marijuana, synthetic cannabinoids, or any controlled substance under the laws of any state, the District of Columbia, or the United States or its territories, the trial court found that the facts of the case were sufficient for a finding of guilt and disposed of the case pursuant to § 18.2-251 or the substantially similar law of any other state, the District of Columbia, or the United States or its territories.

§ 18.2-308.010. Renewal of concealed handgun permit

A. 1. Persons who previously have held a concealed handgun permit shall be issued, upon application as provided in § 18.2-308.02, a new 5-year permit unless it is found that the applicant is subject to any of the disqualifications set forth in § 18.2-308.09. Persons who previously have been issued a concealed handgun permit pursuant to this article shall not be required to appear in person to apply for a new 5-year permit pursuant to this section, and the application for the new permit may be submitted via the United States mail. The circuit court that receives the application shall promptly notify an applicant if the application is incomplete or if the fee submitted for the permit pursuant to § 18.2-308.03 is incorrect.

2. If a new 5-year permit is issued while an existing permit remains valid, the new 5-year permit shall become effective upon the expiration date of the existing permit, provided that the application is received by the court at least 90 days but no more than 180 days prior to the expiration of the existing permit.

3. Any order denying issuance of the new permit shall be in accordance with subsection A of § 18.2-308.08.

B. If a permit holder is a member of the Virginia National Guard, armed forces of the United States, or the Armed Forces Reserves of the United States, and his 5-year permit expires during an active-duty military deployment outside of the permittee's county or city of residence, such permit shall remain valid for 90 days after the end date of the deployment. In order to establish proof of continued validity of the permit, such a permittee shall carry with him and display, upon request of a law-enforcement officer, a copy of the permittee's deployment orders or other documentation from the permittee's commanding officer that order the permittee to travel outside of his county or city of residence and that indicate the start and end date of such deployment.

§ 18.2-308.011. Replacement permits

A. The clerk of a circuit court that issued a valid concealed handgun permit shall, upon presentation of the valid permit and proof of a new address of residence by the permit holder, issue a replacement permit specifying the permit holder's new address. The clerk of court shall forward the permit holder's new address of residence to the State Police. The State Police may charge a fee not to exceed $ 5, and the clerk of court issuing the replacement permit may charge a fee not to exceed $5. The total amount assessed for processing a replacement permit pursuant to this subsection shall not exceed $10, with such fees to be paid in one sum to the person who receives the information for the replacement permit.

B. The clerk of a circuit court that issued a valid concealed handgun permit shall, upon submission of a notarized statement by the permit holder that the permit was lost or destroyed or that the permit holder has undergone a legal name change, issue a replacement permit. The replacement permit shall have the same expiration date as the permit that was lost, destroyed, or issued to the permit holder under a previous name. The clerk shall issue the replacement permit within 10 business days of receiving the notarized statement and may charge a fee not to exceed $ 5.

§ 18.2-308.012. Prohibited conduct

A. Any person permitted to carry a concealed handgun who is under the influence of alcohol or illegal drugs while carrying such handgun in a public place is guilty of a Class 1 misdemeanor. Conviction of any of the following offenses shall be prima facie evidence, subject to rebuttal, that the person is "under the influence" for purposes of this section: manslaughter in violation of § 18.2-36.1, maiming in violation of § 18.2-51.4, driving while intoxicated in violation of § 18.2-266, public intoxication in violation of § 18.2-388, or driving while intoxicated in violation of § 46.2-341.24. Upon such conviction that court shall revoke the person's permit for a concealed handgun and promptly notify the issuing circuit court. A person convicted of a violation of this subsection shall be ineligible to apply for a concealed handgun permit for a period of 5 years.

B. *(Effective until July 1, 2018)* No person who carries a concealed handgun onto the premises of any restaurant or club as defined in § 4.1-100 for which a license to sell and serve alcoholic beverages for on-premises consumption has been granted by the Virginia Alcoholic Beverage Control Board under Title 4.1 may consume an alcoholic beverage while on the premises. A person who carries a concealed handgun onto the premises of such a restaurant or club and consumes alcoholic beverages is guilty of a Class 2 misdemeanor. However, nothing in this subsection shall apply to a federal, state, or local law-enforcement officer.

B. *(Effective July 1, 2018)* No person who carries a concealed handgun onto the premises of any restaurant or club as defined in § 4.1-100 for which a license to sell and serve alcoholic beverages for on-premises consumption has been granted by the Virginia Alcoholic Beverage Control Authority under Title 4.1 may consume an alcoholic beverage while on the premises. A person who carries a concealed handgun onto the premises of such a restaurant or club and consumes alcoholic beverages is guilty of a Class 2 misdemeanor. However, nothing in this subsection shall apply to a federal, state, or local law-enforcement officer.

§ 18.2-308.013. Suspension or revocation of permit

A. Any person convicted of an offense that would disqualify that person from obtaining a permit under § 18.2-308.09 or who violates subsection C of § 18.2-308.02 shall forfeit his permit for a concealed handgun and surrender it to the court. Upon receipt by the Central Criminal Records Exchange of a record of the arrest, conviction, or occurrence of any other event that would disqualify a person from obtaining a concealed handgun permit under § 18.2-308.09, the Central Criminal Records Exchange shall notify the court having issued the permit of such disqualifying arrest, conviction, or other event. Upon receipt of such notice of a conviction, the court shall revoke the permit of a person disqualified pursuant to this subsection, and shall promptly notify the State Police and the person whose permit was revoked of the revocation.

B. An individual who has a felony charge pending or a charge pending for an offense listed in subdivision 14 or 15 of § 18.2-308.09, holding a permit for a concealed handgun, may have the permit suspended by the court before which such charge is pending or by the court that issued the permit.

C. The court shall revoke the permit of any individual for whom it would be unlawful to purchase, possess, or transport a firearm under § 18.2-308.1:2 or 18.2-308.1:3, and shall promptly notify the State Police and the person whose permit was revoked of the revocation.

§ 18.2-308.014. Reciprocity

A. A valid concealed handgun or concealed weapon permit or license issued by another state shall authorize the holder of such permit or license who is at least 21 years of age to carry a concealed handgun in the Commonwealth, provided **(i)** the issuing authority provides the means for instantaneous verification of the validity of all such permits or licenses issued within that state, accessible 24 hours a day if available; **(ii)** the permit or license holder carries a photo identification issued by a government agency of any state or by the U.S. Department of Defense or U.S. Department of State and displays the permit or license and such identification upon demand by a law-enforcement officer; and **(iii)** the permit or license holder has not previously had a Virginia concealed handgun permit revoked. The Superintendent of State Police shall enter into agreements for reciprocal recognition with such other states that require an agreement to be in place before such state will recognize a Virginia concealed handgun permit as valid in such state. The Attorney General shall provide the Superintendent with any legal assistance or advice necessary for the Superintendent to perform his duties set forth in this subsection. If the Superintendent determines that another state requires that an agreement for reciprocal recognition be executed by the Attorney General or otherwise formally approved by the Attorney General as a condition of such other state's entering into an agreement for reciprocal recognition, the Attorney General shall **(a)** execute such agreement or otherwise formally approve such agreement and **(b)** return to the Superintendent the executed agreement or, in a form deemed acceptable by such other state, documentation of his formal approval of such agreement within 30 days after the Superintendent notifies the Attorney General, in writing, that he is required to execute or otherwise formally approve such agreement.

B. For the purposes of participation in concealed handgun reciprocity agreements with other jurisdictions, the official government-issued law-enforcement identification card issued to an active-duty law-enforcement officer in the Commonwealth who is exempt from obtaining a concealed handgun permit under this article shall be deemed a concealed handgun permit.

§ 18.2-308.016. (Effective until July 1, 2018) Retired law-enforcement officers; carrying a concealed handgun

A. Except as provided in subsection A of § 18.2-308.012, § 18.2-308 shall not apply to:

1. Any State Police officer retired from the Department of State Police, any officer retired from the Division of Capitol Police, any local law-enforcement officer, auxiliary police officer or animal control officer retired from a police department or sheriff's office within the Commonwealth, any special agent retired from the State Corporation Commission or the Virginia Alcoholic Beverage Control Board, any employee with internal investigations authority designated by the Department of Corrections pursuant to subdivision 11 of § 53.1-10 retired from the Department of Corrections, any conservation police officer retired from the Department of Game and Inland Fisheries, any Virginia Marine Police officer retired from the Law Enforcement Division of the Virginia Marine Resources Commission, any campus police officer appointed under Article 3 (§ 23.1-809 et seq.) of Chapter 8 of Title 23.1 retired from a campus police department, any retired member of the enforcement division of the Department of Motor Vehicles appointed pursuant to § 46.2-217, and any retired investigator of the security division of the Virginia Lottery, other than an officer or agent terminated for cause, **(i)** with a service-related disability; **(ii)** following at least 10 years of service with any such law-enforcement agency, commission, board, or any combination thereof; **(iii)** who has reached 55 years of age; or **(iv)** who is on long-term leave from such law-enforcement agency or board due to a service-related injury, provided such officer carries with him written proof of consultation with and favorable review of the need to carry a concealed handgun issued by the chief law-enforcement officer of the last such agency from which the officer retired or the agency that employs the officer or, in the case of special agents, issued by the State Corporation Commission or the Virginia Alcoholic Beverage Control Board. A copy of the proof of consultation and favorable review shall be forwarded by the chief, Commission, or Board to the Department of State Police for entry into the Virginia Criminal Information Network. The chief law-enforcement officer shall not without cause withhold such written proof if the retired law-enforcement officer otherwise meets the requirements of this section. An officer set forth in clause (iv) who receives written proof of consultation to carry a concealed handgun shall surrender such proof of consultation upon return to work or upon termination of employment with the law-enforcement agency. Notice of the surrender shall be forwarded to the Department of State Police for entry into the Virginia Criminal Information Network. However, if such officer retires on disability because of the service-related injury, and would be eligible under clause (i) for written proof of consultation to carry a concealed handgun, he may retain the previously issued written proof of consultation.

2. Any person who is eligible for retirement with at least 20 years of service with a law-enforcement agency, commission, or board mentioned in subdivision 1 who has resigned in good standing from such law-enforcement agency, commission, or board to accept a position covered by a retirement system that is authorized under Title 51.1, provided such person carries with him written proof of consultation with and favorable review of the need to carry a concealed handgun issued by the chief law-enforcement officer of the agency from which he resigned or, in the case of special agents, issued by the State Corporation Commission or the Virginia Alcoholic Beverage Control Board. A copy of the proof of consultation and favorable review shall be forwarded by the chief, Commission, or Board to the Department of

State Police for entry into the Virginia Criminal Information Network. The chief law-enforcement officer shall not without cause withhold such written proof if the law-enforcement officer otherwise meets the requirements of this section.

3. Any State Police officer who is a member of the organized reserve forces of any of the Armed Services of the United States or National Guard, while such officer is called to active military duty, provided such officer carries with him written proof of consultation with and favorable review of the need to carry a concealed handgun issued by the Superintendent of State Police. The proof of consultation and favorable review shall be valid as long as the officer is on active military duty and shall expire when the officer returns to active law-enforcement duty. The issuance of the proof of consultation and favorable review shall be entered into the Virginia Criminal Information Network. The Superintendent of State Police shall not without cause withhold such written proof if the officer is in good standing and is qualified to carry a weapon while on active law-enforcement duty.

B. For purposes of complying with the federal Law Enforcement Officers Safety Act of 2004, a retired or resigned law-enforcement officer who receives proof of consultation and review pursuant to this section shall have the opportunity to annually participate, at the retired or resigned law-enforcement officer's expense, in the same training and testing to carry firearms as is required of active law-enforcement officers in the Commonwealth. If such retired or resigned law-enforcement officer meets the training and qualification standards, the chief law-enforcement officer shall issue the retired or resigned officer certification, valid one year from the date of issuance, indicating that the retired or resigned officer has met the standards of the agency to carry a firearm.

C. A retired or resigned law-enforcement officer who receives proof of consultation and review pursuant to this section may annually participate and meet the training and qualification standards to carry firearms as is required of active law-enforcement officers in the Commonwealth. If such retired or resigned law-enforcement officer meets the training and qualification standards, the chief law-enforcement officer shall issue the retired or resigned officer certification, valid 1 year from the date of issuance, indicating that the retired or resigned officer has met the standards of the Commonwealth to carry a firearm. A copy of the certification indicating that the retired or resigned officer has met the standards of the Commonwealth to carry a firearm shall be forwarded by the chief, Commission, or Board to the Department of State Police for entry into the Virginia Criminal Information Network.

D. For all purposes, including for the purpose of applying the reciprocity provisions of § 18.2-308.014, any person granted the privilege to carry a concealed handgun pursuant to this section, while carrying the proof of consultation and favorable review required, shall be deemed to have been issued a concealed handgun permit.

§ 18.2-308.016. (Effective July 1, 2018) Retired law-enforcement officers; carrying a concealed handgun
A. Except as provided in subsection A of § 18.2-308.012, § 18.2-308 shall not apply to:

1. Any State Police officer retired from the Department of State Police, any officer retired from the Division of Capitol Police, any local law-enforcement officer, auxiliary police officer or animal control officer retired from a police department or sheriff's office within the Commonwealth, any special agent retired from the State Corporation Commission or the Virginia Alcoholic Beverage Control Authority, any employee with internal investigations authority designated by the Department of Corrections pursuant to subdivision 11 of § 53.1-10 retired from the Department of Corrections, any conservation police officer retired from the Department of Game and Inland Fisheries, any Virginia Marine Police officer retired from the Law Enforcement Division of the Virginia Marine Resources Commission, any campus police officer appointed under Article 3 (§ 23.1-809 et seq.) of Chapter 8 of Title 23.1 retired from a campus police department, any retired member of the enforcement division of the Department of Motor Vehicles appointed pursuant to § 46.2-217, and any retired investigator of the security division of the Virginia Lottery, other than an officer or agent terminated for cause, (i) with a service-related disability; (ii) following at least 10 years of service with any such law-enforcement agency, commission, board, or any combination thereof; (iii) who has reached 55 years of age; or (iv) who is on long-term leave from such law-enforcement agency or board due to a service-related injury, provided such officer carries with him written proof of consultation with and favorable review of the need to carry a concealed handgun issued by the chief law-enforcement officer of the last such agency from which the officer retired or the agency that employs the officer or, in the case of special agents, issued by the State Corporation Commission or the Virginia Alcoholic Beverage Control Authority. A copy of the proof of consultation and favorable review shall be forwarded by the chief, Commission, or Board to the Department of State Police for entry into the Virginia Criminal Information Network. The chief law-enforcement officer shall not without cause withhold such written proof if the retired law-enforcement officer otherwise meets the requirements of this section. An officer set forth in clause (iv) who receives written proof of consultation to carry a concealed handgun shall surrender such proof of consultation upon return to work or upon termination of employment with the law-enforcement agency. Notice of the surrender shall be forwarded to the Department of State Police for entry into the Virginia Criminal Information Network. However, if such officer retires on disability because of the service-related injury, and would be eligible under clause (i) for written proof of consultation to carry a concealed handgun, he may retain the previously issued written proof of consultation.

2. Any person who is eligible for retirement with at least 20 years of service with a law-enforcement agency, commission, or board mentioned in subdivision 1 who has resigned in good standing from such law-enforcement agency, commission, or board to accept a position covered by a retirement system that is authorized under Title 51.1, provided such person carries with him written proof of consultation with and favorable review of the need to carry a concealed handgun issued by the chief law-enforcement officer of the agency from which he resigned or, in the case of special agents, issued by the State Corporation Commission or the Virginia Alcoholic Beverage Control Authority. A copy of the proof of consultation and favorable review shall be forwarded by the chief, Commission, or Board to the Department of

State Police for entry into the Virginia Criminal Information Network. The chief law-enforcement officer shall not without cause withhold such written proof if the law-enforcement officer otherwise meets the requirements of this section.

3. Any State Police officer who is a member of the organized reserve forces of any of the Armed Services of the United States or National Guard, while such officer is called to active military duty, provided such officer carries with him written proof of consultation with and favorable review of the need to carry a concealed handgun issued by the Superintendent of State Police. The proof of consultation and favorable review shall be valid as long as the officer is on active military duty and shall expire when the officer returns to active law-enforcement duty. The issuance of the proof of consultation and favorable review shall be entered into the Virginia Criminal Information Network. The Superintendent of State Police shall not without cause withhold such written proof if the officer is in good standing and is qualified to carry a weapon while on active law-enforcement duty.

B. For purposes of complying with the federal Law Enforcement Officers Safety Act of 2004, a retired or resigned law-enforcement officer who receives proof of consultation and review pursuant to this section shall have the opportunity to annually participate, at the retired or resigned law-enforcement officer's expense, in the same training and testing to carry firearms as is required of active law-enforcement officers in the Commonwealth. If such retired or resigned law-enforcement officer meets the training and qualification standards, the chief law-enforcement officer shall issue the retired or resigned officer certification, valid 1 year from the date of issuance, indicating that the retired or resigned officer has met the standards of the agency to carry a firearm.

C. A retired or resigned law-enforcement officer who receives proof of consultation and review pursuant to this section may annually participate and meet the training and qualification standards to carry firearms as is required of active law-enforcement officers in the Commonwealth. If such retired or resigned law-enforcement officer meets the training and qualification standards, the chief law-enforcement officer shall issue the retired or resigned officer certification, valid 1 year from the date of issuance, indicating that the retired or resigned officer has met the standards of the Commonwealth to carry a firearm. A copy of the certification indicating that the retired or resigned officer has met the standards of the Commonwealth to carry a firearm shall be forwarded by the chief, Commission, or Board to the Department of State Police for entry into the Virginia Criminal Information Network.

D. For all purposes, including for the purpose of applying the reciprocity provisions of § 18.2-308.014, any person granted the privilege to carry a concealed handgun pursuant to this section, while carrying the proof of consultation and favorable review required, shall be deemed to have been issued a concealed handgun permit.

Article 7. Other Illegal Weapons

§ 18.2-308.1. Possession of firearm, stun weapon, or other weapon on school property prohibited; penalty

B. If any person knowingly possesses any firearm designed or intended to expel a projectile by action of an explosion of a combustible material while such person is upon (i) any public, private or religious elementary, middle or high school, including buildings and grounds; (ii) that portion of any property open to the public and then exclusively used for school-sponsored functions or extracurricular activities while such functions or activities are taking place; or (iii) any school bus owned or operated by any such school, he shall be guilty of a Class 6 felony.

C. If any person knowingly possesses any firearm designed or intended to expel a projectile by action of an explosion of a combustible material within a public, private or religious elementary, middle or high school building and intends to use, or attempts to use, such firearm, or displays such weapon in a threatening manner, such person shall be guilty of a Class 6 felony and sentenced to a mandatory minimum term of imprisonment of 5 years to be served consecutively with any other sentence.

The exemptions set out in §§ 18.2-308 and 18.2-308.016 shall apply, mutatis mutandis, to the provisions of this section. The provisions of this section shall not apply to (i) persons who possess such weapon or weapons as a part of the school's curriculum or activities; … (iii) persons who possess such weapon or weapons as a part of any program sponsored or facilitated by either the school or any organization authorized by the school to conduct its programs either on or off the school premises; (iv) any law-enforcement officer, or retired law-enforcement officer qualified pursuant to subsection C of § 18.2-308.016; (…(vi) a person who possesses an unloaded firearm that is in a closed container, or a knife having a metal blade, in or upon a motor vehicle, or an unloaded shotgun or rifle in a firearms rack in or upon a motor vehicle; (vii) a person who has a valid concealed handgun permit and possesses a concealed handgun while in a motor vehicle in a parking lot, traffic circle, or other means of vehicular ingress or egress to the school; or (viii) an armed security officer, licensed pursuant to Article 4 (§ 9.1-138 et seq.) of Chapter 1 of Title 9.1, hired by a private or religious school for the protection of students and employees as authorized by such school. For the purposes of this paragraph, "weapon" includes a knife having a metal blade of 3 inches or longer and "closed container" includes a locked vehicle trunk.

As used in this section:

"Stun weapon" means any device that emits a momentary or pulsed output, which is electrical, audible, optical or electromagnetic in nature and which is designed to temporarily incapacitate a person.

§ 18.2-308.1:1. Purchase, possession or transportation of firearms by persons acquitted by reason of insanity; penalty

A. It shall be unlawful for any person acquitted by reason of insanity and committed to the custody of the Commissioner of Behavioral Health and Developmental Services, pursuant to Chapter 11.1 (§ 19.2-182.2 et seq.) of Title 19.2, on a charge of treason, any felony or any offense punishable as a misdemeanor under Title 54.1 or a Class 1 or Class 2 misdemeanor under this title, except those misdemeanor violations of (i) Article 2 (§ 18.2-266 et seq.) of Chapter 7 of this title, (ii) Article 2 (§ 18.2-415 et seq.) of Chapter 9 of this title, or (iii) § 18.2-119, or (iv) an ordinance of any county, city, or town similar to the offenses specified in (i), (ii), or (iii), to knowingly and intentionally purchase, possess, or transport any firearm. A violation of this subsection shall be punishable as a Class 1 misdemeanor.

B. Any person so acquitted may, upon discharge from the custody of the Commissioner, petition the general district court in the city or county in which he resides to restore his right to purchase, possess or transport a firearm. A copy of the petition shall be mailed or delivered to the attorney for the Commonwealth for the jurisdiction where the petition was filed who shall be entitled to respond and represent the interests of the Commonwealth. The court shall conduct a hearing if requested by either party. If the court determines, after receiving and considering evidence concerning the circumstances regarding the disability referred to in subsection A and the person's criminal history, treatment record, and reputation as developed through character witness statements, testimony, or other character evidence, that the person will not be likely to act in a manner dangerous to public safety and that the granting of the relief would not be contrary to the public interest, the court shall grant the petition. Any person denied relief by the general district court may petition the circuit court for a de novo review of the denial. Upon a grant of relief in any court, the court shall enter a written order granting the petition, in which event the provisions of subsection A do not apply. The clerk of court shall certify and forward forthwith to the Central Criminal Records Exchange, on a form provided by the Exchange, a copy of any such order.

C. As used in this section, "treatment record" shall include copies of health records detailing the petitioner's psychiatric history, which shall include the records pertaining to the commitment or adjudication that is the subject of the request for relief pursuant to this section.

§ 18.2-308.1:2. Purchase, possession or transportation of firearm by persons adjudicated legally incompetent or mentally incapacitated; penalty

A. It shall be unlawful for any person who has been adjudicated (i) legally incompetent pursuant to former § 37.1-128.02 or former § 37.1-134, (ii) mentally incapacitated pursuant to former § 37.1-128.1 or former § 37.1-132 or (iii) incapacitated pursuant to Chapter 20 (§ 64.2-2000 et seq.) of Title 64.2 to purchase, possess, or transport any firearm. A violation of this subsection shall be punishable as a Class 1 misdemeanor.

B. Any person whose competency or capacity has been restored pursuant to former § 37.1-134.1, former § 37.2-1012, or § 64.2-2012 may petition the general district court in the city or county in which he resides to restore his right to purchase, possess or transport a firearm. A copy of the petition shall be mailed or delivered to the attorney for the Commonwealth for the jurisdiction where the petition was filed who shall be entitled to respond and represent the interests of the Commonwealth. The court shall conduct a hearing if requested by either party. If the court determines, after receiving and considering evidence concerning the circumstances regarding the disability referred to in subsection A and the person's criminal history, treatment record, and reputation as developed through character witness statements, testimony, or other character evidence, that the person will not be likely to act in a manner dangerous to public safety and that the granting of the relief would not be contrary to the public interest, the court shall grant the petition. Any person denied relief by the general district court may petition the circuit court for a de novo review of the denial. Upon a grant of relief in any court, the court shall enter a written order granting the petition, in which event the provisions of subsection A do not apply. The clerk of court shall certify and forward forthwith to the Central Criminal Records Exchange, on a form provided by the Exchange, a copy of any such order.

C. As used in this section, "treatment record" shall include copies of health records detailing the petitioner's psychiatric history, which shall include the records pertaining to the commitment or adjudication that is the subject of the request for relief pursuant to this section.

§ 18.2-308.1:3. Purchase, possession or transportation of firearm by persons involuntarily admitted or ordered to outpatient treatment; penalty

A. It shall be unlawful for any person involuntarily admitted to a facility or ordered to mandatory outpatient treatment pursuant to § 19.2-169.2, involuntarily admitted to a facility or ordered to mandatory outpatient treatment as the result of a commitment hearing pursuant to Article 5 (§ 37.2-814 et seq.) of Chapter 8 of Title 37.2, or who was the subject of a temporary detention order pursuant to § 37.2-809 and subsequently agreed to voluntary admission pursuant to § 37.2-805 to purchase, possess or transport a firearm. A violation of this subsection shall be punishable as a Class 1 misdemeanor.

B. Any person prohibited from purchasing, possessing or transporting firearms under this section may, at any time following his release from involuntary admission to a facility, his release from an order of mandatory outpatient treatment, or his release from voluntary admission pursuant to § 37.2-805 following the issuance of a temporary detention order, petition the general district court in the city or county in which he resides to restore his right to purchase, possess or transport a firearm. A copy of the petition shall be mailed or delivered to the attorney for the Commonwealth for the jurisdiction where the petition was filed who shall be entitled to respond and represent the interests of the Commonwealth. The court shall conduct a hearing if requested by either party. If the court determines, after receiving and considering evidence concerning the circumstances regarding the disabilities referred to in subsection A and the person's criminal history, treatment record, and reputation as developed through character witness statements, testimony, or other character evidence, that the person will not likely act in a manner dangerous to public safety and that granting the relief would not be contrary to the public interest, the court shall grant the petition. Any person denied relief by the general district court may petition the circuit court for a de novo review of the denial. Upon a grant of relief in any court, the court shall enter a written order granting the petition, in which event the provisions of subsection A do not apply. The clerk of court shall certify and forward forthwith to the Central Criminal Records Exchange, on a form provided by the Exchange, a copy of any such order.

C. As used in this section, "treatment record" shall include copies of health records detailing the petitioner's psychiatric history, which shall include the records pertaining to the commitment or adjudication that is the subject of the request for relief pursuant to this section.

§ 18.2-308.1:4. Purchase or transportation of firearm by persons subject to protective orders; penalties

A. It is unlawful for any person who is subject to **(i)** a protective order entered pursuant to § 16.1-253.1, 16.1-253.4, 16.1-278.2, 16.1-279.1, 19.2-152.8, 19.2-152.9, or 19.2-152.10; **(ii)** an order issued pursuant to subsection B of § 20-103; **(iii)** an order entered pursuant to subsection E of § 18.2-60.3; **(iv)** a preliminary protective order entered pursuant to subsection F of § 16.1-253 where a petition alleging abuse or neglect has been filed; or **(v)** an order issued by a tribunal of another state, the United States or any of its territories, possessions, or commonwealths, or the District of Columbia pursuant to a statute that is substantially similar to those cited in clauses (i), (ii), (iii), or (iv) to purchase or transport any firearm while the order is in effect. Any person with a concealed handgun permit shall be prohibited from carrying any concealed firearm, and shall surrender his permit to the court entering the order, for the duration of any protective order referred to herein. A violation of this subsection is a Class 1 misdemeanor.

B. In addition to the prohibition set forth in subsection A, it is unlawful for any person who is subject to a protective order entered pursuant to § 16.1-279.1 or an order issued by a tribunal of another state, the United States or any of its territories, possessions, or commonwealths, or the District of Columbia pursuant to a statute that is substantially similar to § 16.1-279.1 to knowingly possess any firearm while the order is in effect, provided that for a period of 24 hours after being served with a protective order in accordance with subsection C of § 16.1-279.1 such person may continue to possess and, notwithstanding the provisions of subsection A, transport any firearm possessed by such person at the time of service for the purposes of selling or transferring any such firearm to any person who is not otherwise prohibited by law from possessing such firearm. A violation of this subsection is a Class 6 felony.

§ 18.2-308.1:5. Purchase or transportation of firearm by persons convicted of certain drug offenses prohibited.

Any person who, within a 36-consecutive-month period, has been convicted of 2 misdemeanor offenses under subsection B of former § 18.2-248.1:1, § 18.2-250 or 18.2-250.1 shall be ineligible to purchase or transport a handgun. However, upon expiration of a period of 5 years from the date of the second conviction and provided the person has not been convicted of any such offense within that period, the ineligibility shall be removed.

§ 18.2-308.2. Possession or transportation of firearms, firearms ammunition, stun weapons, explosives or concealed weapons by convicted felons; penalties; petition for permit; when issued

A. It shall be unlawful for **(i)** any person who has been convicted of a felony; **(ii)** any person adjudicated delinquent as a juvenile 14 years of age or older at the time of the offense of murder in violation of § 18.2-31 or 18.2-32, kidnapping in violation of § 18.2-47, robbery by the threat or presentation of firearms in violation of § 18.2-58, or rape in violation of § 18.2-61; or **(iii)** any person under the age of 29 who was adjudicated delinquent as a juvenile 14 years of age or older at the time of the offense of a delinquent act which would be a felony if committed by an adult, other than those felonies set forth in clause (ii), whether such conviction or adjudication occurred under the laws of the Commonwealth, or any other state, the District of Columbia, the United States or any territory thereof, to knowingly and intentionally possess or transport any firearm or ammunition for a firearm, any stun weapon as defined by § 18.2-308.1, or any explosive material, or to knowingly and intentionally carry about his person, hidden from common observation, any weapon described in subsection A of § 18.2-308. However, such person may possess in his residence or the curtilage thereof a stun weapon as defined by § 18.2-308.1. Any person who violates this section shall be guilty of a Class 6 felony. However, any person who violates this section by knowingly and intentionally possessing or transporting any firearm and who was previously convicted of a violent felony as defined in § 17.1-805 shall be sentenced to a mandatory minimum term of imprisonment of 5 years. Any person who violates this section by knowingly and intentionally possessing or transporting any firearm and who was previously convicted of any other felony within the prior 10 years shall be sentenced to a mandatory minimum term of imprisonment of 2 years. The mandatory minimum terms of imprisonment prescribed for violations of this section shall be served consecutively with any other sentence.

B. The prohibitions of subsection A shall not apply to **(i)** any person who possesses a firearm, ammunition for a firearm, explosive material or other weapon while carrying out his duties as a member of the Armed Forces of the United States or of the National Guard of Virginia or of any other state, **(ii)** any law-enforcement officer in the performance of his duties, **(iii)** any person who has been pardoned or whose political disabilities have been removed pursuant to Article V, Section 12 of the Constitution of Virginia provided the Governor, in the document granting the pardon or removing the person's political disabilities, may expressly place conditions upon the reinstatement of the person's right to ship, transport, possess or receive firearms, **(iv)** any person whose right to possess firearms or ammunition has been restored under the law of another state subject to conditions placed upon the reinstatement of the person's right to ship, transport, possess, or receive firearms by such state, or **(v)** any person adjudicated delinquent as a juvenile who has completed a term of service of no less than 2 years in the Armed Forces of the United States and, if such person has been discharged from the Armed Forces of the United States, received an honorable discharge and who is not otherwise prohibited under clause (i) or (ii) of subsection A.

C. Any person prohibited from possessing, transporting, or carrying a firearm, ammunition for a firearm, or a stun weapon under subsection A may petition the circuit court of the jurisdiction in which he resides or, if the person is not a resident of the Commonwealth, the circuit court of any county or city where such person was last convicted of a felony or adjudicated delinquent of a disqualifying offense pursuant to subsection A, for a permit to possess or carry a firearm, ammunition for a firearm, or a stun weapon; however, no person who has been convicted of a felony shall be qualified to petition for such a permit unless his civil rights have been restored by the Governor or other appropriate authority. A copy of the petition shall be mailed or delivered to the attorney for the Commonwealth for the jurisdiction where the petition was filed who shall be entitled to respond and represent the interests of the Commonwealth. The court shall conduct a hearing if requested by either party. The court may, in its discretion and for good cause shown, grant such petition and issue a permit. The provisions of this section relating to firearms, ammunition for a firearm, and stun weapons shall not apply to any person who has been granted a permit pursuant to this subsection.

C1. Any person who was prohibited from possessing, transporting or carrying explosive material under subsection A may possess, transport or carry such explosive material if his right to possess, transport or carry explosive material has been restored pursuant to federal law.

D. For the purpose of this section:

"Ammunition for a firearm" means the combination of a cartridge, projectile, primer, or propellant designed for use in a firearm other than an antique firearm as defined in § 18.2-308.2:2.

"Explosive material" means any chemical compound mixture, or device, the primary or common purpose of which is to function by explosion; the term includes, but is not limited to, dynamite and other high explosives, black powder, pellet powder, smokeless gun powder, detonators, blasting caps and detonating cord but shall not include fireworks or permissible fireworks as defined in § 27-95.

§ 18.2-308.2:01. Possession or transportation of certain firearms by certain persons

A. It shall be unlawful for any person who is not a citizen of the United States or who is not a person lawfully admitted for permanent residence to knowingly and intentionally possess or transport any assault firearm or to knowingly and intentionally carry about his person, hidden from common observation, an assault firearm.

B. It shall be unlawful for any person who is not a citizen of the United States and who is not lawfully present in the United States to knowingly and intentionally possess or transport any firearm or to knowingly and intentionally carry about his person, hidden from common observation, any firearm. A violation of this section shall be punishable as a Class 6 felony.

C. For purposes of this section, *"assault firearm"* means any semi-automatic center-fire rifle or pistol that expels single or multiple projectiles by action of an explosion of a combustible material and is equipped at the time of the offense with a magazine which will hold more than 20 rounds of ammunition or designed by the manufacturer to accommodate a silencer or equipped with a folding stock.

§ 18.2-308.2:1. Prohibiting the selling, etc., of firearms to certain persons.

Any person who sells, barters, gives or furnishes, or has in his possession or under his control with the intent of selling, bartering, giving or furnishing, any firearm to any person he knows is prohibited from possessing or transporting a firearm pursuant to § 18.2-308.1:1, 18.2-308.1:2, 18.2-308.1:3, 18.2-308.2, subsection B of § 18.2-308.2:01, or § 18.2-308.7 shall be guilty of a Class 4 felony. However, this prohibition shall not be applicable when the person convicted of the felony, adjudicated delinquent or acquitted by reason of insanity has **(i)** been issued a permit pursuant to subsection C of § 18.2-308.2 or been granted relief pursuant to subsection B of § 18.2-308.1:1, or § 18.2-308.1:2 or 18.2-308.1:3 **(ii)** been pardoned or had his political disabilities removed in accordance with subsection B of § 18.2-308.2 or **(iii)** obtained a permit to ship, transport, possess or receive firearms pursuant to the laws of the United States.

§ 18.2-308.2:2. Criminal history record information check required for the transfer of certain firearms

A. Any person purchasing from a dealer a firearm as herein defined shall consent in writing, on a form to be provided by the Department of State Police, to have the dealer obtain criminal history record information. Such form shall include only the written consent; the name, birth date, gender, race, citizenship, and social security number and/or any other identification number; the number of firearms by category intended to be sold, rented, traded, or transferred; and answers by the applicant to the following questions: **(i)** has the applicant been convicted of a felony offense or found guilty or adjudicated delinquent as a juvenile 14 years of age or older at the time of the offense of a delinquent act that would be a felony if committed by an adult; **(ii)** is the applicant subject to a court order restraining the applicant from harassing, stalking, or threatening the applicant's child or intimate partner, or a child of such partner, or is the applicant subject to a protective order; and **(iii)** has the applicant ever been acquitted by reason of insanity and prohibited from purchasing, possessing or transporting a firearm pursuant to § 18.2-308.1:1 or any substantially similar law of any other jurisdiction, been adjudicated legally incompetent, mentally incapacitated or adjudicated an incapacitated person and prohibited from purchasing a firearm pursuant to § 18.2-308.1:2 or any substantially similar law of any other jurisdiction, or been involuntarily admitted to an inpatient facility or involuntarily ordered to outpatient mental health treatment and prohibited from purchasing a firearm pursuant to § 18.2-308.1:3 or any substantially similar law of any other jurisdiction.

B. 1. No dealer shall sell, rent, trade or transfer from his inventory any such firearm to any other person who is a resident of Virginia until he has **(i)** obtained written consent and the other information on the consent form specified in subsection A, and provided the Department of State Police with the name, birth date, gender, race, citizenship, and social security and/or any other identification number and the number of firearms by category intended to be sold, rented, traded or transferred and **(ii)** requested criminal history record information by a telephone call to or other communication authorized by the State Police and is authorized by subdivision 2 to complete the sale or other such transfer. To establish personal identification and residence in Virginia for purposes of this section, a dealer must require any prospective purchaser to present 1 photo-identification form issued by a governmental agency of the Commonwealth or by the United States Department of Defense that demonstrates that the prospective purchaser resides in Virginia. For the purposes of this section and establishment of residency for firearm purchase, residency of a member of the armed forces shall include both the state in which the member's permanent duty post is located and any nearby state in which the member resides and from which he commutes to the permanent duty post. A member of the armed forces whose photo identification issued by the Department of Defense does not have a Virginia address may establish his Virginia residency with such photo identification and either permanent orders assigning the purchaser to a duty post, including the Pentagon, in Virginia or the purchaser's Leave and Earnings Statement. When the photo identification presented to a dealer by the prospective purchaser is a driver's license or other photo identification issued by the Department of Motor Vehicles, and such identification form contains a date of issue, the dealer shall not, except for a renewed driver's license or other photo identification issued by the Department of Motor Vehicles, sell or otherwise transfer a firearm to the prospective purchaser until 30 days after the date of issue of an original or duplicate driver's license unless the prospective purchaser also presents a copy of his Virginia Department of Motor Vehicles driver's record showing that the original date of issue of the driver's license was more than 30 days prior to the attempted purchase.

In addition, no dealer shall sell, rent, trade, or transfer from his inventory any assault firearm to any person who is not a citizen of the United States or who is not a person lawfully admitted for permanent residence.

Upon receipt of the request for a criminal history record information check, the State Police shall (a) review its criminal history record information to determine if the buyer or transferee is prohibited from possessing or transporting a firearm by state or federal law, (b) inform the dealer if its record indicates that the buyer or transferee is so prohibited, and (c) provide the dealer with a unique reference number for that inquiry.

2. The State Police shall provide its response to the requesting dealer during the dealer's request, or by return call without delay. If the criminal history record information check indicates the prospective purchaser or transferee has a disqualifying criminal record or has been acquitted by reason of insanity and committed to the custody of the Commissioner of Behavioral Health and Developmental Services, the State Police shall have until the end of the dealer's next business day to advise the dealer if its records indicate the buyer or transferee is prohibited from possessing or transporting a firearm by state or federal law. If not so advised by the end of the dealer's next business day, a dealer who has fulfilled the requirements of subdivision 1 may immediately complete the sale or transfer and shall not be deemed in violation of this section with respect to such sale or transfer. In case of electronic failure or other circumstances beyond the control of the State Police, the dealer shall be advised immediately of the reason for such delay and be given an estimate of the length of such delay. After such notification, the State Police shall, as soon as possible but in no event later than the end of the dealer's next business day, inform the requesting dealer if its records indicate the buyer or transferee is prohibited from possessing or transporting a firearm by state or federal law. A dealer who fulfills the requirements of subdivision 1 and is told by the State Police that a response will not be available by the end of the dealer's next business day may immediately complete the sale or transfer and shall not be deemed in violation of this section with respect to such sale or transfer.

3. Except as required by subsection D of § 9.1-132, the State Police shall not maintain records longer than 30 days, except for multiple handgun transactions for which records shall be maintained for 12 months, from any dealer's request for a criminal history record information check pertaining to a buyer or transferee who is not found to be prohibited from possessing and transporting a firearm under state or federal law. However, the log on requests made may be maintained for a period of 12 months, and such log shall consist of the name of the purchaser, the dealer identification number, the unique approval number and the transaction date.

4. On the last day of the week following the sale or transfer of any firearm, the dealer shall mail or deliver the written consent form required by subsection A to the Department of State Police. The State Police shall immediately initiate a search of all available criminal history record information to determine if the purchaser is prohibited from possessing or transporting a firearm under state or federal law. If the search discloses information indicating that the buyer or transferee is so prohibited from possessing or transporting a firearm, the State Police shall inform the chief law-enforcement officer in the jurisdiction where the sale or transfer occurred and the dealer without delay.

5. Notwithstanding any other provisions of this section, rifles and shotguns may be purchased by persons who are citizens of the United States or persons lawfully admitted for permanent residence but residents of other states under the terms of subsections A and B upon furnishing the dealer with 1 photo-identification form issued by a governmental agency of the person's state of residence and 1 other form of identification determined to be acceptable by the Department of Criminal Justice Services.

6. For the purposes of this subsection, the phrase "dealer's next business day" shall not include December 25.
C. No dealer shall sell, rent, trade or transfer from his inventory any firearm, except when the transaction involves a rifle or a shotgun and can be accomplished pursuant to the provisions of subdivision B 5 to any person who is not a resident of Virginia unless he has first obtained from the Department of State Police a report indicating that a search of all available criminal history record information has not disclosed that the person is prohibited from possessing or transporting a firearm under state or federal law. The dealer shall obtain the required report by mailing or delivering the written consent form required under subsection A to the State Police within 24 hours of its execution. If the dealer has complied with the provisions of this subsection and has not received the required report from the State Police within 10 days from the date the written consent form was mailed to the Department of State Police, he shall not be deemed in violation of this section

for thereafter completing the sale or transfer.

D. Nothing herein shall prevent a resident of the Commonwealth, at his option, from buying, renting or receiving a firearm from a dealer in Virginia by obtaining a criminal history record information check through the dealer as provided in subsection C.

E. If any buyer or transferee is denied the right to purchase a firearm under this section, he may exercise his right of access to and review and correction of criminal history record information under § 9.1-132 or institute a civil action as provided in § 9.1-135, provided any such action is initiated within 30 days of such denial.

F. Any dealer who willfully and intentionally requests, obtains, or seeks to obtain criminal history record information under false pretenses, or who willfully and intentionally disseminates or seeks to disseminate criminal history record information except as authorized in this section shall be guilty of a Class 2 misdemeanor.

G. For purposes of this section:

"Actual buyer" means a person who executes the consent form required in subsection B or C, or other such firearm transaction records as may be required by federal law.

"Antique firearm" means:

1. Any firearm (including any firearm with a matchlock, flintlock, percussion cap, or similar type of ignition system) manufactured in or before 1898;

2. Any replica of any firearm described in subdivision 1 of this definition if such replica **(i)** is not designed or redesigned for using rimfire or conventional centerfire fixed ammunition or **(ii)** uses rimfire or conventional centerfire fixed ammunition that is no longer manufactured in the United States and that is not readily available in the ordinary channels of commercial trade;

3. Any muzzle-loading rifle, muzzle-loading shotgun, or muzzle-loading pistol that is designed to use black powder, or a black powder substitute, and that cannot use fixed ammunition. For purposes of this subdivision, the term "antique firearm" shall not include any weapon that incorporates a firearm frame or receiver, any firearm that is converted into a muzzle-loading weapon, or any muzzle-loading weapon that can be readily converted to fire fixed ammunition by replacing the barrel, bolt, breech-block, or any combination thereof; or

4. Any curio or relic as defined in this subsection.

"Assault firearm" means any semi-automatic center-fire rifle or pistol which expels single or multiple projectiles by action of an explosion of a combustible material and is equipped at the time of the offense with a magazine which will hold more than 20 rounds of ammunition or designed by the manufacturer to accommodate a silencer or equipped with a folding stock.

"Curios or relics" means firearms that are of special interest to collectors by reason of some quality other than is associated with firearms intended for sporting use or as offensive or defensive weapons. To be recognized as curios or relics, firearms must fall within one of the following categories:

1. Firearms that were manufactured at least 50 years prior to the current date, which use rimfire or conventional centerfire fixed ammunition that is no longer manufactured in the United States and that is not readily available in the ordinary channels of commercial trade, but not including replicas thereof;

2. Firearms that are certified by the curator of a municipal, state, or federal museum that exhibits firearms to be curios or relics of museum interest; and

3. Any other firearms that derive a substantial part of their monetary value from the fact that they are novel, rare, bizarre, or because of their association with some historical figure, period, or event. Proof of qualification of a particular firearm under this category may be established by evidence of present value and evidence that like firearms are not available except as collectors' items, or that the value of like firearms available in ordinary commercial channels is substantially less.

"Dealer" means any person licensed as a dealer pursuant to 18 U.S.C. § 921 et seq.

"Firearm" means any handgun, shotgun, or rifle that will or is designed to or may readily be converted to expel single or multiple projectiles by action of an explosion of a combustible material.

"Handgun" means any pistol or revolver or other firearm originally designed, made and intended to fire single or multiple projectiles by means of an explosion of a combustible material from 1 or more barrels when held in one hand.

"Lawfully admitted for permanent residence" means the status of having been lawfully accorded the privilege of residing permanently in the United States as an immigrant in accordance with the immigration laws, such status not having changed.

H. The Department of Criminal Justice Services shall promulgate regulations to ensure the identity, confidentiality and security of all records and data provided by the Department of State Police pursuant to this section.

I. The provisions of this section shall not apply to **(i)** transactions between persons who are licensed as firearms importers or collectors, manufacturers or dealers pursuant to 18 U.S.C. § 921 et seq.; **(ii)** purchases by or sales to any law-enforcement officer or agent of the United States, the Commonwealth or any local government, or any campus police officer appointed under Article 3 (§ 23.1-809 et seq.) of Chapter 8 of Title 23.1; or **(iii)** antique firearms, curios or relics.

J. The provisions of this section shall not apply to restrict purchase, trade or transfer of firearms by a resident of Virginia when the resident of Virginia makes such purchase, trade or transfer in another state, in which case the laws and regulations of that state and the United States governing the purchase, trade or transfer of firearms shall apply. A National Instant Criminal Background Check System (NICS) check shall be performed prior to such purchase, trade or transfer of firearms.

J1. All licensed firearms dealers shall collect a fee of $2 for every transaction for which a criminal history record information check is required pursuant to this section, except that a fee of $5 shall be collected for every transaction involving an out-of-state resident. Such fee shall be transmitted to the Department of State Police by the last day of the month following the sale for deposit in a special fund for use by the State Police to offset the cost of conducting criminal history record information checks under the provisions of this section.

K. Any person willfully and intentionally making a materially false statement on the consent form required in subsection B or C or on such firearm transaction records as may be required by federal law, shall be guilty of a Class 5 felony.

L. Except as provided in § 18.2-308.2:1, any dealer who willfully and intentionally sells, rents, trades or transfers a firearm in violation of this section shall be guilty of a Class 6 felony.

L1. Any person who attempts to solicit, persuade, encourage, or entice any dealer to transfer or otherwise convey a firearm other than to the actual buyer, as well as any other person who willfully and intentionally aids or abets such person, shall be guilty of a Class 6 felony. This subsection shall not apply to a federal law-enforcement officer or a law-enforcement officer as defined in § 9.1-101, in the performance of his official duties, or other person under his direct supervision.

M. Any person who purchases a firearm with the intent to **(i)** resell or otherwise provide such firearm to any person who he knows or has reason to believe is ineligible to purchase or otherwise receive from a dealer a firearm for whatever reason or **(ii)** transport such firearm out of the Commonwealth to be resold or otherwise provided to another person who the transferor knows is ineligible to purchase or otherwise receive a firearm, shall be guilty of a Class 4 felony and sentenced to a mandatory minimum term of imprisonment of 1 year. However, if the violation of this subsection involves such a transfer of more than 1 firearm, the person shall be sentenced to a mandatory minimum term of imprisonment of 5 years. The prohibitions of this subsection shall not apply to the purchase of a firearm by a person for the lawful use, possession, or transport thereof, pursuant to § 18.2-308.7, by his child, grandchild, or individual for whom he is the legal guardian if such child, grandchild, or individual is ineligible, solely because of his age, to purchase a firearm.

N. Any person who is ineligible to purchase or otherwise receive or possess a firearm in the Commonwealth who solicits, employs or assists any person in violating subsection M shall be guilty of a Class 4 felony and shall be sentenced to a mandatory minimum term of imprisonment of 5 years.

O. Any mandatory minimum sentence imposed under this section shall be served consecutively with any other sentence.

P. All driver's licenses issued on or after July 1, 1994, shall carry a letter designation indicating whether the driver's license is an original, duplicate or renewed driver's license.

Q. Prior to selling, renting, trading, or transferring any firearm owned by the dealer but not in his inventory to any other person, a dealer may require such other person to consent to have the dealer obtain criminal history record information to determine if such other person is prohibited from possessing or transporting a firearm by state or federal law. The Department of State Police shall establish policies and procedures in accordance with 28 C.F.R. § 25.6 to permit such determinations to be made by the Department of State Police, and the processes established for making such determinations shall conform to the provisions of this section.

§ 18.2-308.2:3. Criminal background check required for employees of a gun dealer to transfer firearms; exemptions; penalties

A. No person, corporation, or proprietorship licensed as a firearms dealer pursuant to 18 U.S.C. § 921 et seq. shall employ any person to act as a seller, whether full-time or part-time, permanent, temporary, paid or unpaid, for the transfer of firearms under § 18.2-308.2:2, if such employee would be prohibited from possessing a firearm under § 18.2-308.1:1, 18.2-308.1:2, or 18.2-308.1:3, subsection B of § 18.2-308.1:4, or § 18.2-308.2 or 18.2-308.2:01 or is an illegal alien, or is prohibited from purchasing or transporting a firearm pursuant to subsection A of § 18.2-308.1:4 or § 18.2-308.1:5.

B. Prior to permitting an applicant to begin employment, the dealer shall obtain a written statement or affirmation from the applicant that he is not disqualified from possessing a firearm and shall submit the applicant's fingerprints and personal descriptive information to the Central Criminal Records Exchange to be forwarded to the Federal Bureau of Investigation (FBI) for the purpose of obtaining national criminal history record information regarding the applicant.

C. ...Within 5 working days of the employee's next birthday, after August 1, 2000, the dealer shall submit the employee's fingerprints and personal descriptive information to the Central Criminal Records Exchange to be forwarded to the Federal Bureau of Investigation (FBI) for the purpose of obtaining national criminal history record information regarding the request.

C1. In lieu of submitting fingerprints pursuant to this section, any dealer holding a valid federal firearms license (FFL) issued by the Bureau of Alcohol, Tobacco and Firearms (ATF) may submit a sworn and notarized affidavit to the Department of State Police on a form provided by the Department, stating that the dealer has been subjected to a record check prior to the issuance and that the FFL was issued by the ATF. The affidavit may also contain the names of any employees that have been subjected to a record check and approved by the ATF. This exemption shall apply regardless of whether the FFL was issued in the name of the dealer or in the name of the business. The affidavit shall contain the valid FFL number, state the name of each person requesting the exemption, together with each person's identifying information, including their social security number and the following statement: "I hereby swear, under the penalty of perjury, that as a condition of obtaining a federal firearms license, each person requesting an exemption in this affidavit has been subjected to a fingerprint identification check by the Bureau of Alcohol, Tobacco and Firearms and the Bureau of Alcohol, Tobacco and Firearms subsequently determined that each person satisfied the requirements of 18 U.S.C. § 921 et seq. I understand that any person convicted of making a false statement in this affidavit is guilty of a Class 5 felony and that in addition to any other penalties imposed by law, a conviction under this section shall result in the forfeiture of my federal firearms license."

D. The Department of State Police, upon receipt of an individual's record or notification that no record exists, shall submit an eligibility report to the requesting dealer within 30 days of the applicant beginning his duties for new employees or within 30 days of the applicant's birthday for a person employed prior to July 1, 2000.

E. If any applicant is denied employment because of information appearing on the criminal history record and the applicant disputes the information upon which the denial was based, the Central Criminal Records Exchange shall, upon written request, furnish to the applicant the procedures for obtaining a copy of the criminal history record from the Federal Bureau of Investigation. The information provided to the dealer shall not be disseminated except as provided in this section.

F. The applicant shall bear the cost of obtaining the criminal history record unless the dealer, at his option, decides to pay such cost.

G. Upon receipt of the request for a criminal history record information check, the State Police shall establish a unique number for that firearm seller. Beginning September 1, 2001, the firearm seller's signature, firearm seller's number and the dealer's identification number shall be on all firearm transaction forms. The State Police shall void the firearm seller's number when a disqualifying record is discovered. The State Police may suspend a firearm seller's identification number upon the arrest of the firearm seller for a potentially disqualifying crime.

H. This section shall not restrict the transfer of a firearm at any place other than at a dealership or at any event required to be registered as a gun show.

I. Any person who willfully and intentionally requests, obtains, or seeks to obtain criminal history record information under false pretenses, or who willfully and intentionally disseminates or seeks to disseminate criminal history record information except as authorized by this section and § 18.2-308.2:2, shall be guilty of a Class 2 misdemeanor.

J. Any person willfully and intentionally making a materially false statement on the personal descriptive information required in this section shall be guilty of a Class 5 felony. Any person who offers for transfer any firearm in violation of this section shall be guilty of a Class 1 misdemeanor. Any dealer who willfully and knowingly employs or permits a person to act as a firearm seller in violation of this section shall be guilty of a Class 1 misdemeanor.

K. There is no civil liability for any seller for the actions of any purchaser or subsequent transferee of a firearm lawfully transferred pursuant to this section.

L. The provisions of this section requiring a seller's background check shall not apply to a licensed dealer.

M. Any person who willfully and intentionally makes a false statement in the affidavit as set out in subdivision C 1 shall be guilty of a Class 5 felony.

N. For purposes of this section:

"Dealer" means any person, corporation or proprietorship licensed as a dealer pursuant to 18 U.S.C. § 921 et seq.

"Firearm" means any handgun, shotgun, or rifle that will or is designed to or may readily be converted to expel single or multiple projectiles by action of an explosion of a combustible material.

"Place of business" means any place or premises where a dealer may lawfully transfer firearms.

"Seller" means for the purpose of any single sale of a firearm any person who is a dealer or an agent of a dealer, who may lawfully transfer firearms and who actually performs the criminal background check in accordance with the provisions of § 18.2-308.2:2.

"Transfer" means any act performed with intent to sell, rent, barter, trade or otherwise transfer ownership or permanent possession of a firearm at the place of business of a dealer.

§ 18.2-308.2:4. Firearm verification check; penalty

A. For the purposes of this section:

"Dealer" means any person licensed as a dealer pursuant to 18 U.S.C. § 921 et seq.

"Department" means the Department of State Police.

"Firearm" means any handgun, shotgun, or rifle that will or is designed to or may readily be converted to expel single or multiple projectiles by action of an explosion of a combustible material.

B. A dealer who is receiving by sale, transfer, or trade a firearm from a person who is not a dealer may choose to obtain a verification check from the Department to determine if the firearm has been reported to a law-enforcement agency as lost or stolen. If a dealer chooses to obtain a verification check, the procedures in this section shall be followed.

C. The person selling, transferring, or trading the firearm to the dealer shall present a valid photo identification issued by a state or federal governmental agency and shall consent in writing, on a form to be provided by the Department, to have the dealer obtain a verification check to determine if the firearm has been reported to a law-enforcement agency as lost or stolen. Such form shall include only the written consent; the name, address, birth date, gender, race, and verifiable government identification number on the photo identification presented by the person selling, transferring, or trading the firearm; and the serial number, caliber, make, and, if available, model of the firearm.

D. A dealer shall **(i)** obtain written consent and identifying information on the consent form specified in subsection C; **(ii)** provide the Department with the serial number, caliber, make, and, if available, model of the firearm intended to be sold, traded, or transferred to the dealer; **(iii)** request a verification check by telephone or other manner authorized by the Department; and **(iv)** receive information from the Department as to whether the firearm has been reported to a law-enforcement agency as lost or stolen.

To establish personal identification and residence for purposes of this section, a dealer shall require a prospective transferee to present 1 photo-identification form containing a verifiable identification number issued by a governmental agency of the Commonwealth, a similar photo-identification form from another state government or by the U.S. Department of Defense, or other documentation of residence determined acceptable by the Department.

E. Upon receipt of the request for a verification check, the Department shall **(i)** query firearms databases to determine if the firearm has been reported to a law-enforcement agency as lost or stolen, **(ii)** inform the dealer if the firearm has been reported to a law-enforcement agency as lost or stolen, and **(iii)** provide the dealer with a unique response for that inquiry. The Department shall provide its response to the requesting dealer electronically or by return call without delay. If the verification check discloses that the firearm cannot be lawfully sold, transferred, or traded, the Department shall have until the end of the dealer's next business day to advise the dealer that its records indicate the firearm cannot be lawfully sold, transferred, or traded pursuant to state or federal law.

In the case of electronic failure or other circumstances beyond the control of the Department, the dealer shall be advised immediately of the reason for such delay and be given an estimate of the length of such delay. After such notification, the Department shall, as soon as possible but in no event later than the end of the dealer's next business day, inform the requesting dealer if the firearm cannot be lawfully sold, transferred, or traded pursuant to state or federal law.

F. The Department shall maintain a log of requests made for a period of 12 months from the date the request was made, consisting of the serial number, caliber, make, and, if available, model of the firearm; the dealer identification number; and the transaction date.

G. The dealer shall maintain the consent form for a period of 12 months from the date of the transaction if the firearm is determined to be lost or stolen. If the firearm is determined not to be lost or stolen, the consent form shall be destroyed by the dealer within 2 weeks from the date of such determination.

H. The Superintendent of State Police shall promulgate regulations to ensure the identity, confidentiality, and security of all records and data provided pursuant to this section.

I. The provisions of this section shall not apply to transactions between persons who are licensed as firearms importers, manufacturers, or dealers pursuant to 18 U.S.C. § 921 et seq.

J. Any person who willfully and intentionally makes a material false statement on the consent form is guilty of a Class 1 misdemeanor.

§ 18.2-308.3. Use or attempted use of restricted ammunition in commission or attempted commission of crimes prohibited; penalty

A. When used in this section:

"Restricted firearm ammunition" applies to bullets, projectiles or other types of ammunition that are: **(i)** coated with or contain, in whole or in part, polytetrafluorethylene or a similar product, **(ii)** commonly known as "KTW" bullets or "French Arcanes," or **(iii)** any cartridges containing bullets coated with a plastic substance with other than lead or lead alloy cores, jacketed bullets with other than lead or lead alloy cores, or cartridges of which the bullet itself is wholly comprised of a metal or metal alloy other than lead. This definition shall not be construed to include shotgun shells or solid plastic bullets.

B. It shall be unlawful for any person to knowingly use or attempt to use restricted firearm ammunition while committing or attempting to commit a crime. Violation of this section shall constitute a separate and distinct felony and any person found guilty thereof shall be guilty of a Class 5 felony.

§ 18.2-308.4. Possession of firearms while in possession of certain substances

A. It shall be unlawful for any person unlawfully in possession of a controlled substance classified in Schedule I or II of the Drug Control Act (§ 54.1-3400 et seq.) of Title 54.1 to simultaneously with knowledge and intent possess any firearm. A violation of this subsection is a Class 6 felony and constitutes a separate and distinct felony.

B. It shall be unlawful for any person unlawfully in possession of a controlled substance classified in Schedule I or II of the Drug Control Act (§ 54.1-3400 et seq.) to simultaneously with knowledge and intent possess any firearm on or about his person. A violation of this subsection is a Class 6 felony and constitutes a separate and distinct felony and any person convicted hereunder shall be sentenced to a mandatory minimum term of imprisonment of 2 years. Such punishment shall be separate and apart from, and shall be made to run consecutively with, any punishment received for the commission of the primary felony.

C. It shall be unlawful for any person to possess, use, or attempt to use any pistol, shotgun, rifle, or other firearm or display such weapon in a threatening manner while committing or attempting to commit the illegal manufacture, sale, distribution, or the possession with the intent to manufacture, sell, or distribute a controlled substance classified in Schedule I or Schedule II of the Drug Control Act (§ 54.1-3400 et seq.) or more than one pound of marijuana. A violation of this subsection is a Class 6 felony, and constitutes a separate and distinct felony and any person convicted hereunder shall be sentenced to a mandatory minimum term of imprisonment of 5 years. Such punishment shall be separate and apart from, and shall be made to run consecutively with, any punishment received for the commission of the primary felony.

§ 18.2-308.5. Manufacture, import, sale, transfer or possession of plastic firearm prohibited.
It shall be unlawful for any person to manufacture, import, sell, transfer or possess any plastic firearm. As used in this section, *"plastic firearm"* means any firearm, including machine guns and sawed-off shotguns as defined in this chapter, containing less than 3.7 ounces of electromagnetically detectable metal in the barrel, slide, cylinder, frame or receiver of which, when subjected to inspection by X-ray machines commonly used at airports, does not generate an image that accurately depicts its shape. A violation of this section shall be punishable as a Class 5 felony.

§ 18.2-308.7. Possession or transportation of certain firearms by persons under the age of 18; penalty. It shall be unlawful for any person under 18 years of age to knowingly and intentionally possess or transport a handgun or assault firearm anywhere in the Commonwealth. For the purposes of this section, "handgun" means any pistol or revolver or other firearm originally designed, made and intended to fire single or multiple projectiles by means of an explosion of a combustible material from 1 or more barrels when held in one hand and "assault firearm" means any (i) semi-automatic centerfire rifle or pistol which expels single or multiple projectiles by action of an explosion of a combustible material and is equipped at the time of the offense with a magazine which will hold more than 20 rounds of ammunition or designed by the manufacturer to accommodate a silencer or equipped with a folding stock or (ii) shotgun with a magazine which will hold more than 7 rounds of the longest ammunition for which it is chambered. A violation of this section shall be a Class 1 misdemeanor.

This section shall not apply to:

1. Any person (i) while in his home or on his property; (ii) while in the home or on the property of his parent, grandparent, or legal guardian; or (iii) while on the property of another who has provided prior permission, and with the prior permission of his parent or legal guardian if the person has the landowner's written permission on his person while on such property;

2. Any person who, while accompanied by an adult, is at, or going to and from, a lawful shooting range or firearms educational class, provided that the weapons are unloaded while being transported;

3. Any person actually engaged in lawful hunting or going to and from a hunting area or preserve, provided that the weapons are unloaded while being transported; and

4. Any person while carrying out his duties in the Armed Forces of the United States or the National Guard of this Commonwealth or any other state.

§ 18.2-308.8. Importation, sale, possession or transfer of Striker 12's prohibited; penalty. It shall be unlawful for any person to import, sell, possess or transfer the following firearms: the Striker 12, commonly called a *"streetsweeper,"* or any semi-automatic folding stock shotgun of like kind with a spring tension drum magazine capable of holding 12 shotgun shells. A violation of this section shall be punishable as a Class 6 felony.

§ 18.2-309. Furnishing certain weapons to minors; penalty
B. If any person sells, barters, gives or furnishes, or causes to be sold, bartered, given or furnished, to any minor a handgun, having good cause to believe him to be a minor, such person shall be guilty of a Class 6 felony. This subsection shall not apply to any transfer made between family members or for the purpose of engaging in a sporting event or activity.

§ 18.2-311.1. Removing, altering, etc., serial number or other identification on firearm. Any person, firm, association or corporation who or which intentionally removes, defaces, alters, changes, destroys or obliterates in any manner or way or who or which causes to be removed, defaced, altered, changed, destroyed or obliterated in any manner or way the name of the maker, model, manufacturer's or serial number, or any other mark or identification on any pistol, shotgun, rifle, machine gun or any other firearm shall be guilty of a Class 1 misdemeanor.

§ 18.2-311.2. Third conviction of firearm offenses; penalty. On a third or subsequent conviction of any offense contained in Article 4, 5, 6, or 7 of Chapter 7 (§ 18.2-247 et seq.) of Title 18.2, which would ordinarily be punished as a Class 1 misdemeanor, where it is alleged in the information or indictment on which the person is convicted, that (i) such person has been twice previously convicted of a violation of any Class 1 misdemeanor or felony offense contained in either Article 4, 5, 6, or 7 of Chapter 7 of Title 18.2 or § 18.2-53.1, or of a substantially similar offense under the law of any other jurisdiction of the United States, and (ii) each such violation occurred on a different date, such person shall be guilty of a Class 6 felony.

Chapter 10. Crimes Against the Administration of Justice
Article 7. Escape of, Communications with and Deliveries to Prisoners

§ 18.2-474.1. Delivery of drugs, firearms, explosives, etc., to prisoners or committed persons
Notwithstanding the provisions of § 18.2-474, any person who shall willfully in any manner deliver, attempt to deliver, or conspire with another to deliver to any prisoner confined under authority of the Commonwealth of Virginia, or of any political subdivision thereof, or to any person committed to the Department of Juvenile Justice in any juvenile correctional center, any drug which is a controlled substance regulated by the Drug Control Act in Chapter 34 (§ 54.1-3400 et seq.) of Title 54.1 or marijuana is guilty of a Class 5 felony. Any person who shall willfully in any manner so deliver or attempt to deliver or conspire to deliver to any such prisoner or confined or committed person, firearms, ammunitions, or explosives of any nature is guilty of a Class 3 felony.
Nothing herein contained shall be construed to repeal or amend § 18.2-473.

TITLE 19.2. Criminal Procedure
Chapter 22.2. Miscellaneous Forfeiture Provisions

§ 19.2-386.27. Forfeiture of firearms carried in violation of Article 6.1 (§ 18.2-307.1 et seq.). Any weapon used in the commission of a violation of Article 6.1 (§ 18.2-307.1 et seq.) of Chapter 7 of Title 18.2 shall be forfeited to the Commonwealth and may be seized by an officer as forfeited, and such as may be needed for police officers, conservators of the peace, and the Department of Forensic Science shall be devoted to that purpose, subject to any registration requirements of federal law, and the remainder shall be disposed of as provided in § 19.2-386.29.

§ 19.2-386.28. Forfeiture of weapons that are concealed, possessed, transported or carried in violation of law.

Any firearm, stun weapon as defined by § 18.2-308.1, or any weapon concealed, possessed, transported or carried in violation of § 18.2-283.1, 18.2-287.01, 18.2-287.4, 18.2-308.1:2, 18.2-308.1:3, 18.2-308.1:4, 18.2-308.2, 18.2-308.2:01, 18.2-308.2:1, 18.2-308.4, 18.2-308.5, 18.2-308.7, or 18.2-308.8 shall be forfeited to the Commonwealth and disposed of as provided in § 19.2-386.29.

§ 19.2-386.29. Forfeiture of certain weapons used in commission of criminal offense

All pistols, shotguns, rifles, ... and other weapons used by any person in the commission of a criminal offense, shall, upon conviction of such person, be forfeited to the Commonwealth by order of the court trying the case. The court shall dispose of such weapons as it deems proper by entry of an order of record. Such disposition may include the destruction of the weapons or, subject to any registration requirements of federal law, sale of the firearms to a licensed dealer in such firearms in accordance with the provisions of Chapter 22.1 (§ 19.2-386.1 et seq.) regarding sale of property forfeited to the Commonwealth.

The court may authorize the seizing law-enforcement agency to use the weapon for a period of time as specified in the order. When the seizing agency ceases to so use the weapon, it shall be disposed of as otherwise provided in this section.

However, upon petition to the court and notice to the attorney for the Commonwealth, the court, upon good cause shown, shall return any such weapon to its lawful owner after conclusion of all relevant proceedings if such owner (i) did not know and had no reason to know of the conduct giving rise to the forfeiture and (ii) is not otherwise prohibited by law from possessing the weapon. The owner shall acknowledge in a sworn affidavit to be filed with the record in the case or cases that he has retaken possession of the weapon involved.

TITLE 52. Police (State)
Chapter 1. Department of State Police

§ 52-4.4. Duties relating to criminal history record information checks required by licensed firearms dealers. The

Superintendent of the Department of State Police shall establish a toll-free telephone number which shall be operational 7 days a week between the hours of 8:00 a.m. and 10:00 p.m., except December 25, for purposes of responding to inquiries from licensed firearms dealers, as such term is defined in 18 U.S.C. § 921 et seq., pursuant to the provisions of § 18.2-308.2:2. The Department shall hire and train such personnel as are necessary to administer the provisions of this section.

§ 52-11.5. Disposal of unclaimed firearms or other weapons in possession of the State Police. Subject to the

provisions of § 19.2-386.29, the State Police may destroy unclaimed firearms and other weapons that have been in the possession of the Department for a period of more than 120 days and that have been determined by the Superintendent or his designee to be unsuitable to be placed in service with the Department. For the purposes of this section, "unclaimed firearms and other weapons" means any firearm or other weapon belonging to another that has been acquired by a law-enforcement officer pursuant to his duties, that is not needed in any criminal prosecution, that has not been claimed by its rightful owner and that the State Treasurer has indicated will be declined if remitted under the Uniform Disposition of Unclaimed Property Act (§ 55-210.1 et seq.).

At the discretion of the Superintendent or his designee, unclaimed firearms or other weapons may be destroyed by any means that render the firearms or other weapons permanently inoperable. Prior to the destruction of such firearms or other weapons, the Superintendent or his designee shall comply with the notice provisions contained in § 52-11.4.

In lieu of destroying any such unclaimed firearm, the Superintendent or his designee may donate the firearm to the Department of Forensic Science, upon agreement of the Department of Forensic Science.

TITLE 54.1. Professions and Occupations
Subtitle V. Occupations Regulated by Local Governing Bodies
Chapter 42. Dealers in Firearms

§ 54.1-4200. Definitions. For the purpose of this chapter, unless the context requires a different meaning:

"Dealer in firearms" means (i) any person, firm, partnership, or corporation engaged in the business of selling, trading or transferring firearms at wholesale or retail; (ii) any person, firm, partnership, or corporation engaged in the business of making or fitting special barrels, stocks, or trigger mechanisms to firearms; or (iii) any person, firm, partnership, or corporation that is a pawnbroker.

"Engaged in business" means as applied to a dealer in firearms a person, firm, partnership, or corporation that devotes time, attention, and labor to dealing in firearms as a regular course of trade or business with the principal objective of livelihood and profit through repetitive purchase or resale of firearms, but such term shall not involve a person who makes occasional sales, exchanges, or purchases of firearms for the enhancement of a personal collection or for a hobby, or who sells all or part of his personal collection of firearms.

"Firearms show" means any gathering or exhibition, open to the public, not occurring on the permanent premises of a

dealer in firearms, conducted principally for the purposes of exchanging, selling or trading firearms as defined in § 18.2-308.2:2.

§ 54.1-4201. Inspection of records
A. Every dealer in firearms shall keep at his place of business, for not less than a period of 2 years, the original consent form required to be completed by § 18.2-308.2:2 for each firearm sale.

B. Every dealer in firearms shall admit to his place of business during regular business hours the chief law-enforcement officer, or his designee, of the jurisdiction in which the dealer is located, or any law-enforcement official of the Commonwealth, and shall permit such law-enforcement officer, in the course of a bona fide criminal investigation, to examine and copy those federal and state records related to the acquisition or disposition of a particular firearm required by this section. This section shall not be construed to authorize the seizure of any records.

§ 54.1-4201.1. Notification by sponsor of firearms show to State Police and local law-enforcement authorities required; records; penalty
A. No promoter of a firearms show shall hold such show without giving notice at least 30 days prior to the show to the State Police and the sheriff or chief of police of the locality in which the firearms show will be held. The notice shall be given on a form provided by the State Police. A separate notice shall be required for each firearms show.

"Promoter" means every person, firm, corporation, club, association, or organization holding a firearms show in the Commonwealth.

The promoter shall maintain for the duration of the show a list of all vendors or exhibitors in the show for immediate inspection by any law-enforcement authorities, and within 5 days after the conclusion of the show, by mail, by hand, by email, or by fax, transmit a copy of the complete vendor or exhibitor list to the law-enforcement authorities to which the 30-day prior notice was required. The vendor or exhibitor list shall contain the full name and residence address and the business name and address, if any, of the vendors or exhibitors.

B. A willful violation of this section shall be a Class 3 misdemeanor.

C. The provisions of this section shall not apply to firearms shows held in any town with a population of not less than 1,995 and not more than 2,010, according to the 1990 United States census.

§ 54.1-4201.2. Firearm transactions by persons other than dealers; voluntary background checks
A. The Department of State Police shall be available at every firearms show held in the Commonwealth to make determinations in accordance with the procedures set out in § 18.2-308.2:2 of whether a prospective purchaser or transferee is prohibited under state or federal law from possessing a firearm. The Department of State Police shall establish policies and procedures in accordance with 28 C.F.R. § 25.6 to permit such determinations to be made by the Department of State Police.

Unless otherwise required by state or federal law, any party involved in the transaction may decide whether or not to have such a determination made.

The Department of State Police may charge a reasonable fee for the determination.

B. The promoter, as defined in § 54.1-4201.1, shall give the Department of State Police notice of the time and location of a firearms show at least 30 days prior to the show. The promoter shall provide the Department of State Police with adequate space, at no charge, to conduct such prohibition determinations. The promoter shall ensure that a notice that such determinations are available is prominently displayed at the show.

C. No person who sells or transfers a firearm at a firearms show after receiving a determination from the Department of State Police that the purchaser or transferee is not prohibited by state or federal law from possessing a firearm shall be liable for selling or transferring a firearm to such person.

D. The provisions of § 18.2-308.2:2, including definitions, procedures, and prohibitions, shall apply, mutatis mutandis, to the provisions of this section.

§ 54.1-4202. Penalties for violation of the provisions of this chapter.
Any person convicted of a first offense for willfully violating the provisions of this chapter shall be guilty of a Class 2 misdemeanor. Any person convicted of a second or subsequent offense under the provisions of this chapter shall be guilty of a Class 1 misdemeanor.

TITLE 59.1. Trade and Commerce
Chapter 11.1. Firearms

§ 59.1-148.3. (Effective until July 1, 2018) Purchase of handguns or other weapons of certain officers
A. The Department of State Police, the Department of Game and Inland Fisheries, the Department of Alcoholic Beverage Control, the Virginia Lottery, the Marine Resources Commission, the Capitol Police, the Department of Conservation and Recreation, the Department of Forestry, any sheriff, any regional jail board or authority, and any local police department may allow any full-time sworn law-enforcement officer, deputy, or regional jail officer, a local fire department may allow any full-time sworn fire marshal, the Department of Motor Vehicles may allow any law-enforcement officer, any institution of higher learning named in § 23.1-1100 may allow any campus police officer appointed pursuant to Article 3 (§ 23.1-809 et seq.) of Chapter 8 of Title 23.1, retiring on or after July 1, 1991, and the Department of Corrections may allow any employee with internal investigations authority designated by the Department of Corrections pursuant to subdivision 11 of § 53.1-10 who retires **(i)** after at least 10 years of service, **(ii)** at 70 years of age or older, or **(iii)** as a result of a service-incurred disability or who is receiving long-term disability payments for a service-incurred disability with no expectation of

returning to the employment where he incurred the disability to purchase the service handgun issued or previously issued to him by the agency or institution at a price of $1. If the previously issued weapon is no longer available, a weapon of like kind may be substituted for that weapon. This privilege shall also extend to any former Superintendent of the Department of State Police who leaves service after a minimum of 5 years. This privilege shall also extend to any person listed in this subsection who is eligible for retirement with at least 10 years of service who resigns on or after July 1, 1991, in good standing from one of the agencies listed in this section to accept a position covered by the Virginia Retirement System. Other weapons issued by the agencies listed in this subsection for personal duty use of an officer may, with approval of the agency head, be sold to the officer subject to the qualifications of this section at a fair market price determined as in subsection B, so long as the weapon is a type and configuration that can be purchased at a regular hardware or sporting goods store by a private citizen without restrictions other than the instant background check.

B. The agencies listed in subsection A may allow any full-time sworn law-enforcement officer who retires with 5 or more years of service, but less than 10, to purchase the service handgun issued to him by the agency at a price equivalent to the weapon's fair market value on the date of the officer's retirement. Any full-time sworn law-enforcement officer employed by any of the agencies listed in subsection A who is retired for disability as a result of a nonservice-incurred disability may purchase the service handgun issued to him by the agency at a price equivalent to the weapon's fair market value on the date of the officer's retirement. Determinations of fair market value may be made by reference to a recognized pricing guide.

C. The agencies listed in subsection A may allow the immediate survivor of any full-time sworn law-enforcement officer **(i)** who is killed in the line of duty or **(ii)** who dies in service and has at least 10 years of service to purchase the service handgun issued to the officer by the agency at a price of $1.

D. The governing board of any institution of higher learning named in § 23.1-1100 may allow any campus police officer appointed pursuant to Article 3 (§ 23.1-809 et seq.) of Chapter 8 of Title 23.1 who retires on or after July 1, 1991, to purchase the service handgun issued to him at a price equivalent to the weapon's fair market value on the date of the officer's retirement. Determinations of fair market value may be made by reference to a recognized pricing guide.

E. Any officer who at the time of his retirement is a full-time sworn law-enforcement officer with a state agency listed in subsection A, when the agency allows purchases of service handguns, and who retires after 10 years of state service, even if a portion of his service was with another state agency, may purchase the service handgun issued to him by the agency from which he retires at a price of $1.

F. The sheriff of Hanover County may allow any auxiliary or volunteer deputy sheriff with a minimum of 10 years of service, upon leaving office, to purchase for $1 the service handgun issued to him.

G. Any sheriff or local police department, in accordance with written authorization or approval from the local governing body, may allow any auxiliary law-enforcement officer with more than 10 years of service to purchase the service handgun issued to him by the agency at a price that is equivalent to or less than the weapon's fair market value on the date of purchase by the officer.

H. The agencies listed in subsection A may allow any full-time sworn law-enforcement officer currently employed by the agency to purchase his service handgun, with the approval of the chief law-enforcement officer of the agency, at a fair market price. This subsection shall only apply when the agency has purchased new service handguns for its officers, and the handgun subject to the sale is no longer used by the agency or officer in the course of duty.

§ 59.1-148.3. (Effective July 1, 2018) Purchase of handguns or other weapons of certain officers

A. The Department of State Police, the Department of Game and Inland Fisheries, the Virginia Alcoholic Beverage Control Authority, the Virginia Lottery, the Marine Resources Commission, the Capitol Police, the Department of Conservation and Recreation, the Department of Forestry, any sheriff, any regional jail board or authority, and any local police department may allow any full-time sworn law-enforcement officer, deputy, or regional jail officer, a local fire department may allow any full-time sworn fire marshal, the Department of Motor Vehicles may allow any law-enforcement officer, any institution of higher learning named in § 23.1-1100 may allow any campus police officer appointed pursuant to Article 3 (§ 23.1-809 et seq.) of Chapter 8 of Title 23.1, retiring on or after July 1, 1991, and the Department of Corrections may allow any employee with internal investigations authority designated by the Department of Corrections pursuant to subdivision 11 of § 53.1-10 who retires **(i)** after at least 10 years of service, **(ii)** at 70 years of age or older, or **(iii)** as a result of a service-incurred disability or who is receiving long-term disability payments for a service-incurred disability with no expectation of returning to the employment where he incurred the disability to purchase the service handgun issued or previously issued to him by the agency or institution at a price of $1. If the previously issued weapon is no longer available, a weapon of like kind may be substituted for that weapon. This privilege shall also extend to any former Superintendent of the Department of State Police who leaves service after a minimum of 5 years. This privilege shall also extend to any person listed in this subsection who is eligible for retirement with at least 10 years of service who resigns on or after July 1, 1991, in good standing from one of the agencies listed in this section to accept a position covered by the Virginia Retirement System. Other weapons issued by the agencies listed in this subsection for personal duty use of an officer may, with approval of the agency head, be sold to the officer subject to the qualifications of this section at a fair market price determined as in subsection B, so long as the weapon is a type and configuration that can be purchased at a regular hardware or sporting goods store by a private citizen without restrictions other than the instant background check.

B. The agencies listed in subsection A may allow any full-time sworn law-enforcement officer who retires with 5 or more years of service, but less than 10, to purchase the service handgun issued to him by the agency at a price equivalent to the weapon's fair market value on the date of the officer's retirement. Any full-time sworn law-enforcement officer employed by any of the agencies listed in subsection A who is retired for disability as a result of a nonservice-incurred disability may purchase the service handgun issued to him by the agency at a price equivalent to the weapon's fair market value on the date of the officer's retirement. Determinations of fair market value may be made by reference to a recognized pricing guide.

C. The agencies listed in subsection A may allow the immediate survivor of any full-time sworn law-enforcement officer **(i)** who is killed in the line of duty or **(ii)** who dies in service and has at least 10 years of service to purchase the service handgun issued to the officer by the agency at a price of $1.

D. The governing board of any institution of higher learning named in § 23.1-1100 may allow any campus police officer appointed pursuant to Article 3 (§ 23.1-809 et seq.) of Chapter 8 of Title 23.1 who retires on or after July 1, 1991, to purchase the service handgun issued to him at a price equivalent to the weapon's fair market value on the date of the officer's retirement. Determinations of fair market value may be made by reference to a recognized pricing guide.

E. Any officer who at the time of his retirement is a full-time sworn law-enforcement officer with a state agency listed in subsection A, when the agency allows purchases of service handguns, and who retires after 10 years of state service, even if a portion of his service was with another state agency, may purchase the service handgun issued to him by the agency from which he retires at a price of $1.

F. The sheriff of Hanover County may allow any auxiliary or volunteer deputy sheriff with a minimum of 10 years of service, upon leaving office, to purchase for $1 the service handgun issued to him.

G. Any sheriff or local police department, in accordance with written authorization or approval from the local governing body, may allow any auxiliary law-enforcement officer with more than 10 years of service to purchase the service handgun issued to him by the agency at a price that is equivalent to or less than the weapon's fair market value on the date of purchase by the officer.

H. The agencies listed in subsection A may allow any full-time sworn law-enforcement officer currently employed by the agency to purchase his service handgun, with the approval of the chief law-enforcement officer of the agency, at a fair market price. This subsection shall only apply when the agency has purchased new service handguns for its officers, and the handgun subject to the sale is no longer used by the agency or officer in the course of duty.

§ 59.1-148.4. Sale of firearms by law-enforcement agencies prohibited; exception. A law-enforcement agency of this Commonwealth shall not sell or trade any firearm owned and used or otherwise lawfully in its possession except **(i)** to another law-enforcement agency of the Commonwealth, **(ii)** to a licensed firearms dealer, **(iii)** to the persons as provided in § 59.1-148.3 or **(iv)** as authorized by a court in accordance with § 19.2-386.29.

West Virginia Code
Current through 2016 Regular Session and First Extraordinary Session of the West Virginia Legislature

Office of the Attorney General
West Virginia State Capitol Building 1
Room 26-E
1900 Kanawha Boulevard
Charleston, WV 25305-9924
Voice: (304) 558-2021
http://www.ago.wv.gov/Pages/default.aspx

Louisville Field Division
600 Dr. Martin Luther King Jr.
Place, Suite 500
Louisville, Kentucky 40202
Voice: (502) 753-3400
https://www.atf.gov/louisville-field-division

PROTECTING THE PUBLIC
SERVING OUR NATION

Table of Contents

Chapter 8. Municipal Corporations.
Article 12. General and Specific Powers, Duties and Allied Relations of Municipalities, Governing Bodies and Municipal Officers and Employees; Suits Against Municipalities.
Part III. General Powers of Municipalities and Governing Bodies.

§ 8-12-5. General powers of every municipality and the governing body thereof. In addition to the powers and authority granted by: **(i)** The Constitution of this State; **(ii)** other provisions of this chapter; **(iii)** other general law; and **(iv)** any charter, and to the extent not inconsistent or in conflict with any of the foregoing except special legislative charters, every municipality and the governing body thereof shall have plenary power and authority therein by ordinance or resolution, as the case may require, and by appropriate action based thereon:

(16) To arrest, convict and punish any individual for carrying about his or her person any revolver or other pistol, ... or any other dangerous or other deadly weapon of like kind or character: Provided, That with respect to any firearm a municipality may only arrest, convict and punish someone if they are in violation of an ordinance authorized by subsection 5-a of this article, a state law proscribing certain conduct with a firearm or applicable federal law;

§ 8-12-5a. Limitations upon municipalities' power to restrict the purchase, possession, transfer, ownership, carrying, transport, sale and storage of certain weapons and ammunition.
(a) Except as provided by the provisions of this section and the provisions of § 8-12-5 of this article, neither a municipality nor the governing body of any municipality may, by ordinance or otherwise, limit the right of any person to purchase, possess, transfer, own, carry, transport, sell or store any revolver, pistol, rifle or shotgun or any ammunition or ammunition components to be used therewith nor to so regulate the keeping of gunpowder so as to directly or indirectly prohibit the ownership of the ammunition in any manner inconsistent with or in conflict with state law.
(b) For the purposes of this section:
  (1) "Municipally owned or operated building" means any building that is used for the business of the municipality, such as a courthouse, city hall, convention center, administrative building or other similar municipal building used for a municipal purpose permitted by state law: Provided, That "municipally owned or operated building" does not include a building owned by a municipality that is leased to a private entity where the municipality primarily serves as a property owner receiving rental payments.
  (2) "Municipally owned recreation facility" means any municipal swimming pool, recreation center, sports facility, facility housing an after-school program or other similar facility where children are regularly present.
(c) (1) A municipality may enact and enforce an ordinance or ordinances that prohibit or regulate the carrying or possessing of a firearm in municipally owned or operated buildings.
  (2) A municipality may enact and enforce an ordinance or ordinances that prohibit a person from carrying or possessing a firearm openly or that is not lawfully concealed in a municipally owned recreation facility: Provided, That a municipality may not prohibit a person with a valid concealed handgun permit from carrying an otherwise lawfully possessed firearm into a municipally owned recreation facility and securely storing the firearm out of view and access to others during their time at the municipally owned recreation facility.
  (3) A person may keep an otherwise lawfully possessed firearm in a motor vehicle in municipal public parking facilities if the vehicle is locked and the firearm is out of view.
  (4) A municipality may not prohibit or regulate the carrying or possessing of a firearm on municipally owned or operated property other than municipally owned or operated buildings and municipally owned recreation facilities pursuant to subdivisions (1) and (2) of this section: Provided, That a municipality may prohibit persons who do not have a valid concealed handgun license from carrying or possessing a firearm on municipally owned or operated property.
(d) It shall be an absolute defense to an action for an alleged violation of an ordinance authorized by this section prohibiting or regulating the possession of a firearm that the person: **(1)** Upon being requested to do so, left the premises with the firearm or temporarily relinquished the firearm in response to being informed that his or her possession of the firearm was contrary to municipal ordinance; and **(2)** but for the municipal ordinance the person was lawfully in possession of the firearm.
(e) Any municipality that enacts an ordinance regulating or prohibiting the carrying or possessing of a firearm pursuant to subsection (c) of this section shall prominently post a clear statement at each entrance to all applicable municipally owned or operated buildings or municipally owned recreation facilities setting forth the terms of the regulation or prohibition.
(f) Redress for an alleged violation of this section may be sought through the provisions of chapter 53 [§§ 53-1-1 et seq.] of this code, which may include the awarding of reasonable attorneys fees and costs.
(g) Upon the effective date of this section, § 61-7-14 of this code is inapplicable to municipalities. For the purposes of that section, municipalities may not be considered a person charged with the care, custody and control of real property.
(h) This section does not:
  (1) Impair the authority of any municipality, or the governing body thereof, to enact any ordinance or resolution respecting the power to arrest, convict and punish any individual under the provisions of subdivision (16), section 5 of this article or from enforcing any such ordinance or resolution;
  (2) Authorize municipalities to restrict the carrying or possessing of firearms, which are otherwise lawfully possessed, on public streets and sidewalks of the municipality: Provided, That whenever pedestrian or vehicular traffic is prohibited in an area of a municipality for the purpose of a temporary event of limited duration, not to exceed 14 days, which is authorized by a municipality, a municipality may prohibit persons who do not have a valid concealed handgun license from possessing a firearm in the area where the event is held; or
  (3) Limit the authority of a municipality to restrict the commercial use of real estate in designated areas through planning or zoning ordinances.

Chapter 61. Crimes and Their Punishment.
Article 7. Dangerous Weapons.

§ 61-7-2. Definitions. As used in this article, unless the context otherwise requires:
(7) "Pistol" means a short firearm having a chamber which is integral with the barrel, designed to be aimed and fired by the use of a single hand.
(8) "Revolver" means a short firearm having a cylinder of several chambers that are brought successively into line with the barrel to be discharged, designed to be aimed and fired by the use of a single hand.

(9) "**Deadly weapon**" means an instrument which is designed to be used to produce serious bodily injury or death or is readily adaptable to such use. The term "deadly weapon" shall include, but not be limited to, the instruments defined in subdivisions (1) through (8), inclusive, of this section or other deadly weapons of like kind or character which may be easily concealed on or about the person. … Notwithstanding any other provision of this section, the term "deadly weapon" does not include any item or material owned by the school or county board, intended for curricular use, and used by the student at the time of the alleged offense solely for curricular purposes.

(10) "**Concealed**" means hidden from ordinary observation so as to prevent disclosure or recognition. A deadly weapon is concealed when it is carried on or about the person in such a manner that another person in the ordinary course of events would not be placed on notice that the deadly weapon was being carried. For purposes of concealed handgun licensees, a licensee shall be deemed to be carrying on or about his or her person while in or on a motor vehicle if the firearm is located in a storage area in or on the motor vehicle.

(11) "**Firearm**" means any weapon which will expel a projectile by action of an explosion.

§ 61-7-3. Carrying a deadly weapon without provisional license or other authorization by persons under twenty-one years of age; penalties.

(a) Any person under 21 years of age and not otherwise prohibited from possessing firearms under § 61-7-7 of this article who carries a concealed deadly weapon, without a state license or other lawful authorization established under the provisions of this code, is guilty of a misdemeanor and, upon conviction thereof, shall be fined not less than $100 nor more than $1,000 and may be imprisoned in jail for not more than 12 months for the first offense; but upon conviction of a second or subsequent offense, he or she is guilty of a felony and, upon conviction thereof, shall be imprisoned in t a state correctional facility not less than 1 nor more than 5 years and fined not less than $1,000 nor more than $5,000.

(b) The prosecuting attorney in all cases shall ascertain whether or not the charge made by the grand jury is a first offense or is a second or subsequent offense and, if it is a second or subsequent offense, it shall be so stated in the indictment returned, and the prosecuting attorney shall introduce the record evidence before the trial court of such second or subsequent offense and may not be permitted to use discretion in introducing evidence to prove the same on the trial.

§ 61-7-4. License to carry deadly weapons; how obtained.

(a) Except as provided in subsection (h) of this section, any person desiring to obtain a state license to carry a concealed deadly weapon shall apply to the sheriff of his or her county for the license, and pay to the sheriff, at the time of application, a fee of $75, of which $15 …. Concealed weapons license may only be issued for pistols and revolvers. Each applicant shall file with the sheriff a complete application, as prepared by the Superintendent of the West Virginia State Police, in writing, duly verified, which sets forth only the following licensing requirements:

(1) The applicant's full name, date of birth, Social Security number, a description of the applicant's physical features, the applicant's place of birth, the applicant's country of citizenship and, if the applicant is not a United States citizen, any alien or admission number issued by the United States Bureau of Immigration and Customs Enforcement, and any basis, if applicable, for an exception to the prohibitions of 18 U. S. C. § 922(g)(5)(B);

(2) That, on the date the application is made, the applicant is a bona fide United States citizen or legal resident thereof and resident of this state and of the county in which the application is made and has a valid driver's license or other state-issued photo identification showing the residence;

(3) That the applicant is 21 years of age or older;

(4) That the applicant is not addicted to alcohol, a controlled substance or a drug and is not an unlawful user thereof as evidenced by either of the following within the 3 years immediately prior to the application:

    (A) Residential or court-ordered treatment for alcoholism or alcohol detoxification or drug treatment; or

    (B) Two or more convictions for driving while under the influence or driving while impaired;

(5) That the applicant has not been convicted of a felony unless the conviction has been expunged or set aside or the applicant's civil rights have been restored or the applicant has been unconditionally pardoned for the offense;

(6) That the applicant has not been convicted of a misdemeanor crime of violence other than an offense set forth in subdivision (7) of this section in the 5 years immediately preceding the application;

(7) That the applicant has not been convicted of a misdemeanor crime of domestic violence as defined in 18 U. S. C. § 921(a)(33), or a misdemeanor offense of assault or battery either under § 61-2-28 of this chapter or subsection (b) or (c), § 61-2-9 of this chapter in which the victim was a current or former spouse, current or former sexual or intimate partner, person with whom the defendant cohabits or has cohabited, a parent or guardian, the defendant's child or ward or a member of the defendant's household at the time of the offense, or a misdemeanor offense with similar essential elements in a jurisdiction other than this state;

(8) That the applicant is not under indictment for a felony offense or is not currently serving a sentence of confinement, parole, probation or other court-ordered supervision imposed by a court of any jurisdiction or is the subject of an emergency or temporary domestic violence protective order or is the subject of a final domestic violence protective order entered by a court of any jurisdiction;

(9) That the applicant has not been adjudicated to be mentally incompetent or involuntarily committed to a mental institution. If the applicant has been adjudicated mentally incompetent or involuntarily committed the applicant must provide a court order reflecting that the applicant is no longer under such disability and the applicant's right to possess or receive a firearm has been restored;

(10) That the applicant is not prohibited under the provisions of § 61-7-7 of this article or federal law, including 18 U. S. C. § 922(g) or (n), from receiving, possessing or transporting a firearm;

(11) That the applicant has qualified under the minimum requirements set forth in subsection (d) of this section for handling and firing the weapon: Provided, That this requirement shall be waived in the case of a renewal applicant who has previously qualified; and

(12) That the applicant authorizes the sheriff of the county, or his or her designee, to conduct an investigation relative to the information contained in the application.

(b) For both initial and renewal applications, the sheriff shall conduct an investigation including a nationwide criminal background check consisting of inquiries of the National Instant Criminal Background Check System, the West Virginia criminal history record responses and the National Interstate Identification Index and shall review the information received in order to verify that the information required in subsection (a) of this section is true and correct. A license may not be issued unless the issuing sheriff has verified through the National Instant Criminal Background Check System that the information available to him or her does not indicate that receipt or possession of a firearm by the applicant would be in violation of the provisions of section 7 of this article or federal law, including 18 U. S. C. § 922(g) or (n).

(d) All persons applying for a license must complete a training course in handling and firing a handgun, which includes the actual live firing of ammunition by the applicant. The successful completion of any of the following courses fulfills this training requirement: Provided, That the completed course includes the actual live firing of ammunition by the applicant:

(1) Any official National Rifle Association handgun safety or training course;

(2) Any handgun safety or training course or class available to the general public offered by an official law-enforcement organization, community college, junior college, college or private or public institution or organization or handgun training school utilizing instructors certified by the institution;

(3) Any handgun training or safety course or class conducted by a handgun instructor certified as such by the state or by the National Rifle Association;

(4) Any handgun training or safety course or class conducted by any branch of the United States military, reserve or National Guard or proof of other handgun qualification received while serving in any branch of the United States military, reserve or National Guard.

A photocopy of a certificate of completion of any of the courses or classes or an affidavit from the instructor, school, club, organization or group that conducted or taught the course or class attesting to the successful completion of the course or class by the applicant or a copy of any document which shows successful completion of the course or class is evidence of qualification under this section and shall include the instructor's name, signature and NRA or state instructor identification number, if applicable.

(e) All concealed weapons license applications must be notarized by a notary public duly licensed under §§ 29-4-1 et seq. of this code. Falsification of any portion of the application constitutes false swearing and is punishable under § 61-5-2 of this code.

(f) The sheriff shall issue a license unless he or she determines that the application is incomplete, that it contains statements that are materially false or incorrect or that applicant otherwise does not meet the requirements set forth in this section. The sheriff shall issue, reissue or deny the license within 45 days after the application is filed if all required background checks authorized by this section are completed.

(g) Before any approved license is issued or is effective, the applicant shall pay to the sheriff a fee in the amount of $ 25 which the sheriff shall forward to the Superintendent of the West Virginia State Police within 30 days of receipt. The license is valid for 5 years throughout the state, unless sooner revoked.

(h) Each license shall contain the full name and address of the licensee and a space upon which the signature of the licensee shall be signed with pen and ink. The issuing sheriff shall sign and attach his or her seal to all license cards. The sheriff shall provide to each new licensee a duplicate license card, in size similar to other state identification cards and licenses, suitable for carrying in a wallet, and the license card is considered a license for the purposes of this section. All duplicate license cards issued on or after July 1, 2017, shall be uniform across all 55 counties in size, appearance and information and shall feature a photograph of the licensee.

(i) The Superintendent of the West Virginia State Police, in cooperation with the West Virginia Sheriffs' Bureau of Professional Standards, shall prepare uniform applications for licenses and license cards showing that the license has been granted and shall do any other act required to be done to protect the state and see to the enforcement of this section.

(j) If an application is denied, the specific reasons for the denial shall be stated by the sheriff denying the application. Any person denied a license may file, in the circuit court of the county in which the application was made, a petition seeking review of the denial. The petition shall be filed within 30 days of the denial. The court shall then determine whether the applicant is entitled to the issuance of a license under the criteria set forth in this section. The applicant may be represented by counsel, but in no case is the court required to appoint counsel for an applicant. The final order of the court shall include the court's findings of fact and conclusions of law. If the final order upholds the denial, the applicant may file an appeal in accordance with the Rules of Appellate Procedure of the Supreme Court of Appeals. If the findings of fact and conclusions of law of the court fail to uphold the denial, the applicant may be entitled to reasonable costs and attorney's fees, payable by the sheriff's office which issued the denial.

(k) If a license is lost or destroyed, the person to whom the license was issued may obtain a duplicate or substitute license for a fee of $5 by filing a notarized statement with the sheriff indicating that the license has been lost or destroyed.

(l) Whenever any person after applying for and receiving a concealed weapon license moves from the address named in the application to another county within the state, the license remains valid for the remainder of the 5 years unless the sheriff of the new county has determined that the person is no longer eligible for a concealed weapon license under this article, and the sheriff shall issue a new license bearing the person's new address and the original expiration date for a fee not to exceed $5: Provided, That the licensee, within 20 days thereafter, notifies the sheriff in the new county of residence in writing of the old and new addresses.

(m) The sheriff shall, immediately after the license is granted as aforesaid, furnish the Superintendent of the West Virginia State Police a certified copy of the approved application. The sheriff shall furnish to the Superintendent of the West Virginia State Police at any time so requested a certified list of all licenses issued in the county. The Superintendent of the West Virginia State Police shall maintain a registry of all persons who have been issued concealed weapons licenses.

(n) The sheriff shall deny any application or revoke any existing license upon determination that any of the licensing application requirements established in this section have been violated by the licensee.

(o) A person who is engaged in the receipt, review or in the issuance or revocation of a concealed weapon license does not incur any civil liability as the result of the lawful performance of his or her duties under this article.

(p) Notwithstanding subsection (a) of this section, with respect to application by a former law-enforcement officer honorably retired from agencies governed by §§ 7-14-1 et seq. of this code; §§ 8-14-1 et seq. of this code; §§ 15-2-1 et seq. of this code; and §§ 20-7-1 et seq. of this code, an honorably retired officer is exempt from payment of fees and costs as otherwise required by this section. All other application and background check requirements set forth in this section are applicable to these applicants.

(q) Information collected under this section, including applications, supporting documents, permits, renewals or any other information that would identify an applicant for or holder of a concealed weapon license, is confidential: Provided: That this information may be disclosed to a law-enforcement agency or officer: **(i)** To determine the validity of a license; **(ii)** to assist in a criminal investigation or prosecution; or **(iii)** for other lawful law-enforcement purposes. A person who violates this subsection is guilty of a misdemeanor and, upon conviction thereof, shall be fined not less than $50 or more than $200 for each offense.

(r) A person who pays fees for training or application pursuant to this article after the effective date of this section is entitled to a tax credit equal to the amount actually paid for training not to exceed $50: Provided, That if such training was provided for free or for less than $50, then such tax credit may be applied to the fees associated with the initial application.

(s) Except as restricted or prohibited by the provisions of this article or as otherwise prohibited by law, the issuance of a concealed weapon license issued in accordance with the provisions of this section authorizes the holder of the license to carry a concealed pistol or revolver on the lands or waters of this state.

§ 61-7-4a. Provisional license to carry deadly weapons; how obtained.

(a) Any person who is at least 18 years of age and less than 21 years of age who desires to obtain a state license to carry a concealed deadly weapon shall apply to the sheriff of his or her county for a provisional license, and pay to the sheriff, at the time of application, a fee of $25, of which $5 of that amount shall be deposited in the Courthouse Facilities Improvement Fund created by § 29-26-6 of this code. Provisional licenses may only be issued for pistols or revolvers. Each applicant shall file with the sheriff a complete application, as prepared by the Superintendent of the West Virginia State Police, in writing, duly verified, which sets forth only the following licensing requirements:

(1) The applicant's full name, date of birth, Social Security number, a description of the applicant's physical features, the applicant's place of birth, the applicant's country of citizenship and, if the applicant is not a United States citizen, any alien or admission number issued by the United States Bureau of Immigration and Customs Enforcement, and any basis, if applicable, for an exception to the prohibitions of 18 U. S. C. § 922(g)(5)(B);

(2) That, on the date the application is made, the applicant is a bona fide resident of this state and of the county in which the application is made and has a valid driver's license or other state-issued photo identification showing the residence;

(3) That the applicant is at least 18 years of age and less than 21 years of age;

(4) That the applicant is not addicted to alcohol, a controlled substance or a drug and is not an unlawful user thereof as evidenced by either of the following within the 3 years immediately prior to the application:

   (A) Residential or court-ordered treatment for alcoholism or alcohol detoxification or drug treatment; or

   (B) Two or more convictions for driving while under the influence or driving while impaired;

(5) That the applicant has not been convicted of a felony unless the conviction has been expunged or set aside, or the applicant's civil rights have been restored or the applicant has been unconditionally pardoned for the offense;

(6) That the applicant has not been convicted of a misdemeanor crime of violence other than an offense set forth in subdivision (7) of this section within 5 years immediately preceding the application;

(7) That the applicant has not been convicted of a misdemeanor crime of domestic violence as defined in 18 U. S. C. § 921(a)(33), or a misdemeanor offense of assault or battery under either §61-2-28 of this chapter or subsection (b) or (c), §61-2-9 of this chapter in which the victim was a current or former spouse, current or former sexual or intimate partner, person with whom the defendant cohabits or has cohabited, a parent or guardian, the defendant's child or ward or a member of the defendant's household at the time of the offense, or a misdemeanor offense with similar essential elements in a jurisdiction other than this state;

(8) That the applicant is not under indictment for a felony offense or is not currently serving a sentence of confinement, parole, probation or other court-ordered supervision imposed by a court of any jurisdiction, or is the subject of an

emergency or temporary domestic violence protective order or is the subject of a final domestic violence protective order entered by a court of any jurisdiction;

(9) That the applicant has not been adjudicated to be mentally incompetent or involuntarily committed to a mental institution. If the applicant has been adjudicated mentally incompetent or involuntarily committed, the applicant must provide a court order reflecting that the applicant is no longer under such disability and the applicant's right to possess or receive a firearm has been restored;

(10) That the applicant is not prohibited under § 7 of this article or federal law, including 18 U. S. C. § 922(g) or (n), from receiving, possessing or transporting a firearm;

(11) That the applicant has qualified under the minimum requirements set forth in subsection (d) of this section for handling and firing the weapon;

(12) That the applicant authorizes the sheriff of the county, or his or her designee, to conduct an investigation relative to the information contained in the application.

(b) For provisional license applications, the sheriff shall conduct an investigation including a nationwide criminal background check consisting of inquiries of the National Instant Criminal Background Check System, the West Virginia criminal history record responses and the National Interstate Identification Index, and shall review the information received in order to verify that the information required in subsection (a) of this section is true and correct. A provisional license may not be issued unless the issuing sheriff has verified through the National Instant Criminal Background Check System that the information available does not indicate that receipt of or possession of a firearm by the applicant would be in violation of the provisions of section 7 of this article or federal law, including 18 U. S. C. § 922(g) or (n).

(d) All persons applying for a provisional license must complete a training course in handling and firing a handgun, which includes the actual live firing of ammunition by the applicant. The successful completion of any of the following courses fulfills this training requirement: Provided, That the completed course included the actual live firing of ammunition by the applicant:

(1) Any official National Rifle Association handgun safety or training course;

(2) Any handgun safety or training course or class available to the general public offered by an official law-enforcement organization, community college, junior college, college, or private or public institution, or organization or handgun training school utilizing instructors certified by the institution;

(3) Any handgun training or safety course or class conducted by a handgun instructor certified as such by the state or by the National Rifle Association;

(4) Any proof of current or former service in the United States armed forces, armed forces reserves or National Guard.

A photocopy of a certificate of completion of any of the courses or classes or an affidavit from the instructor, school, club, organization or group that conducted or taught the course or class attesting to the successful completion of the course or class by the applicant, or a copy of any document which shows successful completion of the course or class, is evidence of qualification under this section. Certificates, affidavits or other documents submitted to show completion of a course or class shall include instructor information and proof of instructor certification, including, if applicable, the instructor's NRA instructor certification number.

(e) All provisional license applications must be notarized by a notary public duly licensed under §§29-4-1 et seq. of this code. Falsification of any portion of the application constitutes false swearing and is punishable under §61-5-2 of this chapter.

(f) The sheriff shall issue a provisional license unless the sheriff determines that the application is incomplete, that it contains statements that are materially false or incorrect or that applicant otherwise does not meet the requirements set forth in this section. The sheriff shall issue, reissue or deny the license within 45 days after the application is filed once all required background checks authorized by this section are completed.

(g) Before any approved license is issued or is effective, the applicant shall pay to the sheriff a fee in the amount of $15 which the sheriff shall forward to the Superintendent of the West Virginia State Police within 30 days of receipt. The provisional license is valid until the licensee turns 21 years of age, unless sooner revoked.

(h) Each provisional license shall contain the full name and address of the licensee and a space upon which the signature of the licensee shall be signed with pen and ink. The issuing sheriff shall sign and attach his or her seal to all provisional license cards. The sheriff shall provide to each new licensee a duplicate license card, in size similar to other state identification cards and licenses, suitable for carrying in a wallet, and the license card is considered a license for the purposes of this section. Duplicate license cards issued shall be uniform across all 55 counties in size, appearance and information and must feature a photograph of the licensee. The provisional license shall be readily distinguishable from a license issued pursuant to § 61-7-4 of this article and shall state: "NOT NICS EXEMPT. This license confers the same rights and privileges to carry a concealed pistol or revolver on the lands or waters of this state as a license issued pursuant to § 61-7-4 of this code, except that this license does not satisfy the requirements of 18 U. S. C. § 922(t)(3). A NICS check must be performed prior to purchase of a firearm from a federally licensed firearm dealer."

(i) The Superintendent of the West Virginia State Police, in coordination with the West Virginia Sheriffs' Bureau of Professional Standards, shall prepare uniform applications for provisional licenses and license cards showing that the license has been granted and shall perform any other act required to protect the state and to enforce of section.

(j) If an application is denied, the specific reasons for the denial shall be stated by the sheriff denying the application. Any person denied a provisional license may file, in the circuit court of the county in which the application was made, a petition seeking review of the denial. The petition shall be filed within 30 days of the denial. The court shall then determine whether the applicant is entitled to the issuance of a provisional license under the criteria set forth in this section. The applicant may be represented by counsel, but in no case is the court required to appoint counsel for an applicant. The final order of the court shall include the court's findings of fact and conclusions of law. If the final order upholds the denial, the applicant may file an appeal in accordance with the Rules of Appellate Procedure of the Supreme Court of Appeals. If the findings of fact and conclusions of law of the court fail to uphold the denial, the applicant may be entitled to reasonable costs and attorney's fees, payable by the sheriff's office which issued the denial.

(k) If a provisional license is lost or destroyed, the person to whom the license was issued may obtain a duplicate or substitute license for a fee of $5 by filing a notarized statement with the sheriff indicating that the license has been lost or destroyed.

(l) Whenever any person after applying for and receiving a provisional concealed weapon license moves from the address named in the application to another county within the state, the license remains valid until the licensee turns 21 years of age unless the sheriff of the new county has determined that the person is no longer eligible for a provisional concealed weapon license under this article, and the sheriff shall issue a new provisional license bearing the person's new address and the original expiration date for a fee not to exceed $5: Provided, That the licensee within 20 days thereafter notifies the sheriff in the new county of residence in writing of the old and new addresses.

(m) The sheriff shall, immediately after the provisional license is granted, furnish the Superintendent of the West Virginia State Police a certified copy of the approved application. The sheriff shall furnish to the Superintendent of the West Virginia State Police, at any time so requested, a certified list of all provisional licenses issued in the county. The Superintendent of the West Virginia State Police shall maintain a registry of all persons who have been issued provisional concealed weapon licenses.

(n) The sheriff shall deny any application or revoke any existing provisional license upon determination that any of the licensing application requirements established in this section have been violated by the licensee.

(o) A person who is engaged in the receipt, review or in the issuance or revocation of a concealed weapon provisional license does not incur any civil liability as the result of the lawful performance of his or her duties under this article.

(p) Information collected under this section, including applications, supporting documents, permits, renewals, or any other information that would identify an applicant for or holder of a concealed weapon provisional license, is confidential: Provided. That this information may be disclosed to a law enforcement agency or officer: **(i)** To determine the validity of a provisional license; **(ii)** to assist in a criminal investigation or prosecution; or **(iii)** for other lawful law-enforcement purposes. A person who violates this subsection is guilty of a misdemeanor and, upon conviction thereof, shall be fined not less than $50 or more than $200 for each offense.

(q) Except as restricted or prohibited by the provisions of this article or as otherwise prohibited by law, the issuance of a provisional concealed weapon license issued in accordance with the provisions of this section authorizes the holder of the license to carry a concealed pistol or revolver on the lands or waters of this state.

§ 61-7-5. Revocation of license.
A license to carry a deadly weapon shall be deemed revoked at such time as the person licensed becomes unable to meet the criteria for initial licensure set forth in section 4 of this article. Any person licensed under the provisions of this article shall immediately surrender his or her license to the issuing sheriff upon becoming ineligible for continued licensure.

§ 61-7-6. Exceptions as to prohibitions against carrying concealed handguns for persons at least eighteen years of age and fewer than twenty-one years of age; exemptions from licensing fees.
(a) The provisions in section 3 of this article do not apply to any person at least 18 years of age and fewer than 21 years of age who is:

(1) Carrying a deadly weapon upon his or her own premises;

(2) Carrying a firearm, unloaded, from the place of purchase to his or her home, residence or place of business or to a place of repair and back to his or her home, residence or place of business; or

(3) Possessing a firearm while hunting in a lawful manner or while traveling from his or her home, residence or place of business to a hunting site and returning to his or her home, residence or place of business;

(4) A member of a properly organized target-shooting club authorized by law to obtain firearms by purchase or requisition from this state or from the United States for the purpose of target practice from carrying any pistol, as defined in this article, unloaded, from his or her home, residence or place of business to a place of target practice and from any place of target practice back to his or her home, residence or place of business, for using any such weapon at a place of target practice in training and improving his or her skill in the use of the weapons;

(5) A law-enforcement officer or law-enforcement official or chief executive as defined in § 30-29-1 of this code;

(6) An employee of the West Virginia Division of Corrections duly appointed pursuant to § 25-1-11c of this code while the employee is on duty;

(7) A member of the United States armed forces, reserve or National Guard;

(8) A resident of another state who holds a valid permit or license to possess or carry a handgun issued by a state or a political subdivision subject to the provisions and limitations set forth in § 61-7-6a of this article;

(9) A federal law-enforcement officer or federal police officer authorized to carry a weapon in the performance of the officer's duty; and

(10) A parole officer appointed pursuant to § 62-12-14 of this code in the performance of his or her duties.

(b) The following judicial officers and prosecutors and staff are exempt from paying any application fees or licensure fees required under this article. However, they shall make application and satisfy all licensure and handgun safety and training requirements to obtain a license as set forth in § 61-7-4 of this article:

(1) Any justice of the Supreme Court of Appeals of West Virginia;

(2) Any circuit judge;

(3) Any retired justice or retired circuit judge designated senior status by the Supreme Court of Appeals of West Virginia;

(4) Any family court judge;

(5) Any magistrate;

(6) Any prosecuting attorney;

(7) Any assistant prosecuting attorney; or

(8) Any duly appointed investigator employed by a prosecuting attorney.

§ 61-7-6a. Reciprocity and recognition; out-of-state concealed handgun permits.

(a) A valid out-of-state permit or license to possess or carry a handgun is valid in this state for the carrying of a concealed handgun, if the following conditions are met:

(1) The permit or license holder is 21 years of age or older;

(2) The permit or license is in his or her immediate possession;

(3) The permit or license holder is not a resident of the State of West Virginia; and

(4) The Attorney General has been notified by the Governor of the other state that the other state allows residents of West Virginia who are licensed in West Virginia to carry a concealed handgun to carry a concealed handgun in that state or the Attorney General has entered into a written reciprocity agreement with the appropriate official of the other state whereby the state agrees to honor West Virginia concealed handgun licenses in return for same treatment in this state.

(b) A holder of a valid permit or license from another state who is authorized to carry a concealed handgun in this state pursuant to provisions of this section is subject to the same laws and restrictions with respect to carrying a concealed handgun as a resident of West Virginia who is so permitted and must carry the concealed handgun in compliance with the laws of this state.

(c) A license or permit from another state is not valid in this state if the holder is or becomes prohibited by law from possessing a firearm.

(d) The West Virginia Attorney General shall seek to obtain recognition of West Virginia concealed handgun licenses and enter into and execute reciprocity agreements on behalf of the State of West Virginia with states for the recognition of concealed handgun permits issued pursuant to this article.

(e) The West Virginia State Police shall maintain a registry of states with which the State of West Virginia has entered into reciprocity agreements or which recognize West Virginia concealed handgun licenses on the criminal information network and make the registry available to law-enforcement officers for investigative purposes.

(f) Every 12 months after the effective date of this section, the West Virginia Attorney General shall make written inquiry of the concealed handgun licensing or permitting authorities in each other state as to: **(i)** Whether a West Virginia resident may carry a concealed handgun in their state based upon having a valid West Virginia concealed handgun permit; and **(ii)** whether a West Virginia resident may carry a concealed handgun in that state based upon having a valid West Virginia concealed handgun permit, pursuant to the laws of that state or by the execution of a valid reciprocity agreement between the states.

(g) The West Virginia State Police shall make available to the public a list of states which have entered into reciprocity agreements with the State of West Virginia or that allow residents of West Virginia who are licensed in West Virginia to carry a concealed handgun to carry a concealed handgun in that state.

§ 61-7-7. Persons prohibited from possessing firearms; classifications; right of nonprohibited persons over twenty-one years of age to carry concealed deadly weapons; offenses and penalties; reinstatement of rights to possess; offenses; penalties.

(a) Except as provided in this section, no person shall possess a firearm, as such is defined in § 61-7-2 of this article, who:

(1) Has been convicted in any court of a crime punishable by imprisonment for a term exceeding o1 year;

(2) Is habitually addicted to alcohol;

(3) Is an unlawful user of or habitually addicted to any controlled substance;

(4) Has been adjudicated to be mentally incompetent or who has been involuntarily committed to a mental institution pursuant to the provisions of §§ 27-1-1 et seq. of this code or in similar law of another jurisdiction: Provided, That once an individual has been adjudicated as a mental defective or involuntarily committed to a mental institution, he or she shall be duly notified that they are to immediately surrender any firearms in their ownership or possession: Provided, however, That the mental hygiene commissioner or circuit judge shall first make a determination of the appropriate public or private individual or entity to act as conservator for the surrendered property;

(5) Is an alien illegally or unlawfully in the United States;

(6) Has been discharged from the armed forces under dishonorable conditions;

(7) Is subject to a domestic violence protective order that:

(A) Was issued after a hearing of which such person received actual notice and at which such person had an opportunity to participate;

(B) Restrains such person from harassing, stalking or threatening an intimate partner of such person or child of such intimate partner or person, or engaging in other conduct that would place an intimate partner in reasonable fear of bodily injury to the partner or child; and

(C) (i) Includes a finding that such person represents a credible threat to the physical safety of such intimate partner or child; or

(ii) By its terms explicitly prohibits the use, attempted use or threatened use of physical force against such intimate partner or child that would reasonably be expected to cause bodily injury; or

(8) Has been convicted of a misdemeanor offense of assault or battery either under the provisions of § 61-2-28 of this chapter or the provisions of subsection (b) or (c), § 61-2-9 of said article or a federal or state statute with the same essential elements in which the victim was a current or former spouse, current or former sexual or intimate partner, person with whom the defendant has a child in common, person with whom the defendant cohabits or has cohabited, a parent or guardian, the defendant's child or ward or a member of the defendant's household at the time of the offense or has been convicted in any court of any jurisdiction of a comparable misdemeanor crime of domestic violence.

Any person who violates the provisions of this subsection shall be guilty of a misdemeanor and, upon conviction thereof, shall be fined not less than $100 nor more than $1,000 or confined in the county jail for not less than 90 days nor more than 1 year, or both.

(b) Notwithstanding the provisions of subsection (a) of this section, any person:

(1) Who has been convicted in this state or any other jurisdiction of a felony crime of violence against the person of another or of a felony sexual offense; or

(2) Who has been convicted in this state or any other jurisdiction of a felony controlled substance offense involving a Schedule I controlled substance other than marijuana, a Schedule II or a Schedule III controlled substance as such are defined in § 60A-2-204, § 60A-2-205 and § 60A-2-206 of this code and who possesses a firearm as such is defined in section 2 of this article shall be guilty of a felony and, upon conviction thereof, shall be confined in a state correctional facility for not more than 5 years or fined not more than $5,000, or both. The provisions of subsection (f) of this section shall not apply to persons convicted of offenses referred to in this subsection or to persons convicted of a violation of this subsection.

(c) Any person may carry a concealed deadly weapon without a license therefor who is:

(1) At least 21 years of age;

(2) A United States citizen or legal resident thereof;

(3) Not prohibited from possessing a firearm under the provisions of this section; and

(4) Not prohibited from possessing a firearm under the provisions of 18 U. S. C. § 922(g) or (n).

(d) As a separate and additional offense to the offense provided for in subsection (a) of this section, and in addition to any other offenses outlined in this code, and except as provided by subsection (e) of this section, any person prohibited by subsection (a) of this section from possessing a firearm who carries a concealed firearm is guilty of a felony and, upon conviction thereof, shall be confined in a state correctional facility for not more than 3 years or fined not more than $5,000, or both.

(e) As a separate and additional offense to the offense described in subsection (b) of this section, and in additional to any other offenses outlined in this code, any person prohibited by subsection (b) of this section from possessing a firearm who carries a concealed firearm is guilty of a felony and, upon conviction thereof, shall be confined in a state correctional facility for not more than 10 years or fined not more than $10,000, or both.

(f) Any person prohibited from possessing a firearm by the provisions of subsection (a) of this section may petition the circuit court of the county in which he or she resides to regain the ability to possess a firearm and if the court finds by clear and convincing evidence that the person is competent and capable of exercising the responsibility concomitant with the possession of a firearm, the court may enter an order allowing the person to possess a firearm if such possession would not violate any federal law: Provided, That a person prohibited from possessing a firearm by the provisions of subdivision (4), subsection (a) of this section may petition to regain the ability to possess a firearm in accordance with the provisions of § 61-7A-5 of this chapter.

(g) Any person who has been convicted of an offense which disqualifies him or her from possessing a firearm by virtue of a criminal conviction whose conviction was expunged or set aside or who subsequent thereto receives an unconditional pardon for said offense shall not be prohibited from possessing a firearm by the provisions of the section.

§ 61-7-8. Possession of deadly weapons by minors; prohibitions. Notwithstanding any other provision of this article to the contrary, a person under the age of 18 years who is not married or otherwise emancipated shall not possess or carry concealed or openly any deadly weapon: Provided, That a minor may possess a firearm upon premises owned by said minor or his family or on the premises of another with the permission of his or her parent or guardian and in the case of property other than his or her own or that of his family, with the permission of the owner or lessee of such property: Provided, however, That nothing in this section shall prohibit a minor from possessing a firearm while hunting in a lawful manner or while traveling from a place where he or she may lawfully possess a deadly weapon, to a hunting site, and returning to a place where he or she may lawfully possess such weapon.

A violation of this section by a person under the age of 18 years shall subject the child to the jurisdiction of the circuit court under the provisions of §§ 49-5-1 et seq. of this code, and such minor may be proceeded against in the same manner as if he or she had committed an act which if committed by an adult would be a crime, and may be adjudicated delinquent.

§ 61-7-9. Possession of machine guns, penalties. It shall be unlawful for any person to carry, transport, or have in his possession, any machine gun, submachine gun, or any other fully automatic weapon unless he or she has fully complied with applicable federal statutes and all applicable rules and regulations of the Secretary of the Treasury of the United States relating to such firearms.

Any person who violates the provision of this section shall be guilty of a misdemeanor, and, upon conviction thereof, shall be fined not less than $1,000 nor more than $5,000, or shall be confined in the county jail for not less than 90 days nor more than 1 year, or both.

§ 61-7-10. Display of deadly weapons for sale or hire; sale to prohibited persons; penalties.

(a) A person may not publicly display and offer for rent or sale, or, where the person is other than a natural person, knowingly permit an employee thereof to publicly display and offer for rent or sale, to any passersby on any street, road or alley, any deadly weapon, machine gun, submachine gun or other fully automatic weapon, any rifle, shotgun or ammunition for same.

(b) Any person who violates the provisions of subsections (a) or (c) of this section shall be guilty of a misdemeanor, and, upon conviction thereof, shall be fined not more than $5,000 or shall be confined in the county jail for not more than 1 year, or both fined and confined, except that where the person violating the provisions of said subsections is other than a natural person, such person shall be fined not more than $10,000.

(c) A person may not knowingly sell, rent, give or lend, or, where the person is other than a natural person, knowingly permit an employee thereof to knowingly sell, rent, give or lend, any deadly weapon other than a firearm to a person prohibited from possessing a deadly weapon other than a firearm by any provision of this article.

(d) a person may not knowingly sell, rent, give or lend, or where the person is other than a natural person, knowingly permit an employee thereof to knowingly sell, rent give or lend a firearm or ammunition to a person prohibited by any provision of this article or the provisions of 18 U. S. C.§ 922.

(e) Any person who violates any of the provisions of subsection (d) of this section is guilty of a felony, and, upon conviction thereof, shall be fined not more than $100,000 imprisoned in a state correctional facility for a definite term of years of not less than 3 years nor more than 10 years, or both fined and imprisoned, except that where the person committing an offense punishable under this subsection is other than a natural person, such person shall be fined not more than $250,000.

(f) Any person who knowingly solicits, persuades, encourages or entices a licensed dealer or private seller of firearms or ammunition to transfer a firearm or ammunition under circumstances which the person knows would violate the laws of this state or the United States is guilty of a felony. Any person who willfully procures another to engage in conduct prohibited by this subsection shall be punished as a principal. This subsection does not apply to a law-enforcement officer acting in his or her official capacity. Any person who violates the provisions of this subsection is guilty of a felony, and upon conviction thereof, shall be fined not more than $5,000, imprisoned in a state correctional facility for a definite term or not less than 1 year nor more than 5 years, or both fined and imprisoned.

§ 61-7-11. Brandishing deadly weapons; threatening or causing breach of the peace; penalties. It shall be unlawful for any person armed with a firearm or other deadly weapon, whether licensed to carry the same or not, to carry, brandish or use such weapon in a way or manner to cause, or threaten, a breach of the peace. Any person violating this section shall be guilty of a misdemeanor, and, upon conviction thereof, shall be fined not less than $50 nor more than $1,000, or shall be confined in the county jail not less than 90 days nor more than 1 year, or both.

§ 61-7-11a. Possessing deadly weapons on premises of educational facilities; reports by school principals; suspension of driver's license; possessing deadly weapons on premises housing courts of law and family law courts.

(a) The Legislature finds that the safety and welfare of the citizens of this state are inextricably dependent upon assurances of safety for children attending and persons employed by schools in this state and for persons employed by the judicial department of this state. It is for the purpose of providing assurances of safety that subsections (b), (g) and (h) of this section are enacted as a reasonable regulation of the manner in which citizens may exercise the rights accorded to them pursuant to § 22, article 3 of the Constitution of the State of West Virginia.

(b) (1) It is unlawful for a person to possess a firearm or other deadly weapon on a school bus as defined in § 17A-1-1 of this code, or in or on a public primary or secondary education building, structure, facility or grounds including a vocational education building, structure, facility or grounds where secondary vocational education programs are conducted or at a school-sponsored function, or in or on a private primary or secondary education building, structure or facility: Provided, That it shall not be unlawful to possesses a firearm or other deadly weapon on or in a private primary or secondary education building, structure or facility when such institution has adopted written policies allowing for possession of firearms on or in the institution's buildings, structures or facilities.

(2) This subsection does not apply to:

(A) A law-enforcement officer employed by a federal, state, county or municipal law-enforcement agency;

(B) Any probation officer appointed pursuant to § 62-12-5 of this code in the performance of his or her duties;

(C) A retired law-enforcement officer who:

(i) Is employed by a state, county or municipal law-enforcement agency;

(ii) Is covered for liability purposes by his or her employer;

(iii) Is authorized by a county board of education and the school principal to serve as security for a school;

(iv) Meets all the requirements to carry a firearm as a qualified retired law-enforcement officer under the Law-Enforcement Officer Safety Act of 2004, as amended, pursuant to 18 U. S. C. § 926C(c); and

(v) Meets all of the requirements for handling and using a firearm established by his or her employer, and has qualified with his or her firearm to those requirements;

(D) A person specifically authorized by the board of Education of the county or principal of the school where the property is located to conduct programs with valid educational purposes;

(E) A person who, as otherwise permitted by the provisions of this article, possesses an unloaded firearm or deadly weapon in a motor vehicle or leaves an unloaded firearm or deadly weapon in a locked motor vehicle;

(F) Programs or raffles conducted with the approval of the county board of education or school which include the display of unloaded firearms;

(G) The official mascot of West Virginia University, commonly known as the Mountaineer, acting in his or her official capacity; or

(H) The official mascot of Parkersburg South High School, commonly known as the Patriot, acting in his or her official capacity.

(3) A person violating this subsection is guilty of a felony and, upon conviction thereof, shall be imprisoned in a state correctional facility for a definite term of years of not less than 2 years nor more than 10 years, or fined not more than $5,000, or both fined and imprisoned.

(c) A school principal subject to the authority of the State Board of Education who discovers a violation of subsection (b) of this section shall report the violation as soon as possible to:

(1) The State Superintendent of Schools. The State Board of Education shall keep and maintain these reports and may prescribe rules establishing policy and procedures for making and delivering the reports as required by this subsection; and

(2) The appropriate local office of the State Police, county sheriff or municipal police agency.

(d) In addition to the methods of disposition provided by §§ 49-5-1 et seq. of this code, a court which adjudicates a person who is 14 years of age or older as delinquent for a violation of subsection (b) of this section may order the Division of Motor Vehicles to suspend a driver's license or instruction permit issued to the person for a period of time as the court considers appropriate, not to extend beyond the person's 19th birthday. If the person has not been issued a driver's license or instruction permit by this state, a court may order the Division of Motor Vehicles to deny the person's application for a license or permit for a period of time as the court considers appropriate, not to extend beyond the person's 19th birthday. A suspension ordered by the court pursuant to this subsection is effective upon the date of entry of the order. Where the court orders the suspension of a driver's license or instruction permit pursuant to this subsection, the court shall confiscate any driver's license or instruction permit in the adjudicated person's possession and forward to the Division of Motor Vehicles.

(e) (1) If a person 18 years of age or older is convicted of violating subsection (b) of this section, and if the person does not act to appeal the conviction within the time periods described in subdivision (2) of this subsection, the person's license or privilege to operate a motor vehicle in this state shall be revoked in accordance with the provisions of this section.

(2) The clerk of the court in which the person is convicted as described in subdivision (1) of this subsection shall forward to the commissioner a transcript of the judgment of conviction. If the conviction is the judgment of a magistrate court, the magistrate court clerk shall forward the transcript when the person convicted has not requested an appeal within 20 days of the sentencing for the conviction. If the conviction is the judgment of a circuit court, the circuit clerk shall forward a transcript of the judgment of conviction when the person convicted has not filed a notice of intent to file a petition for appeal or writ of error within 30 days after the judgment was entered.

(3) If, upon examination of the transcript of the judgment of conviction, the commissioner determines that the person was convicted as described in subdivision (1) of this subsection, the commissioner shall make and enter an order revoking the person's license or privilege to operate a motor vehicle in this state for a period of 1 year or, in the event the person is a student enrolled in a secondary school, for a period of 1 year or until the person's 20th birthday, whichever is the greater period. The order shall contain the reasons for the revocation and the revocation period. The order of suspension shall advise the person that because of the receipt of the court's transcript, a presumption exists that the person named in the order of suspension is the same person named in the transcript. The commissioner may grant an administrative hearing which substantially complies with the requirements of the provisions of § 17C-5A-2 of this code upon a preliminary showing that a possibility exists that the person named in the notice of conviction is not the same person whose license is being suspended. The request for hearing shall be made within 10 days after receipt of a copy of the order of suspension. The sole purpose of this hearing is for the person requesting the hearing to present evidence that he or she is not the person named in the notice. If the commissioner grants an administrative hearing, the commissioner shall stay the license suspension pending the commissioner's order resulting from the hearing.

(4) For the purposes of this subsection, a person is convicted when he or she enters a plea of guilty or is found guilty by a court or jury.

(f) (1) It is unlawful for a parent, guardian or custodian of a person less than 18 years of age who knows that the person is in violation of subsection (b) of this section or has reasonable cause to believe that the person's violation of subsection (b) is imminent, to fail to immediately report his or her knowledge or belief to the appropriate school or law-enforcement officials.

(2) A person violating this subsection is guilty of a misdemeanor and, upon conviction thereof, shall be fined not more than $1,000, or shall be confined in jail not more than 1 year, or both fined and confined.

(g) (1) It is unlawful for a person to possess a firearm or other deadly weapon on the premises of a court of law, including family courts.

(2) This subsection does not apply to:

(A) A law-enforcement officer acting in his or her official capacity; and

(B) A person exempted from the provisions of this subsection by order of record entered by a court with jurisdiction over the premises or offices.

(3) A person violating this subsection is guilty of a misdemeanor and, upon conviction thereof, shall be fined not more than $1,000, or shall be confined in jail not more than 1 year, or both fined and confined.

(h) (1) It is unlawful for a person to possess a firearm or other deadly weapon on the premises of a court of law, including family courts, with the intent to commit a crime.

(2) A person violating this subsection is guilty of a felony and, upon conviction thereof, shall be imprisoned in a state correctional facility for a definite term of years of not less than 2 years nor more than 10 years, or fined not more than $5,000, or both fined and imprisoned.

(i) Nothing in this section may be construed to be in conflict with the provisions of federal law.

§ 61-7-12. Wanton endangerment involving a firearm.

Any person who wantonly performs any act with a firearm which creates a substantial risk of death or serious bodily injury to another shall be guilty of a felony, and, upon conviction thereof, shall be confined in the penitentiary for a definite term of years of not less than 1 year nor more than 5 years, or, in the discretion of the court, confined in the county jail for not more than 1 year, or fined not less than $250 nor more than $2,500, or both.

For purposes of this section, the term "firearm" shall have the same meaning ascribed to such term as set forth in § 61-7-2 of this article.

§ 61-7-14. Right of certain persons to limit possession of firearms on premises.

Notwithstanding the provisions of this article, any owner, lessee or other person charged with the care, custody and control of real property may prohibit the carrying openly or concealing of any firearm or deadly weapon on property under his or her domain: Provided, That for purposes of this section "person" means an individual or any entity which may acquire title to real property.

Any person carrying or possessing a firearm or other deadly weapon on the property of another who refuses to temporarily relinquish possession of such firearm or other deadly weapon, upon being requested to do so, or to leave such premises, while in possession of such firearm or other deadly weapon, shall be guilty of a misdemeanor, and, upon conviction thereof, shall be fined not more than $1,000 or confined in the county jail not more than 6 months, or both: Provided, That the provisions of this section shall not apply to those persons set forth in subsections (3) through (6), § 61-7-6 of this code while such persons are acting in an official capacity: Provided, however, That under no circumstances may any person possess or carry or cause the possession or carrying of any firearm or other deadly weapon on the premises of any primary or secondary educational facility in this state unless such person is a law-enforcement officer or he or she has the express written permission of the county school superintendent.

§ 61-7-15a. Use or presentation of a firearm during commission of a felony; penalties.

As a separate and distinct offense, and in addition to any and all other offenses provided for in this code, any person who, while engaged in the commission of a felony, uses or presents a firearm shall be guilty of a felony and, upon conviction, shall be imprisoned in a state correctional facility for not more than 10 years.

§ 61-7-16. Chief officer certification to transfer or make certain firearms; definitions; appeal.

(a) When certification of a chief law-enforcement officer is required by federal law or regulation for the making, transfer, receipt or possession of a firearm, the chief law-enforcement officer shall, within 30 days of receipt of such a request, provide such certification upon determining that to his or her knowledge the applicant is not prohibited by federal, state or local law from making, transferring, receiving or possessing the firearm for which application is being made and is not the subject of a proceeding that could result in the applicant being prohibited by law from receiving or possessing a firearm. If the chief law-enforcement officer is unable to make a certification as contemplated by this section, he or she shall provide the applicant written notification of the action setting forth the reasons therefor.

(b) For purposes of this section:

(1) "Chief law-enforcement officer" means any official, or his or her designee, that the Bureau of Alcohol, Tobacco, Firearms and Explosives, or any successor agency, identifies by regulation or otherwise as eligible to provide the required law-enforcement certification for the making, transfer, receipt or possession of a firearm.

(2) "Certification" means written confirmation by the chief law-enforcement officer necessary under federal law that the applicant seeking to make, transfer, receive or possess a firearm is not to the chief law-enforcement officer's knowledge prohibited by federal, state or local law from making, transferring, receiving or possessing the designated firearm.

(3) "Firearm" has the same meaning as provided in the National Firearms Act, 26 U.S.C. § 5845 (a).

(c) Chief law-enforcement officers and their designees who act in good faith are immune from liability arising from any act or omission related to certifying a responsible person.

(d) An applicant whose request for certification is denied may appeal the chief law-enforcement officer's decision to the circuit court of the applicant's county of residence. If the circuit court finds that the applicant is not prohibited by law from making, transferring, receiving or possessing a firearm and is not the subject of a proceeding that could result in prohibition, the circuit court shall order the chief law-enforcement officer to issue the certification and may award costs and reasonable attorney's fees to the applicant.

(e) A generalized objection to persons or entities making, transferring, receiving or possessing firearms or particular types of firearms which may be lawfully made, transferred, received or possessed does not constitute a valid basis for refusing certification.

(f) In making the certification decision the chief law-enforcement officer shall require of the applicant only such information as is necessary to identify the applicant for purposes of this section or to determine the disposition of an arrest or proceeding relevant to the applicant's eligibility to lawfully possess or receive a firearm.

§ 61-7-17. Construction of article. Nothing in this article should be construed to abrogate or modify statutory provisions and common law decisions related to defense of self or others.

Article 7A. State Mental Health Registry; Reporting of Persons Proscribed from Firearm Possession Due to Mental Condition to the National Instant Criminal Background Check System; Definitions; Reporting Requirements; Reinstatement of Rights Procedures.

§ 61-7A-2. Definitions. As used in this article and as the terms are deemed to mean in 18 U. S. C. § 922(g) and §61-7-7 of this chapter as each exists as of January 31, 2008:

(1) "A person adjudicated as a mental defective" means a person who has been determined by a duly authorized court, tribunal, board or other entity to be mentally ill to the point where he or she has been found to be incompetent to stand trial due to mental illness or insanity, has been found not guilty in a criminal proceeding by reason of mental illness or insanity or has been determined to be unable to handle his or her own affairs due to mental illness or insanity. A child under 14 years of age is not considered "a person adjudicated as a mental defective" for purposes of this article.

(2) "Committed to a mental institution" means to have been involuntarily committed for treatment pursuant to the provisions of §§27-1-1 et seq. of this code. Children under 14 years of age are not considered "committed to a mental institution" for purposes of this article. "Committed to a mental institution" does not mean voluntary admission for mental health treatment.

(3) "Mental institution" means any facility or part of a facility used for the treatment of persons committed for treatment of mental illness.

§ 61-7A-3. Persons whose names are to be supplied to the central state mental health registry.

(a) The Superintendent of the West Virginia State Police and the Secretary of the Department of Health and Human Resources, or their designees, shall cooperate with the circuit clerk of each county and Administrator of the West Virginia Supreme Court of Appeals in compiling and maintaining a database containing the names and identifying information of persons who have been adjudicated to be mentally defective or who have been committed to a mental institution. The registry shall be maintained by the Administrator of the Supreme Court of Appeals or the superintendent of the West Virginia State Police.

(b) The name of any person who has been adjudicated to be mentally defective or who has been committed to a mental institution shall be provided to the Administrator of the Supreme Court of Appeals or the Superintendent of the West Virginia State Police for inclusion in the central state mental health registry. Upon receipt of the information being received by the central state mental health registry it may be transmitted to the National Instant Criminal Background Check System and to county sheriffs;

(c) The Secretary of Department of Human Resources and the circuit clerk of each county shall, as soon as practicable after the effective date of this article, supply to the Administrator of the Supreme Court of Appeals or the Superintendent of the West Virginia State Police for inclusion in the central state mental health registry the name and identifying information required by the provisions of subsection (d) of this section of all persons covered by the provisions of this article and shall on an ongoing basis continue to provide such information as it is developed;

(d) The central state mental health registry shall contain the name, address at the time of commitment or adjudication, date of birth, date of commitment or adjudication of all persons who have been adjudicated to be mentally defective or who have been committed to a mental institution.

(e) The central state mental health registry shall provide only such information about a person on the registry to county sheriffs and the National Instant Criminal Background Check System as is necessary to identify registrants; and

(f) On or before January 1, 2010, the central state mental health registry shall contain the name, address at the time of commitment or adjudication, date of birth, date of commitment or adjudication and any other identifying characteristics of all persons who have been adjudicated to be mentally defective or who have been committed to a mental institution. Under no circumstances shall the registry contain information relating to any diagnosis or treatment provided.

(g) To the extent the central state mental health registry contains the names of any children under 14 years of age on the effective date of this article, the Administrator of the West Virginia Supreme Court of Appeals shall take whatever steps are necessary to remove those individuals from the central state mental health registry.

§ 61-7A-4. Confidentiality; limits on use of registry information.

(a) Notwithstanding any provision of this code to the contrary, the Superintendent of the State Police, the Secretary of the Department of Health and Human Resources, the circuit clerks, and the Administrator of the Supreme Court of Appeals may provide notice to the central state mental health registry and the National Instant Criminal Background Check System established pursuant to Section 103(d) of the Brady Handgun Violence Protection Act, 18 U. S. C. § 922, that a person: **(i)** Has been involuntarily committed to a mental institution; **(ii)** has been adjudicated as a mental defective; or **(iii)** has regained the ability to possess a firearm by order of a circuit court in a proceeding under §61-7A-5 of this article.

(b) The information contained in the central state mental health registry is to be used solely for the purpose of records checks related to firearms purchases and for eligibility for a state license or permit to possess or carry a concealed firearm.

(c) Whenever a person's name and other identifying information has been added to the central state mental health registry, a review of the state concealed handgun registry shall be undertaken and if such review reveals that the person possesses a current concealed handgun license, the sheriff of the county issuing the concealed handgun license shall be informed of the person's change in status.

§ 61-7A-5. Petition to regain right to possess firearms.

(a) Any person who is prohibited from possessing a firearm pursuant to the provisions of § 61-7-7 of this chapter or by provisions of federal law by virtue solely of having previously been adjudicated to be mentally defective or to having a prior involuntary commitment to a mental institution pursuant to §§ 27-1-1 et seq. of this code may petition the circuit court of the county of his or her residence to regain the ability to lawfully possess a firearm.

(b) Petitioners prohibited from possession of firearms due to a mental health disability, must include in the petition for relief from disability:

(1) A listing of facilities and location addresses of all prior mental health treatment received by petitioner;

(2) An authorization, signed by the petitioner, for release of mental health records to the prosecuting attorney of the county; and

(3) A verified certificate of mental health examination by a licensed psychologist or psychiatrist occurring within 30 days prior to filing of the petition which supports that the petitioner is competent and not likely to act in a manner dangerous to public safety.

(c) The court may only consider petitions for relief due to mental health adjudications or commitments that occurred in this state, and only give the relief specifically requested in the petition.

(d) In determining whether to grant the petition, the court shall receive and consider at a minimum evidence:

(1) Concerning the circumstances regarding the firearms disabilities imposed by 18 U.S.C. § 922(g)(4);

(2) The petitioner's record which must include the petitioner's mental health and criminal history records; and

(3) The petitioner's reputation developed through character witness statements, testimony, or other character evidence.

(e) If the court finds by clear and convincing evidence that the person is competent and capable of exercising the responsibilities concomitant with the possession of a firearm, will not be likely to act in a manner dangerous to public safety, and that granting the relief will not be contrary to public interest, the court may enter an order allowing the petitioner to possess a firearm. If the order denies petitioner's ability to possess a firearm, the petitioner may appeal the denial, which appeal is to include the record of the circuit court rendering the decision.

(g) The prosecuting attorney or one of his or her assistants shall represent the state in all proceedings for relief to regain firearm rights and provide the court the petitioner's criminal history records.

(h) The written petition, certificate, mental health or substance abuse treatment records and any papers or documents containing substance abuse or mental health information of the petitioner, filed with the circuit court, are confidential. These documents may not be open to inspection by any person other than the prosecuting attorney or one of his or her assistants only for purposes of representing the state in and during these proceedings and by the petitioner and his or her counsel. No other person may inspect these documents, except upon authorization of the petitioner or his or her legal representative or by order of the court, and these records may not be published except upon the authorization of the petitioner or his or her legal representative.

(i) The circuit clerk of each county shall provide the Superintendent of the West Virginia State Police, or his or her designee, and the Administrator of the West Virginia Supreme Court of Appeals, or his or her designee, with a certified copy of any order entered pursuant to the provisions of this section which removes a petitioner's prohibition to possess firearms. If the order restores the petitioner's ability to possess a firearm, petitioner's name shall be promptly removed from the central state mental health registry and the superintendent or administrator shall forthwith inform the Federal Bureau of Investigation, the United States Attorney General, or other federal entity operating the National Instant Criminal Background Check System of the court action.

89150324R00171

Made in the USA
Lexington, KY
23 May 2018